Behind Closed Doors

PART 2

What did they think ten years of proceedings would do to a family?

Dean Marlo

ISBN: 9798376964200

Dedication

For Ma/Nan
Your strength, kindness and generosity carries through to us even now.

Preface

Copyright of mentioned characters, quotes and songs belongs to the owners.

The names and identifying details have been changed; any likeness to people or locations, past or present, is accidental.

Everything referenced in this book happened. We could probably carry on to this day, but for the sake of all involved, our story ends in an official sense; there will be an epilogue to bring you up to date.

For the benefit of the narrative, solicitors' letters and so forth have been listed chronologically, although I did not receive the majority on the dates recorded. My solicitor was kind enough to forward me all correspondences, which is how they are included in my documentation of a family's struggle with the Family Courts.

I can confirm, as of publishing this, I do not have a criminal record and have never been cautioned by the police. Although there were so many challenges we faced as a family, my children did have happy times in their childhoods, and those are the moments that carried me through as well.

Despite the events of Behind Closed Doors Part 1, this remains a tale of disbelief, nightmares, lies and deceit, with serious failures across the board.

For anyone affected by domestic violence, sexual assault, child abuse and mental health conditions, these are all subjects that are discussed within this book. These issues touch so many lives yet, sadly, we still need to do more to bring about real systemic change and an adjustment in our values as a society.

Codes of Practice

For solicitors, members of Resolution are required to:
Conduct matters in a constructive and non-confrontational way.
Avoid use of inflammatory language, both written and spoken.
Retain professional objectivity and respect for everyone involved.
Take into account the long-term consequences of actions and communications as well as the short-term implications.
Encourage clients to put the best interests of the children first.
Emphasise to clients the importance of being open and honest in all dealings.
Make clients aware of the benefits of behaving in a civilised way.
Keep financial and children issues separate.
Ensure that consideration is given to balancing the benefits of any steps against the likely costs – financial or emotional.
Inform clients of the options, eg counselling, family therapy, round table negotiations, mediation, collaborative law and court proceedings.
Abide by the Resolution Guides to Good Practice.
This Code should be read in conjunction with the Law Society's family law Protocol. All solicitors are subject to the Solicitors Practice Rules.

Family law Protocol (Children):
Emphasise the need for parents to accept parental responsibility for their children
Aim to promote the child's welfare as the paramount consideration
Encourage separation of addressing the children's needs from those of the parents
Encourage the use of mediation and other dispute resolution options
Provide information about local support/guidance services
Provide information about parenting apart

The principles of judicial conduct:
Judicial independence is a prerequisite to the rule of law and a fundamental guarantee of a fair trial. A judge shall therefore uphold and exemplify judicial independence in both its individual and institutional aspects.
Impartiality is essential to the proper discharge of the judicial office. It applies not only to the decision itself but also to the process by which the decision is made.
Integrity is essential to the proper discharge of the judicial office. Guide to Judicial Conduct 8 Published in March 2013, amended in July 2016 Introduction
Propriety, and the appearance of propriety, are essential to the performance of all of the activities of the judge.
Ensuring equality of treatment to all before the courts is essential to the due performance of the judicial office.
Competence and diligence are prerequisites to the due performance of judicial office.

The Children Act 1989 states that children's welfare should be the paramount concern of the courts. It also specifies that any delays in the system processes will have a detrimental impact on a child's welfare. The court should take into account the child's wishes; physical, emotional and educational needs; age; sex; background circumstances; the likely effect of change on the child; the harm the child has suffered or is likely to suffer; parent's ability to meet the child's needs and the powers available to the court.

How did we get here?

Orders and Applications
25 November 1999 / Application for Parental Rights
24 March 2000 – Order
20 July 2000 – Application for a Residence Order
18 August 2000 – Order
22 August 2000 – Application for a penal notice
24 August 2000 – Order
10 October 2000 – Order and schedule
27 October 2001 – Application to enforce Residence Order and Application for a penal notice
5 November 2001 – Application to vary Residence Order
19 November 2001 – Order
18 December 2003 – Application to vary Residence Order
15 January 2004 – Order
11 February 2004 – Application for a Residence Order
19 February 2004 – Order
27 February 2004 – Application for a penal notice
2 March 2004 – Order
19 March 2004 – Order
27 April 2004 – Application to enforce and vary Order
28 April 2004 – Application to vary Shared Residence Order
29 April 2004 – Order
27 May 2004 – Order
24 June 2004 – Order
5 August 2004 – Order
Statements
5 December 1999 – Statement of the Applicant Father
17 February 2000 – Statement of Ms Hyde
11 August 2000 – Statement of the Applicant Father
15 August 2000 – Statement of Ms Hyde
7 September 2000 – Statement of Mrs Jackson
27 September 2000 – Statement of Ms Hyde
30 September 2000 – Statement of Ms Marlo
2 October 2000 – Statement of the Applicant
29 October 2001 – Statement of the Applicant
16 November 2001 – Statement of the respondent
5 March 2004 – Statement of the Applicant
19 March 2004 – Statement of the respondent
11 May 2004 – Statement of Mrs Jackson
14 May 2004 – Statement of the Applicant

15 May 2004 – Statement of Mr Jackson
17 May 2004 – Statement of Ms Jackson
25 May 2004 – Statement of the respondent
20 May 2004 – Statement of the respondent
Reports
3 February 2000 – Welfare report
9 August 2000 – Report of Dr Russ
26 September 2000 – Report from the Police
28 September 2000 – Report from Social Services
5 October 2000 – Psychiatric Report of Dr Borah
9 October 2000 – Report of Dr Russ
18 September 2003 – Report from the Police
15 June 2004 – Cafcass report
Other documents
8 August 2000 – Acknowledgement
29 August 2000 – Letter from children's GP
5 September 2000 – Letter from children's GP
7 September 2001 – Letter from Dr Russ
9 November 2001 – Letter from the Mental Health Partnership
15 May 2004 – Riverbank School letter
7 July 2004 – County Council letter
July 2004 – Northview Grove School academic report on Hayley Marlo
24 August 2006 – Letter from the Child Legal Guidance
10 August 2006 – Acknowledgement

2005

Survival

At the end of December, I sat down and reflected on the past four years, and receiving sole residence of Hayley, Alice and Lara in August. The dust was settling and I felt confident about our future. As I looked around my office where in the past would be technical drawings, specifications and quotations, four years on, and I saw nothing but folders full of solicitor's letters, court orders, court expert's reports, and the rest of the bullshit that comprises the Family Courts process.

I considered that I had three choices:

First, to leave the folders in my office, not being able to let go and have the past fester in my future.

Second, shred and destroy all of the papers. (Part of me does want to remove the ordeal, which I believe might give me closure, and that is something I desperately need.)

Third, box everything up and put them in the loft, out of sight.

I know I want peace for my family and to get on with my life, so I spent half the morning moving the boxes into the loft. I must admit as I closed the hatch, I felt a sense of relief; I now realise that part of the euphoria was leaving the spiders behind, but I add it to my good feeling about removing the folders.

Speaking of business, Simon is an old school friend and has been with me from the beginning, when I started my company up. Due to the never-ending family court proceedings, and the demands placed on me throughout by the process, since early 2002 Simon had taken on more responsibilities in running my company.

The company has a good reputation which, to be honest, in those years had been kept intact due to Simon organising the work on site when I was unavailable, because I was looking after my children in and out of the residence order, having solicitor meetings, writing letters and many dreaded court hearings - all of which had taken a toll on me and affected my ability to run the company.

Simon took over in 2004, registering the company as limited and getting the hire purchase set up on my old van. I needed to concentrate on Hayley, Alice and Lara and a new year ahead; we agreed I would work for him on a part time basis. Even though it made me sad to see the company I had built over 20 years out of my hands, it was - in part - a relief.

Being parttime and doing the school run, however, means that I am probably going to need to work every Saturday, as it will be my only opportunity to work a full day (except for when the children are at their mother's for weekend contact). Ma comes down every weekend to see the children anyway, but I had a word with Ma, just to check she wouldn't mind looking after them, as I might have to work. Ma was of course more than pleased to help out whenever she can; we both knew the children would be happy spending the time with their nan.

Starting the year

1 January

At 10.30am, I received a phone call from Ruth; she asked me if I would have a word with Alice, as Alice had been rude to her the previous night and she 'would not stand for it'. I told Ruth I would speak to Alice.

Calling Alice, she explained she had a falling out with her mother and her mother's friend, Bernard, over a TV program that was on at midnight, and her mother had told Bernard to 'take' Alice upstairs to her room. Alice stated that her mother and Bernard had repeatedly belittled her, and they carried on in the morning.

Alice asked if she could come home.

I tried to emphasise to Alice that she should stick with her sisters as it's only one more night, and that how her mother spoke to her was wrong, but she should have listened and gone to bed.

(It has previously become apparent that Ruth allows the children to stay up far too late. At weekends, Ruth appears to be entertaining and allowing Hayley, Alice and Lara to do as they wish, for as long as they wish, providing they do not disturb Ruth.)

However, clearly, Alice felt troubled and unhappy about being there, the arguments with her mother are increasing, and so I phoned Ruth back. She already knew that Alice did not want to stay with her any longer, and we agreed for me to pick Alice up.

Also in the call, Ruth ranted about her annoyance at having to drive to McDonalds to handover the children and suggested we meet at the local shops bottle bank instead; I agreed, having not wanted to handover in the parking lot of a fast-food restaurant anyway.

Ruth's requests

13 January

Ruth phoned to speak to the children and then to me. She requested changing several weekends due to holiday arrangements she'd made and I asked her to write to me with the dates that she wanted.

Ruth has always organised the children's contact around her needs and lifestyle; despite not agreeing, I understand that is up to her – it is not the relationship I want as a parent to Hayley, Alice and Lara.

I also inquired if the children have their own passports, as I intend to take them on holiday later in the year; Ruth said she wasn't sure and would get back to me.

Ruth's weekend contact

17 January

It was Ruth's weekend contact, but Hayley had a dentist appointment in the morning and had asked for me to take her instead of her mother. We arranged to meet at the bottle bank of the local shops.

At 9:10am Monday, as I sat at the bottle bank waiting, Hayley phoned me and stated that she had just woken up and everyone was still in bed asleep, so she was going to wake them then be on her way. I told Hayley I'd see her soon.

While I don't approve of Ruth's habits, Hayley doesn't need me to tell her it's abnormal; she is at an age where she is noticing more and more.

Hayley had her check-up and I dropped her to school.

I got home to a letter from the Family Tax Credit Department stating that 'someone' else is claiming for Hayley, Alice and Lara on their application form, and would I please send any information I have to establish who should be receiving the benefit.

(Ruth will find any way to make my life difficult, no matter the potential impact on our children.)

A letter from Ruth – Margaritaville

8 February

18th January 2005

Dear Dean,

Following our telephone conversation, I am writing as requested to confirm the dates we discussed.

I will be away on the w/e 12th & 13th Feb 05 and would like to exchange those dates for either the w/e of 19th & 20th March 05, i.e. taking the children out of school on the Friday and Monday, or change the w/e for a couple of days in the May half term.

Alice's b'day falls in my week which means I can't take the girls away. I would like to suggest that either you keep the children from school on 12pm on 12th April and I have my weeks holiday in the middle and then you have a few days at the end, or we swop the weeks, i.e. you have the 1st and I have the 2nd, which is not ideal for me as I want to take them skiing and it is already late in the season.

I look forward to hearing from you soon.

Regards,

Despite the date written on the letter, it was the 8th of February when Mrs Hart from Riverbank School asked me to pick up this letter handed into reception by Ruth. I did wonder why Ruth had not posted it through my door.

Ruth has already informed Riverbank that I will be picking up Alice and Lara from school on Friday 11th February and returning them on the 14th. I have not agreed to any of the dates that are listed in her letter, because I was waiting for her to confirm what weekends she was supposed changing – she has just done it anyway.

The children have told me that Ruth has a new boyfriend, and that this holiday she has booked for two weeks is to go with him to Thailand. This isn't about her missing her children and a mother's contact, this is about dictating her children's lives and contact around her life, as in the past.

I don't have a problem with changing arrangements to benefit the children, but how long will it be before it is once again thrown in my face that I do not communicate or encourage the children to see their mother?

Mr MP

28 February

May I apologise for my delay in contacting you. Your personal efforts and considerations, regarding my concerns for the welfare and stability of my three young daughters, is appreciated.

I am very happy that in the Town County Courts on the 5th August 2004, it was ordered that Hayley, Alice and Lara were to continue to reside with me; Judge Chips granted a sole residency order in my favour. I cannot express my relief as a father who just wants to get on with my children.

Through the unnecessary hardship and manipulation that I have witnessed, I must express to you the desperate need for sensible and meaningful changes within our system and the attitude towards mothers and fathers as parents. Antiquated ideals and legislation do nothing for the role of parenting in today's world, yet as we consider ourselves a forward-looking society and country, our family law does not reflect the true value of both parents in a child's life.

Parents and their children have never needed a Family Courts that is used as a battleground, where honesty, morals and standards fall to the side; drawn into a world of deception and double standards.

The Family Courts started with fathers solely being granted custody of children, which wasn't right. Throughout time, campaigning had to be done by women to achieve equality. It appears we have gone the other way, wherein a mother's position means more than a father's – we must be able to do better for children and families across the country to treat parents equally.

In 1999, I applied to the Family Courts because I wanted to be a dad and believed that I could provide a good standard of care for my children. Each time I have come into the Family Courts, I have been there representing my children and their welfare.

Thank you for enclosing a copy of the Lord Chancellor and Secretary of State for Constitutional Affairs' letter, 4th August 2004.

It is written with self-assurance that 'The Lord Chancellor and Secretary of State for Constitutional Affairs have a firm expectation that a magistrate will conduct themselves in such a way as to command the confidence of the community which they serve'.

During my dealings with the DCA, I have been lied to, they made up stories to suit themselves, have been dismissive and, on several occasions, sent me down the garden path.

I have no confidence in the accountability or justice in the departments there to investigate serious complaints about the integrity of the legal system itself.

Mrs Jackson, magistrate

This working magistrate has tried to deceive professional people involved, which had the potential to put three children at risk, for her own motives.

It was as a direct result of Mrs Jackson that my children, aged 8, 6 and 2½, were placed under Police Protection, the day after their mother had been sectioned under the Mental Health Act for the fourth time. The additional needless upset caused and what Mrs Jackson put three children through on that day is disgraceful.

Mrs Jackson wrote a letter of complaint to the Children's Legal Services about what my children had said to their Advocate in confidence; this magistrate had no right to undermine the welfare of the children, and again attempt to cover for her daughter's unacceptable behaviour. After the Children's Legal Services received Mrs Jackson's letter, the woman who the children had seen on several occasions was replaced.

Did Mrs Jackson think the abuse the children had talked about with their first advocate would be any different with a new one? Mrs Jackson's letter of complaint I believe shows yet again that she will not accept her daughter needs her help; it has to be recognised that Ms Hyde struggles with day-to-day family situations, which is accompanied by verbal confrontations and aggressive behaviour.

26th April 2004, another incident of abuse occurred towards Hayley and Alice. Hayley had bruises on her arms where she had been grabbed, and Alice had a carpet burn up her spine from where her mother had dragged her across the floor.

I must say that if I had caused any kind of injuries to my children, I would feel ashamed and totally distressed by my actions.

Why was I told that Social Services had worked all night with their legal team, when two children had clearly been physically abused?

I was told by Social Services in April 2004 that I would receive a letter from them, which would explain how Social Services' involvement was instigated under the Child Protection Act, and within 24-hours their concern dropped. To this day, I have received nothing.

Once again, no one seems to care and I can but wonder, that if it was their own children, who were being abused by a parent and failed by organisations set out to protect children, then would they be outraged?

It was enough for my children with what was going on in the background, without Social Services bursting in and within 24 hours dismissing them; Hayley was left waiting after school for a case worker to pick her up and take her to the doctors for an examination with her sisters.

Just another example of an organisation that acted inadequately and not in the children's best interests. Why?

I went to the Family Courts after Ms Hyde withheld my contact with my children, and on the 24th March 2000 Judge Baxter ordered every other weekend contact, but Lara was not allowed to stay overnight with her sisters and dad. Despite caring for and loving Lara, it hurts me when I think that Judge Baxter felt it necessary to deprive three children and their father in such a way. At the time, Lara was 2 years old; according to Judge Baxter's court order, Lara could not have overnight stay until she was 5 years old. I had done nothing but be there for, look after and love my three children as any decent father would.

Why was my love and care for Lara dismissed by Judge Baxter? I believe it was heartless, needless and immoral.

15th January 2004, and we were back before Judge Baxter, where he humiliated Mrs

Millar, who was at the hearing as my McKenzie Friend, for no reason. This I believe to be unacceptable behaviour from a judge or any moral person - the bully was the person who already had all the power in the room.

At the residency hearing August 2004, Ms Hyde's barrister made a very strong point to Judge Chips that I had made complaints to the DCA, the LSC and the Ombudsman.

I wrote to the Law Society in April 2002 about Smitch Law as a firm and Mrs Mason as a solicitor, due to their ongoing interference and harassment of court orders and myself, and the stability of three children. Six months later, I received a reply stating 'the Law Society do not deal with my type of complaints'.

According to the Law Society, Mrs Mason was acting within the boundaries of family law and in the interests of her client.

I wrote to the Legal Services Ombudsman concerning the Law Society and the fact that I have endured over three and a half years of aggressive attitude from a solicitor.

The Ombudsman have written to me, telling me that the needless lies, deceit, confusion and sadness brought into my children's lives, by a self-serving solicitor, was and is acceptable, and that there was no evidence of professional misconduct.

I would like to ask, Mr Rowe, for what reason did I feel the desperation, the sense of hopelessness, the need, and it goes on, to write many letters, on many occasions to you, our PM, the LCD, the DCA, and more?

All my letters have been honest accounts of proceedings, and I have evidently not set-out to complain about anyone's conduct. How can my complaints to the appropriate authorities, relating to several individuals, be used to discredit my character?

The love and care that I show my children today is the same love and care that I have shown them all their lives. Yet, the system has continually tried to destabilize my fatherhood, while ignoring the support Ms Hyde requires, which would remove the need for our family to be involved in the court system in the first place. With help for her mental health, we should have had joint residency from the outset, and it should have been at the recommendation of the institution so-called 'the Family Courts'.

As it stands, we have organisations such as the DCA and the Law Society who condone the dishonest and immoral behaviour. This has got to be considered shameful and unacceptable by the system itself towards children. I believe that no child should be placed in this position by people working within the Justice System and family law.

Once again, thank you for your support with my children. I hope you are well and I look forward to seeing you soon.

Yours respectfully…

To Ruth

2/3 March

As discussed, I am prepared to swap the second week of the holidays with you. I shall make Hayley, Alice and Lara available at the bottle bank on the 16th April at 12pm. Alice and Lara have Monday 25th April off school, if you would like to meet at the bottle bank at 12pm on that day please inform me.

Also, would you please let me know about Hayley, Alice and Lara's passports?

Yours sincerely…

I'd already told the children we were going to Disney and that I just needed to finalise the dates. After agreeing to Ruth's changes, I contacted the holiday company and the only times available for a holiday to Disney was Thursday to Thursday; meaning the children would miss school – I hope the schools will allow them off for those days.

3 March

Dear Mr Church/Mrs Tran,

I am writing to ask if Alice and Lara/Hayley may be excused from school on April 7/8th 2005.

We have planned a family holiday at Disneyland Paris for six nights. Unfortunately, I have had to book our stay in Disneyland from Thursday to Thursday.

I believe Alice and Lara/Hayley would benefit from this break and I am sorry that I must ask for time off from school.

I hope that you have no objection to my request, and may I assure you of my best intentions at all times.

Thank you for your attention with this matter.

Yours sincerely…

Smitch to me direct

3 March

We refer to our letter 20th December 2004 and note that we have not heard from you in response.

Our client has had to seek advice from us again concerning the court order made on the 5th August 2004, with regard to her contact with the children.

We understand that you are unable to communicate with our client and she believes that you may be intending to take the children away for the first half of Easter holidays.

The court order clearly provides that our client should have contact with the children for the first week of the Easter holidays.

Our client spoke to you six weeks ago, asking you to confirm when you were intending to take the children on holiday so that she could make arrangements herself.

We understand also that you have requested that the children's passports are given to you, as we understand that the younger children are on the passports of our client.

Our client is saddened that you are unable to communicate with her in a courteous manner.

We would be grateful if you would please respond within 5 days confirming the dates when you intend to take the children on holiday and also with confirmation that when the children are returned to our client, their passports are available so that our client can also take the children abroad on holiday.

We would strongly recommend that you seek your own independent legal advice with regard to the contents of this letter.

Ms Hyde wouldn't tell me if the children had their own passports... It's another matter that should not need solicitor involvement; what in the context of this letter would require them to 'strongly recommend' I seek legal advice'? Am I breaking the law, or being detrimental the court order and my children's welfare?

Ms Hyde knows the schedule is written that I have the first week and she has the second week of Easter, as that is why she wrote to me herself in the first place. I have swopped many days and weekends at her request, yet it is made out that we never agree.

The word 'Disney' and their resorts conjures up some great images, and the possibilities of some good times with your children; for some reason, this normal parenting function must be turned into something involving solicitors and their suggestions of something sinister or detrimental to the children.

It is shameful that this law firm can interfere in a family's dynamics, in such a way that they are directly involving themselves in every aspect of a family's affairs.

I can feel the bowels of hell stirring...

As per usual, Ruth has punctuated her demands with the looming threat of Smitch Law's interference in a court order, our children's childhoods and my life.

Smitch Law react in their normal big bully way, with wild cries of some injustice. Ruth is then unavailable for her weekend contact with her children, not in accordance with the court order.

Since 6th August 2004, all three of my children are doing very well at home and at school. Hayley's school report is excellent. Alice is excitedly preparing herself for secondary school and Lara has just been awarded a Memorial Cup, which is presented each year to a pupil of the school that stands out for their friendliness, politeness and their positive attitude.

I would like to ask Smitch Law to stop interfering and undermining three young children that have a right to be left alone and be able to get on with their lives.

Smitch Law have spent four years abusing their position to destabilise the welfare of three young children and their father; they demonstrate the very worst that a family law solicitor could be.

I believe that enough is enough. Ruth's allegations are clearly made-up stories, which, as history shows, are a part of her mental health condition, yet Smitch Law's letters continue to be aggressive and unhelpful, in their attempt to disrupt the normality that we have been able to hold onto within our family.

I am complying with the court order, why should I be threatened and bullied?

Another Letter to Ruth

24 March

As discussed, Hayley, Alice, Lara and myself will be going on holiday to Disneyland Paris on the 7th of April 2005.

If I may suggest, I shall make available Hayley, Alice and Lara at the bottle bank on Friday the 15th of April at 12pm, and you return Alice and Lara to me at the bottle bank on Monday the 25th of April at 12pm, as it is a non–pupil day for them; Hayley should go to school as normal.

I am pleased that you have informed me that Hayley has a passport and confirm we have agreed you will provide Alice with a passport and I shall apply for Lara's.

As discussed, and as in the past, I am happy for you to change the weekend schedule, so long as it does not interfere with Hayley, Alice and Lara's stability and your requests are within reason.

Yours sincerely…

Still writing to Melissa

28 March

Please find changes to Ms Hyde's contact, as requested by her:

27th October 2004 – Wednesday 12pm contact with the children to Thursday 28th at 2pm.

3rd January 2005 – Contact with children from 12pm on Wednesday 5th January to 12pm Monday 3rd January.

11/14th & 25/28th February 2005 – Ms Hyde misses two contact weekends with the children due to being on holiday.

24th March 2005 – Contact with the children 12pm Friday 25th March and not 12pm Thursday 24th March.

28th March 2005 – Monday handover of the children at 1pm and not 12pm

2nd September 2005 – Ms Hyde to drop the children on Friday 2nd September and not Monday 5th September.

Despite my agreements to several of her changes, Ms Hyde phones the home phone at 10pm/10.30pm, leaving verbal abuse on the answer machine. She threatens me with 'Smitch Law' and 'what they are going to do with you, when they get you back into court'.

I have done nothing but comply with the court order and also Ms Hyde's requests to have or return the children, to suit herself – I have sole residency, and Ms Hyde has contact/half holidays; I do not begrudge or withhold Ms Hyde any extra time, but I do question how it can be Ms Hyde and her solicitor who dictate the court ordered schedule.

If I had not agreed with Ms Hyde's request to exchange the Easter two-week half term, I would have booked my holiday within the holiday period.

Due to the instability, confusion, abuse and threats that have been placed in our lives as a result of Ms Hyde's never satisfied chopping and changing, I must ask you, please, to insist that Ms Hyde keeps to the court schedule in the future.

The court schedule, on occasions, unfortunately does not run to suit one or both parents. I have tried to help Ms Hyde on many occasions with her residency periods; this evidently is still not good enough for her.

I am happy and prepared to have Hayley, Alice and Lara when Ms Hyde is not available. However, as you are aware, I am working part-time, and I have to be organised and know beforehand when the children are with their mother throughout the year. Is this not the reason for the court residency schedules?

The schedule should not be for Ms Hyde and Smitch Law to change or dictate; Mrs Mason hounded our residency for 4 years, and it looks like she is back on the hunt.

Ms Hyde has the same time with our children for school holidays as I do; she should be able to organise a holiday for the children that does not interfere with the court schedule or their time at school. (Her changes put me in a position where my choices were to cancel my children's holiday to Disney, or book Thursday-Thursday – I do not mean to be hypocritical.)

Hayley, Alice and Lara have been caught up over the past four years in the dishonest and detrimental game overseen by an institution that proclaims the importance of stability and welfare in a child's life. These so-called professionals have quite clearly brought nothing more than legal manoeuvring and sadness into their lives.

The Family Courts' inability to see the clear aggression and pressure that is placed on innocent children and their parents is a failure of the people that work within the system, who are entrusted to ensure honesty, morals and standards are upheld.

Yours sincerely…

Timing

28 March

At 11am, Hayley called saying that her mother has said she will be dropping them back at 2pm instead of 12pm, but that she would be phoning me to confirm this. We chatted for a minute, before Hayley said she had to get ready to go to lunch.

Hearing nothing from Ruth, at 12:30pm I tried her number; with no pick up, I called Hayley back. When I asked what was happening, as I couldn't get through to Ruth, Hayley sighed and said that their mother hadn't taken them to lunch, and that she, Alice and Lara had told their mother if she will not drop them back at 1pm, they will walk home.

Shortly after, Ruth called saying she was busy this afternoon, and she dropped the children at the bottle bank at 1pm.

Melissa Writes to Mrs Mason

30 March

We have been consulted by Mr Marlo and have before us a copy of your letter to him dated 3rd March 2005, that it appears may have crossed with my confirmatory letter to Ms Hyde dated 2nd March 2005, with additional correspondence both between Mr Marlo and your client, and yourselves to Mr Marlo.

Mr Marlo is fed up with both your continued diatribe against him and Ms Hyde's continuing attempts to create confusion and disharmony, unnecessarily. His only concern is that his children have the opportunity to thrive within a stable family routine and maintain their relationship with both of their parents.

Continued allegations and attempts to litigate by correspondence serve no purpose other than inflaming the situation, inevitably putting the girls' peaceful existence with their father, at risk.

On Mr Marlo's behalf, we ask you to stop it.

For that reason, I do not propose to respond fully to any of your correspondence. However, in the event that Ms Hyde seeks to return to court, I will give evidence relating in the correct venue.

The current position is that since the order was made last August, Mr Marlo has accommodated a number of requests made by Ms Hyde to alter the schedule of contact with the children, to suit Ms Hyde's work and holiday arrangements and plans. In the spirit of working together to promote the children's welfare, Mr Marlo agrees with Ms Hyde's requested alterations and relinquished periods of contact.

The children will be spending the first week of the Easter school holiday with Mr Marlo to enable Ms Hyde to take them away on holiday in the second half of the Easter school holiday; Mr Marlo will be delivering the children at 12pm at the bottle bank on Saturday, April 16th. On Monday, 25th April, Alice and Lara have non–pupil day, however Hayley should be at school.

Mr Marlo understands that Ms Hyde and the children will not return to the UK until late on 24th April. Mr Marlo will expect to collect all three children from the bottle bank at 12 noon on Monday 25th April, unless, of course, Hayley attends school on that day, in which case Mr Marlo will expect her to return home after school.

At the conclusion of the Easter school holiday, Mr Marlo believes it will be best for everyone, and not least the children, for the regime of their contact with Ms Hyde to revert to that seen as in their best interests by the court. Ms Hyde is therefore due to have the children for weekend staying contact commencing again on Friday, after school, 29th April and alternate weekends through to the June half–term holiday when she will have the children from Friday, after school, 27th May through to 12 noon on Wednesday, 1st June 2005. As in the past, Mr Marlo is happy to accommodate any additional contact requested by the children.

One request that Mr Marlo would make is that Ms Hyde desist from telephoning after she finishes work in the evening. The phone ringing between about 10pm and 10.30pm is not conducive to the children's sleep pattern and simply serves to disrupt. Ms Hyde may phone before 9pm, if she so chooses.

Finally, Mr Marlo hopes that there will be no necessity for either Mr Marlo or Ms Hyde to consult solicitors in the future with respect to their daughters and should like to suggest to Ms Hyde that keeping communication simple and in writing, in respect of non–emergency matters, will be of the greatest assistance in future, ensuring clarity is maintained.

(Arr Melissa, making a clear case for calm and easing tensions – take a breath and we're back in the room. It is a relief, sometimes I wonder if it's just me, to read Melissa's concerns for how damaging the constant involvement of Smitch Law and Mrs Mason have been, and their attempts to manipulate me and my children's residency.)

Smitch to me

31 March

We refer to our letter to you dated 3ʳᵈ March and your response to our client dated 30ᵗʰ March (copy attached).

Our client is most concerned that she has not yet received the undertaking requested from you, as to exactly when you will be returning from Disneyland with the children and that you will be returning Hayley's passport to our client so that she can then take the children on holiday approximately two days later.

Our client has already confirmed to you that she will be leaving for her holiday with the children on 17ᵗʰ April returning late on 24ᵗʰ April or the early hours of the 25ᵗʰ April. Our client would like to take one of the six nights she is owed to keep the children overnight on 25ᵗʰ April and return them to school on the 26ᵗʰ April.

Our client understands from the children that the trip to Disney is for a week—please confirm.

Our client is now away until Monday 4ᵗʰ but wishes to reassure you that she wants the children to go on the holiday to Disney and will provide you with Hayley's passport early next week, provided the undertaking sought in this letter has been received.

So Smitch Law's client is on holiday; Ms Hyde knew all of my holiday arrangements as we had discussed it on the phone and I had written to her. Anyway, if I do not tell their client what day we arrive back, and if I do not confirm, Ms Hyde and Smitch Law are suggesting, what? That Ms Hyde will not hand over Hayley's passport and therefore prevent not only Hayley from going on holiday, but the whole family – as we would not be going if Hayley was not on board.

Hayley had asked her mother for her passport herself, as she was excited and had it on her list of things to pack. As Hayley knows it is part of going abroad, yet again, she saw her mother withholding something that was hers and that she needs for her holiday, without any reason.

Hayley was upset and could not understand why her mother wanted to continue to cause trouble; we are now at the mercy of Ms Hyde's reliability, with three days on the countdown. Meanwhile, I'm being accused of withholding the children's passports, preventing them from going on holiday with their mother, in the future, when that is what Ms Hyde is doing right now.

This is the same behaviour I experienced living with someone who has bipolar disorder – Ms Hyde goes to Smitch Law with her own manifested version of the situation, and puts the blame on anything to justify her position.

Melissa's request to 'stop continued allegations and attempts to litigate by correspondence', is disregarded, and Smitch ploughs on regardless. Surely, Smitch Law must conduct themselves in compliance with honesty, morals and standards, in their duty to their client and the *children* involved, as this is *family* law?

Throughout, Smitch Law have acted like a divorce lawyer, wherein it is all about gathering possessions and maximizing their client's gains, but this is children's matters, and they are not objects to be bartered about. In truth, they aren't even benefitting their client, as Ms Hyde has no need for solicitor involvement – I have no interest in stopping the children from seeing her, to go on holiday or otherwise.

Letter to Ms Hyde

3 April

As discussed, Hayley, Alice, Lara and myself will be going on holiday to Disneyland Paris on the 7th of April. We are due back on the 13th April.

I shall ensure that my mobile phone is switched on, following the court appointed days, Thursday 7th and Monday 11th between 6pm and 8pm. I believe that Hayley and Alice are taking their mobiles and as normal you can phone them as you please.

Yours sincerely…

From Mr MP

6 April

Dear Mr Marlo,

Thank you for your account of the experiences of your children and yourself, particularly in the way in which 'the system' failed for some period of time. It is a great relief and joy that it did eventually come to the correct conclusion, though I fully appreciate the pain this has left.

As mentioned, when my secretary, Beverly, spoke to you, please find enclosed a copy of the letter I received from BBC Radio 4 who are searching for cases of injustice or wrong–doing. It may be that your experiences may be helpful to their programme.

With a General Election now called, there are no MPs until after then. Though I am unable to act on your behalf during this period, hopefully all goes well then, I would like to be kept updated of your situation and any way in which I may assist further.

All the best to you and your daughters.

Yours sincerely…

Dear Mr Rowe,

Would you like to help with a new series of Face the Facts, Radio 4's award winning investigative programme presented by John Waite?

We're on the look–out for cases which might merit further scrutiny and highlight areas of injustice or wrong–doing. In the past, some of our best programmes have come from suggestions made by Members of Parliament. It might be that you have a constituent who's been raising concerns, or a group of people who've come to you with an issue which needs highlighting. Or you might have local or national suspicions about companies, policies, trends or practices which you think we should investigate.

We're keen to develop ideas now for transmission in our summer series and look forward to hearing from you. The last series included an investigation into an evangelical church offering so called miracle births; a programme highlighting an agency exploiting overseas nurses coming here to carry out NHS work; a report on suspicious deaths at an army base and an expose of the terror tactics employed by animal rights extremists.

If you can help, please e–mail us.

Yours sincerely,

Disney!

7-13 April

This is the first proper family holiday we have had since the family court process began.

We stayed in the Goofy themed ranch hotel – everyone was up and ready to go for when the horses and donkeys were led around in the mornings.

It was a really fun time, and a break we all sorely needed.

From the Council

12 April

Dear Mr Marlo,
FREE SCHOOL MEALS
We understand that your circumstances with regard to your entitlement to Child Tax Credits changed with effect from 12/04/05 and must therefore advise you that your children are no longer entitled to receive Free School Meals and you must pay for any school meals taken after this date.

Since the investigation into who is entitled to Child Tax Credits, and after sending my financial details and proof of sole residency, I received a letter on the 15th of March, stating the evidence I provided was not sufficient to prove I was in receipt of CTC – as a result, I now find that I am no longer entitled to free school meals for Alice and Lara. I do believe the people making these decisions should think about what position people are in to begin with, to be requesting free school meals for their children.

(It is another expense I will attempt to work more to budget for, but it brings back memories of standing in the Post Office and being told I had to handover the child benefit book along with my milk tokens for Lara, because, due to a counter claim by Ms Hyde, they had been cancelled.)

BBC Radio 4

14 April

Would you please look through my compiled documents and consider the instability placed in the lives of three children and their family by the court system.

My family's case is an example of the needless and detrimental attitude that is having a far reaching and damaging effect on the stability and welfare of children within our communities.

May I thank you for telephoning me on Wednesday 13th April. I have enclosed my letter sent to Mr Rowe MP, which details the harassment and pressure placed in our lives as a family.

In my case, the Family Court System, and certain individuals working within it, have abused the ethical code and their position; their behaviour and performance has quite clearly failed three children.

I do hope that you consider our case worthy of your programme and understand the injustices that have occurred. Perhaps with accountability of the wrong-doings, meaningful changes can be made for the benefit of people across the country.

I do not know why a system that proclaims honesty, morals and standards let my family down in this way, but I do not believe our case is an exception – apart from the fact I have extensively documented the entire shameful process.

Yours sincerely…

Melissa to me

15 April

Further to our conversation today, please find enclosed a copy of the two faxes that I received from Mrs Mason, together with a copy of my letter in response.

Whilst writing, I also confirm that you will need to collect the children on 25ᵗʰ April at the bottle bank.

15 April

We refer to previous correspondence and in particular with regard to our client's holiday contact with the children, which commences tomorrow.

Our client is asking that your client arrange to deliver Hayley's passport to this office by 2pm today in order that there is no further confrontation between our clients tomorrow.

Our client instructs us that she will be returning during the early hours of 25ᵗʰ April and as such she would like to keep the children overnight until 26ᵗʰ April when she would return the children to school.

We have considered the court order of 6ᵗʰ August 2004 and would refer you to paragraph 4 of that Order which provides for handover in relation to holidays to be at 6pm if the holiday consists of an even number of days.

Our client instructs us that she has not invoked this part of the order, but will be doing so now.

We will be writing to you further with regards to the other issues that you have raised in earlier correspondence but please confirm by return that your client will drop Hayley's passport to these offices by 2pm and that the handover for the children will be on 25ᵗʰ April at 6pm at the bottle bank.

Yours sincerely,

Sometimes it appears that court orders are written under the influence of an astrological soothsayer; hand over time is 6pm if a holiday has even days, and what if it is odd? It is so unnecessarily complicated, insisted by someone who cannot handle complications.

Mrs Mason continues to show her professional prowess within the field and the children's passports can be found at the offices of Smitch Law in the future – I cannot be trusted with the children's passports, but I can be trusted with the responsibility of caring for the children…

Will there ever be a court order and residency schedule that Smitch Law and Mrs Mason, on behalf of their client, could not manipulate or mishandle?

They have managed to find a new thing to pick at, to waste months on unnecessary letters, Legal Aid and their purse are back on the scene, for something that isn't an issue. Despite knowing that we as two parents, and our children, need normality, routine and to settle down as a family.

How have I got into this position?

For some reason, Ms Hyde wants to make an issue about Hayley's passport, so, here's Mrs Mason, ready to throw down the accusation of there being some kind of altercation should Ms Hyde and I meet. I'm all for avoiding confrontation but Mrs Mason is interfering and meddling when there is no need – is it possible for solicitors to advise their client to listen and communicate, rather than alternating between allegations and demands?

Through her solicitor letters, Mrs Mason's attitude has almost brought me to my knees before, and I was sure I would not let it happen again... All parents have to organise situations, and these should not be unnecessarily lorded over by solicitors. Mrs Mason should not be involved in what is a matter of passing a passport to each other.

If on the other hand, Mrs Mason had any evidence that I am spiteful and vindictive, or proof that, unlike what had been agreed, I will not handover Hayley's passport or will abuse Ms Hyde (thus ruining my children's holiday with their mother, upsetting my relationship with them and bringing more strife into my life – than I already have - from Ms Hyde) I would expect many letters of condemnation and demands from Mrs Mason, court applications and hearings – all quite understandable and justifiable.

Repeatedly, Smitch Law refuse to give me the credit of a decent parent and have never written to me in a respectful way; it is always threats, false allegations and contradictory demands. They refuse to accept that I am a responsible father of three children, or acknowledge the impact Ms Hyde's mental health condition has, as her mood and judgment fluctuates. After four years of duty to their client, might it not be time for a different approach?

No, it is evident they have no interest in not being involved and, as in the past, they always find a reason to act on Ms Hyde's demands.

15 April

We refer to your fax dated 15th April, upon which we have obtained our client's instructions.

We confirm that our client will not be delivering Hayley's passport to your office by 2pm today as Mr Marlo has confirmed that the passport will be with Hayley tomorrow morning when the children are dropped off at the bottle bank, and he contends your client always knew this would be the case, as he is quite happy for the children to have a nice holiday with their mother.

With regards to your client keeping the children overnight until 26th April, our client has confirmed that he would like to stick to the court order of 5th August 2004, upon which he will be expecting to pick the children up at 6pm 25th April at the bottle bank.

We should be grateful if you could let your client know, and confirm in writing to us by return that your client is happy to comply with our client's request.

15 April

Thank you for your fax dated 15th April.

We can confirm that we have advised our client that your client will deliver Hayley's passport to her tomorrow, when the children are dropped off for the commencement of contact.

Our client will hand the children back to your client on the 25th April at 6pm at the bottle bank.

What is going on?

10/11 May

10th

I received a phone call from Social Services; the woman introduced herself as Karen, and stated that Ms Hyde has raised several concerns about Hayley, Alice and Lara to the Children's Mental Health Team. The CMHT have made a referral to Social Services regarding the welfare of all the children within my care and about the behaviour of all three children. I asked if she could explain.

She stated:

(1) 'All three children's behaviour is getting worse.'

(2) 'All three children sleep in the same bedroom.'

(3) 'There have been significant difficulties with managing access and sticking to previously arranged timetables.'

(4) 'Hayley is showing signs of distress and this is evident in Hayley's changing and aggressive behaviour.'

Karen went on to say, 'I understand that you are sharing access of your children at the moment.'

Dumbfounded by Ms Hyde's other allegations, I snapped back to reality and replied that I have had sole residency of our children since August 2004, and Ms Hyde has our children every other weekend and for half the school holidays.

I do not understand why Social Services would not be aware of the custody and residency of three young children who sadly have been involved with them before.

By her own reckoning, personality, effort and courage, Hayley is not at all violent in her nature; Hayley has overcome the pressure, instability and injustices that have been unfairly placed within her childhood, and is overall a happy and kind person. I have witnessed what Hayley has been through and I am very proud of her for not allowing the sadness inherent from her experiences to change her outlook on her life and life itself.

Alice is enjoying her last year at primary school and is a social, confident and witty child – there is no evidence that her behaviour is bad, let alone getting worse. Despite many sad and difficult years, Alice has an outgoing and loving personality.

I feel totally hurt that anyone (Ms Hyde) could imply that Lara is trouble at all – I have never seen Lara's behaviour change from being happy and polite, with a calm and understanding nature. Lara is lively and bright, despite years of upset in her life; she enjoys learning and going to school, and is liked by all the teachers and her peers.

Karen from Social Services ended the call by stating that she would like to interview Hayley, Alice and Lara at their schools on Friday.

There was nothing I could say in return. I am not opposed to Social Services or any children's organisation contacting me or the children; I have nothing to hide and am proud of the parent I try my best to be, but I do nonetheless believe that the false allegations Ms Hyde puts forth about me, only results in further abnormality in the children's lives.

One phone call to the schools, and the children's disposition and current situation could have been verified, which would have also shed light on Ms Hyde's false accusations.

(I feel like it is often forgotten that while everything occurring in the background has been having an effect, within the Family Courts, social services and so on, we are still just a family, with three children who are growing up, going through the universal highs and lows like everyone else.)

I phoned Melissa and explained to her the disbelief and shock I felt after receiving Social Services' call. I stated that Alice has her SATS on Friday and she needs to be settled and calm – not have thoughts of Social Services on her mind.

If Social Services do not know that children are doing their SATS this week, I would suggest that they do their homework, and unless there is evidence of mental or physical abuse, they should not interfere.

Melissa stated that she would phone Social Services and follow up on the details of the referral.

11th

Melissa phoned and explained that Social Services were informing me first and then contacting the schools; they have agreed to talk to Mr Church before requesting to talk to the children.

Social Services have not confirmed this to me and, once again, without Melissa following up, would I have been told what is going on with my children?

Schooling

26 May

I received a call from Mrs Sparrow, Hayley's assistant Head of House from Northview Grove, who stated that after an interview with Ms Hyde, it has been decided that Hayley may benefit from counselling at an organisation named 'Yes'. I asked Mrs Sparrow if Hayley was doing ok at school, as I hadn't noticed any changes at home.

Mrs Sparrow stated that she has Hayley for one class and believes she is acting like a normal 13-year-old, but Ms Hyde informed her that Hayley needs help coping with the loss of her great grandmother. (Pincher.)

Not believing that but deciding to move on, I asked why I was not informed of Ms Hyde's meeting, concerning the mental stability of our daughter, to which Mrs Sparrow replied that when Ms Hyde came into the school, she informed her 'Mr Marlo could not make it'.

Ms Hyde did not inform me of her appointment at Northview Grove and I was totally unaware that she thought Hayley was affected by her great grandmother dying; I believe that Hayley and I have a good relationship, where she is comfortable sharing her problems with me.

(I didn't want to press the issue for Hayley, but feel I would be failing as a dad to not check in, if she is upset or not doing well.)

Later that day I asked Hayley if she's doing alright in herself and Hayley replied, 'Yeah.' We talked a little about school and her friends, and I asked if there was anyone she wanted to talk to, like she had in the past, about what is going on. Hayley's nose scrunched up, 'What, like social services?'

I said, 'No, counselling, Mrs Sparrow called today and it was mentioned.'

Hayley replied that she doesn't need to talk to anyone right now and, despite my lack of mention, that she does not know what her mother is talking about.

Dear Melissa – Ms Hyde's Behaviour

28 May

I feel that I must write to you once again with deep concern for my three daughters.

On one hand, Social Services felt it necessary to contact me and propose interviewing my children within three days, and on the other hand, I asked Mr Church, of Riverbank Primary School, yesterday, if Social Services had been in contact, and he replied they had not.

I have experienced, been told and read the nightmare stories of Social Services' inability to act in the appropriate manner, letting down children and families.

The mental pressure and harassment that Ms Hyde cultivates is disgraceful, unnecessary and totally detrimental to our children's wellbeing.

It concerns me to think that Northview Grove were quite happy for Hayley to receive counselling, at the behest of Ms Hyde's perceived sadness in Hayley, when neither Hayley, the school nor I see her having any problems. This is confirmed by the fact the school have never contacted me with concerns for Hayley's emotional or educational wellbeing, and have said the counselling is at Ms Hyde's request.

Yours sincerely…

Dean Marlo

To Ms Hyde

20 June

Please find enclosed, the schedule for 2005/2006. If you have any requests to exchange a weekend, would you please put this in writing and I shall be happy to look into it.

Riverbank School have a non–pupil day on the 11th July. I will meet Alice and Lara at the bottle bank at 12pm on that Monday.

As discussed, I have relayed your contact numbers on Alice's registration form for Northview Grove.

Yours sincerely…

Milestone: Alice goes to Northview Grove

September

Amid all that has gone on, somewhere in there I am also simply a parent, proud of my little girl growing up.

Alice was a bit unsure about Northview, as some of her friends were going to Horizon Academy, a different feeder school. Unfortunately, while I was willing to talk to Alice more about where she wanted to go, Alice told me that her mother had told her, 'Northview is where you are going.'

It was a surprise and another bout of sadness that during the conversation with Alice, Hayley had admitted that she would have rather gone to Horizon Academy, as some of her friends also did, and that it was mostly at her mother's insistence that she went along with Northview Grove. I asked why she hadn't mentioned it to me, as I would have supported her. Horizon Academy is a few neighbourhoods over from Northview, but it would work out about the same to drive there. Sighing, Hayley said that their mother had already been giving her so much grief over going to Northview, she just didn't want to make things worse.

(I will always be frustrated by Ruth's attitude. Horizon ranks higher than Northview in our area, and is the other main school Riverbank feeds to. As far as I can see, Ruth wanted Hayley to go to Northview, and similarly Alice, so she no longer has to get up for the school run. Once Lara is of age, Ruth will be able to wave the responsibility entirely by insisting Lara goes to Northview; it is selfish when this should be about our children's wishes and futures.)

Luckily, Alice is the kind of person that people flock to, and although she is at times shy, she gets along with others easily. She also has her own mobile and, if going by the number of times she's appeared at my elbow to ask to top her phone up, she can still talk to and organise to meet her friends that are going to Horizon.

It's a proud moment, but it also brings a slight wave of sadness over me. Ruth has wasted so much of my life with my children, and as two out of three are now in secondary school… All the special times we had together while the children were young and the opportunities to do more, slip away so quickly.

Nearly had a heart-attack

1 December

I booked a go karting party for Lara's 8th birthday, everything was going great; Lara had been around the track and *loved it.*

Next thing I know, Lara's collapsing down the fire escape after going out for some air, and I felt my entire stomach drop with her.

An ambulance was called, Lara hit her head on the first step and slipped through the handrail to the ground below. I held her and she was conscious but making no sense — Hayley and Alice crowded around and we awaited the ambulance.

The paramedic lifted Lara up and transported her to the gurney; Hayley and Alice wanted to come with us but only one person was allowed in the back of the ambulance.

Lara was, is, fine and she was diagnosed low blood pressure which led to her passing out, and the fall had left her with a slight concussion. Once she was settled into a hospital bed, I let out the breath I felt like I'd been holding since the sickening moment she went ragdoll. Lara had to be woken every two hours but she is *alright.*

I knew I had to inform Ruth, however, I couldn't use my mobile in the hospital and I felt unable to leave Lara's side.

Rob, my brother, drove Hayley, Alice and Ma up to the hospital and as soon as they arrived, I left Lara to phone Ruth. I told her what had happened as well as that Lara was ok. She yelled down the phone about my lack of care, for my horrible idea to take Lara go-karting and so on. I informed her the visiting hours end at 4pm, and that I was going to stay with Lara overnight in the hospital. Ruth hung up.

Ma, Hayley and Alice had kindly gathered the presents Lara's friends had brought to the go-karting centre and arranged them around the bottom of Lara's bed for her to see when she woke up. We all shared a hug, then Ma, Hayley and Alice left with Rob, who gave them a lift home, with Ma staying overnight to look after them.

Ruth arrived at 10pm and stayed for 15 minutes before she was asked to leave.

2006

Business

8 January

Simon and I have happily worked together for the past two years, and he gained a lucrative contract with a large housing association to fix solar panels onto many of their properties. Simon explained he was interested in specialising in the industry, as the work appears to be ongoing, with few competitors offering the services. He asked if I wanted my company back, because he intends to start a new business that solely fits solar panels.

I was thrilled and never envisaged getting my company back. Feeling excited and confident that this was the beginning of a Good Thing™, I looked forward to regaining my financial position, which would only benefit the children and us as a family.

Simon and I sat down, went through and completed the process of changing the company's details, ownership of the company, appointing myself new company director and ownership of the company's assets i.e. one car and one 2 year old van on hire purchase.

When I informed the children we would be getting a nicer car and van, they couldn't wait to go out for a drive. I had visions of family holidays and days out, and generally just enjoying being a family.

Simon will always remain a good friend, and we agreed to meet up when we get a chance.

Mother's contact weekend

20 January

During Ruth's weekend contact, between 7 and 8pm, I received a distressing call from Hayley; both Hayley and Alice were crying and stated that they were walking home, having left their mother's. I told them to stay where they were and I would come and pick them up.

Hayley and Alice had red blotchy faces and eyes puffed up, they were both sobbing and looked dreadful, to the degree where I had to stop the car and get in the back to give them a hug.

Alice told me that she was jumping on an indoor trampoline and calling her mother a 'ditcher' for going on holiday to Australia with her boyfriend, Bernard, and not being here for several of their weekend contacts. Both Hayley and Alice said that Hayley hadn't joined in with Alice, although she agreed.

Alice stated that Bernard, rushed up to her and shoved her chest sending her across the room, landing on the floor.

Hayley had been sitting on the settee and watched it happen. Then Ruth turned to Hayley, grabbed her arm and started to drag her off the settee, telling her to 'get out'. Alice ran up the stairs to her bedroom, their mother let go of Hayley and followed behind Alice, shouting 'get out of my house'.

Hayley watched Bernard go up the stairs and could hear Alice screaming, 'Get out of my room!'

Hayley went to help Alice. Bernard was standing by Alice's bed and her mother was struggling with Alice on the ground, trying to prevent Alice from using her mobile. Alice was screaming at both their mother and Bernard to get out of her bedroom.

When Hayley went to get their mother off Alice, Bernard told their mother to leave them and go back downstairs.

Their mother stood up, and said, 'I want both of you out of my house! Go on get out! Have your fucking father deal with you!'

(Lara heard the whole incident, as did the neighbours, but stayed in a separate room and did not leave with Hayley and Alice.)

Horrified at yet another episode of unacceptable abuse, I asked Hayley and Alice if they wanted to report what happened; they said yes, and I drove us to the police station to report the incident.

Of course, I want to ask Bernard what right he had to use physical force on my daughter… However, I do not want to be involved in Ruth's life, we are separated and my only interest is our children. As usual, I have to rely on the system to do the right thing.

At the police station, we were asked to wait in a room; after an hour, I went back to the reception to ask when my children were going to be seen, and the officer stated that they were trying to organize for a female police officer to speak to them.

(I tried not to think about Lara, who just doesn't want to cause trouble. I understand her not coming with Hayley and Alice, however it still doesn't feel good to know she is on her own with her mother, when Ruth is in this state of mind. Lara's never said her mother gets as cross with her as she does Hayley and Alice, but I worry. It is also upsetting that Ruth will no doubt use Lara remaining with her as evidence that Hayley and Alice are liars, or that I'm coaching them – and the cycle begins anew.)

Another fifteen minutes later, two male officers came into the room, apologising that no female officers were available. They listened to and re–assured Hayley and Alice but said, regarding Bernard – which really, isn't the whole of it – 'It will be his word against your word'. The officer said, 'Have a think over the weekend, give us a ring on Monday and if you still feel it is necessary, we will have a chat with him.'

It didn't feel adequate, but the girls were exhausted, upset and wanted to go home.

I thought about the situation and discussed with Hayley and Alice what they wanted to do. I didn't believe that the incident should be brushed aside and Hayley and Alice were adamant that Bernard had pushed Alice, so I called the police station on the Monday morning and asked to speak to the officers who were involved; the receptionist stated that both officers were off-duty until Wednesday.

A letter from Ruth

22 January

Dear Dean,

Please find listed below the dates and telephone numbers for when I am away in case of any emergencies with the children.

I fly out to Australia on the 25th January 2006 and will return late on the 11th February.

As discussed on numerous occasions since the end of November, 5th January and most recently today, I am very disappointed that Hayley's passport has not been renewed. I have had many conversations with you on this subject where you have said that you will renew it or give it to me so that I can. You are well aware that it expires in March and that I wished to book a holiday in advance in January for a break in the Easter holidays. It is obvious that Hayley cannot travel without a passport. By refusing Hayley a new passport you are denying us all a family holiday. The holiday should already have been booked and if it is not booked within the next few weeks then it will become too expensive for me to travel. As you know, I always book my holidays early so that it is affordable for me.

Will you please confirm to me that you will either renew the passport and give it to me to enable me to book, or give the old passport to me to enable me to renew it.

I am further disappointed that over the last few weeks you refuse to speak to me on the phone and insist on making Alice mediate for you, and also that when I do try to discuss any issues with you that you hang up. None of the children should be involved with issues that concern arrangements between the two of us.

I would appreciate a reply to this letter in no later than 14 days.

Yours sincerely,

There is some confusion here, as Ruth already has the children's passports, being the last person to take them on holiday abroad in 2005. I have repeatedly informed Ruth that I will be happy to get a new passport for Hayley, but she has Hayley's old one and I need it for the application.

As always, I try my best to communicate with Ms Hyde and had thought things were largely going smoothly, but I admit that when she becomes verbally abusive on the phone, I do not endure her tirades. The problem with talking to Ruth is that because of her mental health condition, she will manifest ideas and scenarios that simply aren't true, such as that I have Hayley's passport, and is convinced, will scream until she is red in the face, that this is fact.

To clear some of the debts I had accumulated, I took out a loan for £5000. When planning on taking the loan out, I included a holiday for the children. They deserved a break, and what better than a snowy escape?

I informed Ruth that I am going to book a skiing holiday with the children for the beginning of February, as I was unable to now book it within the half term.

(At around 3 am, I heard the letterbox flap and went to the door to find Hayley's old passport had been pushed through. In the morning I sent it off to be renewed.)

Letter from Ruth

24 January

Dear Dean,

I have decided that the safest place for Alice and Lara's passports is for them to be kept with my solicitor. That way, if there is any kind of accident or event that either delays or prevents my return you will know where they are.

In future, if all passports are kept with the solicitor, then they are readily accessible as soon as either of us wishes to travel. If they are always returned after use there can be no problem with either of us booking holidays.

Yours sincerely,

Ruth and Bernard are taking a two–week holiday to Australia and my children's passports will be with Smitch Law. What sort of parents are we, where one would withhold and therefore prevent the other from taking the children on holiday? There's no evidence I have ever been like this, yet the reason Smitch Law are still involved, and by the looks of it will be until Lara is 16, is because Ruth is manipulating the situation through her solicitor.

As far as the court order is concerned, we as parents should be able to handle passport handovers, because it's never been an issue, and what can I say in the face of my children's passports being kept with a solicitor rather than their mum or dad? It again undermines and condemns my involvement as my children's father, as though I am either a criminal or a heartless bastard or both, where Ruth can get away with implying it.

The mental erosion continues, with another baseless demand that seeks to discredit my ability to be a responsible parent. I am made to feel like a criminal, a rotten father.

(Is this normal, or am I just fucking abnormal?)

To the schools – time off

25 January

Dear Mr Church/Mrs Tran,

I am writing to ask if Lara/Hayley and Alice may be absent from school on the 6th February / 10th February 2006. I apologise for requesting the days of school.

If you have any questions concerning the above please do not hesitate to contact me.

Thank you for your attention with this matter.

Yours sincerely…

Northview about Alice

26 January

Dear Mr Marlo,
Lateness; Alice Marlo, 7OK
I would like to make you aware that Alice has received a late mark in the register on 5 occasions since the start of term. This persistent lateness can only be detrimental to Alice's education, causing a disrupted start to the day for your daughter's whole tutor group and often results in important information about forthcoming events being missed during tutorial time or assembly. I have enclosed a copy of the pattern of lateness.
11-11-05 – PM – Late
21-11-05 – PM – Late
09-12-05 – AM – Late
16-12-05 – AM – Late
19-12-05 – PM – Late
I would like to ask for your support in encouraging your daughter to adhere to the school rules with regard to time keeping so as to ensure they do not receive more late marks in the register.
If the lateness continues, I will have no alternative but to refer Alice to the Education Welfare Officer as it is considered an unauthorised absence for that part of the day that has been missed.
Yours sincerely,

I had a talk with Alice about punctuality and, as it is a new term, I said if she curbs her lateness she can pick out a new mobile phone for her birthday.

Skiing Holiday

6 – 10 February

Despite her letter claiming she was leaving Alice and Lara's passports at Smitch Law's offices, I was informed by Mrs Hart that Ruth had dropped them into reception.

Prior to Ruth going to Australia, I informed her that we would all have our mobiles with us on holiday to France, as we normally would at home. Ruth still hasn't phoned the children or my mobile.

Hayley has a fear of flying, like I do, but said I make her feel safe, and by holding her hand, it made me feel better too as the plane dipped. Alice doesn't like flying either, but managed ok and Lara, who describes the best bit as the take-off and landing because it's like a rollercoaster, enjoyed herself immensely.

The children and I have had loads of fun on the Alps and, as predicted, they are far more adept at skiing than I am - I found myself in the 'better off watching' class.

Consequences

14 February

On Ruth's return from holiday, both Hayley and Alice have refused to go to hers for the contact weekend, due to Bernard pushing Alice and their mother grabbing Hayley, which they are both still hesitant and upset about. Lara has continued contact as per the order; I never feel easy about Lara going by herself to her mother's, but what can I do, as long as Lara wants to go? While Lara didn't witness the incident, she did hear it all kicking off and things escalating, which I believe Lara has normalised, as her mother has never handled disagreements calmly.

Lara has said to me before, that she is aware that as long as she is getting on quietly with what she's doing, her mother is less likely to become enraged. I also believe it is clear to see, whereas both Hayley and Alice at the same age were already engaging in arguments with their mother, Lara removes herself from the room and avoids the confrontation. Whilst I firmly do not place any blame on Hayley and Alice, as they are both growing children, with Ruth's short fuse and muddled state of mind at times, it certainly does not help home life for anyone.

I phoned Mr Ellwood from Cafcass and explained the situation. I took his advice on board and tried to encourage Hayley and Alice, by suggesting they start off with just having dinner at their mother's. However, they both stated they wanted reassurances from their mother, but she has denied both her own and Bernard's behaviour.

I do not want to break the court order but understand Hayley and Alice's reasons for not wanting to go for contact at the present time.

Knowing full well, when headed back into the Family Courts, I will be made to feel like I am a criminal for standing by my children and not invalidating their feelings or wellbeing, again I await Smitch Law's padded envelope to hit the doormat, with false allegations and threats of penal notice applications. A highly paid barrister will present a very convincing case to the judge about how I am preventing the children from having contact with their mother, the judge will then stare wildly in my direction, and agree with their learned friend.

It appears to be easier to scorn a father, in order to ignore the elephant in the room, and this has always been Ruth's severity of bipolar, which has a direct effect on the person she is day by day.

Throughout, the Family Courts have shown they do not know how to deal with a family wherein the father is not the problem – it cannot be solved by arresting father, or removing his contact with his children; if it is not a father being the aggressor or the one who is physically violent, they have no inclination on how to proceed, despite the answer being very simple: to get Ms Hyde support. Their actual intentions have always been to return the children to their abuser and potentially abusive household, which can only be seen as shameful hypocrisy when we are dealing with children's welfare.

Smitch Law pursing Ms Hyde's applications is another example of a disgraceful moral compass, and needless interference. The children refusing contact with their mother due to an abusive incident (which, given the chance, would resolve with time, as the children mend their relationships, and could be avoided with outside monitoring of Ms Hyde's mental health) or the children wanting more contact with their mother (if they wish, and as I have never stopped them from doing), needn't be written into the court order – it should be accepted as the children's current feelings, with a view to abide by the residence schedule, if appropriate.

Contact

3 March

After having phone contact with Ruth, it was arranged for Hayley and Alice to go round their mother's for a couple of hours; I dropped Hayley and Alice off at 6pm.

Within one hour, Alice phoned me to come and get her, after she had a falling out with her mother.

Hayley stayed until 8pm, when I picked her up as arranged.

Tea, after school

15 March

On Wednesday, Ruth called asking if I would drop Hayley, Alice and Lara to her for tea after school. I agreed and dropped them off at 5pm and picked them up at 8pm.

Later, Ruth phoned and spoke to Hayley, Alice and Lara. (Hayley explained after that her mother was going to a party and was asking if they would like to go.) Hayley told her mother that it was fine, and that she and Alice will see her Saturday morning instead; I heard Hayley say they were not coming until lunch time, and state that both she and Alice had things to do on Friday.

Ruth demanded to speak to me, hurling abuse about Hayley and Alice not coming to hers for the weekend. I asked Ruth to hold on and asked Hayley and Alice if they were sure they did not want to go on Friday after school; they both replied 'no'.

Ruth continued on the phone, insisting that we have always swapped Mother's Day weekend. Despite knowing that would go in one ear and out the other, I replied that I have no problem with her having the children, but it is up to them if they wish to go. She hung up.

Dean Marlo

Another letter from Ruth and my reply

17 March

Dear Dean,

It is with regret that I have to write this kind of letter again concerning contact.

Since you have had full custody, eighteen months now, I do not have much time to spend with the children and the time I do have is precious and shouldn't be minimised by yourself.

When I was away in Australia and you had an extra contact weekend, I asked you for a weekend in return anytime between then and the end of December 06 and you said to me that you had things planned on every weekend; I find this very hard to believe.

Also concerning my trip to Australia, I gave you a letter informing you of the dates when I was travelling, contact number and email address in case of an emergency. Whilst I was away, you took the children out of school for a week and out of the country for a week's skiing holiday and didn't tell me. I think it is perfectly reasonable for you to inform me if you are travelling abroad with the children. I have always taken the trouble to do so and we have always called you on arrival. You knew well before I left for Australia that you would be going skiing.

You also did not encourage the children to come to see me for my half of half term. Only Lara came so you had extra contact time with Hayley and Alice.

There is now another contact weekend 18/19th March which as per the schedule (court order for alternate weekend contact) should be my contact weekend. You have said that the children won't be coming, this is unrelated to the following Mother's Day weekend yet you seem to be using this as an excuse for not letting me see the children two weekends in a row.

As previously discussed, I said to you that I would like Friday 24th as an extra contact night as I am going away with the children for the weekend. I didn't expect that you would decide that I should lose the previous weekend in order for me to enjoy Mother's Day weekend. In the past, if Father's Day has fallen on one of my weekends, I have always assumed that you would have contact with the children, including the night, in addition to the court schedule.

Recently, it was Hayley's birthday and this year she should have been with me yet you again decided that instead of coming from school on Friday, she would be with you and I collect her in the morning. When I came to collect her, you had gone to work and your mother was babysitting.

It seems that all too regularly you are changing the court order but always in your favour and you seem unable to allow even one swapped weekend but always retain extra time for yourself.

The Easter holidays are only two weeks away and I spoke with you to confirm the dates. You were quite clear that I was having the first week as per the schedule and I asked you several times; yet 2 days later, at 7.10am on 14 March as I was leaving for work you insisted on having a conversation to change the weeks. I have spoken with you in the past and have said that I am quite happy to swop provided I have enough notice. I have to inform my employer in advance when I can and can't work and two weeks is just not enough.

Could you please contact me within the next few days to confirm whether you want to change the schedule? Please let me remind you that any changes to the court order must be put in writing. We need to inform each other of any changes so that we can plan in advance.

48

To Ruth,

As discussed, I agree to exchange Mother's Day weekend 25th/26th for the weekend 18th /19th March.

On the phone, I suggested that you have contact on the weekend 1st /2nd of April, but you have declined.

I shall make the children available on the 10th April at 12pm at the bottle bank.

Yours sincerely,

Dean Marlo

Arrangements

24-26 March

It is as jarring to exist in a state of extremes as it is to read it.

In the past, it is Ruth who has had a problem with Father's Day/Mother's Day arrangements, going from certain hours on the day, to swapping whole weekends, regardless of what she had already argued for in court.

Lara went to Ruth's for the whole weekend; Hayley and Alice went to stay on the Saturday. They called on Sunday to wish Ma a happy Mother's Day and said they were staying overnight at Lindsay's, one of their mother's step-sisters.

From Ruth

29 March

Dear Dean,

Thank you for your hand delivered letter, received Sunday 26th March 6.35pm. The contact weekend was already over.

Re your first paragraph. There was never any discussion to exchange the Mother's Day weekend. As referred to in my previous letter, if Mother's or Father's Day falls upon the other persons non-contact weekend we have always assumed that it is an extra contact night for that person in addition to the court schedule; I have already lost a whole weekend while I was away plus five days during the Christmas holidays.

Re your second paragraph. You rang me at 2pm on 24th March suggesting that I have contact on the following weekend 1st and 2nd April. I have been in my present job for eighteen months and I would like to remind you again that my work schedule operates one to two weeks in advance making it difficult for me to change at such short notice. So, while I appreciated the offer, I would like to make it clear that the weekend was not declined out of choice but due to short term work commitments.

Therefore, I need at least three weeks' notice in future. However, in this instance I have fortunately managed to cancel some of my work and will pick the children up from school as discussed.

Yours sincerely,

Dean Marlo

Ruth's half term contact

8/9 April

8th

Lara has been at her mother's for half term; Hayley and Alice still do not follow contact with her per the order.

It was around 6pm, when Hayley said that her mother had been phoning her several times during the day, asking her and Alice to sleepover, and saying that they would be allowed two friends to stay over as well. Hayley asked if I thought it was a good idea and I said if she'd like to go, she'll have her friends there and if anything happens, she can call me.

Hayley phoned her mother back to say that they were going to come, but first had to pack and walk to meet their friends.

At 7:30pm, Hayley, Alice and friends came through the door and asked if I would drop them off, which I said yes. Hayley's mobile rang and she told her mother that they were on their way now. As I walked out of the front door, my mobile rang. Ruth told me that her house was not a hotel, and she was not happy about them turning up so late.

(What can I do about it, I'm just the driver!)

I told Ruth that I was in the car dropping them off now; Ruth said that it was not good enough and hung up.

I dropped Hayley, Alice and friends to Ruth's, and drove home.

Not long after, I was woken from dozing on the settee by the phone; I answered and it was the police. They said they obtained my number from Ms Hyde and asked if Hayley and Alice were with me; I informed the officer I had dropped the children to their mother's earlier in the evening. The officer stated they received a call from Ms Hyde, who has made allegations that they have been violent towards her and were now missing. I told the officer that I would jump into my car and go and look for them. I took his phone number so that if I found them, I could ring him back.

Whilst I was driving along a route that I thought Hayley and Alice would use, I received a further phone call from the police informing me that Hayley and Alice were back at their mother's. They asked me to park up the road from Ms Hyde's and an officer will come and talk with me.

As I sat in the car, an officer followed by Hayley and Alice came towards me. The officer asked me to take Hayley and Alice home with me as it looked like the issue wasn't going to be resolved, to which I said of course.

Back home, Hayley explained what happened.

They said goodbye to me, knocked on their mother's door and she let all four of them in. Hayley took her bag up to her bedroom and came back, where Alice and their friends were waiting. Their mother was telling Alice that her house isn't a hotel; Hayley took a front door key off the hook and as they started to walk out, their mother asked where they thought they were going.

Hayley replied, 'We are going to the shops for snacks.'

Their mother said, 'You are not going up the shops now.'

Hayley told her mother that she was, her mother asked for the key back and as Hayley said 'no', her mother grabbed her throat by her collar and pulled it together, choking her. Hayley told her mother that she 'could not breathe' and her mother had said, 'Good.'

Her mother put pressure on her neck and took her to the ground. Hayley tried to punch her to get her to let go, and Alice tried to pull her off Hayley. Managing to break her mother's grip on her collar, Hayley pushed herself up and the children *ran* out of her house.

I called the police officer, and relayed what Hayley had told me. They advised me to have Hayley speak to Social Services or Child Legal Guidance.

After comforting Hayley, I had a conversation with her and Alice about the way they spoke to their mother before she hurt Hayley, and that they need to ask before going out, for example.

(I am conflicted, as I think the children knowing that their mother has a mental health condition and being able to understand the reason she reacts certain ways would benefit their relationships overall. However, I don't know how to get the words out right and I think it should be a conversation between Ruth and the children. I'm fully aware that my involvement on the subject would backfire if the children talk to their mother about it and she misinterprets my intention to avoid conflict, as she does with everything else.)

The next day, Hayley told me that she had called CLG about her mother's behaviour.

9th

I got a call from Lara – and was worried that she was in trouble – but instead, Lara excitedly said that her mother had taken her out to get kittens; they had gotten two, but Lara said that her mother has told her one is specifically hers. Lara has named her kitten 'Wotsit' and the other kitten 'Maisy'.

I asked about Wotsit for a few minutes and checked that Lara was ok, after what happened with Hayley. Lara said she had kept out of the way. She had heard her mother downstairs with Bernard all night, but did not see her mother until mid-morning, when she had announced she could get a kitten, 'because I am good girl'.

I said goodbye to Lara and Wotsit, who Lara had brought to the phone; although pleased for Lara to be happy, her mother's manipulation and behaviour overrides any jubilation I feel.

I'm just a kid

As promised, I got Alice a new mobile for her birthday and Lara took Alice's old one, so really there is no longer any need for telephone contact times or for Ruth to call the children through my phone.

Not long ago, Hayley brought home a new friend, Chloe; she is 15 years old, in the year above Hayley at Northview, and was accompanied by three 15–year–old boys. They are all from the local area, apart from one boy who jumps on a bus to school and back again late in the evening.

Hayley and her new friends would come home after school and hang out in her room or play in the garden on the trampoline, and at the weekend they would all go to town and then sleep over.

Chloe and the boys were polite, laughed and messed about for many hours. One day I found cigarette butts thrown down the back of the shed. Having already had the talk about the dangers of cigarettes/nicotine with Hayley, I trusted that she was not doing the smoking. I told Hayley that her friends are all welcome, but I do not want to have them smoking at our home or in our garden. Hayley understood and apologised.

A few weeks passed, and Chloe and the boys stopped coming round. I asked Hayley if everything was ok, and why her friends hadn't been over. Hayley stated that she was still friends with Chloe, but she didn't want to hang around with her.

I believe Hayley had felt the pressure from the new environment granted by older friends and how they behaved; smoking and staying out late. I was proud of her for removing herself from the situation, as I know how hard peer pressure can be and it can be a struggle to find a good friend group.

Court Orders

3 May

A representative from Child Legal Guidance came to talk to Hayley and Alice about changing the existing court order. Hayley and Alice would like off the court order entirely, with the view of remaining in my full custody, and being able to choose when they go to their mother's.

Parenting

13/14 May

I have booked a holiday to Disney for the 12th of August; I hope it is something we can all look forward to in the summer.

Alice came into the kitchen and asked if she could go round her new friend's granddad's house to sleepover. (The new friend is Hayley's old friend Chloe, which I have mixed feelings about both as Alice is 3 years younger, and that it is someone Hayley had knocked about with, and that must be weird for her.)

I told Alice that she is 12-years-old and too young to sleepover at a 15-year-olds; Hayley stopped hanging out with Chloe, not that I know the exact reasons but I know Chloe smoked and that's not something Alice needs to be introduced to, and I don't know her granddad at all. As a compromise, I told Alice that I was happy for her and Chloe to sleepover at home. Alice argued the point for 5 to 10 minutes and then stated that she was going to the shops.

While Alice was out, I went to Hayley's bedroom and asked her about Alice wanting to sleepover at Chloe's granddad's. Hayley shook her head and said, 'You know Chloe smokes and takes drugs?'

(Not the drug taking part!)

The surprise must have shown on my face because Hayley explained that's why she stopped hanging out with Chloe.

Hayley told me that she had been invited to one of these sleepovers at Chloe's granddad's and that alcohol and drugs were taken there, which is the reason why Chloe invites her friends to his; her granddad drinks until he falls asleep and has a police tag.

I was slightly shocked at the casual delivery Hayley gave, because although I am not naïve enough to think children at school don't partake in all sorts of things, I didn't realise how close my children were to it. It went without saying, but I made sure to give Hayley a hug and thanked her for being the person she is.

Lara had a friend, Maisy, over to stay the night and they were busy playing in the sitting room. Returning from the shops, Alice started to argue and insist that she was going to this sleepover at Chloe's granddad's. Alice kept walking in and out of the sitting room disrupting Lara and her friend despite me asking her to either invite Chloe here or come and sit down; I believe this was in attempt to make me cave in to her disruptive behaviour for the sake of everyone.

(This is, sadly, a tactic, deployed by a not-even-teenager. If I say 'you can go' it cancels out my previous reasoning and boundaries I've set for her as a parent. However, not letting her go means she continues to talk at me and disturb Lara and Maisy, which doesn't send either of them a positive message.)

I listened to Alice and her attitude for another 10 minutes, and then I told Alice again that she can have Chloe sleepover here or I can drop her home later.

Alice replied, 'Fine, I'm going to my mother's.'

I said to Alice that her mother will not allow her to sleepover with someone that she doesn't know, and that she can't use her mother when I do not allow her to behave as she wants.

Walking out the room, Alice said, 'I don't care,' and phoned her mother. Alice came back into the kitchen and said, 'I am going to my mother's now, she's going to call you.'

As if by magic, my phone rang and I explained to Ruth the situation with Alice. I felt relieved as Ruth agreed that Alice should not be allowed to stay out with Chloe and it was also reassuring that Ruth thought Alice needed to find a different friend group.

We agreed that Alice would stay at hers tonight. Within 10 minutes, without a goodbye, Alice announced that her mother was outside and she was off.

If I had let Alice go to this granddad's for a sleepover, at the age of 12, I would lose any hope of guidance with Alice as she grows up. Alice's perception of herself is already older and more mature than she actually is. I can only hope Ruth is true to her word and doesn't let Alice go.

14th

At around 10am, Lara, Maisy and I were walking into Sainsbury's to do a weekly shop – and maybe get some comics – Alice called my mobile and stated that she was going to stay with her mother until 12pm.

Come 1:30 pm, Maisy had gone home and I tried Alice's and Ruth's phones several times, but no one picked up. Nearly half an hour later, Alice called me to say that she would be home in 20 minutes.

Alice walked through the door at 3.10pm.

I called hello to Alice but she didn't reply; I heard her walk down the hall and I followed as she went into Hayley's bedroom. Alice, out of nowhere, called Hayley a 'twat'. I told Alice not to talk to Hayley like that and to not come home and start trouble; there was simply no need for it. Alice kicked off at Hayley and me. She finished by turning to me and saying, 'What are you going to do about it?'

I told Alice that if she was not prepared to act in a decent and proper way, then she can go to her room and calm down. Alice wandered from room to room and said, 'I might as well go back to my mother's.' Before I could reply, Alice's phone was in her hand and she had called her mother. Moments later, my phone rang. Ruth loudly declared that as I am going to antagonise Alice, she is on her way to collect her. I asked Alice to watch a film with Hayley, Lara and myself but she replied, 'My mother is on her way.'

Although I was hoping Alice would come home, at 7:30 pm Alice called stating that she was going to sleep at her mother's and probably would on Monday night as well. I asked Alice if she would come for a chat after school on Monday; Alice replied, 'Okay.'

9pm, Hayley, Lara and I were all in bed, when I heard the home phone ring. I let it go through to the answer machine as I always take my mobile to bed. Minutes passed; Hayley knocked and came into my bedroom, saying it was her mother on the phone and she had called her mobile to ask her to give me a message. Hayley looked uncomfortable; she said, 'Alice is never coming round again.'

I said to Hayley that I am sorry her mother had called her to say that, and gave her a hug goodnight. I got up and sat in my office. More mind games or a sad bout of pre-teenage rebellion, exacerbated by Alice's realisation and ability to switch homes?

Alice's Schooling

15 May

Monday, I said goodbye to Hayley, dropped Lara to school and headed to work. Northview Grove called and I was told that Alice was late for school; she had come in with Chloe and they both looked tired. I explained that there had been a disagreement and as a result Alice stayed at her mother's over the weekend. I mentioned that I have arranged to talk to Alice after school today about this weekend and keeping to boundaries, and will also reiterate the importance of her being on time for school.

Alice came home after school and we sat in the living room to talk. I said to Alice that I thought it would be a good idea for her to settle down at home and go with Lara this weekend to her mothers, as it is her mother's weekend contact.

Alice stated, 'My mother has said I can live with her if I want to.'

(As I've always said, I will stand by my children's wishes, however it did hurt to hear and so–)

I asked Alice if that is what she wants; Alice shrugged and looked away. Then Alice asked if she could use the phone – I had thought it was strange I hadn't seen her mobile in her hand every 10 seconds – she rang her mother and said, 'I'm ready.'

(This talk was never going to end well, with a prearranged pick-up service if Alice didn't hear what she wanted.)

Feeling sad and knowing that Alice was now giving me the silent treatment, I walked into the garden and sat down, trying to work out what had happened over the past 48 hours. After several minutes, I figured it was worth trying to talk to Alice again, however, as I walked into the hall, Alice came out of her bedroom and stated that she was off. I was half way through 'I love you, Alice' when the front door slammed; no goodbye.

Waiting a few hours, until after dinner, homework and games with Hayley and Lara, I phoned Ruth to discuss Alice's worsening attitude but Ruth cut me off and said, 'It is disgraceful how you have treated Alice and no wonder she does not want to live with you.'

I asked Ruth if she had forgotten why Alice went to hers on Saturday, and reiterated that Alice cannot be able to change residence because she doesn't like a decision either of us makes as responsible parents.

Ruth replied, 'You have been bullying Alice just like you did to me and that is why she does not want to live with you!'

Knowing that refuting her accusations leads nowhere, I said to Ruth that telling Alice she would pick her up from mine today did not help matters, as Alice seemed ready to go from the moment she came in. Alice needs to realise her age – despite the social pressures, the advent of instant messaging and whatever a 'Bebo' is – she is a child and doesn't care about our role as parents to make responsible decisions for her; *she is a child* and therefore cannot do as she wants – particularly when that involves alcohol or drugs!

Ruth denied what I was saying, belittling me in the process, and hung up on me.

Incredulity

17 May

One of Lara's friends' mothers and I arranged for me to take Lara and her daughter to an indoor play centre after school. Just as I was preparing to leave work to ensure I was there on time to collect them, I received a call from Mrs Hart at Riverbank School to say that Lara was not feeling very well and Lara was asking if I could come and get her. Mrs Hart also stated that Ms Hyde had tuned up at school and was not so politely requesting that I meet her in Mr Church's office to discuss vague sounding 'matters'.

I told Mrs Hart I would be there for Lara but that I would schedule with Mr Church to discuss what points Ms Hyde has raised. I was not prepared to be summoned by Ms Hyde to be eviscerated in front of Mr Church, as I believe anything to do with Alice and what is going on with Ms Hyde, has no relevance to him or Lara at Riverbank.

Calling Lara's friend's mother, I rearranged going to the play centre for another day.

7:30pm, I tried ringing Alice but she didn't pick up. I called Ruth's phone and asked to speak to Alice but Ruth refused and put the phone down.

I did go and see Mr Church the next day and he told me that Ms Hyde believed Lara is being bullied at home. Seeing my shock and confusion, he reassured me that he had not seen any evidence or changes in Lara's wellbeing or her attitude around school with teachers and friends.

Mrs Mason to me

18 May

We refer to previous correspondence and have been instructed by our client that Alice came to live with her on Saturday 13th May.

We understand that Alice is wishing to remain with our client and our client is happy for Alice to remain with her until matters can be resolved between you.

We have discussed with our client and she has agreed that it would be premature to make an application to the court in respect of the residence of Alice and she would prefer to reassess the situation in a while.

In the meantime, however, our client would be grateful if you would please arrange to ensure that the child benefit book in respect of Alice is given to her so that she is able to claim this while Alice is residing with her.

We would be grateful if you would please respond to this letter as soon as possible.

I paid Ms Hyde the Child Benefit for Alice for this week by cheque, but I am not prepared to contact the Child Benefit Agency until I can talk to Alice properly about where Alice wants to live, because this is, to me, an example of growing up rebellion and not an actual desire to change households.

(Mrs Mason requests I give her client the Child Benefit, and I guess it makes no difference to a self-serving solicitor that her client has paid no maintenance since 2004.

The reality is, if Ms Hyde had been granted sole residency, CSA would have contacted me immediately to ensure I was providing financially for my children, as a father, and back-paid Ms Hyde for any time she was solely taking care of the children prior to the order. It is an expectation for a father to be paying maintenance, yet Ms Hyde can not only avoid paying but also, within days, can use a solicitor, funded by Legal Aid, to request Alice's Child Benefit.)

Smitch are inflammatory as always and should be advising their client to be a parent to Alice and talk to her about her attitude – Alice has not left home due to abuse; I have no problem with Alice living with her mother; I have given Ms Hyde the benefit for Alice and would inform the CSA if Alice wants to make the change permanent.

I have never heard of a solicitor getting involved or being helpful in a child's development and becoming a teenager; parents are there to help guide their children through these changes in their lives, with calm support and trying to keep them on track, even if this appears to be at a distance.

It is upsetting for me to see Alice behaving in this way; she has fallen out with Hayley and Lara for no reason, and it seems so sudden that the situation at home could go from caring to confrontational.

It's that slow erosion again, where I am a person and parent that is going through my own emotional turmoil… If you had asked me six days ago, would Alice act like she has, I would have laughed. I am not laughing now, and have a letter from Mrs Mason to confirm the sad situation I find Alice, myself and our family dynamic in.

From Northview, about Alice

19 May

Dear Mr Marlo,
ACADEMIC DETENTION
Pupil: Alice Marlo, 7OK
Alice has been placed in this detention for the following reason(s), failure to attend a faculty detention on 18ᵗʰ May.
The detention will take place on: Thursday 25ᵗʰ May 2006 at 3:15pm and will last for 45 minutes.

Like a bad penny spins around and around

21/22 May

Sunday 21st

Getting no response on any of the children's mobiles, I tried the home phone but received 10 minutes of verbal abuse from Ruth until I heard Lara in the background asking to talk to me. I told Lara that her rabbit has given birth and we chatted for a bit before Ruth took the phone away. I was mid-way through asking Lara if she wanted to pop in to see them, when Ruth hung up.

Although sad that even happy events have to be abnormal, I accepted the dismissal and got on in the office. Shortly after, Hayley rang and said she had to be quick, as they are not allowed to use the house phone and her mother has taken their mobiles; Hayley told me she loved me and had to go.

Again I'm worried, but I don't see a way of addressing what's going on in my children's lives.

Monday 22nd

I received a call at work from Northview, stating Hayley is unwell and requesting I collect her. I phoned Ma and asked if she was available to come over and be with Hayley, and as she said yes, I left my gear on site and picked Hayley up. Ma arrived shortly after I got Hayley set up on the settee, and I thanked her as I headed back out to work.

At 11 am Ruth left a message on the answer machine stating that Lara is ill, not at school and that she would drop Lara off at the bottle bank at 1pm. Ruth did not phone my mobile, she just left the message on the answer machine; it was only the fact that Hayley was also off school ill, that I received the message from Ma.

I packed up and drove to the bottle bank at 1 pm. Ruth pulled up with Lara. Alice also jumped out of her car; Ruth said that Alice was not feeling well and she wanted to see the baby rabbits. (I'm starting to suspect all three children have caught 'baby rabbit fever' – although they do look tired, perhaps it was another long night.)

Through her car window Ruth stated, 'I will pick Alice up in half an hour.'

On the way home, Alice kept repeating to Lara that the rabbits are hers.

(With bad luck, a house move and illness, plus one from their mother's, the children each having a rabbit somehow ended up with Alice having two rabbits, Sweep and Pippin, in different cages. However, Alice, due to either her age or temperament, lacks the responsibility to care for her pets consistently. I suggested to Alice that if she gave Lara one of her rabbits, then I would only have to moan about her watering, feeding and cleaning out one rabbit; Alice thought it was a good idea. And here we are, now realising Pippin was pregnant.)

I told Alice there are seven babies and they can all enjoy caring for them.

As everyone settled in, Alice walked into the kitchen and announced, again, to Hayley and Lara that all the rabbits are hers. I reminded Alice that she had given Pippin to Lara a month ago, due to not wanting to look after her. It has been Lara and Ma who have cared for both rabbits on many occasions.

Alice walked into the garden to see the rabbits. Hayley, Lara and I had a house meeting and it was decided Alice could have all of the rabbits bar two babies. Neither Hayley nor Lara wanted an argument with Alice; I find it difficult to manage Alice's behaviour as she has a state of extremes – such as calling her mother when I enforce a rule she doesn't like. Without Ruth's support, I fear this will only escalate as Alice grows up.

Alice came back into the kitchen and I told Alice that Hayley and Lara have agreed that she could have all of the rabbits but they are going to choose one each. Alice replied, 'No way! They are all mine!'

Hayley and Lara were saying to Alice, 'That's not fair!'

I told Alice that she can share and will still have five baby rabbits to look after - there is no need for her attitude towards her sisters.

Alice said, 'I don't care, they are mine and I'm having all of them.'

Ending the conversation, Alice took out her phone, dialled her mother, stated 'come now' and walked out of the front door, without saying goodbye.

Ma, Hayley, Lara and I settled back down in the living room. (I couldn't help the feeling that the other shoe was about to drop)

At 3pm, Ruth rang the house phone and asked to speak to Lara. I heard as I passed the phone over Ruth state to Lara that all of the rabbits are going to hers and that the rabbits are Alice's. Lara, bless her, told her mother that the fair thing to do, was for us to keep two of the babies. Ruth repeated that all of the rabbits are coming to hers, that Lara would see them at hers and that she was sure Alice would let her have one.

(Sorry Hayley, it looks like you're not included in this.)

Again, Lara replied surely the best thing to do is for us to just keep two. Ruth told Lara to get me. Lara gave me the phone back.

With a raised voice, Ruth told me, 'The rabbits are Alice's and she has had both of the parent rabbits from birth, so the rabbits are hers. I will be collecting them and Lara can pick one of the babies.'

I told Ruth that Alice had given Lara Pippin as she didn't want the responsibility of looking after her, and how Alice is acting is childish. Ruth stated she would be round at a vague and ominous time 'later' and hung up.

Ma, Hayley, Lara and I were sat down at the dinner table when the phone rang and Hayley got up to answer it. Hayley said, 'We are having tea.' She frowned, then turned to me saying, 'Our mother is coming now to collect the rabbits.'

I requested the phone from Hayley, who gladly gave it up, and told Ruth that she should have given me a time so that we could organise the rabbits. (I'd already conceded the rabbits as the 'other shoe.') Ruth replied that she wanted the rabbits put on my drive and all of Alice's stuff 'right now', and she would also be dropping Hayley's old wooden bunkbed over and will leave it on the drive.

I told Ruth that I would not be breaking Alice's bedroom apart within days of Alice and I having had a disagreement, and that if Alice truly wishes to stay with her, I will have a talk with Alice about where she wants to live and where she wants her belongings.

Ruth stated, 'Alice and I will see you soon.'

Twenty minutes later, Alice knocked at the front door. I opened the door for Alice and she walked past me saying, 'We need to arrange a day for my mother to collect my rabbits and for me to take my stuff.'

Lara, despite me asking her to let it be for the moment, was prepared to say that she thought it was unfair that Alice wasn't interested in Pippin until she had the baby rabbits, and so she followed Alice and me to Alice's bedroom.

I explained to Alice that her attitude towards the rabbits and her sisters has been unreasonable; that she cannot decide something is hers after not wanting to take care of it; finally, that I only want her to be happy, but I also want her to understand that if she wants to live with her mother that is not a problem, but she needs to settle down in a home both for herself and her schooling.

With regard to Pipin, Alice replied, 'Well that shows you how stupid Lara really is.'

The situation wasn't really improving. I told Lara to go start her homework, and said to Alice that she should have a think about her attitude and behaviour, and come back tomorrow to organise her belongings.

(I know it was not the best thing I could have said, but I was fed up with Alice's selfishness and the trouble over nothing, coupled with the verbal abuse and instability brought by Ruth on her behalf. I'm still living with the aftershocks of Ruth's impact on my life; I try to mitigate their mother's behaviour coming through, but it's tough and our family life has become a nightmare again.)

I said to Alice that she needs to look at how she is behaving and treating the people around her; Pippin having babies should be a happy and exciting time.

Alice replied, 'Whatever,' and slammed the front door as she left.

Ma headed home and about ten minutes went by. Hayley was in the garden, checking on the rabbits, Lara was in the sitting room and I was in the kitchen washing up… Someone began bashing on the front door as if they were intent on bringing it down.

I opened the door slightly and saw Ruth. Ruth pushed the door out of my hand and rushed into the doorway, shouting, 'You are a fucking cunt!'

On the bounce-back of the hinges, I managed to grab the door and tried to close it. Ruth put both arms against the door, preventing me from shutting it. I didn't want to hurt Ruth but I sure didn't want her in my house either. After several attempts of bracketing the door against my foot, so at least she wouldn't gain any land, and asking Ruth to *please* get out of the way, she backed off and I managed to close the door.

Lara stood at the door of the sitting room; we looked at each other and could hear Ruth still yelling 'you are a fucking cunt' and that 'Alice is going to get her fucking rabbits'. As Ruth began another round, Lara and I heard a loud thud.

I went to the sitting room window and saw Ruth kicking the side door of my van. Lara came and stood by me and watched, shocked like I was, as her mother kicked my van; punctuating each kick by shouting 'you are a fucking cunt'. Re-entering my body and returning to the moment, I told Lara to come away from the window and noticed Hayley in the hallway. She suggested watching something on her laptop with Lara, and I gave her a grateful smile and hug.

I called the police. Ruth continued to shout verbal abuse in the background and as she got into her car, I saw Alice in the passenger seat – Alice must have witnessed her mother's appalling behaviour too.

The police came and took pictures of the damage to the van and I gave a statement. It felt like this day would never end.

Later that evening, I received a call from the police and they stated that at first Ruth had denied causing any damage to the vehicle, but finally admitted to it.

It was almost 9pm when the house phone rang. I let it go through to the answering machine. Ruth ranted down the phone that she had been waiting for the police to come; they are now at hers; the police are coming round with her to ensure that she takes the rabbits and Alice's belongings. Ruth warned me to get Alice's stuff out of her bedroom and on the drive 'or else'. Having already spoken to the police, I texted Ruth that nothing is going anywhere tonight, and we can discuss arrangements in the morning.

An hour passed without incident.

Hayley, Lara and I were in bed when I heard someone throwing something on to the drive. I looked out of my bedroom window as someone knocked on the front door. I got up, followed by Hayley, and found Alice at the door.

(It was strange to wish that Ruth would never come to my house again, and at the same time hope that Ruth is at least here and that Alice hadn't walked home at this time of night.)

Once more, Alice walked past me without a hello and said, 'I need a pair of joggers for P.E. in the morning.'

Alice went into her room for 5 minutes before reappearing and saying that she could not find them anywhere. I know she has more than one set of joggers, so I suggested she take a different pair. Alice said no.

Hayley suggested to Alice that she has P. E. first period and that Alice could borrow hers after her lesson. Alice shrugged her shoulder and turned around. I asked Alice as she left if we could have a chat after school tomorrow.

Alice replied, 'I have detention.'

I said, 'What about Wednesday?'

Alice handed me a letter and replied, 'Detention, but I'll ring you I guess.'

22 May

Dear Mr Marlo,
PASTORAL DETENTION
Pupil: Alice Marlo, 7OK
Alice has been placed in this detention for the following reason(s), persistent lateness.
The detention will take place on: Wednesday 24th May 2006 at 3:15pm in House area and will last for 45 minutes.
Yours sincerely,
(Please sign and return the slip below to the House office, acknowledging the Pastoral Detention and that you will ensure Alice attends.)

Eternity

23 May

Down on my long list of what I find hard to take on board, is the fact that Ruth, Mrs Mason and Smitch Law have continually placed unacceptable behaviour at my feet, not only through the letters that landed on my hall floor, but also in front of judges in the Family Courts. The judge was supposed to evaluate if I was or if I was not the sort of person that was capable of such disgraceful behaviour.

It also concerns me as a father that if I *had* acted like Ruth, using foul language and bringing violence to her home and causing damage to her vehicle, Ruth and Smitch Law would have tried anything – and I do mean anything – to bring my disgraceful behaviour to a judge and, I suspect, I would not be allowed to see my children and be regarded as a violent man in today's society; someone to avoid; to be kept at a distance; an undesirable person to care for children.

I have had years of abuse, hurtful lies and mental torment in my life from Ruth and Smitch Law's letters and attitude, a magistrate, a judge, a barrister and all the way to some so-called Lord, and not leaving out unforgettable performances from such organisations as the Department of Constitutional Affairs, the Law Society and the Legal Services Ombudsman.

I have had to endure more mental harassment and torment in my life over the past several years, due to these people's disgraceful conduct and dishonesty.

I do live from day–to–day with these people's deceit and it is shameful that Ruth continues to act in the manner that I have been portrayed, while I am threatened by professional people in their attempt to discredit my name and character, and prevent a loving father from having proper contact with my children.

Why is Ruth's behaviour acceptable?

Do they think it is easy, having to stand there as Ruth calls me a 'fucking cunt', at least ten times, in front of Lara? Do they think I do not care that Ruth can show up at my property, demonise my name, kick my work van and do so in front of our children?

I phoned Melissa and explained what had happened the day/evening before, I expressed to Melissa the behaviour and foul language that was being witnessed by all our children, especially Lara aged 8, and the sheer instability that Ruth's behaviour was placing in all of our day to day lives, again.

I asked Melissa if we could look at an injunction, preventing Ms Hyde from coming to our home and behaving in such a disgraceful way. Melissa told me because Ms Hyde had a mental health record, she thought it unlikely the courts would look at my case, but she made an appointment for me to go and see her.

After receiving a quotation of £550 for the damage to my vehicle door, I got in touch with my insurance company to see if they would pay for the repairs. They have told me that if I claim for the damage through my insurance, I would lose my no claims bonus and this would cost me a minimum of £50 per year.

Ruth caused the damage to my vehicle and I believe that Ruth should be held responsible for her actions, which may prevent her from acting in a similar way in the future.

It is not only the persistence of Ruth's abhorrent behaviour and the impact on our children witnessing such things, it the statement it makes to me. That van and my ability to go to work in it is the reason there is a roof over our children's heads, lunch in their bags, toys in their rooms, petrol in the car and everything else. Without my business, I would never made it through all the family court hearings since 1999. For her to kick my van, all these years later, is another insult to everything I've worked so hard to build.

I can't – don't want to – spend the rest of my life with this as my reality at my door.

Ruth continues to try and bring abnormality into my life and our children's lives; three sisters are upset, Alice is shirking responsibility and manners like water to a duck's back, and there's £550 worth of damage to my works van, all over a sleepover and some bunnies?

Ruth has made no effort to back me up with regards to Alice's behaviour, and what is Alice supposed to think, when her mother has taken the position that the rabbits should all be hers? Ruth has made no attempt to encourage Alice to discuss the situation or think about how her behaviour is affecting the whole family.

(How can we be six years on and I feel like nothing at all has changed? Ruth's manipulation of Alice that caused so much upset in her young life has returned to take a swipe at her teenage life, too. And, as usual, everyone else must deal with the consequences and fallout.)

Dean Marlo

From Northview, re Alice

24 May

Dear Mr Marlo,
MAJOR DETENTION
Pupil: Alice Marlo, 7OK
I regret to inform you that your child's behaviour has been such that we have had to place them in major detention on Friday 26th May 2006 at 3:15 in the Main Hall.

Such punishment is only given for serious offences or for cases where less serious misconduct continues persistently. In this case, the punishment is given for being offsite at lunchtime without permission on 19th May.

I write in order to make you aware of the position and hope that you will support the school and encourage more satisfactory conduct from your child in the future.

Should you wish to discuss the matter further, would you please arrange an appointment to see your child's Head of House.

Yours sincerely…

Regression

26 - 31 May

26th

I went to Parstons' office and spoke to Melissa – regardless of her lack of faith in my likely success, I don't believe Ruth's behaviour should be permissible or excused. If her mental health issues are causing her to behave in this way, then she needs help and monitoring; the children and I should not have to suffer her manic aggressive episodes; Alice definitely does not need an erratic home life when she is already testing boundaries.

After school, Hayley mentioned that her mother has bought Alice a mobile phone and Alice had given Hayley her new number.

Feeling like once more Alice is being alienated from me, but with a side of teenage rebellion instead of childhood innocence, I worry for Alice. Ruth is manipulating her and that truly sickens me.

Hayley gave me Alice's number and, as Alice is probably walking home to Ruth's still, I thought I would try to get in touch with her. The phone rang but it was Ruth who answered; I asked to speak to Alice and Ruth stated, 'Do not phone Alice on this number! You should phone me if you have anything to say to Alice.'

I reminded her that every time I ask to speak to Alice, she either puts the phone down or refuses. Ruth put the phone down.

Ten minutes later, I received a text from Ruth stating that if I want to speak to Alice, I have to ask her first – for her permission.

The screen dimmed. I closed my eyes.

29th

Ruth phoned and asked if I could drop Lara off at the bottle bank at 1pm instead of 12pm on Wednesday. I told her that it was fine, Ruth interrupted, 'Well actually 1.30.'

I replied okay, that is fine.

30th

Ruth phoned and said she wanted to confirm one thing, 'You will be at the bottle back with Lara at 2pm tomorrow.' The time had changed again, I took note but didn't bat an eye at responding ok. Ruth went on, 'The rabbits are coming to mine and you can leave them on my drive. I am organising for the police to be here, because that is the fairest way.'

I told Ruth the police are not interested in the rabbits, and have more important things to be doing.

Ruth stated, 'They will be here.'

She went on for one or two-minutes ranting and more verbal abuse, with highlights including:

'I want all of Alice's stuff left on your drive!'

'Alice is not coming back!'

'You *will* drop the rabbits off … Or expect the police on your doorstep, or somebody who will *do you in.*'

This conversation I have on tape.

It would appear that it is acceptable and I am expected to endure this behaviour towards myself, which in turn has an impact on our children, plus, I have the worry of another incident manifesting and taking over our lives again, or Alice getting hurt.

Also, if Ruth had not made such a nightmare of the Alice situation, I would, at least, be talking to Alice now and reached an understanding with her; Alice may have taken on board that as her dad I love and care for her, and that my responsibilities as a parent are not always going to align with what she wants.

(It feels strange writing this out, this is surely something almost every parent has experienced? Rebellion? Children defying rules? The only difference here is that inexplicably Ruth has decided that keeping Alice in her favour is more important than Alice's stability and maturity necessary to understand boundaries put in place for her welfare. Alice is only 12.)

31st

I dropped Lara off at the bottle bank at 2pm, as requested by Ruth. There was no mention of rabbits; Ruth did not climb out of her car to search my boot for the cage or bunnies under my seats. (As I had feared.) Lara waved one more time before jumping into Ruth's car and she pulled off.

Damien

1 - 6 June

Ruth phoned with more verbal abuse, yelling, 'You are the Devil's son! Your real name is Damien! You are a part of 666 and you owe me £40,000!'

This call I have on tape.

I sent Melissa an e-mail, like it's a ritual now. Ruth's behaviour continues to effect me, while I continue to be a dad to our children.

2nd

7.15pm Alice came round with a friend. I told Alice that we really need to sit down and have a chat.

Alice replied, 'How about now?'

I thought it would be better if we sat down together when she was not with a friend, but if it's the best we can do… I said let's have a house meeting.

Despite me having very little contact with Alice at all, either by phone or at home, Alice is barely out of children's size shoes and is making decisions that are affecting her life; at the top of all that, she needs to let everyone know where it is she wants to live permanently.

I asked Alice if she wants to live with her mother.

Alice replied, 'I never said that I am living with her… But I don't know because I have heard about you being violent and hurting our mother.'

(By not being that way by nature and never retaliating; enduring and tolerating every disruption, provocation, aggression – my only hope left is that my children grow up knowing right from wrong, seeing their dad walk away in the face of confrontation, and trust that their dad loves them, nothing more, nothing less.)

I reminded Alice that she has been there on many occasions, and knows that I have never got involved with the constant verbal and threatening behaviour from her mother and that, in all of her time with me, she has never seen me act that way towards her mother or anyone.

Alice replied, 'I only have your word for that.'

(Two-strikes to the jugular. Alice can't really believe that, can she?)

I told Alice that this conversation had gotten off track, but in her head and heart, she knows that I have never behaved aggressive or violently. Alice said, 'Do I?'

Sighing, I asked Alice if she had seen the side of my van.

Alice replied, 'I was in the car but didn't see, and our mother said that she did not touch the van and that after we left, you went outside and damaged the van yourself.'

(Strike three, time to tap out.)

I told Alice that her mother has been cautioned by the police, and that I have never lied to her. (Let alone faked £550 worth of damage to my own works vehicle; even if I was that way inclined, I would have no need to 'make Ms Hyde look bad' as her actions speak for themselves.)

Alice said, with the confidence of someone whose knowledge of the justice system comes from 'Eastenders' and 'The Bill', 'Yes, cautioned Dad. It does not mean she did it.'

I told Alice that Lara and I stood at the sitting room window and had watched her mother kick the van.

Alice replied, 'Dad it has nothing to do with me.'

I know that this incident had nothing to do with Alice, it was an example of the behaviour that she can verify happened – that it was not my word up against her mother's, but that her sisters had witnessed their mother's behaviour.

Alice left to go and play with her friend in her room, before returning to her mother's in the afternoon.

3rd

I received through the post a letter which included a bank statement of mine, dated 1 September 1999, which Ruth must have taken from the letter box of our old home at the time.

Ruth wrote a note with the statement: 'Maybe this will jog your memory.'

I believe she is referring to the £40,000 she claims I owe her from the sale of our children's home. (At the risk of rehashing matters discussed 'Behind Closed Doors', I owed Ruth nothing then, and nothing now.)

5th

Monday, 8 am, I saw Hayley off to school and I drove half an hour to the site where I had the responsibility of refurbishing a large part of a mansion. (As a lad from a council estate, who was told he had little hope of achieving anything in the future, it still blows my mind when heading down the 200 yard drive.)

Lara has a non–pupil day today, so I packed up my tools and left to meet Lara and Ruth at the bottle bank for 12 pm. At 11.30, as I arrived home, I received a call from Ruth who stated that she would be dropping Lara off at the bottle bank at 1pm. I said 12pm was the agreed time and Ruth replied that I had an extra two-hours when I dropped Lara off on Wednesday; I couldn't believe it.

I reminded Ruth she had requested Lara be dropped later and that I thought it was due to her work. Ruth stated that she had wasted her time, having to go to Northview Grove School about Alice and that she wanted another hour with Lara. I had little choice but to say oaky. Ruth asked if I had received her letter and I replied no. (I said no because I do not want to incessantly be abused by Ruth about anything and everything.) Ruth went on, stating that someone from Northview Grove had written 'bitch' on Alice's school blazer and when she drops Lara off at the bottle bank, she wants £50 from me as she has had to replace it. She put the phone down.

I spent a moment thinking about the job I could have pushed on with, and decided to go shopping, which would allow Lara and I to go straight home when I pick her up.

I parked by the bottle bank at 12.55pm. At 1:10 pm, I received a call from Ruth stating that they are on their way. Ten minutes went by before Ruth pulled up. Lara got out of Ruth's car and jumped into the back. I, as usual, stayed in the car. I was about to start my engine when Ruth got out of her car and came up to my window.

Ruth was demanding that I give her £50; I asked for the receipt. (I have no problem providing for my children, but I go through the process of ensuring everything is done properly, to prevent any false allegations.)

Lara and I sat there and watched Ruth push her face up against the window, her nostrils flared, yelling, 'I want my fucking fifty-pounds for Alice's fucking blazer.'

The language was disgraceful and once again Lara could clearly hear and see her mother, along with everyone else in the vicinity. I asked Ruth to stop swearing, but she just carried on. I started my engine and Ruth walked away shouting more verbal abuse.

Back home, with Lara settled in, I phoned Parstons to ask if Melissa had received my e-mail; I was told that Melissa was on holiday for two weeks and that I could speak to Mrs Glover, senior partner, or Mr Buckley, intern. I said I would get back to them.

In the way that it seems to happen, Alice's disapproval at not being allowed a sleepover and the subsequent incidents because of the rabbits has faded into the background; Ruth escalates everything without knowing what it is she is causing trouble over. Last month it was my works van, today it's her face print on the window of my car.
6th

I have received a letter from the Child Benefit Agency due to a duplicate claim; this is following daily phone calls where Ruth has demanded I give her Alice's Child Benefit. I have paid her the weekly amount that she would receive for Alice, but Alice still needs to decide where she is going to live. If Alice makes the decision to live with Ruth, then of course I have no problem giving Ruth the Child Benefit for Alice.

However, now Ruth has forced the situation anyway – my Child Benefit for all three children has been suspended pending a review.

Policing

9 June

8.25am Lara and I were sitting at the kitchen table practising her times tables before we leave at 8.30am. My work colleague, Cole, pulled his car onto our drive and knocked on the front door; as I let him in, he said he thinks Ruth has pulled up outside. I looked out of the door and saw Ruth advancing.

She was shouting, 'You are a fucking cunt!'

I quickly closed the front door, and could see Ruth standing in the porch through the glass. 'You are a fucking cunt! Where's my fifty pounds?! Alice is your daughter and you should treat her like one!'

Lara had been ready to go, but she stood by Cole and could hear clearly hear her mother. This verbal abuse and bad language went on for several minutes, even as I spoke to Ruth through the closed door, asking for her to stop swearing and leave – finally, I said if she doesn't go, I will phone the police.

Ruth replied, 'Good we need the police here to deal with your fucking behaviour and I am going nowhere.'

I felt that I had no choice but to actually phone the police. It was not what I wanted as this would continue the disruption in Lara's life and her day at school.

On the phone to the police, the operator asked me several questions and it suddenly became quiet outside. The operator asked if Ruth was still there, and I said I can no longer see her.

I opened the front door and, to my considerable relief, I relayed to the operator that Ruth was gone. We arranged for a police officer to come and see me at 5:30pm.

Cole and I went outside and looked at our vehicles for damage. As we walked back to the front door, I noticed that Ruth had scratched the Devil's mark (a pentagram, and I only know what it is because of Ruth's previous episodes) into the bricks of the porch.

The house where we currently live is a rented property, Ruth knows this, and it is disgraceful that she can come to someone's home and deface it as she has.

I dropped Lara to school and decided to call off work.

Every day this week, I have woken up in the morning and been determined to phone Parstons, but I have weakened as time has passed. I just could not face the disappointment and frustration in trying to express to a solicitor that Ruth and her behaviour is breaking me down.

I relinquished my fears, and phoned Parstons, asking the receptionist if she could confirm when Melissa was coming back from her holiday; she informed me that Melissa is back on the 26th June.

I felt desperate to speak to a solicitor to try and stop the disgraceful behaviour and bad language brought to our home and into our children's lives, to this day, by Ruth. Any sort of normality I have achieved for myself and stability provided for my children, Ruth has tried to disrupt.

I spoke to Mrs Glover, and she suggested I make an application for an injunction against Ms Hyde; I asked her to please prepare to do so.

Ruth phoned my mobile ten times throughout the day but I refused to answer the calls from her. Why should I put up with more verbal abuse from Ruth? I listened to the first voicemail, in case it was an emergency, but it was clear these calls were simply to harass and disrupt.

The truth is I do not want to phone the police, I do not want to phone my solicitor and I am deeply sorry that I am troubling any of them. I am finding it hard to cope and manage with the level of trouble at my home and the constant abuse from Ruth.

I do feel depressed and mentally drained and totally fraught by Ruth's behaviour, and the fact that it all seems totally acceptable towards my children and myself.

My personal life is made a misery by Ruth's attitude, foul language and false allegations. I believe that it has been deplorable what Lara, Alice and Hayley have been through, seen and heard because of their mother.

What's more, I have done nothing to warrant these reactions from her; I take good care of our children; I make adjustments based on her plans; I pay whatever receipt she thrusts in my face; I do not interfere in her life; I do not call her unnecessarily; I am not abusive; I am not violent – yet I feel her overbearing presence and influence over my life just as much as I did over a decade ago.

5 pm I cooked Hayley and Lara tea. I didn't much feel like eating and prepared myself for the police visit.

They never showed up.

At 7 pm there was a knock at the door. I straightened my jumper and took a deep breath, preparing myself for police involvement in my life.

Standing in the doorway, was Alice and a friend.

'My mother has thrown me out,' Alice said.

As I welcomed Alice and friend in, I thought about what being 'thrown out' could entail, and asked what had happened.

After school, Alice went out and when she came home, she and her mother had argued, which ended with her mother marching her to the door shouting, 'Get out of my house and don't come back!'

Ruth once again has placed me in a very difficult position; for the first two to three weeks Ruth refused to allow me to talk to Alice, and Alice made no effort to contact me. My calls went unanswered as did my texts.

I had mentally prepared for when Alice was willing to talk and wanted some involvement with me to arrange for Alice and I to go and sit with a counsellor, and talk about the situation that we have found ourselves in. For my part, I would hope that Alice could realise that she cannot disrupt everyone's lives, because she cannot always have what she wants or get her own way, and that some advice could be given to me, to help deescalate Alice before she decides to call her mother.

Despite being kicked out from her mother's, Alice was in high spirits. Alice wheedled that she had arranged with her mother to sleepover at her friend's and she asked if it was alright for her to still do so. I agreed as I thought it would give me time to talk to Hayley and Lara about the situation and Alice walking in, stating that she is back. Both Hayley and Lara had realised the fact that Alice's behaviour was bad and hurtful, and expressed that her attitude was hard to live with.

It is difficult; as Alice's parent, I want Alice home and to get her back on track, because I love her and there is no need for her to be acting this way. At the same time, I am a parent to Hayley and Lara too; I have to take into account their emotional development and understanding of the situation, whilst having little choice but to allow Alice back into our home without properly addressing her behaviour over the last few weeks.

To be honest, I had been expecting a call from Ruth to follow Alice's return, but none came.

My stomach was twisting due to the lack of food, and I phoned the police to see if they were still coming round. The operator stated that being Friday night, they were busy early and she would leave a note for an officer to come and see me tomorrow.

Twenty minutes later, the phone rang and it was a police officer; we had a long chat and he gave me a quick response number in case of any more disturbance or trouble from Ruth at our home. He also told me that if a person has a mental health record, it does not permit them to make someone's life a misery, harass someone or break the peace or law in anyway and, if a solicitor could not do anything for me, then he suggested that I get back in touch with the police and they would look into harassment.

Tricky business

12–15 June

Monday 12th
Alice has returned to residing at home. (Thankfully, the rabbits did not in fact go to Ruth's.) Alice told me that every day she was with her mother, her mother would hound her to call me and ask for her Child Benefit.

I had to call Alice's doctor to ask for some new hay fever tablets; the receptionist stated that Ms Hyde had been in that morning and asked for the same. I told the woman that if Ms Hyde has organised to get the tablets, I will contact her to pick them up.

I tried calling but Ruth didn't answer.

(Because of how bad Alice's hay fever can be, we get her tablets on prescription; it is likely I will be buying her more, which is both an unnecessary expense, and her mother making Alice's life difficult.)

Tuesday 13th
In the morning, Alice told me that she had phoned her mother and asked her to drop her hay fever tablets into school.

I received a letter from Smitch Law, read the threats within and didn't look at it again.

Wednesday 14th
It was around 4.30pm when Alice arrived home from school, coming through the door on the phone to her mother and asking why she had not dropped her tablets off. Ruth told Alice that she would drop them round in half an hour. I asked Alice to keep an eye out for her mother, as I do not particularly want her to come to our door. Alice rode her bike around the area outside our house for the first half an hour but came in after she had called her mother three times already to ask where she was.

Later, there was a knock on the front door and I checked my clock, it was 9.40pm. I looked out of my bedroom window and saw Ruth's car. I met Alice in the hallway, where Alice stated, 'I bet that's our mother.'

I confirmed that it was and Alice went to the front door. I heard Ruth have a go at Alice, even after Alice closed the door. I asked Alice if she had got her tablets and Alice replied, 'Yes, but my mother has not given me all of them, she has cut sections off the packet which means I only have enough for 3 days.'

Thursday 15th
6.30pm Alice phoned her mother and asked her if she would drop the rest of her hay fever tablets into school; her mother said if she gets time, she will.

I finally got through to Mrs Glover at Parstons; I told her what my children and I were going through and the contents of Smitch's letter. She told me to 'ignore the silly letter'.

So I burnt it – I obviously was not in a good place.

To Ms Hyde

16 June

Re: Father's Day 18th June 2006.
Would you please make Lara available at the bottle bank at 10am Sunday on your next contact weekend, Friday 30th June 2006.
Would you also confirm in writing your contact arrangements for your birthday.
Yours sincerely…

While dropping Lara at Riverbank, I gave Mrs Hart the letter to give to Ruth.
I would drop it round to Ruth's, but given her behaviour and the likelihood that she will deny the letter was even written, I have to include third parties like Mrs Hart to bear witness to me communicating.
I asked Alice if she was going to her mother's for the weekend; Alice replied no.
Friday after school and on Saturday, Alice repeatedly phoned Ruth as she was going to run out of her hay fever tablets. Alice told me that she had left several messages on her mother's home phone and mobile as she was not answering either.
I suppose it was just wishful thinking that Mrs Glover would phone me on Thursday and also that she would phone me on Friday. Wishful thinking that I might receive a call of reassurance that the abuse of my family and myself was totally unacceptable and would be looked into.

Father's Day

18 June

In the morning, Alice phoned her mother several times, but she didn't pick up; around 9am, Ruth called and Alice asked for the rest of her tablets. Having come into the kitchen, I heard from where I was standing as Ruth demanded Alice to 'get your father'.

Alice said, 'No, I just need my tablets. It's Father's Day and I don't want you having a go at him!'

(It is difficult, navigating the waters of being a parent with the constant storm Ruth brings into our lives. It cannot help the children's relationship with their mother but Hayley and Alice have always stood up to her, and increasingly, as they are older now, they defend me when it comes to their mother's verbal abuse and behaviour. I do not want my children to be involved; I have always tried to show them to walk away from bad situations and to not answer being shouted at by yelling back.

It mostly feels like only Lara has picked this up – apart from occasionally with Alice – and I can't help but attribute that to having less awareness and understanding because of her age. Lara has been fortunate to have lived with a greater influence of the family dynamic I always wanted to have – calm, loving and fun. Hayley and Alice had a lot of difficult early years and it is frustratingly sad that I see the same behaviour, incidents and sadness continue in their relationship with their mother.)

Scowling, Alice put the phone against her hand and told me her mother is insisting on talking to me.

I just could not face it; apart from it being Father's Day, I am drained and fed up with the abuse.

Alice said goodbye to her mother and we shared a hug. The constant seesaw of emotions is overwhelming, and even as I comfort my daughter, there is no comfort for myself – Ruth's behaviour has already gone on too long, and appears destined to carry on.

Someone knocked the door, and we all knew it could only be Ruth. Alice answered, hoping that her mother brought her tablets. Ruth told Alice to get me; I walked to the door and asked Ruth if she had Alice's tablets, and, if not, would she please leave my property.

Out of nowhere, Ruth said, 'You will not be getting any money from me for that van.'

I told Ruth to please give Alice her tablets and that I would see her and Lara at the bottle bank at 10am.

Ruth stated, '10.30, you asshole.'

I reminded Ruth that I had written to her and that I asked her to drop Lara at 10am.

Ruth sneered, 'See you at 10.30, little boy.'

Repeating that I would see Ruth at 10am as previously arranged, I closed the front door. Alice and I stood in the hall, and for the next minute or two, Ruth continued shouting verbal abuse.

Exhausted with the trouble at my door again, I told Ruth through the closed door that if she did not leave, I would phone the police. Ruth hurled more abuse. As I began to dial, the shadow moved from the porch; I walked to the front room window to check and saw Ruth getting into her car.

Just before 10am, Alice and I arrived at the bottle bank. At 10.10, I started to pull off as I had arranged to pick Hayley up at 10.15; Hayley had slept over with friends the night before but wanted to be home for Father's Day. Suddenly, Ruth drove around the corner. Lara jumped out of her car, borderline while it was still moving, followed by Ruth.

As Lara opened the door and climbed in, Ruth held the door open, planting her head and upper body inside the car to have a go at Alice, preventing Lara from closing the door. Lara moved to the next seat over, to get away.

Alice had reached back for the door handle, telling her mother to get out of the way so that we could go, but Ruth just carried on. I asked Ruth to please let us go as we needed to meet Hayley. With a motion that made the car frame rattle, Ruth reared back and slammed the door. As she passed Alice, she was still yelling and banged on the window with her fist.

I pulled off and was relieved to get away.

My Statement

20 June

I, Dean Marlo, make oath and say as follows:

I am the applicant herein and I make this statement consisting of 5 pages believing it's content to be true and in support of my application, without notice to the respondent, for Non–Molestation and Occupation Orders pursuant to Sections 33 and 42 of the Family Law Act 1996 in the terms of the draft order annexed to my application.

The respondent and I are associated persons, having previously cohabited. We have never been married to each other, although we are the parents of three children; Hayley Marlo, born 1992, Alice Marlo, born 1994, and Lara Marlo, born 1997. I am the sole tenant of a rented property; the respondent has no rights under the tenancy.

2. The respondent and I have been involved in family law proceedings, regarding our three children. The children initially lived with the respondent, with contact afforded to me. The respondent suffers with mental health problems and, in July 2000, was sectioned for the fourth time under the Mental Health Act. The children came to live with me. On the respondent's release in August 2000, the children remained with myself. Court proceedings were issued, and an interim shared residence order was put in place whereby the children alternated weekly between us. In October 2000, a shared residence order was put in place whereby the children spent six weeks with each of us. This arrangement broke down, with both the respondent and I making allegations against the other. I issued an application for sole residence of our children in December 2003. At the directions hearing in January 2004, the respondent indicated she also wished to apply for sole residence of all three children. In April 2004, by consent, an interim residence order was made in my favour. In August 2004, a residence order was granted in my favour in respect of all three children, with contact to the respondent. I refer to this Order exhibited hereto marked 'DTM1' at pages 1– 3.

3. Since the residence order and defined contact to the respondent was made, which provided for further or other contact to be agreed between the parties in writing, there has been substantial difficulties with the conduct of the respondent when trying to discuss with her alternative or additional contact. By way of example only, I cite the following events, which have taken place over the last two months, in the presence the children.

4. On Monday 22nd May 2006, after the respondent and I had spoken over the phone, at 6pm in relation to a dispute of how to divide the baby rabbits between our children, the respondent turned up at my front door bashing it and shouting you are a 'fucking cunt'. After I refused to allow the respondent to enter my property to take the rabbits, I heard a loud thud. I looked out of the window and saw the respondent kicking the side of my van door while at the same time shouting/screaming at the top of her voice, 'you fucking cunt'. Lara, who is 8 years old, was standing next to me watching and listening to everything that the respondent was doing until I told her to come away from the window and phoned the police.

The police arrived at my property that evening and took pictures of the damage that the respondent had caused to my van. Please refer to pages 4 and 5 of the exhibits marked 'DTM1'; police incident number attached. Later I received a call from the police who said that they had spoken to the respondent, who at first denied causing any damage to my van, but then admitted to it. The police confirmed that the respondent was cautioned. The cost of repairing the damage caused by the respondent came to £550. Please refer to page 6 of the exhibits marked 'DTM1' for the garage's quote.

5. On Thursday 23rd May 2006, at 6.10pm, I received a phone call from the respondent stating that she was coming over to collect the rabbits and Alice's belongings, and expected to find everything on my drive. I told the respondent if she came to my property, I would call the police. The respondent ignored what I said and replied 'I am on my way'.

At 8:50pm, I received another call from the respondent who was using obscene language and threatened that she is waiting for the police to turn up so that they can accompany her over to my property. The respondent hung up the phone.

At 9:40pm, I heard a knock at the front door; when I answered it, Alice was standing there asking to get some tracksuit bottoms for school in the morning. I could not see the respondent, but believe she was sitting in her car waiting.

6. On 29th May 2006, I received a phone call from the respondent asking me if I could drop Lara off at the bottle bank at 1pm instead of 12pm on Wednesday, 31st May. I replied that's fine, and the respondent changed it to 1:30pm; I agreed.

7. On 30th May 2006, I received a further phone call from the respondent screaming about the rabbits and demanding that they are on my doorstep for her to collect or expect the police or 'somebody who will do you in'. I was subjected to further verbal abuse until finally the respondent hung up.

8. On Thursday 1st June 2006, I received a phone call from the respondent stating that I was the 'Devil's son'; my name was 'Damien'; I was part of '666' and further verbal abuse before she finally hung up.

These calls I have on tape.

9. On Monday 5th June 2006, I received a phone call from the respondent at 11:30am stating that she would be dropping Lara off at the bottle bank at 1pm, rather than 12:00am (as agreed in the order made on 5th August 2004). I replied that the time to drop Lara off was 12pm. The respondent stated that she had wasted her time going to Northview Grove with respect to Alice, and that she wanted another hour with Lara, I reluctantly agreed; Ms Hyde stated she wanted £50 to replace Alice's blazer which had been defaced.

I arrived at the bottle bank at 12:55pm. The respondent arrived late with Lara. Lara got out of the respondent's car and into the back of mine. The respondent came over to the window of my car and demanded that I give her £50. I asked for the receipt and the respondent replied, 'I want that fucking £50 for Alice's fucking blazer.'

Lara was again being subjected to the respondent's intimidating and foul behaviour. I asked the respondent to stop swearing and started my engine. The respondent stepped away but continued to verbally abuse me.

10. On 9th June 2006, at 8:30am I was getting ready to leave the house and take Lara to school when my work colleague arrived and stated that he saw the respondent pull up

outside the house. When I saw the respondent walking up the drive-way, I shut the front door. The respondent was shouting 'you fucking cunt' amongst other verbal abuse for a several minutes; once again, Lara was present. I told the respondent that if she did not stop swearing and leave my property, I would call the police. It went quiet and we believed that the respondent had left. My colleague and I went outside to check our vehicles for any damage and noticed that the respondent had engraved a pentagram onto the brickwork of the porch. Please refer to page 6 of the exhibits marked 'DTM1'.

I received a further ten phone calls on my mobile from the respondent throughout that day, although I refused to answer them.

At 7pm that evening, Alice turned up at my house stating that the respondent had thrown her out.

11. On the 18th June 2006, Alice contacted her mother to drop off her hay fever tablets. At 9:30am the respondent arrived at my property with the tablets. The respondent demanded to talk to me so I went to the door, and she stated that I would not be getting any money for the damage she has caused to my van. I told the respondent that I would see her and Lara at the bottle bank at 10am. The respondent replied, '10:30, you asshole.'

I closed the door and the respondent remained outside on my doorstep screaming verbal abuse for the next several minutes. I repeated to the respondent that if she did not leave, I would phone the police. The respondent left my property.

12. The respondent's behaviour has become unpredictable and unstable. I am particularly very worried and anxious that our daughters may be harmed in some way due to the highly stressful situation brought about by the respondent's behaviour. My children and I have been subjected to numerous phone calls, threats, intimidation and verbal abuse. I am emotionally drained and extremely concerned that the respondent's behaviour is causing our children emotional harm. I cannot endure any further aggressive or violent behaviour from the respondent whether it is in the children's presence, or not.

13. I am extremely fearful of how the respondent will react to my application, and it is for the reasons set out above, that I make my application for the protection of the court, without notice to the respondent.

In all the circumstances I ask the court to grant me the relief I seek under Sections 33 and 42 of the Family Law Act 1996, in the terms of the draft order annexed hereto.

Dean Marlo

Court – Justice?

21st June 2006 / Town Family County Courts
Father's application – injunction against Ms Hyde

Judge Baxter orders a hearing for the 23rd June 2006, both parties to be present.

There is no excuse for arriving at someone's home and using foul language, defacing the brickwork on the property nor for causing criminal damage to a vehicle -all witnessed by children.
If I had done any of the above, I would already be spending time in a cell.

The Judge looking down

21 June

Mr Buckley and I lodged my application, went into the waiting room and sat down. Mrs Glover came in and sat down with us, mentioning that we have two judges in today. Several minutes later, a court usher came into the room and stated that the case would be heard next door – in the family court side, rather than the criminal side. Mrs Glover asked the usher who was sitting on the bench today and the usher replied, 'Judge Baxter.'

My heart sank.

Within a split second, Mr Buckley and Mrs Glover were walking me towards the door – I considered making a run for it, even looking for a hole in the ground to fall in, after all, this was the judge I had written to the DCA about.

(I did not think it was appropriate for Judge Baxter to be looking at my case, but hey, I still have nothing to hide.)

We all walked into the family court side of the building, I noticed that the whole place was deserted; no sad or angry faces; no solicitors; no barristers; no tumbleweed; nothing!

It was about 1.10pm, and after convincing myself that I was not going to be crucified again, I barely had time to express my thoughts and fears to Mr Buckley and Mrs Glover, when the usher announced that Judge Baxter was ready to see us.

For the first five minutes, I could only pickup one or two words that Judge Baxter was saying, as he was mumbling; I was unsure if it was to himself or if he was addressing someone in the court room.

Judge Baxter focused on Mr Buckley and announced, 'I do not feel that there is any danger of things getting worse, I will see both parties on Friday 23rd June 2006.'

He did not even speak to me. We did not discuss my statement, and he made no effort to try and evaluate the level of disruption and disorder still occurring because of Ms Hyde's flagrant disregard for basic decency.

Throughout, Judge Baxter has acted like a tyrant when dealing with my children's welfare and stability, our case and towards myself. If alarm bells aren't ringing in his head, the fact I am still standing before him – with more evidence of Mrs Hyde's unpredictable behaviour and mental instability – then I despair.

I had to laugh (inside of course) when Judge Baxter declared 'I do not feel that there is any danger of things getting worse' – has Judge Baxter become a clairvoyant or is he a fucking comedian working on his material?

(I sincerely hope that any decent person would read 'I am extremely fearful of how the respondent is going to react' and seek to provide protection for the person and children who are involved. I still don't believe Judge Baxter has a moral bone in his body, and that he shouldn't be presiding over family law.)

Either way, if I did not laugh, I would cry.

The Mediation Services

21 June

Dear Mr Marlo,

Ms Hyde has attended an initial appointment with a mediator. Mediation is an opportunity for you and your former partner to negotiate in a secure environment. It can help you to sort out the practical and financial arrangements you need to make, for example contact with children and division of assets. Mediators are impartial and are there to facilitate your discussions. Mediation can help you find a way forward, reduce bitterness and improve communication.

We would like to invite you to attend an assessment meeting for which there will be no charge, where you can find out more about mediation. During your information meeting, a decision can be made whether mediation is suitable for your situation. If you decide to go ahead with mediation and you are concerned about violent or abusive behaviour, tell us and we can plan appointments with your safety in mind.

Part of the first appointment will be used to check your eligibility for Community Legal Services Funding for mediation. If you qualify for the public funding, mediation will cost you nothing. Please check the enclosed pack to see what information you need to bring. The information pack also gives details of our charges if you are found not to be eligible for Community Legal Service Funding. Attending this meeting will not commit you to mediation, just to talking to us about whether it would be helpful.

We hope you will agree to come along and find out more about the mediation process and look forward to hearing from you.

Yours sincerely,

If I am beginning to sound inconsiderate, standoffish or, heaven forbid, difficult, it is because I have endured four years of court hearings and Ms Hyde's dictation, behaviour and abuse of my children and myself.

Just this year, I have had to stand back as Ms Hyde influences Alice through negative aspects of her lifestyle; the children and I have been screamed at in our car and at our home; my van has shoe prints worth £550 indented in the door – Ms Hyde and I do not need *mediation*. Ms Hyde needs to put her children first and get on with her life, so that the rest of us may do the same while we are all still young enough to enjoy it.

I've had well over a decade of Ms Hyde's abuse and I just want to be a father to my children.

Melissa's back, back again

21 June

Further to your recent instructions, I am writing to thank you for retaining me and in order to provide you with some important information at this stage in the proceedings. This letter sets out the terms upon which you are engaging this firm's services.

The Legal Help and Help at Court Legal Advice and Assistance Scheme is available immediately to assist clients who are on particularly low incomes or in receipt of certain state benefits.

The scheme is limited in scope to a maximum of £500, and for 'family' work carried out under this scheme our hourly rates are as follows:

Preparation, Attendance file & personal 'Family Work' – £50.05. All other work – £47.80.
Travel/Waiting 'Family Work' – £28.05. All other work – £26.80.
Letters Written/Telephone Calls – £3.95. All other work – £3.75.
All the above is subject to VAT.

Whilst the Legal Services Commission have placed a limit of £500, we are required to carry out cost/benefit tests and are required to follow guidelines. For example, acting for a petitioner in a divorce should not require us to work anymore than 3–4 hours, and if it does, we are required to justify this and to notify you.

I anticipate the work I require to carry out for you under the 'Legal Help' scheme to be 4 hours. If I anticipate going above this limit, I shall advise you in writing.

I abhor the involvement of solicitors in my life (not Melissa specifically of course, but the institution) but I feel hopeless to wade through the hearings without some sort of legal representation and support.

If Parstons charges basically £4 per letter, no wonder Smitch Law has been generating letters needlessly, when the two parties should have been encouraged to sort out matters between themselves, like most of the people in this country, who coexist together or not, without the need of a solicitor.

Dear Melissa

22 June

I applied to the courts to prevent Ms Hyde from turning up at my children's home at her will and being abusive, aggressive and violent. I am getting nothing more from applying for this injunction than peace of mind and to be able to feel safe from the verbal and physical abuse that Ms Hyde unleashes.

The judgements that have been placed in my life from people working within the system are quite clearly dishonest and immoral. I believe that any honest and decent member of our community would feel just as I do, used and abused.

I have only heard poor excuses for why this behaviour cannot be addressed, yet I find that Ms Hyde's word is recurrently used as fact. The chaos and upset are so extreme, and I must ask why the system allows these people to abuse my children's childhoods and myself as a parent.

It is clear that Ms Hyde's behaviour and the incidents that she has had with Hayley and Alice have resulted in all three children's wellbeing and stability being once more threatened. I do believe this is linked to her bipolar disorder, and the community mental health team need to be involved to support Ms Hyde; the inability or wilful ignorance of numerous judges and Mrs Mason to understand her mental health condition has dragged this situation on.

Melissa to me – Legal Aid

22 June

Dear Mr Marlo,

Public Funding and the Exercise of Devolved Powers

I confirm that I have sent your application for public funding to the Legal Services Commission following exercise of Devolved Powers, and what follows is an explanation of how the Public Funding Scheme works.

Before granting public funding, the Commission decides whether: –

If in all the circumstances there are reasonable grounds for the case to continue.

AND

Your disposable income and your capital are inside the limits laid down by the regulations.

Limits on Public Funding

Even if your application is successful, the Commission may set a limit on the amount of work that we can do to start with. Your case is then considered again and the Commission decides whether it is reasonable for your funding to continue. If the decision is positive, the limit can be increased.

Payment of Contributions

Depending on your financial situation, you may be offered public funding on condition that you pay a monthly contribution.

The Commission will notify you of the amount you need to pay and will not issue a Certificate until you have paid the first month's contribution. I cannot do any public funding work for you until the Certificate has been issued.

The monthly contribution must be paid each month while the Certificate is in operation. The Commission tell me if you do not pay, then I can do no more publicly funded work until the contributions are brought up to date.

Changes in your Finances or your Address

The Legal Services Commission Area Office MUST be told if your financial circumstances (income and capital) change or if you change your address.

An improvement in your finances may mean that you either have to pay a monthly contribution if you are not already paying one or have to pay a higher contribution. If your financial circumstances worsen, any contribution you are paying may be lowered or it may be stopped altogether.

Cost Consequences of Public Funding

If the Commission grants a certificate, then legal costs for work within any limits, which have been made, will be paid by the Commission. 'Legal costs' means charges for my time and disbursements such as Court fees or experts reports. Therefore, you are not invoiced by me for work done under the terms of the Certificate.

Costs Estimate

It is not possible to state exactly what the final cost figure will be. On the information I have now, I estimate that the final cost figure should be between £1,200 and £1,500.

If your Case is Successful

If you are successful, the general rule is that the successful party has their costs paid by the losing party.

However, in practice, quite often the costs paid by the losing party do not cover the total of the costs incurred by the successful party.

Any difference is 'clawed back' by the Commission from any money or property you have 'preserved' or obtained as a result of the work done for you. This is the 'Statutory Charge'. Please refer to 'Paying Back the Legal Services Commission – The Statutory Charge' the leaflet which I have already given you. 'Preserved' means that you keep something valuable that you might otherwise not have kept, for example a share in a house.

Because of the Statutory Charge, public funding is not necessarily free.

If your Case is not Successful

Should your claim fail, then it is possible for the Court to order you to pay your opponent's costs. However, because you are publicly funded you have some protection. The law provides that an order for costs against a publicly funded party must not exceed the amount (if any) which they consider it reasonable for that party to pay. The Court considers the circumstances of both parties and their conduct during the dispute.

The Court will usually order costs against a losing publicly funded party but will direct that that order cannot be enforced without the consent of the Court. That is the winner has to apply to the Court to take enforcement action to recover their costs.

Because of the protection mentioned above the Court may or may not give consent. If consent is not given, your opponent can apply again in the future if the loser's circumstances improve.

Discharge of Revocation of your Legal Services Commission Certificate

In most cases once a matter is over, we simply apply for your Certificate to be discharged.

Occasionally, a Certificate is revoked by the Commission. An example would be if your application was found to contain an untrue statement.

The differences between discharge and revocation are very important. On discharge you are publicly funded until the date of the discharge and only pay the Commission if the Statutory Charge applies.

On revocation, you will be regarded as never having been publicly funded and therefore be obliged to pay back to the Commission any costs paid by them on your behalf.

IT IS VITAL TO KEEP THE COMMISSION UP TO DATE WITH YOUR CIRCUMSTANCES AND REPLY QUICKLY TO ANY CORRESPONDENCE FROM THEM.

I shall contact you as soon as I hear from the Commission about your application.

I apologise for such a long letter but the law and the rules regarding public funding are both lengthy and quite complicated. If you need further explanation, please do not hesitate to contact me.

Yours sincerely…

Court – Can't you see?

23rd June 2006 / Town Family County Courts
Father's application – injunction against Ms Hyde

Judge Baxter orders no contact between both parents – save through solicitors – and children to walk to respective parents' homes for residency, contact and holidays.

Essentially, Judge Baxter dismissed Ms Hyde's behaviour and the criminal damage caused by her at the children's home and witnessed by Lara. Judge Baxter told me to, 'Get on with the residency.'

Judge Baxter – Nominated for his performance as 'Bruce' (Jaws, 1975) and nominee for the British Comedy Awards 2006

At 9.30am, I met Mr Buckley in the family court side of the court building; fifteen minutes later, he expressed his concern that Ms Hyde had still not turned up, and that the judge may start another case, which could go on for several hours. Ten minutes after that, I was informed Ms Hyde, followed by her mother Mrs Jackson, had arrived, and my barrister Mr Barrett went to have a word with her counsel.

It was not long before Mr Barrett came back, and he stated that Ms Hyde had not got a barrister, she was representing herself, and that she told him she had a tape that she wanted Judge Baxter to listen to. I told Mr Barrett that I have nothing to hide.

The usher announced that Judge Baxter was ready for us; Ms Hyde walked into the courtroom with Mrs Jackson behind her. Entering once everyone was in position, Judge Baxter stated, 'I realise that it was very short notice for Ms Hyde to gain a barrister.'

After looking through the typed notes of the hearing, I obviously did not need a barrister either; due to Judge Baxter's attitude with Mr Barrett, my worries about my children's stability and the continuation of Ms Hyde's abusive and aggressive behaviour were outright dismissed or ignored. No one had invited, encouraged or provoked Ms Hyde to come to our home, for any reason. Due to Ms Hyde's behaviour, instability and chaos was brought into our lives. I didn't want to phone the police and have them at my door. I did not want to get involved with solicitors, or take Ms Hyde to court. I did these things because of the nightmare unfolding once again in my children's lives and mine.

When Alice went to live with her mother from the 13th May to the 9th June, we had two incidents at the bottle bank. Judge Baxter jumps to some conclusion that we have problems when we meet, and this clearly had not been the case for the majority of the time since the order was made in 2004. I have met Ms Hyde on occasions in the playground at Lara's school and at sports days and other events, without trouble or fuss.

The disgraceful behaviour that I had no choice but to come to the court to address began in January after the trampoline incident, and not as Judge Baxter suggested, 'at any meeting or opportunity'. This may be because Ms Hyde's bipolar disorder occurs in episodes – there are periods when she is reasonable towards our children.

Mr Barrett stated to Judge Baxter that my application is in relation to Ms Hyde coming to my house and causing criminal damage. Judge Baxter said that he would deal with that on the assumption that there is 'no need for the parties to meet'. We are the parents of three children at various stages of development, by necessity there is going to be overlap there, and it is vital that Ms Hyde and I do not backpedal. Judge Baxter, once again, takes the complete wrong approach to our family.

Judge Baxter mocked my pictures of the evidence, as if the £550 worth of damage to the door and the defacing of the brickwork to the porch, on a rented property, was a joke!

The reason we were standing in court was moved on from so swiftly I almost got whiplash, as Judge Baxter queried Ms Hyde's dissatisfaction with contact arrangements. Prior, Judge Baxter refused to allow Mr Barrett to explain that Hayley and Alice, because of the behaviour of Ms Hyde towards them, were not currently having weekend contact.

In January, when Hayley and Alice stated that they did not want to return to Ms Hyde's, I phoned Cafcass and spoke to Mr Ellwood, who told me not to force them but to try and encourage Hayley and Alice, to which I have. Ms Hyde has had every opportunity to talk to several organisations concerning Hayley and Alice not wanting weekend contact and complying with the court order, rather than return us to court. I believe she chose not to do so, because of her own violent behaviour in the *several* incidents with Hayley and Alice.

When Alice went to her mother's, I spoke to Melissa, and she was trying to make contact with the Children's Legal Centre to ask if Alice would like to arrange to meet with me and talk to someone. I had tried to contact Alice many times by phone, but she either did not answer or Ms Hyde refused. On one occasion, Ms Hyde sent me a text reaffirming what she'd shouted on the phone: if I wanted to talk to Alice then I must ask her for her permission first. (This text I still have.) I believe it was a golden opportunity for Ms Hyde to back me up as a parent, help Alice as a mum and parent, and use the opportunity to try and level the ground she had lost with Alice, over the disputes and incidences that had occurred between herself, Alice and Hayley.

Instead, Ms Hyde started making abusive phone calls to our home and making false allegations about Hayley and myself bullying Alice. As the weeks passed, I believe Ms Hyde's behaviour was deteriorating and she was becoming more abusive and aggressive.

I have never prevented Ms Hyde from phone contact with Hayley, Alice or Lara. I had, up to the half term (the Hayley and Ms Hyde incident), arranged and dropped off Hayley and Alice to Ms Hyde's several times, and swapped Mothering Sunday with Ms Hyde, as she and the children were going away for a weekend party.

After the incident in April, Hayley and Alice have made it clear to me that they did not want to stay over with their mother, although they have occasionally called in at hers.

I do not make any fuss, cause trouble or problems as I want my children to have a good relationship with their mother; it is whether their mother is capable of consistently providing a good relationship for them that I'm worried about – and if not, can all these outside organisations involved in our family ensure she receives support?

I have not tried to prevent Lara from her weekend contact with her mother, evidently, as Lara has continued contact where Hayley and Alice have not. All three children have their own complicated relationships with their mother, and it is not my place to make decisions that impact that for them. As long as they're safe and happy, I'm happy.

Judge Baxter's statement that 'it does get to the heart of the issue' is unfounded, and once again I feel that it is me that is being held responsible for Ms Hyde's behaviour and actions. As Judge Baxter had now turned this hearing for an injunction into several family court issues, I believe it is an injustice that he would not allow my barrister or myself to reply to his unfounded comments and beliefs.

My children have all been through this before, and it is an unsettling and unsure time for any child to have in their lives. We do not need a return to court hearings extending for monthly periods over residency. Judge Baxter had nothing but what Ms Hyde had told him this morning – none of which was relevant to this hearing and was totally without evidence of any kind.

It is suggested by Judge Baxter that if Ms Hyde is dissatisfied with the contact arrangements, she should go to her solicitor. Is that the same as me going to my solicitor, getting advice and asking to make the appropriate application for this injunction?

Mrs Jackson, who was or still is a magistrate and accompanied Ms Hyde at this so-called hearing for an injunction, was well aware of the procedure. You would have thought, from the previous statements of 'truth', set before judges by this 'Justice to the Peace', any decent grandmother would have encouraged and helped their daughter sort out her contact with Hayley and Alice, if she truly was so concerned. After all, she has not seen her grandchildren for months. (Hayley 7 months, and Alice from 20th January to the 13th May, and from 9th June onwards.) Mrs Jackson has had every opportunity to contact Hayley and Alice on their mobiles, to talk or arrange meeting, or the home phone, but she has not done so.

How can this judge be so far from the truth and also so far away from the reason that I made the application, which was to try and prevent Ms Hyde's disgraceful behaviour at our home and in front of the children? The dents in my van door and the word 'cunt' being added to my daughter's vocabulary was the reason I was at this hearing today.

I believe that the heart of the issue is and has always been the conduct of Ms Hyde, and Judge Baxter's inability to have any understanding of the disgraceful behaviour which has been placed in three children's lives, yet again.

I also believe that it is shameful how a judge can repeatedly ignore, dismiss and, with ease, shift any wrong doing and blatantly discredit and denounce the person/parent who has shown stability, reliability, patience and understanding, not only with my children but also with Ms Hyde, despite such provocation from Ms Hyde's condition over the years, and on more than one occasion, condemnation from judges in the Family Courts.

Ms Hyde stated to Judge Baxter that the root of this problem is when Alice was 'kicked out by her father' and stayed with her for a month. The evening Alice chose to walk out of our home, I called Ms Hyde and explained to her why Alice was upset. Alice is reaching her teenage years, and I believe that she was testing the water, as all children growing up do. Standing my ground as a sensible parent has caused me many problems, problems that I believe would not exist if Ms Hyde had done her role as a parent to Alice.

When Judge Baxter asked Ms Hyde to provide an undertaking not to visit my home, Ms Hyde stated she wanted an undertaking from me as well. (Arr the old bartering system.) I shook my head; it was with disbelief at the farce that was being played out. He became very irritated indeed at my human response of shaking my head; I was not shouting or using foul language, I was not scratching the side of his desk or causing criminal damage to the courtroom. He made further derogatory comments aimed towards my conduct and character, insulting the effort that I have put into my children and the situations with Ms Hyde.

Judge Baxter did not address Ms Hyde's disgraceful behaviour in any way. He did not suggest that it was unacceptable under any circumstances, and he showed no care for the damage Ms Hyde has caused, physically and emotionally to her children.

Mr Buckley's typed notes of the hearing

23 June

BA – Mr Barrett, my barrister
JB – Judge Baxter

BA: I am here on behalf of the applicant Mr Marlo on an application for non-molestation and occupation orders, the respondent is here in person.

JB: Yes, I looked at this application on an ex–parte basis but rejected it the other day and requested that you all come back once notice has been served on the respondent. An occupation order I believe in this circumstance is not relevant as the respondent has not lived or is living in the applicant's current accommodation do you agree?

BA: I agree your Honour the respondent has not been in occupation of the applicant's accommodation. Whilst negotiations were taking place, Ms Hyde informed me that she has a tape. Unfortunately, we had limited time to talk, however I understand she wants the court to hear the tape, although I have not heard it.

Ms Hyde: This is not true.

JB: Is there a tape?

Ms Hyde: There is a tape which is completely different to when I was arrested and completely different to my statement.

JB: What? The taped interview was not submitted?

Ms Hyde: No.

BA: Missed, client speaking to Judge Baxter.

JB: What amounts to your client's statement are allegations which are connected with contact, yes? The order was made by Judge Chips which involves Hayley, 14, Alice, 12, Lara, 8 years, residing with him and a contact order was dealt with in the summer of 2004, quite complicated. It provides for alternate weekends and half the holidays from the sounds of things most of this order has gone under the bridge; handover to take place at McDonalds.

(No, my application has no relevance to the contact. Ms Hyde was not at my property to handover the children, this was an unprovoked incident, which was why my application had been to the criminal court, not the Family Courts.)

BA: This is no longer the case your honour, handover now takes place at the bottle bank during school holidays; during school term time it takes place at the children's school and my client is not in attendance.

Ms Hyde: No, your honour.

JB: Contain yourself Miss – you will have your say once I have spoken with Mr BA to understand exactly what his position is! Now I will change the order from McDonalds to the bottle bank. Mr BA, is there a problem with contact?

(Oh, thank you, your Honour; that was the third thing on my list of why I was here today in court, to make sure the judge changes the existing order and piece of paper to set the handover of the children at McDonalds to the new destination, the bottle bank.

That was number three sorted, just the criminal damage to a works van and a rented property to go…)

BA: Hayley and Alice have not been going to Ms Hyde's due to the violence used against them the last time. I believe the last they saw their mother was on Mothering Sunday; these are the two eldest girls; I understand that Lara does attend. The problem is with Ms Hyde's ability to control herself, which has caused problems in the past.

JB: In relation to contact is there any reason why Ms Hyde should visit your client's home other than at the bottle bank? The reason I ask is with respect to paragraph 5 of your client's statement is that this is the only time they both actually come face to face and there are problems.

(Good to see Judge Baxter has got to paragraph 5 in my statement, yet the problem was not with the handovers.

Again, I felt like a criminal with police at my door and trouble down the road for my neighbours, all because of Ms Hyde.)

BA: Yes, your honour at the bottle bank.

JB: Your client also has made complaints in relation to phone calls and her coming to the house. As far as I am concerned there is no need for her to do either one of these. I also find complaints with respect to the bottle bank. What actually happens, where is the bottle bank?

BA: Just down the road, a few hundred yards.

JB: There is no need for the Applicant to go to the bottle bank. They are all old enough.

BA: Missed again, as client interrupting Judge Baxter.

(Good old father, interrupting the emperor. I didn't want my 8-year-old daughter to walk by herself along several busy roads.)

JB: Is there any reason why there cannot be a solution from not allowing these people to meet?

(We've gotten so completely off track, now as two parents, we are not allowed to meet, diminishing any chance of bringing Ms Hyde to account for her unacceptable actions, or for us to ever try to get on as a separated family; he's essentially saying these two parents are as bad as each other.)

BA: My client's application is in relation to Ms Hyde coming to his house.

JB: Yes, I will deal with that on the assumption that there is no need for the parties to meet. This also relates to the bottle bank. There is no need for your client to take the children to the bottle bank. You are seeking an order from stopping her from coming to his home.

(Three penal notices placed on me by the family court judges – Judge Baxter himself bestowing me with at least one – without any evidence; simply for turning up on that day in court. In each of the applications against me, there was no criminal damage, aggressive or violent behaviour, and yet Ms Hyde is beyond reproach; she can vandalise my van and a rented property, and behave in such a way that no adult should, let alone in front of children.)

BA: And damage.

JB: What on the brickwork, what is it?

BA: The sign of the Devil your honour.

JB: This means nothing to me, take a seat. Ms Hyde first of all, I get the impression that you are not happy with the current contact arrangements?

(It shouldn't matter what the symbol means, the point is Ms Hyde scratched it into the brickwork of my rented property – oh well, better find out why she wasn't happy…)

Ms Hyde: Yes, your Honour.

JB: Do you have a solicitor?

Ms Hyde: Yes, I do but Mrs Mason is on holiday and there was no one to come to today's hearing with me.

(Poor, defenceless Ms Hyde, charged with criminal damage with no one to defend her. Not that she needs Mrs Mason here, what with the Fat Controller as a judge, who has already dismissed everything that we've been put through, in addition to seeing the evidence.)

JB: I am not capable (well he said it!) *to deal with contact today however, I can vary the drop off and collection from McDonalds to the bottle bank, by consent. If you are dissatisfied with the arrangements regarding contact you need to go to your solicitors, get advice and ask them to make the appropriate applications.*

(Is Judge Baxter preparing his jokes for his first show at the Apollo? How can he be suggesting Ms Hyde bring us back to court concerning residency, when we are standing in his courtroom, regarding an injunction, due to one of us causing criminal damage? This would be understandable, if the person he was suggesting to seek legal advice, was not in fact the person who had been cautioned by the police!)

Ms Hyde: I have a letter written by my solicitor addressed to the respondent in relation to contact, would you like to see it your Honour?

JB: Yes. Unless it has a direct relation to the offence involved in these proceedings.

BA: I have not seen this letter your honour.

(Not court protocol.)

JB: Neither have I which is why I am wanting to read it now. (Judge Baxter reads the letter and passes it to Mr BA.)

JB: Well, this is not the best letter written by Mrs Mason; however, it does get to the heart of the issue. Mrs Mason needs to put an application in on your behalf rather than writing insufficient letters. Now to the problem in hand. In general terms do you contest parts or all of Mr Marlo's statement?

(Not one of Mrs Mason's best letters? Who is Judge Baxter, Mrs Mason's editor in chief? I felt myself looking around for the cameras and film crew; there was no way I was standing in a courtroom, having applied for an injunction against Ms Hyde for kicking the door of my work van and scratching a Devil symbol on a property, all in front of our children, only to have Mrs Mason – on holiday but still interfering with proceedings, going to incredible lengths to defend her client; as it would appear, she is on call for Ms Hyde 52 weeks of the year – have an off day in letter writing, but nonetheless get to the heart of the issue, which is what to Judge Baxter?

That Ms Hyde needs help with her parenting, as he suggested in 2000 but decided was too late for in early 2004? No, clearly this is a classic case of a father's intent to make a mother's life difficult.

Six years of hell from Smitch Law, Mrs Mason, Ms Hyde and the Family Courts, one badly written solicitor's letter later, and we've found the root of the matter. Mrs Mason managed it and she wasn't even in the fucking country!)

Ms Hyde: Part of it, however the root of this problem is when Alice was kicked out by her father and stayed with me for a whole month in May.

JB: I understand it from the application that the children had not seen you at all?

BA: May I interrupt your Honour. It is the two eldest that have not seen their mother since Mothering Sunday.

JB: Yes, however Ms Hyde is saying that she has seen and has had Alice stay with her for a month. Now this is either true or it is not. Mr BA have the two eldest children seen their mother after Mothering Sunday?

(Mr BA talks to client.)

BA: Yes, your Honour, I understand that Alice did stay with her mother during May, I apologise having told the court that it was Mothering Sunday when the children last saw their mother.

(The context of Alice staying at her mother's in May would go above Judge Baxter's head anyway. Alice was pushing boundaries that needed to be addressed by both Ms Hyde and myself, by going to her mother's because I would not let her sleepover with a friend's granddad with a police tag. Instead of supporting my setting of that boundary, Ms Hyde used Alice's rebellion as an opportunity to influence my residency and make a case to go back to court, as well as to pressure both Alice and me for Alice's Child Benefit.

In the background, Alice's behaviour at school had dipped while staying at her mother's.)

JB: It is not fair for me to try all of the evidence today-

(It is not fair to the children or me to continue the farce but here we go again; Judge Baxter has seen the evidence, there is no more to bring to the table regarding Ms Hyde's behaviour at my children's home. If Judge Baxter *was* looking for evidence concerning contact of the children with Ms Hyde, then we were all in the wrong hearing.)

-however what I can do is adjourn and give Ms Hyde the chance to put a statement, however I believe I have got to deal with this now. Ms Hyde, I will need your undivided attention! Now it seems necessary for there to be no communication between these two parties as it seems this is when problems arise, apart from communication via solicitors. I would therefore like Ms Hyde to provide an undertaking not to visit the home.

Ms Hyde: I want an undertaking as well.

JB: It seems Mr BA that your client is shaking his head, however I believe that with cross undertaking, it will provide for a balance between these two people who are as bad as each other.

(Judge Baxter, back on stage at the Apollo. With all seriousness, this comment hurt and shocked me because, over the years within the Family Courts, there has been no evidence provided against me suggesting I am replicating Ms Hyde's behaviour.

This comment by Judge Baxter served no purpose, only giving Ms Hyde the confidence that she can behave in any manner on her reign of disruption, and not only would there be no consequences against her, she could see me reprimanded for her behaviour. It is an unjust statement to make, one that is very easy for someone who clearly doesn't care either way.

I would love to see Judge Baxter's evidence of any of the above.

It can't be right that Ms Hyde can stand before a judge, with a criminal damage charge, and see that I will be looked upon in equal measure as the issue for the family, despite all of the incidences involving Ms Hyde.

It should be about the behaviour of the person and the person's actions that determines how they are treated. This very judge put a penal notice on me for standing by my daughter in 2000; how exactly do you think I would have been treated by Judge Baxter if I had kicked and dented Ms Hyde's car door?)

JB: Both clients shall not to loiter in the vicinity or communicate… Mr BA will you tell your client to stop shaking his head, it is really irritating me!

(Unfortunately, it was a human reaction on my part; when someone is talking such bullshit, and you're not allowed to utter a word, for fear of flames coming from Judge Baxter's nostrils; as a father to three children, trying to raise them in some state of normality and happiness, yet perpetually thrown by Ms Hyde's bipolar and personality; as a person, just some council estate kid, standing before someone who has to be referred to as your Honour, when there's nothing honourable about any of it...

'The prisoner who now stands before you,

Was caught red–handed showing feelings,

Showing feelings of an almost human nature,

This will not do.')

JB: Is your client prepared to agree?

(I was being asked to agree to something I hadn't ever done, which is bring trouble to Ms Hyde's door – there's family court justice for you.)

(Mr BA takes instructions.)

BA: My client is prepared to make the undertakings.

JB: Yes (Judge Baxter interrupted) less self–righteous, so upon the respondent Ms Hyde undertaking paragraph 1 not in any way to communicate with Mr Marlo save through her solicitors Smitch Law and…

Ms Hyde: What happens about illness? He never tells me; he leaves it until four o'clock.

JB: I daresay he does let you know. Paragraph 2 not to enter, re–enter, visit or loiter in the vicinity of his address and upon Mr Marlo undertaking paragraph 1 nor in any way to communicate with the respondent Ms Hyde, save through his solicitor Parstons, and paragraph 2 not to enter, re–enter, visit or loiter in the vicinity of Ms Hyde's address.

(Judge Baxter's high and almighty order is to encourage solicitor involvement in this family – it would be a breach of a court order for me to, say, text Ms Hyde about something that Lara wants from her residence; I could be penalised. If Lara texts her mother to ask herself, we're involving children in making arrangements – have we found the family court paradox?

Also, who's paying for these solicitors to be involved? It is a waste of the public purse, or puts unnecessary pressure on a parent with sole residency of three children!

We have a new one for the list of accusations I have had placed on me – everyone tick 'loitering' off their 'Bad Fathers Resume' bingo card. I must be close to a full house, with the top prize of a prison cell for the weekend, bed and full board.)

JB: Just out of mild interest, can you help me with the geography of your address, Ms Hyde?

Ms Hyde: It is in equal distance to the bottle bank as it is to the Mr Marlo's house.

JB: So, you are half a mile apart?

Ms Hyde: Yes, but the only other problem is phone contact. What happens if the children are ill?

JB: If the children are ill, Mr Marlo is bound to tell the Headteacher.

Ms Hyde: But he doesn't, he never tells the Headteacher.

(Again, a baseless lie by Ms Hyde but a detrimental accusation against me. Mr Church has written many letters of commendation as to my upbringing of the children, and my communication with the school – however, I couldn't shake my head, let alone remind Judge Baxter of this fact. So the stage is set: I don't communicate with anyone.)

JB: All I'm saying Ms Hyde is if the Headteacher knows that the children are unwell and not in attendance at school then he will tell you, which I will not look as being in breach of this Order. (Judge Baxter interrupted by client.) Both of you have the classic ability to cause problems!

(I had been quiet as a mouse so far, only shaking my head and twitching my whiskers; the only classic ability I have is being dragged into other people's lies, deception and agendas. It's a rubbish superpower, but Marvel is lacking in superheroes that are good at pissing people off.)

JB: On those undertakings, it is ordered that one, there be no Order for costs, save detailed assessment of the publicly funded costs of the Applicant Mr Marlo. You say Ms Hyde that Mrs Mason is on holiday, when is she back?

Ms Hyde: Monday week.

JB: May I suggest that you go and see Mrs Mason so that you can make an application and get into court with respect to contact.

(Is Judge Baxter on commission, filtering customers to Mrs Mason at Smitch Law?)

Ms Hyde: Does it have to be dealt with by Judge Chips, as I would like you to deal with it your Honour?

(Does Ms Hyde must think she has some favour with this judge, to say such a thing? Meanwhile, I had fallen off my chair and awaited Judge Baxter's response.)

JB: (Missed, Judge Baxter interrupted by client.) …well I have never had that before where I have been asked in open Court for my assistance in another application, however it's possible or it may be his Honour Judge Chips, I don't know. I will leave it at that.

This is not how a judge, impartial and unbiased, should have responded to Ms Hyde blatantly requesting for him to reside on our case – in Ms Hyde's eyes, Judge Chips had ruled for me to have Sole Residency, and Judge Baxter, throughout, has punished me and my children, while being sympathetic to her demands, regardless of the evidence before him to suggest otherwise.

So, my application to prevent someone from repeating violent behaviour at my children's home, according to Judge Baxter's wealth of experience as a judge (and comedian), has concluded with:

An undertaking by myself to not communicate with Ms Hyde or visit her property – no loitering, either.

Any communications to be passed through solicitors – Smitch Law being cordially invited to disrupt the children's lives for potentially years to come.

The encouragement, based on Ms Hyde's unhappiness with existing arrangements, to contact the not-so-great letter writer and solicitor on retainer, Mrs Mason, to issue further applications.

Mediation Appointment

29 June

Dear Mr Marlo,
An assessment appointment has been made for you on Tuesday 4 July at 12.30pm at the above address. Your mediator will be Rachel Mars. Another mediator may be present.
This appointment is free – if you are unable to keep it, please let us know immediately. As a charity, a cancelled appointment threatens the future of our service.
Mediation will cost you nothing if you are eligible for Community Legal Service Funding. Part of this appointment is to assess you for Public Funding. If you do not attend – your entitlement may be affected.
We look forward to seeing you.

Dean Marlo

Lara's sports day

29 June

As we were having breakfast, I asked Lara if her mother had spoken to her about picking her up after sports day for Ruth's birthday. Lara replied that her mother had not mentioned it.

At about 3pm, as I sat watching Lara's sports day, I received a call. I answered the phone and it was Smitch Law; a solicitor announced himself and stated that he had been instructed by Ms Hyde to inform me– I interrupted him and stated that any information he has to say should be relayed to my solicitor, not me.

It should not be acceptable for Ruth's solicitors to contact me direct; I do believe that this is a form of harassment. I was at Lara's sports day and Ruth knows this – she should have been there too.

Five or so minutes later, I received a call from Melissa, who said that Smitch Law had been in contact, and Ruth has stated she will be taking Lara after her sports day.

I wrote to Ruth on the 16th June and asked for her to inform me and Lara what her plans were. Ruth, via Smitch Law, decides to inform me, leaving Lara in the wind, 15 minutes before the events finish.

After the last race, I ran across the track and over to Lara. Such is the way of everything involving Ruth, I was dealing with happiness and pride, as well as sadness, because I had to inform Lara that her mother is picking her up. It is not right; it is not normal and it is unsettling for an eight–year–old child to be unaware of what is going on in their life.

102

No fireworks allowed

4 July

I attended the mediation appointment at 12:30pm, as requested.

I gathered all of the letters of communication I had and any details that showed we were able to get on and organise arrangements for our children.

We spent 10 minutes assessing whether I would need to pay for any further meetings and moved on to how I thought Ms Hyde and myself could resolve our issues; they said that I would be surprised how sitting down with Ms Hyde and a mediator could resolve many of the problems we had.

I asked if I could have two minutes to explain; I told them that the issue has not been acrimony as much as it is the effect Ms Hyde's condition has on her ability to make reasonable judgements. We have made changes, re-organised the holidays or weekends for special events, which only becomes an issue when Ms Hyde's mental health deteriorates or perceives myself to be in the wrong – resulting in Ms Hyde contacting her solicitors.

While I am willing to speak and compromise with Ms Hyde, I am not prepared to sit in a room with her and defend myself against her false allegations, which have only ever clouded the situation.

I said that if perhaps Ms Hyde herself was being mediated (in the absence of a mental health team) they could help her to cope with her children or find an organisation that could.

They told me that I have their number and if at any time I changed my mind, I could call them.

(I asked myself, do I need mediation meetings, just to say Ms Hyde should comply with the court order and be there for her children?

I cannot express the desperation I feel… Seven years since Ruth and I separated, and she still has a huge detrimental impact on my day-to-day life.

I know this is in part to do with Ruth's bipolar disorder, yet, as throughout, people and organisations jump on Ms Hyde's merry-go-round and we start again on square one.)

Dean Marlo

Mason to Melissa – rackets at the ready

10 July

We refer to the hearing before his Honour Judge Baxter on the 23rd June 2006 and have now obtained a copy of the order which confirms that cross undertakings were given by our respective clients.

Our client instructs us that she has been endeavouring to obtain confirmation from your client that both Alice and Lara will be coming with her on holiday to Egypt in the first week of August.

Could your client please confirm that Alice and Lara will be coming on that holiday.

There have been problems in the past with regards to holidays which have resulted in our client losing money when the children have not come for the planned trip.

We would ask that you please respond to this letter as your client has failed to respond to any correspondence that has been sent to him this year.

You will appreciate that there has to be lines of communication between the solicitors given the undertakings that have now been made and our client does require a response as soon as possible.

(Oh dear, Mr Marlo is not responding to my letters, one can but wonder why!)

Hayley has been adamant from the inception of Ms Hyde's Egypt holiday that she doesn't want to fly and therefore doesn't want to go, and Lara has been certain that she wants to go. For Alice, she shares Hayley's fear of flying and, as Hayley has also commented, she is apprehensive of her mother's behaviour, which is volatile in their home setting – let alone miles away. Lara considers herself 'unlikely to set her mother off' and has no fear of airplanes; even I would have liked to see the pyramids and more of what Egypt has to offer.

All of the above Ms Hyde is aware of, because the children have spoken to her, as I have on the phone, but it normally ends up with abuse and accusations that I will not let the children go on holiday. I repeat what Hayley and Alice had told me, and that Lara has always been on board, but she will not have it, shouting, 'You are stopping the children from having a holiday with their mother!'

The only outlier is Alice, who is uncertain – again, most predominantly, due to her mother's behaviour.

There has never been a holiday wherein one or more of the children have not gone with the respective parent, and it is a bizarre allegation only presented to attempt to add credibility to the implication that I go out of my way to make Ms Hyde's life difficult – when in reality, the opposite is true.

Admittedly, I had a great time sitting there watching one of Smitch Law's letters go up in flames. I try to keep my carbon emissions to a minimum, but this was a personal 'kick in the bollocks' to Mrs Mason, also on behalf of all fathers who had to respond to letters containing nothing more than threats from a solicitor.

I know if there is one thing that gets up Smitch Law and Mrs Mason's noses, it is to let them know that they are not of importance to me or my children.

(Smitch Law are a law firm of dictators, and dictators do not like being ignored.)

'Why is a solicitor getting involved at all?' is the real question – apart from some ridiculous order.

Is it because one of their client's children does not like flying?

Is it because another one of their client's children is concerned about their mother's behaviour?

Or is it none of the above? Perhaps Mrs Mason could tell us.

The children and their parent's situation when flying to go on holiday, is only a question Ms Hyde and her children can answer. Why write to me, when many children and adults have a fear of flying?

Ms Hyde knew Lara wanted to go and that Hayley did not want to go. Ms Hyde need only have spoken to Alice to discuss with her daughter her holiday plans, like any normal parent would.

My family's day to day lives are made into something inexplicable, strange and absurd, when many of the things are normal in other families, and don't require solicitor involvement.

Dean Marlo

Accidents

11 July

We had some great fun this summer. I bought a giant swimming pool for the children and while Ma and the children loved to swim in it, it quickly became the largest ammo stock of water balloons for an entire neighbourhood of children who would be racing around the back garden, in battle. Come July though, it needed cleaning out; me, Ma and Alice took it on.

Ma grabbed a mop and stepped into the pool. At the same time, she slipped and fell.

It was a whirlwind of the ambulance and us following to the hospital, to make sure Ma was alright. By the time we got there, Ma had been given a dose of morphine, which turned her into even more of a comedian; under the circumstances, we ended up laughing more than crying.

Unfortunately, the x-rays came back and Ma had broken her leg, requiring surgery.

The children and I agreed we would go to see Ma every day after school, and would make sure to gather some things to bring her comfort.

As soon as we got home, Lara got her drawing pencils out, to decorate the walls by Ma's hospital bed. Hayley and Alice discussed what books and word search puzzles to take, and, despite it being a sad situation, I felt proud of the love our family have for each other.

Mason to Melissa – Three letters in one day

14 July

Extremely Urgent
We refer to previous correspondence and look forward to hearing from you, by return, to confirm that contact will be taking place today with all three children.
We look forward to hearing from you, please by 12 noon today.

We thank you for your letter dated 13th July and we look forward to hearing from you, please, as soon as possible.

We thank you for your fax of today's date and look forward to hearing from you with regard to the holiday to Egypt.

(Unfortunately, Melissa's replies to Mrs Mason of July 13th and 14th are MIA.)

Summertime sadness

17 July

Ruth's weekend contact just passed, and although Hayley and Alice went on the Friday night, they came home on Saturday. Fortunately, I was in the office and not on site. I asked them if everything was alright; they said that their mother was going out on Bernard's sailing boat and they didn't want to go, so they came home.

I asked if Lara had gone with their mother, and Hayley said, 'Yes, she didn't want to go either but our mother wouldn't let Lara come with us.'

When I picked Lara up from school on Monday, I listened as Lara told me about her weekend. She was upset as she hadn't wanted to go with her mother and Bernard on his boat, and while Hayley and Alice had been able to choose, she was forced by her mother to stay with her. Lara explained that she spent the entire time below deck, whilst her mother and Bernard had drinks. When they got back to land, Lara said to her mother, 'I don't understand why I couldn't have gone to Dad's, when you didn't want me here anyway.'

I asked how her mother responded and Lara smiled sadly; imitating her mother's voice she said, 'Don't be silly and say horrible things, we had a wonderful time!'

I gave Lara a hug and told her next time her mother is going boating to call me and I would try and speak to her, to see if she will let her come home and be dropped back later.

Ms Hyde's application (C2/C1)

18 July

C2

I am applying for residence orders in respect of Alice and Lara and in the interim for my contact with all three children to be enforced.

Domestic abuse, violence or harm

Do you believe that the children named above have suffered or at risk of suffering any harm from any of the following; any form of domestic violence; violence within the household; child abduction; other conduct or behaviour by any person who is or has been involved in caring for the child(ren) or lives with, or has contact with, the child(ren)?

Yes.

Your reason(s) for applying and any plans for the child(ren)

There have been long running proceedings with regard to Hayley, Alice and Lara. On 5 August 2004 his Honour Judge Chips made an order for all three children to live with Mr Marlo and for me to have defined contact. There have been lots of problems with regard to my contact with the children, with Mr Marlo refusing to comply with Court Orders, him failing to keep me advised of serious issues relating to the children, him removing the children from the jurisdiction without even informing me and in May 2006 Alice came to live with me. Alice left Mr Marlo's home on 13th May 2006 and stayed with me until 9th June 2006. During that time Alice did not have any contact with Mr Marlo which was her choice.

I have been advised by Alice and Hayley's school that their attendance is very poor and both the children are missing a lot of school. I have attendance records to confirm this. Lara has had 51 absences from school this year, since the start of school in September 2005, which I think is excessive.

Alice's behaviour has deteriorated since she has been living with Mr Marlo and she has been in trouble at school and at Martial Arts because of her aggression. I am very concerned about her and also with regard to Lara. Alice has now been referred for anger management at her school.

I have been very concerned about Mr Marlo's care of the children and the fact that his dog had bitten the children on several occasions requiring medical attention.

I have not had contact with Hayley for months and Mr Marlo fails to encourage her to have any contact with me since Mother's Day. Mr Marlo tries to cut me out of the children's lives by preventing contact, refusing to keep me informed about important matters relating to the children and generally making my life as difficult as possible.

I believe that it is not in the children's best interests to continue to reside with Mr Marlo. I have to accept that because of Hayley's age then she should be able to live where she wishes but I firmly believe that Alice and Hayley would benefit from living with me and having contact with Mr Marlo.

Why is it that when Alice refused contact with me, it was 'her choice', however when Hayley and Alice similarly refuse contact with Ms Hyde (due to abuse!) Ms Hyde applies to court and is successful?

That's not a copying error, Ms Hyde wrote 'Alice and Hayley' rather than 'Alice and

---

Lara' at the end of her application to court for sole residence of Alice and Lara…

This reminds me of the early 2000s, where Hayley was similarly swept to the side and forgotten about, so long as Ms Hyde gets Alice and Lara out of the deal. My heart breaks for Hayley; she loves Ma like a mum, but I know that doesn't replace the real thing, especially when her mother openly disregards years of abuse, turmoil and sadness in Hayley's young life at 15, just as she did when Hayley was 8.

These are not the wishes of any of the children; they all know their mother's household is volatile, an environment where you walk on eggshells because you don't know if their mother is going to be affectionate or abusive. I will continue to be supportive when any of the children desire to have contact, or sleepover for extra periods, but I will not bet my children's lives on Ms Hyde's ability to be stable and treat them as a parent should. She completely omits the incident where she strangled Hayley in front of Alice and two of their friends. It is shameful behaviour.

I am once again living on a knife edge, and fail to see how Ms Hyde's applications can be justified when, apart from Ms Hyde's dissatisfaction, no organisation or one person have ever come to the conclusion that the children being in my care has an adverse effect on them or their wellbeing.

I wish I was someone capable of making my voice heard, of telling my children's story and have anyone understand how thoroughly Ms Hyde has ripped us all apart – it makes my skin crawl to be looked down on by a judge and told I am just as bad, when all I have ever wanted is for my children to have a good childhood.

This feels like a very, very long year already.

C1
Further Information
Social Services have been involved with the family as a result of problems in the past. Mr Trumpton and Christa Banner of Social Services have had involvement with the children in the past but there is no current involvement. The Police have also been called out in recent months as a result of problems with both Hayley and Alice.

Incidents of abuse, violence or harm
There have been a number of incidents with regard to Mr Marlo being abusive and threatening to me often in front of the children. When I lived with Mr Marlo, he was both verbally and physically aggressive to me and the children have seen incidents between us.

Even after Mr Marlo and I separated he continued to be abusive and threatening to me and he often swears at me and makes derogatory comments about me in front of the children.

I have been very concerned about the effect of this behaviour on the children and have suggested to Mr Marlo that the children should have some form of counselling. Mr Marlo does not agree with me.

I continue to be fearful that the children will be at risk of emotional harm from Mr Marlo because of his unpredictable behaviour and his temper.

Mr Marlo did apply to the County Court in June 2006 for an injunction order against me claiming that I had been abusive and threatening to him. I deny that I acted in this manner and at Court on 23 June 2006 no order was made on the application for the injunction although both Mr Marlo and myself had to give undertakings to the court not to communicate at all or to attend at each other's homes.

Involvement of the child(ren)
All of the children have witnessed arguments between Mr Marlo and myself and they are well aware of Mr Marlo's feelings towards me. I believe that Alice has been severely affected by such behaviour. She is displaying signs of aggression herself; she has been in trouble at school because of this and she has been excluded from her Marital Arts class because of this behaviour.

Steps or orders required to protect you and the children
I am hopeful that the undertakings given by both Mr Marlo and myself will assist but I still have concerns about the emotional welfare of the children while they are living with Mr Marlo. As a result of the undertakings being given, I am hopeful that the children will not be made to communicate with me direct regarding the contact arrangements, which will take the pressure off the children.

It is evident that Mrs Mason needs to advise her client as a human being and not an open purse, to encourage Ms Hyde to seek help. It has to come from an unbiased (in Ms Hyde's eyes) person – since the beginning, and certainly with varying degrees of escalation, my questioning of Ms Hyde's behaviour and judgement is always misconstrued in her mind, and I am generally reserved to be blamed.

Every parent finds challenges when raising their children, but I firmly believe that Ms Hyde needs support due to the additional stresses of her bipolar disorder, and this is what would have a real positive impact on our children's lives, as well as our ability to get on with each other.

How can she deny it and Judge Baxter dismiss her criminal damage, when she was cautioned by the police?

Take a bow Judge Baxter, I knew, *even at the time*, that the undertaking I had to take for having my van kicked in and letterbox sworn at would be turned around to imply my behaviour is as Ms Hyde claims. Basically, Judge Baxter gave Mrs Mason and Ms Hyde a joker card, which is the last thing our family needed, because he could have stopped the problems from evolving to where we are now, at that hearing.

My response

In the past, Social Services have been involved due to allegations made by the children in respect of the manner in which the Applicant, Ms Hyde, cares for them and incidents of abuse.

Most recently, I was phoned on 10 May 2005 by Social Services, who informed me that the children's Mental Health Team have referred the children to Social Services as a result of concerns expressed by Ms Hyde to them. Those were understood to be that 'all three children's behaviour is getting worse'; 'all three children sleep in the same bedroom'; 'there are difficulties with managing access and sticking to previously arranged timetables'. However, the social worker appeared to be unaware of what the residency and contact arrangements actually were. I have had no further communication from, or with, Social Services.

Contrary to her claim, police involvement in recent months has been due to Ms Hyde's behaviour, and not my own or the children's behaviour.

Ms Hyde and I have not lived together since 1999, which was, to my knowledge, before the last occasion that Ms Hyde was sectioned under the Mental Health Act.

Since the order providing for the children to reside with me was made in August 2004, I have only met with Ms Hyde at pre–arranged handover venues during school holidays and have not left my vehicle. Instead, Ms Hyde has, on occasions such as in May and June this year, been verbally abusive to me through an open window or door of my car, while the children have been moving from one vehicle to the other.

I recently sought an injunction against Ms Hyde, who had been turning up at my home being abusive and aggressive, and on one occasion, in full view of Lara, caused criminal damage to my vehicle; as a result Ms Hyde was cautioned by the police.

In respect of the suggested counselling for the children, I discussed this at length with Hayley's teacher, Mrs Sparrow, in May 2005 as a result of Mrs Sparrow informing me that she had a meeting with Ms Hyde, at Ms Hyde's request, regarding Hayley's mental stability and welfare. Mrs Sparrow told me that Ms Hyde had informed her that I 'could not make' the appointment. The truth was I had no knowledge of the appointment. The Applicant apparently informed the school that she was concerned as she thought that Hayley was affected by her great grandmother dying.

The children have previously been seen at CFCS, who did not consider any work with the children was necessary.

Sometime around the year 2000, as a result of a report or letter, I believe from Ms Hyde's psychiatrist, there was a suggestion that the children may benefit from counselling. I understood this suggestion was made at a time shortly after the children's separation from Ms Hyde when she was sectioned under the Mental Health Act and when they subsequently resided with Ms Hyde. The children attended the Children and Families Counselling Services in late 2002/early 2003 and saw Mr Guall, and the recommendation was that no assistance was needed.

Apart from my phone conversation with Hayley's teacher, Mrs Sparrow, in May 2005,

I have not been approached by anyone with respect to counselling for my children.

In so far as risk of emotional harm to the children, especially from my allegedly unpredictable behaviour and temper, any risk of harm to the children stems from Ms Hyde's abusive and erratic conduct, which is exacerbated by her mental health condition.

I have written conformation of my commitment to my children from the schools, and no incidents involving myself with the police, as well as character witnesses from customers to neighbours, which I believe provides evidence to refute the way Ms Hyde has portrayed me throughout court proceedings. There has been no intervention by either schools, Social Services or the police due to my conduct or care of the children.

Regarding the injunction proceedings in June 2006, and the resulting cross–undertakings, I understood these to have been made to keep the parties on an equal footing. As handovers have, when we have facilitated it, taken place at a neutral venue for more than two years and the children are now of an age to be able to walk between the two parental homes; I was prepared to proceed with cross–undertakings that neither party attend at the other's home and that there be no direct communication between the parties. However, I still believe Lara, 8, is too young to be walking by herself.

The children have never witnessed arguments between Ms Hyde and myself, as I have never responded to Ms Hyde in kind. There have been incidents since May 2006, when Ms Hyde has turned up at our home and been verbally abusive, and caused criminal damage.

Other incidents have arisen when Ms Hyde has 'had a go' at me, either through an open vehicle window or door, as the children have been changing vehicles. The children may have also overheard Ms Hyde 'having a go' at me over the phone or on the answering machine. It may of course be that Ms Hyde perceives my refusal to acquiesce to demands from her, as an argument. I have annexed hereto marked 'DTM 1' to 'DTM 6' copies of letters, regarding changing arrangements in the period March 2005 to 16 June 2006 showing the parties' ability to communicate and generally alter arrangements without 'argument'.

The allegation that Alice is displaying signs of aggression, having been in trouble at school and excluded from her Martial Arts class because of this behaviour, is incorrect. The statement by Ms Hyde that she believes Alice is displaying signs of aggression because Alice has been severely affected by witnessing arguments between myself and Ms Hyde is incorrect. Whilst Ms Hyde states that the children are 'well aware' of my 'feelings towards' Ms Hyde, she fails to state what those feelings are, in her view. By contrast, one or more of the children have been exposed in May and June this year to a number of incidents where Ms Hyde has berated me, sworn at me, called me a 'fucking cunt', an 'asshole', aggressively and repeatedly kicked my vehicle, to name a few examples.

Contrary to the children being 'well aware' of my 'feelings towards' Ms Hyde; they are well aware of Ms Hyde's feelings towards their father. Hayley and Alice have also been on the receiving end of violence from either Ms Hyde or her boyfriend while in Ms Hyde's care, which were also overheard or witnessed by Lara.

I have annexed hereto marked 'DTM 7' a letter from the Martial Arts School. In fact, as told by the instructors at the school regarding Hayley and Alice, the respect issue arose out of Alice's desire to chew gum during class, which was a health and safety risk. I have not been able to communicate with Alice's school since receipt of Ms Hyde's application. I do believe, however, that Alice had a particularly difficult period in school during the month that she resided with Ms Hyde, from 13 May to 9 June this year.

I annex hereto at pages 'DTM 8' to 'DTM 17', copies of the children's school reports for the last academic year. I believe that any difficulties arising this year are as a result of Alice growing up and issues in Alice's relationship with her mother, as well as Alice deciding to live where she wanted, and pick up sticks when she did not get her own way.

I am not sure if Alice's behaviour was fully playing one parent off another; I had no communication with Alice during most of her time spent at her mother's. Alice was not interested in her sisters, Nan nor Dad.

The children are not asked by me to take responsibility for making any contact arrangements. The contact arrangements are clear and in accordance with the court order. Difficulties that took place earlier this year between Hayley and Alice and Ms Hyde, while the children were with Ms Hyde, are outside my full knowledge as I was not present. As a result of those difficulties, both Hayley and Alice do not always follow their scheduled contact times with Ms Hyde, although generally they visit Ms Hyde when Lara has a contact weekend.

All three of the children have mobile phones that Ms Hyde may initiate contact with them on at any time, and vice versa, in addition to court ordered telephone contact.

I believe that the residency schedule and court order should remain as it is, however, I have no issue with Ms Hyde having more contact as long as the children are happy, safe and continue to do well at school. I would therefore suggest the clauses be added: for additional contact with Ms Hyde to be arranged before the dates suggested, and if the children refuse contact due to an abusive incident, the issue cannot be brought before the court as contempt of the order.

End of hospital

19 July

After a week in the hospital, Ma was discharged.

Before I had a chance to speak to Hayley, Alice and Lara, they had already set up a bed for Ma, a spare bottom bunk in one of their rooms. I appreciated their caring natures, but said we'd have to talk to Nan first.

We offered Ma to come live with us while she is recovering, however, Ma has always been an independent person, and said she would be more comfortable in her own flat, which luckily is on the ground floor. Rob lives nearby, and we of course will visit her every day still; we took Ma home and got her settled.

Smitch to Melissa

19 July

We refer to your letter dated 18th July 2006, upon which we have taken our client's instructions.

First our client is due to have the children from after school on Monday, 24th July through until 14th August.

Our client is unable to swap weekends as your client is suggesting at such short notice, and she expects Alice and Lara to come to her after school on Monday and she will then have six days to speak with Alice about whether she intends to travel to Egypt on 1st August.

Our client is, therefore, not able to agree to your client's proposals and we look forward to hearing from you, by return, that our client will have contact in accordance with the court order.

Our client also instructs us that she is unable to consider contact in September as the schedule for September onwards has not yet been agreed

Our client has been asking your client since May of this year to agree the schedule but he has failed to deal with this.

We look forward to hearing from you with a proposed schedule for September 2006 for the next 12 months.

Yours faithfully,

So, one solicitor's letter demanding I inform her whether Alice will be going on holiday, and another for Mrs Mason to tell me that Ms Hyde will have six days to talk to Alice about going to Egypt.

(Public funding being used as money for old rope.)

From Martial Arts Instructor

20 July

To whom it may concern,

I am writing to you regarding the reason for Miss Alice Marlo having her licence revoked for two weeks from our Martial Arts School. Alice was never violent or aggressive towards anybody at the club. The licence was revoked due to no respect to MAS instructors, after refusing to remove her chewing gum.

If there are any further queries about this matter, please do not hesitate to contact me.

Yours sincerely,

Sam

MA Instructor

Smitch to Parstons, come in Parstons

24 July

Smitch serves:
We refer to our letter dated 19th July 2006 and look forward to hearing from you by return that our client is to have the children from after school today until 14th August 2006.
Yours faithfully,

Parstons returns:
We thank you for your letter of 19 July 2006, informing us that Ms Hyde was unable to swop the weekend of 12/13 August for 22/23 July. Mr Marlo had been hopeful that Ms Hyde would agree and offered in addition the first weekend of September 2006, so as to enable Lara to accompany him, Hayley and Alice on holiday, when they go on 12 August. It was understood that Ms Hyde's planned holiday is for one week commencing on 1 August 2006, and, as previously when requested by Ms Hyde, Mr Marlo has agreed to swop weekends (the last occasion being to enable Ms Hyde to have a contact weekend on the weekend of Mothering Sunday this year) he had believed Ms Hyde would reciprocate.
With respect to the schedule for contact over the next academic year, the school holiday's will be the reverse, so that for example next summer, contact will take place during the second part of the holiday. The alternate weekend contact recommences on 9/10 September.
Would you please obtain Ms Hyde's further instructions regarding weekend of 12/13 August. As 22/23 July has now passed and was not, in any event, agreeable to Ms Hyde as a swopped weekend, will Ms Hyde agree to having either a couple of days in the last week of August after the bank holiday, or the first weekend of September? Additionally, would you please ensure that full details, including flights and accommodation address for the holiday to Egypt are provided at some stage this week, so that Mr Marlo knows travel details and where Lara and Alice (should she accompany Lara) will be staying. We anticipate providing you with Mr Marlo's holiday details in the week commencing 7 August, for onward transmission to Ms Hyde.
We await hearing from you.

Smitch backhands:
We thank you for your fax of today's date upon which we have taken our client's instructions.
Our client was unaware that your client had booked a holiday with the children during her period of contact.
Our client is very unhappy that your client should do this but does not want to upset the children by insisting that they stay with her during the summer contact that has been ordered.
Could you please provide, by return, details of your client's holiday with the children including documentary evidence as to when that holiday was booked and confirmation of the times that the children will be travelling.
Our client will return the children to your client on 12th August to enable them to go on holiday and she is requesting an extra weekend with the children in September which dates we will confirm shortly.
Our client is expecting to collect Lara from school today and we would ask that you please confirm that

this is agreed.

Our client also instructs us that your client has not contacted her previously in an attempt to swop contact weekends and the first mention of this was last week.

We look forward to hearing from you.

Yours faithfully,

Parstons volleys:

We thank you for your second letter of today's date and having spoken with Mr Marlo we can confirm Ms Hyde is expected to collect Lara from school today and now enclose copy details regarding the holiday on 12 August 2006.

You will note from this that the booking provides for departure on the train at Ashford in Kent, at 10:20am on 12 August 2006. Mr Marlo believes that to be on the safe side, the children would need to leave with him by 7am. Will this be convenient for Ms Hyde or would it be preferable to her, for Lara, and any other of the children, to return to Mr Marlo the previous evening, at say, 6pm or another time up to about 9pm? We await hearing from you in this respect.

Mr Marlo has obtained documents as herewith detailing travel and hotel, with hotel telephone number handwritten at the top. We look forward to receiving Ms Hyde's travel and accommodation details, at her earliest opportunity, please.

Mr Marlo made the booking in May, he believed in accordance with the children's end of term dates. Both Hayley and Alice broke up on Friday, and in the normal course of events, Lara would have ordinarily been expected to break up on this same date. This summer, it transpires, this was not the case. Mr Marlo wishes to assure Ms Hyde that he had no intention of usurping any of the children's holiday contact and awaits details as to the weekend or dates Ms Hyde wishes to have contact, to make up for this coming weekend.

Yours faithfully,

Smitch lobs:

We thank you for your letter dated 24th July 2006, upon which we have taken our client's instructions.

Our client has advised us that the schedule for 2005/2006 clearly shows the children should have been with our client until 14th August.

Our client will return the children to your client by 7pm on 11th August in order that they can leave early for their holiday the following morning.

Our client will be providing us with details in respect of her holiday to Egypt and we will forward these to you.

In the meantime, we would ask that you please explain how your client is intending to take the children out of the country given that we currently hold the passports for Alice and Lara?

We are instructed that your client has taken the children out of the country earlier this year without our client's knowledge or consent and without the passports that we currently hold.

We look forward to hearing from you in this regard.

Yours faithfully,

Partsons rackets:

Thank you for your third letter, received by fax, today. We shall let Mr Marlo know to expect the children by 7pm on 11 August 2006 and await hearing from you as Ms Hyde's alternative date/s for

September contact.

In so far as the content of the remainder of your letter is concerned, we shall, of course, obtain instructions. In the absence of the same, however, we would state that clearly as Ms Hyde requires the children's passports for their holiday to Egypt, perhaps Mr Marlo anticipated that Ms Hyde, when returning the children after their holiday and in the knowledge they were going on holiday to France with him, would ensure the children had their passports with them. Now that you have identified this possible issue, for which we are grateful, perhaps you would confirm with Ms Hyde that this is the case.

We look forward to receiving details of the holiday to Egypt, at your earliest convenience, and to clarification with respect to the children's passports.

Yours faithfully,

(Is this a justifiable and reasonable expense for legal aid to be funding? My guess is that Judge Baxter is getting a cut and has been requested to perform at Smitch Law's Christmas ball; up on stage, making everyone laugh.)

Feeling that I had hit another low, in addition to the worry of forthcoming hearings, unable to sleep, I decided to stay up all night and relay my thoughts to paper.

I would like to ask Mrs Mason to explain what right she has to insinuate she will withhold Alice and Lara's passports, when I have sole residency and it is supposedly the scenario we were avoiding by Ms Hyde insisting it is the 'safest place'.

Mrs Mason has no authority to hold these documents, yet this dictator felt it her position to do so. I believe that Mrs Mason's client lost joint residency of her children in 2004 because Judge Chips saw through the lies and the constant trouble Ms Hyde brought into all of our lives, including her own.

Smitch Law are acting in exactly the same way, the only difference is Mrs Mason is not an appointed guardian or related to my children. Also, Mrs Mason knows she is protected by her own, the Law Society and the Supervision of Solicitors, despite clearly hounding a family for years; she believes she is untouchable and can act as she wishes just as long as she states 'on behalf of her client'.

(Who's watching the Watchers?)

Mrs Mason is a horrible person – there I have said it – and an appalling family law solicitor, who has stamped her nasty personality into my family's lives. For many years, Mrs Mason has shown total disregard to the emotional wellbeing of three children and any court order.

I feel overwhelmed and suffocated by the legal entanglement, and the sheer ease by which the dishonesty and interference is allowed to prevail. I do find it difficult to understand how this solicitor can act in such a distressing way towards me as a parent and three young children.

When I complained about Smitch Law and Mrs Mason's detrimental behaviour, the instability they were bringing into my children's lives, the emotional pressure I felt as a parent, the fact they were immorally working against a family court order and surmounting a massive cost to legal aid - I thought at least the hostile and controlling behaviour would stop.

(Give a dog a bone, and here we are again.)

A proper administration of justice and one of those fundamental tenets, a pillar of fairness, is to ensure honesty, morals and standards are paramount in any investigation carried out by those who find themselves with the privilege of overseeing justice. My hope is that what my family and many other decent parents suffered in the hands of shameless people involved in family law, as relayed in 'Behind Closed Doors', can be an insight into the needless corruption found within the system.

I do hope that the misery documented in my files will one day serve as a reminder to all involved in family law that they must conduct themselves in compliance with ethical codes of practice, and the understanding should be that the behaviour, attitude and determination of all involved must be in the interests of the children.

In years past, we were a happy family, despite the challenges brought on by the children's mother having a severe mental health condition.

In the Family Courts, it is not a criminal court, and we as a family had committed no crimes. For most of the family court hearings I attended, they served one purpose, and this was to relay disinformation, which amounted to defamation of my character and ability to look after my children – within four years, I went from every other weekend contact only to sole residency.

It must be seen as unethical for a third party to interfere in a detrimental way in parents' and their children's lives.

Blinded by self-importance and greed, Smitch Law and Mrs Mason have had so many opportunities to recognise a parent with mental health problems and help them, through the NHS and her mental health team.

(Clearly, Smitch Law and Mrs Mason do not give a fuck.)

Years ago, I was told that Smitch Law did not like to lose a case and this may have a bearing on their behaviour to this day. It is evident, Mrs Mason, in and out of court, will say and do anything to get the children back with her client.

Is it this ethos to win that drives Mrs Mason's hounding and immoral behaviour, or is it contempt for children, family law, honesty, morals and standards?

Court – the unknown variable

28th July 2006 / Venray Family County Courts
Mother's application – sole residency of all three children

Smitch Law's barrister suggests that a Child Psychologist report is competed, and Mr Marlo's, as well as the children's, medical records are reviewed. Judge Recorder Jadin agrees.

Hearing listed for 8 August 2006 be adjourned and re–listed on Friday 25 August 2006 at 10am at the Venray County Court, with a time estimate of 1 hour.

This hearing is taking place in Venray, a nearby city with a two hour round trip by car. My legal funding only covered the injunction proceedings; so, despite numerous letters regarding holiday plans, neither Melissa nor I were informed and I was therefore not represented at this hearing.

Family Holidays

1 – 9 August

Lara left to go to Egypt with her mother; Hayley and Alice refused to go, owing to their fear of flying and the continuing poor relationship with their mother. (Despite Smitch's hounding of me for the details of our holiday, I was never informed about the details of where in Egypt Lara is going or staying. While worrying, there is little I can effectively do about it.)

Ma was recovering well from her broken leg, but unfortunately while Lara was away, as Ma transitioned from a wheelchair to a walker, something went wrong and she had to call an ambulance.

At the hospital, they confirmed that she had broken her leg again, and caused another fracture further up; this was however due to the wrong sized rod being used in the operation.

Hayley and Alice asked again if Ma would like to stay with us when she can come out of hospital, and we could help her recover; Ma said that she would love to, and would looking forward to spending the time with us.

We told Ma we would visit her every day, to keep her spirits up.

On the way home from the hospital, we bought a adjustable bed. Hayley and Alice set it up in the living room, in preparation. It felt good to see the children coming together to care for their nan, and repaying the love and care their nan has shown them all their lives.

Two days before Lara was due back, Ruth allowed Lara to use her mobile to phone me; Lara asked how Nan was and I told her that nan had a fall but was doing well.

Lara was so upset she wasn't there to look after her nan, but I told her not to worry, as she would be back soon and Nan would want her to have fun on holiday. I asked about the pyramids and any history she has learned while over there; Lara went quiet before she told me they had gone passed the pyramids in a bus, but her mother had said they would not have time to see them.

I know this meant a lot to Lara, who is bright and keen to learn about the world around her.

(Another great holiday for Ruth, with Lara just dragged along.)

Dean Marlo

From Riverbank School

3 August

To whom it may concern,

Please note that there has been an error on Lara's school report for 2005/06. The 'Number of Unauthorised Absences' should read zero and the figure shown i.e., 51 half days, are the number of Authorised Absences for the academic year.

Mr Marlo has correctly followed the school policy in notifying the school on all occasions when Lara was absent.

I would also like to add that Lara has enjoyed a happy, successful and settled school year. In fact, this has been the case over the past two years where her home life has been more stable and consistent.

Yours sincerely…

I don't have enough words to express how thankful I am for people involved like Mr Church. I will put this letter to the judge and hopefully he will find it significant and put a stop to the disinformation being falsely presented to the Family Courts at every hearing.

I know that without the help from people like Mr Church, who are prepared to take the time to write letters in an honest and meaningful way, I would have been submerged by the false allegations without evidence, bantered about within the Family Courts by Ms Hyde, Mrs Jackson and Mrs Mason.

I understand the process of a solicitor or a barrister being the person presenting the case on behalf of their client, but there must be relevance and truth in what they are suggesting. With serious issues, such as abuse, aggressive behaviour and manipulation within family and children matters, evidence to the fact must be seen as vital to the accusation.

Meeting MP

4 August

Melissa wrote to inform me she has applied for public funding on my behalf; now we wait for the commission's decision.

I made an appointment with Mr Rowe, MP, to relay my concerns as to the injustice that I have once more experienced with Judge Baxter in the courts.

As in the past, I have spoken to Mr Rowe about the conduct and behaviour of several members of the judiciary. I talk to Mr Rowe because he is my only line to having the dishonesty and instability not be for nothing – some days, I do feel I have failed as a dad, and I wonder if my efforts have only made things worse. Every day, I hope the sadness we have all experienced can be used by organisations and ministers to make meaningful changes, and prevent this happening to other families.

I do not want Mr Rowe to hold my hand nor do I want to use his name when it suits, I simply would like to be treated honestly and fairly, and for my children's lives to mean something to the people working within the system.

From Mr MP Rowe

7 August

Dear Mr Marlo,

Further to your latest appointment at my Advice Bureau, as promised I have written to the Lord Chancellor to request that the performance of Judge Baxter is monitored. I enclose a copy for your information. I will contact you again when I get a response.

While obviously things are considerably better for you than when you first contacted me several years ago to see my support bureau, I recognise that your former partner continues to cause you unhappiness. I am sorry to hear this but, as explained, it is for your legal representative and the courts to deal with this situation. As an MP, I have no jurisdiction over the decisions and actions of the court.

I do hope that issues of concern will be resolved in your favour. Best wishes.

Yours sincerely…

Dear Lord Chancellor,

Is there a system for checking the performance of Judges?

Your records will confirm that I had cause to complain in the past about Judge Baxter as a result of concerns raised with me by different constituents involved in unrelated cases. Regrettably, 'the system' took no appreciable action as far as I could see.

I was therefore somewhat relieved when I heard that Judge Baxter had retired. However, I gather that he has come out of retirement! And I have just received another complaint about his performance.

Has Judge Baxter retired or not? If he has not, I do urge you to use whatever powers and influence you have to get someone to check his performance. I trust that this can be done. Many thanks.

Yours sincerely…

Dropping problems

11 August

Ruth phoned Hayley, for reasons known only herself, and told her that she would drop Lara off at the bottle bank at 7pm. Hayley told me; I texted Ruth to confirm and received no reply.

At 6.50pm, I drove with Hayley and Alice to the bottle bank and parked up. We waited nearly half an hour before Lara scampered out of Ruth's car, and we went to visit Ma.

Melissa also wrote to me:

Further to our recent meeting and phone conversations, I now enclose, for your information, copies of the documents that have been lodged at Court today on your behalf. I confirm that I have also served Smitch Law with copies of the same documents, on your behalf.

Hopefully, we will soon have a response to your recent application for Public Funding Legal Aid certificate at which stage, provided you are granted a certificate, I will formally go on the record as acting on your behalf in these Children Act Proceedings.

Should you hear from the Legal Services Commission with any queries in relation to your application, please make sure you respond to them straightaway, and also let me know. If neither you nor I have heard anything by 22nd August, I shall need to look at trying to obtain emergency funding for you to be represented at the Hearing listed on the 25th August.

Dean Marlo

My Application (C1) Form

Further information
Involvement with outside authorities and organisations
Social Services were involved in April 2004. Mr Trumpton was involved for a short period – a matter of days. There is no current involvement. Social Services' involvement is documented in these proceedings in relation to Ms Hyde's applications for enforcement and variation of the shared residence order and my application for variation of the same order, made on 27 and 28 April 2004, respectively. Social Services were also involved on 10 May 2005 on receipt of a referral from CMHT about the children and made phone enquires to me, but I have heard nothing further.

The Police have been involved since 20 January 2006, in relation to several incidents; further information may be obtained from them via the incident numbers included:

On 20 January 2006, Alice and Hayley alleged that they had been assaulted by Ms Hyde and her boyfriend, while at Ms Hyde's home. PC's Byrd and Mullins are the names of the officers whom Alice and Hayley spoke to. There was minimal involvement; the officers informed that it was their word against the boyfriend's.

On 8 April 2006, I received a phone call from the Police between 8:30pm and 9:00pm informing Ms Hyde had made a complaint to the Police that Hayley and Alice had been violent towards her, and were missing. Whilst I was driving along a route that I thought Hayley and Alice would use, I received a further phone call from the police informing me that Hayley and Alice were at their mother's and asking if an officer could speak to me. I parked near Ms Hyde's home and Hayley and Alice came out. The officer asked if Hayley and Alice could go home with me, which they did.

Hayley informed me that she was forced to the ground by Ms Hyde holding on to her collar so tight that she could not breathe properly. The only way Hayley could get free was by trying to push her mother off and Alice trying to pull their mother away from Hayley. I have had no further involvement with the police, relating.

On 22 May 2006, Ms Hyde turned up, uninvited, to my home. Hayley was in the garden and Lara was inside and heard Ms Hyde shouting abuse at me, calling me a 'fucking cunt'. Lara saw Ms Hyde repeatedly kicking the side door of my van. Ms Hyde was cautioned by the police and admitted to causing criminal damage.

Incidents of abuse, violence or harm
On 22 April 2004, Hayley suffered bruising; Alice a graze to her spine. Hayley is believed to have gone to Alice's aid when Ms Hyde dragged Alice across the floor, to remove Alice's trousers during a disagreement. This caused the carpet burn to Alice and bruising to Hayley when she intervened. Hayley and Alice were seen by their GP.

On 20 January 2006, Hayley and Alice, in distressed states, called, asking me to come and collect them from the street where they were walking. I was informed by Hayley and Alice that they had left Ms Hyde's home because Alice had been shoved by Ms Hyde's boyfriend, with such force that she flew across the room, landing on the floor. Both Hayley and Alice informed me that Alice had called their mother a 'ditcher' for choosing

128

to go on holiday to Australia instead of having them for weekend contact, causing the boyfriend to assault Alice and Ms Hyde to grab Hayley by the arm, dragging her off the sofa where she was sitting. Hayley has told me that she followed Alice, Ms Hyde and her boyfriend upstairs into Alice's room where Alice had run after being assaulted. Hayley saw their mother struggling with Alice; Hayley believed that their mother was trying to prevent Alice from using her mobile phone.

I did not witness the above, which all occurred when the children were in Ms Hyde's care. On the last two occasions, neither Hayley nor Alice sought any medical treatment.

Involvement of the child(ren)

As well as the above, Ms Hyde has been aggressive and verbally abusive to me in front of one or more of the children. Specifically, on 21.5.2006, when Ms Hyde was shouting and swearing outside my home and causing criminal damage; on 5.6.2006, when Ms Hyde was swearing loudly and verbally abusing me in front of Hayley and Lara; on 9.6.2006, when Ms Hyde was shouting abuse and swearing loudly outside my home at 8am, in the presence of Lara; on 18.6.2006, when discussing time for handover of Lara, Ms Hyde called me an 'asshole' in front of Alice.

Hayley and Alice have been affected more than Lara. They have memoires of when Ms Hyde's mental health was very bad in the late 1990's and early 2000's. They are developing as individuals and identify more clearly what they see as intolerable behaviour. If they think something is unfair, they say so, and if there has been an incident at their mother's, they refuse contact for a period.

They are dealing with the situation by visiting Ms Hyde during Lara's contact and expressing a desire for peace to get on with their lives. Lara is younger but I am sure she is taking it all in and may, if Ms Hyde does not modify her behaviour, react in the same way as her sisters.

Witnesses

Instances reported to the Police, may be clarified by the Police Civil Evidence Unit and there was an independent witness present at my home on 9 June 2006, who would provide supporting evidence.

I also believe that Hayley and Alice have an Advocate through the CFCS and the Children and Youths Advocacy Service, who they have been confiding in.

Medical treatment or other assessment of the child(ren)

The children have seen their doctor after several of the incidents.

There was a referral a number of years ago when Mr Guall at CFCS who advised that they did not need counselling or therapy, they needed stability and consistency.

Steps or orders required to protect you and the child(ren)

Continuation of the current, simple regime of contact as set out in the order made in August 2004, enabling the children to maintain their relationships with Ms Hyde.

Parenting classes or support for Ms Hyde, to help her manage the way she treats our children.

In Hayley and Alice's case, steps to enable them to resolve issues that they have with Ms Hyde which should enable them to rebuild and maintain their relationships.

Any orders shall enable the children to have normalcy and consistency in their lives.

An end to court proceedings.

Holidays

12-19 August

It was unfortunate that we'd booked a holiday to Disneyland Paris, before Ma had broken her leg. Talking to Ma, she said she would be fine and did not want us to miss the holiday; as Rob had been coming over to see her anyway, he said he would take care of Ma and Sully while we were away.

We stayed in the main hotel – it was stunning and once more a totally different world. It was lovely to see the children enjoy themselves, even as we spent hours in the queues. Memorably, my hat was lost to the surroundings of Thunder Mountain.

Hayley, Alice, Lara and I were immersed in the Disney setting, with all the fun and magic this holiday provided.

It feels a far cry from the unknown that awaits when we get home.

Dear Melissa, re: Mrs Mason's letter

20 August

Re: Smitch Law's letter from Mrs Mason 13 June 2006. (MIA, but you will get the gist from my response.)

Hayley and Alice have not reinitiated regular weekend contact due to the behaviour and conduct of Ms Hyde and her boyfriend. They have reported several incidents involving physical abuse and violence.

Lara has maintained weekend contact with her mother to date.

I find Smitch Law's letters once again to be false and unhelpful; they are trying their utmost to manipulate the situation at any cost – as per usual, it is the children that are impacted.

Smitch Law should clarify what they are stating in their letters; Lara has continued, in accordance with the court order, her weekend and holiday contact with their client. (When, that is, their client is available for her weekend contact with Lara.) However, Smitch Law are content in writing none of the children are having regular contact with their mother and Ms Hyde is quite happy to twist the truth.

If I thought it would get me anywhere, I would write again to the Law Society; Smitch Law's letter writing has been unerringly immoral and deceitful.

Ms Hyde is well aware why Hayley and Alice have not wanted to go to hers for weekend contact and I believe Lara has done well to keep a level-head, and do what she wants with regards to her contact with her mother.

(Lara, unlike Hayley and Alice, has been fortunate to spend her conscious years with Ms Hyde only in small bursts; she has always had the stability and juxtaposition of how our home is compared to her mother's; Lara, to my knowledge, does not challenge her mother's unreasonable behaviour, whereas Hayley and Alice have grown up to.)

I have talked to Hayley and Alice about seeing their mother, but what can I do if for their own reasons they do not want to go? And what parent would knowingly send their children to a parent that is clearly physically and mentally abusing them? If being pulled across the floor and being strangled is not abuse, then what is?

This is the cycle I find myself in everyday; I am anxious for my children when in their mother's care, because the signs are there that she is not coping or treating them appropriately. However, when the children do want to have contact with their mother, they seem happy to do so; I have no desire in stopping them from doing what they want to do. There's no one I can talk to for advice, no organisation to relay my concerns that will approach Ms Hyde in a way that befits her diagnosis, as support and not as an accusation, even though she has abused the children on too many occasions.

Judge Baxter once referred to Ms Hyde's mental health condition deteriorating as not a case of if, but a case of when; that tension is what hangs over our family daily.

I have in no way tried to prevent Lara from her weekend contact with her mother. This is not to say that I am not worried about Lara when with her mother.

Ms Hyde asked me if I would meet her and discuss the situation with Hayley and Alice, this I agreed to, but Ms Hyde never got back to me.

I informed Ms Hyde as soon as possible when Lara went into hospital.

I informed Ms Hyde of our skiing holiday before she went to Australia; she could have contacted the children on their mobiles or through my own, however, she did not.

I have never prevented Hayley, Alice or Lara from going on holiday with their mother; I renewed Hayley's passport and (thought) I had come to an agreement with Ms Hyde where she would get Alice's passport and I would get Lara's. Ms Hyde made so much nuisance and trouble over the money for Alice's passport, I just gave up and paid her.

I was unhappy to be informed that Alice and Lara's passports were being held by Smitch Law and that they were with them for 'safe keeping'. I would like this rectified because I have a right to look after my children's passports, and also the right to stop the silly games played by Ms Hyde and Mrs Mason.

If Ms Hyde or Smitch Law have any evidence to suggest that I have or would withhold my children's passports, then I ask them to produce this or hand over my children's passports, so my children and I can try and live a normal life as best as we can.

I did not reply to Smitch Law's letters because I do not see the point of writing in circles.

I have never told my children to keep anything a secret from anyone, including Ms Hyde, and I feel once again that Ms Hyde attempts to discredit me in any way she can.

I have informed and communicated with Ms Hyde as best as it is possible.

Ms Hyde is constantly over the top and ends up being verbally abusive. I cannot and do not want to put up with it; I have had conversations with Ms Hyde and we have organized things and sorted things out, but there always seems to be trouble around the corner.

As to Ms Hyde stating that I am, 'unable to discuss matters in a calm and reasonable manner', to this day I tape my calls with Ms Hyde, and I am happy for anyone to listen to them. You can work out exactly who is unable to communicate in a calm and reasonable manner.

(No… I forgot that would be too easy, in this stupid game that has gone on for years of my life.)

For being so antagonising and unreasonable, I do seem to let Ms Hyde have almost all of her requests!

When the children want more contact with their mother, it has been arranged and if this extended to the children wanting weekly or monthly periods, I still don't believe we as two parents should need a judge's piece of paper to detail it. I have no interest in withholding the children or money from Ms Hyde; it is Ms Hyde's dissatisfaction that drives the solicitor wagon, court interference and changes to the order. In truth, the scenario of the children wanting extended contact with their mother hasn't occurred and that is because we never have the opportunity to get that far, before there is another incident of abuse when the children are in her care.

There are enough bad feelings between Ms Hyde, Hayley and Alice, and what is clear is these bad feelings have arisen due to Ms Hyde's behaviour and conduct with her daughters.

Ms Hyde's application for residence of Alice and Lara has not been thought through. In my opinion, the success of this application would only worsen the children's feelings towards their mother.

Hayley, Alice and Lara have all seen me walk away and avoid the abuse and aggression year after year; they have never seen their father retaliate.

Lara is eight years old and, I believe, loves her dad because of the loving, caring and stable home life she has. By Lara's age, Hayley and Alice had already been through so much upset with their mother, what with Ms Hyde being sectioned four times and her disgraceful behaviour resurfacing for months throughout their childhoods.

My concern is that Lara shall become distracted from the smashing person that she is and once again it is mindless and an injustice to put Lara through the emotional torment of being torn away from a loving home and a caring father, who has maintained the stability and care in Lara's life since she was born.

This hearing should be about Ms Hyde's contact with Hayley and Alice, and addressing the cause of the issues, i.e., her behaviour. In the long term, it should be about preventing Lara from having the same experiences her sisters have.

It should be stressed to the Family Courts that our family has been through all of this and it was decided that I was the one capable of ensuring our children's welfare, to which I have done.

I am tired of having to constantly defend my conduct and ability to be a decent father and person. Ms Hyde's allegations and applications have no evidence to support them; it is just on Ms Hyde's word, meanwhile she is abusing our children.

As Judge Chips stated in his summing up in 2004, Mrs Jackson, Smitch Law and Mrs Mason listened to the stories that Ms Hyde was telling them, but they did not really know what was going on.

It is disgraceful and shameful that Hayley, Alice and Lara have had their childhoods constantly torn apart and messed around, by the words and behaviour of their mother.

I do not believe that Hayley, Alice nor Lara would want to live with their mother on a full-time basis.

As before, I am prepared to continue to try and encourage the resolution of Hayley and Alice's situation with their mother. I am aware that the Child Legal Guidance have been trying to organise a meeting with a mediator, Hayley, Alice and Ms Hyde.

If Ms Hyde is determined to go back to court, then I believe that it should be for her concerns about her weekend and holiday contact with Hayley and Alice, and not a sole residency application on the basis my care is inadequate, as suggested.

Alice and Lara – Letters to court

21 August

Dear Sir or Madam,

My name is Alice Marlo and I believe that my mother has applied for full residency of me and my little sister Lara I stand strongly that I do not wish too go back to our mothers because on many incidents she has injured me and my sister Hayley. In April 2004 she pulled me across the floor and I got a massive carpet burn on my back and on the 20th January her boyfriend shouted in my face and pushed me off an exercise trampoline I slid into a huge Wicca basket all I did was shout ditcher because our mother was off to Australia on another one of her holidays. And so many more incidents from when I was little to where I am now I believe that children should be able to grow up as normal and should not have all the trouble and strife in there lives and try to be kids for as long as they can. I hope you will read this and take my points into consideration thank you.

Alice Marlo

I might not be perfect yet I no I am not but violence is not the answer by far.

Dear Judge,

I am here by writing you this letter to inform you about the following,

I wish for the court order to stay how it is now; I go to my mothers every other weekend and for the rest of the time with my father.

I also wish for the school holidays to stay the same, which also means I am with my father this Christmas, my mother next year and so on.

I don't wish anymore hassle against my father or mother.

Yours sincerely

Lara Marlo

Melissa to me

22 August

Further to our phone conversation yesterday, I enclose a copy of a letter I have sent to Smitch Law, on your behalf and for your information. I also enclose a copy of the Order listing the hearing, this week, for Friday 25th August at 10am. Would you please let me know whether you would like us to meet at the Court, at say, 9.45am, or whether you would like to meet me at the office, at 9.30am?

Additionally, please note that the Hearing is listed as a Directions Hearing. This means that I will need to discuss with Ms Hyde's legal representatives what directions Ms Hyde will be seeking.

I would say that it is unlikely proceedings brought forward to challenge the decision of a residency order will be successful, as any future judge would view it as undermining a learned colleague's ruling, however it may be that Ms Hyde will continue regardless.

I would suggest that a Cafcass report, detailing Hayley and Alice's wishes and feelings about their contact with their mother is needed.

Full statements will also be needed from both you and Ms Hyde, and, in relation to Lara, the Cafcass officer will also need to include her and make any recommendations in relation to Lara in the same report as should be prepared in relation to Hayley and Alice. Would you please give this some thought, so that we can discuss it before the Hearing on Friday?

I do not want to bring my children back into the family court arena, but someone or some organisation, like Cafcass, needs to get a grip on what is going on in the children's lives.

I phoned Melissa and agreed with her Cafcass suggestion, in the hope this would bring an end to court experts and proceedings for our family.

Melissa writes to Mrs Mason

22 August

Further to recent correspondence, we have now obtained Mr Marlo's instructions.

He is agreeable, as previously proposed, to contact taking place on the weekend of 1/3rd September and wishes to re–iterate his thanks to Ms Hyde for agreeing the swop. Mr Marlo suggests handover time on Friday, 1st September at 12 noon. The children will walk to their mother's.

Additionally, we understand that Hayley and Alice are to return to school on Monday 4th September, whereas Lara does not return to school until the following day, Tuesday 5th September. Hayley and Alice can walk back to their father's at the conclusion of contact.

On Monday 4th September, Mr Marlo proposes the drop off take place at some time between 9am and 12 noon, as is convenient to Ms Hyde, at the bottle bank with both Ms Hyde and Mr Marlo remaining in their respective vehicles. (Mr Marlo is opposed to allow Lara to walk on her own along what can be busy streets.) Perhaps you would take Ms Hyde's instructions and revert to us with her preferred time for handover to take place on Monday 4th September, so that we may inform Mr Marlo.

With respect to the schedule of contact for next academic year, it is believed that Ms Hyde has made a mistake with the alternate halves of the October half–term holiday.

We understand Ms Hyde to be due the second half of the holiday this year, having the first half of the holiday last year. Perhaps, as the first weekend of September is now going to be a contact weekend, we could suggest that the alternate weekend's flow from that, then it will come right for October half–term holiday and the remainder of the schedule remains as is.

In addition, we believe there is a minor error at the Easter weekend 2007. We are able to confirm Mr Marlo's agreement to the rest of Ms Hyde's schedule for the next academic year. We await hearing from you as to whether or not Ms Hyde agrees contact weekend for September and October 2006 should be 2/3rd September, 16/17th September, 30/1st Sept/October, 14/15th October, half–term holiday 25/29th October and Easter 2007, 9/ 15th April.

(Melissa, trying to make it clear for everyone to follow and end this nightmare.)

From the Legal Services Commission

24 August

Dear Mr Marlo,
We have assessed your income after outgoings as over £30,000.
This means you are not entitled to public funding.
You cannot appeal against this decision. Attached is a copy of the breakdown of assessment. This will show you how we have calculated your means assessment. If you have any queries regarding this, please refer, in the first instance, to the booklet 'Means 1 – The Guide' which you should have received when completing your means assessment forms.
If you have further queries, or if you feel we have made a mistake, please write to us with the relevant details and we will review your case. Please provide this information by 7 September 2006. If your circumstances have changed since you completed your assessment forms, we are unable to review your case. If this is the situation and you still require the benefit of public funding, you need to see your solicitor to make a fresh application.
You may want to speak to your solicitor before you reply to us.
Yours sincerely,

That figure is largely made up of my 'business capital' – the assets of the company like the van... which is not disposable to me, because if I sell the van to pay the court fees, I can't go to work anymore!

Am I being forced into becoming unemployed to gain legal aid, to keep another barrister at work?

I do wonder how many vans it might take to end this façade, as I have not got the normal currency i.e. pounds, dollars and pence, it's down to breaking my company up.

They do not care if I end up raising my three children below the poverty line, scratching about on benefits; doing nothing more than barely surviving. It is a trap, and the system is among the legs trying to kick you off the ladder. I am proud and lucky to run my own business, to have the ability to work and achieve a standard of living for my children – these hearings go beyond my ability as a parent, and has consumed every aspect of my life.

Courts for reports

25th August 2006 / Town Family County Courts
Mother's application – sole residency

On the request of the Applicant Ms Hyde, Judge Recorder Jadin ordered that a Child Psychologist prepare a report as well as the medical records of the family to be sent to the courts via Smitch Law.

Judge Recorder Jadin states Ms Hyde's Legal Aid will meet half of the cost for the report, and Mr Marlo is to pay the remainder.

I was requested to sign a document in court to say I would pay half for the Child Psychologist's report, and found myself doing so just to get out of the building – despite knowing I can't afford it.

The Hearing (25th August)

At 9.30am, I met Melissa outside the Town family court building.

We found an empty waiting room, where Melissa left me to go and speak to Mrs Mason. When Melissa returned, she stated that Ms Hyde is applying for joint residency of Alice and Lara, and Mrs Mason is going down the road of asking the judge for a psychologist report on Hayley, Alice, Lara and myself. Melissa also stated that Mrs Mason had been given a letter from Child Legal Guidance, and that she said she would photo–copy the letter.

The bundle provided by Mrs Mason to the court consisted of almost 600 pages; ranging from penal notices placed on me 2000/2001/2004, to Mr and Mrs Jackson's statements of 2004.

Although in the past I have been willing to agree to any requests and demands, we have been through interviews with Cafcass and various similar organisations, when ordered by the Family Courts – the trouble remains not because of the children, but Ms Hyde, who the court already knows has bipolar.

Ms Hyde suffered from mental health problems before we met. Since I have known Ms Hyde, she has been sectioned under the Mental Health Act four times, for at least a month's treatment. Ms Hyde smashed up our homes when becoming ill, has continually shouted, screamed at as well as physically and mentally abused our children. Without provocation, Ms Hyde has arrived at the children's home, being verbally and physically aggressive. In May, Ms Hyde was cautioned for causing criminal damage to my vehicle by the police.

So much of my children's lives has been turned upside down by Ms Hyde's behaviour and attitude, yet over countless hearings the blame is shifted to three children and their father who have been trying to get on with our lives.

Ms Hyde seems to play the system to her personal requirements and whims, without any consideration for the children; she refuses to see it is her behaviour which has caused the problems in her relationships with them. (As do the family court judges.) Her accusations against me have been proven false, and the only issues the children have ever brought up have been due to their mother's care. Especially in 2004, when Judge Chips made it clear that full investigations had been done into all of the allegations about the children's welfare and stability.

(I am now fully aware that justice and the ability to recognise and provide assistance as necessary for someone with a mental health condition, is beyond the scope of the judges and courts.)

Despite the false allegations made by Ms Hyde, which was why we were here today, neither Social Services nor the police have been involved with Hayley, Alice or Lara while they have been in my care, due to my conduct or parenting. 2005 was one of the calmest years we've had, with the children doing well at school and getting on with their childhoods.

Melissa agreed with my view that prior to the judge instructing a psychologist, a

Cafcass report would have been sufficient, but explained that if I do not agree to Ms Hyde's demands, then it would be likely the Cafcass report would suggest us all being seen by a psychologist anyway, which could take a further 3 months.

Between two fires, an extension of the emotional stress and disruption in all my children's lives, I had to agree to the child psychologist's report being done.

Melissa also stated that because my public funding is in question, I will be expected to pay for this psychologist to interview us all, which she estimated the cost would be £1,500 to £2,000... In addition to the fee to obtain my family's medical records.

Forget between two fires, now on fire myself- I asked if there was a possibility that the judge would see reason, and deem the suggestion unnecessary. How can I be asked to pay the costs to satisfy Ms Hyde, when I have the responsibility of looking after our children in the interim? (Regardless of whether I hope, for my children's happiness and welfare, and my fatherhood, that Ms Hyde does not get sole residency.)

Hayley and Alice are at an age where they have their own advocates, with whom they have had several meetings to which I am not a party to.

I have just endured 3 years of financial hardship, and there are many things that the children need in their lives that the £1,500 to £2,000 could be better spent on.

Once again, I am left with no choice but to agree to something that I feel very strongly against. Melissa went to speak to Mrs Mason and it was announced that the judge was ready to see us.

Mrs Mason stood up and began, 'I have been told that Mr Marlo was unaware of Child Legal Guidance's involvement and I find this hard to believe; Alice had gone to live with my client for a month and my client is unaware of the reasons why she did, but there must have been a huge row between Mr Marlo and Alice.'

The judge stated that they did not want to get into the 'tos and fros' of the case.

Hayley and Alice have not had contact weekends with their mother because of her behaviour and attitude towards them, but this was not talked about, and the truth and facts of why we were at this hearing were not discussed.

In contrast, I sat there in a family courtroom listening to Mrs Mason state to a judge baseless remarks concerning my conduct, character and what is in fact happening in three children's lives.

I believe that Mrs Mason's statements to the judge were made to aggravate the situation. This so-called professional family law solicitor has continued to have a disruptive effect, and with her aggressive correspondence, I must ask if I will ever be left alone to be a parent?

To me, it is not in the children's best interests to be dishonest in an attempt to justify their client's application to the court.

This is not the first time that Smitch Law has put false allegations and their client before the welfare of the children.

Ms Hyde was well aware of the situation and the full reasons why Alice had gone to live with her. Alice stayed with her mother from the 13th May until 9th June, when her mother 'kicked' her out, and has had limited contact since. Still, I received a letter from Smitch Law on the 14th June (MIA), stating that Alice has decided to live with her mother.

Any honest and decent parent would understand that I was acting in the best interests of my 12-year-old daughter by not allowing Alice to go to that sleepover; I was setting a sensible boundary to protect her from a potentially harmful situation. Standing my ground with Alice has worked (at present) as she has not made any unreasonable requests and has recurrently returned home at our agreed time when out playing with her friends on the estate or when she goes into town.

Mrs Mason clearly uses the situation to mislead the judge.

We were in court for the interests, welfare and stability of three children and not to denounce, condemn or cast doubt on any one party or parent for the sake of it. If Mrs Mason had any evidence to corroborate her claims, she would present an actual case and not just flimflam that makes a decent parent's life near impossible.

After the hearing, Melissa asked if I would return to the waiting room as Ms Hyde had requested changes to the forthcoming weekend schedule; Ms Hyde wanted to alter all of the contact weekends through September and October. I told Melissa that I was not happy to change all the weekends, as it brought instability and confusion into an easy-to-follow regime of alternative weekends each year. (As best as possible.)

Due to Mrs Mason's oar, alterations now, mean problems in the future.

From Melissa (and LSC)

25 August

Dear Mr Marlo,

Further to our attendance at court this morning, I enclose my typed notes of the directions given by Judge Recorder Jadin, for your information. I have slightly altered the wording, and believe it should now make more sense. When I receive the court sealed/typed order, I shall of course send you a copy straight away.

I have also spoken again to the Legal Services Commission, chasing a copy of the letter they received from Smitch Law. Suffice it to say that when I got back to my office, at lunchtime today, there was no sign of a copy from either the Legal Services Commission or Smitch Law.

You are going to very kindly spend the weekend colouring in schedules for this year and next year! (Two for this year, please.) I do appreciate you doing this. If you are able to let me have the three coloured schedules by Tuesday 29th August 2006, it would be even more appreciated.

Please be aware that I shall be speaking with your accountant early next week, and may also need to write to him again. The Legal Services Commission have now asked for specific information from him and if he does not cover it in his reply to my letter faxed to him yesterday, I inevitably will have to ask him to do so. I will be in contact with you next week.

In the meantime, may I remind you that Ms Hyde is now insisting that handover takes place at the bottle bank (she does not want the girls to walk) and the next weekend contact has been agreed as being from 12 noon on Friday, 1 September 2006 until 12 noon on Monday, 4 September 2006 (in respect of Lara).

Ms Hyde expects Hayley and Alice, should they see her on that weekend, to return to you on the Sunday evening, as they start school again on the Monday. In addition, you have agreed that Ms Hyde will have contact on the following weekend, 8/10 September 2006. This was in hope that she would then agree to revert to the proper fortnightly schedule commencing the next weekend, 15/17 September 2006. I will be communicating with Mrs Mason in respect of this, next week – hence my request to you for the coloured schedules.

I look forward to speaking with you again next week.

Yours sincerely…

Please find attached, a copy letter I have received from the Legal Services Commission regarding a letter sent to them by Smitch Law on 23rd August.

Re: Mr Marlo

We act for Ms Hyde in respect of court proceedings concerning her three children.

Mr Marlo is the ex–partner of Ms Hyde, Father of all three children and Mr Marlo is represented by Melissa Brenna of Parstons Law.

Melissa/Parstons Law firm have served us with Notice of Issue of Mr Marlo's public funding certificate, a copy of which is attached, but there is no certificate reference provided, although the certificate appears to have been granted on 21st June 2006.

Our client has asked that we write to you to make representations with regard to the granting of public funding to Mr Marlo.

1. *Ms Hyde instructs us that Mr Marlo has had two holidays abroad this year with all of the children. In February 2006 and the other in August 2006. In February, Mr Marlo took the children skiing in France and in August to Disneyland Paris, staying at one of the top hotels. Our client, who has worked in the travel industry, has advised us that these holidays would have cost several thousand pounds each.*

2. *Mr Marlo owns a car registered in 2001 and our client believes the car is worth in excess of £8,000.*

3. *Mr Marlo works in construction and in the past has been a director of companies. It is understood that his business is limited and is registered at Mr Marlo's home address, although Mr Marlo is not named as a director.*

4. *Ms Hyde has explained that Mr Marlo seems to have a very good lifestyle, spending money freely on the children and enjoying meals out regularly.*

We would be grateful if you would please consider these representations and revert to us in due course.

(This is a Mrs Mason and Smitch Law tactic and request - when does the bullshit end? Mrs Mason knows, and it will be when her client regains residence of her children, by hook or by crook.)

I am single parent financially recovering from family court involvement, with sole residence of three children, working hard for a family holiday, and yes we as a family had two fun packed holidays in one year.

Smitch Law are manipulative and are simply trying to place a parent at a disadvantage within family court proceedings. They want to be the only solicitor in the room; without representation, both they and I know that I would be there just to make the numbers up, basically an extra in a Family Courts Production.

As relayed, it looks like I am up to my old tricks, forging children's passports and public funding certificates; I must have made a mistake and forgot the reference number.

Also, no mention of Ms Hyde's holiday to Australia for 2-weeks and then Egypt?

(Look, I don't want to get into a tit-for-tat, but they brought it up!

Further to things that are an expectation for me and a free pass for Ms Hyde, I was never informed about the details of her trip to Egypt with Lara, and accepted that when I was at least able to talk to her on the phone. Smitch Law, before trying to pick fault with a respondent, and relaying such information, should ensure that their own client behaves to the standard they are suggesting, and disclose their own client's affairs to the LSC.)

I have worked hard since I gained sole residency of my children, and with the help of Ma, I manage to provide a standard of living for my family. I know we are not going to be rich, but we are better off than many single parent families, simply because my mum cares, and I am in a position to fit my work around being there for my children.

I have never heard of a parent's holidays with their children being used in such a derogatory way; we are a family consisting of three young children that have been put through hell by a system that is supposed to ensure the welfare and stability of children, and a mother who, quite simply, still needs support from a doctor and not an unscrupulous solicitor; meaningful help is something the Family Court System has proved itself unable to provide.

My three children have every right to be taken skiing and to Disneyland, as most parents do, or sadly can only wish to take their children on such adventures.

I as a parent struggle on occasions through the year, as one never knows the extent of the financial commitment children bring, and what expense is around the corner – shoes, school trips, etc. It is a poor fantasy to suggest I am rolling in money, as I barely make ends meet each week like many other parents do. Some weeks are good, and some go backwards.

I started my business in the 80's and have never worked for any other company.

Besides Disney in 2005 – which was also on a loan – since 2000, my children had not had a proper holiday together, and we'd been through 4 years of family court hearings. (Caravan holidays in England will always hold a place in the children's hearts – Disap-Pontins, the beach and a pier, but again with the upheaval the last few years had been, I hoped to make up for lost time even though Hayley and Alice are growing up fast, and Disney, I consider to be, the ultimate children's holiday.) Yet Smitch Law finds these important events and experiences in a child's upbringing and development as some form of wrongdoing.

My options:

Sit at home with Hayley, Alice and Lara, and explain to them that I cannot afford to go on holiday, because I know that money needs to be saved, just in case we go back to court and I want to be legally represented.

Take Hayley, Alice and Lara on holiday and watch them having fun and being allowed to be children.

(Fuck our legal system, the family court and of course Smitch Law's dagger in three more children's lives.)

Yes, the children, their nan and I do go to an expensive restaurant on each of their birthdays, while throughout the year, if we go out, it is down to the 'Hungry Horse' with a free desert and treasure map with crowns.

I have to work hard for a week to earn the sort of money these people are charging for one day; at the cost of my family and to the detriment of my children's daily lives.

As a father, I took my children on holiday and I understand that without Legal Aid, which historically I don't have a great track record of keeping, I will have to face the legal system on my own.

I am of the understanding that with court applications and legal aid, they determine if the case is justifiable and the likelihood of the applicant being successful – where I find I fall at the first fence, Ms Hyde routinely runs the course. It seems to be felt by all concerned that Ms Hyde is a dead cert and all of her applications are justified.

I had been put through the family court process and came out the other side with sole residence of three young children, yet, two years later, Ms Hyde is still being permitted to instil the chaos she had leading up to 2004.

Dear Melissa, re: the Witch Hunt

1. I was borderline bankrupt from 2002 to 2005, while still providing for my children. I believe that Hayley, Alice and Lara have missed out on many of the basic things that children deserve. I have struggled to meet their needs at school and outside activities. I have relied on the financial support of Ma and, between us over the years, we have saved our change in several bottles, stood in the freezing cold at many bootsales, and I took out a loan.

2. Simon, previous director, bought the car on hire purchase and when I took over, it was an asset of the company, to which I do have the shared use of and keep up the repayments for. It is not worth £8,000 and I was unaware Ms Hyde is a used car salesman, as well as a travel expert.

3. I have enclosed a copy of a letter from Companies House which states that I am a director and that the company is registered at the Chairman's address. I am told that basic information is available on their website, but there is a fee to gaining certain information. Quite clearly, Ms Hyde nor Mrs Mason are prepared to pay the cost to establish that I am a director of the company, and the misleading allegation based on false information in this paragraph from Smitch Law is clear to see.

4. Do I not have the right to try and bring a standard of living to my children? Do I have to regulate my life and the type of holidays that I take my children on?

I take Lara to school at 8.45am; I then go to work and return to meet Lara at 3pm. I work most Saturdays when I have weekend contact with Hayley, Alice and Lara, and I always work Saturdays and Sundays when the children are at their mother's for her weekend contact. (Though I have had to adjust for Hayley and Alice being home.) I am trying and it is difficult.

Why should I work hard, or the taxpayer, to pay for unnecessary court costs and for a psychologist? I have done nothing but try and continue the stability and care in my three children's lives.

Neither Social Services nor the police have been involved with Hayley, Alice or Lara when they have been in my care; the schools have seen a positive improvement in the children's education and mind-set since I was granted sole residency; this has not changed, apart from for Alice testing boundaries, which was exacerbated by her mother's attitude.

From MP Rowe

29 August

Dear Mr Marlo,
Please find enclosed a copy of the acknowledgement I have received from the Department for Constitutional Affairs.
They are currently investigating this matter. I will contact you again when I receive a full response. Best wishes.
Yours sincerely…

Dear Mr Rowe,
I refer to your letter of 7 August 2006, addressed to Lord Hedges, Secretary of State, about complaint regarding performance of judges.
Your letter was received on 10 August 2006 and the Minister aims to reply within 20 working days. However, if we anticipate a delay, I will inform you as soon as possible.
I shall also contact your again if, after considering your letter further, it appears that another Department may deal with it more appropriately.
Yours sincerely,
Correspondence Officer

Dear Mr Rowe,
Thank you for your letter of 7 August 2006, addressed to the Lord Chancellor, concerning His Honour Judge Baxter, in which you pose the question: is there a system for checking the performance of judges?
Since the implementation of the Constitutional Reform Act 2005, which came into effect on 3 April 2006, the Lord Chancellor and Lord Chief Justice hold joint responsibility for all judicial complaints and conduct matters. Your comments raise a number of issues which they may wish to consider further. Please accept my assurance that this matter is receiving attention and that a full response will follow as soon as possible.
Yours sincerely,
Office for Judicial Complaints

Melissa writes

5 September

Further to our phone conversation, late this afternoon, in haste I enclose copies of my letter to Child Legal Guidance, the Order made by Judge Recorder Jadin, and my letter to Smitch Law, for your information.

Please note that we have to finalise a statement for you next week. Would you please ensure that you will be available to come in to my office at some time on Friday 15th September to approve and sign your statement? It will need to be at some time before 2pm.

Weeks after the hearing, I was hounded with letters by Smitch Law (MIA) for the £2,500. I wrote to Smitch Law and explained that I did not have £2,500, and would not put my children's upbringing into finical difficulty by paying for a Child Psychologist.

Dear Mrs Mason,

We thank you for your copious correspondence received over the course of the past few working days, by both fax and hand delivery. We are only responding in this letter to matters concerning the schedule for Residence and Contact over the coming academic year and our letter to Child Legal Guidance in pursuance of the order made by Judge Recorder Jadin on the 25th August 2006.

We now enclose Mr Marlo's coloured schedule and await hearing from you in respect of contact weekends in the period 15th September to the October half–term.

Mr Marlo will expect Ms Hyde to collect Lara from school on Friday 8th September, and for contact to take place on that weekend. Mr Marlo then believes that if he has the following two weekends before resumption of alternate weekends, this will bring the routine into line for October half–term. May we please hear from you once you have had the opportunity of obtaining Ms Hyde's instructions.

We also enclose, by way of service upon you, copy of our letter to Child Legal Guidance. Kindly acknowledge safe receipt.

To whom it may concern,

This firm has acted for Hayley and Alice's father in the past in respect of the family proceedings and we are currently assisting him in respect of an application made by the children's mother, Ms Hyde, to vary the residence and defined contact order made in the County Court in August 2004.

Judge Recorder Jadin, on the 25th August 2006, ordered this firm to send you a copy of the order made on that date and to invite you to consider whether an application should be made to join all of the children, or any of them, to the proceedings. We enclose a copy of the order as made.

Kindly acknowledge safe receipt of this letter and the order.

Dean Marlo

The court order – 25th August

The parties do file their statements of evidence by 4pm on 15th September 2006.

That a joint letter of instruction be agreed and sent to Mrs Lydia Sanders, Consultant Psychologist to prepare a psychological assessment to the family dynamics and relationships of the Applicant Mother, Respondent Father and the children, such letter to be sent by 15th September 2006.

The Applicant and Respondent do provide an authority for the release of their medical records and the children's medical records, including psychiatric records in the case of Applicant Mother, by 4pm on 1st September 2006.

Mrs Sander do report with regard to the psychological assessment by 15th December 2006. Such report to be filed with the court and on both parties solicitors.

The consultant psychologist do have leave to see the children for the purpose of preparing her report and for the case papers to be released to her.

There be a further directions hearing at 10am on 4th January 2007, at the Town County Court, with a time estimate of 1 hour.

It is certified that the instruction of the consultant psychologist be deemed to be a necessary and just expense to be covered by the parties public funding certificates.

The Respondent's solicitors shall send a copy of the order to Child Legal Guidance and shall invite them to consider whether an application should be made to join the children or any of them to these proceedings. A copy of the letter send to CLG shall be provided to the Applicant's solicitors.

Costs in the application.

Melissa writes to me

11/12 September

11 September

In haste, I enclose your original schedule for this current academic year. I should appreciate it if you would please phone the office and leave a message for me that you have safely received your original schedule.

I also confirm that I shall tell Smitch Law that you will collect Lara from school on both 15th and 22nd of September, and that Ms Hyde's next contact weekend will be 29th September; thereafter running on alternate weekends.

I look forward to speaking with you again on Thursday 14th September regarding your statement.

12th

After speaking to Melissa on the phone, she informed me that the psychologist Mrs Sanders has stated that she would not be able to complete the necessary report until later, likely February 2007.

I asked Melissa if we could change to having Cafcass interview the children and myself instead, which would still be a 3–month wait. Melissa stated the Child Psychologist's report has been ordered, and it therefore has to be Mrs Sanders.

As I am not able to receive Legal Aid, thanks Mrs Mason, I asked Melissa what costs I am looking at to be legally represented; she replied with an estimate of £5,000 plus. The price of bringing more instability into three children's lives will be £10,000 plus, for two solicitors, and that is without the payment for the psychologist.

Dear Mr Rowe,

12 September

Thank you for your letters 7th August and 29th August concerning Judge Baxter's behaviour and performance. I feel that I must write to you again.

25th August 2006

This hearing regarded Ms Hyde applying for joint residency of Alice and Lara, and before we sat in front of the judge, she insisted that Hayley, Alice, Lara and I need to be seen by a psychologist. Melissa advised that if I did not agree to Ms Hyde's demands, then the judge would likely agree with Ms Hyde's legal representative, in any case.

Due to the fact that my public funding is once again in question, half of the cost for the psychologist report, £1,500 to £2,000, is required to be paid by me. Why should I be asked to pay the costs to satisfy Ms Hyde and the Family Courts' lack of insight into the situation?

Hayley and Alice have not had contact weekends with their mother because of her behaviour and attitude towards them, and they have their own advocates, with whom they have seen several times.

The £2,000 could be better spent on the many things that the children need in their day to day lives. Once again, I was left with no choice but to agree to something that I felt very strongly against.

In the courtroom, Mrs Mason stood up and stated to the judge: 'I have been told that Mr Marlo was unaware of Child Legal Guidance's involvement and I find this hard to believe; Alice had gone to live with her mother for a month and my client was unaware of the reasons why she did, but there must have been a huge row between Mr Marlo and Alice.'

Mrs Mason's speculation was made without fact, was unprofessional and not what decent parents need in the Family Courts. How can a solicitor make false allegations to a judge in an attempt to mislead them from what is in fact going on in three children's lives?

The whole system falls apart if there is no evidence to substantiate the accusations solicitors and barristers are making and present to a judge.

This solicitor's attitude was senseless and antagonistic; within her opening statement, Mrs Mason has *again* falsely justified their client's unreasonable demands, while providing an excuse for Ms Hyde to drag out court hearings.

Social Services or the children's schools haven't recommended a psychological report done on the children, yet Smitch Law, based on Ms Hyde's word, can instigate another three months of pressure on a family.

Alice stayed with her mother from the 13th May until 9th June, and Ms Hyde was well aware why Alice came to her initially, as we discussed it at the time. On the 14th June, I received a letter from Smitch Law stating that Alice has decided to live with her mother.

I am fed up with the dishonesty and the games that Smitch Law seem happy to play in the Family Courts.

How can I not complain?

I was in court once again representing my children's best interests and welfare. I have continued to bring consistency and stability into all my children's lives, and cannot accept the behaviour that I was needlessly subjected to, to this day, inside and out of the family court walls.

12ᵗʰ September 2006

Melissa informed me that the psychologist Mrs Sanders will not be able to complete the necessary reports until as late as February 2007. As I am not able to receive Legal Aid, I asked Melissa what cost I would be looking at to have her representation; Melissa estimated £5,000, plus.

I am knowingly agreeing to more emotional instability into my family's lives, and I'm financially bringing us to our knees in the process. I really don't know who the Family Courts think they're helping. Certainly not three young children.

For the money spent on legal advice and court appearances of Smitch Law alone, it would have been a fraction of the cost to arrange some form of help for a parent who clearly needs it, and in the process bring meaningful change to three children's lives.

Melissa forwarded me a copy of a letter sent to the Legal Services Commission by Smitch Law, acting on behalf of Ms Hyde, please find enclosed, along with my response.

Thank you for your time and attention.

Yours sincerely…

Melissa writes to Smitch Law

13 September

We write with reference to your fax dated 12ᵗʰ September.

It was our understanding that at court it was agreed Ms Hyde would have contact with the children for the first two weekends in September, if Mr Marlo then had the following two weekends before resumption of alternate weekend contact, as this would bring the routine in line with October half–term.

We therefore confirm that in line with the agreement actually reached at court, Mr Marlo will be having contact with the children this coming weekend. He too has already made arrangements.

Mr Marlo will expect Ms Hyde to collect Lara from school on Friday 29ᵗʰ September, and for contact to take place on that weekend.

Unfortunately, I was getting sick of Smitch Law's interference in my life, and as the small piece of gratification I could get, that letter was one that made it to the bin.

Melissa passes to me

15 September

I refer to our phone conversation this morning and enclose, for your information, copy of the correspondence I have faxed to the Legal Services Commission, regarding your eligibility for Public Funding, the notice to show cause regarding your business interest, and the response to Ms Hyde's representations to the Legal Services Commission.

I do hope that you have a good weekend. We need to speak early next week and finalize your statement.

Yours sincerely,

Dear Sirs,

Re: Mr Dean Marlo

We refer to our phone conversation with customer services and thank the Commission for the extension to 15 September 2006, to enable response to both enquires contained in your letter to Mr Marlo, dated 24 August 2006, and the notice to show cause. Please accept this letter as the continuation to reply to show cause, enclosed herewith, in addition to a letter from Mr Marlo's accountants dated 8 September 2006.

Firstly, we had understood the application to have been made to discharge Mr Marlo's prior Public Funding Certificates, following conclusion of Children Act proceedings in August 2004. Clearly your records do not reflect that, hence this full response to notice to show cause.

In addition, as the certificate under the above reference number has not been discharged, please also consider in light of the content of this letter and enclosures, whether Mr Marlo remains entitled in respect of means to the benefits of said certificate continuing. We fully address the questions of both Mr Marlo's income and capital herein, in light of the relevant guidance and further information provided by the accountant.

Please note we are responding under separate cover (enclosed herewith) with respect to the representations made to yourselves on behalf of the other party as a result of their application to vary the current Residence/Contact Order as made in August 2004 and which, we believe needs to be read in conjunction with this letter, for the purposes of the Commission's review of Mr Marlo's funding.

Reply to Show Cause

As stated above, we were under the impression that previous certificates had been discharged; the question of residence of the children having been settled and lengthy judgement given, in August 2004. Mr Marlo therefore did not believe (and nor did we) that the change to his circumstances, which took place in January this year, was to be reported to the Commission in respect of previous certificates.

Mr Marlo became a shareholder and company director on 8 January 2006. Mr Marlo has not received any dividend and does not have sole control of any retained profit. Please refer to the enclosed copy letter from his accountant. Please note the CLSMEANSIC was incorrectly completed by the accountant who referred to the company's accounts for year ending 31 October 2005 and which were absolutely nothing to do with Mr Marlo when completing page 4 of the form, on the application for a Public Funding certificate in August 2006.

In respect of the company's retained profit, again, please note the content of the accountant's letter. Of the retained earnings, the bulk are fixed assets, and which are an inherent part of the business. It is our understanding that the accounts to 31 October 2005, reflected liquid and realisable retained earnings of £3951. At the very most, on 8 January 2006, as a 50% shareholder, Mr Marlo can only be said to have the potential of a benefit of half that figure, amounting to £1975.50. It was on this basis that we undertook our own financial assessment of Mr Marlo's means to assess him under the Legal Help and Help at Court Scheme.

In reply to your second question, as it is only this current year that Mr Marlo has been a shareholder and company director, please refer to the L17 provided with his application in August, for salary information. No dividend has been paid so far this year.

There are no company accounts yet made up for this current year, which ends on 31 October 2006. As Mr Marlo has not previously been a shareholder or company director, there are no company accounts that he can provide you with, although you were provided with a copy of the company's accounts year ending 31 October 2005, in connection with Mr Marlo's application for Public Funding, made in August.

The information that Mr Marlo has provided to the Commission with respect to the company, is the only information that is available from accounts made up to 31 October 2005, when he was not a shareholder or company director. On the basis of that information, and at this stage we would question whether the Commission has undertaken the financial assessment from a biased position as a result of the representations made to the Commission on behalf of the opponent in previous and current proceedings, resulting in you assessing Mr Marlo as having been a shareholder and company director during the year that the provided accounts related to.

Of course, we realise that the accountant's erroneous completion of the CLSMEANSIC has not assisted in the Commission being able to base its assessment on Mr Marlo's actual financial circumstances. The Commission was however advised of this prior to issue of the notice to show cause.

In so far as the Income and Capital Assessment on Mr Marlo's application made in August is concerned, please advise as a matter of the utmost urgency how you wish Mr Marlo to proceed in light of the following:

The accountant's admitted error, previously notified to the Commission by phone, in completion of the CLSMEANSIC;

The application of the CLS Financial Regulations 2000 as amended, specifically:

Under Regulation 5(6) a client is not eligible for legal representation if his disposable income exceeds £632 per month and (a) his disposable capital exceeds £8000. Mr Marlo believes that the Commission has made an error in its calculation of both his income and disposable capital, and seeks a review of that decision in accordance with the Commission's correspondence dated 24 August 2006 and subsequent extension of time from 7 September to 15 September 2006, in which to reply to the notice to show cause.

What specific further information (in the event it is found the following regulations apply to Mr Marlo) is required to enable proper consideration to be given under Regulation 31(1) applying Regulation 31(2), as to both the capital amount that the Commission considers Mr Marlo could withdraw from the assets of the business without substantially impairing its profits or normal development and what sum, he could borrow on the security of his interest in the business without substantially injuring it's commercial credit.

Whether in relation to the company's fixed assets Regulation 26 applies, in so far as if the resource of a capital nature does not consist of money, it's value shall be taken to be (a) the amount which that resource would realise if sold, or (b) the value assessed in such other manner as appears to the assessing authority to be equitable and also considering the application of Regulations 30, 30A and 31, what further information may be required from Mr Marlo.

We await hearing, on Mr Marlo's behalf, as a matter of urgency, what the Commission considers shall be the best way in which to proceed in order to ensure that the Commission has all the information it requires to undertake its review.

Yours faithfully,

Please refer to attached correspondence for answers to specific questions.

Dear Sirs,

Re: Mr Dean Marlo

Thank you for providing copy of representations made on Ms Hyde's behalf, by Smitch Law to yourselves with respect to Mr Marlo receiving the benefit of Public Funding.

In light of the history of this matter we consider it necessary to respond fully, as follows:

In June 2006, Mr Marlo sought help from this firm, following various alleged incidents involving Ms Hyde and also police attendance and alleged criminal damage by Ms Hyde to a vehicle parked outside Mr Marlo's home. There was a clear deterioration in the situation and in the family supervisor's absence from the office, there was an erroneous attempt by the Senior Partner and junior fee earners to exercise devolved powers in what was perceived as an emergency situation.

This resulted in Mr Marlo being served with Notice of issue of Emergency funding, however, upon the supervisor's return to the office, the application to the Commission was not proceeded with and no claim made against the Commission relating. This was due to the fact that in Mr Marlo's particular circumstances, exercise of devolved powers was inappropriate as a faxed emergency application should have been made, initially, as well as there having been a failure in respect of correct forms having been completed and submitted within 5 working days of the purported exercise of devolved powers to the Commission.

With respect to the inferences contained in Smitch Law's letter, that Mr Marlo's means excluded him from the ambit of the Public Funding Scheme, we comment as follows:

We undertook a full means assessment on the basis of his circumstances from when they changed on 8 January 2006 and found that he qualified in respect of both capital and income, however, there would likely be monthly contribution in respect of any certificate;

In so far as the holidays that Mr Marlo has had with the children this year are concerned, we would ask if a parent is to now be penalised for being frugal to enable holidays to be taken? Are applicants for Public Funding excluded because they accept gifts of a holiday abroad? If so, then perhaps we should mention that Ms Hyde has similarly benefitted from at least one holiday abroad this year, paid for, we understand by her partner. Mr Marlo, however, accepts that that is the case and makes no representation relating, to yourselves.

The car is not registered to Mr Marlo. It is a motor vehicle that the company has through hire purchase and ownership remains with the hire purchase company. It is primarily used by the Chairman.

Mr Marlo works part–time (he has responsibility for the children pursuant to the Residence Order made in August 2004) and is paid a salary, full details of which have been provided on form L17. Mr Marlo became a shareholder and company director on 8 January 2006, from the good will of a long-term friend who needed to dispose of his interest in the company. Mr Marlo's home, which is rented and in respect of which he receives Housing Benefit, is not the registered address of the company, and has never been so.

With respect to Ms Hyde's view that Mr Marlo seems to have a very good lifestyle, spending money freely on the children and enjoying meals out regularly, this is a view that Ms Hyde appears to have held for an extended length of time, and which raised itself again earlier this year, with Ms Hyde making financial demands of Mr Marlo for £40,000 that she seemed to believe he owed her from about 1999. We would, at this juncture, point out that some parents prefer to minimise the amount of money they spend on themselves and instead prefer to ensure their children's needs are met.

Please be aware that Mr Marlo considers these representations (which from his recollection, Ms Hyde has made previously to the Commission) to be evidence of Ms Hyde's continued implacable hostility towards him.

We trust that the above is sufficient as comments on said representations and await hearing from the Commission as to any next steps.

Yours faithfully....

8 September 2006

Dear Mrs Brenna,

Further to your correspondence of last week, my apologies that I have not replied sooner but I have been out of the office for most of this week.

We can confirm that Mr Marlo only became the company director and shareholder on 8 January 2006. He was therefore, not paid a tax-free company dividend of £11,000 in the year ending 31 October 2005.

We are not able to comment on what level of dividend may or may not be paid in future years. We would also like to point out that although the company has retained earnings of £31,339 this is made up in the main (£27,388) of fixed assets that are unlikely to be realisable at that value.

Mr Marlo has asked us to confirm that we should be able to prepare the 2006 accounts within one month of receiving the paperwork from the company.

Yours sincerely,

Accountant

From Legal Services Commission (forwarded)

25 September

Dear Sirs,
Your client Dean Marlo
I refer to your faxed letters of 15ᵗʰ September about our assessment of Mr Marlo's means.
Mr Marlo's earlier certificates were discharged, but we are trying to decide if we should revoke them instead.
For our practical purposes the information the accountant put in the MEANS1C was correct. Mr Marlo has taken over the business from his predecessor so the information about his predecessor is an indication of what he may earn himself. We must assume that a similar dividend will be available this year, and that at least part of the money is available now, unless the accountant can confirm that a dividend cannot be paid. The accountant quite properly is unable to comment on this year's dividend; I doubt he has seen the necessary documents, but Mr Marlo could make them available if he is convinced that he will not be able to take a dividend.
We would expect Mr Marlo to be able to borrow against his share of the company's assets. We could disregard his share only if he provided documents to show that he has made credible attempts to borrow against the assets and been refused.
We will also need accounts covering the life of the company to allow us to attempt to predict future earnings and the current value of the business.
In addition, and mainly to enable us to consider whether or not we should revoke the earlier certificates, we need the enclosed schedule of assistance to be completed, signed and dated by Mr Marlo. In answer to your question, 'Are applicants for Public Funding to be excluded because they accept gifts of a holiday abroad?' I must answer: yes, quite possibly. It is disappointing that Mr Marlo told us on page seven of his MEANS1 that no–one had given him financial help when by your account they had.
In summary we need:
A credible account of what dividend is expected this year.
Good evidence that he cannot borrow against his assets.
Company accounts covering the life of the company.
The completed schedule of Assistance.
Another MEANS1C correctly completed by the company accountant.
If we get the above information, in the unlikely event that once we have examined it Mr Marlo appears to be financially eligible for public funding, we will have to refer the application to the forensic scientists in our head office's Special Investigation Unit. This is not because Smitch Law made representations against his eligibility, but because that is how we deal with all applications from company directors and shareholders – the LSC's experiences is that they are only very rarely eligible.
Yours sincerely,
Senior Case Worker

How can it be assumed that what my predecessor earned will be the same the next year, or that the funds would be enough to cover the cost of being a single parent with three children, working between 9:30am to 2:30pm, in order to the do the school run? I wasn't going to ship my children out in the place of work, like sadly many parents have to; my business gives me the ability to adapt around the children's needs.

Being there for the children means not working full time, and I cannot understand how LSC can write with this tone to a single parent, who is going to work but clearly also doesn't have the funds to afford solicitor's costs and representation in court.

I am a proud man, and did not want to relay the fact that at the age of 44, with three children, my mum provided the money for our holiday.

From CLG to Northview

5 October

Dear Mrs Tran,

We are instructed on behalf of Alice in family proceedings. I enclose herewith a copy of her authority to act for your records.

We have been discussing with Alice how things are going for her at school. Alice seemed very positive and requested that we contact you to see how things have been going recently, in particular attendance and discipline.

Alice also mentioned that during year 7, she underwent a test for dyslexia but she has not yet been notified of the result. I wonder whether this is something you could look into.

If you need any further information from us, do please contact us at the above address. In the meantime, we look forward to hearing from you in the near future.

Yours sincerely...

Dean Marlo

Courts – A letter

6th October 2006 / Town Family County Courts

Upon reading a letter from Smitch Law dated 3rd October 2006, Judge Randall orders a hearing at 10am on the 23rd October 2006, time estimate 30 minutes, to consider the current directions and time table.

From LSC

17 October

Dear Mr Marlo,
Your Legal Aid
Please find attached a copy of your certificate for Legal Aid. A letter has also been sent to your solicitor. The attached information sheet tells you more about legal aid, but if you have any further questions, please contact our specialist team on the number at the top of this letter. When you call, please have your case reference ready.
Yours sincerely,
Regional Director

After hanging me upside down for three weeks to check my pockets for loose change, I'm granted Legal Aid!

I'm expecting the ground to open up at any moment.

(Or for my Legal Aid to be rescinded.)

Dean Marlo

Alice's Form Tutor – Northview Grove

18 October

Re: Alice Marlo 8OK
Dear Mr Marlo,
We have great pleasure in informing you that Alice has now received a total of 25 House Points across her curriculum areas.
This is very good news and I am sure you will want to congratulate Alice on doing so well.
We hope that she will continue to work well throughout the year to build up her House Points total further.
Well done, Alice!
Yours sincerely,

Hayley and Alice's wishes to the Judge

21 October

Dear Sir/Madam

Please find enclosed a copy of myself and Alice's wishes. Alice and I tried to email this letter to our advocate at CFCS but it failed to send several times. Alice and I feel very disappointed that after speaking to Angela and informing her of are efforts to send this email Angela stated that it was to late and she could not be involved in Mondays hearing.

Despite this Alice and I put a copy of are email in the post 1st class. We both feel that is very important that the judge is aware of are wishes.

Hayley and Alice Marlo

To Angela,

This is what we tried to send you in an email but our email was not working:

Hello its Alice and Hayley Marlo,

Hope you are ok we are writing to you about are orders for you to follow about what we want to happen

We want to not have a court order to go round our mothers but if we want we can go see are little sister Lara round her house when ever we want as long as it is convieiont.

Thank you.

Hayley and Alice Marlo

Dean Marlo

Court – the illusive 'final' hearing

23rd October 2006 / Town Family County Courts
Mother's application – Joint residency

Ms Hyde withdraws her application for sole residency, changing to join residency and the judge orders for Mrs Sanders' report to be filed by 16th February 2007; costs of the report be paid by Ms Hyde's public funding certificate.
Further directions hearing set for 12th March 2007.

The real reason for this hearing was to allow Smitch Law to ask the judge for my half of the bill for the Child Psychologist to be put onto Ms Hyde's Legal Aid in order to get the Child Psychologist's report done. Judge Neely agreed.

I do not have the money, refused to pay, and therefore the report would not be funded. It was a setup by Mrs Mason, under the pretext of Ms Hyde withdrawing her sole residence for joint residence.

On the 28th July, Ms Hyde had us all back in the family court to apply for sole residency; Smitch Law asked for the child psychologist because Ms Hyde was reportedly concerned about the children's welfare in my residence. In Ms Hyde's applications, she has asked them to intervene due to me being allegedly both verbally and physically aggressive; that the children are deeply traumatised by living with me and my behaviour - with no evidence provided, just Ms Hyde's word, year after year.

Months later, with the children happy in my residency and my refusal to fund the report, a directions hearing is set-up solely to ensure the report is done.

It is a part of Ms Hyde's mental health condition, to believe that everyone else has a problem and not herself. This should be recognised by the courts; Ms Hyde is waiting at the side-lines to have her 'aha' moment, when I have nothing to hide and this will only shed further light on the children's abnormal situation with their mother.

By the order of the very court I was standing in, I had the responsibility of three young children and yet, would be earning nothing while everyone else in the courtroom was being paid by public funded Legal Aid.

I was being tried, and my family sentenced, by unjust people, when what my family needs is an end to proceedings and peace; I want to get on with life with my children, and work to provide a good standard of living for my family.

I, and many other parents and family members, rely on the Family Courts for honesty, morals and standards within children matters. Instead of a resolution, families are torn apart by dishonesty, immoral behaviour, and a mockery of standards.

Melissa to me

23 October

Further to our attendance at court this morning, I enclose a typed note of the Order that was agreed and endorsed by His Honour Judge Neely. I also wish to clarify that:

1. *Ms Hyde is not continuing with her application to vary the residency order, or seeking residence of either Alice or Lara;*
2. *Ms Hyde is continuing with her application to achieve contact with Hayley and Alice, however the emphasis will be on the Chartered Clinical Psychologist meeting with the children, Ms Hyde and yourself to see if she can help smooth the path, see what has gone wrong, and look at what, if any, help the children need in rationalizing and maintaining their relationship with Ms Hyde;*
3. *You need to go into the Surgery and authorize disclosure of the children's medical records (and yours) to me so that I can get them copied and provided to the Psychologist.*
4. *Contact is to continue and the schedule that you prepared, with the exception of the Easter holidays, and has been incorporated into the order. I enclose coloured schedule incorporating this change to the Easter holiday.*

Judge Neely's Order –

1. *The Applicant Ms Hyde do have leave to withdraw her Application for a Residency Order.*
2. *That paragraph 1 of the Order dated 25th August 2006 be discharged;*
3. *That paragraph 2 of the Order dated 25th August 2006 be amended so that the letter of instruction to the Psychologist sent by Wednesday 25th October 2006.*
4. *That paragraph 4 of the Order dated 25th August 2006 be amended so that the Psychologist report is filed by 16th February 2007. The cost of the report to be paid for by the Applicant's public funding certificate;*
5. *There be a further Directions Hearing on the first open date after 1st of March 2007.*
6. *The parties have agreed the attached schedule which sets out the periods of residence/contact for the period September 2006 – September 2007;*
7. *Costs in the Application.*

From MP Rowe

24 October

Dear Mr Marlo,

Please find enclosed a copy of the response I have received from the Secretary of State for Constitutional Affairs, Lord Hedges of Thornton.

Hopefully you will find the Minister's comments to be of interest. I look forward to receiving your comments. Best wishes.

Yours sincerely…

Dear Mr Rowe,

Judges Accountability

Thank you for your letter of 7 August. You ask me whether there is a system for checking the performance of judges. You indicate that you have received complaints about the performance of His Honour Judge Baxter and you seek clarification on whether or not he has retired. I apologise for the delay in this reply.

Judges of course sit in public hearings every day and are subject to a certain degree of scrutiny in that way. Their judicial decisions may also be subject to an appeal to the higher courts and assessed accordingly. Additionally, some appraisal and monitoring schemes are in place for fee paid judges. The Deputy District Judges scheme, for example, has now been extended to all circuits. This means all Deputy District Judges in civil courts in England and Wales are appraised.

Appraisal schemes are also in place for Deputy District Judges in Magistrates Courts and in some tribunals and I will be considering the extension to other full–time appointments in due course. Most of the full–time appointments are made from among those who have served in a part–time capacity in the relevant jurisdiction, and therefore their suitability and competence in that capacity will have had to be proven before appointment is made.

When complaints are made about the personal conduct of a judge, I do instruct my officials to make enquires, which generally include drawing the matter to the attention of the judge concerned and giving him or her the opportunity to comment. Each complaint is dealt with individually and I am determined to ensure that judges uphold the standards of conduct that the public expects of them. However, I must emphasise that I am unable to investigate decisions made in a judicial capacity as this would violate the concept of judicial impartiality.

Arrangements are in place with the judiciary to ensure that, when any concerns arise about a judge's health or capacity to conduct judicial business, these are brought promptly to my attention. I will then decide what, if any, remedial action is required.

I turn to your questions about Judge Baxter. While I am unable to comment upon your current concerns, I can confirm that he retired as a Circuit Judge on 30 June 2003. Since that time, he has continued to sit in retirement as a Deputy Circuit Judge. In accordance with established procedure, this arrangement is subject to annual review and I can confirm that his current tenure extends to 30 June 2007.

I should of course be interested to hear about your current concerns, should you wish to bring them to my attention.

From LSC

5 November

Dear Mr Marlo,

Our file for your application has been closed. This is because the application was rejected more than 90 days ago as it was not properly completed and we have not received the correctly completed application and/or the requested supporting documentation.

If public funding is still required, a fresh application must be made.

If you have any questions about this letter, you should phone this office and your call will be passed to a member of staff who will assist you. To enable us to deal with your enquiry, please be ready to tell us your case reference number.

A copy of this letter has been sent to your solicitor.

Yours sincerely,

Regional Director

Dean Marlo

The Cat Sketch

10 November

After Patch… Hayley, Alice and Lara asked if they could have a kitten. It was agreed that to stop the arguments over the kitten they would have one each to look after and care for.

(I know I'm probably setting myself up for this next one, but my theory is that cats are safer – having to put Patch down and lie to my children about him being on a farm, to this day, still haunts me. Despite my brain trying to rationalise everything, I don't want anyone hurt and although cats scratch, the children have experience with their mother's cats…)

We went to a Cat Rescue and the children were lucky, as three 8-month-old kittens needed rehoming together.

The litter tray has entered the house.

Housing Services

14 November

Dear Sir/Madam,

Further to my visit to your office, please find a list of my outgoings and my circumstances, which prevents my ability to pay the £714.29.

Income (month basis):

Housing Benefits – £390.52

Work and Child Tax Credits – £635.68

Child Benefit – £163.40

Working wages – £480.00

Total – £1,669.40

Outgoings (month basis):

Rent – £795.00

Gas – £50.00

Electricity – £46.00

School dinners – £216.00 (three children, 24 days)

Telephone – £20.00

Council Tax – £19.00

Anglian Water – £41.30

Petrol (to take Lara to school) – £20.00

Total – £1,207.30

This leaves me with £462.10 per month; £115.52 per week for food shopping and children's clothes.

As my three children are getting older, the personal needs of the two older children have increased.

In July and August, my mum broke her leg twice and for several weeks the children and I would visit her in the evening at hospital. Due to the parking charge, I found that over the three weeks visiting my mum I had spent over £90. This was unforeseen and resulted in a short fall in money that I had available each week.

I do not want to default with my payments and am requesting an extension.

Yours faithfully…

Dear Mr Rowe

1 December

Thank you for your letters 24th October regarding Judge Baxter.

The hearing for an injunction

I believe that my rights as a victim were not respected in court. Ms Hyde was not reprimanded in any way for her behaviour, neither verbally nor officially. It was her violence towards myself and our children that was the issue and not mine, yet we were both equally penalised.

For the first 18 months of my sole residency, we had a peaceful life; it only took 3 weeks to return us to the chaos Ms Hyde used to cause when we were co–habiting and when we had joint residency.

I feel that Judge Baxter's attitude towards me was unjustified and inappropriate. Owing to Judge Baxter's performance and me shaking my head, he has thrown our family back into the Family Courts, simply because he would not accept the issues remain due to the behaviour of Ms Hyde towards the children and myself.

Surely judges have a duty to prevent the court's time being wasted on cases that are being brought back needlessly.

I am the parent that two years ago was judged to be the best suited to raise my children; it is unjust that such an important ruling can be so easily questioned.

As the stabilising influence in my daughters' lives, I feel the direction that has been implemented is unfair on our family life and their emotional wellbeing.

In August 2004, Judge Chips told me to get on with raising my children and continue to provide for their welfare and stability, to which I have done.

Judge Baxter failed to address the issues that the hearing was about and I believe this is a repeat of Judge Baxter's inappropriate behaviour and performance as a judge in the Family Courts.

Over the years, I have kept a record of the incidents caused by Ms Hyde's behaviour and mental instability, also that of Judge Baxter's behaviour, his directions and rulings. I have relayed many of these incidents with Ms Hyde in my statements to Judge Baxter and the family court; on one occasion, Judge Baxter hadn't read my statement 'because it was too long' and in June, Judge Baxter claimed not to be able to see the criminal damage in the photographs provided, which the police had cautioned Ms Hyde for.

I find myself and my children with needless emotional worry and uncertainty in our family life. I have done nothing to Ms Hyde, just put up with her disgraceful behaviour towards our children and myself over many years.

Quite clearly the family court has not considered the emotional well–being of the children, over the petty bureaucracy involved during the hearings.

On the 18th of October, Melissa told me that Ms Hyde had applied to the Family Courts for a hearing for directions, which would be held on the 23rd October. At this hearing, Ms Hyde withdrew her application for sole residency, changing to joint residency of Alice and Lara, while ensuring the child psychologist report will be completed.

I cannot understand how Ms Hyde was allowed to petition the family court for sole residency of Alice and Lara in the first place; there have been ongoing difficulties with Hayley and Alice's contact due to her treatment of them. Even with her weekend contact, there have been numerous incidences of the children being taken to school late, or not at all.

I am certain that had Ms Hyde and my position as parents been reversed, I would not have been able to make such demands as she has.

Once again, I will fully cooperate with all directions issued by the Family Courts and hope that the meeting with a psychologist will achieve some sort of closure to another unsettling period in three childhoods.

2000/2006

The difficulties in our children's lives have been due to their mother's disgraceful behaviour and attitude, and a history of recurring mental health problems. I also believe that it is quite clear that much of the trouble has been intensified by Smitch Law's overzealous advice to their client.

The Family Courts' attitude towards me as a caring father is disgraceful; Judge Baxter in particular has had every opportunity to help our family, to support Ms Hyde and ensure the welfare of three innocent children. Instead, he has continually been downright rude, criticizing and denouncing the effort that I have shown my children, the Family Courts and Ms Hyde over the years.

Years of false allegations have been placed at my feet, never with evidence, and quite clearly are used to form a case, and request a hearing. I do feel very strongly that Smitch Law have incessantly exaggerated and inflamed any situation possible. This may be beneficial to them but is detrimental to the children, who should be everyone's main concern.

Neither parents nor children should have their lives disrupted or placed in uncertain circumstances by the manipulative manoeuvring of unscrupulous law firms.

The Family Courts should be focused on the children's welfare and stability of a family, and mindful of antagonistic solicitors. The children do not benefit from this going on in the background; the only ones to benefit are the self–serving firms of solicitors who, if my case is typical, generate an awful lot of work for themselves and the Family Courts. This is also a shameful drain on taxpayers funding Legal Aid.

I strongly believe that my children's case should be looked into, not only the performance and attitude of Judge Baxter, but also the cost of the manipulation that has been brought into three children's lives by an overzealous solicitor and the Family Courts.

I appreciate all the assistance you have given me.

Yours sincerely…

Court expert requesting medical records

4/13 December

4 December

Dear Mr Marlo,

We have been requested for copies of Hayley/Alice/Lara's medical records.

It is apparent that some people do not fully understand what is to be released. We would prefer to be absolutely sure that this is understood before we do so.

What will be released to the solicitor is the entire contents of the medical records which are held in this Practice. These will contain:

The written records made by all of the GPs you have had since your notes started (perhaps since birth).

Copies of all letters from your GP to hospital since the notes first started.

Copies of all letters and results of tests and of examinations from any hospital you might have attended ever since the start of the Medical Records.

Letters from other bodies such as the DSS and Social Services if such have been sent to your doctor at any time.

Medical notes include psychological and psychiatric illness as well as physical illness.

If you are happy for us to continue with this process then please sign the bottom of the letter, return it to the Practice and we shall deal with the matter as promptly as we can.

If you have changed your mind please let us know. We will NOT automatically send the medical records if we do not hear from you.

Yours sincerely…

Why doesn't the psychiatrist gather the documents and write to the surgery to request the information she wants to know? It shouldn't be passed through a solicitor; surely a trained psychiatrist and the GP could have a meaningful conversation and organise the relevant details as necessary.

Signing the document and returning it also involves paying the fees to have the records copied and sent – it is another expense shoehorned into my finances, which I am reluctant, for so many reasons, to acquiesce to.

Mrs Mason has done nothing but persecute every aspect of my being, and I'm not comfortable for anyone, let alone the continuing plague on my life, to look through something personal. It is not that I have anything to hide, which will be proven, it is that I am a person who has a right to privacy - the Family Courts have had my life and my children's lives under a microscope for years.

Smitch Law have and are trying anything to find a problem with me; they are hell-bent on discovering any information that they can use to discredit me as a person and my ability to be a parent to my children. Mrs Mason is not expected to comment first hand on the contents of my medical records, and therefore she should not have been given the task of passing them on to the psychiatrist on the basis of my right to privacy. I feel it is harassment endorsed by family law and the Family Courts. It was this very person, Mrs

Mason, who ensured I was not legally represented at these hearings.

I just want to be here for my children, yet I am made to feel that I have committed a crime, where my basic rights are removed and I am identified as someone working against the family court system. As a single father, I am one of the minority who has sole residence of my three children, but my children's mother has the Family Courts in her favour, with the mentality being that fathers are all aggressive, trouble in a mother's life, have no real importance in their children's development and are oblivious to a child's emotional and physical needs.

I feel this way and I *have* sole residency – my heart goes out to all the dads not seeing their children.

13 December

Dear Mr Marlo,

As you will know, I have been asked by the court to provide an assessment to help in the questions about contact between your daughters and Ms Hyde, their mother.

I would like to arrange an initial visit to meet with you all. We can then arrange for further appointments. I can visit on Friday 5th January at around 10am. Please could you contact me to confirm the arrangements or to arrange another time?

Yours sincerely…

Only twenty-three more days before I reset my clock to the next countdown and deadline. If I did not love my children, I would walk away and let Ms Hyde and the Family Courts get on with it. I wonder who Ms Hyde, Mrs Mason and the judges would find to blame for the abuse a parent is inflicting on three children then.

(Probably the ghost of an absent father.)

Dean Marlo

Northview Grove

18 December

Re: Alice 8OK

Dear Mr Marlo,

We have great pleasure in informing you that Alice has now received a total of 50 House Points across her curriculum areas.

We are pleased to see that Alice is continuing to build on her earlier success and I am sure that you will also want to congratulate and encourage her further.

We hope that she will continue to work this positively and co-operatively across all areas.

Well done, Alice!

Yours sincerely...

Hayley's Advocate's (CLG) Application

19 December

Your reason(s) for applying and any plans for the child(ren)
Hayley is the child of the Applicant and Respondent in ongoing proceedings and makes this application by her litigation friend and advocate. Hayley lives with her father Dean Marlo, Respondent in the current proceedings. There is an Order for contact with her mother, Ruth Hyde, the Applicant in these proceedings.
Due to difficulties Hayley has had with her mother during contact, Hayley seeks discharge of the order for contact. Neither the Applicant nor Respondent reflect Hayley's view and she therefore seeks leave to be joined as a Respondent acting by her litigation friend in order that her views can be represented to the court.

Further Information
Social Services have been involved with the family as a result of problems in the past. There is no current involvement.

Incidents of abuse, violence or harm
Hayley's mother has been violent to Hayley and also has shouted and caused arguments.

Involvement of the child(ren)
Hayley and the other children have witnessed such outbursts as detailed above.

Steps or orders required to protect you and the child(ren)
Hayley is hopeful that the order she seeks, i.e., discharge of the order for contact will protect her and her sisters.

It amazes me that a court would not read this application, and feel something towards three children that are clearly experiencing difficulties at their mother's; Hayley and Alice still aren't having regular contact with her.

Hayley is but a child, and it should not be her responsibility to protect her sisters from her mother's behaviour, when there are people in positions to help Ms Hyde, with the possibility of improving the relationship she has with her three daughters.

A realisation from the courts, that Ms Hyde's mental health condition continues to affect her judgement and ability to cope with her children at any age, would ensure that she accepts and attends the support available, because she isn't going to do so willingly; her bipolar makes her believe it is everyone else that is not acting rationally.

Avoidance of getting Ms Hyde parenting classes and mental health support, has lead us to court involvement still in 2007.

My counter to Ms Hyde's application for sole residency is to persist with the existing order, which means I have sole residency of our three children, and although Hayley knows her wishes always stand first and foremost, I understand why she wants to be free from the pressure to return to her mother's at any point under a judge's court order.

The courts should look at the history, and understand there is no evidence of me preventing the children from contact with their mother, and, as in the past, I'm more than happy to arrange contact to suit Ms Hyde or the children's wishes. There should be provisions in place for when the children site mistreatment, wherein Ms Hyde cannot return the family to court, to enforce contact of children she's abusing; it is then up to the children and their relationships with their mother, to initiate contact again.

If Ms Hyde receives help, there's a good chance of peace for our family and her contact with her children would not be disrupted, because the incidents would be less likely to occur, or there would be support to guide her through a mental health episode. Even if it does not reach the extent of being sectioned, her behaviour during these periods is unacceptable and may lead to full mania if unsupervised, which is not a good outcome for anyone, as the children have experienced in the past and should not be forced into reliving.

2007

Dean Marlo

Notice to the schools

4 January

Dear Mr Church/Mrs Tran,
Lara/Hayley and Alice have an appointment with a child psychologist on Friday 5th January in the morning, as explained in my call to you. I shall drop Lara/Hayley and Alice to school after lunch.

If you have any questions concerning the above, please do not hesitate to contact me. Thank you for your attention with this matter.
Yours sincerely…

The Child Psychologist Interview

5 January

Mrs Sanders came to talk to Hayley, Alice, Lara and myself.

We had to do all sorts of activities, including a timeline, which was honestly sadder and more difficult than it should have been. It's simultaneously been a very long time and no time at all; Hayley and Alice's childhoods were plagued with so much.

The children spoke to Mrs Sanders in their bedrooms on their own. Meanwhile I made a coffee, sat in the kitchen, looking at the pictures decorating the walls; written work from school; art they've drawn for me; many of our favourite photos picked out from our albums.

Mrs Sanders and I then had a conversation, and after, I thought about the man I was in 2000, walking out of Mrs Odam's office and feeling confident I had proven worthy of being part of my children's lives. Seven years on, I hope this report accurately reflects our family and the reasons why there are problems.

Hayley, Alice and Lara have missed a morning from school just to meet Ruth's demands; as usual, the children are the ones disrupted.

Dean Marlo

Courts – Removing Hayley

9th January 2007 / Town Family County Courts
Hayley's application – removal from the order

Hearing for the application made by Child Legal Guidance for Hayley to be removed from the court order, matter listed for 16th February 2007.

Cycles

10 – 18 January

Wednesday 10th
Ruth and I arrange for her to pick Lara up after school and have tea. Ruth dropped Lara home at 7:30pm.

Monday 15th
For Ruth's weekend contact, Lara stayed over Friday to Monday morning, as usual, Hayley stayed on Sunday night only and Alice came home on Sunday. Apparently, the reason for this was Ruth had taken Alice clothes shopping on Saturday, and was going to take Hayley on Sunday.

I asked Alice why they were not all going shopping together, and what about Lara; she replied, 'I don't know, our mother makes the rules.'

In November, Alice wanted to go with the school on a mystery trip to Belgium and France; in December I made the first payment of £35. Today, over breakfast, Alice stated she didn't want to go on the trip anymore. I asked Alice if she is sure, as she might change her mind closer to the time – Alice said she has fallen out with the people in her group.

After I waved Alice off to school, I received a call from Riverbank stating Lara isn't at school. I tried to call Ruth several times but she did not pick up.

Mid-morning, I received a phone call from Northview Grove stating that Hayley was not in school and they were now unaware where Alice was, after she registered in her form. I rang Hayley with no pick up so tried Alice; she explained that she spoke to Hayley and she was still round her mother's, so that's where Alice went.

Thursday 18th
Alice stayed with Ruth from the 15th to the 18th of January, coming home after school on the 18th.

I'd received another call from Northview Grove; Alice had received an intervention for truancy from lesson and leaving the school grounds. I had a discussion with Alice about a separate call from Northview, reporting that she had been late to school every morning this week; she looked tired but rolled her eyes and said she wasn't 'that late'. While I was reminding Alice that school is important, especially as she moves up the years, she was absorbed by her phone and left the room.

Dean Marlo

Northview Letter

16 January

Level 3 Intervention / Mathematics
Pupil: Alice Marlo, 8OK
Dear Mr Marlo,
I am writing to inform you that Alice's behaviour has warranted a Level 3 intervention. The reason for this decision is, truancy from lesson, 15th January 2007, period 2.
As a result, your daughter will need to attend a meeting with the Cluster Group leaders, named above, in the House area on Thursday 18th January 2007 at 3:15. This meeting may involve strategies such as completing missed work or discussing consequences of poor behaviour. The maximum duration will be one hour, therefore your daughter will be released by 4:15pm.
Level three sanctions are recorded centrally in the school and will form part of the student's record. Alice will be monitored for a short period following this in order to ensure that she has settled down and the issue is fully resolved.
We seek to work with parents to achieve the highest standards of behaviour and achievement from our students in the interests of their positive development.
Yours sincerely,

Between Teachers – re: Alice

19 January

From: Receptionist
To: Mrs Sparrow
Cc: Mr Garrett
Could someone please call mum asap. She says that Alice is now as from today going to be living with mum 2 days a week. Apparently there are court proceedings going on and a solicitor involved. She is not happy as she is not getting any of the letters she is supposed to get about detentions etc. she is also really angry with Alice's English teacher for things she has said to her. Her number is enclosed.

From: Mrs Sparrow
To: Assistant Head of House
Maurice,
Maybe you could find out what's happened.

From: Assistant Head of House
To: Learning Support
Cc: Mrs Sparrow
Spoke to Alice's mum. Her English teacher did a spelling test with the group and told them that if they did not get 5 marks they would be in detention.
She is concerned that staff have not been informed about Alice's dyslexia (apparently she has been trying to get her tested for over a year, which Maurice believes she is referring to testing carried out by school) and she is just about to be tested. There are no problems in the ED MED SOC or SEN list, so I assume that the teacher was unaware of her difficulties.
Please can you ring Mrs Marlo to update her on the current situation. I confirm correspondence is listed to be sent to both parents.
Many thanks,

Boundaries and arrangements

19 January

At approximately 12pm, I received yet another phone call from Northview Grove, who stated that Alice was in the medical room, refusing to return to class, and asked whether I was available to collect her. I informed them that I was at work, but I would be along within half an hour at most. I packed up site and jumped into my van.

Ten minutes later, Northview Grove phoned again, and stated that Alice has asked them to contact her mother instead. I said that I was on the way and would be along shortly.

I picked Alice up and asked how she was feeling. She gave me mostly the cold shoulder for my question, just stating 'ill'. I do not like doubting my children's honesty, but Alice's relationship with school has been rocky recently, and I don't believe Alice was truly unwell. (She flicked about with the radio to pick a song and started texting on her phone.)

I told Alice that I would have to go back to work, if Ma is available. Alice replied, 'Why did you pick me up? I could have walked to my mother's.'

I told Alice that she was not going to use her mother as an excuse to get out of school. Alice went into her bedroom and came out stating, 'I have phoned my mother and she is going to pick me up now.'

Then, Alice walked out of the front door.

In the evening, I got a call from Ruth claiming Hayley is hanging around outside her house with several of her friends, refusing to come in or to leave, and will I pick Hayley up. I agreed to do so and collected Hayley, who was there on her own when I arrived; she said she didn't want to go inside, after her mother had refused to let her friends in.

Alice stayed with Ruth from Friday 19th through to the 22nd, Monday. Alice was late for school on Monday morning.

Northview EP

22 January

Dear Mr Marlo,
Please find enclosed a copy of the report following the visit of Ms Helen Little, assistant Educational Psychologist on 7.12.06.
I will discuss this report with Mr Gabriel Vine, Educational Psychologist, to ascertain whether further testing may be appropriate. You will see this does not give a diagnosis of dyslexia but staff have been made aware of the low reading and comprehension ages and the difficulty they may present in Alice's learning. In the meantime, I have placed Alice on the Special Educational Needs List under School Action for Moderate Learning Difficulties.
Please contact me if you have any queries.
Yours sincerely,

Alice's Advocate's Application

24 January

Your reason(s) for applying and any plans for the child(ren)

Alice is the child of the Applicant and Respondent in ongoing proceedings and makes this application by her litigation friend and advocate. Alice lives with her father Dean Marlo, Respondent in the current proceedings. There is an Order for contact with her mother, Ruth Hyde, the Applicant in these proceedings.

Due to difficulties Alice has had with her mother during contact, Alice seeks discharge of the order for contact. Neither the Applicant nor Respondent reflect Alice's view and she therefore seeks leave to be joined as a Respondent acting by her litigation friend in order that her views can be represented to the court.

Further Information

Social Services have had involvement with the family in the past. There is no current involvement.

Incidents of abuse, violence or harm

Alice's mother has been violent towards Alice and verbally abusive and caused arguments.

Involvement of the child(ren)

Alice and the other children have witnessed and been subject of aggression and violence as set out above.

Steps or orders required to protect the child(ren).

Alice is hopeful that the order she seeks will protect her and her sisters.

Arranging tea

24/27 January

Wednesday 24th
Ruth and I arranged for Hayley, Alice and Lara to go for tea; she dropped them home at 8pm.

Lara came through the door holding some brochures for a private school, which Ruth had given her. Apparently, Ruth thinks Lara would be happier in a boarding school.

I asked Lara if she wanted to change schools, and she looked sad.

'No Dad,' Lara said, 'but I didn't want to say that to Mum.'

Ruth really does frustrate me. Riverbank is a great Primary School, and Lara only has two years left there. Lara is popular with her class, gets on well with her teachers and has always had smashing year reports.

Not only that, but who would be funding this private tutorage? I can't afford it, even if Lara did want to go.

I will not support Ruth's desire to create problems where they do not exist.

I also doubt Ruth's intentions; of course, I do not want Lara locked away for weeks or months (as I see it) in a boarding school, and it appears if Ruth cannot have sole residency herself, she is prepared to send Lara away, so neither of us have residency. I know Lara is clever, but there are several great schools and colleges close by, which would allow Lara to be challenged in her education and still have her family in her life.

Ruth is aware that Mr Church is very willing to praise my parenting and is happy to relay in writing the truth about my conduct within the school. I cannot help thinking that this is just an extra attempt to manipulate my ability to refute what she continually suggests to the courts. Mr Church had seen Hayley and Alice in the past, and now Lara, as well as interacting with both Ruth and myself. I will always be thankful that Mr Church cares for the welfare of Hayley, Alice and Lara, and has always been prepared to show it.

Saturday 27th
Hayley and Alice informed me that their mother has booked a holiday to go to Spain in the April half-term.

Meanwhile, the taxpayer pays for Ruth's legal team.

Lara did not seem as excited, stating the holiday will consist of the beach and the bar - I had to grimace as Lara finished with 'and not in that order'.

Child Benefits

2/4 February

2nd

With the psychologist report upcoming, I find myself wishing away time despite what that means for enjoying my children's childhood, just to get to the end of the court hearings.

Recently, Ruth has started picking Alice up from our home in the morning, at around 8am, to 'wash her hair'. Sadly, it is Alice that has decided she will not wash her hair when showering at home – this is encouraged by her mother who will pick her up at any time.

After numerous sporadic morning pickups, I received a call from Northview Grove stating that Alice has arrived at school wearing her pyjamas for the second time this week. I had to explain that Alice is spending mornings at her mother's, which has left me in a difficult position; when I have spoken to Alice about her behaviour, she reacts by getting her mother to pick her up, or staying at her mother's and having no contact with me.

I have tried, but Alice has a taxi waiting in the wings and her mother would rather cause problems for Alice's education than act like a responsible parent. Despite having sole residency and welcoming Ruth being a mother to our children, I cannot understand how Ruth continues to disrupt Alice, in particular, as she seeks her mother out if I challenge her behaviour. Alice staying with her mother would not be a problem, if Ruth was committed to being a parent and I wasn't receiving calls from Northview.

Ruth phoned and asked me if I would contact the CBA to organise for her to receive Alice's Child Benefit. I stated that at the present time Alice is abiding by the court order (apart from mornings) and while I didn't mind giving Ruth the money when Alice was staying with her, I currently need it to care for the children. Ruth began shouting about how much I owe her, so I hung up.

4th

Hayley and Alice informed me that they were going to Asda at 6pm with their mother for holiday clothes; jeans, tops etc. When they came home, Hayley and Alice told me that their mother spent over £200. Please understand, I do not mind what amount Ruth is spending on our children. I say good luck to her, but I cannot comprehend the fact that I once again have been placed in a position of emotional and financial worry.

The stability that I have worked hard to achieve in my children's lives and my own, has once again been ambushed and I find myself down on the side of the road, trying desperately hard to figure out how and why I keep getting my legs taken out, and how all the people involved just carry on; knowing full–well the difficulty they have asserted in my life for no justifiable reason.

Just to finish me off, Hayley said that her mother had kept going on about the child benefits, and how it was unfair for her.

Court – Alice's removal

6th February 2007 / Town Family County Courts
Alice's application – removal from the court order

Application made by Child Legal Guidance; Alice would also like to be removed from the court order. Judge Baxter orders for the hearing to discuss both Hayley and Alice's applications to be held on 16th February, with representatives for Ms Hyde, Mr Marlo and the children only to attend.

The order states 'file and serve on each other and solicitors' – I had hoped Judge Baxter would have noticed I was sat in court alone. I waited for the crowd (Ms Hyde's legal team) to disperse from the room and left on my own.

It is funny that my children are legally represented, but I am not. Once more Judge Baxter fails to realise his ruling leaves one party unrepresented at this hearing. At least the children's solicitor should be able to relay via the advocate the children's wishes, and I will not have to hear Mrs Mason or one of her many barristers claim, 'These are not the views of the children your honour, this is the view of Mr Marlo.'

(Small mercies; little steps.)

Making arrangements for the children

7/9 February

7th

Ruth and I arranged for Hayley, Alice and Lara to go to hers for tea; Ruth dropped them home at 8pm.

9th

At half-term, Lara stayed with her mother for the duration, while Alice and Hayley slept over for only two nights.

Courts – evaluated

16th February 2007 / Town Family County Courts
Hayley and Alice's applications – removal from the court order

Applications heard to discharge Hayley and Alice from the current contact orders are adjourned until 12th March 2007 at 10am. Mrs Sanders has completed her evaluation and report of the children and Mr Marlo, which is to be seen by the solicitor and counsel for Ms Hyde and Mr Marlo (who is not legally represented). The parents shall file and serve on each other and the solicitors for the children, a position statement by 4pm 2nd March 2007.

Judge Yergin orders there are to be no further proceedings and a final hearing on the 12th March.

(Arr frabjous day, I thought another final hearing date would never come!)

The psychologist's report.

Dean,
The court seems to have done it again and sent it to my office, instead of to you.
Regards,
Melissa

Psychological Report
Hayley Marlo – D.O.B March 1992
Alice Marlo – D.O.B April 1994
Lara Marlo – D.O.B December 1997
Report prepared by: L.Sanders
B.Sc., M.Sc., Dip. Clin., B.Ps.S., A.F.B.Ps.S
Reason for referral
I have been instructed by Mrs Mason, solicitor for Ms Hyde and Ms Brenna, solicitor for Mr Marlo, to make an assessment, providing information concerning:
The family dynamics and relationships of Ms Hyde, Mr Marlo and the children, with particular regard to contact issues.
Sources of information
Documents (Listed in appendix 1)
The medical records of Mr Marlo and the children were requested but have not been received.
Discussion with the following people:
Mrs L Mason, solicitor for Ms Hyde.
Mr Church, Headteacher Riverbank Primary School.
Mrs Sparrow, Head of House, Northview Grove School.
Visits and observations
Mr Marlo, Hayley, Alice and Lara together – 05.01.07.
Hayley Marlo (at home) – 05.01.07.
Alice Marlo (at home) – 05.01.07
Lara Marlo (at home) – 05.01.07.
Ms Hyde – 19.01.07/30.01.07.
Alice Marlo (at mother's house) – 19.01.07.
Hayley Marlo (at school) – 06.02.07.
Lara Marlo (at school) – 05.02.07.
Mr Marlo – 05.02.07.
Background information and chronology
Family structure.
Ruth Hyde. Date of Birth (DoB) 06.64. *Ex–partner to Dean Marlo, mother of Hayley, Alice & Lara Marlo.*
Dean Marlo. DoB 02.62. *Ex–partner to Ruth Hyde, father of Hayley, Alice & Lara Marlo.*
Hayley Marlo. DoB 03.92. *Daughter of Ruth Hyde & Mr Marlo, sister to Alice & Lara.*
Alice Marlo. DoB 04.94. *Daughter of Ruth Hyde & Mr Marlo, sister to Hayley & Lara.*

Lara Marlo. DoB 12.97. *Daughter of Ruth Hyde and Mr Marlo and sister to Hayley and Alice.*

Chronology:

The following chronology is drawn from the documents provided, dates may not be exact and there may be differing views of the events by the parties.

1986

Ms Hyde, aged 21, had brief episode acute disturbance and hospital admission while travelling abroad.

1987

Ms Hyde, aged 22, had brief episode acute disturbance and hospital admission while travelling abroad.

1991

Ms Hyde ended apparently physically abusive relationship.

Ms Hyde and Mr Marlo began their relationship.

November, *Ms Hyde consults her doctor following an alleged incident of physical violence.*

December, *Ms Hyde removed from GP list because of rudeness.*

1992

Hayley born.

1993

June, *Ms Hyde admitted to psychiatric hospital for one month, manic and aggressive behaviour.*

October, *Ms Hyde discusses marital problems with her doctor.*

1994

Alice born.

1995

Ms Hyde had a two-month admission to psychiatric hospital.

1997

December, *Lara born.*

Ms Hyde consulted doctor about marital problems, doctor records 'children not at risk.'

Ms Hyde admitted to psychiatric hospital with puerperal psychosis.

1998

February, *Ms Hyde discharged from hospital.*

June, *Ms Hyde discharged from outpatient clinic.*

November, *Mr Marlo contact family doctor as Ms Hyde's mental state deteriorating.*

1999

November, *Mr Marlo referred self to Cannabis Support Group for assistance with drug use.*

November/December, *Ms Hyde and Mr Marlo separate. Children live with their mother.*

2000

July, *Ms Hyde admitted to psychiatric hospital, children stayed overnight with maternal grandparents. Hayley wanting to be with her father.*

August/September, *Interim shared residence order. Children going between both parents' houses. Hayley refusing to return to her mother, disruptive behaviour from Hayley and Alice.*

October, *Shared residence order made.*

2001

December, *Ms Hyde's GP records problems with children due to shared residency.*

2004

May, *Order for residence with Mr Marlo made.*

May, *Ms Hyde had admission, mood variability.*

2006

May, Psychiatrist noted 'symptoms of irritable mania' and concerns as Alice is staying with Ms Hyde. Ms Hyde admitted committing an act of Criminal Damage.

This is where, if I had a barrister, help for Ms Hyde could be mandated – her mental health condition affects her judgement and how she conducts herself on a daily basis, and is intensified during manic episodes. These incidents are a clear indicator she needs support, and not the family court circus.

How can a clinical psychologist document Ms Hyde's behaviour and not conclude that she needs the involvement of a mental health team, for her own benefit and the children, who are growing up fast and are subject to emotional and physical abuse?

All of this has been encouraged to continue, because the narrative has been persistently pushed that I am just another aggressive and violent man, and the cause of Ms Hyde's bipolar disorder, which is banded about without evidence.

Family Background

Following the ending of the relationship of Mr Marlo and Ms Hyde in 1999, there have been long running proceedings consisting of allegations and counter allegations which are detailed in the documents of the court bundle provided and listed in Appendix 1.

This has been an acrimonious case and I do not intend to list the difficulties experienced here. It is sufficient to identify difficulties concerning communicating significant information about the children, allegations of physical abuse on Ms Hyde and her partner's part, and contact difficulties. There was a relatively steady and calm period between 2004 and 2006.

Mr Marlo

Introduction and observations

Mr Marlo was co–operative with the assessment and was well oriented as to time and place. I did not carry out any formal psychological testing, however, he did not appear to have any difficulties in his overall level of cognitive functioning.

Mr Marlo phoned in response to my letter concerning the assessment and queried that the appointment involved taking the girls out of school; he suggested that the interviews could take place in Riverbank Primary School, where the Headteacher had offered a room.

I confirmed that it did involve time from school and explained my reasons for the intended home visit. There was a long silence and as it was unclear what Mr Marlo's response was. I re–iterated the reasons for the situation and eventually he agreed. On my visit, he apologised and said he had not meant to be awkward. I identified his underlying anxiety about the process and he was able to acknowledge this.

Mr Marlo appeared weary and rather flat emotionally in both interviews. He was calm throughout the interview and interaction with the girls, warming up and appearing more relaxed later in the assessment.

Mr Marlo is self–employed and is trained as a builder. He stated he tries to fit his work in around the school routines but, if necessary, his mother has babysat. He voiced his sense of grievance about not being granted Legal Aid and felt penalised for trying to have a role in his children's lives.

Interview

Relationships in the family

Mr Marlo described the last few years as a relatively calm period. The girls had been going regularly to contact with their mother until a year ago when the issue of her holiday had arisen and her partner had backed her up in a disagreement with Hayley and Alice. This apparently resulted in a physical incident between Ms Hyde's partner and Alice, and Ms Hyde and Hayley; the two older girls stopped visiting.

During this period, Lara has continued to have contact but the two older girls had not wanted to, although Hayley had stayed in contact by phone. Mr Marlo was not willing to force them and realised they would come round in their own time. This was now happening and he thought it would be better if it became settled again into a routine.

Throughout both interviews, he was clear he did not know what happened in incidents between the children and their mother, and emphasised there was always two sides. He did not run down or criticise Ms Hyde, although he brought up several of the difficult incidents, which had occurred. He thought it important for Ms Hyde to handle any situations in a 'calm' manner and be firm, especially with Alice.

Children

Mr Marlo clearly cares deeply for his children. He was grateful for Hayley and Lara's calm temperaments as this helped influence Alice, who was very changeable. He thought many of the conflicts in the family arose around Alice and recently Hayley had come to a similar conclusion. Otherwise, they were normal children coming into their adolescence, with all the changes this involved.

Hayley was of the age when family activities did not interest her as much as going out with her friends, and he was having to set limits with which she complied. He talked over his intention to set a time limit for a disco she wanted to attend, and had encouraged Hayley to talk to Mrs Sparrow at school about whether she thought this was a reasonable time.

We discussed the incident when he had intervened to move Hayley, with her friends, from sitting outside near her mother's house. He was not aware she had been so angry with Alice that she had been saying she wanted her adopted.

Alice was the one he was most concerned about, as she was not as old as she appeared or thought herself to be. She did not accept limits as easily as Hayley and he had talked to her about 'using' her mother at these times; he acknowledged she had the potential to play one parent off against the other.

In the recent situation when Alice had gone to stay with her mother, Mr Marlo's version of events was very different from Alice's (8.2.19). He had collected her from school, as she was unwell. She had not been happy with him talking to her about not going to school or his needing to return to work; as a consequence, she had decided to go to her mother's house.

Mr Marlo described Alice as having a tendency to 'go for the jugular'; she was intense, could be very rude and provoking. It was clear there are rivalries between the girls and he did not want Alice to damage her relationships with her sisters. Alice was very changeable, at home and in her friendships at school.

Lara was seen as older than her age, but was still young and became upset by Alice's rivalry and teasing. He advised her to ignore the provocation from Alice, but she found that hard. He thought she was missing out on the family activities they used to do as her two older sisters were beginning to want to spend more time with their friends.

Mr Marlo stated that Lara had recently brought home some brochures about a private school, which her mother had given her. Apart from the financial implications, his view was she was doing well at her primary school where she had friends and it would be too unsettling for her to move at this stage.

Information from school

Mrs Sparrow, Head of House Northview Grove School, stated that Mr Marlo had been calm, helpful and responsive parent. He always informed the school of any absences and appeared concerned for his daughters' interests.

Mr Church, Headteacher of Riverbank Primary School, had not experienced any difficulties with Mr Marlo and the last two years had been a 'calm period'. Lara was on time for school and Mr Marlo consistently informed the school if she was ill and when she would return. He thought Mr Marlo clearly loved his children and they did not seem to play him up; instead, they had seemed more organised and settled since the change of custody. He thought the children 'remarkably well adjusted'.

Ways forward

Mr Marlo thought the girls needed stability and no further changes. He agreed there needed to be common ground rules and both he and Ms Hyde had to know where the children were. He agreed that any arrangements to stay with Ms Hyde should be made in advance and that Alice, in particular, had to realise that her mother could not always be there as she worked too. He felt Ms Hyde needed to be firm with Alice.

Summary

Mr Marlo clearly loves his daughters and wants stability for them. Emotionally he was very flat and controlled and was able to discuss the difficulties and conflicts in a calm and reasonable manner. He was able to acknowledge there were always two sides to be taken into account and there were points of agreement between himself and Ms Hyde.

His ability to manage the situation for the girls responsibly and consistently was borne out by staff at both schools. Although Mr Marlo was very calm throughout this assessment, it is clear from papers contained in the bundle (social worker – page 509, and Cafcass – page 131), the complaints he made about Ms Hyde's mother and Ms Hyde's barrister, that he has the capacity to become aggressive and pursue a grievance intently.

It is likely, with his own childhood background of traumatic incidents of control and abuse (Ms Hyde's medical notes, 07.07.93), he developed a style of attachment in which control was the only safe option, whether by care giving or punitively. This surfaced in his relationship with Ms Hyde but to a much lesser extent with the children. His emotional style is cut off (hypo–arousal) which after a certain degree of conflict or provocation could result in an aggressive outburst.

Writing formal letters of complaint to the appropriate organisations is now deemed an 'aggressive' action. People who genuinely have endured an injustice, tend to be unable to sweep it under the rug and move on.

What actual evidence does this psychologist have of me behaving this way, let alone having an 'aggressive outburst'? Or that 'control is the only safe option'?

I have put up with so much, only some of which she touches on in her report; despite those provocations being bad enough, I have hid behind doors, stayed in the car and never gone out to meet Ms Hyde when she has brought trouble to my door and when exchanging the children, whether at home, the McDonald's car park or the bottle bank.

Where, in the above, can this psychiatrist infer an aggressive person?

Am I being aggressive as I sit here at my desk, documenting what is going on in my life, day after day, year after year, constantly writing when I am not sure if anyone actually cares, or if anyone might even read what I have found within the walls of the Family Courts?

My notion of someone being aggressive would be, jumping into my car and instigating confrontation with Ms Hyde, Mrs Mason, Judge Baxter and numerus barristers. That is the stereotypical view of someone brought up on a council estate, but even coming from a deprived area, all of my friends have grown up to be decent people and not violent thugs, as portrayed.

Ms Hyde kicked my van in, which started proceedings in 2006 – I stood inside my house with Lara and Hayley, merely witnessing Ms Hyde's aggression. My reaction, was to not get involved and call the police.

I would like to ask if anyone wants to watch as criminal damage takes place to their vehicle? Do Smitch Law, Ms Hyde and this psychologist, consider me requesting Ms Hyde stop kicking my van, an escalation of my supposed aggression?

As usual, Ms Hyde's conduct came out of the blue and was over within minutes; all we could do, which as a family is all we've ever done, is stand back in shock and wait for her to leave.

There is something deeply wrong with the psychologist citing Ms Hyde's medical notes from July 1993, height of mania, as the source of information on *my* childhood. If that background is necessary, I believe the psychologist should have spoken to me myself about it and gained the information… Despite having an abusive father, I still had the love from my mum; the knitted jumpers (which I still receive alongside my children); the Christmases huddled around the tree playing Monopoly; the knowing looks she'd give me when I came home covered in mud from a game of football.

As great as it is that humans have spent a long time studying the brain and personalities, we do not fit explicitly into the boxes of two extremes. If I am *hypo-arousal* I am emotionally deficit except for anger, which I suppose means Ms Hyde is *hyper-arousal* which means she's emotionally erratic and not prone to anger? Humans are not cut and dry like that. I am exhausted after ten years of Ms Hyde making all our lives miserable, and I want the court hearings to end; I love my children dearly and support all their interests; I have never had an aggressive outburst. But that does not fit the picture.

His style is very different from Ms Hyde's and the ending of their relationship has affected them both deeply. Unfortunately, this has resulted in their being unable to negotiate a more neutral position in parenting.

Ms Hyde's behaviour during her pregnancy of Lara, and after, broke me; the years prior with Hayley and Alice seemed mild by comparison.

I was heartbroken when she took the children and stopped me from seeing them. I felt overwhelming relief that I was away from Ms Hyde.

What about the previous statement that since I gained sole residency in 2004, there had been a 'calm period'?

In the face of another person who has all the power to change my children's residency, and down a long line of unscrupulous performances by so–called professionals – I'm still standing here saying I have only ever wanted to be a father to my children.

Mr Marlo's obvious affection for his daughters and his detached emotional style has provided a stability, if at time with a little insensitive, which they needed after the upheavals caused by their mother's ill health.

I love my children with everything I am; yet, this love is called insensitive. I don't *understand*– before and after Ruth was sectioned, I was there for Hayley, Alice and Lara with love, care and support. I was not planning or scheming behind the Ms Hyde's back, aiming to prevent the children from seeing their mother, I was not rushing back to court for some special order, I loved my children and have never coached or tried to manipulate their feeling towards their mother.

Strengths

Mr Marlo clearly loves his children.
He has provided stability in his children's lives.

He co–operated with the assessment.

He has been a responsible and consistent parent in his dealings with the children's schooling.

He was able to discuss the issues in this assessment calmly and acknowledge the differences which exist between Ms Hyde and himself.

He appears to be able to focus on demands of the present moment and immediate future.

Staff in both schools have seen him handle the children reasonably and effectively.

He has common areas of agreement with Ms Hyde about the children's behaviour and its management.

Concerns

Mr Marlo's cut off emotional style can lack sensitivity to his daughters' complex range of changeable feelings.

Really, what is she implying here? Am I a robot built in a depot, or just another crab in a bucket; a man; emotionless and, more–so, incapable of understanding the feelings of my children?

He has the potential for aggressive behaviour with adults.

This statement has no right to be there, and it fucking *hurts*. I wrote letters of complaint to the appropriate organisations; Ms Hyde has abused and continued to abuse my children and myself, doctors, staff, strangers at shops.

His sense of grievance can fuel the conflict with Ms Hyde.

Ms Hyde is a fire that needn't any fuel, and the implication that I am – what? taunting? – aggravating Ms Hyde to prolong a conflict I've never wanted anything to do with, after all these years, is beyond words. It is exhausting, frustrating enough to tears, because it's so easy for these people to write offhand remarks that damn your sense of person down to your very core.

Ms Hyde

Introductions and observations

Although Ms Hyde was clearly anxious, she was co–operative with the assessment and was well oriented as to time and place. I did not carry out any formal psychological testing, however, Ms Hyde did not appear to have any difficulties in her overall level of cognitive of functioning. She gave me two documents, one a personal statement and the other an article on the dynamics between partners involved in controlling and violent relationships.

She had apparently told her daughters they could tell me things in confidence and was rather taken aback when I said I could not undertake to do this. I explained that the assessment was specifically to put information before the court and that secrets were unhelpful.

On the first visit, when difficulties had arisen between Alice and her father, Ms Hyde was agitated and showing signs of a high level of psychological arousal. Her attention was scattered and she had difficulty focusing on issues, she was unconnected; emotions and ideas occurred, her flow was interrupted and diverted. In dealing with Alice, she was unclear in her communications and while saying she was not pressuring her daughter to see me, she clearly was.

On my second visit, Ms Hyde was much calmer and more relaxed. Whilst there was less pressure of speech, the same pattern of scattered attention was evident; it was hard for Ms Hyde to focus and follow through an idea. However, she again showed evident heightened physiological arousal when discussing the difficulties between Mr Marlo and herself.

Ms Hyde frequently became absorbed in repeating the difficulties and grievances in her relationship and I had to persistently return the focus to the present time and options. In reporting conversations about differences in parenting style, Ms Hyde appeared to concentrate on problem listing and blaming rather than seeking solutions.

At times her thinking was over generalised and she made absolute statements, which did not fully reflect the situation, e.g., 'Lara has had to do without me at all.' When I pointed out that Lara had experienced a consistent relationship even if not living with her, Ms Hyde repeated her assertion and could not adjust her perception. Her main focus was on the difficulties and when situations had gone relatively smoothly.

'…Over generalised and she made absolute statements, which did not fully reflect the situation.' Oh, you mean like 'Mr Marlo is aggressive, has physically abused both me and the children and has done everything he can to destroy my family?'

Everyone involved now knows Ms Hyde's full mental health history, and here the psychologist lists the way her condition manifests in day-to-day life. Yet, I still cannot be certain what conclusion Mrs Sanders will reach.

'…Repeated her assertion and could not adjust her perception.' – Which is why it is incredibly difficult to compromise or reason with her; once she has decided something, that is 'fact', and anyone who says otherwise is an arse who she will fight tooth and nail to validate her distorted point.

Interview

Relationships in family

Ms Hyde concentrated on her experiences of her relationship with Mr Marlo and her concerns that the same pattern was being replicated with the children. She thought they were unable to express their wishes freely to him and he unduly restricted the at home, often in trivial matters. She described a competitive element between them in relationship to the children about who was the good or better parent.

Ms Hyde was concerned that Mr Marlo was not encouraging and supporting the children in their relationship with her and particularly around contact. She was of the opinion that he was actively interfering and making it hard for the girls to have contact. The difficulties Ms Hyde listed included; making arrangements for attractive activities scheduled for her contact weekend; interrupting contact by 'continually' texting or phone calls; reports of Mr Marlo making negative statements about her to the girls. At the same time, Ms Hyde made allegations of Mr Marlo being absent during his contact weekends and evenings and not ensuring the children were adequately supervised or fed.

I would hope that if Mrs Sanders had met the man described above, she would have recognised the emotional manipulation and heard from the children that this occurs. Instead, I have to work Saturdays, sometimes often and sometimes more occasionally, to support my family. When the children are at their mother's, we may exchange a goodnight text, or if they need to ask about something they call, but I certainly don't 'continually' contact them – they have their own lives to be getting on with at their mother's and I take the opportunity to work Sunday as well.

I have already had the conundrum of whether I am a father who is always at work and the children have a few extra toys, or it's a brand butter rather than the company basics range; or, a father who stays home with my children, relies on the system for support and therefore the children's childhood experiences are less exciting, and they know certain school trips and activities are out of the question.

(Why the elite in modern society are allowed to get away with keeping the system this way, I've yet to figure out. I was waiting for the revolution in the crowds of a Greenpeace rally 20 years ago.)

Due to being fortunate with my business, and how I've had to adapt in primordial soup to survive, I try to balance the seesaw. I do rely on the top up Child Benefit gives – although if the courts were out of my life, maybe I could work my way out of that one too – and I go to work on Saturday, leaving the children with Ma, who they love dearly, even as Hayley and Alice have grown up and arranged to go out instead (I leave a note, have a nice day and love to you all) and come home in time to cook dinner.

During the week, I work half the amount of time during the day because I am dedicated and *want* to be there for Lara's school run. I am there because it feels good being there for Lara in the school playground and I know Lara feels the same, as I did for Hayley and Alice. (All part of my low-something and coldness towards my attachment with my children.) As many parents find, there is a sense of joy as your child or children run across the playground, and throw their arms around you; this joy is still there as your children grow up, apart from you find you are more of a drop off point for their school books, items of clothing and PE bag as they run off to see their friends.

In Ms Hyde's eyes, I'm damned if I am involved in my children's lives and damned for when I can't be there.

Towards the end of the conversation, however, Ms Hyde stated that up until April 2006 contact had generally been satisfactory. She thought the situation had deteriorated from the time when she had told the girls of her intended trip to Australia with her new partner. At this point, Alice, in particular, had reacted intensely, expressing strong feelings of rejection and abandonment and called her mother a 'ditcher'.

By Ms Hyde's own admission, the last year of difficulties, incidents and court hearings, all stemmed from her going on holiday, and the reaction of Hayley and Alice. This hearkens back to how Ms Hyde interacts with her children – she did not inform them beforehand she was going to book a holiday, she announced that she *was* going on holiday and would miss contact time. At the end of the day, despite everything she has put the children through, they love her as their mum, and Ms Hyde cannot even appreciate that.

It appears that the relationship between her daughters and her new partner, which had previously been good, had changed after this and an incident when he had supported her. Ms Hyde did not appear to understand Alice's response reflected the underlying insecurity in her relationship with her mother.

Ms Hyde described how contact would be all right for several months, then there would be an incident and a period of not communicating and then returning to the previous level. Despite this longer–term perspective when difficulties arose, it was clear that Ms Hyde lost this overall view and old grievances and emotional responses were reactivated. Even in a period of relative stability, she was unable to acknowledge the improvement because she was already anticipating the difficulties ahead.

Ms Hyde was able to acknowledge that her episodes of mental ill health had an impact on her daughters but was unable to identify in what way and at the same time said they would have been 'too young to remember'. She acknowledged incidents when she had 'flipped' such as the time she had kicked Mr Marlo's van, but did not appear to recognise these would have an impact on the children. Ms Hyde went on to say the experience had made her stronger, she knew her limits, recognised when she was taking on too much and had more empathy with the difficulties of others. However, she still thought she had 'lost custody for no particular reason'.

Ms Hyde now acknowledges she did kick the van, which is contrary to what she wrote in her application to court, where she denies it. Notably, someone who 'flipped' and caused criminal damage does not constitute being called aggressive or unacceptable.

Also, here is confirmation, Ms Hyde continues to show no insight to the children's feelings, or how her behaviour has an effect on them in the long term; she believes the traumatic events are exclusive to her being actually sectioned, and has no concept of the months before and after, where her behaviour was still manic, and since, regardless of whether or not she has been sectioned, episodes have occurred and this is clear through the children's reluctance to have contact with her.

I know I am only here to make the numbers up, but no one considers the effect all of Ms Hyde's behaviour has had on me, yet I am able to maintain a reasonable dialogue with her, even though I have every right to be disgusted by the way she treats our children, and how the whole situation has drained me. I don't want a medal, just acknowledgement that Ms Hyde needs help and the family is under the influence of how Ms Hyde's bipolar presents.

(As I understand, the meaning of myself as a father within the Family Courts is only to be emotionless, aggressive and detached.)

Children

Ms Hyde clearly loves her children and is concerned for their wellbeing. She was most concerned about Alice because of the times she had difficulties with her father and had come to live with her mother both last year for a month and currently for a weekend. We discussed the ground rules for Alice's unscheduled stays. Alice's emotional temperament was similar to Ms Hyde's and we discussed the difficulties which emerged between them because of this; it was clear that they both tended to spark off each other. She thought Mr Marlo favoured Alice and placed her in the position of family spokesperson.

I love all my children equally. They're obviously individuals and have different needs, but Hayley, Alice and Lara are amazing children. Alice, whose temperament at times mirrors Ms Hyde's, does not wait for permission and will loudly inform anyone what she has problems with. I said it before, but when Alice called her mother because I'd enforced a boundary she didn't like, Ms Hyde should've backed me up as a parent; not allowed Alice to escape responsibility and circumvent rules that would be the same for Hayley or Lara if they were in Alice's situation.

And now here, Ms Hyde uses Alice as a scapegoat and justification, when in actual fact it is her bad parenting choice that led to Alice staying with her for a month, which coincided with Alice's behaviour at school deteriorating.

Ms Hyde's responses have sometimes been unhelpful, as in the comment she had made to Alice after some misbehaviour during her stay last year, 'If you are going to behave like that you might as well go to your father's.' This had precipitated Alice's return to her father.

More recently when Alice was swearing Ms Hyde had said, 'Do that again and you won't have anyone here, I'm not putting up with you.' Alice had stormed off upstairs. When she came down later, Alice said she wanted a drink in a reportedly aggressive way and Ms Hyde had not replied.

Giving Alice the silent treatment, is Ms Hyde the child or the adult here?

When I talked about being able to make calm, bridging statements at times like this rather than being emotionally reactive, Ms Hyde was unable to understand the difference.

She also reported saying another time, 'You chose to live with your dad,' which had a blaming quality and could only exacerbate the situation. Ms Hyde seemed unaware how statements like these had an impact on the children and made them reluctant about contact.

Ms Hyde held views contrary to the information given to me by the school; she was concerned about

Alice's performance and thought she was not putting in enough effort. However, the recent testing showed how much effort Alice had put in to gain satisfactory grades despite her reading difficulties. Ms Hyde was also worried about the number of absences of both Hayley and Alice, and the times they appeared to have been absent at the same time. When she showed me the records, part of this perception was due to a misreading of the symbols used. I suggested that she speak to the school about her concerns.

Ms Hyde was also concerned about the lack of supervision both Hayley and Alice had from their father in the evenings and gave examples of them being on the streets in the evenings and getting into trouble.

Recently, while Ms Hyde was at work, Hayley had come to her house with friends. When Alice had refused to let her into the house following her mother's rules, Hayley and her friends had sat outside a neighbour's house creating a disturbance. Mr Marlo had to intervene and apparently Hayley had been very angry. She had said Alice 'was not a member of the family' and she wanted both Alice and Lara adopted. Ms Hyde said while Hayley was generally quiet, she could lose her temper and took after her father in this.

Of all the behaviour Hayley witnessed, and is old enough to unfortunately remember, lack of emotional control and loud outbursts are not from her father.

There had been a recent incident at school with Hayley, which had been out of character, and Hayley had been upset at being in trouble. Hayley was reported to be low in mood and negative about herself and her life. We discussed how sensitive and reactive adolescents could be and Hayley's generally good record at school. I suggested that it was important to emphasise this, help Hayley to calm, see the positives in herself and retain a realistic perception.

Hayley was such a sweet and goofy child, and being a teenager first out of her siblings, with everything going on in the background, is difficult for her. We talk often, and I believe if this low mood persists, she will speak to me about it, as she has with other things in the past. Hayley's been through a lot, and she needs to remember she doesn't have to be like her mother, or Alice, to be liked and heard, she just needs to be herself.

Ms Hyde reported that Lara was on the gifted register, although this was not confirmed by Lara's Headteacher. She thought this contributed to her being more able to see situations more clearly than her older two sisters. She reported that Lara had been a little tearful after seeing me and thought I had 'hit a few chords with her'. More recently, Lara had apparently said she had handed me two letters expressing her wishes; I was puzzled and wondered if she had confused me with someone else as she had not handed any letters to me. When I checked with Lara, this apparently referred to a letter she had written a considerable time ago.

Ms Hyde reported Lara feeling that 'no—one was listening'. She had replied, 'You probably don't feel that,' and had continued to persuade her daughter out of her expressed feelings, a more sensitive listening approach is needed especially at times like these.

Gaslighting a nine-year-old. Classy.

She thought the girls were confused and felt guilty about saying negative things about her to their father.

How does she know what is said in our house? This is an accusation that paints her as the victim to not only my 'abusive behaviour' but bullying from her three children. We get on with our lives, we do not sit in a prayer-circle badmouthing their mother.

We discussed the complaints and rivalries between the three girls and how their very different temperaments brought them into conflict.

Information from school

Mrs Sparrow, Head of House Northview Grove School, had mostly phone contact with Ms Hyde, often when there were difficulties in contact. Ms Hyde tended to worry that Hayley and Alice were not doing well at school and this was as a result of difficulties with their father. The school did not consider the level of absence of either girl sufficient to require any action.

Mr Church, Headteacher at Riverbank Primary School, had seen the children with Ms Hyde and they were said to 'play her up'. There had been times when it had been difficult at school with Ms Hyde because of her emotional state.

Ways forward

Ms Hyde strongly thought she should have joint custody. In her view, this would give the children clear permission to have contact with her, have a closer relationship with the schools and provide some financial assistance for her with the children. I asked whether this would lead to even more difficulties in joint decision making and communication but Ms Hyde dismissed this concern.

I understand to the outside observer, it may appear the children 'play' their mother up, but I think that unfairly neglects the fact that Ms Hyde has bipolar disorder, and this makes keeping calm and many other aspects of parenting challenging for her.

The children have never needed 'permission'; when Hayley and Alice choose not to have contact due to either verbal or physical abuse, Lara has continued per her wishes to do so. When the children or Ms Hyde have requested additional contact, we have arranged for them to go.

Ms Hyde said she and Mr Marlo backed each other up about rudeness and behaviour, this is a positive area of agreement, which hopefully could be built upon. We discussed the importance of common ground rules for the girls. Both parents needed to know where the girls were and notice of where they were staying for the night. Ms Hyde stated the girls had to get their father's agreement and she needed a days' notice of them coming to stay as they had to accommodate her work schedule and plans. The issue of sleepovers during the week needed to be settled as during term time; the children needed their sleep.

The communications between Ms Hyde and Mr Marlo about the girls was clearly vital both for their safety and to co-ordinate activities. The order not to communicate directly was resulting in communications being channelled through the girls, which was emotionally difficult for them. We discussed less direct but speedy methods such as texts or emails, but Ms Hyde was pessimistic about Mr Marlo using these.

The communication problem was introduced by the courts, on the suggestion of Smitch Law, on behalf of their client. We were always going to need to communicate, and have done so since that order; it's only when the conversations break down due to Ms Hyde having an ongoing mental health condition, that things become difficult.

(I don't want to point the finger, except to actually achieve help for our family situation. For many years, not only have I had to defend myself as a person, I've never managed to convince anyone that I haven't acted in a way that was detrimental towards Ms Hyde, as a partner and a mother, or my children, or Ms Hyde's relationship with her children. This reality has been overlooked, dismissed, and the contrary used against me without evidence or witness to such behaviour.)

We're almost to the end of Ms Hyde's evaluation, and despite the conduct described, there is no suggestion that Ms Hyde is capable of an 'aggressive outburst'. Yet, the incidents referenced have all resulted in Hayley and Alice not having contact due to physical abuse, as well as the emotional abuse of the entire family.

I wish Ms Hyde *would* text, but for her, communication isn't worth doing unless she can get verbally agitated and high on that angry feeling.

Summary

Ms Hyde has a legacy of emotional difficulties from the past e.g., separation of her parents and sexual abuse from her stepfather (medical notes, discharge summaries May 1993 and March 1998). She acknowledges that while her mother has been practically supportive, she has been unable to offer emotional understanding and support. Unsurprisingly, Ms Hyde has an anxious attachment pattern and the styles of emotional relating between Mr Marlo and Ms Hyde were an extremely difficult mix, resulting in conflict which included incidents of aggression verbal and probably physical.

Where is the evidence of me responding in kind to Ms Hyde's verbal or physical aggression? It's unjust to write such a thing based on psychological concepts and not the facts of the case before her.

An extremely difficult mix, wherein upon our separation, Ms Hyde emptied the house of all the belongings and moved out with the children; shortly after, we went on holiday together as a separated family to the Dinosaur Park; I bought her a car, brand new, for her use with the children; I provided maintenance cheques; I babysat my children when Ms Hyde had plans…

In the initial months after our separation, things were looking positive for our children's future, as two parents who were no longer together but had the potential to equally provide love and care. Even with Ms Hyde's mental health condition, we could have arranged for me to have the care of the children during these periods, with her able to see them as much as she was able, until she has received help and could cope with the children's needs.

There was no need for events to take place the way they did, given my support for Ms Hyde during her periods of illness when we were in a relationship, and my care of my children, as at times a single father during those episodes, proved I was capable of having equal contact as the children's mother.

They all ignore the seven years we were together, where I was not abusing Ms Hyde or her illness, I was there looking after her, as someone I loved, and our three children. I have always been willing to compromise, work with and support Ms Hyde, just as I have always been asking for the outside help to properly do so.

This all comes back to the same misunderstanding as this psychologist is having, which is that I do not comprehend the ways in which Ms Hyde's bipolar affects her.

She will be fine, mostly, for a few weeks, and then her judgement and conduct becomes questionable again; this is exacerbated by the fact she is not, to my knowledge and based on the children's reactions, receiving help, or being monitored when the children bring up her behaviour towards them.

The focus is instead: why isn't this mother having contact with her children? The conclusion drawn is that the father is the problem, which is the same incorrect narrative they've used to try to resolve our family's issues before, and it hasn't worked, because they need to be addressing the children's reports of abuse at their mother's.

I'd like to think this psychologist, having reviewed our family's documentation, would have read Hayley and Alice's applications for removal from the court order. This clearly indicates problems at home with Ms Hyde and there should be more concern both for Hayley and Alice, but also for Lara, as she approaches the age that is already proving to be challenging for her mother.

Ms Hyde's medical history indicates an intermittent psychological vulnerability, and is more susceptible to relational stresses. She appears to have been particularly vulnerable psychologically in the postnatal period and two of the episodes of mental ill health were precipitated by the birth. Without sensitive, close support and understanding at these times, she struggled emotionally and an episode of mental illness was precipitated.

I don't know if it is solely the failing of the understanding at the time, or something else, but in 1993, when Ms Hyde was discharged for the first time during our relationship, we both needed to be sat down with by her doctor or mental health team, and the risks associated with pregnancy and Ms Hyde's condition should have been discussed. At the time, I wasn't aware of Ms Hyde's mental health history, but those doctors had access to her records and would have therefore been aware her condition pre-dates having children, and while obviously the changes during pregnancy may exacerbate her condition, it should have at least been acknowledged that her issues were underlining.

I love Hayley, Alice and Lara, and wouldn't change having them, but if I had been told about Ms Hyde's bipolar disorder, we could have at least both been prepared and got her the support she needed, instead of it being terrifying as a partner and a parent with young children around, when Ms Hyde's episodes took over. Due to the fact we weren't married, even though we lived together and had children, I was not privy to her diagnosis and Ms Hyde, who clearly does not acknowledge that she has a problem, did not discuss her condition with me; leaving me unaware of what to do while Ms Hyde's behaviour was so erratic and emotionally gutting.

Again, Mrs Jackson kept quiet and did not have the decency even for her grandchildren to help her daughter, instead choosing to relay that I was an abusive and aggressive man; a proper psychopath; the reason her daughter would become ill.

The consequent losses involved in the break–up of her partnership, the change of residence of the children and the difficulties in contact have affected her deeply. The continuing conflict and legal battle have contributed to her ongoing sense of grievance and she has been unable to move on emotionally.

Ms Hyde has been unable to let anyone else move on at all.

If a red flag is not blowing in the wind after a judge has read this, and it is not evident that proceedings should stop, then I fail to see the point of anything in this report.

Ms Hyde clearly loves and wants the best for her daughters. However, emotionally and physiologically, Ms Hyde is very reactive with difficulty in holding focused attention. In situations of conflict or challenge, she easily becomes hyper–aroused and has difficulty in managing these emotions.

In past situations, her basic fight defence has been activated and she has been unable to hold back the verbal and physical outbursts.

I can't even imagine how scathing the report would be if I, a man, was described as unable to holdback any form of outburst – I was described as aggressive and all I've done is write letters! I do not think it would be paired up with applying for joint residency, the waste of this psychologist's time and the rinsing of the Legal Aid purse.

Her limited range of tolerance for emotional situations and reactivity present obstacles to her responding calmly and managing situations involving the children in a consistent and effective manner. She has limited ability to identify the boundary between her feelings and those of the children, and sees their opinions and reactions as solely due to her husband's influence, rather than the cumulative impact of the past experiences in their lives.

(Between paragraphs 16 and 18, we have gotten married.)

Even though it appears all I am capable of is complaining, and I find fault in every report made, I do commend Mrs Sanders for being polite and genuinely interested when talking to myself and the children – she wasn't just phoning it in. For the most part, I agree with what she has said, and she does outline Ms Hyde's behaviour as it is in our day-to-day lives; this is what we need to bring an end to proceedings in the Family Courts.

Strengths

Ms Hyde clearly loves her daughters.

She cooperated fully with the assessment.

She has substantially contributed to the positive development of her children.

She can be sensitive to the emotions of her daughters at times.

She wishes to broaden their experiences.

Concerns

Ms Hyde is highly reactive and has difficulty focusing on the present issues calmly.

She has difficulty separating out her feelings from those of her daughters'.

She focuses on past grievances rather than current issues.

She ascribes views and opinions held by her daughters as shaped by their father rather than their own experiences.

She has physically and mentally abused the children in the past, and her mental state would indicate there is risk of reoccurrence... Just in case Judge Baxter is sitting in the chair for this hearing and skips forward to the summaries only.

Hayley Marlo

Observations

Hayley is a calm and friendly young teenager who related well. She appeared calm, thoughtful and was able to express herself clearly.

Mrs Sanders relays Hayley's attributes and qualities, which Ms Hyde cannot see in any of her children.

On our first meeting, she acknowledged feeling nervous about talking to me and appeared very edgy when talking about her mother. On our second meeting, although having toothache, she talked more freely.

Interview

Hayley clearly has a good relationship with her father and with whom she feels safe and special. She said she could say anything to him and would turn to him if troubled. Although he had not said so, Hayley worried her father might be lonely if she and her sisters were all away with her mother, as a consequence she would phone him at these times. She was obviously sensitive to the feelings of others and takes on, to some degree, responsibility for helping them.

Hayley talked about the relationships between her sisters. Although there were disagreements, which could be intense, and at times became physical, they were short lived and soon forgotten. She acknowledged she would say Alice was adopted or wanted her to be adopted when she was worked up but this soon passed. She thought the main differences were with Alice who enjoyed fashion and concentrated on her appearance whereas she and Lara were more tomboys.

Hayley acknowledged feeling 'down' at the moment; there were disagreements between some of her closest friends and the negatives at school were getting to her. However, she was also able to list the positive relationships she had at school with certain staff members.

Hayley openly stated she did not like having a court order for contact with her mother; she wanted to be able to choose when she went. She stayed over at her mother's house when Lara was there. She did not go on her own; if she visited, she liked to take a friend as that eased the situation for her. She preferred to call in on a more casual basis to see her mother, for shorter periods, several times a week. She thought phone contact was satisfactory.

She recognised that the relationship with her mother was better when Alice was not there, as she was the one who tended to cause arguments. At these times, Hayley would then get pulled into it and Lara would become upset and cry.

Hayley discussed how changeable she found her mother; she would say one thing and then later say something different. She wanted her mother to be more consistent so she could begin to trust what she said. When the situation was calm then she had a 'good mum' who did things to make her happy such as making nice things for her to eat.

However, Hayley had a divided view of her mother and said 'lots of me thinks she is a bad mum' and referred to her trying to 'strangle her' in the past. It is clear that past events have a strong influence on her feelings of safety and trust with her mother. I asked what she would want to say to her mother, Hayley replied, 'No hitting or cornering me.' She wanted to be able to talk things through calmly. If her mother came to their house, she should avoid causing arguments. Hayley also thought her mother said things about her father which 'did not need to be said' and she wanted her mother to 'stop blaming things on Dad'.

I couldn't do Mrs Sanders job and write this clinical report where a child is telling you that she doesn't like being alone with her mother for a myriad of reasons. Being strangled and cornered shouldn't be an experience for any child, and not being able to trust her mother is so sad, because I have had to watch the children love their mother, and it not be understood by Ms Hyde; their mother could have received help years ago.

As someone who loves their mum, I wouldn't wish for my children to have a bad relationship with theirs, and I've only ever wanted Ms Hyde to be a good mum to our children, as I try my best to be a good dad.

Someone, implement the parenting help ordered for Ms Hyde in 2000 – please!

Hayley had mixed views about Bernard, her mother's new partner. She used to like him but after an incident when she stated she saw him push Alice, she had been wary of him. She had felt he was taking her mother away from her and her reaction to their trip to Australia had shown this.

Hayley thought she could manage conflict with her mother better now and walk away or if necessary, ask Bernard to help calm the situation. So, although Hayley had reservations about Bernard and had withdrawn from the relationship with him, she still saw he could be a source of support if needed.

I asked about any conflicting arrangements when it was her mother's contact weekend. Hayley said there were sometimes conflict with wanting to do things with her friends. It was clear from what she said that as she develops and becomes independent this is increasingly likely to be the case.

Hayley had strong views about her maternal grandparents calling them 'evil' because they 'shut me in their house' and had taken sides. She described how she and her sisters had been caught up in the scene of confrontation with her father while in her grandparents' house. She and Alice had been trying to get to him and being prevented from doing so; she admitted it had been 'really scary'.

She said her maternal grandparents wrongly believed things about her father. These incidents appear to have had a strong impact on her and the opinions she has formed. She described feeling more at ease with her paternal grandmother, with whom she felt special and loved. She thought her paternal grandmother took a more neutral view.

Hayley had another resentment about the way she felt her mother had chosen her secondary school without giving her any choice. She did not particularly like it but accepted the decision. I asked her about her support network for when she needed to talk about her feelings. She responded that her Head of House and tutor were supportive. Hayley also values Alice's support; at school she has not always been able to stand up for herself at times and has welcomed her younger sister's direct and challenging style which has offered her protection.

I asked about Hayley's future plans. She is considering as either a physical education teacher at primary school level or a signer for deaf people. She became much more relaxed and her enthusiasm for signing was obvious. She became interested in this because one of her friends is deaf. Hayley had found it rewarding to help her be understood; she said, 'I feel like I'm someone and feel happy helping.'

Information from School

I met with Mrs Sparrow, Head of House at Northview Grove School, who has known Hayley for over three years. Hayley was said to show 'fair effort' across all her subjects and her work was progressing satisfactorily. Hayley was viewed as potential vice prefect but had not quite met the standards in dress; these were only minor details, but ones she would have to enforce herself if she were in a more responsible position. It was evident that Hayley's abilities, temperament and contribution to the school was appreciated.

Mrs Sparrow described Hayley as 'a lovely girl' who had good relationships with both staff and her peers. Mrs Sparrow described Hayley as being a little tearful at times, particularly if there had been an incident at home and seemed in need of some adult care and support. Her tutor tried to meet her at the beginning of the day, cheer her up and ensure that her day began well. Mrs Sparrow thought that generally, Hayley responded as any normal teenager would.

Summary

Hayley is a quiet and thoughtful adolescent who enjoys making a contribution and helping others. She is liked and respected for this at school. She dislikes confrontation, wants a quiet life and has difficulty at times in being assertive. She is affectionate and loyal to both her sisters and her father. Although there are the normal conflicts in relationships with her sisters, these are short lived.

As the eldest, Hayley has experienced more of the upheavals within the family than her sisters and has been a protective factor for them. However, the emotional uncertainty and conflict has affected her and as a consequence she values consistency and stability. She appears to have difficulty in asserting her needs at times and can feel over-responsible for other's feelings. The variability in her mother's mood and behaviour is stressful and difficult for Hayley to manage and it has undermined her confidence in their relationship.

The impact of past events has shaped her views and she sees them from the emotional perspective of a young person who was frightened and felt the loss of security in her life. I found no evidence of alienation in her views of her mother but some hints of it in her views of her maternal grandparents, but the foundation of these seemed to be the traumatic scene of separation from her father who she loved and being 'imprisoned' in their house.

Hayley needs stability, support and encouragement for her growing independence, but within a framework of clear limits. She will need the understanding and guidance to deal with the emotional changes of adolescence and negotiate the changing allegiances, conflict and competition which emerge in friendships.

Strengths

Hayley is a quiet, reflective young person.
She relates well and could express her views clearly.
She is affectionate and loyal to her sisters.

She has a close relationship with her father.
She enjoys helping others.

Concerns

Hayley finds the variability in her mother difficult to manage and it has undermined her trust in their relationship.
She has difficulty standing up for herself with others and is vulnerable to being bullied.
She has difficulty in letting the effects of past incidents go.
She is vehemently against her maternal grandparents for what she sees as their part in the family conflict.

Alice Marlo

Observations

Alice is a lively, volatile young teenager who looks older than her nearly thirteen years. She is a confident and dominant figure in the family, evident in her exchanges in the family tasks and the views of others.

Alice expressed her views freely to me and clearly did not hold back expressing herself within the family. She was focussed on getting her views across, had a combative attitude and would contradict others without carefully listening to their viewpoint.

Interviews

First meeting

Alice said she visited her mother when Lara was staying. She said this was for Lara; Alice thought her younger sister became lonely there as she had when staying last year. Alice had gone to live with her mother as a result of conflict with her father about staying with a friend in what he had thought were unsuitable circumstances.

I asked about this stay and Alice said although her mother had 'done lots of stuff' she only wanted to remember the good parts. She thought her mother 'not a good mother' because of the priority she gave to her boyfriend. Alice said, 'She can be kind but it is like walking on eggshells.'

She had several strategies for visiting her mother and minimise the difficulties between them. The first was based on how she felt and the level of self-control she could manage, which she expressed as 'I won't go if I know I'll start an argument and then Mum will start arguing'. Another was using the support of neutral others such as visiting with a friend or if she knew there was someone outside.

How can alarm bells not be ringing for this psychologist that not one, but two children have coping mechanisms, including ensuring they are not *alone* with their own mother but with a friend, because they have lived with their mother's behaviour their whole lives? Two children have 'expressed' strategies on dealing with their mother and that is just not how it should be. I wish reading these harrowing words from my children (that aren't a surprise but are nonetheless upsetting) meant that support for Ms Hyde, parenting courses and monitoring would finally be put into place. It's not fair for the children to have spent their whole lives dealing with the forefront of Ms Hyde's mental health or behavioural issues, meanwhile the Family Courts and the experts crammed into the witness box tiptoe around calling Ms Hyde's behaviour out; I've lost my voice and cramped my hand trying to get anyone to listen, so it is left to *children–*

It was clear she realised the volatile relationship with her mother. She acknowledged her part in their disagreements and that their similar fiery temperaments made conflict more likely.

Alice is not the adult in this situation; while it is commendable of Alice to recognise her own behaviour, the 'conflicts' (read incidences of physical and/or mental abuse) do not fall on Alice's twelve–year–old shoulders.

This was confirmed by the observations of her sisters and father. Alice said she 'could guarantee there would be an argument' if she went for a meal at her mother's house. I asked who would be responsible for starting this and, with endearing candour, she said, 'half and half.' She thought that neither she nor her mother were good at 'letting things go'.

Alice wished for a stable relationship with her mother and acknowledged there had been an improvement but she had found her mother's unreliability difficult when they had been living with her. Her wishes were for her mother 'not to shout or hit'.

With both Hayley and Alice indicating they love their mother and are struggling with the volatility and physical abuse her mental health condition contributes towards, it should be a clear sign for this psychologist to implement something to help Ms Hyde, while her relationships with her children are still salvageable; before Lara gets to an age where she is included more in the physical abuse and so the children may have a good childhood, even though there have been rough patches.

Alice did not like 'being bossed' by her mother's partner; instead, she wanted her mother to take responsibility for discipline when she visited. She also wanted her mother not to talk to her about her dad, this clearly upset her and she would come to his defence resulting in conflict between them.

Alice talked about school and her difficulties with a particular teacher which she felt 'picked' on her, especially if she was feeling moody. She said 'I find it hard to go to school and act normal when this is happening in the background, it builds up inside.' She found it hard to concentrate and, from her description of events, to respond calmly to authority at these times.

Alice also can get into conflict with her peers because of her outspokenness. She recognised Hayley's difficulties in standing up for herself and readily acted in her defence.

I asked about the anger management help she had received. She was fairly dismissive of it as there had only been a few sessions. She described being given the opportunity to talk over worries but there had not been a specific focus to emotional and anger management skills which could be very useful for her. She thought it would help if she was able to use the time out system and remove herself from the classroom when wound up but, according to her, had been unable to access the scheme.

Alice had several grievances about fairness within the family, one which revolved around sharing responsibilities e.g., tasks at home and taking care of the rabbit. According to Alice, when Lara stayed with her mother these devolved to her; she felt strongly that Lara should have to do more on her return in repayment. She expressed a very definitive and rigid perspective, wanted situations to be fair and equitable with little flexibility for negotiation. This is a common view at her developmental level and in children caught up in parental disputes.

It is not a parental dispute, this is about incidents happening when the children are in their mother's residency, and then refuse to have contact.

Second meeting

This was unscheduled; Alice was at her mother's house when I called as a result of a conflict with her father. Alice was clearly distracted and unsure what to do, she kept coming in and out of the room and refused to eat any breakfast. Ms Hyde was trying to persuade her to talk to me before returning to school.

I saw Alice in her room and as she talked, she began to calm. She had felt unwell and wanted to be absent from school, she acknowledged she had recently truanted from school and her father had said she had had too many days off. The argument had grown heated between them and Mr Marlo was reported to have said, 'sort yourself and your stuff out' meaning ready to go to her mother's house.

Alice described feeling shocked and surprised because when they argued, her father was always calm. At this point, Mr Marlo tried to persuade her to stay but she had refused.

We discussed the importance of her having a calm down time at her mother's house and then resolving the disagreement with her father. Alice stated she did not want to 'abuse' the situation with her mother and was clearly aware that this could lead to further difficulties between her parents. We discussed using the idea of time out at home where she needed to be left alone to calm herself.

Following on from the previous discussion I had with her at home, we also talked about getting a time out card at school to allow her to leave a situation to gain control of her feelings and remain in school, rather than absenting herself which only led to more trouble for her. She was unsure how to get this and arrangements were made for her to see her Head of House about this.

Information from school

Mrs Sparrow said Alice was showing 'good effort' across all her subjects; her grades were just below the 'good' grade and she was performing well. Recently, Alice had been assessed by the Educational Psychology Service and found to have a reading age of eight years and four months and a reading comprehension age of six years and eleven months; this is four years, four months and five years, nine months below her chronological age respectively.

As a result, the school was offering Alice extra assistance through learning support, and had changed the emphasis for her in French, a subject which she had been showing frustration. This information also helped to explain the areas of difficulty such as spelling, which she had recently refused to do.

Alice was said to get on well with the majority of the staff although she could be awkward and had been rude at times. She tended to mix with others who were not necessarily a good influence. Intermittently, her temper would show but she would respond well to Hayley at these times. She was said to have had a bad phase in the Christmas term and had intermittently truanted class, most recently the previous week. Recently she had been given a time out card to use, which allowed her to leave a lesson for a short period to gain control of herself and calm down.

Summary

Alice is a volatile and impetuous young teenager with a lively temperament. She had a clear view of the difficulties this posed her both with her mother and authority at school. To her credit she recognised that she was equally responsible for the conflictual nature of the relationship with her mother and she had a number of sensible strategies for minimising this conflict.

Alice was clear she would only accept discipline from her mother and not her partner. However, any discipline is unlikely to be welcomed unless delivered in a fair, firm and calm manner.

Alice is affectionate and demonstrative to her sisters but unaware of the stresses in their relationship to which her temperament contributes greatly. Despite her differences with Lara, she is fiercely protective of both her and Hayley.

Alice was very perceptive of the emotional impact, of the long-standing conflict in her family. She easily becomes emotionally activated and struggles with self-control; she requires assistance to help her develop a range of skills in this area. As she moves into adolescence, she is likely to test the limits considerably and it will be important that the adults in her life give her consistent boundaries in a firm and calm manner.

Strengths

Alice is a lively young adolescent who communicates her feelings and wishes directly.

She took responsibility for her part in the volatile nature of her relationship with her mother.

She had several sensible strategies and suggestions for minimising the conflict between them.

She was perceptive of the impact the family stress was having on her at school.

She is willing to ask for help.

Dean Marlo

Concerns

Alice can be challenging, particularly to authority and requires firm limits.
She has a volatile temperament and could use some emotional management strategies.
She focuses on issues of unfairness and has difficulty letting past situations go.
She is dominant in the family and unaware of her impact on her sisters.

Lara Marlo

Observations

Lara is very adult for her age. She made good eye contact, talked to me freely and related well. In the family task, she watched Hayley and Alice closely as they shared memories which excluded her. However, she was also extremely assertive, in a quiet way, about her own memories.

First interview

Lara was clear that she wanted 'no more changes' and to continue staying contact with her mother. Apart from seeing her mother, she was explicit that this gave her time away from Alice whom she found difficult. Lara was closer to Hayley, who she described as 'the best sister ever'.

Lara talked about the activities she did when staying with her mother such as cycling, having friends to stay and her computer. However, at times she was bored and missed many of her belongings which were in her bedroom at home. Sometimes Hayley and Alice would call in.

Lara said her mother was 'calm normally, unless we do something wrong or when Alice became stroppy'. She described herself as the 'good one' although at times she did get told off which she thought was fair.

Lara said it was hard to get her mother to play with her at times, she was too busy or wanted to have a cup of tea or cigarette, although she was now giving up smoking. She enjoyed it when they played games together such as backgammon.

Lara talked about her mother's partner. She wanted to keep on the good side of her mother so she pretended to like him. She clearly did not want to do anything which would upset people and so make it difficult for herself.

We talked about what she would like to happen. She became a little tearful as she said she wanted them to be 'like a normal family' but she knew it would not happen. If her mother and father were together for any time there would be fights; they could not talk to each other without getting caught up in disputes and 'games'. Lara was clear about the differences between her parents. Her father did not like her mother and did not talk about her, whereas her mother did not like her father and talked badly about him.

Lara said her father did not talk about the situation with her mother; he only talked about issues which came up at court and their views so he could represent these to the court. She said he does not 'let on how he feels'. About the differences between her parents she said, 'I'm so used to it now but sometimes at school it gets to me.' The comparisons with the family situations her peers brought it home to her.

Lara thought her opinion was often not asked for or included as she was the youngest in the family. She said, 'They forget I'm here and think they can do what they like.' She was close to her father and Hayley but Alice was changeable and very reactive; Lara thought she and Hayley were the calmer ones.

Lara talked about school where she had 'the best teacher'. However, she was having difficulty with one girl who seemed determined to join her group of friends and would not accept Lara's rebuffs. This girl seemed to be splitting up Lara's group of friends and causing her some distress.

Lara described herself as 'happy' but added poignantly she sometimes thought, 'What my life could have been, it's not their fault (parents) the world is how it is. You just dream it in your dreams.'

Second interview

Lara again talked about the arguments and difficulties she has with Alice. Although her mother and

212

father gave her the same advice, to ignore her, she found this just made Alice worse. Lara described Alice as 'being two faced'. She would say things against her mother and then go stay with her; she also 'added things which were not true'. Her version of events leading up to Alice's recent stay with her mother was that Mr Marlo had taken some privileges from her, Alice 'blew up' and said she was going to her mother's. Lara clearly stated her father did not 'throw Alice out'.

In a similar way Hayley had reacted, apparently uncharacteristically, to some sanctions and had become very angry. This resulted in her saying she wanted to be an only child and her sisters to be adopted. Lara said Hayley tried to remain in the good books with both parents and tried to shield Alice. Hayley had encouraged Lara not to tell their father about Alice truanting, but, as Lara observed, he was bound to find out, which he did from the school. It was easy to see why Lara enjoyed staying on her own with her mother, she described it as a 'sister free zone'.

I asked Lara about how easy it was for her to say what she wanted and to talk about good times she had with either parent. She said, 'No-one tells me, but I don't want to insult or hurt anyone,' and so she was careful in what she said, did not want to upset or alarm anyone and so withheld small details.

I asked about the letters her mother had mentioned to me (6.2.11.). Lara said her mother had got it muddled, it had been in the past when she had given her father a letter to give to the judge at court. She seemed unsurprised at her mother's confusion of events.

Lara was pleased that her paternal grandmother was now well enough to come and stay again and this helped when Mr Marlo had to go out to work. I asked about any activities that were arranged and clashed with her contact weekends. She said there were no special activities; Hayley and Alice went out.

Lara said, with fervour, she just wanted to grow up and be able to decide for herself where she went and what she could go, instead of having to ask permission. She was chafing against being the youngest and the limitations this imposed on her.

Information from school

Mr Church is Lara's Headteacher; he reported the school had not experienced any difficulties with Mr Marlo, and the last two years had been a 'calm period'. Lara was on time for school and Mr Marlo consistently informed the school if she was ill and when she would return.

Mr Church described Lara as having settled well and she was a 'loyal and bright little girl'. She was a very able child who had the capacity to do very well at school. She was a good negotiator and he thought I would have a very sensible discussion with her. Lara was popular with others and was able to talk out her differences. His only concern was that she could manage any pressure from her mother.

Summary

Lara is a bright nine–year–old girl who is rather battle weary after the years of acrimonious disputes between her parents and changes of court orders. She has a realistic, adult perspective of the conflict between her parents and sees they are unable to change the situation. She has adapted by behaving well, thinking things through and negotiating. She has had to grow up early in her life and make compromises in her spontaneity. Lara is careful about expressing her views and holds a lot inside rather than speak out in case she aggravates the situation. Although she is capable of being assertive, it was difficult for her. She has an underlying sadness which only surfaces intermittently but which she poignantly expressed to me.

The strengths Lara has developed are evident at school where she is seen as a good negotiator and able to view situations from the perspective of others. She is very loyal and her social life is extremely important to her as a result of the discord in her family. Consequently, any difficulties and shifting allegiances between friends affects her deeply.

Lara was explicit that she wanted no further changes, she had adapted to the situation and preferred not to have to deal with further upheavals. She was content with the regular contact she had with her mother, although it was not easy being in a different place from her belongings and every day activities.

I suppose it might be implied, but it appears it is never outright asked of the children if they are happy living with their dad; the only mention made in terms of Lara, concerns where her stuff is. Isn't asking if the child is happy where they're living important, when ascertaining their wishes and feelings?

Strengths

Lara is a bright and perceptive child.
She is loyal to her family and close to her older sister.
She sees other's viewpoints and has strong negotiating skills most evident at school.
She is a sociable girl and her friendships are extremely important to her.
She related well and was able to articulate her views clearly.

Concerns

Lara has had to become more adult than her nine years.
She has adapted to the conflict by behaving well and giving the needs of others priority.
Her underlying sadness about the family situation surfaces intermittently and leaves her vulnerable to discord in her friendships and in future relationships.

Discussion

The differing allegations, counter allegations and problems around contact have been detailed in the bundle and I will not emphasise them here; this assessment is not about apportioning blame. Hayley, Alice and Lara are lovely, capable young people and both parents have substantially contributed to their development. This is a credit to them both as they have struggled within their relationship.

The struggle isn't our relationship – that ship sailed years ago – it is with Ms Hyde's on-going bipolar disorder and ability to cope with her three children. The children would be following the schedule, and Ms Hyde and I would be happily interacting only for arrangements if she wasn't abusing the children.

I wasn't hoping for the report to conclude Ms Hyde be sent away or never see her children again, I simply believe Ms Hyde needs to receive support with her parenting, which is affected by her mental health condition.

We know how influential childhood attachments and traumatic experiences are in determining future adult styles of emotional management and relationships. There is substantial evidence of the major role played by psychological regulation, both emotional and physiological, in determining our ability to function effectively (Gendhart 2004, Schore 2003). If we are able to remain within our 'window of tolerance' (see Appendix 2) we can react effectively and adaptively to changing and challenging circumstances. If, however, a person has poor emotional management skills they become dysregulated and become either hyper–aroused where the primary defences of fight or flight are activated. If the arousal continues to be high and overwhelming, the person moves into a shutdown, (hypo–arousal) where they become detached emotionally. However, a person in hypo–arousal can move quickly into fight with increasing stress. (See explanatory diagram Appendix 2.)

The experiences in their childhood have directly shaped Ms Hyde's and Mr Marlo's very different styles of attachment and emotional relating. Ms Hyde has a characteristically reactive (hyper–aroused) style and Mr Marlo a detached (hypo–aroused) style which can move rapidly into a fight defence when feeling under threat. Both parents can move into verbally aggressive and, at times, physically aggressive responses.

Please provide literally any evidence – testimony, police records, school reports, ex–

neighbours, customers, the children's friends' parents – other than letters from Smitch Law and Ms Hyde's unending defamation campaign against me, backed by conflict of interest herself Mrs Jackson and Co., that I have ever been verbally or physically aggressive towards anyone; again, I am cut down at the knees with allegations written as fact by someone who met me twice.

I wish I had a time machine to take this psychiatrist back to my children's tear–streaked faces; Ms Hyde trashing homes; the screaming that would go on for hours; three sweet little girls absolutely *crushed* by all the behaviour that is neatly tied up as 'Ms Hyde's hyper–aroused style'.

And once the doctor ('B.Sc., M.Sc., Dip. Clin., B.Ps.S., A.F.B.Ps.S') has sat in a room for hours, having been shouted back at every attempt of intervention, and has wiped the tears from the cheeks of three children caused by nothing and ending with them being told they are *wretched*; once they have seen bin bags full of Christmas toys on Boxing Day and food piled high on the roof of the car; smacked arms and legs and bottoms; as soon as that psychiatrist has tried calling Social Services, a GP and Ms Hyde's mother; when that psychiatrist is on their knees begging for someone to take a look at what is happening behind closed doors and *help*, then I would bring her back to this moment and honestly ask how she thinks it feels to read these words.

It is 2007. I've been asking for someone to look into Ms Hyde's behaviour for so long two of our children are virtually grown. I still have heartache from when she was 14, telling me of how her mother had strangled her and taken her to the floor, I could picture a 4–year–old Hayley with fat tears rolling down her red cheeks showing me a smack mark that hurts. That's not something I'd expect this doctor to imagine I am capable of, what with my lacking in the emotions department; the overwhelming guilt that my little girl has grown up but she's put down by the same old hurt.

I am tired to the bone, but I am still standing here. Ms Hyde has abused not only our three children, but myself and Ma and anyone who holds me in any sort of esteem. I know this is about our three children and no matter what Ms Hyde does to me, no matter how much I wish, after every incident of abuse at their mother's, I could keep them far, far away from her, I stand beside them and reassure them that I will always be here for them; that they should have contact with their mother; that their opinion on their lives matters and that abuse such as Ms Hyde has made normal for us all is not normal at all.

I want to be allowed to be a father to my children and get on with my life, as I have tried to do throughout.

I just–

I don't think differing styles really cuts it.

Ms Hyde's episodes of mental ill health were of extreme dysregulated states and within these times she was both unaware of her behaviour and the effects on others.

The loss of the partnership and the ensuing acrimonious conflict has left both with a sense of grievance. Whilst an emotionally intimate partnership can be ended the parenting relationship persists and the ability to move on to more neutral, present child focussed collaboration is required. Past issues can never be addressed through the children and can be exceedingly damaging for them. How relationships are negotiated now will be very influential in the children's future relationships with their parents, their own partnerships and parenting styles.

The writing is on the wall, the acrimony is one sided. Can someone tell me where my grievance is? I have sole residency, the support of my children's schools and the love of my three children as their father. My concerns are for my children's welfare and that is not a grievance.

The children clearly love both their parents but have obviously been affected by the disruptions to their care taking, the frightening episodes of mental ill health of their mother and the inadvertent neglect or lack of appropriate responsiveness as stated by Dr Russ (Page 446, para 3). In addition, they may have been witness to, and central to, the ongoing conflict between their parents with all the emotional turmoil and conflicting loyalties this raises. Any competition for the children's affection or allegiance only increases the possibility of the parents being split and manipulated either consciously or unconsciously by the children. Mr Marlo and Ms Hyde need to be able to provide clear boundaries and a united front if they are to monitor effectively the whereabouts of the children for safety.

Can we reflect back to Ms Hyde's quoted words of 'the children are too young to remember' for a moment, and really consider the mindset of someone in the present day who still, despite 6 sections under her belt, does not believe her long-term mental health issues affect her children? Not even acknowledgement, consideration, for her children? As she has already stated, the children know the differences between their parents. I have no desire to create a competition between Ms Hyde and I – I just want to be a good parent to my children. This seems to be a wild concept within the Family Courts.

Like Dr Borah (page 485, para 15.3), I found little evidence of coaching of the children's views by Mr Marlo and little parental alienation. Instead, their views reflect their own experiences of their mother which they find hard to integrate into a whole.

Again, if I had legal representation, paragraphs like this could refute many of Ms Hyde's false allegations; regardless of it being written in this report, which is due to be read by a judge, a barrister would have read this for what it was, and made sure Ms Hyde's counsel could not incessantly imply that I am damaging my children's relationship with their mother.

This was clearly expressed by Hayley who said, 'when things are OK, I've got a good Mum who tries to make me happy' and then 'a lot of me thinks she's a bad Mum who tried to strangle me'.

It is heart-breaking, as I sit here at my desk writing my responses until 2 o'clock in the morning, to read this. If help for Ms Hyde is implemented, there will be no need for her to apply to the courts because the children are refusing contact, as her receiving mental health support would prevent the situations from escalating to the point where she harms her children. I also can't help finding it incredible, that this phycologist can write Ms Hyde had strangled Hayley, and it doesn't mean anything. There are no alarm bells and there is no compassion for the fact the children are put in this position by their mother, when there have been so many opportunities, i.e. the Family Courts, to avoid this abuse happening. If the roles were reversed… Hey, it's mum's behaviour in question – what can you do?

This demonstrates her struggle to hold together the extremes of experience she has had with her mother. In a similar way, her views of her grandparents have been shaped by her own perspective of the traumatic events at their house, their apparent siding with her mother and may be in part, in picking up on her father's animosity towards them.

Both parents need to see beyond their own differences and disputes, to see the situation through their children's eyes and help secure a positive and realistic relationship with the other parent. This means both parents have to refrain from discussing their views of the other parent, or making assumptions based on their past experiences in front of the children. When a dispute, emergency or crisis occurs (as with Alice recently) it is important that both parents remain calm, not take sides and encourage the children to work on and resolve any difficulties they have with the other parent. Both parents could benefit from learning to respond with sensitivity and ensure their own reactions are not escalating the situation for a child, to use 'cool down' times with the children and themselves and defuse the tensions and conflicts between the children. In particular, Ms Hyde could benefit from therapeutic assistance in this.

All three girls were consistent in their wishes to stay with their father, for no further changes to be made, in wanting contact with their mother but wanting a choice. They consistently identified their mother's emotional variability and volatility difficult factors for them to manage and found strategies to reduce the stress of such contact. None of them showed signs of being afraid or wary with their father, all were affectionate and at ease with him. They held positive views of both parents and loved them both.

(Thank you, Mrs Sanders.)

Living with Mr Marlo has provided a stable base for the children; this is reflected both in the consistent observations from school staff that the children are calmer and more organised, and in the children's own statements.

Alongside this emotionally more stable base, they need the contact with Ms Hyde as she has very different views and experiences to offer them. Over the coming adolescent years, all three girls will need the understanding and support of a female model and relationship. She has an influential part to play, as her daughters mature and become independent young women making steps into serious intimate relationships.

This paragraph makes me uncomfortable. The implication that the most important part of parenting Ms Hyde is commended for is being a woman and having experienced adolescence as one. As a 40–something year old man, who has been in relationships with women and a committed father of three daughters, the idea that I would be incapable of discussing periods, getting sanitary towels, talking about relationships, or supporting my children emotionally, is insulting. I don't need to have a uterus to empathise with pain you can do nothing but suffer through. Are there questions I can't answer? Absolutely. However, I have access to the internet and the children also have Ma, who is a positive female presence in their life. I'm not besmirching Ms Hyde's role as a mother, but if we were to be a sum of our parts, please do not tell me that deciding factors in parenting can really be from such out–dated ideologies.

Secondly, my children are 14, 12 and 9 – can we not talk about them like the most important things about their near futures aren't school, college and healthy friendships, and that they don't already – Lara included – have sex education at school?

She's talking about crossing bridges years in the future, when Ms Hyde can't get her children to school on time consistently every other weekend.

Both parents will need to have clear, consistent ground rules e.g., sleepovers, time back home, keeping parents informed, and the ability to withstand the normal rejection and variability of adolescence. If they are unable to achieve this on their own, then mediation could be considered.

Currently, both parties are meant to communicate only through their solicitors because of past acrimony. This has several unfortunate effects, one being that more communication is channelled through the children which places them in an emotionally stressful position between the parents, exposes them unnecessarily to adult concerns and presents opportunities for manipulation.

Hayley and Alice, as they have clearly indicated through applications to court and discussions with Mrs Sanders, organise their periods of contact with their mother – because of their mother's volatility, this contact is often sporadic and best left for them to discuss with their mother anyway. I write to Ms Hyde and communicate with her when necessary, which I know isn't really in the interests of regaining any normality with Ms Hyde, but it's what Judge Baxter left us with. At the end of the day, I also know Ms Hyde uses me as a verbal whipping post and Judge Baxter's stupidity at least gave one less avenue for Ms Hyde to start confrontation. (In truth, it didn't; even when only listening to Ms Hyde's verbal degradation on the answering machine, I still feel low.)

At times it is essential that the parents communicate immediately and directly, e.g., as to a child's whereabouts for safety reasons. Under these circumstances communication through solicitors is not viable. Generally, the court orders to avoid direct confrontation are helpful and should remain. However, the current directions about communications should be re–considered and possibly varied to take into account these issues. Encouragement to use more emotionally neutral channels such as texts and emails could be considered for non–urgent communications.

Judge Baxter strikes again. One of these days, the court will listen to a tape of a conversation between Ms Hyde and myself, and the truth about who is the aggressor will come out; until such time, we have to deal with solicitor involvement at the direction of a family court judge, which you don't need to be a child psychologist to know is not what our family needs.

I know, as the children do, dealing with their mother is hard work if nigh on impossible; treading on egg shells would be a good analogy. I have never been cautioned by the police or found outside Ms Hyde's home making her live a misery, there are no telephone records that show I hound Ms Hyde, and the evidence that could be provided shows that I do communicate and agree with many of her requests for contact with Hayley, Alice and Lara.

On occasion I have to stick up for my children and myself, as I am aware that given the chance, Ms Hyde will walk all over me just to get her own way, but I do this by writing letters to my MP or talking to Melissa, not harassing Ms Hyde.

Let's forget, for one moment, that I am a nasty bastard;

Some weeks and months, Ms Hyde seems fine and then, out of the blue, she is not happy about something – it's like being on a roller-coaster. I have lived with and have known Ruth and her bipolar disorder for 16 years; she does not recognise when she is being unreasonable or verbally and physically abusive; she has difficulty in assessing her response and behaviour to any normal situation.

To suggest that I am encouraging this behaviour by Ms Hyde is an insult to the fact that my children and I have already been through so much. It does hurt when a psychologist suggests I have a detrimental part in what is going on in our lives; the only part I have ever played is one of asking to be left alone. If I am a criminal or trying to fuck someone's life up, show me the evidence and I will do my time. If not, please leave me and my children to get on with our lives.

It sounds like the decent and right thing to do, but I find my family imbedded in a world of deceit, where, despite strong evidence indicating it would benefit everyone in the situation, getting Ms Hyde help is not the priority. Instead, it's making unfound statements that there is ongoing conflict between both parents; this ongoing conflict, is Ms Hyde, Smitch Law and Mrs Mason harassing a court order and me as a parent.

I do not write Mrs Mason derogatory letters in response to her own antagonistic and constant demands. I just file them. (Ok, true, I burnt a couple.)

(I am not sure if burning solicitor letters would be seen as yet another one of my aggressive tendencies. I do not invite people round to witness the event, along with a free barbeque; at those times, I am drained and feel so low, it is my moment of defiance to what is going on in my life, and I do feel slightly better as I sit there on my own, watching the bullshit go up in flames.)

Recommendations

These recommendations are offered to the court:

The current situation concerning residence and contact remain.

Any variation to overall agreements and predictable events be communicated as at present.

Consideration of using other neutral means to communicate over more short-term arrangements and direct communication over matters of urgency.

If common ground rules cannot be achieved in this manner mediation should be considered.

Ms Hyde could benefit from therapeutic assistance with emotional management.

I understand that my duty, as an expert witness, is to the Court. I have complied with that duty. This report includes all matters relevant to the issues on which my expert evidence is given. I have given details in this report of any matters, which may affect the validity of this report. To the best of my knowledge and belief, the statements contained in this report are true and correct.

L Sanders

I know I have ripped into Mrs Sanders' report throughout, and it probably comes across as 'Mr Marlo isn't happy again' – I do appreciate Mrs Sanders' findings (you could say I am over the moon) and believe she has captured the dynamics in our family to an extent. I fully understand Mrs Sanders cannot completely comprehend what has been detailed in my documentation of the years as they've passed, as she had limited time and insight into our daily lives. However, I feel the Family Courts have picked our family up again, held us all in limbo for months; they will have a look, ignore the abuse reported about Ms Hyde, blame both parents and put us down in the same position – meanwhile, three children will still be at risk.

Dean Marlo

Melissa with the order for me

19 February

Please find enclosed a copy of the order made by his honour Judge Yergin, on 16th February 2007.

I confirm that I have sent forms out to your accountant and should appreciate your contacting him, perhaps on Wednesday, just to chivvy him along! In the meantime, while we are waiting for those forms to be prepared, we do need to arrange to meet so that we may fully and properly discuss the Child Psychologist report and prepare a Position Statement for you.

The deadline for the Position Statement is 2nd March. I leave it to you to let me know whether there is one day that is convenient, between now and the 2nd March, for you to come and see me. I presume that it would be on a bad weather day. If I do not hear from you, and it's pouring with rain one day, I will try to contact you to see if you are available.

I have not heard from Smitch Law as to any proposals Ms Hyde may have for finalizing matters. I will let you know if I do but, in the meantime, just await our next meeting.

Melissa, bless her heart, has seen me sinking in shark infested waters and offered a life-raft in the form of her expertise for free, if I am not granted Legal Aid. I am, as ever, grateful for the legal assistance. Melissa requested if possible we meet on Saturday mornings; I understood she had actual cases to deal with and she was doing me a great favour by inviting me in at a time when she is catching up on work.

What's best for our children

23 – 26 February

Friday 23rd
Ruth's contact; Lara and Alice go for the weekend, while Hayley stays over Saturday night.

Monday 26th
Approximately 6pm, Alice phoned and stated that she was going to sleep at her mother's tonight; I told Alice that I would like her to come home and keep to a routine. Alice stated that it makes no difference. I asked Alice if she had asked her mother and Alice replied, 'She wants me to stay.'

I asked Alice to pass the phone to her mother so I could confirm it was alright with her, but Alice replied that she did not want to, as I would try and persuade her mother not to let her stay.

I told Alice that if it was okay with her mother then I have no problem. Ruth came onto the phone and stated that she has told Alice that she could stay tonight but she is busy the rest of the week. I stated to Ruth that I have no problem with Alice wanting to stay, but Alice does need to have a routine, for her health and schooling.

Ruth replied, 'I have told Alice that I am busy the rest of the week, so she cannot come over.'

It's the right solution for the wrong reasons; Ruth should be mindful of Alice's difficulties with learning in some aspects and want to support Alice by not allowing her to pick days where she changes residence on a whim; she needs stability. However, it is of course to do with Ruth's lifestyle and whether or not it is convenient for her to have Alice stay.

Northview re, Alice

27 February

Level 3 Intervention/Mathematics
Pupil: Alice Marlo, 8OK
Dear Mr Marlo,
I am writing to inform you that Alice's behaviour has warranted a Level 3 intervention. The reason for this decision is, truancy from lesson, 26th February 2007, period 4.
As a result, your daughter will need to attend a meeting with the Cluster Group leaders, named above, in the House area on Thursday 1st March 2007 at 3:15. This meeting may involve strategies such as completing missed work or discussing consequences of poor behaviour. The maximum duration will be one hour, therefore your daughter will be released by 4:15pm.
Yours sincerely,

Birthday bliss

27 February

I arranged with Hayley and Alice to meet Lara and myself at the bottle bank after school. We needed to go shopping at Sainsbury's and all three wanted to go into town after as it is my birthday tomorrow.

As Lara and I got into the car, my mobile rang; the receptionist from Northview Grove stated that Alice had left her phone at school, and it was in the office to be collected tomorrow. I drove to the shops by the bottle bank and saw Alice standing outside. Lara and I walked around to where Alice was; I told her phone was in the reception at Northview, and she could collect it tomorrow. Alice was upset about her phone and started talking to her friend who came out of the shop next door. I asked Alice if she was coming with us to Sainsbury's and then to town, Alice told me that she would go home with her friend Britney, and would meet us there before we went to town.

Hayley arrived and we went shopping.

Once home, Hayley, Alice and Lara helped bring in the groceries and I started packing it away. I heard Hayley ask Lara where she wanted her something put and, for some reason, Alice told Hayley to get out of Lara's room.

Several more words were exchanged when I heard Hayley say, 'Why don't you go back to our mother's!'

Alice stormed out of Lara's room and into the kitchen stating that she is going to her mother's. I told Alice not to listen to Hayley, and to get ready while I had a word with her. Alice replied, 'I'm not going,' and walked into her bedroom with the house phone in hand. Having been left by Alice, I found Hayley and spoke to her about saying hurtful things she doesn't mean that she knew would upset Alice.

While I was asking Hayley to apologise, Alice burst out of her room and walked out of the front door. I went out to speak to Alice, but she was gone. I reached for my mobile to call her, and remembered Alice didn't have her phone.

Sighing, I told Hayley that I understood that Alice's behaviour was unnecessary in the first place, and that I also understood she needs to stand her ground with Alice. However, I reiterated that what she said did not help the situation.

Hayley stormed off stating, 'Why should Alice be allowed to throw me out of Lara's room?'

I left Hayley to calm down, and finished unpacking the shopping. Several minutes later, Hayley came back into the kitchen and said sorry, and that she realised that Alice leaving was not what I wanted and was not the best start to my birthday. I told her I know that love, and that she would be better off ignoring Alice than getting involved.

The house phone rang and I picked it up. Ruth stated that she had Alice sitting in her car, and that Alice has informed her Hayley and Lara are excluding her from my birthday and the family, and saying things like she should live with her mother. I replied that the disagreement had been about Hayley being in Lara's room, and that it was all three of the girls' idea to go into town to get some bits for my birthday; I have told Hayley off, and she will apologise to Alice for saying what she did.

Ruth stated she would drop Alice back at 9 pm. I told Ruth that we were, as I said, going into town. She replied, 'Alice does not want to come.'

I asked if I could speak to Alice, but Ruth refused.

Hayley, Lara and I headed to town. I gave it an hour, phoned Ruth and asked if I could speak to Alice. Ruth repeated that Alice did not want to talk to me. I told Ruth that she should be encouraging Alice to apologise to Hayley for starting the argument and to listen to Hayley's apology.

All Ruth has done is give Alice an opportunity to elongate a silly argument that would, normally, quickly have been gotten over. Within minutes of a disagreement between two siblings, Ruth had driven round, picked up Alice and then refused to allow me to talk to her.

There does seem to be a pattern that on every special occasion, a problem appears to manifest.

Ruth didn't drop Alice off at 9pm, and didn't contact me.

(Not that I am particularly surprised, however I mention it because it is a school day, and I am repeatedly accused of a lack of communication; yet, outside of those documents, I am the one left in the dark about what is going on.)

Hip-Hip-Hooray

28 February – 2 March

Wednesday 28th

Alice came home after school. Ma came down and we stayed in for my birthday; although Hayley and Lara attempted to set up the games/cake they had organised, Alice refused to take part with them and was very frosty towards all of us.

Thursday 1st

Mr Caldwell from Northview Grove called me informing that Hayley has been involved in a disturbance with some other pupils in a case of bullying and the police had been called. When I asked what had happened, he reported that a group had been bullying someone; Hayley and a friend had walked up to the scene when they were accused of starting trouble by the other children. I asked if Hayley was ok, and he stated she had gone to her next class.

Hayley was upset after school because the girls who had accused her and her friend of starting trouble were normally the girls that were bullying Hayley and her friends. We talked about the bullies and what happened, and I tried to reassure Hayley that she would not be in trouble and to stay away from the girls involved.

When it came to the time Alice would usually arrive home from school, and she didn't come through the door, I began to worry. I tried telephoning Alice's mobile and Ruth throughout the evening, but no one answered. I must presume that Alice is staying at her mother's, so I texted Alice that I hope she is alright, I love her and to come home and talk.

Neither Ruth nor Alice got back to me.

Friday 2nd

Mrs Tran phoned me after the police had been to the school; she informed me that the school and the police have stated that they are aware Hayley was not involved, and that Hayley and a friend had turned up after the incident. Mrs Tran made it clear to me that the teachers were well aware of the troublemakers in the school, and Hayley was not one of them.

Mrs Tran also stated that Hayley had got herself worked up, 'She believes that the police will not see the big picture and her friends will get into trouble.'

The phone was then passed to Hayley and I tried to tell Hayley that the bullies were not worth tears and I would see her soon, but it had been an emotional day for her. Mrs Tran suggested that Hayley came home and have a quiet rest of the day, and start again tomorrow. I appreciated Mrs Tran's understanding and offered to pick Hayley up but Hayley said she would walk home to clear her head.

From NGS

2 March

I am writing to inform you that Alice will be placed in our ISC (Internal Support Centre) for a period of one day(s) on Monday, 5 March, 2007, and will be working in isolation on a one-to-one basis with a member of staff.

The reason for Alice being placed in the ISC is rudeness to a member of the office staff.

The ISC facility is covered by closed-circuit security for the safety of students and staff.

Alice will be returned to normal lessons after serving her ISC but will continue to be on a report for a period of time. Should the report prove unsatisfactory Alice may well have to return to the ISC or indeed face other sanctions, subject to the circumstances.

Should you wish to discuss this matter further, please contact me at school through the usual channels.

Yours sincerely,

It is difficult for me to know how to approach Alice and bring her behaviour back on track, when any attempt I make to discuss issues, I'm met with either 'I'm going to my mother's' or 'my mother is picking me up'.

Apples, trees and other metaphors

3/4 March

3rd

Hayley and I had a talk about her having a sleepover tonight, and the fact that due to work pressure, I had to be on site in the morning, which is Hayley's birthday, but would be home by noon. Even after talking to Hayley, I still felt guilty that I would not be there in the morning to wish her a happy birthday; though I know Hayley will have her friends to wake up with, and Lara and Nan too.

Hayley wanted to go out with her friends on the estate, and we arranged for her to be home at 1pm for lunch. Lara, Ma and I spent the day drawing sharks and reading through one of her marine biology books. When 1 o'clock came, Hayley and her friends walked through the door with various Spar bags filled with snacks, ready for a movie night.

At 6pm, Ruth phoned and stated that she was dropping Alice off at 7.30pm.

Fifteen minutes late, Alice came through the door with a friend, who I recognised as Britney from the shops the other day. Alice went into her room, got changed and came with Britney into the living room asking what time she had to be in. I told Alice as it wasn't a school night, if they remained close to home, she could stay out until 8pm, and asked for Britney's parent's number as, if they were late, I would be calling them. Alice put up a bit of a fuss, but Britney wrote the number down and they disappeared out the front door.

(For those of you wondering why, when Alice's behaviour has been rude at best, I was not calling Britney's parents to pick her up and talking to Alice about the situation… I wish I had a good answer. What it mostly boils down to though, is this year has not had the best start, and today was a peaceful, good day. While I don't appreciate being used like a doormat, I do not want to argue with anyone, including my children; sensible boundaries were set and I just want peace in our lives.

The result of a comment to Alice about Britney would either be Alice walking out of the door to who knows where, or calling her mother to pick her up; either way, we go backwards rather than forwards. Clearly, Alice needs a different approach to parenting than her sisters.)

It was almost 8pm and I received a call from Cole who thought he had seen Alice in town, waiting for a bus. In disbelief, I thanked Cole and called Alice's mobile. When Alice picked up, I asked her where she was. She said that she and Britney had wanted to go to town; I began to say that she is supposed to be home by 8pm, but Alice cut me off, saying, 'It doesn't matter, we will be home soon,' and hung up.

I called the number Britney had written down, and her dad answered. I asked if Britney is allowed into town at night; he told me that he was led to believe that she was staying at Ruth's, and he was not happy that his daughter was in town.

I hoped having spoken to Britney's dad and organising for Britney to be picked up when they arrived back, that Alice would see reason and it would be confirmation from another parent that, at the age of 12-years-old, it is unsafe and inappropriate for them to be in town at night; doubly so for not informing anyone.

Alice and Britney came home at 8.45pm. Before Alice could disappear into her room, I told Alice that it was not acceptable to be in town at this time of night nor was it what we had agreed to before she went out. Alice just dismissed me and went into her room.

I asked Britney to phone her dad and tell him she was ok. Meanwhile I checked on Lara, who was finishing her game on the Playstation in the living room with Ma, and knocked on Hayley's bedroom door, ducking my head in when she responded. I checked if they needed anything, said happy birthday for tomorrow and gave her a hug before leaving her and her friends to it.

Alice came out of her room and asked me why I had asked Britney to call her dad, as well as stating that Britney is not allowed to sleepover now. I told Alice that I had explained if she wasn't home on time I would call Britney's parents, and that Britney's dad had agreed it was unacceptable for them both to be in town at this time of night. Alice replied, 'This is why I do not what to live here!'

She slammed her bedroom door.

Lara and Ma went to bed; I waited for Britney's dad, before knocking on Alice's door and seeing Britney out. Alice remained in her room and didn't say a word to me when I went back to say goodnight.

Her words from earlier stung and with it being Hayley's birthday, which we only get to celebrate together every other year, I went to sleep, desperately hoping that tomorrow would be better.

It was 12.30am when Alice came into my bedroom and stated that her mother is going to pick her up. I told Alice that it was the time for sleep and if Alice wanted to go to her mother's, she could speak to her about it at a reasonable time in the morning.

Alice said, 'My mother is coming, so bye.'

I got up to attempt to talk Alice, or at least ensure she actually gets in her mother's car, but Alice went back to her room.

Unable to fall back asleep, I waited to hear the front door open. At 1.10am, my mobile rang. Ruth asked me to explain why Alice has been on the phone with her asking to be picked up. I went through the events of the day; stating that Alice had not come back at the time she and I had agreed, that her and Britney were in town at night and that she had not told me she was even going into town.

Ruth said nothing about supporting the boundary I had set for Alice, or about the fact it was a Saturday night, which means drunkards and partiers are getting started and that is not a safe environment for two pre-teen girls who think they're older than they are. What Ruth did say was, 'These children are crying out to be with their mother!'

Frustrated, tired and needing to be up for work in a couple of hours, I replied that this was not the time for that discussion, and what is important is for Alice understand and respect the boundaries – which will not be achieved if Ruth picks her up.

Ruth responded with verbal abuse about how awful a father I am, and I ended the call by asking, again, that Ruth please by all means talk to Alice but do not pick her up and allow Alice to switch houses in the middle of the night, as that is escalating much further than giving Alice a 'time-out'.

Several times after Ruth's call, Alice came in and asked if I would take her round her mother's, as she can't pick her up because she has had too much to drink; each time I replied that I would like for Alice to go to her room and get some sleep, and reminded her it is Hayley's birthday, so we should all be celebrating together.

At 1.25am, Ruth phoned again and had a go at me for 'preventing' Alice from going to hers. Ruth stated, 'This is the behaviour that no one sees, preventing my daughter from seeing her mother.'

Feeling more exhausted now than tired, I felt I had no alternative but to put the phone down.

I went into Alice's room, and she immediately asked me if I will take her to her mother's. I replied again, that if she still felt that way in the morning, I would be leaving for work at 5:30, so if she is up, then we can discuss her going to her mother's; if not, I can take her when I get back from work – despite knowing full well Alice would be out the door, as soon as her mother is awake. Alice was not too polite, so I left her to it.

I couldn't sleep, and ended up in the office.

At 3am, I poked my head around Alice's door and found that she had fallen asleep in her bed.

4th

Alice was not awake at 5:30am, so I wrote out the usual notes for the children, with a 'happy birthday' for Hayley and a promise to talk to Alice.

I managed to get home from work slightly earlier, and Hayley and her friends were having a late breakfast. Alice refused to come out of her room. We celebrated Hayley's birthday with music, cards and the opening of her presents.

At 1pm, Hayley's friends went home as we were having a family meal at Murdock's.

Throwing the taps on for a quick bath, I knocked on Alice's bedroom door. Instead of being called in, Alice's door opened and she almost walked into me as she stated her mother is picking her up in ten minutes, so if I want to talk, now is the time.

I asked Alice to stay because we are all going out for a meal to celebrate Hayley's birthday, she should be there and we all want her to be there. Alice stated that she had better things to do and if I was going to try and persuade her, she would leave right now and stand at the top of the road to wait for her mother.

I said no more.

Although, inside, I was frustrated that Ruth knowingly encourages Alice to be selfish on Hayley's birthday, doing what she wants, and incites the bad feeling between them as sisters, when she should want Alice to be there for Hayley. Hayley has always made the effort for Alice on her birthday.

By Ruth's actions, she's widening the gap between all our children; Alice would have gotten over her silly attitude, and we could have all enjoyed Hayley's celebrations. Instead, as soon as Alice is not happy, or things are not going her way, Ruth has given Alice, 12 years old, the ability to be collected at a phone call's notice.

Hayley, Lara, Ma and I had a nice meal at Murdock's but it was the first birthday we could spend all together that we haven't; I know Hayley is upset by Alice's actions.

Dean Marlo

Being a parent... Is hard

Everyone goes through their teens – for a child and their parents this is a new experience, with highs and lows for all concerned. There is no hard or fast rule to how it will affect each person.

Out of all my children, it is Alice that is primed for a rebellious teenage stage; Alice is strong willed, thinks she is older than she is and, overnight, was happy to break boundaries that I had set for her, believing she could behave as she wanted, and have no routine; fliting between homes and bunking off school.

Over the years, I could see that Alice has a different temperament to Hayley and Lara. It has been Alice at the forefront of standing up to her mother's behaviour, verbally retaliating on the telephone and defending herself and her sisters. Alice always gives as good as she gets, whereas Hayley, who is usually roped in trying to protect Alice, and Lara keep out of the way, avoiding confrontation with their mother.

It is hard for me to comprehend where the Alice with 25 house points and a big smile on her face, as she knew her Nan and I would be pleased as punch, had gone. I have treated all three of my daughters the same, yet Alice dismisses the love and care she has been shown by her sisters, Nan and myself.

No matter how hard I try, I cannot talk Alice round; there is no next level i.e. shouting, slapping or dragging, and I am not going to stand in front of the door to prevent Alice from leaving – that is not how a parent should react, and behaving as such would only heighten the situations and give Alice cause for real resentment.

Alice and I never have slanging matches when she breaks boundaries or tells me she is off to her mother's. I do not want to fall out with Alice, so my best option for our relationship is not to defy Alice's actions with an iron fist, instead, when I do have the opportunity, I talk and explain to Alice why her behaviour is disappointing and not in her best interests.

Sadly, as many parents that have been through this with their children will know, talking calmly to a teenage rebel is like trying to put a fire out with a water pistol… You can only hope they take on board that you love them and will be here for them.

Alice is not the first child to act in this way and she will not be the last; what makes Alice's and my situation as a parent worse, is the fact that Big Brother, the Family Courts, are always in the background. Any day, week, or month, I could be summoned to court to explain and defend why Alice is rebelling at home and school. As in the past, the court façade will be played out, and it will be my parenting that is in question.

From NGS (To Ms Hyde, forwarded)

5 March

Thank you for meeting with me and Mrs Sparrow this morning. I have made the following arrangements:

Mrs Sparrow will discuss Hayley and Alice's absence with our Educational Welfare Officer.

Mrs Hayden, Head of Learning Support, will see Alice to reassess her possible needs with regards to dyslexia.

I have asked staff who teach Alice to be aware of her learning needs.

I have asked our office to send letters from the school to both Mr Marlo and Ms Hyde.

Melissa to me

5 March

Further to our meeting on Thursday last week, please find copy of your Position Statement as lodged at court and served on Child Legal Guidance.

I managed to speak to Ms Hyde's legal representative on Friday afternoon. Ms Hyde has not yet finalized her Position Statement and I am expecting to exchange the Position Statement with Mrs Mason, I hope, on Tuesday. I was content to give Ms Hyde a bit of additional time. She has a lot of difficult issues to deal with, arising from the Psychologist report, and I believe it only fair that Ms Hyde has time needed to come to terms with the content of that report, before I apply any pressure in trying to sort out exactly what is going to happen.

Mrs Mason informed me that she has drafted Ms Hyde's Position Statement. She needs to know that Ms Hyde agrees to it, before Mrs Mason and I can discuss the way forward. In the overall circumstances, I had to agree with Mrs Mason that is really the only way to proceed.

If we do not get a 'plan' agreed before Monday's Hearing, I will not be too concerned. We need to be at court for as near to 9.15am as possible. I realise that you many need to get Lara to school, and may well arrive at court a little after 9.15am. That will not be a problem. I will start negotiations with Mrs Mason, and Hayley and Alice's legal representative.

In the meantime, while I realise that you and Ms Hyde do discuss making arrangements for the children over the phone, please think about whether you will also agree to email communication with her. Please also think about the circumstances in which you would agree to Alice going to stay with her mother (i.e., if there is a repeat of last week's events.) Primarily, I should have thought that non–school next days would be OK, but what about if there is an upset during the school week? What kind of upset would it need for Alice to go to Ms Hyde?

Would it be better if you contact Ms Hyde in the event of an upset and inform her so that Alice then goes to her? (These are just suggestions – the aim of the exercise is really to prevent Alice from playing you one off against the other and toing and froing all the time just on a whim.)

I will contact you as soon as I receive Ms Hyde's Statement and arrange a time with you, when we can discuss the content of her Position Statement as well as your thoughts on setting boundaries for Alice.

My Position Statement (March)

I, having read the report of Mrs Sanders and being aware of the learned judge's comments made on 16 February 2007, and regarding the likelihood of discharge of the order for contact in respect particularly of Hayley and possibly Alice, believe that careful consideration needs to be given to how appropriate boundaries regulating particularly Alice's behaviour can be maintained in the absence of a framework for contact.

I believe that the report of Mrs Sanders accurately reflects Alice's need for consistent boundaries and that Alice is already testing the limits that I endeavour to maintain.

By way of example, on 27 February 2007, Alice and Hayley had a disagreement, at home after school, and I tried to resolve the situation but Alice had called her mother and was picked up. With Alice in her car, Ms Hyde called; I explained how I had been in the process of dealing with the situation when Alice had walked out, and Ms Hyde responded that Alice wanted to stay with her. I tried to contact Alice in the evening, but she did not answer her phone and Ms Hyde informed me Alice didn't want to talk to me.

I believe this is an example of Alice using one parent to push the boundaries set by the other parent. Ordinarily, if there is a disagreement in my home between the children, it is over within ten minutes. I am very worried that the stability Alice has benefitted from over the past few years will be eroded if there is no consistency in the way both parents deal with this kind of situation.

I do not believe that Alice making rushed decisions, in the heat of the moment, which her parents acquiesce to, are always in Alice's best interests. Whilst I accept the advice given by Mrs Sanders, for Alice to have 'time out', I do not believe it to be in Alice's best interests to achieve this by rushing to Ms Hyde's home on any and every occasion; however, I acknowledge that there may be occasions where it may be appropriate for Alice to achieve 'time out' at her mother's home.

I believe situations need to be dealt with there and then so that any bad behaviour can be addressed. I have absolutely no problem or difficulty with any of the children spending time with Ms Hyde. The problems and difficulties arise from how allowing Hayley and Alice to, effectively, do what they want, when they want, can fit easily into a stable, structured home and school life.

I believe that Lara's contact regime should remain as it has over the past few years but believe that the boundaries regulating Hayley and Alice's contact, especially so that Alice cannot truant easily from school again or develop the habit of running away from situations by announcing that she is going to her mother's, need to be fixed.

I would like to suggest that Ms Hyde and I enter into a written agreement governing how we, as parents, will maintain consistent boundaries for all three children, but I am aware that such an agreement would not be enforceable.

In light of issues addressed in Mrs Sanders' report, I remain concerned that consistent parenting of the girls could be jeopardised into the future and I welcome the opportunity of discussing with Ms Hyde, the steps that both she and I should take if future difficulties arise, without having the necessity of seeking the court's intervention.

Northview re, Hayley & Alice

6 March

Level 3 Intervention/Expressive Arts
Pupil: Alice Marlo, 8OK
Dear Mr Marlo,
I am writing to inform you that Alice's behaviour has warranted a Level 3 intervention. The reason for this decision is, repeated failure to follow reasonable instructions, 2ᵗʰ March 2007, period 4.
As a result, your daughter will need to attend a meeting with the Cluster Group leaders, named above, in the House area on Thursday 8ᵗʰ March 2007 at 3:15pm. This meeting may involve strategies such as completing missed work or discussing consequences of poor behaviour. The maximum duration will be one hour, therefore your daughter will be released by 4:15pm.
Yours sincerely,

Level 3 Intervention/Expressive Arts
Pupil: Hayley Marlo, 10TU
Dear Mr Marlo,
I am writing to inform you that Hayley's behaviour has warranted a Level 3 intervention. The reason for this decision is, repeated failure to follow reasonable instructions, 5ᵗʰ March 2007, period 2.
As a result, your daughter will need to attend a meeting with the Cluster Group leaders, named above, in the House area on Thursday 8ᵗʰ March 2007 at 3:15pm. This meeting may involve strategies such as completing missed work or discussing consequences of poor behaviour. The maximum duration will be one hour, therefore your daughter will be released by 4:15pm.
Yours sincerely,

Both of them getting detentions, for the same reasons in the same subjects – should I be buying a lottery ticket?

When I spoke to Hayley about why she got the detention, she told me she was just being silly and reminded me it is only her first one. (I used that myself, on my first one with Ma, so I couldn't fault her, although, with what's going on with Alice, I did feel a shiver down my spine.)

Northview; Alice; Exclusion

6 March

Dear Mr Marlo,

Pupil: Alice Marlo, 8OK

I am writing to inform you that I have today excluded from school your daughter for two school day(s) from Wednesday, 7 March to Thursday, 8 March, 2007. Alice should return to school on Friday, 9 March, 2007 following an interview with Mr Caldwell/Mrs Sparrow.

The reason for Alice's exclusion is persistent refusal to co-operate with a member of staff, including senior staff, persistent refusal to follow instructions, rudeness to staff. Mr Caldwell/Mrs Sparrow will talk to you and Alice about the situation Friday, 9 March, 2007 at 8.15am. If this is not convenient, please contact the school to arrange an alternative appointment.

The Chairman of the Discipline Committee has been notified. You have the right to make representations to the Governing Body and should you wish to do so please write to Mrs M Clegg, Clerk for the Governing Body, c/o Northview Grove School. The Governors' Pupil Discipline Committee meets as required.

You have the right to see a copy of your daughter's school record upon written request to the Headteacher.

Your daughter's Head of House will ensure that she is given work to do while at home. Please return any work due to school to be marked. No work will be given for 1 day exclusions.

The school website provides a variety of coursework for students via the internet, which students may access if excluded from school. If you do not have internet facilities then your local Library provides them and you can access our website from there.

Should you have any other queries regarding this situation you may contact the school Educational Welfare Officer – Ms J Musk.

We regard it as an essential part of the exclusion that Alice is not to be on or near the school site at any time during the exclusion period.

Yours sincerely,

Alice hasn't been home since Hayley's birthday; I have sent her a text in the mornings and given her a call in the evenings, with no answer or response. Despite some attitude problems, Alice is a loving and caring daughter, and it is a shock to come to the realisation that she has cut off her contact with me and her sisters.

As her dad, I'm worried about Alice's attitude and behaviour, but do not know how to address it; I have tried to talk to Ruth about the situation, however she has been more interested in criticising me.

Ms Hyde's Statement, March 2007

7 March

I, Ruth Hyde, make this statement believing it to be true and knowing that it will be placed before the court in evidence.

I refer to the order of his honour Judge Yergin, dated 16th February 2007.

I have had the opportunity of considering the report of Mrs Sanders very carefully. I saw Mrs Sanders on two occasions namely 19 January 2007 from 10am until 12.20pm. Alice was actually with me at that time as a result of an argument with the respondent and so it wasn't possible to spend all of that time discussing matters one to one with Mrs Sanders. Mrs Sanders also spent about 45 minutes alone with Alice in her bedroom. I then saw Mrs Sanders on 20 January 2007 for about three hours and I felt that this meeting went better because there were no distractions and I was able to speak with her freely. I also phoned Lydia the following day to ask if I could speak again but Lydia thought it would not be necessary.

I feel that I did not have sufficient time to speak to Mrs Sanders about what my concerns were. I felt that I had to explain the history so that she had a good idea of what had gone on in the past but Mrs Sanders wanted to focus on the present and the future. Mrs Sanders has stated in her report that I focus on past grievances rather than current issues but so much has gone on in the past that clearly has affected how we all are now. There are lots of issues that have not been addressed properly and I wanted to explain this.

Whilst there was an inaccuracy in Mrs Sanders's report with regard to the chronology, I am pleased to see that this has now been rectified and that it is clear that I was not admitted to hospital in April 2003 as first stated. This mistake has made me feel very unhappy with the report generally. I also note that in the chronology there is at May 2004, 'Ms Hyde had admission, mood variability'. I was not admitted to hospital in May 2004 and I have no idea where this information has come from.

I can also confirm that my stepfather has not sexually abused me. There was one occasion when I was about 12 years old when my stepfather was drunk and he tried to kiss me.

I am also concerned that Mrs Sanders did not have the opportunity of reading either the medical notes of the respondent or of the children. These were ordered by the court but the respondent did not obtain the notes and I feel that in order that the report can be fully completed then Mrs Sanders needs to see these reports. Mrs Sanders has had the benefit of reading all of my notes but none for the respondent or the children.

I am happy to say that both Hayley and Alice have been having more contact with me in recent weeks and both children have been staying overnight with me. Hayley stayed over for the first time on New Year's Day but prior to that she had stayed with me once on the Mother's Day weekend when we went to Cornwall to stay with my sister.

I am worried, however, that contact has only been taking place in recent weeks because the respondent is aware of these ongoing proceedings and he is encouraging the children to have contact. I am fearful that once these proceedings are over that the respondent will revert back to how it has been, namely that Hayley and Alice will not come for contact.

I have always been concerned in the past that Hayley and Alice have felt torn between wanting to see me and knowing how the respondent will feel if they actually have contact with me. I refer to paragraph

7.2 of Mrs Sanders' report in which she clearly states that Hayley worries about the respondent and the fact that he may be lonely when the children are with me. I have raised this in the past and the fact that the respondent is telling the children how they are his world, that he does not need a girlfriend and that all he wants is his own mother and the children. I do not believe that this is a healthy attitude to have.

At paragraph 9.2.7 of Mrs Sanders's report Lara states to Mrs Sanders that the respondent did not talk about me to the children but he did talk about the issues which came up in court. I do not believe that this is at all appropriate and the children do not need to know what is said about them in court. The respondent does not like me and it is only in very recent times that the children have been coming for contact because of these ongoing proceedings.

I have to accept that Hayley and Alice, given their ages, do not want to be the subject of a court order and I would be agreeable to an order for reasonable contact to take place between me and Hayley and Alice, but for the contact to take place during the times when Lara is with me.

I have had Hayley and Alice turn up at my property on a number of occasions when I have been working or when I have made other arrangements and it is difficult for me to explain to the children that I cannot always be there for them. By way of example, on 26 February 2007 I received a phone call from Hayley saying that the respondent had to go to work and could she please come to my home for half an hour before school so she did not have to be on her own. I was due to be working that day but agreed to collect Hayley who came round for half an hour and then I took Hayley to school. Alice and Lara were already with me as they had stayed for contact over the weekend. Both Alice and Lara were ill over the weekend and I took both children to the doctor on 26 February 2007. I am very concerned about Alice because she is not sleeping properly and her menstrual cycle is irregular. Alice is also not eating properly. The doctor on 25 February 2007 told me that he thinks Alice is suffering with stress. I had to call the doctor out to Alice on Sunday 25 February 2007 because she was so poorly.

If Hayley and Alice wish to have contact with me then I would of course be delighted but I would wish them to come for contact on the weekends when Lara is with me or during the holidays when I have holiday contact with Lara. If they want to see me at other times then they need to give me notice. I have given both Hayley and Alice a key to my home but on the understanding that they must phone me if they arrive and I am not there.

I am aware that Hayley and Alice have been spending a lot of time wandering the streets at night when they should have been in the care of the respondent. I do not believe it is safe for the children to be out late at night. Hayley has already got into trouble recently for picking on other children and I feel that she needs to have boundaries set so that she does not get into trouble again.

In recent weeks, Alice has been spending more and more time with me and she has not wanted to go home to the respondent. Alice has told me that she and the respondent have been arguing and I have tried to encourage Alice to speak with the respondent about the issues.

On Monday 26 February 2007, Alice was staying with me and I had arranged for her to go to the doctor's because she was feeling unwell. Before we went to the doctors, Alice told me that she didn't have any shoes to wear. I called the school to check whether Alice could go into school in trainers but was told that she hadn't had suitable shoes for over a week and she must come to school in shoes. I took Alice out that morning to buy shoes so that she would not get into trouble at school. After Alice had been to the doctors I took her to school and agreed to collect her in the afternoon. Alice advised me that she wanted to stay with me and this was agreed with the respondent.

Alice has spent more nights with me since January than with the respondent. I cannot force her to go back to live with the respondent but it is a very difficult position for me to be in. From what I have read from the documents filed by Child Legal Guidance, both Hayley and Alice have indicated that they do not want any orders with regard to contact as they would wish to be able to see me when they like. This is not borne out by Alice's behaviour and the fact that she has chosen herself to spend the majority of her time with me at my home. It is difficult for me because I do not get any support from the respondent who simply gets annoyed and becomes abusive and I am struggling financially to manage. The respondent gets all the benefits for the children including tax credits and I am trying to manage on just my earnings.

I am also very concerned that the respondent still continues to keep me in the dark about important matters relating to the children. On Friday 2 March 2007, I phoned Northview Grove School to discuss Alice's health with Mr Caldwell. Mr Caldwell asked if I was ringing about Hayley and the incident that had taken place the day before. I did not know what Mr Caldwell was talking about but he then told me that Hayley had been involved in a disturbance with some other pupils on 1 March 2007 and the police had been called. The police came to the school on Friday 2 March 2007 to interview the children and the respondent was asked to collect Hayley at 10.30am to take her home. The respondent did not phone me to let me know what was happening and I had to find out via the school. I am dismayed that, yet again, he does not think that I should be informed of incidents which are clearly very important. The respondent has still not informed me of this incident.

I would ask the court to consider making a Shared Residence Order in respect of Lara and to consider what should happen with respect of Alice. I appreciate that Hayley is of an age where she can make her own decisions and that perhaps she should not be subject to an order, but Alice is not yet 13 and would ask the court to consider making a Shared Residence Order in respect of Alice as well. I think Lara would benefit from having a Shared Residence Order. She has told me on a number of occasions that she would like to spend equal amounts of time with both me and the respondent and I wish the girls to know that they have two homes with two parents who love them very much.

My main concern has been the way the respondent refuses to keep me informed with regard to important matters relating to the children and the fact that he refuses to discuss anything with me as previously set out.

My solicitors have sent numerous letters to the respondent and to his solicitors but only very rarely do they respond.

It has been very frustrating for me that it is not even possible to agree schedules for forthcoming contact and I would ask the court to make an order that the schedules are agreed well in advance and that in addition the respondent give the following undertakings: –

That he will ensure that he notifies me immediately with regard to the children having accidents or becoming ill or in the event of problems concerning the children e.g., Hayley being questioned by the police very recently and Alice being excluded from school.

That he will release the children's passports to me at least one week before any planned trip abroad.

That he will advise me well in advance of any holiday that he plans to take with the children out of the jurisdiction and that he will provide me with contact details while he is away in case of an emergency.

The schedule for contact/shared residence needs to be agreed by the end of the summer term at the latest. I would be able to send the respondent my proposed schedule each year by 1 April and would state that this gives the respondent three months to come back with any alterations or agree the same. If the respondent does not agree with the schedule by the end of the summer term, then I would ask that my schedule be agreed.

I understand that solicitors cannot be involved for the next 7 years but I am still concerned, in view of the respondent's actions in the past, that every year I will have to seek legal advice just to get the respondent to agree the schedule. This cannot continue.

I do not think that the proposals I am making are at all unreasonable. Whilst I accept that Hayley and Lara will continue to live with the respondent, I am still their mother and I have felt that the respondent has tried to push me out of their lives by refusing to speak with me, taking the children on holiday out of school without even informing me and not even letting me know when the children have had quite serious accidents until sometime after the event. Alice has decided that she wishes to spend much more time with me and I worry that her relationship with the respondent is very fragile.

I also have grave concerns about Alice and her behaviour. Whilst I understand that Mrs Sanders has made suggestions about how both the respondent and I deal with Alice, I feel that her problems are much deeper than anyone believes. There is now produced to me and marked 'RH1' a copy of letters from Alice's school to myself and the respondent dated 19 July 2006 and 12 October 2006 which clearly sets out the school's concerns about her behaviour. There is now produced to me and marked 'RH2' a further letter from the school dated 23 January 2007 which raises concern about Alice truanting from class. I know that Alice has spent a lot of time off school and her attitude, on occasions, can be appalling.

I have seen from Mrs Sanders' report that the respondent struggles to cope with Alice's behaviour, and both Hayley and Lara are obviously very affected by this.

I would hope that the respondent and I can agree about Alice receiving some help for her problems by way of counselling or something similar but we both need to work together to do this. Alice needs to know that she cannot just run backwards and forwards between her father and me and that she needs to have some routine and security in her life.

I am pleased to note that the respondent has finally confirmed that he is agreeable to the undertakings that we have given to the Court being varied so that we may communicate in respect of matters relating to the children. However, I would not wish the undertakings to be discharged in their entirety as I am concerned that the respondent will revert to his aggressive behaviour if the undertakings are discharged. The undertakings can simply be varied to say that we cannot communicate save for matters relating to the children.

With regard to the recommendation about mediation, I can confirm that in June 2006 I was referred by my solicitor to mediation in the hope that we could resolve the issues between us and avoid further litigation. The respondent refused to even go for the intake assessment and so it was impossible to try and discuss matters with him.

For all of these reasons, I wish the court to set down a hearing to consider what should happen with regard to whether there should be a Shared Residence Order in respect of Lara and Alice. I would want Mrs Sanders to come to court to be asked questions about how she has reached her conclusions and also for an addendum report to be ordered once Mrs Sanders has had to opportunity of considering the medical notes of the respondent and the children.

I realise that ongoing proceedings are not in anyone's interests but I firmly believe that there are a lot of inaccuracies in Mrs Sanders' report and that the court needs to hear evidence from her and also from myself and the respondent before a decision can be made which will be in the children's best interest.

Signed,

Dean Marlo

Exhibits referred to in Ms Hyde's statement

19.07.2006

Dear Ms Hyde,

Following an appraisal of the Summer Term assessment scores, we are writing to express our concern over Alice's unacceptable effort in certain areas.

Achievement is, of course, directly related to the effort put in and obviously we do not wish to see any of our pupils underachieve. We will be reviewing progress next term and expect to see greater commitment to those areas which require more effort. We are sure you will wish to work in partnership with us to ensure this happens.

Should you wish to discuss this letter, please do not hesitate to contact me at the school.

Yours sincerely,

Mrs Sparrow

Head of Okikiolu House, Northview Grove School

12.10.2006

Dear Mr Marlo,

Re: Alice Marlo – 8OK

Your daughter's behaviour around school recently has given cause for concern. As well as various reported incidents of non-co-operation there seems to be a lot of screaming going on.

We have identified three students in 8OK as being disruptive and are removing two of them from Okikiolu House. Alice will remain in Okikiolu House where we hope she will settle down and behave herself as expected.

Yours sincerely,

J Garrett

Deputy Headteacher, Northview Grove School

23.01.2007

Dear Mr Marlo,

I am writing to inform you that Alice's behaviour has warranted a level 3 Intervention. The reason for this decision is: Truancy from a lesson on 15th January 2007, period 2.

As a result, your daughter will need to attend a meeting with the group leaders, named above, on Thursday 25th January 2007 at 3:15. This meeting may involve strategies such as completing missed work or discussing consequences of poor behaviour. The maximum duration will be one hour; therefore, your daughter will be released by 4:15pm.

Level 3 sanctions are recorded centrally in the school and will form part of the student's record. Alice will be monitored for a short period following this in order to ensure that she has settled down and the issue is fully resolved.

It is not necessary at this point to convene a meeting with you, however, should you require further information please ring the Lead Teacher or Head of House named below.

When did living get so complicated?

6 – 9 March

Tuesday 6th

Alice is still staying at her mother's. However, as far as the school know, I have sole residency and so it was me they called to inform me that Alice has been excluded from school on the 7th and 8th of March. The reason: persistent refusal to co–operate with members of staff. Alice will be allowed back in school Friday 9th. I informed them that Alice is currently residing with her mother, but I can come and collect her.

I was told Alice has asked them to contact her mother, and I heard no more.

Wednesday 7th

I received a call from Mrs Sparrow of Northview Grove, and she told me that Ms Hyde has sent Alice to school informing her that she can be placed in the ISC; Mrs Sparrow reiterated that Alice has been excluded from school and that is what it means. Again, I offered to collect her, but was informed that Alice has requested for her mother to be contacted.

After speaking to Mrs Sparrow, my phone went off almost immediately. Melissa was on the other end stating she has received a fax from Smitch Law; Ms Hyde has contested the child psychologist's report.

(Arr the latest bombshell!

If the Family Courts are going to look into her dissatisfaction with the report, they will have to re-read Mrs Sanders' comments:

'The continuing conflict and legal battle have contributed to her ongoing sense of grievance and she has been unable to move on emotionally.'

'Ms Hyde is very reactive with difficulty in holding focused attention. In situations of conflict or challenge, she easily becomes hyper–aroused and has difficulty in managing these emotions.'

'In past situations, her basic fight defence has been activated and she has been unable to hold back the verbal and physical outbursts.')

Thursday 8th

I received a call from Melissa about the hearing on Monday; she assured me that even though I am not in receipt of Legal Aid, she will still come to court and into the hearing to give me support and advice. Melissa stated that it was a shame I had no funding or that I could not raise the sufficient amount to hire a barrister, as she thought that with one, there would be hope of settling and closing several issues. I asked how much instructing one would cost... Melissa replied £600 – £700.

I sat at my desk for the next three-quarters of an hour, remembering how emotionally draining the past experiences of numerous court appearances had been. Having to endure listening to misleading and untrue allegations about myself and my ability to be a good parent.

I couldn't bear to face it again; I phoned one of my friends to ask if he and his wife could lend me £600 – £700. My friend stated that if I was to call around tonight, his wife would be there with a cheque. I thanked them both, and discussed a time frame I could pay them back in (even though they tried to wave me off).

Friday 9th

Although I had borrowed £600, Melissa called to inform me she had found a barrister who could be there given the short notice, but the fees were £800 plus VAT. I reluctantly paid on my credit card, and used the cheque for £600 that I had borrowed to reduce my personal overdraft.

Alice, Ruth and myself had to attend an appointment at Northview Grove regarding Alice's behaviour. Alice looked tired and bored throughout, while Ruth argued it is the school's inability to help Alice with her dyslexia that has resulted in her disruption at school.

From NGS

8/9 March

8 March

Dear Mr Marlo,

Following my meeting with Ms Hyde on 5th March, I have made enquires with regard to the four areas that were discussed.

Mrs Sparrow, Head of House, discussed Alice's and Hayley's absence with our Educational Welfare Officer and has been assured that there is no problem with their attendance at school.

Mrs Hayden, Head of Learning Support, had already written to Ms Hyde on 22nd January enclosing a report of the assessment done by the Assistant Educational Psychologist on 7th December 2006. There was, therefore, no need to reassess Alice's needs.

All staff who teach Alice have been made aware of her learning needs by Mrs Hayden.

Enquires in our school office confirm that all correspondence from the school has always been sent to both Mr Marlo and Ms Hyde. A note has been made to ensure that this practice continues.

Yours sincerely,
Mrs Tran

9 March
Dear Mr Marlo,
Pupil: Alice Marlo, 8OK
Please find the home-school agreement, required to be signed by Alice.

I agree to abide by the School's Classroom Rules which are:
To treat others with consideration and respect;
To listen when it is others turn to talk;
To follow instructions from teachers and other staff;
To sort out difficulties without making matters worse;
To ask for help appropriately if you need it;
To do your best to behave in a way which allows others to learn.

I agree that I will: not persistently refuse to co-operate with a member of staff, including senior staff, not persistently refuse to follow instructions; not be rude to staff.

I understand that failure to comply with these conditions may result in further and more serious action being taken by the school.

To Melissa, reply to Ms Hyde's statement March 2007

Trying to kiss a 12–year–old girl is *sexual assault*. Even though Ms Hyde had told me about the abuse, explaining comments made throughout her childhood like 'if you want to take things further let me know', I still feel shocked and horrified to read it. When Ms Hyde and I cohabited, I questioned Mrs Jackson about Mr Jackson and the allegations; Mrs Jackson told me that her daughter had made up dreadful stories about anyone from an early age.

(We'll have to bench the residency hearings; a full investigation should be made concerning Ms Hyde's allegation written in her *own statement*. Are we not in the Family Courts? It is unacceptable for the Family Courts to ignore and dismiss this allegation against a man that has access and contact with my children. Like any normal parent, I do not want my children taken over to the Jackson's house or be anywhere near a potential paedophile.

Mrs Mason clearly cherry-picks what comprises an allegation of abuse and what the appropriate responses should be.)

Between Ms Hyde, Mrs Jackson and Smitch Law they have repeatedly lied, deceived and denounced a loving and caring father, who over many years has continued to show patience and understanding with Ms Hyde's behaviour and mental health. Meanwhile, they protected and defended a man who attempted to sexually abuse his step-daughter?

Has this law firm taken over as 'Big Brother'? Every aspect of my life has already been under scrutiny and yet is still being consumed by Mrs Mason and the Family Courts, simply because I am here for my children. The medical records were not produced because, having no legal aid, the court deemed that I had the responsibility of paying for the copies that would be sent to Mrs Mason.

I would rather spend the money on my children.

The judge placed financial pressure on me as a single parent. It had been this very court which gave me sole residency of three children. As in 2004, there was no evidence brought to the court hearings of Ms Hyde's assertions, nor would any be found in the family's medical records – last seen in 2004.

These hearings exist due to Mrs Mason relaying made up stories on behalf of her client, requesting a child psychologist report and our medical records. Now to top it off, after all of the months of uncertainly and anxiety, Ms Hyde has contested the report, which will prolong proceedings.

This is to me, clearly, down to Ms Hyde's mental health condition – she is unable to empathise with her children's feelings, comes to twisted conclusions, denies her involvement in incidents and does not recall how she has behaved.

Despite having all of the worry and pressure of no legal aid and not being in a position to pay for proper legal representation, I have not turned nasty or vindictive towards Ms Hyde. I have had no letters from Smitch Law claiming harassment; you would have thought according to my reputation and past behaviour as reported to the Family Courts, I would have been making Ms Hyde's life unbearable.

This has not happened simply because I am not the cause of trouble in our family and despite what Ms Hyde's counsel have stated with full conviction to several judges at too many court hearings – I am simply trying to get on.

I hope that between Ms Hyde and myself, we can give our children good childhoods.

However, I must question how I have been penalized as a single parent with three children, when I have: the responsibility to provide financially and care for my children; to work hard to make ends meet each week; tried to improve my family's position by not being reliant on benefits, as well as working around my children's school times and their needs.

Ms Hyde continues to receive Legal Aid and to bring instability into her children's lives and my own.

When Ms Hyde told me that she would like to take the children to her step-sister's on Mother's Day weekend, I had no problem and the children went.

This once again was a clear indication that I have never had problems with Ms Hyde's contact with her children, as the child psychologist reported she saw no evidence of; I do not have the mind to make things difficult or try and spoil Ms Hyde's time with her daughters.

Ms Hyde states that contact has only been taking place in recent weeks due to proceedings and that she is worried about contact in the future. I have never stopped any of the children from having contact with their mother, as shown by Lara's ongoing contact in accordance with the court order; Hayley and Alice, at Ms Hyde's own admission, stay at her home as they wish – why are we in court?

I think all three children have done well living in a home where one of their parents has ongoing and unmonitored mental health problems. Hayley and Alice are growing up and I think it is not in the realms of fantasy that as the children get older, they would spend less time with an abusive parent and an unstable home life. Bar Alice's current disposition, which is part of teenage rebellion.

I have never asked Lara why she still wants contact with her mother; if Lara is happy to go, then I am happy to put my concerns for Lara to the back of my mind, as I want Lara to have a relationship with her mother, as I tried with Hayley and Alice.

As made clear in Mrs Sanders's report, Ms Hyde cannot comprehend and will not accept that the children have their own minds and their attitude reflects the behaviour and attitude shown to them, and, as individuals, they each have their own relationship with their mother.

From August 2004, Hayley, Alice and Lara had gone on weekend and holiday contact with Ms Hyde - this was without issue. In the early part of 2006, several incidences happened at Ms Hyde's home and Hayley and Alice stated that they did not want to put up with the level of aggression that they received when staying with their mother.

Ms Hyde has continually denied anything happening on the occasions that Hayley and Alice have referred to, and gives her children no credit; Hayley and Alice have acted of their own volition based on their experiences, and not, as Ms Hyde suggests, under my influence.

At the time of the incidents, I phoned Ms Hyde to try and calm things down but Ms Hyde was on full throttle and more interested in accusing me of not allowing her daughters to visit her. When Alice stayed with her mother and refused contact with me, not due to abuse of any form but due to not getting her own way, I did not serve Ms Hyde with a court application – although unhappy about not seeing Alice and worried about her schooling, it was down to Alice and Ms Hyde.

I phoned Mr Ellwood from Cafcass and talked to him. I arranged on several occasions with Ms Hyde to drop Hayley, Alice and Lara round for tea after school.

I have continued to try and regain some stability between Hayley, Alice and their mother, but Ms Hyde has never made anything easy. I believe it is now Ms Hyde that has changed her attitude towards the children, which is encouraging Hayley and Alice to go.

Hayley is a loving and caring person/daughter. Hayley sometimes phones me between 8.30pm and 9.30pm to talk about what she has done that day; Hayley asks if I am all right and we say goodnight, and that is it. A daughter communicating with her parent. Hayley has sleepovers at Ms Hyde's or is out with her friends, as many normal children are. Hayley may show concern because she cares, but I am glad to say that Hayley gets on with her life, she is not moping over her dad; she is doing her best to have fun and enjoy her childhood.

I do not talk to our children about what has gone on in court but I do ask them about their feelings, what their needs are and what they want to see happen.

Ms Hyde is stating that Lara should have contact per the order 2004, and Hayley and Alice can visit, as long as it is during the times when Lara is with her. So that's all three children under the order of 2004? Then she changes to shared residency of Alice and Lara, neither of whom have said that's what they want, nor is it the recommendation of the child psychologist.

I am sorry but I am on the side of parents that believe and make it clear to their children, that I am always pleased to see them and over the past three years (during Ms Hyde's weekend contact) Hayley and Alice popped home to say hello or to get something many times. On some occasions, Hayley or Alice have gone into their bedrooms, played some music and stated that they were off round their mother's.

I haven't had much time to talk to Alice, given the volatility of the previous months, but if she is suffering with her periods, it is a discussion for Alice and her doctor, not the Family Courts.

I believe the rest of Alice's apparent illness is a result of staying up far too late; Alice has shown signs of being rundown (evident in Alice's behaviour at school); when I have seen Alice, she has been tired and irritable. Alice's answer to my clarification of inappropriate behaviour has been to phone her mother and leave.

When Alice was at home, she rarely went out in the evening; six out of seven nights, Alice would be home with Lara and myself or in her room. When Hayley does go out, she is always back at the time we have agreed. Hayley has continued to respect and respond to the boundaries that I set for her; Hayley is a smashing daughter and she is aware that I am grateful for her behaviour and attitude towards boundaries that have to be set.

Hayley has not got into trouble recently for picking on other children and once again

I am disgusted that Ms Hyde will use false allegations concerning her own daughter, as some sort of misleading indication that something is wrong with Hayley.

Northview Grove and the police have stated that they know Hayley was not involved. Mrs Tran phoned me the next day the police came to the school to talk to the children, stating that Hayley had got herself worked up and suggested that Hayley came home for her emotional wellbeing – Hayley was not sent home due to bad behaviour.

Ms Hyde distorts any truth or happening to suit herself, in her ceaseless attempts to disrupt and discredit my ability to be a parent.

Ms Hyde expresses concern that I am not at home in the evenings or at the weekends, and that she also worries how the children are eating. Apart from being untrue, it is a bizarre allegation to make. (Is she there, or constantly parked outside of our home? Again, there is no evidence to the allegation.) It is quite clear that throughout Ms Hyde's statement of 'truths', she has attempted to make me appear to be the worst parent and person in the world.

The Family Courts should find it obvious, the vast difference between these allegations and what has been conveyed by the children's schools, the Cafcass officers and reports in 2004, and, now in 2007, the child psychologist's report.

In Ms Hyde's 'Supplemental Information Form/Form C1A/Town County Court' 21st July 2006, she states –

'Mr Marlo did apply to the Town County Court in June 2006 for an injunction order against me, claiming that I had been abusive and threatening to him. I deny that I acted in this manner and at Court on the 23rd June 2006 no order was made on the application for the injunction, although both Mr Marlo and myself had to give undertakings to the court not to communicate with each other at all or to attend each other's home.'

In Mrs Sanders's report, 6.2.5, Ms Hyde confirms that she caused criminal damage to my vehicle. So, she lied in her application, and this should have been an indictor to all involved that Ms Hyde's statements are unreliable. (I make the point, but I am not sure it matters or is deemed relevant to the Family Courts or the process of gaining court proceedings.)

Mrs Sanders's report also confirms that I have consistently informed the schools if the children are ill and when they will be coming back. Mr Church of Riverbank Primary has written several letters confirming this fact, yet Ms Hyde can continue to use it as a point of contention. Mr Church's letters to the court have never expelled the notion, and I can only guess the conformation from Mrs Sanders will have the same effect.

I would like the family court to appreciate that every day I take Lara to school on time. I go to work, and am back on time to collect Lara – without fail. I am at home from then on and cook dinner for the family every evening.

When I have to work on a Saturday, Lara is always doing a project with her nan, whether it be trips to town or the library, knitting, sewing, painting – as Hayley and Alice enjoyed their time with their nan and myself at Lara's age.

I have not used my children as a reason not to work and as you can imagine it takes a great deal of effort to organise my work in the construction industry, come home, be there for my children and be a good dad.

As a caring parent, I was reinforcing to Alice that it is unacceptable to bunk off school.

I believe Ms Hyde has done nothing more than encourage Alice to stay off school and remain at hers, where she does not enforce suitable rules. Alice has become rude and her attitude towards school and her teachers has deteriorated. I have received several calls from Ms Hyde stating that she is taking Alice to the doctors because Alice is suffering from stress and depression.

I am not a doctor but I do know my daughter; up until 2007 – barring Alice wanting to sleep at a 15-year-old's grandfather's who had a tag in 2006 – Alice was a caring and loving child, who was doing well at school; she was outspoken but not rude or spiteful. Since, I believe that Alice has acted like many children coming up to her teens. Being only a couple of years younger, Alice saw Hayley start her teenage years, going out more and spending her pocket money in town and also witnessed the changes in her sister; with the advent of 'Bebo', their phones and being at secondary school, Alice has always seen herself as older than she is. To her credit, Hayley is handling her changes and teens brilliantly, and it was just wishful thinking on my part that Alice would be the same.

Alice has tested the boundaries and Ms Hyde has reinforced her choice to leave my home to get her own way. In a family situation where there is not an entirely different house and parent to be in the favour of, Alice would sit in her room, think about the situation and we'd have talked about it. I never get the opportunity to deescalate Alice as Ms Hyde is already waiting outside. She does not use the time to talk to Alice about her issues, or encourage her to take responsibility of her actions by accepting what rule I have set (as long as it's reasonable). Instead, Ms Hyde uses Alice to claim that I am an incompetent father, and Alice uses the free house with less strict rules to her advantage. This is playing one parent off on another, as unfortunately some children in Alice's position do, but that is only feasible because Ms Hyde allows her to.

I personally believe that Ms Hyde's attitude and behaviour towards Alice has not helped Alice through this time in her life. Alice's schooling has suffered; this I believe to be partly due to staying with Ms Hyde on school nights.

Alice had requested £20 for a pair of school shoes, which gave me the opportunity to see her for a few moments and try to arrange for her to come home to talk properly; Alice had taken the money and rushed out the door saying she would get the shoes in town with her mother on Saturday.

Paragraph 19 can be debunked by letters from Northview Grove and Riverbank School.

In 2004, the judge ruled that I was the parent most capable to have sole custody; matters were fully investigated and I do not believe residency should be brought into question, as Ms Hyde has again provided no evidence that my parenting is detrimental, nor that the children want to change the residency, as they said to Mrs Sanders.

I am concerned about Ms Hyde suggesting of joint residency for Lara, as she has enjoyed her 3 years of stability with me and regular weekend contact with her mother. Lara is clearly happy with residency as it is and is aware she can have contact with her mother whenever she wishes.

Hayley knows I've never stopped her from having any kind of contact she wanted with her mother, same for Alice – they both want off the court order to not allow their mother to control their living arrangements, and to stop their mother taking me back to court after an incident of abuse in her home disrupts their contact.

I do not believe a joint residency order is what Alice wants; she is enjoying the situation with her mother now, however as the psychologist described and the past shows, Ms Hyde cannot control herself, and arguments have the potential to escalate to the point where Alice is not safe.

There are already too many incidents recently where disagreements have ended physically: Alice being pushed off the trampoline, Hayley being dragged off the sofa or being strangled and taken to the floor – I am, as always, only concerned. I feel that I should be outraged by Ruth's behaviour towards our children, and I am, but any intervention on my part for my children's welfare, as previously, has led nowhere.

And, when Hayley and Alice decide to resume contact after the incidents, they get on with their relationships with their mother. The children have all accepted that Ms Hyde's behaviour is the way it is, and I believe it has been normalised for them by the lack of any serious attempts to help Ms Hyde with her condition. I do not deny the children's mother contact, but it must be realised that without outside involvement, Ms Hyde's parenting is a ticking time bomb – just a case of what will set her off next time, and when.

Bipolar is classified as periods of highs and lows. There are times when Ms Hyde is and can be pleasant on the phone, but it is never a given and, over the years, I have come to accept that it is also never a given what she will disagree with and cause an issue over. I have maintained my position of not responding in kind and avoiding confrontation, and have found no alternative but to endure, due to the lack of support for Ms Hyde, the solicitor's letters, verbally abusive phone calls and the turmoil our children experience as a result.

I do find it strange that I have sole residency, yet Mrs Mason, under the instruction of Ms Hyde, is the one proposing schedules and demanding I agree to them.

When I completed the schedules for 2006/2007, I was pleased to see alternate weekends had worked out almost perfectly. Ms Hyde stated that she had one or two days to discuss; I saw no problems with this and gave her the schedule for 2006/2007 to make her amendments.

Then, Ms Hyde rejected this schedule and produced her own, making several changes to the routine of contact. It could not have been any more straightforward; I knew that there may be some weekends and days Ms Hyde and I would talk about, but there really shouldn't be a large number of adjustments to be made, and the current order specifies every other weekend contact and half school holidays to Ms Hyde. Once again, Ms Hyde is attempting to overcomplicate and manipulate a very simple arrangement.

I do not think that the children wanting extra contact with Ms Hyde needs to be written onto a schedule, when it has already been going on without the need for it to be ordered. Outside of the family court's scope, it has acted as an indicator of how well their relationship with their mother is going and what Ms Hyde's current temperament is. Clearly, they want contact with their mother, and this only doesn't occur after she has been abusive towards them; the children know they have a safe and loving home with me, so the question for all of them has always been: 'how is our mother treating us right now?' Due to Ms Hyde's ongoing disorder, I believe that the children choosing to go for contact when they feel comfortable makes sense, as Ms Hyde at times cannot cope, and

I think their relationships would benefit from the flexibility.

(Lara has the most balanced temperament of our children, which I believe is due to not growing up and being conscious in as much of a volatile environment, like Hayley and Alice were.)

I have informed Ms Hyde, at the first opportunity of the children's accidents and being ill.

As to the letter from Northview Grove that Ms Hyde has marked 'RH2', dated 23rd January 2007 re Alice truanting from class on the 15th January - Alice was excluded from school because she found out that Hayley was not at school and was still at Ms Hyde's. Alice walked out of school and went to her mother's.

Each year, I have received a letter from Northview Grove School asking me to complete and confirm phone numbers and addresses. (This form I believe to be a standard form sent to every parent.) Each year, I have filled in this form, along with Ms Hyde's phone number and address, and I am aware that Northview Grove School do send duplicate letters to Ms Hyde, as they have confirmed. When I have talked to Northview Grove, I have been told that they have already or were going to phone Ms Hyde. Again, we are not the first separated family to exist, and this I believe is standard protocol.

Looking through the way my children's case has been handled by the Family Courts and the legal system, I believe that this hearing is again not about three children, it is clearly Smitch Law's desire to win a case, on behalf of their client, at any cost.

It is farcical for the psychologist to suggest Ms Hyde and I had a competition to see 'who is the best parent', although I have witnessed solicitors and barristers behaving in this way.

As I asked myself after the first incident, and on every occasion ever since, why, from the very start of the children missing their contact, weren't the children simply asked why they did not want to go to their mother's? The incidents of abuse would be relayed and the solution clear for all to see - get Ms Hyde parenting help. Instead of that, Mrs Mason makes out that I am the most manipulative person in the world, and that there is something wrong with my parenting; she is relentless in her endeavour to suggest any accusation she can against me. It is unacceptable, without the evidence to support it, to submit such assertions to a judge.

Placing instability in a family's lives is merely part of the game that is played out by so called professional people, all under the veil of 'we have a duty and moral obligation to the children involved in court proceedings and the welfare and stability of children must be paramount'.

Mrs Mason has plagued me and my children from the very start. She has never let things settle down and I know the argument will be that Ms Hyde walked through Smitch Law's doors, but the way Mrs Mason has conducted herself in representing Ms Hyde has been deplorable.

It is also a total fallacy, played out by Ms Hyde and Mrs Mason, that I have in anyway tried to prevent Ms Hyde from going on holiday with our children.

I received numerous letters from Smitch Law with false and misleading allegations regarding the passports, which is an example of Ms Hyde's ability to over–complicate any simple task, and another opportunity for Smitch Law to write to me. Mrs Mason does her best to dramatize and condemn 'my' behaviour, as verbally relayed to them by Ms Hyde. I am just a normal, honest and decent father to my children… I am not a criminal, yet I am made to believe I cannot be trusted with matters relating to my children, even handing over their passports.

I have followed all of Ms Hyde's and Smitch Law's requests to relay my holiday details and contact numbers. Whereas, I am always left unaware of the actual details of Ms Hyde's holidays. I have letters from Smitch Law stating that their client is taking the children to Spain or Egypt, but I get no location or hotel phone number.

I do not believe the Family Courts, nor solicitors, need to be involved in Ms Hyde and myself agreeing alternate weekend contact and half school holidays. Each year, I have made it clear to Ms Hyde that I am more than happy to receive a letter from her indicating weekends and times she would like to change.

I have not only shown Ms Hyde honesty and fairness when completing the yearly schedule, I have also shown Ms Hyde, our children and the court order respect and consideration at all times.

Reading through the many letters that I have received from Smitch Law, it is quite clear that between Ms Hyde and Mrs Mason, they have only wanted to prolong the trouble over made-up and misleading allegations.

Ms Hyde made similar allegations in her statement for the hearing in 2004. These were proven unsubstantiated and this is once again the case.

Alice's bad behaviour at school is aggravated by Ms Hyde's inability to keep to a sensible routine. Late nights and oversleeping in the morning do not provide Alice a good example, at a time when rebelling against routines and sensibility is how Alice is acting out.

Mrs Sparrow from Northview Grove School has told me that Alice behaves perfectly well in 80% of her classes, and that Alice has behaviour problems in only some lessons, with some teachers, which may be down to the different groups of children in her classes for different subjects.

I believe Mrs Sanders' report indicated that I have no more problems than any ordinary parent with the children's behaviour. I do not struggle to cope with Alice's behaviour; I *do* struggle to communicate with Alice when she drops out of our home to stay with Ms Hyde.

It was Judge Baxter and Ms Hyde that were so insistent on 'undertakings' in 2006, which ordered no contact between two parents with three children and a court order to comply to.

I spoke to you about Judge Baxter's ruling, and I made it clear that Ms Hyde and I need to talk and communicate for the sake of our children, like normal parents; we need to organise holidays and outside activities. I mentioned this clause to Mrs Sanders, and discussed the thoughtless attitude of Judge Baxter. Mrs Sanders agreed that we would always need to have a line of communication available, and this judgement was not in the best interest of the children. (But was in the interests of the solicitors, i.e. Mrs Mason and Smitch Law.)

Ms Hyde states that she does not wish the undertakings to be discharged in their entirety, as she is concerned that I will revert to my 'aggressive behaviour'. I would like the Family Courts to actually acknowledge that Ms Hyde's aggressive behaviour was the reason for these undertakings. I have never been antagonistic towards Ms Hyde, and this has been made clear throughout.

I would also like the Family Courts to recognise that Ms Hyde has repeatedly used the police, solicitors, Family Courts and even our children in a personal vendetta against myself.

I did attend the mediation meeting on the 4th July 2006 at 12.30pm without Ms Hyde, but I felt it would not help in this situation. Having read Ms Hyde's statement, I believe it was the right decision, as she continues to show she is incapable of making sound judgements and information gets confused in her mind, which only brings to the surface Ms Hyde's dissatisfaction that I have any responsibility for our children.

The final straw and to top it all, I would have to pay for mediation - which I can't afford! I do not want to spend money satisfying Ms Hyde and her desire to publicly ostracise me in front of a third party, without any evidence to what she's saying. In reality, the relationships of Hayley, Alice and Ms Hyde need counselling. I can but wonder how, with all of the court hearings, experts and guardians, this has not been put in place.

(I know it's 'too late' for parenting classes – arr good old Judge Baxter, maybe counselling can be organised. Or are we out of time?)

I believe I have been a good father and parent, and that the sole residency awarded to me by the family court has no reason to change, when I provide for the best interests of the children. Mrs Sanders and both schools support this opinion.

It was Smitch Law that asked for a child psychologist report. Now that the report has come out with a supportive view of keeping the children with me, they decide to contest it; I see no justification in challenging Mrs Sanders' conclusions. Surely, Legal Aid cannot pay for the report, and then pay for the person who did not get the conclusion they wanted, to contest the report they requested?

I know that my medical records have to be produced to the court – would it be possible for you to forward them to Mrs Sanders instead of Mrs Mason?

(I am anxious it could affect my residency, in the ineffective and biased Kangaroo Family Courts I'm accountable to.)

As always, I appreciate your help.

Kittens

11 March

At 5pm, Lara phoned me from her mother's and told me that Wotsit has had kittens. We chatted about the experience she had and how small they were before she excitedly went back to them. Later, at 7.30pm, Ruth phoned me and said Lara wants to stay on Monday night to look after the new kittens. I said no problem.

On this contact weekend of Ruth's, Lara stayed the whole weekend, plus Monday night, Hayley only on Saturday night, while Alice still hasn't come home.

Court – acts

12th March 2007 / Town Family County Courts
Mother's application – joint residency of Alice and Lara
Hayley/Alice's application – removal from court order

Ms Hyde contests the child psychologist's report, so the hearing is adjourned and Judge Yergin deferred the case to the Principal Register of Family Division the Strand London.

Judge Yergin orders Mrs Sanders to attend the High Court for the first day of the final hearing at the Royal Courts Strand London; with a time estimate of 2 days before a High Court Judge.

Hayley Marlo is discharged from all previous orders save for the order granting parental responsibility to Mr Marlo; the application for Alice to be discharged to be dealt with by the trial judge at the commencement of the final hearing.

The day of the hearing

12 March

At 9:15am, I met Melissa and Mr Carey (my barrister) at court, ready for the hearing at 10.

We talked about the case and I gave Melissa the children's passports, as requested by Ruth/Smitch Law. I only have Hayley and Lara's passports, because when I requested the children's passports in 2006 from Ruth for our holiday, Ruth withheld Alice's – which did not matter at the time, as, lucky enough, all three children are still on my passport until 2008.

We were all called in and Judge Yergin said that he hoped to close these proceedings today, but he believed that Ms Hyde 'wanted her day in court'. Hayley's legal representative asked the Judge for Hayley to be removed from the court order, which the Judge agreed.

(Due to Ms Hyde contesting the report, the judge has to send us to London because of legalities that I do not understand. I thought this was going to be the final hearing, which made sense for me to have a barrister at – instead, I've basically paid for him to turn up and do nothing, as proceedings are halted until London.)

After the hearing, Melissa, Mr Carey and I went into one of the small waiting rooms; Melissa asked if I would mind leaving the room as Mrs Mason was on her way to sit down and go through Ms Hyde's latest requests to change the residency schedule.

I got up and left the room. Standing outside the door, Hayley and Alice's legal representative, Miss Novak, walked past me, smiled, said hello and found a seat further down. Mrs Mason came out of one of the waiting rooms, unaware I was standing in the corridor, and walked over to talk with Miss Novak.

From where I was, I clearly heard Mrs Mason ask, 'Do you know what dates you are available? As you heard, the case from hell is going to need two days in London.'

She talked some more and turned to walk towards me. I felt shocked and I tried to compose myself; I knew I had to say something but I was still trying to comprehend what had just been said. I asked Mrs Mason what she meant by her statement 'the case from hell', and she apologised, claiming what she had meant to say was 'this difficult case'.

Mrs Mason entered the room with Melissa. I asked myself why this person is so hateful towards my family, my children and me. Another 10 minutes passed, where I tried to make sense of the orchestrators of so much of our family's 'difficulties' and 'hellish' proceedings, when they're the ones who dragged us here. What Mrs Mason and Smitch Law want is certainly not an end to proceedings.

I believe this is another example of uncaring and unprofessional behaviour and attitude from Mrs Mason; this has been her performance throughout the proceedings.

(I know, where is my aggressive behaviour that has been written about for years within these four walls. Mrs Mason has treated me and my children's welfare like dirt, and I believe it is befitting that I should hear Mrs Mason say what she did.)

Mrs Mason has touched every bone and nerve in my body; she either does not care, or she is so far up her own arse, she cannot see the carnage and hurt her dishonest behaviour has caused my family.

Melissa came out of the room and told me that when Mrs Mason came in, she apologised, as she believed she might have 'upset' her client.

For what my children and myself have been put through and witnessed over the years, just to bring normality into our lives, it has been an uphill struggle, trying to keep up with what was going on in the background and maintain the stability that my children need and deserve.

How can Mrs Mason, without thought or care, refer to my children's case as 'the case from hell'?

The only upside, besides Hayley's life now being free from court influence, is that Melissa told me Mrs Mason has agreed for her to pass on my medical records.

Having wasted my time at court, I picked Lara up after school and was asking about her day; Lara told me she and Alice had missed the morning at school and that Cruella de Vil had taken her in at 11am.

I asked if they were unwell, and Lara had said no, her mother had gotten up late and then had to go to court, so she had to call someone to take her. There's no excuse, the hearing was at 10am, for Ruth not taking Lara to school - it's partly Lara's wellbeing the proceedings are supposed to cover!

Not long later, Hayley called to say that she was going clothes shopping with her mother after school and they would be back late.

In the evening, Hayley texted to say she was staying the night at her mother's.

Typed notes of Hearing on 12 March 2007

Dear Dean,

I enclose typed notes of the hearing. This is abbreviated – you saw my handwritten notes!! I am sure however it accurately reflects what occurred at the Hearing on 12th March – Melissa.

The children are going on holiday to Spain with Ms Hyde at Easter and Hayley and Lara's passports were handed to their mother, in court, by counsel for Mr Marlo, Mr Carey.

11am called in before his honour Judge Yergin.

Mr Porter, barrister for Ms Hyde, introduced the case and referred to HHJ Yergin seeing advocates only on 16 February 2007, and giving a pretty firm indication that would not be minded to make an order regarding Hayley and most likely Alice, too. Had expected the hearing today to be the final hearing.

HHJ Yergin agreed and said there had been too much litigation.

Mr Porter continued stating that the difficulty Ms Hyde has in resolving matters is that his instructions are, in respect of the two eldest children, she does not believe that the view accords with Alice's wishes, as Alice has been living with her for the majority of the time this year.

[Residence to Mr Marlo and a permissive contact order to Ms Hyde.]

For Hayley, matters have moved on since Mrs Sanders' report; Hayley, police involved at school. Alice remains living with mother.

Ms Hyde's proposal for Lara is to be with her from Friday to Tuesday morning and on a Wednesday for tea, and half of the school holidays. Shared residence and likewise with Alice who should be encouraged to spend time with Ms Hyde at the same times as Lara.

Alice has been seen by the GP and she is suffering from stress.

Whilst the court is concerned at long proceedings, it is not a straightforward case. It is a high-risk case especially in respect of Hayley and Alice.

HHJ Yergin then stated he was not surprised given all the litigation.

Mr Porter continued by stating that things were getting worse rather than better. It is too early for the court to step out. He continued, and took issue with the children's representation by Child Legal Guidance, suggesting that the court should appoint a guardian, and instruct a representative on behalf of Hayley and Alice, stating that Child Legal Guidance were acting on Hayley and Alice's instructions rather than in their best interests. [Which is what a guardian would do, act in Hayley and Alice's best interests.]

HHJ Yergin then told Mr Porter that his client does not want to end the proceedings. She wants 5 days in the High Court. If it is to be done then it has to be done properly.

Mr Porter continued that Mrs Sanders' report should be objectively fair and raised concerns about the report – no medical records for the children or Mr Marlo. Ms Hyde believes that there are untrue matters recorded in her medical records which have clouded Mrs Sanders' judgement. Ms Hyde says those matters have clouded Mrs Sanders' view and she is concerned that the children may have seen or have access to Mrs Sanders' report. There are a number of matters that [Mr Porter] I am instructed to challenge in Mrs Sanders' report. There is the question of the separate representation of Hayley and Alice; the conclusions of Mrs Sanders. It is not a matter where one can easily apply pressure [to settle].

Mr Carey then addressed HHJ Yergin on behalf of Mr Marlo, informing that his instructions are to conclude the proceedings, if at all possible, today. Mr Marlo is very concerned about Alice, in particular, she has just recently been suspended from school and is getting into all sorts of trouble at school. Mr Marlo takes the view that she needs help, and that things need to be settled for her. The existing residence order should stay as it is with permissive contact order for Hayley.

Miss Novak, counsel for Hayley and Alice informed that they had been seen separately by their solicitor, on Friday. Hayley confirmed that what she wants is for things to stay as they are, to have reasonable contact with Ms Hyde and that she wanted to have contact with Ms Hyde when Lara was there. Hayley feels she is able to make the decision.

Alice went to Ms Hyde on 4 March (this is where Ms Hyde disagreed and there was some discussion between her, her counsel and Mrs Mason) and was excluded on 7/8 March and is now on school report. Both parents attended a meeting at school on 9 March regarding Alice's behaviour.

Alice made it quite clear that although at the moment she is living with Ms Hyde, she does not want the residence order to change. She feels a lot of pressure is being put on her about where to live and deciding on residence.

HHJ Yergin then stated that Ms Hyde is determined to have a hearing. She wants Mrs Sanders here in a vague attempt to persuade her to change one or two words of a paragraph…

Mr Carey informed that if there was to be a further hearing, Mr Marlo would need sufficient time; he has had his public funding withdrawn following a letter from Ms Hyde's solicitors.

HHJ Yergin indicated that he knew the difficulties but said that there was no option other than for there to be a final hearing, unsatisfactory though it may be.

Miss Novak suggested that appointment of a guardian for Hayley and Alice was not necessary.

HHJ Yergin expressed concern that appointment of a guardian would mean a considerable delay.

Miss Novak continued that the court would be able to deal with what was in the children's best interests.

HHJ Yergin indicated that he thought it may have been arguable in the past that the children should be separately represented through a guardian, but not now.

Mr Carey suggested discharging the order in respect of Hayley as it was the most uncontroversial. Mr Porter agreed.

HHJ Yergin discharged all orders in respect of Hayley, with Mr Marlo to retain the Parental Responsibility order.

There was then considerable discussion about who could sit as a High Court Judge to hear Alice's application to be joined as a party to proceedings. The proposal ultimately being for a local Judge to sit as a High Court Judge to consider Alice's application, then transfer the case back to the County Court and go on to hear the final hearing, with a total of a two-day time estimate. It is hoped this will take place locally, at the Town County Court.

So, we're taking the judge with us, and going from a 6-mile round trip to 200 miles, just to change the building?

Arrangements for kittens

13 - 18 March

Tuesday 13th
Ruth phoned and stated that she couldn't have Lara tomorrow (Wednesday), so she wants Lara to go round on Thursday, however, on Thursday, Hayley has a performance with her signing club at school at the Town Arts Centre, where various schools and colleges do a routine or song and donations are given to the local deaf association. I'm incredibly proud of her; sadly, there are only four tickets per child, so Ma can't come.

I know Lara is excited and thrilled with the kittens, and I agreed for Ruth to pick Lara up after school on Thursday and bring her to Hayley's performance. Ruth also stated that she would be dropping Hayley off to me at 12pm, as she was not at school today.

I was on site, and called Ma to ask if she was available to come down to be there for Hayley. Ma got on the bus, I texted Hayley to let her know Nan would be there and I carried on at work.

Thursday 15th
During breakfast, Hayley told me that she would phone me at 6.30pm to find out where I was sitting at her performance. Hayley went to school, I dropped Lara at Riverbank and went to work.

Halfway through the morning, I received a call from Northview, asking for an explanation as to why Alice wasn't at school. I replied, again, that Alice has been staying with her mother and mentioned that I am worried about the routine she is getting into. When Alice stays at her mother's, she appears to lack a bed time and a set wake-up time, which is reflected by her attendance at school.

At 6pm, as I drove to the Arts Centre, Hayley phoned me. Unable to pull over I let it ring through and arrived in the parking lot. I called Hayley back, and she asked if Lara was with me; Hayley said she knew her mother was picking Lara up from school, but that her mother had told her she was going to phone me, so that I could pick Lara up on the way through. I replied that I had not received a call. Hayley stated that she would phone her mother and I told Hayley that I would stay parked.

Ruth did call, asking if I would get Lara, Alice and herself tickets; she would drive down to the Art Centre and meet me there.

As I joined the queue for tickets, my phone went off. Ruth stated that Alice is 'being stupid', has locked herself in the toilet and is stating that she is not coming now, 'so do not get her a ticket'.

I asked Ruth if she would ask Alice to talk to me; Ruth did so, but Alice was not interested. I told Ruth that Ma is at home at our house, and she could drop Alice with Ma. (Although Ma would have loved to be there to support Hayley.)

Several people along the queue later, and my phone rang again. Ruth told me that Alice wanted to come now, so would I please get her a ticket. I agreed and was glad that Alice had changed her mind.

I was at the head of the queue, when I got yet another call. (My anxiety levels were peaked by the constant attention brought to myself with my phone ringing every other minute.) Ruth stated that due to Alice's behaviour, she was dropping Alice at my home to stay with Ma and told me not to get her a ticket. There was not much I could do about the situation, but I resolved to buy Alice a ticket any way.

I bought the tickets, in the hope that Alice would show up alongside Ruth despite her last call, and went to find a seat. I texted Hayley to let her know where we would be and wished her good luck.

Ruth and only Lara arrived 30 minutes late for the show, and I had to leave to give Ruth the tickets. She followed me to our seats and we sat down.

In the break, Ruth had seen someone that she knew and disappeared into the crowd. Hayley and her friends came over to ask if they could have some money to buy a drink; Lara asked if she could go with Hayley. I gave Hayley and Lara £10 and they vanished. Ruth rematerialized and asked where Lara was, and I explained that Lara was with Hayley getting a drink.

I know that this is sounding like a magic show but, wait for it, drum roll, please… Ruth then disappeared once again.

As if by magic, Lara and Ruth returned, and sat down. After a few moments, Lara turned to me and in a quiet voice, with her bottom lip to one side, she said, 'Dad, our mother ordered herself a drink. She took the £10 off me and gave me the change back.' Lara's bottom lip extended even further as she announced, 'I think you paid for her drink.'

I laughed and told Lara that I didn't mind, but thanks for telling me where my money was going.

At the end of the show, Ruth made no mention of paying for her ticket. I did not expect the money, but the offer would have been appreciated; I've read through her latest statement of condemnation of me just a week ago, and yet she still takes liberties. In court I am portrayed as trouble; a violent man, who is constantly verbally abusive… Well, here we are, apart from Alice, all sitting down, ready to watch Hayley perform.

From a distance, who would believe this family 'from hell' is in the depths of court proceedings?

Left alone, this is how we should have been as parents: getting on in the interests of our children. Ruth's mental health could have been managed, or at least acknowledged within the Family Courts; taken seriously, and followed through with help for that parent. Instead, we have had seven years of Mrs Mason and Smitch Law hounding and manipulating any family situation, and the courts left the door wide open.

Friday 16th

While I was waiting for Lara to come out of her class, one of Lara's friends' mum, Sophie, came over to me. We exchanged some small talk before she said she was sorry to bring this up, but Ruth had sat next to her in the children's assembly yesterday. Ruth has been saying to several parents that I am a 'drug dealer' and her children were not safe around me or my home.

Sophie laughed and said, 'You're not a drug dealer, are you?'

It was a strange conversation to be having in the school playground, but I assured Sophie I have nothing to do with drugs – I looked around furtively and told Sophie to meet me behind the bicycle shed in ten minutes, and we both laughed.

Sophie's children are almost the same age as Hayley, Alice and Lara respectively, and they have all been round to play/sleepover and vice versa for years – at both Ruth's and my home. Consequently, Sophie told me she did not believe some random accusation about my character, and she replied to Ruth, 'All three of my daughters go round and have sleepovers at Dean's with Hayley, Alice and Lara and there have never been any problems of any kind.'

Ruth's allegation is untrue and totally detrimental to my credibility with other parents within school, despite it being false. This is not the first time Ruth has made allegations to other parents about my behaviour and character; this is just a continuation of Ruth's determination to lie, deceive and discredit my name and character in anyway and with anyone. There's nothing I can do about it because she can say damning remarks with no consequences, and the jury of peers, which is predominantly mothers on the playground, cast their judgement.

Once again, I am concerned that Lara's childhood and social development with her school friends has constantly been threatened by Ruth's false and misleading comments and statements about me.

This is the world I live in: it was only yesterday Ruth and I were sitting next to each other, almost clinking our glasses, as Ruth threw her wine down her neck.

Sunday 18th

It was around 9.30 at night, and Hayley, Lara and myself had gone to bed. The house phone rang and Alice asked if she could come over to pick up her history book for school. I said of course and asked how she was getting here.

Alice replied that her mother is bringing her.

I got up and waited until 20 past 10 before Alice walked through the door, did not return my hello, got her book and left.

Dean Marlo

Melissa still writes to me

19 March

Firstly, I enclose a copy of the order made on the 12th March, for your information.

I also enclose a document to be filled out for the Legal Services, together with a copy marked as such and on which I have handwritten notes to help you in completing the original. Please do your best with this form. I have already filled some bits in on it. If you need to see me about it, please contact me. Alternatively, we could discuss any query relating to this form on the phone.

I am also communicating with your accountant about the form that is needed from him for the Legal Services Commission. It is my proposal that we use these forms not only to try to obtain you funding now, for the remainder of the case, but to rectify the previous revocation of your certificate. You will see that there is a schedule of assistance that I have prepared and which is attached to the back of the document I have provided you.

Also enclosed is a letter of authority for you to please complete with your GP details, sign and date and return to me, so that I may obtain your medical records from your GP and photocopy them to forward to the psychologist, in accordance with the court order 12th March 2007.

Despite having nothing to hide in my medical records, I still feel it is Mrs Mason prolonging the game she is playing – I am only fortunate that Melissa has been so understanding.

The financial cost is another I just have to accept, as the court has ordered it.

Northview School Action

20 March

Dear Mr Marlo,

Alice's review is now due and in preparation we are gathering current information on her progress in all areas of the school. Alice will be asked to complete a review form.

Alice will be reviewed on Thursday 26th April. If you would like the opportunity to come into the school on that date and be involved in this review please telephone the Learning Support Administrator, who will organise a convenient time.

Yours sincerely,

Dean Marlo

Trouble's never far behind

20 – 21 March

Tuesday 20th
Ruth arranged for Hayley, Alice and Heather, Alice's friend, to go clothes shopping at Tesco after school.

When Hayley got home, she told me about the trip.

When they arrived at Tesco, Alice went off with her friend while Hayley chose some clothes and went into the changing rooms. Hayley heard someone having a go at someone, so she changed and came out of the room. Ruth, Alice and Heather were being asked to leave the shop, by the store manager and a security guard.

Ruth was shouting, 'My daughter is in the changing room.'

Hayley caught up with them as they were being escorted out and they got into Ruth's car. As they drove out of the car park and down the road, the next minute the police had flashed their blue lights and pointed through the window for Ruth to pull over.

Hayley said that it was so embarrassing as the police took everyone's name, and read Ruth, Alice and Heather the riot act; the police stated to her mother that the manager told them that if this type of incident ever happens again, then Ruth will end up being banned from the store.

Wednesday 21st
Ruth picked up Lara from school for tea and dropped her home at 8.15pm. It amazes me how much Lara has learned already, and the details she gives about each kitten.

Dear Mr Rowe,

22 March

I was pleased and relieved in February to receive the report prepared by Mrs Sanders the child psychologist. In her report she recommended that all three children should remain with me.

Melissa told me that on the 16th of February 2007 there was to be a hearing covering Mrs Sanders's report; this was to be with legal representatives only. After this hearing, Melissa phoned me and stated Judge Yergin made it clear that there were to be no more court hearings, bar the final hearing on March 12th, and that the children were to continue living with their father.

(Hoo-ray! Hoo-ray!)

On the 7th March 2007, Melissa phoned and informed me that Ms Hyde was contesting Mrs Sanders' report and the judge at the hearing would have no alternative but to send the case to the High Court. The next day, Melissa called again; she assured me she would come to the hearing to give advice, but she thought that with a good barrister, several issues could be dealt with.

Having endured listening to misleading and untrue allegations about myself and my ability to be a good parent for too long, I asked a friend for a loan to instruct a barrister. The cost was £800 plus VAT.

On the 12th March 2007, I met Melissa and Mr Carey, my barrister, at the court.

We were all called in and the judge said that he hoped to close these proceedings today, however he believed that Ms Hyde wanted her day in court. (And so we were ordered to give Ms Hyde her day in the High Court.) The judge also removed Hayley from the order, which is what Hayley wanted.

After the hearing, I overheard Mrs Mason speaking to the children's legal representative, where she asked, 'Do you know what dates you are available? As you heard, the case from hell is going to need two days in London.'

I asked Mrs Mason what she meant by 'the case from hell', and she apologised and said what she had meant to say was 'this difficult case'.

This was very unprofessional conduct by Mrs Mason in the heart of the family court building, and is just another example of her uncaring and unscrupulous behaviour – this is the attitude that has been shown throughout proceedings. Never mind the fact it has always been Smitch Law's and Mrs Mason's hostile attitude that has continued to shape the road our family's case has been on.

I have, as any honest person and caring parent would, stood up for my children's welfare and stability, and I believe that these people and the system have let down three children.

It is quite clear that these people have lied and misled to suit themselves. This I first raised awareness of to the Law Society in 2002; Mrs Mason and Smitch Law's position has not changed.

Please understand that I am not deliberately bringing up the past, I am trying to express to you that as a person and a parent, I do not believe that we deserve Mrs Mason referring to our family as a 'case from hell', not when Ms Hyde with Mrs Mason's playbook dragged us there!

I enclose only several reasons why I feel that I cannot accept this unprofessional behaviour and disregard to my children.

On many occasions, Judge Baxter made me feel as uncomfortable as he could, and his attitude towards me as a caring father was as disgraceful in 2000, as it was flippant in 2006. He has continually been downright rude, criticizing and he denounced the effort that I have shown my children, Ms Hyde and the Family Courts over the years.

I still condemn Judge Baxter for his behaviour and attitude towards Mrs Millar in January 2004.

I would also say that due to Judge Baxter's attitude and behaviour, he has not helped overall in his job to safeguard three children's lives.

In June 2006, I applied to the courts to prevent Ms Hyde from turning up at our home, at her will and being abusive, aggressive and violent. I wanted nothing more from applying for an injunction than peace of mind and to be able to feel safe from the verbal and physical abuse that Ms Hyde continues to unleash on our homes, as well as towards our children and myself.

At the hearing on 21st June 2006, Judge Baxter stated that he did not feel that there was any danger of things getting worse and that he would see both parties on 23rd June 2006.

Back in court on the 23rd June 2006, my barrister explained to Judge Baxter that Hayley and Alice have not had proper weekend contact with their mother due to violence used against them, however Lara still went for contact; he stated that the problem was with Ms Hyde's ability to control herself, which has caused problems in the past.

Judge Baxter stated that he would deal with that on the assumption that there is no need for the parties to meet, or communicate without solicitors. Again, I do not believe this was the right position for Judge Baxter to have taken.

Judge Baxter looked at the photographic evidence that I had provided; he mocked my pictures, as if going berserk in front of your children, causing £550 worth of damage to a van door and defacing the brickwork on a rented property, was a joke.

After the incident of the 31st March 2006, when Hayley was taken to the ground by her throat, Hayley and Alice made it clear to me that they did not want to stay over with their mother.

I do want my children to have a good relationship with their mother – with the court unwilling to implement help for Ms Hyde, the children take it upon themselves to introduce boundaries for contact with her. While I think it is something my daughters should not have to do, I commend them for being willing to try with their mother despite Ms Hyde never showing any form of acknowledgement or change.

Once more in a family court building that I entered for *help*, I found that it was me being held reasonable for Ms Hyde's actions; on this occasion, it was also Ms Hyde's behaviour towards Hayley and Alice that Ms Hyde and Judge Baxter twisted the truth of.

As Judge Baxter had turned the hearing for an injunction against further criminal damage occurring at my property into several family court issues, it was an injustice that Judge Baxter did not allow my barrister or myself reply to his unfounded comments and beliefs.

I know it is a long process to go through it all, but I reiterate to you in my letter today: my children have all been through this before, and it is an unsettling and unsure time for any child to have in their lives.

Quite clearly, one cannot base any truth or fact in what Smitch Law's letters state. (After all, a solicitor is acting on behalf of their client, and are only repeating what their client is telling them). Anyone can go into a solicitor (especially if Legal Aid funded) and have a letter written to someone about something that did not happen.

The proof is in the evidence; police incident numbers; neighbours' testimonies; photos; witnesses.

I believe that in this case Judge Baxter's inability to 'judge' with some common decency is quite clear; Judge Baxter's assumptions were immoral and insulting, not only to me but also to my children and the years of abuse, from all quarters, we have endured.

At the end of the hearing in June, Judge Baxter adjourned, and asked Ms Hyde to provide an undertaking not to visit my home. Ms Hyde stated to the Judge that she wanted an undertaking as well.

Judge Baxter stated to my barrister, 'Your client is shaking his head, however with cross undertakings it will provide a balance between these two people who are as bad as each other.'

I believe that time and time again I have shown my ability to act in an honest and decent manner, regardless of the provocations Ms Hyde has come up with.

I was only shaking my head, Mr Rowe; I was not shouting or using foul language, I was not scratching the brickwork on someone's house or causing criminal damage to someone's vehicle.

The real issue was Ms Hyde's disgraceful behaviour brought to our home, the criminal damage, which was carried out in front of the children, and not about encouraging Ms Hyde and Smitch Law to make further unsubstantiated claims against me, or further court applications. I want to get on with my children's lives.

It was another opportunity to ensure help for Ms Hyde; Judge Baxter is aware of our case, as in 2000, he himself had stated that with regard to Ms Hyde's mental health condition, reoccurrence 'wasn't a case of if, it was a case of when'. He should have understood that what had unfolded and had been brought to his attention, was one incident of many, where Ms Hyde's mental health condition was influencing her unacceptable behaviour. While the Family Courts many not have been equipped to deal with someone with a mental health condition, they were in a position to assist in finding organisations that may be able to help Ms Hyde.

(I thought I was in the Twilight Zone, watching a judge inspect the boot prints indented into my van door in a photograph, and ask me what he's supposed to be looking at. Even when I've got the police report and confirmation Ms Hyde has been cautioned, I am made to feel like I'm blowing all of this out of proportion. I provide for our daughters with that van. It is only the love of my children that gives me the strength to endure the constant erosion I find myself entangled in.)

As you well know, I wrote to the DCA about Judge Baxter's attitude in 2004 – the times may change but the hammer stays the same. In February 2004, in my first letter I stated that Judge Baxter has made it quite clear that this is not about three young children; this is about a piece of paper; *his* court order. Judge Baxter showed no interest to how the children had been getting on with their residency and schedule, and no interest in their stability within his proposed schedule.

Tell me, why am I still writing to you about Judge Baxter in 2007? Because, I know I have better things to do, and I cannot figure out why my family's situation continues to be tumultuous.

No clear and honest investigation was ever carried out concerning the performance of magistrate Mrs Jackson and this is evident in the DCA's letter of 24th June 2003. They state the opposite to the police and the Headteacher of Riverbank Primary; the DCA felt justified to lie to me in their letter and dismiss any inappropriate behaviour on Mrs Jackson's behalf.

Mrs Jackson, standing magistrate, wrote a letter of complaint, based on what three at risk children told a children's advocate. Upon receiving the complaint, the advocate who the children had seen on several occasions, who was polite and professional, was replaced. I'm sure Mrs Jackson never gave it another thought, but Hayley, Alice and Lara could not understand why their advocate changed.

Mrs Jackson uses her position as an entitlement to act immorally and, by protecting her daughter who needs help, not only dismissed the abuse her own grandchildren had suffered but also condemned their father in the process.

Mrs Jackson's false allegations came to light in every statement she put before the court, however was most prominent when she spoke to Mr Ellwood, the Cafcass officer. At the hearing on the 25th June 2004, Mr Ellwood stated that Mrs Jackson had, in a phone call to him, first informed him she was a magistrate, then stated 'Mr Marlo is a psychopath'.

All I wanted after the separation of my family was to see my children and reassure them that I was there for them. That was it!

Despite all of the above, I have got on with my children and the Family Courts' sole residency order.

In February 2004, I wrote a letter of complaint to the Bar Council, regarding the behaviour and performance of the barrister Mr Ween in the Family Courts.

By April, the commissioner had decided my complaint was to be investigated. On the 10th May, I was notified by the Bar Council that Mr Ween would be sworn in as a District Judge on the 17th May, therefore falling outside the Bar Council's jurisdiction. They sent me a letter on the 17th, stating that if I wished to proceed with my complaint, I should address it to the DCA.

When I wrote to the DCA, and on the 23rd June received a reply, I was informed my complaint had nothing to do with them. This went backwards and forwards between the DCA and the Bar Council for several months until the DCA finally decided it was their responsibility.

Mrs Mason sent the Professional Conduct and Complaints Committee a letter that was misleading about my complaint against Mr Ween. She managed to condemn me and exonerate Mr Ween on the notes of someone who wasn't even in the room.

On the 21st October 2004, I received a letter from the DCA stating that there was no case of inappropriate behaviour by neither Mr Ween nor Judge Baxter.

The truth is a paralegal witnessed and heard Mr Ween blatantly lie to me.

At the hearing of the 25th July 2004, another of Ms Hyde's barristers stated to the judge that I had made many complaints about several people and all of my complaints had been investigated. This statement by a barrister to the judge was not true – I didn't receive the letter of dismissal for two complaints until October – and was deliberately misleading in a hearing for sole residency; what relevance did my complaints have to the hearing for my children's welfare?

So-called professionals in family law have clearly forgotten that they have a duty to 'children' and to ensure that their behaviour is in children's best interests.

Despite all that has happened, I have got on with my children and the Family Courts sole residency order.

In 2002, Smitch Law wrote to the Legal Aid Department questioning my entitlement for Legal Aid. This was regarding the family court hearing for joint residency of Hayley, Alice and Lara. My solicitor at the family court told me that I would have to pay £800 for representation at the hearing that followed my Legal Aid being suspended. I had to agree despite having financial difficulties at the time.

Due to Smitch Law, on behalf of their client, my legal aid was wrongly rescinded causing me extra worry and financial hardship.

Once again in 2006, Smitch Law placed uncertainty in my family's lives by falsely challenging my receipt of Legal Aid. Not only did I have the worry of more court appearances, but also the strain of having to pay for any representation.

I am unable to bring home a full pay packet because I am a single parent, with limited time; I am fortunate to organize my work around my children's schooling, however a one–day job takes me two–days.

I know that we are not going to get rich, but I am trying to bring a standard of living to our family. I am also trying to set an example to my children, concerning working. I have worked to raise my three daughters. Once again, I felt that I was being unfairly punished for this. I could not earn the sort of money needed for sufficient representation, and the sheer volume of court hearings would have sunk anyone's savings or driven them into debt. It is unjust to expect someone to foot the bill for legal representation when the hearings are a farce; no evidence of wrong doing on my part has ever been produced. Even when court experts provide reports, it is not enough to overcome Ms Hyde's ability to pursue applications.

I am trying to raise my three daughters, to which I am told is not easy; yet I feel persecuted, victimised and bullied, by the aggressive attitude towards my family's wellbeing and myself.

It was due to Mrs Mason's overzealous behaviour and attitude, and her letter to the Legal Services Commission, again resulting in my Legal Aid being withdrawn, which created this next chapter of the family court nightmare: I found myself in the Family Courts agreeing to pay half for the Chartered Clinical Psychologist's report, which was estimated at £5,000. I explained I did not know where I was going to get the money from, but felt under pressure to sign anyway.

On this occasion, Smitch Law brought nothing more than financial instability into my life and when this did not achieve what they wanted, they simply headed back to court and manipulated a judge to suit their client's needs.

I believe that there are many two–parent families that only just mange to be financially sound week after week. Smitch Law would be well aware of the distress that their letter to the Legal Service Commission would cause. I do fear that the legal bills will result in placing me into a bankruptcy situation.

I was hounded by Smitch Law (through Melissa, who was not representing me but still in the trenches) for confirmation that I would pay the £2,500. I told Melissa that I could not write a letter of confirmation to Smitch Law, as I was not capable of earning that sort of money within a short–term basis. Melissa told me that she would relay this to Smitch Law.

Several days later and out of the blue, Melissa informed me Ms Hyde had applied for an emergency hearing. On the 23rd October 2006, Ms Hyde withdrew her application for sole residency and Smitch Law requested the judge put the cost of the report onto Ms Hyde's Legal Aid. Judge Neely agreed.

What concerns me, is the orchestration Smitch Law, a solicitor, can carry out not only within the family court building but throughout the entire process. They had a busy month, organising for my legal aid to be revoked, for an unnecessary child psychologist report to be obtained – that Ms Hyde has now contested as it did not rule in her favour – then for the public purse to fund said report and the application to contest it!

(Please do not get me wrong, I do appreciate and am grateful that the worry of trying to earn or find that sort of money has been removed from the back of my head.)

You will remember the court order of October 2000, which devised a schedule of contact under joint residency. Despite the division of residence set out to alternate, there were many issues with keeping to and deciding on the schedules, due to Ms Hyde's demands.

A six weekly residency schedule, as ordered by the Family Courts, had turned into a schedule where the children were staying with one parent for 14 nights and 61 nights with the other. I was happy to have my children for this extended period, but it evidently did not bring consistency to the contact order; several changes were simply to organise Ms Hyde's holiday arrangements, which Smitch Law were more than happy to insert themselves into.

In November 2001, I went back to court because all three children had expressed their thoughts to Social Services about their mother's inability to care for them and incidents of abuse.

Smitch Law have tried to dictate and aggravate every existing court order, and have sent hundreds of letters to Melissa and myself that have been full of false allegations and pure lies; Smitch Law have tried on many occasions to threaten me with written comments.

Even now, they will not take the sensible and moral action to advise their client to concentrate on doing the right thing for her children.

On to the latest proceedings, March 12th 2007 (and on and on and on):

Once again, it appears to have been forgotten the reason family court proceedings started up again in 2006: Hayley and Alice's contact with their mother following incidents of abuse and criminal damage.

The children clearly need stability and consistency, but most importantly to get on with their lives, without court proceedings in the background.

The false allegations that were made by Ms Hyde in her most recent statement, overseen by Mrs Mason, have no evidence to corroborate them – and I simply must endure this?

One last example; Judge Baxter permitted Ms Hyde to shout across the courtroom, 'When the children are ill, he does not phone the schools!'

I shook my head in disbelief and was belittled, yet Ms Hyde is yelling across the courtroom.

It is completely untrue, and both schools relayed I always inform them of absences in the child psychologist's report.

I'm writing to you to inform you what it is like, in the underbelly of the system, to expose the unjust, unhelpful and toxic attitude that surrounds family law.

('Dieu et mon droit', meaning 'God and my right' sounds great on the family crest, until your God is just another human and your rights are debatable.)

My situation now is that Ms Hyde appears to be dictating what is going to happen with Alice and Lara's residence. Alice needs to settle down with a healthy routine at home and at school; Lara needs to not have the interference Hayley and Alice have had in their lives. In itself, it worries and concerns me.

(If anyone gets to call this a case from hell, can I at least throw my name in the pot? Sincerely, no one wants the court involvement to be over more than me.)

Yours respectfully…

Dean Marlo

Hindsight is a bastard

Unfortunately, at the beginning of the year, there were arguments each morning as to whose turn it was to clean out the litter tray. Alice started staying at her mother's and her cat has been left to myself, Hayley and Lara to look after.

Lara's cat was borderline hostile and I could see that she was probably not old enough to handle the care that this particular cat needed. Hayley and Lara looked after their cats, but not without some complaint on occasions. I phoned Alice and told her that we all needed to have a house meeting about the cats, so would she please come home and discuss this.

I arranged the house meeting (Alice did not turn up). I told Hayley and Lara that I thought it would be a good idea to take Alice's cat back to the Cat Rescue Centre, Lara stated that she would like to take her cat back too; Hayley asked if she could keep hers.

I phoned the rescue centre and the woman stated that the kittens would have to be re–homed together.

I apologised to Hayley and Lara and told them that it was bad parenting by me, to get pets and then rehome them.

I called Alice and when she didn't pick up I left a voicemail explaining the decision was that it would be best for the cats to be rehomed; it would be a couple of days for me to have time to take them back, so she can come home and say goodbye. I also texted her the same, in case she ignored the voicemail.

From Ruth

27 March

Dear Dean,
Over the last three months I have incurred considerable expenses looking after Alice:
School dinners –
January 2 weeks @ £2.50 5 days/week – £25.00
February 3 weeks @ £2.50 5 days/week – £37.50
March 4 weeks @ £2.50 5 days/week – £50.00
Total – £112.50
For the days that Alice has been off school due to sickness and two days exclusion, I am still providing a proper meal at home and have had to take time off work; none of the expenses I am listing include medicine, sanitary towels, tights, vitamin tablets or any money toward the cost of home meals, clothing and general expenses incurred in general day to day living.
The necessary items that I have had to purchase are as follows:
School blazer – £29.00
Haircut – £6.00
School shoes – £12.00
School skirts – £13.00
Mobile top up – £10.00
Pocket money @ £8.00 per week – £72.00
As you are in receipt of Child Benefit for Alice, I think it is fair and reasonable that this is passed to me, as discussed with both myself and Alice with you. I suggest you give it directly to Alice at the beginning of the week so that wherever she is staying the night she has money for her school dinners.
I do not receive any tax credits for Alice, I think it is fair that I do.
I have spoken with the Child Benefit Agency and the Tax Credit Office, and they expect in respect of Hayley, Alice and Lara when they are spending their half–terms and holidays or extra time with me and I am the one feeding, clothing and entertaining them, that you pass over the money to me for this period of time.
In the last two years and seven months, you have never given me any money at all.
Yours faithfully,

It is amazing that after well over half a million words, I could write them all again in response to letters like this. Not that I'd be saying anything new; I keep shouting into this void in the hopes that someone can understand, really, what my family are going through.

I shouldn't have to explain that Ruth has, on paper, every other weekend contact and half school holidays; she has no excuse not to be working. Regardless, I have always paid for whatever receipt or letter Ruth has been presented to me. I have not asked in the past *ever* for money from Ruth, not even when it would have made it easier for me to provide for our children.

And the fact she wants Alice on the frontlines of transferring Child Benefit to her!

I'm not a child psychologist, but you don't need to be one to see how Ruth is messing with all of our children's heads.

In response, I wrote a letter and included the cheque for half the amount, as requested:

Please find enclosed a cheque for £58.50 to cover for Alice's Child Benefit, from the 1st March to the 5th April.

I shall ensure you receive Alice's Child Benefit once a week.

Yours sincerely…

Mrs Mason writes to the Child Psychologist

30 March

We refer to previous correspondence and enclose herewith a copy of the order made by his honour Judge Yergin on the 12th March 2007.

We would refer you to paragraph 6 of the order and would ask that you read the copy medical records of Mr Marlo and the children, and, if necessary, please provide an addendum report to confirm if your conclusions or recommendations are affected. We have already provided you with copies of the children's medical notes and we understand that Melissa Brenna will forward you Mr Marlo's notes direct.

You will see that there is to be a two-day hearing with regard to this matter and you are required to attend Court on the first day of the hearing.

We do have your dates of availability but it would be helpful if you could provide us with an estimate for your fees in attending that hearing and preparing the addendum report.

(Amongst all the emotional upset I am feeling, I dared to imagine how I would have felt if I had been forced to pay half of the cost for a now debunked psychologist report…)

What do they expect to find in my medical records? That I had escaped from Area 51? Am I related to the 'Boston strangler'? Is there a list of several service wounds from my time in the SAS?

There is nothing in my medical records that will change the outcome of the report, and Smitch Law are clutching at straws, with all the cost that comes with it, and it has nothing to do Ms Hyde's ability to care for the children or my own.

This amended report and a court appearance will be thousands of pounds taken from Legal Aid. Smitch Law and Mrs Mason requested the report on their client's behalf to be paid for by Legal Aid, now Mrs Mason will use Legal Aid to bring Mrs Sanders to court, to cross-examine her.

It's a circus.

Smitch Law and Mrs Mason show no principles or care towards the family and solely act in the interests of themselves, and secondly their client, who has shown in the past that she is not able to look after the children in a manner that is consistently acceptable. Mrs Mason and the Family Courts know this, because it is written in this report, and all the reports previously! Yet they continue to influence any part of this family, searching, for some reason, for anything to excessively criticize my ability as a parent in a way that is harassing, detrimental and has a direct negative impact on my family's lives.

As a family law firm, Smitch Law and Mrs Mason are acting like a dictator and are facilitated by public funded Legal Aid, which is shameful.

Miles away

29 March – 4 April

Thursday 29th

Alice popped home before school, the children said a final goodbye to the cats and, as requested by Ruth, went to hers after school.

Friday 30th

Ruth, Hayley, Alice and Lara fly to Spain.

Monday 2nd

I received a phone call from Ruth, from Spain; Ruth explained that Alice has locked herself in the toilet, and she asked me to phone Alice and speak to her. I immediately called Alice's mobile, but got no pick up. I also sent her several texts that she did not reply to.

Calling Ruth back, I told her that I couldn't get through. Ruth went to the toilet door, told Alice that I was on the phone and asked her to talk to me. I heard Alice shout 'go away'.

I spoke to Hayley and Lara, who were happy to chat but did not say why Alice had shut herself in the toilet. Lara handed the phone back to Ruth; I said that she should be calm, give Alice 20 minutes to settle down and then try again. I told Ruth to ring me back if she needed to and that I would text Alice to let her know I would call her in an hour.

Shortly after ending the call with Ruth, I received a text from Alice asking me to phone her; through sobs, Alice asked me to come and get her. I had to gently explain I couldn't come to Spain. She said she'd get her mother to put her on a plane, and I could meet her at the airport. Again, I told Alice that she is on holiday, she needs to calm down and resolve the issue with her mother.

An hour later, I phoned Ruth and she told me that all three children were happy playing and doing their own thing.

Wednesday 4th

At 11.30am, Ruth phoned again and aggressively asked if I allow Hayley to tell me to 'fuck off'. I told Ruth of course I do not allow Hayley to swear – not that I have heard Hayley swear anyway – and Ruth responded that I better phone my daughter and tell her that she cannot say it to her mother.

I asked Ruth to pass Hayley the phone; Hayley came on crying. She told me that she knew that it was wrong, but her mother was allowing Alice to do whatever she wanted; whereas she and Lara were not allowed to do the same. I reminded Hayley that swearing at her mother would not change the situation, and told her to try and enjoy the rest of the holiday, as she would be home soon.

Being a parent is already an emotional roller coaster – why is it so difficult for the Family Courts to accept I want my children to be happy? They are on a family holiday and receiving calls like this… I am worried about what is going on and feel even more helpless as they are out of the country.

I try not to allow my anxieties to fester and linger over the fact that before I met Ruth, it was while travelling abroad she experienced two mental health episodes – the way the Family Courts and Mrs Mason have treated Ruth's condition (i.e. by not treating it) has left me feeling unable to call out Ruth's behaviour, not to ostracise her but to get support for her, or defend my children when incidents and situations escalate or are abnormal. I question whether I should be worried, when I know that Ruth's mania leaves her unable to cope with three children, and I question whether I should be doing more for Hayley, Alice and Lara's sake, despite having no clue what it would be.

Who's driving this flying umbrella?

7 – 12 April

Saturday 7th

I left for work at 6.30am and returned home at 6pm. As I drove down the road where I live, I saw Lara and Ruth standing on my drive. I pulled up and said hello, admittedly confused, and Ruth told me that Alice was inside.

I must confess, I had no idea that the children were changing residence at 6pm this Saturday. I know that I should have been aware what was on Ruth's schedule for her contact, and therefore should have considered that because we are running on Ruth's timetable, then things will not be straight forward, normal or as set out in any court order.

Ruth said goodbye to Lara and drove off.

Once inside, I asked Lara if she thought it strange that she wasn't with her mother for the weekend, and Lara explained her mother is going to a party.

It is amazing to me, that even with the undertakings she forced me to agree with, Ruth sees no problem in arriving at my home unannounced. Naturally, I wish we were a cordial split family, but time proves to me again and again that we're not, not with Ruth at the helm. I have no problems with Ruth dropping our children at my home as long as she behaves, and informing me beforehand would be appreciated.

Alice came out of her room to tell me that her mother is taking her to London for her birthday. I acknowledged this and said perhaps Nan or I could give her money for her birthday to spend in London.

This week, Alice stayed at home on the 7th and 8th.

Sunday 8th

My vision of holidays in the car, due to the problems we've had and the children growing up so quickly, have never come to fruition; I decided to sell the company car and get a smaller one. The garage gave me a part exchange, offering £900 for the car – as I was leaving, I thought about the Legal Aid Commission taking under advisement from Mrs Mason, relying on Ms Hyde's estimate that the car is worth £8,000.

Monday 9th

At breakfast, Alice asked if she could sleepover at a friend's tonight; I knew Alice's friend and said yes, asking for the parent's number to check it's alright with them. Alice then stated that she is staying with her mother tomorrow, so she would see me on her birthday.

I asked Alice if she would be celebrating her birthday with Hayley, Lara, Nan and me at home (as we have done, every other year); Alice replied that her mother is taking her shopping in London on her birthday, and they would not be back until late, so she will pop in Wednesday morning and celebrate with us on Thursday.

I told Alice that it would be nice for her to spend her birthday with her sisters, Nan and me, as she can go shopping with her mother anytime but we only get birthdays every other year together. Alice stated, 'You have not organized anything for my birthday.'

It was true; besides a meal at Murdock's, seeing if Alice wanted any friends to stay over, and providing food and music, Alice hadn't given me much chance. I reminded Alice that I hadn't seen her, otherwise I would have been able to organise something.

Ignoring what I said, Alice asked for her birthday money now, so she could spend it shopping in London, and explained she was leaving soon; her mother was dropping Alice at her friend's house. I told Alice when she comes home tomorrow, I'd give her the money with her card. Alice agreed and was out the door.

That evening, around 8.30pm, I received a call from Ruth where she was verbally abusive and told me that Hayley had been over asking to borrow a sanitary towel. Ruth stated, 'You are a useless father and parent. You should be giving me the child benefit and tax credits for Hayley and Alice!'

I put the phone down.

I have tried to cultivate an environment at home where if the children need something, they are comfortable to come to me and ask for it. I have been out for chocolate, hot water bottles and sanitary products for Hayley in the past. I think Hayley was just using a sanitary towel while she was over to see her mum, and once again Ruth has come up with a narrative wherein I am, as usual, a 'useless father'.

Ruth tried phoning several more times but I didn't have the energy to pick it up.

Tuesday 10th

The children have two weeks off school and at breakfast, Lara told me that her mother had arranged with her to go around today and see the kittens. I told her that was alright with me. Lara said her mother stated she was going to call me to agree a time. While we waited for Ruth, we played some football and decided that I would call after lunch if we still hadn't heard from her. With the football match over, Lara sat down to play a game on the computer.

11.30am, Ruth phoned, starting the conversation by telling me it was rude to hang up on her (but not rude to call someone useless?). Deciding not to comment, I asked what time she wanted Lara to come over. Ruth stated that she wants Lara over tomorrow for tea; I told Ruth that Lara thought it was today. Ruth began shouting, 'You cannot just drop Lara off without telling me!'

I told Ruth that Lara informed me this morning we were waiting for her call, otherwise I was going to ring her. (I didn't say that it is also Alice's birthday tomorrow, so we would ordinarily have plans, and isn't she supposed to be in London with Alice?)

Asking again for when Ruth wanted to meet at the bottle bank, Ruth replied, 'It is totally unfair to spring this on me but I suppose Lara can come today. You can drop Lara off to me at 2pm and pick her up at 8pm.'

So much for injunctions, court orders and judge's heartfelt remarks.

Lara came back from her mother's with this letter:

Dean,

Alice's b–day present: Nikon camera

£130 – Camera

£7 – Memory card

£7 – Camera case

Alice has given me £20 towards the camera.

Give me a ring to sort it out.

In response, I prepared an envelope to drop through her door:

To Ruth,

Re: Alice's birthday present

Please find enclosed, a cheque for £72 towards Alice's birthday presents.

Yours sincerely…

Wednesday 11th

Thinking Alice was probably having a lay-in, I texted her happy birthday when I woke up (6:30am) and phoned her at 10.30am. Alice did not pick up or reply.

I spent the day with Lara; Hayley had gone into town with some friends. At 3pm, Hayley called me and said she had just seen Alice.

So much for London, communication and well wishes; I didn't see or hear from Alice on her birthday, and neither did Ma, who had also called Alice, and missed her when she came round today.

The presents and cards sat unopened; the cake uneaten.

Thursday 12th

Again, I tried to contact Alice (as well as through Ruth) to no avail. I knew Ma was coming down today, so I booked an appointment to look at a job just out of town. When I returned, Ma told me that Ruth had been on the phone and had asked Lara several times if she wanted to go round hers; Lara repeatedly told her mother that she did not want to go.

I don't think Ruth, or either parent, should interfere with holiday contact in such a way. Ruth constantly chops and changes the dates and times to suit herself, and bar seeing the kittens because they are growing up quickly, I don't think it's helpful, given our family's history with schedules, to not keep to the stability of the court order. I was only out for a couple of hours, and while Hayley and Alice have a sporadic visiting schedule with their mother, it doesn't help the situation or come across as normal family behaviour because of the disruption Ruth causes around it.

Breaking bad

14 - 16 April

Saturday 14th

At 12pm, Alice called, saying that she is going to pop in and could she have her birthday money, as she, her friend and her mother are going to London. She didn't explain why she hadn't gone to London as planned on her birthday, or why she didn't come home or let us know what was going on.

Alice told me that for her birthday she had gone to a disco called 'Stem' and that her mother picked her up at 12am – bearing in mind it was Alice's 13th birthday.

In January this year, Hayley had asked to go to the same disco for her 15th, and I had said yes, but I would pick her up at 10.30pm. (Due to changes in her friend group at school, Hayley opted to have a quiet one in the end.)

Once again, I don't think Ruth is setting Alice healthy boundaries, and she is certainly not supporting the boundaries I set for Hayley, who is 2 years older than Alice.

(I do myself no favours; however, it is difficult. I am not the sort of person to want to withhold anything from my children. Should Alice be able to walk through the door, give me a hug, open her cards, collect her gift money and head back out? No. However, do I want to mention Alice's attitude and kick off a cycle wherein Alice ignores me, Ruth is on the line calling me a terrible father, which could possibly lead to a 'van door incident' and the atmosphere for everyone is more on edge? No.)

Sunday 15th

With kittens being officially ruled as a bad idea, we have been discussing getting a dog. However, with Alice's movements all over the place, there hasn't been time for us to organise things.

Just before midday, Ruth phoned and asked Lara if she would like to go round hers; Lara said no. At 12.30pm, Ruth called my mobile and told me she will be dropping Alice off at 3pm – at 4.15pm, Alice came through the door.

I told Alice we needed a 'house meeting' as we both needed to know what is going on in her life and the whole family needs confirmation as to what she wants to do and where she wants to live. Alice explained that she did want to come home, but her mother is being nice to her. I said to Alice that it must be good and that I am happy for her, but she still needs stability and both her mother and I need to know where she is living.

This is difficult because unfortunately I believe, and I also believe Alice fears, that Ruth's current attitude towards her will not last. However, I have always encouraged and backed the children's wishes. I told Alice that she needs to really think about the situation we have found ourselves in and she needs to be sure as to where she wants to live. The court involvement cannot continue; whatever order is made next will have to stand.

Alice replied, 'If I come home, would I still be allowed to sleepover at my mother's on Wednesdays and weekends when Lara does not go to hers?'

It hurts me when Alice talks about staying at her mother's when Lara is not there; I love my three children equally, and it is sad to see Alice distancing herself from Lara. Over the years, I have always felt more reassured when Hayley, Alice and Lara had contact with their mother, because they were there for each other. They are well aware their mother's behaviour fluctuates from good-to-bad with verbal outbursts and lack of care towards them; both Hayley and Alice mention visiting their mother when Lara is there because they feel protective of her.

I explained to Alice if she does better at school, i.e. getting to school on time, less detentions and at least makes the effort, then of course I have no problem with that.

Finally, I asked Alice if she understood that we all need routine and consistency in our day–to–day lives, and that when I talk to her about her schooling and attitude, it's because I care and want her to be happy. Alice nodded, gave me a hug and disappeared into her bedroom. After 20 minutes, Alice reappeared and announced that she is changing her bedroom around, which involved me once again taking Alice's bunk bed down and putting her old bed back.

Alice fell asleep with her room looking like a hurricane had hit it.

Monday 16th

It was the start of another day. I mentioned the possibility of getting a new dog over breakfast, which everyone was on board with. The children went to school and I headed to work.

Not long into the day, I received a phone call from Northview Grove, who stated Alice is missing from her lesson. I phoned Alice's number but she didn't answer. I phoned Ruth to ask if she had seen Alice, and Ruth replied without concern, 'Alice does not like her maths teacher and is probably hiding in school.'

In disbelief, I replied Alice shouldn't be hiding and missing lessons just because she doesn't get on with her teacher. Alice is well aware that if she has a problem, then she should sit down and talk to one of us about it; Ruth replied, 'She has to me.'

Ruth stated that she has made an appointment with the school and is sorting it out. I asked if she thinks I shouldn't be told about her asking for a meeting at the school regarding Alice.

Ruth replied, 'You did not even know Alice had a problem with this teacher and once again it has been left to the children's mother to support and sort out the children's problems.'

I told Ruth that I haven't had a proper conversation with Alice for several weeks, through Alice's choice; that shouldn't stop Ruth from communicating with me about Alice's education, as I have sole residency. Ruth hung up.

Feeling at a loss, I got on with work before leaving for Lara.

After school, I tried calling Alice again to find out where she is and what she is doing; this is the opposite of what we discussed yesterday. Thankfully, Alice picked up, she stated that she was at her mother's and would be back soon.

At 5.30pm Alice came through the door with one of her friends, asking if they could stay for tea. I agreed; they disappeared into Alice's room.

As I cooked dinner, the house phone rang and it was Ruth asking to speak to Alice. I knocked on Alice's door and handed the phone over. Alice came into the kitchen after the call and stated that her mother has joined a fitness club and is taking her tonight, so would I take her friend home and drop her off at her mother's after. Alice also stated that because they wouldn't get back until late, she would be sleeping round her mother's tonight.

(I know, I'm being organised by a thirteen-year-old to make her plans come to fruition, however – whether or not it is a school night, or that Alice's behaviour at school today hadn't been good, or that while a pleasant experience for Alice, her education is suffering because of her living habits – it is at Ruth's direction. Saying no would achieve two things, Alice would take her friend by the arm and leave, or I would receive a call from Ruth accusing me of 'stopping' Alice from seeing her mother, and Alice would be picked up by Ruth anyway.

I don't know if it is 'teenagerism' – although Hayley isn't like this – or her mother's influence, but I can't seem to get through to Alice that the period of her life right now is important, and that her flitting between homes is serious. Unfortunately, I cannot enforce any form of boundary on Alice without Ruth's support; therein lies the problem.

I have no issue with Alice wanting more contact with her mother, however I believe that Alice's behaviour since she has started doing so has coincided with getting worse, and therefore it is not in her best interests to be with Ruth full-time. Alice is my daughter and I love her so I want her to be home, but also, I want her to be stable and happy, even if that is at her mother's.)

Irrespective of my feelings on the matter, I dropped Alice's friend home and took Alice to her mother's at 7.30pm. Ruth's car wasn't on the drive, nonetheless, Alice didn't comment on it so I waited for Alice to get in the front door, waved goodbye and drove home.

Mrs Mason and Mrs Sanders

16/17 April

16 April

We enclose herewith our firm's cheque in the sum of £4,117.20 in settlement of your invoice, receipt of which please acknowledge.

Now, that is a lot of money for a psychologist report that Mrs Mason had requested and for their client to reject the conclusions of.

17 April

Thank you for your letter dated 30th March concerning the above family. I have received Mr Marlo's medical notes and those of the children. I estimate that reviewing the notes and providing an addendum is likely to take between three to four hours dependent on the contents and relevance of the notes. I can provide this by 27th April 2007.

I attach a current list of available dates to assist with the timetable of the court hearing. My expenses for appearances are £600 a day and preparation at a rate of £100 per hour plus expenses. Do you know which court this case is to be heard at?

It takes 40 hours plus of hard work to make that sort of money a week; it must be nice to have a job which includes extra for expenses.

Northview Hayley again

17 April

Level 3 Intervention/Information Technology
Pupil: Hayley Marlo, 10TU
Dear Mr Marlo,
I am writing to inform you that Hayley's behaviour has warranted a Level 3 intervention. The reason for this decision is, repeated failure to follow reasonable instructions, 20th March 2007, period 3.
As a result, your daughter will need to attend a meeting with the Cluster Group leaders, named above, in the House area on Thursday 19th April 2007 at 3:15pm. This meeting may involve strategies such as completing missed work or discussing consequences of poor behaviour. The maximum duration will be one hour, therefore your daughter will be released by 4:15pm.
Yours sincerely,

Checking in with Hayley after school, she told me it was 'just classroom banter'.

(I am worried that Hayley could fall into the same patterns as Alice, or that this is in response to Alice's behaviour of late. I'm worried that even though a few detentions aren't the end of the world, in the eyes of the next family court judge… Could it be? What does that mean for Lara, if the general statement 'all three children's behaviour is getting worse' rears up again?

Trying to maintain healthy routines

17 – 19 April

Tuesday 17th

It was another day that Alice hadn't come home after school, and as I heard nothing from her, I gave her a call. Alice said she is having tea at her mother's and they are going to the health club tonight; they would not get back until late, so she is sleeping at her mother's again.

Wednesday 18th

Hayley asked if I would write her a note to allow her out of school for lunch on some days. I told Hayley that I didn't think it was a good idea to have an open-pass to come out of school for lunch but, if she lets me know in the mornings that she wants to do so, I will give her a letter of permission to leave on the day. I could tell Hayley wasn't happy, however she gave me a hug and headed to school.

I dropped Lara at Riverbank and went to work. Not long into the morning, Northview Grove called asking why Alice wasn't at school. Sighing to myself, I explained Alice was at her mother's at the moment.

At 7.15pm, Ruth phoned and stated that she was dropping Alice round in 30 minutes… Over an hour later, Alice came home and went straight to bed, evidently exhausted.

Thursday 19th

While we were eating breakfast, Ruth phoned the home phone and asked to speak to Alice; Alice told her mother that she would be ready in ten minutes and passed the phone to Lara. I asked Alice why her mother was picking her up and Alice replied, 'You refuse to drop me and Hayley to school.'

Both Alice and Hayley have friends who live in nearby, and walk further to school.

I have discussed this with Alice before, and she also knows that we have a routine wherein Lara has breakfast and then we do either maths tables, spelling or reading before we leave, as Hayley and Alice did with me when they were younger. I don't believe it would be fair to Lara to disrupt this, just so that I can drive them to school.

(I am a normal parent with a younger child to consider. Northview Grove is a ten-minute walk away and I am not prepared to encourage my children to be lazy.)

Sensing a losing battle, I asked Alice what she is doing this weekend. Alice said that she is sleeping at her mother's Friday and Saturday, and will come home on Sunday.

We finished eating, and Hayley asked if I would write her a note to allow her out of school at lunchtime today. As I wrote Hayley's letter, Alice stated that her mother had written to Northview Grove allowing Alice to come out of school at any lunch period. Hayley asked why she had to get a letter from me every time…

I told Hayley that it is because I care, and I don't want her to get into trouble out of school or get in a habit of not going back. I changed the subject but I could see that Hayley was not impressed.

Just before 8am, Ruth drove to our home and picked Alice up.

Lara came into the kitchen and asked if it was all right to go round her mother's after school and see the kittens, I said no problem. Ruth dropped Lara back at 7.45pm.

(The injunction hearing is another I can add to the list of 'not worth my attendance'; Ruth appears at my door as she pleases.)

Dean Marlo

From the LSC (nail in the coffin)

20 April

Dear Mr Marlo,
We have assessed your income (after outgoings) as £15,369.72.
This means you are not entitled to public funding.
You cannot appeal against this decision. Attached is a copy of the breakdown of assessment. This will show you have we have calculated your means assessment. If you have any queries regarding this, please refer, in the first instance, to the booklet 'Means 1 – The Guide' which you should have received when completing your means assessment forms. This explains what expenses can and cannot be taken into account in your means assessment. If you do not have this booklet, please ask your solicitor for a copy.
If you have further queries, or if you feel we have made a mistake, please write to us with the relevant details and we will review your case. Please provide this information by 4 May 2007. If your circumstances have changed since you completed your assessment forms, we are unable to review your case. If this is the situation and you still require the benefit of public funding, you need to see your solicitor to make a fresh application.
A copy of this letter has been sent to your solicitor.
Yours sincerely,
Regional Director

Assessment Assumptions and Disregards
Because your own disposable leaves you out of scope of legal aid, I have not yet calculated your disposable capital, and I have not taken into account (under CLS Financial Regulation 11(4)(b)) resources made available to you by your mother.
Your 'other' income is one twelfth each of last year's company dividend and the money your company lent you over the last year. We have been given no reason to believe that the next dividend will be less.
Notes
N/A – Not Assessed
If Out of Scope, the Upper Income Limit used during the computation of this assessment was £672.00
This is the figure that you pay should you be required to make a contribution towards your Public Funding, there is a minimum contribution due and so you may see an annual figure indicated above, but this should be ignored if your monthly contribution is nil (i.e., 0.00).

How, when I run a small construction business which has never had the same turnover year-on-year, can I be assessed on last year's dividend?

To be here for my children, I can only work certain hours; the relentless involvement of solicitors and time spent going through the – seemingly endless – family court process, I can't afford to advertise, therefore, the work we carry out is all from recommendation, which has, of course, had a dramatic effect on the company's turnover.

From MP Rowe

20 April

Dear Mr Marlo,
Further to your phone call to my office today, I am writing to confirm that I have written again to the Lord Chancellor concerning your case. A copy of my letter is enclosed for your assistance.
I have also written to your solicitor to offer her any help which she feels I may be able to provide.
The treatment you and your children have received is clearly unacceptable to which the legal system must share responsibility. When I receive responses, I will contact you again. Best wishes.
Yours sincerely,

Dear Lord,
Since separating from his partner, Mr Marlo and his children have been subjected to a long campaign through the legal system by his ex–partner, Ms Hyde.
Because of the efforts of Ms Hyde, with the help of Legal Aid, Mr Marlo and his children have been subjected to a horrendous period. This included Mr Marlo almost becoming bankrupt, as he was not able to receive financial legal support, but also the demands for a psychological report against Mr Marlo, which proved him to be an excellent father.
For your assistance, I enclose a copy of the dossier my constituent has sent me which details a very distressing experience which remains ongoing at considerable public expense.
I would be grateful for an opportunity for Mr Marlo and myself to have a meeting with you, so that you may be aware of the impact and consequences on families whereby an ex–member may literally make their lives hell through the legal system. As a result, I hope that you will be able to consider measures that may be of help to prevent such distress in the future. Thank you.
Yours sincerely,

Dear Ms Brenna,
Mr Marlo has advised me that you have been representing him concerning the on–going difficulties he has experienced with his ex–partner. I understand that you are attempting to obtain Legal Aid to be able to continue to help him.
I am therefore writing to offer any help you feel that I may be able to provide to Mr Marlo. Your comments would be gratefully received.
Best wishes.
Yours sincerely,

Home life blues

22/23 April

Sunday 22nd

Alice came home and stayed overnight. Just before bedtime, 8.30pm, Ruth called and asked to speak to Lara; Lara asked if she could go see the kittens after school tomorrow, I agreed. I understand that the kittens are going to be sold soon and Lara wants to spend time with them.

Monday 23rd

Alice and Lara went to their mother's after school and Ruth dropped Lara home at 8pm.

Court – the yellow brick road

24th April 2007 / Town Family County Courts
Mother's application – Get the crew to London

The child psychologist files her addendum report, confirming no change in her views for the children to remain in residency with Mr Marlo.

Smitch Law express to the judge that it is vital that Mrs Sanders attends the hearing at the Royal Courts in London.

Judge Yergin rejects the surjection and states, 'Your client does not want to end the proceedings, your client just wants five days in the High Court and only wants Mrs Sanders in court in a vague attempt to persuade her to change her report.'

Despite being comatose throughout the morning's events - somewhat at ease knowing I was there to make the numbers up and the fact this hearing was not about me as such - I soon woke up when I heard Judge Yergin talk about 5 days in London.

I have committed no crime, yet these people are taking over my life; the thought of 5 days of this bullshit, traveling to London and back would drive me crazy, I want to be here for Hayley, Alice and Lara, and this sham is doing nothing more than bringing instability into their lives.

Dean Marlo

Mrs Sanders to Smitch Law – medical records

24 April

Dear Mrs Mason,

Enclosed is the addendum report, covering the medical notes of Mr Marlo and the children. Please confirm its safe receipt. Please send copy to Mr Marlo's solicitor. I also enclose an invoice for this work.

Mr Marlo

1.1. I have seen the medical records for Mr Marlo. These consisted of:
General Practitioner's notes from May 1963 – 21.12.2001.
Patient Summary up to 27.03.2007.
Various letters of referral, and blood test results from 1983 – 23.03.07.

1.2. Over this period Mr Marlo has sustained a variety of physical injuries, which is consistent with his work as a builder. Other entries refer to a range of physical ailments. These do not have any bearing on his psychological state and relationships within the family.

1.3. There is a suggestion, in a letter dated 01.12.67 from a Locum Paediatric Registrar, that Mr Marlo (then aged 5 years 9 months) had suffered from some epileptic type seizures. He was prescribed Phenobarbitone at night and was reported to be 'doing well'. There are no further references to this, suggesting that this was resolved and not a permanent condition.

1.4. Mr Marlo has suffered from episodes of depression as a result of external situations e.g., in May 1976 apparently as a result of his brother marrying into Jehovah's Witnesses; 1980 as a result of his parent's separation. It was noted there was no diurnal variation and no medication was prescribed. Instead, Mr Marlo preferred to deal with it himself.

(This is nothing against any religion; Rob had cut himself off from Ma and me during this period, and having been through a lot together, it was difficult.

My old man raised his hand to Ma, but I was not a little boy anymore; I stood in front of Ma and told that abusive fuck to leave. Ma was upset at what she saw as her family breaking up, and it was hard to know I caused her sadness, even if she deserved better than him anyway.

I do not view myself as ever having depression; things happen in life that have been *depressing* or have caused me moments where I have felt *depressed* but I do not have a mental health condition, and was able to deal with it by working hard on myself to have a moral compass and not be like my father, which was easy really, because I had all of Ma's attributes.)

In 1981 Mr Marlo, aged 19 years, was said to have overdosed on paracetamol (nine tablets) but there was no information as about the reason or advice given.

(This one is a story for worriers; across a day I had taken a one more paracetamol than you're supposed to – I told Ma, and she flustered and fussed so much I ended up at the doctors.)

There was a return of 'mild depressive symptoms' in 1996.

(Five years with Ms Hyde was admittedly starting to get to me; it was more about what she was putting the children through, while I tried to keep them sheltered from it and get Ms Hyde help.

1.5. There are a number of letters detailing Mr Marlo's concerns about Ms Hyde's mental health and the children's welfare. In 1999, Mr Marlo consulted his doctor about his daily use of cannabis and was referred to a drug clinic. He attended the brief contact service for one session and different options to becoming drug free were discussed with him. In 1999, Mr Marlo had a Drug Abuse Screening test, which showed negative across a wide range of drug substances including cannabinoids.

1.6. In summary, Mr Marlo's medical records show him to suffer from episodes of mild depression in response to strain and loss in family relationships. He had regularly used cannabis but the records suggest he sought advice and tests show he was not using cannabis from 1999. He expressed a number of concerns to professionals about the mental health of his partner and the effects on the children.

Hayley Marlo

2.1. I have seen the following:
General Practitioner's records from November 1992 – March 2005.
Patient Summary to the end of 2006.
Assorted letters of referral and advice up to December 2006.

2.2. Hayley's medical notes show a range of ordinary childhood ailments and minor injuries. In April 1996, she was noted not to be sleeping and having behavioural problems over a three–week period; advice about using a star chart was given. In December 2006, during a consultation for headaches it was noted 'all well at home and school'.

2.3. The concerns as to the emotional effects of the discord between the parents was noted. In June 2000, a referral was made to CAFS. The assessment of CAFS stated that the children had been placed with Mr Marlo and 'the children had expressed a wish for this'. The letter went on to say that while the children were suffering emotional distress, CAFS would not offer any further service until the assessment by Social Services was completed.

2.4. The emotional stress due to the alternating residence between parents in 2001 was noted. Another referral to CAFS was made as a result of Ms Hyde's concerns that the children returned from their father 'disturbed, paranoid, stating they hate her and are very aggressive towards her'. Ms Hyde was reportedly reluctant for the children to see a social worker in a neutral venue and again no further service was to be offered until the current assessment, presumably by Social Services, was completed.

2.5. In summary, the medical notes indicate other's concerns about the emotional effects of the discord between her parents. There was little in the notes to indicate overt medical effects on Hayley but it is possible that the frequency of headaches may be due to stress but there is no definite evidence as to their origin.

Alice Marlo

3.1. I have seen the following:
General Practitioner's records from December 1994 – September 2006.
Patient Summary for the same period.
Assorted letters of referral and advice up to February 2007.

3.2. Alice's medical notes show a range of ordinary childhood ailments and minor injuries. Concerns for the emotional effects on Alice and her sisters as a result of her parent's difficult relationship and separation are noted.
In June 2000, a referral to CAFS was made. The assessment of CAFS stated that the children had been placed with Mr Marlo and 'the children had expressed a wish for this'. The letter went on to say

that while the children were suffering emotional distress, CAFS would not offer any further service until the assessment by Social Services was completed.

3.3. The emotional stress due to the alternating residence between parents in 2001 was noted. Another referral to CAFS was made as a result of Ms Hyde's concerns that the children returned from their father 'disturbed, paranoid, stating they hate her and are very aggressive towards her'. Ms Hyde was reportedly reluctant for the children to see a social worker in a neutral venue and again no further service was to be offered until the current assessment, presumably by Social Services, was completed.

3.4. In March 2003, Ms Hyde contacted the doctor about Alice's behaviour on return from her father's house. She was reported to be 'very aggressive, going mad, attacking other children and threatening Mum with a knife – Mum desperate'. Ms Hyde was given advice about firm behavioural management strategies.

3.5. In February 2007 on a home visit (Ambulance OOH service) it was noted that Alice was not co–operative. Ms Hyde indicated that her daughter was 'under a lot of stress with lots of family problems'. She was advised to see her own doctor.

3.6. In summary, the medical notes indicate Alice has shown emotional and behavioural distress resulting from the conflict between her parents.

Lara Marlo

4.1. I have seen the following:
General Practitioner's records from January 1998 – March 2007.
Patient Summary for the same period.
Assorted letters of referral and advice up to December 2006.

4.2. Lara's medical notes show a range of ordinary childhood ailments and minor injuries.

In April 2004, it was recorded, 'Hopeless scenario again. Anger between parents – court case tomorrow – animosity between parents. Social services involved.'

4.3. The concerns as to the emotional effects of the discord between the parents was noted. In June 2000 a referral was made to CAFS. The assessment of CAFS stated that the children had been placed with Mr Marlo and 'the children had expressed a wish for this'. The letter went on to say that while the children were suffering emotional distress, CAFS would not offer any further service until the assessment by Social Services was completed.

4.4. The emotional stress due to the alternating residence between parents in 2001 was noted. Another referral to CAFS was made as a result of Ms Hyde's concerns that the children returned from their father 'disturbed, paranoid, stating they hate her and are very aggressive towards her'. Ms Hyde was reportedly reluctant for the children to see a social worker in a neutral venue and again no further service was to be offered until the current assessment, presumably by Social Services, was completed.

2.5. In summary, there is little to suggest medical effects of the stress on Lara of her parent's prolonged conflict.

I understand that my duty, as an expert witness, is to the court. I have complied with that duty. This report includes all matters relevant to the issues on which my expert evidence is given. I have given details in this report of any matters, which may affect the validity of this report.
L Sanders

Mrs Mason is a human being. (Allegedly.) There must come a time where, as a person, she stops thinking about her career, being a self-serving solicitor, and sees how her involvement is seriously damaging parents and their children. Surely, it must mean something, to read a report again regarding her client's mental health struggles and treatment of her children, and to know that she has played a massive role in exacerbating the misery and destruction of any peace we as a family could have had.

After Mrs Sanders' report, I had thought that court proceedings would finally come to a conclusion. Her views haven't changed, but nor has the Family Courts' ability to draw out proceedings.

(I've talked about my cannabis use before – I got up every morning, ran my business; I had three beautiful children; a nice house and a good standard of living. I did not drink, I came home from work, enjoyed my role as a father and occasionally when the children were in bed asleep, I would have a joint in the garden. Despite many people looking down on me for smoking pot, I would say living with Ruth and her manner, for me personally, it was the only way I survived.)

Northview, Alice with two 'Howlers'

24 April

Level 3 Intervention/Communications
Pupil: Alice Marlo, 8OK
Dear Mr Marlo,
I am writing to inform you that Alice's behaviour has warranted a Level 3 intervention. The reason for this decision is, truancy from school, 23rd April 2007, break time.
As a result, your daughter will need to attend a meeting with the Cluster Group leaders, named above, in the House area on Thursday 26th April 2007 at 3:15. This meeting may involve strategies such as completing missed work or discussing consequences of poor behaviour. The maximum duration will be one hour, therefore your daughter will be released by 4:15pm.
Yours sincerely,

Level 3 Intervention/Mathematics
Pupil: Alice Marlo, 8OK
Dear Mr Marlo,
I am writing to inform you that Alice's behaviour has warranted a Level 3 intervention. The reason for this decision is, repeated lateness.
As a result, your daughter will need to attend a meeting with the Cluster Group leaders, named above, in the House area on Thursday 3rd May 2007 at 3:15. This meeting may involve strategies such as completing missed work or discussing consequences of poor behaviour. The maximum duration will be one hour, therefore your daughter will be released by 4:15pm.
Yours sincerely,

Trouble is a different beast these days

25 April

It was 2pm when Ruth phoned me, and she asked if Lara had singing after school. I replied yes, to which Ruth stated that she is picking Lara up; I said to Ruth that she hadn't arranged with me to do so.

Ruth replied, 'Did Lara not tell you?'

I said no, and told Ruth that I would pick Lara up from singing, ask her if she wants to go to hers, then phone Ruth back to inform her and drop Lara off. Ruth gave some verbal abuse and hung up.

Driving to meet Lara after school, I couldn't think of anything else but finding Ruth in the playground and her causing a scene. Thankfully, Ruth was nowhere in sight and I asked Lara about going to her mother's.

Lara said, 'Sorry dad, I forgot to tell you.'

I asked Lara if she wanted to go and she said yes; I texted Ruth and dropped Lara off.

When I got home, Alice was watching TV in the living room and Hayley was at the kitchen table doing homework. I asked Alice if she had any homework to be getting on with, she said, 'Done it.'

Sceptical, I asked to have a look, and Alice replied, 'The book is at my mother's.'

I made dinner, we all ate and after I sat with Alice back in front of the TV. At 7.45pm, Ruth dropped Lara back.

I told Alice that at 8pm, I would like to turn the TV over so we can watch 'Top Dog', a show Lara has been following recently. Alice hit the roof, yelling that Lara is not going to come home and start to tell her what program she is going to watch. Not understanding why this was an issue, I told Alice that she has a TV in her bedroom if she doesn't want to watch the show.

Alice replied, 'That's right! Throw me out of the living room and into my bedroom.' In disbelief, I asked Alice to be reasonable and said she would probably enjoy the show if she watched it.

Alice said, 'This is why I do not want to live here… Lara gets everything and I get nothing.'

I told Alice that the living room is a family room, and she watched programs like this when she was 9; there is no reason why she can't stay to watch it. Alice stormed out and went into her bedroom.

Lara said, 'We don't have to watch it Dad,' and it didn't feel good to hear.

There are a lot of concessions being the oldest, middle and youngest siblings; different between ages, families and genders. Due to Alice's more overbearing attitude, Lara doesn't have the same childhood experiences that Hayley and Alice had, notwithstanding Ruth's repulsive behaviour at times, and Alice has already forgotten what it's like to be 9.

Minutes later, Alice appeared in the doorway saying her mother is outside and she is staying at hers.

Northview; Alice; Exclusion

26 April

Dear Mr Marlo,
Pupil: Alice Marlo, 8OK
I am writing to inform you that I have today excluded from school your daughter for two school day(s) from Monday, 30 April to Tuesday, 1 May, 2007. Alice should return to school on Wednesday, 2 May, 2007 following an interview with Mrs Hewitt/ Mr Caldwell/Mrs Sparrow.
The reason for Alice's exclusion is throwing a cold drink over her teacher and persistent poor behaviour. Mrs Hewitt/Mrs Sparrow will talk to you and Alice about the situation Wednesday, 2 May, 2007 at 8.15am. If this is not convenient, please contact the school to arrange an alternative appointment.
The Chairman of the Discipline Committee has been notified. You have the right to make representations to the Governing Body; should you wish to do so please write to the Clerk for the Governing Body, c/o Northview Grove School. The Governors' Pupil Discipline Committee meets as required.
You have the right to see a copy of your daughter's school record upon written request to the Headteacher.
Your daughter's Head of House will ensure that she is given work to do while at home. Please return any work due, to school to be marked. No work will be given for 1 day exclusions.
The school website provides a variety of coursework for students via the internet, which students may access if excluded from school. If you do not have internet facilities then your local Library provides them and you can access our website from there.
Should you have any other queries regarding this situation you may contact the school Educational Welfare Officer.
We regard it as an essential part of the exclusion that Alice is not to be on or near the school site at any time during the exclusion period.
Yours sincerely,

Alice came home with this letter; I tried again to talk to Alice about her behaviour, and that she should have spoken to me before letting things get this far.

(All of the trouble at school, is for silly reasons, like uniform – wanting to wear a hoodie under her blazer – or classic class clown stuff. I can see Alice acting out as a result of what is going on in her life, but I find it difficult to know how to help her, because Alice has a get out clause, via her mother, if I attempt to address any of the problems.)

After I had finished speaking, Alice asked for her pocket money. I explained that because she has been excluded, and hasn't made any attempts to reconcile her behaviour – this is not the first attempt to talk about what's going on that we've had – I would not be giving her any pocket money this week, but if she gets back on track, I will add it to the following week's amount.

Alice jumped up, and hurled a load of abuse at me; I know I couldn't be heard, but I tried to explain that she hadn't lost her pocket money, she just needed to do better at school and she'd get it back. Stating she was calling her mother to pick her up, Alice went to her room.

(Ah, the despair.)

I overheard Alice shouting down the hall, 'Why can't you come? Well leave now!'

The rest of the evening, everyone was sort of on edge, even though Alice stayed in her room and their mother did not appear. Alice came out for dinner, said nothing to anyone, and disappeared with her plate.

Later, Ruth still hadn't arrived and when I checked on Alice, she had fallen asleep.

Slippery slopes

27 – 30 April

Friday 27th
When I woke Alice up in the morning, Alice refused to talk to me.

After breakfast, Alice phoned her mother to tell her that she was ready. At 7.50am, Ruth picked Alice up.

Ruth and Alice insisted on this routine, on the occasions Alice stays the night here at home, of picking Alice up in the mornings; Hayley and Alice used to walk to school together, and meet up with friends along the way, and it is another way Ruth has, without realising it, increased the distance forming between them.

Not that Hayley usually wants a lift, as she likes to chat with her friends on the walk, but Hayley has never been offered one by her mother; it seems exclusive to Alice. Again, this is not about Alice having a disagreement while at home, and Ruth providing support as a loving mother, this is about Ruth facilitating disruption to Alice's everyday routine, which is having an effect on everyone.

At about 10am, I received a phone call from Mrs Sparrow from Northview Grove; she explained that while Alice has been excluded from school from Monday, she was expected to come in today. I informed that Alice had gone to her mother's this morning before school.

Ruth didn't contact me to say that Alice wasn't going to school, nor why. It is supposed to be a lift to school; not a day off. I called Ruth and she stated, 'Alice is not at school today because she is depressed, which is a sign of stress.'

I asked Ruth if she knew that Alice had been excluded from school, and Ruth said, 'Yes, I have just been told by Northview Grove and I must say that it is ridiculous that the school have only just phoned to tell me that Alice is not at school today.' Ruth went on, 'I am building up a case against Northview Grove because it is a useless school.'

Feeling unequipped to respond to that, I asked if I could talk to Alice. Ruth passed the phone over, and I asked Alice if she is alright.

Alice replied, 'Yes, fine.'

I said to Alice her mother does not need to build up a case against Northview Grove, as if she needs to talk to her doctor or a counsellor then that is what we need to arrange.

Alice replied, 'I know that dad, but when I was excluded the last time school said that they would send homework and they never did, and we are seeing if they do this time.'

Since Ruth has taken over this situation, she is clearly not focusing on Alice's wellbeing or behaviour, which has not been good recently.

(I would like to warn Northview Grove to keep an eye on the briny, in case Mrs Mason comes swimming up from the depths.)

Saturday 28th
Hayley is sleeping over at her mother's tonight and, as far as I know, so is Alice.

At 8pm, I received a call from Ruth; she explained that she had not seen Alice all day and Alice wasn't answering her phone. I told Ruth I would phone Alice and get back to her. I tried several times with no luck.

About half an hour later, Ruth phoned and said Alice has turned up.

Sunday 29th

When Hayley came home, she said to me, 'Can you believe, Dad, Alice and our mother are acting as if nothing has happened at school? Alice is still rowing with her and doesn't tell her where she is going when she goes out.'

We agreed it wasn't good for Alice.

Monday 30th

I made an appointment with Mrs Sparrow from Northview Grove, predominantly to talk about Alice, but also, because of the hearings, I want confirmation that the police did not come into school to speak to Hayley, and that Hayley was not sent home from school, as relayed in Ruth's 'statement of truth'.

While I was there, Mrs Sparrow asked if I would mind going with her to see Mrs Hewitt, who was dealing with Alice's integration back into school. Mrs Sparrow looked through the teachers' files on Alice, and told me how well Alice is doing in half of her subjects, but she has a total disregard for some teachers and subjects. (i.e. If Alice decides that if she is not going to do something, then she is rude and will not comply with reasonable instructions.)

I explained why I was reluctant to come to meetings with Ms Hyde, because I believed that she would make a scene, to which I did not want to be a part of. As shown in the past, Ruth likes to use me as a catalyst for her own deranged thinking, which will not help Alice's reintegration nor the school with Alice's future. I want to address the concerns for Alice and stand by the school in respect of Alice's behaviour towards her teachers and her education.

Likewise, I am drained and do not want to be repeatedly judged by Ruth's conduct, accused of being 'just as bad as each other'.

Thankfully, Mrs Sparrow said that she understood, and stated it was not necessary for us both to attend the reintegration meeting.

Mrs Hewitt informed me that when she had talked to Ms Hyde, she discussed her coming in for a meeting on Tuesday with Alice for reintegration back into school. However, Ms Hyde told her that it was inconvenient and she would drop off her work schedules to Mrs Hewitt, in order to arrange a suitable time to come in and discuss Alice.

Mrs Hewitt stated that after talking to Ms Hyde on the phone, she felt that Ms Hyde would not accept or understand that Alice was excluded because of her behaviour towards her teachers and around school. Ms Hyde told Mrs Hewitt that she had several issues herself that she wanted to bring up and seek answers for. Mrs Hewitt wondered if I knew what these matters were, I said I do not know.

Mrs Hewitt asked if I would be able to come in with Alice on Wednesday; I said that I can be there, but I'd have to talk to Alice to see whether she would come to the meeting with me. Nodding, she said she would call to finalise the arrangements.

(Such as the issues Ruth wants to bring up with the school, once again Ruth has got her own agenda and she will be heard over the rest. The school have additional support available, but Alice must want to change her behaviour. While Ruth is about to make a scene at school, Alice skates the responsibility and proactive attitude she needs to get back on track. With Ruth not backing the school, it only encourages Alice to disregard the rules and her education; this should be about getting Alice back into school and helping with her learning difficulties while she has the comfort of doing so in a school setting. Ruth seems to be more interested in drawing out the instability in Alice's life.

Again, if Alice is struggling emotionally or with regard to her mental health, we need to find support for her sooner rather than later.)

Getting home from Northview at midday, I tried Alice's mobile – no pick up – and phoned Ruth to ask how Alice is and if I could speak to her. Ruth stated that Alice has just got up, so I can phone her mobile, and Lara had felt ill this morning but she would probably take her to school after lunch.

(I am worried; on Ruth's contact weekends, Lara is ether taken late to school or not at all. Lara comes back from Ruth's tired and I don't want her getting into bad habits.)

Continuing on, Ruth said Alice has told her that she wants to live at hers on Tuesdays, every other Thursday, Fridays and Saturdays, meaning Alice would be home with me on Mondays, Wednesdays, every other Thursday and Sundays. I told Ruth that much chopping around isn't going to bring Alice stability, it would basically make life a mess. It was also not what Alice had stated to me the other day. In response, Ruth went on about 'what a sad old man you are' and so on. This call I have on tape.

It does feel like I'm holding onto the frayed edges of a rope that began untwining years ago; while the Family Courts and experts stand to the side and examine said rope, the children's childhoods become more and more muddled.

(And to be honest, I don't want to point fingers, as that doesn't help. However, in this case, we have already identified several times what the common denominator for instability, abuse and a general lack of care is; until Ruth gets help, that isn't going to change and the children are only getting older.)

I phoned Alice and we arranged for me to pick her up from her mother's after Hayley, Lara and I had been shopping at Sainsbury's – Alice didn't want to come. Lara said she hadn't gone into school today until lunchtime, as her mother had gotten up late.

For dinner, Hayley planned on cooking lasagne, with help from Lara, which she'd learned at school. I picked Alice up and after a lovely meal, Alice told me that she has arranged for Nan to pop down tomorrow because she is not yet back at school.

Alice and I talked about what she was up to and why she's having problems at school. With regards to her reintegration meeting, I asked if she would come with me, since her mother was unavailable. Alice said yes and we had a hug, which brought tears to my eyes.

I gave Alice a pen and paper and asked her to write down what she would like to see happen with contact and her place of home; Alice wrote the following:

Monday – Dad
Tuesday – Mum
Wednesday – Dad
Thursday – Mum & Dad every other week
Friday – Mum
Saturday – Mum
Sunday – Dad

(Two sensible parents could have a schedule for their child like this, and the child could thrive. However, Ruth has shown she doesn't have the consistency to provide the care and attention needed for such contact.)

I told Alice the same as I had her mother, that this arrangement would not bring stability into her life, nor would it be good for her family around her. Alice walked out of the kitchen stating that she was going to phone her mother to come and pick her up. I followed Alice to her bedroom door, trying to talk to her about her proposal, and stated to her again that I have no objection to her sleeping at her mother's on weekdays and every weekend that she chooses, as long as she is showing improvement at school.

Alice replied, 'You asked me to write down what I want to happen and then you have a problem with it!'

I said to Alice that I love her and there is no reason to go down this road.

Alice replied, 'You can shut my door on your way out.'

As I left and shut the door, I joined Hayley and Lara in the living room.

After about 20 minutes, Alice walked straight from her bedroom out the front door. Saddened that Alice has chosen to leave as soon as I say something she doesn't like, but unable to help her understand why it is unreasonable to change homes every other day, I got up to say goodbye and as I opened the door, I watched Alice get into Ruth's car and they drove off.

Dean Marlo

Mrs Mason replies to the psychologist

30 April

Thank you for your letter dated 24th April 2007, together with the addendum report. I have now applied to the Legal Services Commission for payment of your fee note and will let you have the cheque within the next two to three weeks.

(Just another pay day for the Paymaster General, meanwhile, I am treading water with sharks, and there is no Legal Aid in sight.)

Alice

1 - 4 May

Tuesday 1st

It was 11am and I thought I would push my luck and phone Alice; she answered and I asked if she was still popping round to see Nan. Alice replied, 'Yes but I am up town with my mother and we are buying school shirts and stuff.' Alice said she would be over as soon as they were finished.

Alice has four shirts at home, two that were bought recently; I have always bought Hayley, Alice and Lara what they need for school. It is totally unnecessary, as Alice will either be living at home, where her shirts are, or with her mother, and I have no desire to withhold Alice's belongings. I believe it is just part of Ruth's game, wherein she will relay what she has had to pay out for Alice to the family court or provide me with a needless invoice to be paid.

If Ruth is as strapped for cash as she claims to be, it would be straightforward to tell Alice to see her dad and I would have bought what Alice needed or given her the money. (Or Alice could have taken a shirt out of her wardrobe.)

I have made it clear to Ruth, if Alice wants to live with her I am more than happy to give her Alice's Child Benefit. However, when I have asked Alice where she wants to live, Alice has come up with 'I don't know' or the schedule of one day here and one day there. (Backed by her mother, as Alice has stated, 'my mother has not got a problem with this arrangement, it is only you.')

Alice came home to see Nan; she stayed for an hour before being picked up by Ruth.

Close to bedtime, Ruth phoned and asked to speak to Lara; I presume Ruth asked Lara if she wanted to go round on Wednesday because Lara replied 'no' at first and then as she kept asking, Lara said, 'I'm coming round on Saturday and I don't want to come tomorrow.'

Lara leaned back on the sofa and stated her mother wanted to talk to me.

I took the phone and Ruth said, 'I will see you in the morning.'

(Alarm bells began ringing in my head.)

Ruth informed me that she has swopped her shifts around and would be bringing Alice herself to the reintegration appointment.

Knowing the trepidation of being in the same room as Ruth when she is riled up, I decided to speak to Alice, who said her mother has a lot she wants to bring up to the school so she was not worried if I was not there. Ruth took the phone back from Alice and, not wanting to reveal the real reason, I that due to the time of the appointment clashing with when I take Lara to school, I would not be coming with her and Alice. Ruth said I should just get someone else to drop Lara off.

I am not prepared to bring instability into Lara's routine but before I could say so, Ruth cut me off and stated she is going to phone the school tomorrow and tell them that I will be late to 'Alice's very important meeting'.

Wednesday 2nd

This morning, Hayley got up and complained that her throat was hurting and mentioned that one of her friends has glandular fever. I said we'd go to the doctors, but Hayley said she has an exam so she will go to school.

At 8am, I phoned Northview to talk to Mrs Hewitt and I informed her Alice stayed at her mother's last night, so it would be Ms Hyde bringing Alice to the meeting. I informed that I would not be attending because the focus needs to remain on Alice. Mrs Hewitt stated if there was a reason to contact me, she would.

Ten minutes later, Ruth called, stating she had spoken to Mrs Hewitt, who had said she would wait until I got to the meeting. I informed Ruth that I would not be at there, and Mrs Hewitt was aware of this. I then received verbal abuse, claiming I do not care about Alice and that I am a useless father.

Still, Ruth had unsettled me, so I phoned the school back and asked if Alice's appointment had been changed. The receptionist had a quick word with Mrs Hewitt and she stated that the reintegration was for 8.30am, and if Ms Hyde is not there with Alice it will have to be done another day.

I asked the receptionist what does it mean for Alice if Ms Hyde is late; will she be allowed back into school or not? The receptionist stated that she did not know.

I took Lara to school and, on the way back, Hayley phoned me stating that her throat was really hurting. I picked Hayley up from school and took her to the doctors. The doctor told me to keep Hayley off school and we picked up some medication.

Once Hayley was set up on the sofa, I phoned Northview Grove and was told that Ms Hyde had turned up on her own at 8.45am. The whole *point* of the reintegration is for Alice to be there.

I spent the day expecting a call from Ruth that didn't come.

At 8.10pm, Ruth dropped Alice home.

I asked Alice how she got on at school today and Alice told me that she didn't go. When I asked why, Alice stated that her aunt was due to come to her mother's at 8.30pm, but didn't arrive until 12.30am. Alice said, 'I was too tired because I didn't go to bed until 3am.'

Thrown off the discussion of the meeting entirely, unfortunately for relatives, it is very important for Alice to get back into school, and learn at least the basics to aid her in her life; I don't begrudge Alice's relationships with Ruth's family, but I don't think it was in Alice's best interests, or Ruth's, to be up that late on a school night, or miss school to meet her aunt – let alone at the time of Alice's reintegration meeting.

This is the other faucet that Alice uses while staying at her mother's; in our home, there is a routine for bedtime. At Ruth's it does appear Alice can more or less do as she wishes, and while that is like being the king of the castle for a teenager, it is not healthy for Alice short or long-term.

With this in mind, I told Alice that she needs to go to sleep at a proper time and get back into a routine with regards to school. Alice replied, 'I will Dad, I am starting my schedule and this time I am going to keep to it and not sleep at my mother's when I am down to sleep at yours.'

Confused, I asked Alice what schedule she was talking about and Alice said, 'The one where I sleep at yours every other day, and weekends when I want at my mother's.'

Sensing a losing battle with Alice's sleeping arrangements, I instead tried to talk to her about her behaviour at school. Alice stated, 'My mother has told me that you have no room to talk, as you were expelled for punching a boy in the eye, so do not be a hypocrite.'

I told Alice I was not expelled from school for punching anyone, and that sometimes parents are hypocrites simply because they do not want their children to make the same mistakes as we did. (What is Ruth teaching Alice? Instead of encouraging Alice to reform at school, she has used the opportunity to undermine me as a parent and a person.)

Alice replied, 'My mother has told me that she could take me to your school and I would see it in your records.'

I explained to Alice that schools do not keep records from that long ago, and even if they did, it would not read that I'd hurt anyone. Alice looked like she was going to rebut that point as well, so I shook my head and instead said it is time to move on.

Throughout their lives, the children have asked about several stories that their mother has told them about me, all of which are made up in her head. I know that Ruth has also said to Alice that when we lived together, I would beat her up. This is not true and I have never been threatening or aggressive towards Ruth or anyone; no school reports; police intervention; no evidence of Ruth's claim. Yet, these doubts have been put into our children's heads.

(I have relayed that I got a job at the COOP when I was 14, and I started my business in my 20's; I'm both the work force and face of my company. My customers are from word of mouth, and I know that some people are very good at hiding their true behaviour, but I've got neighbours, friends and customers who would act as character witnesses if these accusations ever went anywhere other than things Ruth can say to hurt me, which is stated as fact and moved on from, even though she's talking about me, a person; yes, a man with feelings. When I think Ruth has gone down every avenue she can to harass me, she finds another.)

Leaving my own hurt aside, it can't be healthy for the children to hear such things about one parent from the other…

Alice stood up saying, 'Well, I'm going back to my mother's.'

Calling her mother, Alice was picked up within ten minutes.

Alice will not commit to saying she wants to live with her mother because, I believe, she does not want to; in Alice's immaturity, she wants free reign, to do as she pleases, and Ruth wants to walk into the Family Courts with assertions of discord within my residency.

Not only is Ruth manipulating Alice, I fear for Hayley's attitude and Lara's education in the future.

Sadly, I cannot seem to find a way to help Alice, but I am determined to keep trying and to ensure that I stand by my children, even as the disruption seeps into their childhoods.

Thursday 3rd

In the early evening, Ruth called with several things on her itinerary, 'Firstly, have you received my letter from my solicitors?'

I replied no. Ruth explained that she is going to Australia and taking the children out of school – lo-and-behold communication is possible! Then she went on to talk about

Alice's bedroom; she implied that Lara should not be asking to move into Alice's bedroom. (This call I have on tape.) It has nothing to do with Ruth, as she does not live in our house, but Alice and I have already talked about Lara's request that if Alice is not going to be living here a lot of the time, she would like to move back into that bedroom.

In 2004, when we moved into this rented bungalow, initially, all three girls wanted to share the biggest bedroom; an idealistic dream for about a couple of weeks, before Alice's volatility, Lara's toys and Hayley's interests became a problem one way or another. Alice chose to stay in largest bedroom; Hayley and Lara were happy to share the next biggest bedroom and I stayed in the small bedroom.

After 4 or 5 months of this arrangement, Hayley was getting older and liked to talk to her friends out of her bedroom window after school. Come the end, Lara would rarely use her bedroom to play in, as the room she shared with Hayley had, understandably, started to look like a teenager's bedroom.

Hayley, Alice, Lara and I had a house meeting, and I told Lara that she could move into my bedroom and I would make a bed up in the front room in the evenings.

After several months, Hayley and Lara pulled a house meeting on me, and said they'd talked about me sleeping on a mattress on the floor, and decided to share a room again, so that I could have my bedroom and bed back.

Unfortunately, as time went on, I could see that we were getting back to the days where Hayley spent most of her time in her bedroom and Lara stayed out. To be fair Hayley, Alice and Lara have always enjoyed their bedrooms, and I cannot fault Hayley for how well she shared her space. However, I could see that Lara was missing out on all the things that children do in their bedrooms.

I organised another house meeting, where I proposed buying a sofa bed, and I would go back in the front room. While musical rooms was playing, Alice asked Lara if she could have the room that was mine, which Lara would have been moving back into, in exchange for the big room. Lara was reluctant to give her room up but reckoned that a bigger bedroom would suit her, because of her toys and the space to play. The little room is at the front of the house and, as Hayley does, Alice wanted to be able to speak to her friends through her bedroom window.

Despite Alice claiming Lara to be some sort of favourite, Alice actually has more stuff than Lara, and so a wardrobe and other bits and pieces remained in the big room. This caused some issues as Alice would not respect Lara's space, and so Lara had been wanting to go back to the small room.

I don't mind sleeping in the front room for my children's happiness, however, since the end of last year, Alice has been messing about with where she is sleeping and ultimately living; meanwhile she has control of two rooms in the house. I have never touched Alice's bedroom, nor do Hayley or Lara go in there, but we are all waiting for Alice to decide what she is doing.

On the 4th of May, I wrote to Ruth:

Please find enclosed, a cheque for £36.30 to cover for Alice's Child Benefit, from the 16th April to the 7th May.

Yours sincerely…

Northview to Ms Hyde cc me

3 May

Dear Ms Hyde,

I am writing with regards to your recent phone call to the school requesting that Alice does not take part in Physical Education due to her Hayfever. As Alice's Hayfever will prevent her from going outside for the foreseeable future and as a result will have an impact on her experiences within PE, we will require a doctor's note highlighting that she is unable to go outside and participate.

I have spoken to Alice and requested that she registers with her teacher at the start of every lesson and that she brings her PE kit in case she is able to take part, as for example the class completed an indoor high jump lesson in which Alice could have participated in. For those lessons when Alice is unable to take part in the lesson, I have arranged work for her to complete in the learning centre, this work is set in line with the current activities that she would otherwise be completing practically. Once completed the work will need to be handed into her PE teacher who can then mark her work and set further appropriate tasks.

Should you wish to discuss the matter further, then please do not to hesitate to contact myself at the school.

Yours sincerely,

Melissa

In early 2004, per the order, Ms Hyde received the Child Benefit for Alice and Lara, and myself for Hayley. At this time, for no reason, Ms Hyde applied to the Child Benefits Agency for Hayley's Child Benefit, which resulted in the Child Benefit I received being suspended for several months.

In October 2004, I was awarded sole residency and have received the Child Benefit for all three of my children since.

In May 2006, when Ms Hyde applied to the Child Benefits Agency for Alice's Child Benefit, as Alice stayed with her for three weeks – this resulted in my Child Benefit being suspended. Alice came back to live at home on the 9th of June, but the benefit was suspended until the 28th July. Being in the position of requiring benefits to assist in the care of my children, I phoned the Child Benefits Agency and they informed me they were waiting for confirmation from Ms Hyde.

I believe that this is a continuation of Ms Hyde's behaviour towards me and the fact that she will do anything to bring disruption into my life, wellbeing and my ability to look after our children. Ms Hyde has never offered any financial support toward their up–bringing, before nor since my sole–residency. I have never requested any, instead having chosen not to induce the abuse and trouble any such request would incur.

I have worked hard, though I am only able to do so part time, to achieve the stability in my children's lives and my own, yet the people involved just carry on with their lives, knowing full well the disruption they cause and the financial impact that has on my family.

Repeatedly, throughout their lives, Hayley and Alice have told me that when they are with their mother, she has mentioned to them that I should give her the Child Benefits. This is no longer surprising nor despicable behaviour to me – this is the norm.

I feel that we seem to be in a game played by Ms Hyde and Mrs Mason. The amount of work and money this solicitor has generated out of thin air is morally wrong and dishonest – let alone the redundancy of Smitch Law's job as 'family' law solicitors.

Mrs Mason's overzealous behaviour and attitude towards a single parent with three children, and their letters to the Legal Services Commission, has resulted in my Legal Aid being withdrawn, twice. The first, a ploy to remove my legal representation, giving them the ability to behave as they wished without a barrister on the other side, questioning their conduct. The second is still affecting me a year later; not only have I the worry of more court appearances, but also the strain of having to pay for any representation.

The letter that I received from the Financial Services Commission was extremely worrying, as already my children and I have endured 3 years of financial struggles; we're now headed for court in London.

If Smitch Law were happy that they have ensured the payment of the child psychologist through Ms Hyde's Legal Aid, you would expect them to respect the content of the report.

I cannot express to you the anxiety I've had over the past months regarding the outcome of the Legal Aid situation, and the conclusion of the hearings.

Despite this, as always, I shall remain as the mainstay of my family and will continue to love, care and work hard for my children.

I would like to thank you Melissa for the effort and genuine care you have shown my children and myself over many years, and I appreciate all the time and assistance you have given.

Yours truly...

Dean Marlo

Northview for Hayley

8 May

Pupil: Hayley Marlo, 10TU
Dear Mr Marlo,
Hayley was given an intervention for the reason shown below which was to take place on 19ᵗʰ April 2007.
Reason: Repeated failure to follow reasonable instructions, 20ᵗʰ March 2007, period 3.
As your daughter failed to attend the intervention on that date, it has been rescheduled for the coming Thursday, 10ᵗʰ May 2007, at 3.15pm. Please ensure that Hayley attends the meeting to ensure the matter is resolved.
Yours sincerely,

What Hayley is going through at school can happen with any child; I try and relate to when I got detentions and the issues weren't really serious, they were just teenage behaviour. So, while I had a word with Hayley about listening to her teachers, she assured me 'it's the last one Dad', with a smile on her face and a hug. In the back of my mind, I am still worried.

I know these detention letters are destined for Mrs Mason's court bundle along with Alice's; Mrs Mason and a barrister will claim that all the children are unhappy with father's residency and out of control at school.

(Ouch - that's not true!

Well, I won't have a barrister to refute anything – best I can do is shake my head, despite knowing even that will piss someone off.)

Home life, ch–ch–changes

5 – 9 May

Saturday 5ᵗʰ
The house phone rang at 8.45am, and Lara picked up the phone; it was Ruth. Lara said that her mother stated, 'You can tell your father to drop you off at 9am.' This I did, so Lara could say goodbye to the kittens, who were being rehomed and Ruth dropped Lara back 10.20am.

Tuesday 8ᵗʰ
Alice has remained at her mother's, ignoring my texts and calls.

While I was at work, Northview Grove phoned me and stated that Alice was not at school.

(I spoke to Mrs Hewitt about Alice's reintegration meeting; Ruth has not told me, and I can only hope she will ensure Alice's return to school. I was informed it was agreed for Alice to return on the Tuesday, so she would not have the shock of a full week at school.)

After school, Lara and I were sitting on the settee in the front room watching a shark documentary. The programme finished at 9pm, and just after the phone rang. Lara answered, and after a few moments I heard her say she doesn't want to come round on Wednesday. I could tell that Ruth was having ago at Lara; Lara put the phone to the side of her face and sighed.

Another minute of listening to her mother passed and Lara stated, 'It has nothing to do with Dad! Dad has said nothing to me – why can't you leave dad alone?'

Lara told me her mother said, 'Ok we will talk about Alice's bedroom,' and had a 'real big go' at her about moving into Alice's bedroom. (Which she hasn't; no one has touched Alice's room.)

It is sad because Lara is a happy 9-year-old, who stated after her conversation with her mother, 'There is no way am I moving into my old room… I will stay where I am and out of trouble.'

If any decent parent could hear how Ruth talks to Lara, I believe they would be outraged and appalled to hear the verbal and mental abuse that Ruth has continued in all of her children's lives.

Instead of the end of our relationship meaning the best for our children's childhoods and our own lives, I've watched Ruth's abuse evolve both as Hayley and Alice have gotten older, and in new ways with Lara.

Wednesday 9ᵗʰ
It was around 8pm when Ruth phoned and talked to Hayley and Lara. Lara got upset because her mother told her that Alice wanted to talk to her; Lara stated that Alice had a go at her for 'stealing' her bedroom. As Lara walked down the hall to where I was, I heard Lara tell Alice, 'I'm not in your stupid room, now leave me alone!'

Lara put the phone down and came and sat with me, I looked at Lara and could see in her face she was upset.

Puppy

10 May

I spent the day at work, intermittently trying to get a hold of Alice.

There isn't a good way of doing this; adhering to Alice's treatment of us all as a family punishes Hayley and Lara when they are just trying to get on. So, it is not that I wanted to do this without Alice, or that I'm completely comfortable that we did, but if Alice decided to come home *because* we are getting a puppy then the situation would be no better than it was before either.

If we weren't going back to court, the pressure about Alice's living situation would not be there. Whilst living at her mother's, if her schooling and attitude wasn't so dire, I wouldn't have a problem – even with Alice's crazy hand written living schedule. I still believe it is not that Alice wants to live with her mother, it is that Ruth has been doting toward Alice for this period and is allowing Alice to live like an adult, rather than a child who needs structure and routine.

All Ruth sees is the court hearing approaching, with one of our children living with her, but it's for the wrong reasons and she is so short-sighted, focused on her own agenda of getting the children back, that she can't see that she is sacrificing Alice's stability in an attempt to change the residency.

(I have been told that Ruth lets the children drink alcohol on some occasions. Hayley also admitted that her mother asks her to roll cigarettes before and on car journeys; when she is off school, she rolls her mother a fag as they take Lara to Riverbank.

I know *why* Alice is tired and desires the lifestyle her mother provides, and why I receive so much kick-back from Alice for not running the same household.)

The same goes for Lara; I have done nothing to coach my children's views. Lara is no longer asking for the extra contact with her mother. This is because it wasn't that her mother's behaviour and attitude towards them had improved, there were six kittens.

Again, Ruth proves herself to be too inconsistent to have the children reside with her full time, and that is my main concern. While she may twist Alice's living arrangements and Lara's extra contact into justification for joint residency, she is unable to consistently provide for them every other weekend.

All this to say, I picked Lara up from school and Hayley from home, and we were on the road to getting a puppy. Although I think Collies will always have my heart, we are getting a Golden Retriever, because they're notably sweet, smart dogs.

Hayley and Lara have named her Sully, from Monsters, Inc., and she is (as were her siblings) incredibly cute.

Northview; Alice

11 May

Pupil: Alice Marlo, 8OK
Dear Mr Marlo,
I am writing to inform you that Alice will be placed in our ISC (Internal Support Centre) for a period of one day(s) on Wednesday, 14 May, 2007, and will be working in isolation on a one-to-one basis with a member of staff.
The reason for Alice being placed in the ISC is persistent disruption of lessons.
The ISC facility is covered by closed-circuit security for the safety of students and staff.
Alice will be returned to normal lessons after serving her time in the ISC but will continue to be on a report for a period of time. Should the report prove unsatisfactory Alice may well have to return to the ISC or indeed face other sanctions, subject to the circumstances.
Should you wish to discuss this matter further, please contact me at school through the usual channels.
Yours sincerely,

Ruth's weekend contact – Trouble colours

12 May

It was abnormal to do it without Alice, however her attitude didn't allow me any room to negotiate – I bought Sully as a family pet nonetheless.

Alice phoned from Ruth's and asked if she could come round and see Sully; as I don't have work lined up for this weekend, I asked if Lara could come too (Hayley had texted me to say she was staying at a friend's) and Alice stated that she would ask her mother. A few moments later, Alice stated that her mother said that I will have to pick them up. I told Alice it was not a problem and headed over.

Getting in the car, Alice stated our mother said they only have half an hour because she is taking them out.

Sully was delighted with all the attention, and Lara hid with Sully when it was time to go. I figured the best idea was to bundle Sully into the car as well, and we dropped Alice and Lara back to their mother's and drove home. Shortly after, I was in the office with Sully fast asleep in the chair next to me when Ruth called and yelled, 'You are taking the fucking piss!'

I closed my eyes and took a deep breath, asking Ruth what she wanted.

Ruth replied, 'Get those children back here now, you were supposed to have dropped them off half an hour ago!'

I told Ruth that I had already dropped Alice and Lara back to hers, and watched them go through her front door. Ruth mumbled, 'Well unless they have gone straight into their bedrooms…'

With that, she put the phone down.

I heard nothing more from Ruth.

Thunder bolts and lighting – all within two minutes, placed in my head and life. It's being involved with someone who just wants to abuse you and enjoys being able to shout at someone who has no option but to sit there and normalise being told, 'you are taking the fucking piss'. For sure, I get no pleasure from being talked to in this manner; most of the time it hurts, and I feel harassed and exhausted.

How can I talk to Ma or anyone about the abuse that is going on in my life, being told to 'fuck off' or that I am a 'cunt' and 'not good' for my children? It might fly over my head once or twice, but year after year has eroded me to the very core.

It's the despair, knowing I that have to put up with it and the feelings that follow, which is constantly in the background of my ongoing concerns for Hayley, Alice and Lara.

Per my new routine, on the 15th of May, I wrote to Ruth:

Please find enclosed, a cheque for £12.10 to cover for Alice's Child Benefit from the 7th May to the 14th May.

Yours sincerely…

Mrs Mason writes to the psychologist

16 May

We enclose herewith our firm's cheque in the sum of £350 in settlement of your invoice, of which please acknowledge.

Well removed from Smitch Law, Mrs Mason and Mrs Sanders, I, like most single parent families, am just making ends meet.

Dean Marlo

Northview re – Hayley

18 May

Level 3 Intervention/Information Technology
Pupil: Hayley Marlo, 10TU
Dear Mr Marlo,
I am writing to inform you that Hayley's behaviour has warranted a Level 3 intervention. The reason is, rudeness to staff, 15th May 2007, period 2.
As a result, your daughter will need to attend a meeting with the Cluster Group leaders, named above, in the House area on Thursday 24th May 2007 at 3:15pm. This meeting may involve strategies such as completing missed work or discussing consequences of poor behaviour. The maximum duration will be one hour, therefore your daughter will be released by 4:15pm.
Yours sincerely,

Again, I believe Hayley has done well to grow up and be the person she is; I can see in that process through what she has experienced, things have affected her, most recently through occasional outbursts of challenging rules and requests, resulting in rudeness.

I can but wonder if this is in response to Alice's behaviour and reputation, which Hayley feels the need to prove herself against – and how, if so, I'm going to help both of them.

While I continue to support her as her dad, Hayley knows she is the only one who can choose how she behaves and I hope she will outgrow this, as many teenagers do.

Official notice

21 May

It is ordered there will be a hearing in the High Court London for directions on the 25th June 2007 at 10.30am for 30 minutes.

(Melissa had to forward me the order, because it had been sent to Parstons office… Just more salt in my Legal Aid wounds.)

Dean Marlo

Northview – Alice

22 May

Level 3 Intervention/Technology
Pupil: Alice Marlo, 8OK
Dear Mr Marlo,
I am writing to inform you that Alice's behaviour has warranted a Level 3 intervention. The reason is, unsafe behaviour with technology equipment, 15th May 2007, period 2.
As a result, your daughter will need to attend a meeting with the Cluster Group leaders, named above, in the House area on Thursday 24th May 2007 at 3:15. This meeting may involve strategies such as completing missed work or discussing consequences of poor behaviour. The maximum duration will be one hour, therefore your daughter will be released by 4:15pm.
Yours sincerely,

Mrs Mason to Mrs Sanders

22 May

I enclose herewith a copy of the order made on the 21ˢᵗ May 2007 by the Principal Registry confirming the Hearing date of 25ᵗʰ June 2007 at 10.30am.

Could you please confirm that you will be able to attend the Hearing at the Royal Courts of Justice and I would suggest that you arrange to be there by 9.30am.

Meeting at Northview

23/24 May

23rd

I made an appointment with Mrs Sparrow to discuss Hayley and Alice's behaviour. Mrs Sparrow asked if I minded if two other teachers could be present. I agreed.

In the meeting, I explained that I believed that Alice's poor behaviour over the last several months was due to Alice's attitude and response to boundaries that had been set, resulting in Alice rebelling and spending many weeks moving from one parent to the other, bringing instability into her own life.

Hayley has only recently been getting into trouble over silly things, but obviously I want to avoid her attitude towards others and school similarly deteriorating.

The whole family are exhausted by the ongoing proceedings over the past 7 years, and now we have the opportunity to put an end to any more proceedings being brought before the Family Courts.

I also explained that Ms Hyde's behaviour towards myself over the last few months has been dreadful; without going into any detail, I relayed that Ms Hyde had been verbally aggressive and abusive towards me, and I had no intentions of encouraging her behaviour. Any constructive meeting between Ms Hyde and myself would best be left until after the court proceedings conclude.

As I would like to believe we are very close to the end of family court proceedings, I hope this will finally allow Hayley, Alice and our family to settle down.

All three teachers agreed, told me they understood and thanked me for coming in to explain the situation.

24th

I received a phone call from Child Legal Guidance, who asked me if they could speak to Alice, as they could not get through; I told the woman Alice is currently staying at her mother's. The woman stated it was urgent she speaks to Alice in preparation for the forthcoming hearing on the 25th of June so I gave her Ruth's number (in case she didn't already have it) and said I would try get in touch with Alice to have her call back.

Personal Testimony – our vet

25 May

I have been Mr Marlo's veterinary surgeon for approximately 7 years. Professionally, I have been impressed by Mr Marlo's responsibility towards his pets, sometimes under difficult circumstances. I have been able to use these occasions to form a personal opinion of Mr Marlo and his relationship with his daughters.

Mr Marlo has attended this practise with his 3 daughters, most frequently Lara who expresses aspirations to join my profession. Lara is a delightful girl, polite and confident and very interested. She smiles cheerfully. I have a daughter the same age as Lara and so I have been particularly drawn to the relationship between Mr Marlo and Lara. They have a very strong, understanding relationship, mutually supportive and with tremendous affection for each other. Their relationship is active and functional.

I would be very sad to hear of any mechanism, legal or otherwise, that would challenge the value of the relationship between Mr Marlo and his daughters.

Ruth's contact – half term holiday

25 May

The children are at their mother's for the weekend and then for half term, so it is just me and Sully at home.

It was evening, when I received a call from Ma. She stated that Alice had rung her, upset because she had an argument with her mother; Alice asked Ma if she could come and sleep at hers tonight. Ma said to Alice she should go home and see me, to which Alice replied that she didn't want to. Ma said she told Alice not to be silly, as I would be pleased to see her.

I thanked Ma and told her she had done all that she could, and if Alice phones me, I will let her know what happens.

Since coming off the court order, Hayley generally doesn't spend the full weekend of contact at her mother's, even when Lara does. Hayley had arranged with me to pick her up from her friend's at 9pm. I was getting into the car when Alice and her friend walked around the corner.

Alice told me that she has been arguing with her mother and she had followed Alice and her friend, Amber, from room to room shouting at them; they explained how Ruth went up to Amber and shouted right in her face. They both told Ruth that they were leaving, but Ruth placed herself in front of the door each time they tried to get out.

Alice said that Lara also had a friend over, who witnessed their mother racing back and forth shouting before running upstairs. My heart squeezed at the thought of Lara and her friend, hiding in her room. As always, I want to get her out of the situation but I don't know how.

They told me that Ruth blocked the front door and then the back door and, as she was doing this, she was shouting at them and stating, 'This is your father's fault!' even shouting at Lara, 'This is yours and your father's fault!'

Alice told me that she stated to her mother, 'How did Dad get into this?' at which point she had come away from the door so Alice and Amber made a run for it.

Once again, the children are subject to all of this shouting and emotional abuse, due to Ruth's inability to calm a situation down without aggressive and abusive behaviour. I don't even know what the argument was about, but I know it shouldn't escalate like this and, if Alice and Amber hadn't made it out when they did, it concerns me that really anything could have happened.

My phone went off, and I already knew it was going to be Ruth. She was agitated as she asked if Alice was with me and I told her Alice had just arrived. Ruth went on to tell me that Alice had been swearing at her and she had sent Alice a text telling her to phone her within five minutes, or she would phone Amber's mother. I said to Ruth I will pass my phone to Alice. After Alice had finished talking to her mother, I told her that I was going to pick Hayley up but I'd be back shortly to sit down with her properly and have a chat.

Hayley and I returned home; Hayley went to her room and I sat down with Alice, Amber and Sully in the living room. Alice said, 'Amber has just phoned her mum and if it is ok with you, can she sleepover tonight?'

I said I'd have to speak to Amber's mum myself, but I didn't have a problem with Amber staying.

(The rock and a hard place idiom no longer feels potent enough; perhaps between the devil and the beautiful, briny sea is more fitting?

Alice's behaviour in the past few weeks and months, really since the end of last year, has been dismaying and tough. However, it's been an emotionally difficult night for her, and there are so many factors that go into every decision I make, even though I know my legs are going to be swept from under me by everyone else's choices. If this is an opportunity to get Alice back on track at school, and improve her attitude towards others, then I have to try.)

As Amber pulled her phone out of her pocket, it rang. It was Amber's mum; Amber said that Ruth had phoned her mother and she had to go home now. Amber's mum asked if I would drop Amber home, I said yes.

Hayley came into the living room and sat down. As I quickly texted Ma to let her know Alice was home safe, I heard Hayley ask Alice why she had fallen out with their mother.

Alice replied, 'I don't think I want to talk to you.'

Confused, like I was, Hayley asked, 'Why?'

Alice stated, 'Our mother told me that you and Lara told the Mrs Sanders that you don't like me and it was in her report.'

Hayley stood up and said to Alice, 'I told Mrs Sanders that I don't like the way you act around the house, and towards Lara and me.'

With the damage already done by this allegation, I asked both Hayley and Alice to please stop. I told Alice and Amber to get ready so we could take Amber home.

In the past, I have received letters from Smitch Law accusing me of discussing court details with the children, when the truth of that situation was me explaining what changes could be made, or were, and finding out their opinions and wishes. What Ruth has done, is brought into question the foundations of the sisters' trust and respect for each other.

I am once again deeply worried about Alice's emotional wellbeing; normally, all three children are there for each other if one of them is hurt or in trouble. Ruth has not only discussed something she absolutely shouldn't have with Alice, she has also oversimplified what Hayley and Lara mean. I know my children, and I also know that Hayley, Alice and Lara do on many occasions get on very well. There are disagreements between them but that is normal for any family; Hayley and Lara love Alice as their sister, and only don't appreciate the way she has been treating them recently.

Later that evening, I tried to explain to Alice that it was her behaviour her sisters dislike, not her personally, such as the arguments about rabbits or Lara with her bedroom, which Hayley and Lara have expressed to her a number times previously. Alice nodded and said she is going to bed, and it doesn't take a child psychologist to figure out it is going to take time for Alice to understated her sisters' perspectives of the past few months.

It is not only my relationship, as well as her own, that Ruth has tried to sabotage with our daughters, but their relationships as siblings too. It is diabolical to have been forced, by a self-serving law firm and an incompetent family court system, to watch the domino effect of Ruth's behaviour play out over the years in all of our lives.

Lara stayed with her mother for the full half term period, the 25th through to the 30th May. Hayley slept over at Ruth's on the 28th and 29th May. Alice didn't go back to her mother's at all this week, but did visit during the day on the 31st of May.

(It is difficult for me to comprehend, why, after the abuse they have both received from their mother, Hayley and Alice return. I don't question them on it, but I do question it myself, and worry that Ruth's abusive behaviour has been normalised and is affecting their personalities.

A parent's conduct and mentality plays a huge part in the development of child, obviously, and that has a bearing on the behaviour and attitude learned. The unhealthy relationship Ruth has nurtured with all our children is already having consequences in their lives.

Still, thinking this through doesn't help, because I struggle to understand how to improve our family's dynamics, when we're embroiled in the Family Courts on the road to nowhere again.)

A call to Mrs Mason, logged

29 May

Mrs Sanders confirms she has received this firm's letter and she would be able to attend court on the 25th June, but she wondered what was happening as the time estimated for the Hearing was 30 minutes. I explained that I would double check matters with the court, as the hearing had been listed for 2 days and it was clear that nothing was going to be dealt with within 30 minutes, except for directions.

At the end of this recorded conversation, Mrs Mason indicated, for Legal Aid purposes, this call took 6 minutes.

Mrs Mason, part of a family law firm, were instructing the psychologist to go to the Royal Courts of London, yet did not bother to confirm the timing of the hearing.

(Is that just so they can write and charge for another letter or phone call?)

Ruth pens

1 June

Dear Dean,

I am writing to confirm our various discussions and to make sure that there is no confusion over dates regarding our trip to Cornwall. I would not usually arrange for the children to be taken out of school but in this instance, it is an important family event to celebrate the life of Aunt Pincher, attended by close family and friends at her home village where all of the family enjoyed many summer holidays. It will be a happy event and to that extent will be more of a holiday for the children and on that I, nor they in future years, would want to miss.

Here are the dates:

Thursday 7th June children come to mine from school. Then leave for Cornwall.

Travel back Tuesday 12th June.

Wednesday 13th back to school.

Mr Church is aware of our arrangements and I have notified Mrs Sparrow.

Regards,

Alice's behaviour

1 - 5 June

Friday 1st
Alice asked if she could have a sleepover and if they could sleep in the front room. I replied yes. In the evening, we agreed that she had to be in at 9.15pm; Alice phoned me and stated that she was going to be late. At 9.45pm, Alice and her friend walked through the front door. I told Alice that her behaviour was not good enough and she would have to conduct her sleepover in her bedroom. Alice complained but went into her bedroom.

Saturday 2nd
Alice asked if her friend could sleepover again tonight, and if they could sleep in the front room; I replied yes. Later, Alice wanted to go out, so we agreed they had to be home at 9pm - Alice and her friend came in before 9pm and slept in the front room.

Sunday 3rd
During the day, Alice visited her mother's. When she came home, Alice declared that on school days, she'll come home after school but her mother will pick her up at around 9pm; Alice will then sleep at her mother's and go to school in the mornings.

I told Alice that this is not stability, as she would be hanging about late at night waiting for her mother to turn up, and it is not practical to live from day to day in two places. We have been through this before; for now, she needs to be in one home during the week until her schooling improves. Alice stated that she is fine with it and so is her mother. Again, I tried to explain that her reports reflect the chaos of her living arrangements.

Grabbing her phone, Alice rang her mother and asked for her to pick her up. Even though Alice was now ignoring me, I told Alice that she should not call her mother just because I say something she doesn't agree with – I only want what's best for her, and it is not necessary to leave when we need to talk about things.

Within five minutes, Alice had walked out of the front door into Ruth's car.

I feel like I am on a rollercoaster and Ruth is in the control box; Alice is all over the place and it is difficult to find a solution.

Over the past 4 months, Alice has been rebellious but it has been Ruth's interference and determination to make an issue out of anything. Ruth has picked Alice up within minutes of her having a disagreement with Hayley, Lara or myself, which does not allow for the problem to come to a normal conclusion or be resolved. It is challenging to parent Alice, simply because while I am not prepared to allow Alice to behave in any way she wishes and break boundaries that I have set for both her and Hayley, Ruth manages to insert herself into the family dynamics of our home and she doesn't even live here.

I am aware that the behaviour in a small minority of unfortunate families is extreme, and I believe this is how Ruth would like to see our family and me act. This is simply not the case. I would like the Family Courts to see that the disagreements that happen in our home and between Hayley, Alice and Lara are unfortunately common in many families. Other parents have reassured me that the children will grow out of this.

Hayley on a small number of occasions has been in trouble at school but in all, she is a polite, caring and a thoughtful teenager. While I do not condone the detentions, it is again, a normal possibility for anyone who has a child at secondary school.

Alice's behaviour has become silly and rude; on several occasions, Alice has been pleased to inform me that she is breaking boundaries that I have set for her, which Hayley was still keeping to. However, I believe this behaviour has quite clearly come from Alice playing one parent off against another, and an immature teenage attitude.

Instead of supporting me as we parent our children, as I have sole residency and she weekend contact, Ruth has allowed Alice to behave as she wants, undoing the boundaries and not actually supporting her schooling – no bed time, late mornings, disorganisation and encouragement of such behaviours so long as Alice remains in her home.

Sadly, I believe that Ruth is allowing Alice such freedoms and chaos to give her the ability to go to the forthcoming hearing, and use Alice as a weapon against our family, Mrs Sanders' report and myself.

Monday 4th

This morning Hayley went to school and Lara had a non–pupil day. We spent the morning in the garden with Sully, creating make-shift agility poles and jumps out of whatever we could find.

At 10am, Ma came round and I went shopping at Sainsbury's.

It was 11.45am and I was in the kitchen putting the shopping away, when I heard the front door close. Alice walked into the kitchen, and I asked why she wasn't at school. Sitting down at the table, Alice stated she felt tired so didn't go to school. I reminded Alice that school is important, and that she must make the effort. I didn't suggest her going in at lunchtime, as I could see the bags under her eyes. Instead, we all spent the afternoon in the garden, playing with Lara and Sully, and checking the vegetables, which Lara and I had planted earlier in the year.

After dinner, Alice stated that her mother is picking her up in the morning, as she is going to wash her hair. Although not truly agreeing at all, I said to make sure she gets to school on time.

At about 6.30pm, Alice said she was off to bed, and slept through 'til the morning.

Tuesday 5th

As usual on a school day, at 6:45am, I checked in on Hayley and Alice to make sure they were awake – both have alarms on their phones, but I was a teenager once, and am familiar with 'five more minutes'. Shortly after, Alice came out of her room stating she didn't have time for breakfast as her mother will be here soon.

Hayley finished her cereal and went back to her room to get ready, while I woke Lara up. Alice flitted around the kitchen and hallway before going back to her room; when I asked if there was anything I could get her to eat, Alice repeated that her mother will be here soon. At 7.40am, Ruth picked Alice up.

It seems Ruth and Alice's schedule is standing, as Alice came home after school.

I put talking to Alice about getting into a proper routine to the back of my head, knowing I need a different approach. I am fed up with the subject myself, and I know if I bring it up again it will only achieve Alice walking out.

From MP Mr Rowe

5 June

Dear Mr Marlo,
Please find enclosed a copy of the response I have received from the Ministry of Justice.
My office will be contacting Minister for Family Justice's Diary Secretary to arrange a meeting. I will contact you again when this has been organised. Best wishes.
Yours sincerely,

Dear Mr Rowe MP,
Thank you for your letter of 20 April to the Lord Chancellor, attaching correspondence from your constituent Mr Marlo. This has been passed to me for reply as minister responsible for Family justice.
Mr Marlo raises a number of concerns in his letter, particularly regarding the conduct of a firm of solicitors, the behaviour of a judge, the involvement of a magistrate in his case and the withdrawal of public funding and overall, his distressing experiences within the family court system.
I should advise that it is for the Law Society to deal with complaints regarding solicitors and as such I am unable to help in this matter. However, I would be happy to meet you and Mr Marlo to discuss the concerns he has regarding the family justice system more generally. Please contact my Diary Secretary to arrange a convenient date.
Minister for Family Justice

Worry is a lifestyle

6/7 June

6th

I have been waking up between 2.30am and 3.30am in cold sweats, worrying about all that is going on.

It was only 7am and again Alice stated she did not have time for breakfast. After ten minutes, I asked Alice, standing at her window, if I could get her some cereal quickly – Alice replied, 'No she will be here in a minute.'

Half an hour later, Ruth arrived to pick Alice up.

Despite doing my best to be a good parent and shield my children from it, I live with the anxiety for the conclusion these hearings will bring.

In my desperation, I phoned Melissa. I needed to talk to someone.

I received a letter from Northview about Alice's learning support;

Pupil: Alice Marlo 8OK

Dear Mr Marlo,

The Educational Psychologist is visiting the school on Monday 11th June. It is planned for him to see Alice.

Yours sincerely,

7th

The usual morning routine played out and Alice stated once again that she did not have time for breakfast. It was 7.40am when Ruth arrived to pick Alice up.

Ruth is taking Hayley, Alice and Lara to Cornwall tonight, and they will return to school on Wednesday the 13th June. Ruth has also told me that she intends to take the children to Australia this Christmas. This will mean Hayley, Alice and Lara will miss more school time.

I am happy for the children to have enjoyable holidays with their mother, but I worry; Alice's attitude at school hasn't been fantastic to put it mildly and Hayley has her exams to study for; Mr Church has emphasised to me that the term starting in September 2007 is a very important year for Lara, and it is vital that Lara is present to achieve her full potential and her wishes to pass the Eleven-plus.

To the vet (thank you)

8 June

Firstly, I would like to thank you for the time you have taken to read through several of my letters.

I share your empathy for the needless and shameful attitude shown by the Family Courts and legal system towards parents and their children. It is sad to see genuine parents that are victimised and discriminated against with regards to their children in the Family Courts.

The elected people within our country must see the needless bias and injustice occurring to children and their parents. Quite clearly, we need to remove the prejudice and unjust attitude, behaviour and performance when concerns are brought forward.

Please find enclosed a letter that I propose to send to Gordon Brown PM. I intend to send this letter via Mr Rowe MP; he has been supportive in the past and I am sure that he will endorse this correspondence to Mr Brown.

Due to the Family Courts' attitude and performance, my children and I have not been allowed to get on with our lives. The Family Courts have propagated instability and emotional upset over too many years.

If you would like to add to my letter to Mr Brown, or write one of your own, I would be more than happy to include it in my correspondence to Mr Rowe.

I hope one day what we as parents have gone through with our children will be looked upon as shameful and detrimental to children's wellbeing.

I will not stop trying to bring honesty, morals and standards into innocent children's lives and the lives of their parents. I know you feel the same, and I thank you for that. If I can help you in anyway in the future, then please do not hesitate to contact me.

Mr Rowe

9 June

Many thanks for your reply dated 5th June and the corresponding letter from the Minister for Family Justice. I appreciate once again the efforts you have made in gaining a positive response from them. I look forward to receiving your confirmation of this appointment.

As you are aware, my right to Legal Aid was questioned and on the 20th April I received confirmation I was not entitled to Legal Aid. The LSC have stated that the loan I took out in January 2006 for £5000 has to be included in my sum of earnings of that year.

My children and I had just endured three years of borderline bankruptcy and I was not only able but also willing to work around my children, and therefore I took a loan out to pay off several debts that I had accumulated and make possible a skiing holiday with my children in France.

I have given long consideration to my financial position within my family and I am not prepared to endanger my family's monetary situation further, in order to gain professional representation in what is evidently a continuation of matters that were fully contested in 2004.

I am concerned about the fact that the family court is not keeping me informed as to what is happening in 2007. Melissa was sent the order on 21st May, which should have been addressed to me and regarded the time for the hearing on 25th June.

This episode has been going on since 2006 and from March this year, I had been worrying and waiting for the Family Courts to inform me of the dates for the two–day proceedings in the High Court in London.

On the 9th June, I was unofficially given a one-page copy of the 'index to Ms Hyde's trial bundle', which is 529 pages long – this bundle goes right back to 24th March 2000.

It is very worrying to find that one person has a large bundle of papers all ready for a High Court Hearing in London on the 25th June; I, on the other hand, had not personally received as much as an official notice of the date. If it had not been for Melissa kindly informing me, I would still be unaware.

Court time and Legal Aid funds have already been spent on the issues of 2000 to 2004. I would like to know if the Family Courts are reviewing Judge Chips' ruling of 2004… Is there no double jeopardy in family law? (Please do not tell me.)

I am sickened to read in Ms Hyde's 'Index of the trial bundle' that Mrs Jackson's statements are included.

Mrs Jackson misused her position as Justice of the Peace and brought into question the integrity of a parent who she knew had done nothing but love and care for my children. Throughout proceedings, she tried to deceive the police, a Headteacher, judges, Social Services and the DCA, who are supposed to ensure that those in privileged positions do not abuse their station or people from the community they are there to serve.

In 2006, at Mrs Mason's request on behalf of her client, the judge ordered for Mrs Sanders, Chartered Clinical Psychologist, to report on the family dynamics and relationships of Ms Hyde, myself and the children, with particular regard to contact issues. This I believe Mrs Sanders carried out.

Ms Hyde's decision to contest the report is another example of her inability to get on with her and our children's lives, which is compounded by the malicious attitude and pursuance of Smitch Law.

I have no idea how to relay my position to the High Court; naturally, I fear that the judge will only have in front of them the 'bundle' put together by Mrs Mason. How can I compete with a bundle 529 pages long, which I already know contains false statements?

As in the past, I am also anxious that my dissatisfaction with my family's treatment by people working within the Family Courts, and my subsequent complaints, are going to be used against me at the forthcoming hearings. Please understand that I have only brought my concerns about the inappropriate behaviour my family has received, when necessary, and to the appropriate departments. I wrote letters to the relevant authorities and, undoubtedly, I have not been happy with their findings, but I have moved on, and got on with my children and my life.

From the court papers, I now find out that the hearing is to be at 10.30am in central London. Unlike previous years and occasions, I have received no communication from Smitch Law, despite the fact we're now going to London.

(Arr solicitor's payback... You will not reply to our letters, then we will ensure you are kept in the dark. If I had not contacted Melissa and she had not made the inquiries, Mrs Mason and her client would have been the only ones in court!)

As a parent in the Family Courts, I see disruptions being placed in three young children's lives, while we supposedly focus on their welfare. I will, as I always have, accommodate the court's timetable in an attempt to bring their involvement to an end.

I would like to express to you that it is not easy having this going on in the background of my life, and I am emotionally exhausted by the events over the past 7 years within the Family Courts, just for wanting to provide stability and wellbeing for my children, as any decent parent would – I cannot help but feel guilty of bringing more strife into their lives than if I had walked away from the start. This obviously was not my intention; however, the guilt is still there.

While I try to focus on my family, I am concerned about what is happening within the Family Courts and to what action I should take next.

I therefore enclose a letter for your attention, to Gordon Brown incoming PM, as I feel I have no one else to turn to; I would like to ask you, if you would be so kind as to endorse my letter to Gordon Brown by sending it to him.

I would like to thank you once again for your time and attention. I do appreciate all you have done for my family and myself.

Yours respectfully,

Gordon Brown Incoming PM

9 June

I am writing to you because I believe that you, as a parent yourself and as the Prime Minister, must look at the situation and instability that children, mothers and fathers find themselves in.

I have written many letters over the past seven years about my experience as a father within the Family Court System and hope you would be prepared to give me some of your time; I believe that it would be beneficial to the people of this country and a positive step by a Prime Minister who is prepared to overcome the negative values that still exist within our system, on all fronts.

I would like to make it clear that I am after nothing more than your professional time and understanding, as a human being, a parent, a Member of Parliament and the Prime Minister of our country.

This does not come from a place of political motives or intentions, but from my experiences; I would like to try and help the children and parents in our communities. In turn, I believe this would be a step in the right direction to address how people treat each other generally; healthy relationships between parents are beneficial to stable, happy children.

The sheer energy that is wasted by the ponce and disillusionment of family law as a whole, has allowed solicitors to prey on the stability of the families they're supposed to be assisting. Add in the financial burden, and it is clear actual benefits would be seen if the money was devoted to a better standard of living and rebuilding communities.

There needs to be a positive and fair approach towards the parents entering the Family Courts, with measures in place that protect those who need protecting and safeguard the wellbeing of any child involved.

Understandably, there are many reasons why someone may not be granted joint or sole residency, however I refuse to believe that a majority of men are incapable of caring for, or disinterested in, their children. A good father in a child's life is as important as a good mother in a child's life.

It is morally wrong to alienate one parent from providing for and helping raise their child on the basis of their gender. The Government needs to be at the forefront of helping our society overcome issues that generate discrimination, corruption and abuse.

I have been told on several occasions, by professionals, that the task of addressing the problems the system has is too large for any one-person. However, is that not what MPs, PMs, the idea of governance to begin with, is all about? I am bringing the injustice faced by children and parents in the Family Courts to your attention, as I have with various government bodies. My records show a clear insight into what unfortunately can happen to any caring parent and their children in this country.

I am not Bob Geldof. I am just a common-garden, genuine parent who has gone through hell to have the right to see and be with my children.

It is difficult, I am aware, to fully appreciate a set of situations if you have not gone through them personally, which is why I must express to you the extent of the harassment and uncertainty the system is placing on children and parents. I would like to believe that the system owes me the right to show them the turmoil and sadness that they brought into three young children's lives, because their father wanted to be their dad. For that I have been abused and discriminated against by the Family Courts and the legal system.

The issues raised in my family's story can be used as a springboard to bring a fresh and new approach to children and parents that are unfortunately from separated families. I would like to see guidelines that show people honesty, morals and standards can and will be maintained. In return, this can only result in a huge shift in the attitude and wellbeing of people now and in future generations.

Genuine changes do need to be made in the interests of children's long–term stability and upbringing, which starts with trying to ensure both parents play a role in their children's lives, together or sadly not.

I see and speak to many single mothers who are mentally and physically exhausted from the pressure of being a single parent. I also see fathers that have lost their respect, identity and commitment, due to being wrongly devalued by the Family Courts.

Despite my intentions to be an involved father from the beginning, and that I have had sole residency of my three daughters since 2004, a solicitor made the upbringing of my three children as difficult as they could. This enduring harassment of a single parent, shows no regard for the children's welfare and stability within their childhood or a court order.

I believe that my concerns for the behaviour and performance over the past 7 years by a solicitor should be properly addressed by the Law Society.

Time and time again, I have found my children and myself in a game of deceit by so-called professionals, who have clearly forgotten that they have a moral and ethical duty to children, wherein their actions and performance should be in any child's best interests. After all, this should be the purpose of 'family law', doing right by the children and not acting solely on the wishes of their client, which should be seen in family law as criminal.

In addition, I would like the efforts and thoroughly professional behaviour of Melissa Brenna, Parstons Solicitors, to be recognised.

I have never sat in Mrs Brenna's office and heard her be derogatory towards Ms Hyde, nor has she ever encouraged decisions that may have been beneficial to my position, but could have aggravated the situation. For this I will always be grateful. Mrs Brenna has never forgotten that she is dealing with children and their parents, and has throughout been thoughtful and tactful.

I wish to be clear that this is not a vendetta against a solicitor by a disgruntled opposing party; this is about the systemic failures that are allowing solicitors to exploit children and family situations. I strongly believe that the Law Society and the Family Courts should recognise the fact that some legal representatives are adhering to ethical and moral standards, while some are not.

This is not a request for intervention in my case, I merely believe that the existing attitudes have no place in our society or in the Family Courts. I hope that you will agree.

It would be nice to see some positives come out of my family's negative experiences.

Although I am all too aware that it is a sensitive and difficult area of law, I believe that my records undoubtedly show that this instability and degradation is preserved within the system itself.

Prime Minister, I am sure you would like to be written into the history books for many things but most of all you could inspire real change that does not end when your tenure does, across several social areas of our society.

Maybe, as Prime Minister and most importantly as a parent, you are in a position to equalise the legal bias between 'mother' and 'father' to one as a 'parent'.

For these reasons alone, I would ask you to look into addressing the problems that lie within our system and society; I hope that you would agree that there would be no better place to start than with families.

The majority of the people in our country are hardworking and prepared to make personal allowances to maintain a standard of living in a fair society. I know you will agree that we must continue to look at positive steps and add to the improvements that have already been achieved.

Due to my story, I believe I have much to offer a listening Prime Minister and a committed government. A serious look into my records would assist in highlighting several major problems with the operation of children's welfare.

I sincerely hope that we can meet in the near future and I look forward to a meaningful, honest and constructive conversation with you.

I must express my regards and thanks to my MP Mr Rowe, who, on many occasions, listened and understood the helplessness felt by me and many other parents in our community. Mr Rowe has shown me courtesy and integrity, and in turn I believe that, given the opportunity, a real difference can be made to people's lives today.

I must express that I am after nothing more than stability for my three children, and to prevent this happening to other children and parents.

Yours respectfully...

The Resistance 2007

9/10 June

I met with Melissa and Mr Buckley, pro bono, as Melissa had again been the one to receive the High Court directions letter which should have been addressed to me; she handed it to me and expressed her concerns that the forthcoming hearing will be too much for me to handle on my own, due to the pressure that I am under and have been living with for many years.

Unfortunately, I picked the wrong lotto numbers again, and my letter to the High Court of Justice Family Division was as follows:

'Take notice that I, Dean Marlo, the respondent in the case, act on my own behalf.'

Sunday 10th

While at work, I received a phone call from Hayley in Cornwall; Hayley stated, 'Our mother wants to stay in Cornwall for one more day and we would like to stay as well.'

I told Hayley no problem (realistically, what could I do about it?), to be safe and have fun, and that I look forward to seeing them when they get back.

Forwarded from Mr Church

12 June

To whom it may concern,

Mr Dean Marlo has been known to personnel at this school for the past eleven years. During this time, he has been a very supportive parent to the school, always willing to give freely of his time.

Throughout the years, when the children have resided with him, he has consistently ensured that they have arrived for the start of the school day well organised, in good time and with everything they need. His communication with school has been excellent and he has often helped with class activities during the school day. Without question, Mr Marlo has always followed the procedures and protocol in place.

Hayley and Alice have now moved on to secondary school. The youngest daughter, Lara, is still here at Riverbank School in the year 4 class. She is a bright girl, and with two years left of her primary school education, I feel it is imperative that she continues to benefit from the stable environment that living with her father has given her. I am confident that she will then achieve the high academic results of which she is capable. She is a happy, friendly and mature girl who has a very good rapport with her father.

We hope the above points prove helpful. Please do not hesitate to contact the school should you require any answers to questions.

Signed,

Mr Church (Headteacher)

Mrs Hart (Office Manager/ School Governor)

I still cringe to remember Ms Hyde, on numerous occasions, shouting across the courtroom that I never contact the schools, and the times Mrs Mason and Smitch Law's barristers, have relayed to several judges the same.

Yet one conversation with the Headteacher of Riverbank, from anyone involved, would have provided a greater insight, and not allowed Smitch Law to paint a completely different story, wherein they persistently use it as justification for Ms Hyde requiring solicitor involvement. For some mysterious reason, every judge, bar one – thank you Judge Chips – have held Smitch Law in favour, regardless of a lack of evidence to substantiate their claims.

Without the honesty and integrity of people like Mr Church and Mrs Hart, I would not have been able to challenge the false accusations Ms Hyde and Mrs Mason put forward, repeatedly, without care.

The Hon Family Minister

13 June

I dropped Lara to school, hopped on a train to London (knowing I'd have to be on the return by 1pm to be back in time for her) and met with Mr Rowe and the Minister for Family Justice.

On the journey there, I got lost in thought for a moment. No one was aware I was going to meet my MP and the minister, and I have put in so much effort and time to relay the injustices happening to my family, all while with raising my children, being harassed by Ruth, Smitch Law and the Family Courts. I was now on the way to London, rushed between the school day, in the hope of bringing accountability and honesty to family justice, in a meeting I never expected to actually happen.

I handed the Minister for Family Justice the following letter:

There must be changes in our legislation.

Throughout family court proceedings, the same reasons and excuses were used as to why changes could not be made or investigations carried out; 'we cannot intervene because the case is ongoing and in the hands of the family court judges'.

Unfortunately, that is the whole point, the case is ongoing, which is due to the manipulation of some individuals within the Family Court System. When the behaviour being brought to your attention is blatantly dishonest and not in the interests of children and families, then someone with the authority must step in and stand up for honesty and decency, and ensure family values are imbedded into our Family Courts and family law – which are clearly being abused at the present time.

While I was granted sole residency in 2004, after 4 years of proceedings, it is now 2007, and my family's case has been transferred to the Royal Courts of Justice in London.

In 2002, Smitch Law, on behalf of their client, wrote to the Legal Aid Department questioning my entitlement for Legal Aid; this was regarding the hearing for joint residency of my three daughters Hayley, Alice and Lara, which was brought about after my children's mother had been sectioned under the Mental Health Act for the fourth time. I strongly believe that because of the malicious interference of Smitch Law on behalf of their client, my financial aid was wrongly rescinded. In order to be represented at that hearing, I had to agree to pay £800, despite having financial difficulties at the time. Subsequently, several months later this bill, along with several others, placed me in a position where I almost had to file for bankruptcy.

Once again in 2006, Smitch Law, on behalf of their client, challenged my receipt of Legal Aid; this was regarding my children's mother applying for sole residency, after several abusive incidents involving her and the children at her residence.

The removal of my Legal Aid is just another example of the continuing instability, (this time financial), which Smitch Law has managed to add to my family's day–to–day lives. This is obviously not in the best interests of three young children.

I am unable to bring home a full pay packet because I am a single parent, with limited time; I organize my work around my children's schooling and therefore a one–day job takes me two–days. Not only do I have the worry of more court appearances, but also the strain of having to pay for any representation.

While I am trying to bring a standard of living to my family and set an example to my children concerning working ethics, I feel that I am being unfairly punished for this. Clearly, I cannot earn the sort of money needed for sufficient representation.

I must express the disparity between one parent receiving financial aid and still going on personal holidays abroad and the other taking out a personal loan for a family holiday. I believe that we should be treated equally; this is simply not the case.

If I go down the road of paying for legal representation, this may result in me falling into bankruptcy. Having worked hard to be self-sufficient my whole life and having entered the Family Courts asking for nothing more than to be a dad to my children, it would be incredibly disheartening to be forced into that position.

Several weeks after I had reluctantly agreed in the family court (2006) to pay the estimated £2,500 for a Child Psychologist, and my previous solicitor had informed Smitch Law that I could not comply with their request for conformation of payment, they simply took the matter back to the Family Courts, in an emergency hearing, wherein my children's mother withdrew her application for sole residency, now wanting joint residency, and the full cost of the Child Psychologist, as requested by Mrs Mason, was placed onto her Legal Aid.

Once again, it appears my children's lives and my own are in a game played by Smitch Law. The amount of work and money this solicitor has generated falsely and to the detriment of the children involved, I believe to be morally wrong.

The overall behaviour and performance of this solicitor must be seen as unacceptable and an insult to the welfare of children. Smitch Law did not approach family law with a reasonable evaluation of the situation, and were able to ensure their client's demands, regardless of the welfare of the children and parents involved.

Within the courts, some of these people are genuinely being abused, and they are not being helped. Others are exploiting prejudices and antiquated ideals. Some are lining their pockets while children and genuine parents suffer. And somehow, the Family Court System approves numerous applications...

At which point, I have to ask – what is the point?

It doesn't seem to protect;

Domestic abuse cases against women are still too common; rape prosecutions are close enough to non-existent that *everyone* should be up in arms; victims who are men are scared to speak out, or are humiliated for doing so; Social Services is so overloaded it cannot provide meaningful help for every child who needs it.

It doesn't seem to mediate;

I have given you only some of many examples where Smitch Law's involvement either exacerbated, inflamed or directly influenced the negative result to a situation.

From my perspective, Smitch Law's actions are an amalgamation of their inability to accept that I can be a level–headed parent, and a total disregard towards their client's mental health. We can all agree that court proceedings, whether it be a single hearing or yearlong cases, are a stress on everyone involved; the concerns this would negatively impact Ms Hyde's mental health in any case was mentioned in the first reports ordered in 2000, yet Smitch Law have ploughed on mercilessly.

I do feel victimised and shocked by Smitch Law's attitude towards a single parent who was given the responsibility of three children. Despite the number of letters I have written to various people and organisations, I cannot express to you the worry I've suffered over the past months regarding the outcome of the latest hearings, as I add another year to the compounding anxiety and stress, and ultimately I realise almost a decade has gone by, and with it some of the best years with my children.

Despite this, as always, I shall endeavour to be the mainstay of my family. I will provide love and care, and work hard for my children. What I have been through also leaves me determined to help other children and their parents.

I am asking my government to make the commitment to children and genuine parents, to ensure that welfare and stability are not just buzzwords, but meaningful, across all aspects of the attitudes and behaviour of those working in family law.

Dear PM, Family Justice Minister, MP & Secretary

14 June

Dear MoFJ,

I would like to take this opportunity to thank you for not only making time for my appointment on Wednesday 13th June, but also your kind consideration of my situation.

It was reassuring to come to your department and be treated in such a polite and professional manner; attentive and diligent ministers will certainly be an advantage as we continue to improve the quality of life of the people the legislation governs.

Thank you once again for your time taken with Mr Rowe and myself.

Yours respectfully...

Dear Mr Rowe,

Many thanks for your assistance and support on Wednesday. You are, without a doubt, a caring and sensitive person, and, as my MP, you are a credit to your profession.

The three hours I spent with you on Wednesday was not only pleasurable but also hopefully productive in addressing the situations many parents and children find themselves in.

Once again, I thank you for your time and consideration throughout.

Yours respectfully...

Dear Beverly,

I would like to take this opportunity to thank you personally for your time and efforts in assisting Mr Rowe in his work concerning my family.

I have always found you polite, caring and helpful; you have shown me that you are a kind person.

You are a credit to your profession and no doubt an invaluable member of Mr Rowe's team.

Once again, I would like to thank you on behalf of my children and myself.

Yours respectfully...

Dear PM,

I would like to bring to your attention the efforts Mr Rowe, my local MP, has made on my behalf. Throughout, Mr Rowe has been honest and straight forward with me, he has always given me sound advice and has been tireless in his efforts to assist my children and myself.

I would appreciate it if you would be so kind as to take the time to express your recognition of his dedication in his parliamentary responsibilities to his constituents.

I would also like to take this opportunity to wish you well in your forthcoming term and thank you for your time in considering my request of appreciation to Mr Rowe.

Yours respectfully...

Time, Ticking Away

14-19 June

Thursday 14th
In the playground with Lara, I asked about her day. She told me it was alright, but she'd been late again to school because her mother had not woken up until 10.30am – Lara had gone into her mother's room several times, but spent the morning getting her breakfast and waiting for her mother to get out of bed.

Friday 15th
When I tried to discuss school with Alice, she declared she is going to her mother's, because she doesn't 'get on at me'. Within a phone call, Alice was out the door.

Saturday 16th
Alice stayed at her mother's, while Hayley and Lara did Father's Day preparations; their efforts are as always loving and meaningful, but we all felt Alice's absence.

Sunday 17th
I woke up to a full breakfast and many presents, with Sully charging in to help rip them open. Alice came home at 11am, and we had a lovely day.

At 7.30pm, Ruth picked Alice up.

Monday 18th
Alice came home after school and stayed the night.

Tuesday 19th
After school, Alice asked for a lift to her mother's as she is staying there tonight. I asked Alice if she wanted dinner first; Alice said yes, and I dropped her to her mother's at 5.30pm.

Three hours later, Alice walked through the front door and said she had changed her mind.

We all spent a peaceful evening in.

Mrs Mason writes to Mrs Sanders

15 June

I refer to previous correspondence and write to advise that I have spoken with the Royal Courts of Justice who have confirmed that the forthcoming hearing is for directions only and listed for thirty minutes.

I have faxed Mr Marlo's solicitor to ask if they would agree that there is no need for you to attend that hearing, and as I receive confirmation from them, I will let you know.

I anticipate that the court will now list a two-day hearing sometime after July, and I would be grateful if you would please let me have your dates of availability right through until September.

I'm going to have to go all the way to London for 30 minutes! I was under the impression this hearing was for two days, but we're wasting one day to direct the next day - who's organising this crazy theatre production? While everyone else is getting paid generously for their time, I'm missing two days off work, and have the stress of the hearings, the school run, what the result is going to be – fuck, am I on the right train?

Also, it was because Smitch Law, on their client's behalf, contested her report that Mrs Sanders may have needed to be present, so that they could cross-examine her – why would I want her to be there? I don't want to be there myself, and her addendum report changed nothing.

Mrs Mason knows full well that I am not legally represented, and, as history shows, the solicitors' letters are included as the 'proof' of the accusations Ms Hyde brings forward; Ms Mason conveniently included them in the court bundle.

Mrs Mason still making a service

16 June

2 May

We refer to previous correspondence and note we have not heard from you with regards to Hayley's TB injection which is now overdue. In the absence of hearing from you, our client will now arrange to take Hayley to the doctor herself to ensure that the inoculation is up–to–date.

In the meantime, however, our client instructs us that she wishes to take the two youngest children to Australia on the 2nd December 2007 for a period of three weeks on holiday and to visit family.

Could you please confirm that your client would agree to the children going on holiday and being removed from school for two weeks.

We would be grateful if you would respond as soon as possible as our client needs to book the flights.

When Melissa handed me this letter with an explanation that despite the date, Parstons had only recently received it, she commented that she'd already spoken to Mrs Mason, as well as informing Smitch Law officially, and had made it clear that Parstons no longer represented me, so they should be sending all communication direct to my home address. Melissa has no idea why Smitch Law continue to write to Parstons.

(We're back to unprofessionalism or ignorance – which is worse?)

In the background, Ms Hyde and Mrs Mason are causing so much trouble, anxiety and turmoil in our lives, again; meanwhile, their client is proposing to fly off to Australia.

There is so much going on in my life, but I am not the sort of parent who would miss their child's TB injection; I simply haven't relayed it in a letter to Mrs Mason because Ms Hyde already knows, and she uses the same doctor as the children… Between them, they are still scraping the bottom of the barrel of allegations to throw at me.

(Good old Legal Aid and the level playing field. The whole situation's absurd; one-minute, Legal Aid is paying for a child psychologist report, the next they're paying to contest it in the High Courts of London, and after that it's absolutely essential to the children's welfare that it ensured Ms Hyde's flight plans aren't going to be disrupted.)

Melissa's reply to Mrs Mason:

We enclose, for the sake of clarity, Mr Marlo's written notice of acting in person and take this opportunity to remind you that our involvement was one of trying to assist. We are not on the record.

We have, however, spoken to Mr Marlo about your client's plan to take Alice and Lara to Australia. Mr Marlo has a copy of your letter relating, but queried exactly how much school it is proposed they will miss as your letter is not clear. Lara will be sitting her 11 Plus next year and it will be imperative that her attendance at school in the preceding terms is as full as possible. The children have already had time out from school term, which was extended while they were away, and Mr Marlo is concerned at the amount of time it is proposed will be missed, namely the whole of December in the Autumn term.

Finally, Mr Marlo does not require the psychologist at the directions hearing. It was your client who wished to have the opportunity of questioning the psychologist at the final hearing.

The Principal Registry of the Family Division

19 June

Please find enclosed my position statement for the hearing on 25th June.

I have always put my children first and am grateful for the support of their schools, the court appointed child psychologist and Judge Chips, in their recognition and confirmation of my ability to be an honest and decent parent.

Yours faithfully,

Proceedings have been ongoing since 1999, following the parties' separation, in respect of the three children: Hayley Marlo, born March 1992 and now aged 15 years and 3 months; Alice Marlo, born April 1994 and now aged 13 years and 2 months; Lara Marlo, born December 1997 and now aged 9 years and 6 months.

There has been a period of sole residence to Ms Hyde with defined contact to myself; a period of shared residence where the parties followed a coloured schedule that required revision at the commencement of each school Autumn Term and most recently, since 29 April 2004, a period of sole residence to myself with defined contact to Ms Hyde.

On 5 August 2004, his honour Judge Chips, sitting in the Town County Court, gave a judgement of sole residency to myself, after hearing full evidence from the Cafcass officer, the parties and Ms Hyde's family. No approved transcript of his honour Judge Chips' judgement is available.

Following this judgement and the making of the order on 5 August 2004, there was a relatively settled period until 2006. There were two incidents at Ms Hyde's home involving Hayley and Alice, which resulted in a period when Hayley and Alice were refusing to see or stay with Ms Hyde. In addition, following a number of aggressive outbursts from Ms Hyde, one of which resulted in Ms Hyde being cautioned for criminal damage to a vehicle parked at my home; in June 2006, I sought an injunction under the Family Law Act 1996. In those proceedings, the parties gave cross undertakings to the court, including not to communicate directly with each other.

On 21 July 2006, Ms Hyde made an application to vary the order made on 5 August 2004. At about the same time, Ms Hyde's solicitor wrote to the Legal Services Commission regarding my application for public funding, which has resulted, as in a previous occasion in 2002, in my funding being revoked. I am now not represented in these proceedings, although I have received limited assistance from the law firm who acted on my behalf in relation to previous applications in this matter.

Following the incidents in the earlier part of 2006, the elder two children have been gradually re–building their relationships with Ms Hyde. There has additionally been a report and an addendum report by Mrs Sanders, Chartered Clinical Psychologist, both of which have been filed in these proceedings.

Hayley and Alice, through CLG, issued applications on 9 January 2007 to be joined as parties to these proceedings and for the contact order to be discharged. Their supplemental application forms state that Ms Hyde has been violent towards them and verbally abusive/caused arguments, as well as that Ms Hyde has made allegations in front of them that I have been abusive and threatening to her.

At the directions hearing on 12 March 2007, all previous orders in respect of Hayley, save for the order granting parental responsibility to me, were discharged by consent. The cross undertakings given in June 2006 were varied to enable the parties to communicate directly with respect to the children, without being in breach of their undertakings. Alice's application to be joined as a party was adjourned to be dealt with by the trial judge at the commencement of the final hearing of Ms Hyde's application, with a time estimate of 2 days.

Both prior to and throughout these current proceedings, Lara has maintained contact with Ms Hyde in accordance with the order made on 5 August 2004, with assorted variations as agreed by the parties. Alice currently chooses to come and go between the parties, and appears to have opted to stay with Ms Hyde on weekends when her sisters are not doing so.

All three children have recently enjoyed an extended holiday with Ms Hyde to Cornwall, for which they were taken out of school. Ms Hyde is additionally planning to take the children on holiday to Australia later this year for three weeks, although it is currently unknown whether Ms Hyde has any school summer holiday plans for the children to travel abroad.

(Melissa helped write) My position statement

I believe that these ongoing proceedings are damaging to all three of our children but in particular Alice, who has been experiencing an extremely unsettled period since Mrs Sanders made her report available. I reiterate my position as set out in my previous Position Statement filed in these proceedings and dated 2 March 2007, both in respect of Alice and in respect of the children's contact in the future.

Ms Hyde made her application shortly after I felt I had no alternative but to apply for a Non-Molestation and Occupation order, as a result of what I viewed as a deterioration in Ms Hyde's behaviour towards me in front of the children, and to prevent any further confrontational situation arising at my home.

Ms Hyde's position has changed during the course of these proceedings, and she is now believed to be seeking a Shared Residence Order in respect of Alice and Lara.

I am unable to agree that there should be a Shared Residence Order for many reasons. The foremost of which is due to the ongoing reports from the children after periods of contact with their mother, ranging from lack of care to physical abuse. I believe that there would be greater potential for disruption and difficulty in the future if we were to return to a pattern of shared residence, such as that which was previously in place, and discharged, in April 2004.

Annexed hereto is a copy of a recent letter from Lara's Headteacher at Riverbank Primary School, emphasising in his view the importance of Lara continuing to benefit from the stable environment of the past three years.

Whilst I agree that a degree of flexibility is required when raising children, there should be some structure to the children's lives so that everyone knows what should be happening and when. Without wishing to resurrect issues that were dealt with in previous proceedings, difficulties have arisen when last minute alterations have been sought to contact periods, and I would hope that whatever order the court deems fit to make on Ms Hyde's application, it should be as such as benefit the children's stability and minimise any future confrontation.

I am also concerned that Ms Hyde's overlooked mental health is playing a role in her treatment of our children, ongoing proceedings, and the manner in which they are being conducted on Ms Hyde's behalf. I do not wish to belittle or in any way upset Ms Hyde, but as stated in the beginning of Mrs Sanders' report (Page 32) Ms Hyde's 'episodes of mental ill health were of extreme dysregulated states and within these times she was both unaware of her behaviour and the effects on others'.

Ms Hyde also refers in her statement dated 7 March 2007, at paragraphs 6 and 7, to Mrs Sanders having obtained inaccurate information from somewhere. I simply believe that it may be the case that Ms Hyde, when in an 'extreme dysregulated state', has told her doctor these things and hence they are recorded in her medical records.

The same allegations are levied time and time against me, as I am berated by Ms Hyde for: taking the children out of school to go on holiday; failing to communicate with Ms Hyde; being unable to meet financial demands from Ms Hyde; accused of alienating the children due to Hayley and Alice refusing to see Ms Hyde while Lara maintained regular contact; accused of only encouraging Hayley and Alice to have contact because there are court proceedings – despite there now being no order in place for Hayley, and the only time the children have refused contact is due to incidents of abuse, as reported by the children, involving their mother; by way of a few examples.

In so far as Ms Hyde's application, I believe that Ms Hyde is attempting to re–visit matters that were fully considered by his honour Judge Chips in August 2004, and that are addressed in the judgement given. A copy of both the 'chronology of significant events' and the schedule of 'disputed facts and incidents', completed for that final hearing, are annexed hereto.

I believe that approved transcript of the judgement given by his honour Judge Chips will be an invaluable aid to the court, and potentially reduce the costs associated with both the court's time and Ms Hyde's public funding, by reducing the time estimate for the final hearing. I do not have the financial resources to obtain an approved transcript of the judgement. For these reasons, I would ask that, if at all possible, a copy of the approved transcript of judgement of 5 August 2004, be provided by the court for the final hearing.

Without a solicitor, and without Melissa's generosity of her time and knowledge, if I had written my position statement alone, it certainly wouldn't have sounded like this, and what are probably obvious things to include to Melissa, would have gone completely missed by me.

Dean Marlo

Ongoing

20-22 June

Wednesday 20ᵗʰ

Alice stated to me at breakfast, 'Don't worry Dad, if you get a call from school saying I'm not there. I have to wash my hair at my mother's so I might be late, but I am going in.'

I said to Alice that we all have to keep to a routine and time keeping; this is a part of life.

In reply, Alice said, 'Don't have a go at me just because I want to wash my hair.'

Again trying to establish a boundary, for school at least, I told Alice that if she was late for school, she would be getting no pocket money this week.

Leaving the room, Alice said, 'I don't care.'

Just after 7.30am, Ruth picked Alice up.

Northview called at around 10, to inform me Alice had been late.

Thursday 21ˢᵗ

I received a call from Northview, requesting I collect Alice due to her behaviour at school; they also mentioned Alice had asked for her mother to be called first, but she had not answered.

I picked Alice up and tried to talk about her day, but Alice sat in silence, staring out the window.

Once we got home, Alice shut herself in her bedroom, telling me to 'go away' the several times I tried to talk to her. She briefly resurfaced to take her plate of dinner and shook her head when I asked if she wanted to join us in watching a movie.

I'm worried about Alice and I think she needs someone to talk to. I mentally added it to the list for the office tomorrow, although getting Alice to speak to someone from an organisation might be the difficult task.

Friday 22ⁿᵈ June

In the morning, Alice seemed to be feeling better and ate breakfast with Hayley and Lara at the table. I decided to not broach the topic of contacting an organisation and potentially upset Alice before school, and it felt like a good morning; Hayley and Alice left on time, and Lara smashed her 8-timestables before I dropped her to school.

The children were all with Ruth after school for a charity fun run; when Hayley and Lara came home, they proudly showed me their certificates. Shortly after, I received a text from Alice saying her mother has asked her to stay over.

Mrs Mason faxes

21/22 June

21 June

Dear Mrs Sanders
I enclose a copy of a letter dated 18th June 2007 but received by me on the 20th June 2007 from Mr Marlo's solicitor. You will see that he does not require your attendance at the directions hearing on Monday, and I can confirm that there is no need for you to attend.

21 June

Dear Mr Marlo,
We understand from Parstons that you are now representing yourself and we enclose herewith a draft of the schedule for September 2008 which our client has prepared.
Our client is being represented by barrister of council on 25th June 2007 and it is hoped that the schedule can be agreed, in interim, before a final decision is made in respect of our client's applications concerning the children.

I am not 'now' representing myself – Melissa had informed Mrs Mason she was no longer representing me months ago. Mrs Mason knew, however, that I do not want to play 'Solicitors' Tennis' and she would not therefore get paid per letter in reply. It is just another example of Smitch Law facilitating and encroaching their involvement on every aspect of my family's lives when they choose.

From Mrs Sanders:

22 June

Dear Mrs Mason,
Just to let you know that in the absence of any information to the contrary, I will not be attending the directions hearing on Monday; it would be highly unusual to require an expert for this type of hearing.
Hope all well with you, cheers.

22 June

Dear Mrs Sanders,
Thank you, I did send you a fax earlier confirming that you are not required.

Dean Marlo

Position Statement on behalf of Alice Marlo

22 June

Alice Marlo was born April 1994 and is therefore 13.

The Applicant Ms Hyde is Alice's mother and the Respondent Mr Marlo is her father. Her parents separated in 1999. Alice has an older sister, Hayley (15) and a younger sister, Lara (9). Alice has, in the past, been adversely affected by the conflict between her mother and father and by her mother's mental health problems.

On 5 August 2004 HHJ Chips ordered that Alice and her sisters should reside with their father and should have defined contact with their mother.

In January 2006, Alice was assaulted by her mother's boyfriend, Bernard Craven, while in her mother's home. In April 2006, Alice was involved in another violent incident in her mother's home.

From 13 May 2006 until 9 June 2006, Alice lived with her mother in her home and had no contact with her father. She then returned to her father's home.

In June 2006, Mr Marlo applied to the County Court for injunctions following an incident at his home on 22 May 2006. On 23 June 2006, the parties gave cross–undertakings not to communicate with each other and not to attend at each other's homes.

On 21 July 2006, Ms Hyde applied to the County Court for residence orders in respect of Alice and Lara and for interim contact with all three of her children. Ms Hyde subsequently withdrew her application for a residence order but persisted with her application for enforcement of the contact order.

On 30 November 2006, Alice gave written instructions to her solicitor at Child Legal Guidance to the effect that she did not want a contact order telling her when she must see her mother and that she should be allowed to decide for herself when she had contact with her mother.

In January 2007, Alice's litigation friend, (a child's advocate) applied to the County Court for discharge of the contact order. The case was transferred to the High Court and directions were given on 21 May 2007.

Since 21 May 2007, Alice has spent some time living with her mother but she is currently living with her father. On 21 June 2007, Alice gave instructions that she still wants the residence and contact order to be discharged so that, like Hayley, she can decide where she should live and when she should visit. She anticipates living with her father and having staying contact with her mother at weekends and sometimes during the week. She also wishes to intervene in the proceedings because she has had such contradictory reports of what has happened in Court in the past that she would welcome the opportunity to understand what is really happening.

The Court may only grant Alice leave to make an application if it is satisfied that she has sufficient understanding to make the proposed application (Children Act 1989 S10(8).

Such applications should be approached cautiously since, once a child is party to proceedings between warring parents, she will be exposed to hearing evidence which it might be better for her not to hear and may have to be cross–examined (Re N (Contact: Minor seeking Leave to Defend and Removal of Guardian) [2003] 1 FLR 652 Coleridge J). However, sometimes children whose parents are in conflict need a voice and sometimes they need more than that i.e. someone who is able to orchestrate an investigation of the case of their behalf (per Hale LJ as she then was in Re A (Contact: Separate Representation)

354

[2001] 1 FLR 715 at p.721 and per Wall J, as he then was, in Re H (Contact Order) [2002] 1 FLR 22 at p.36 and in Re M (Intractable Contact Dispute: Interim Care Order) [2003] 2 FLR 636 at p.640)

The Court should have regard to the likelihood of success of the proposed application (Re SC (A Minor) (Leave to seek Residence Order) [1994] 1 FLR 96 Booth J and Re Lara (Residence: Child's Application for Leave) [1995] 1 FLR 927 Stuart–White J).

The principles set out by Sir Thomas Bingham MR in Re S (A Minor) (Independent Representation) [1993] 2 FLR 437 are equally applicable in these circumstances.

Kevin Briggs

Throughout, it has been mentioned that there have been incidents of violence involving Ms Hyde, which are the reasons for Alice's periods of not having contact with her mother. When Alice went to stay with her mother, there was no description given of abuse on my behalf as to the reason why, and this should mean something to the judge who reads Alice's application.

The crux of this situation can be summarised in two key points:

'...she did not want a contact order telling her when she must see her mother...'

As in the past, what is crucial is that none of the children, understandably, want to be forced into having contact with their mother after she has been abusive – that is the only reason contact stops with her in the first place. Ms Hyde is not able to empathise with her children's feelings and perceives everything through the myopic lens of her own warped perspective. I was not stopping the children, they simply didn't want to go, and Ms Hyde has taken me back to court repeatedly due to the consequences of her own actions towards the children; as also in the past, the children have sought their mother out to fix their relationships and this would have happened without court intervention, which, in truth, has only applied to Lara for the past year.

'...she should be allowed to decide for herself when she had contact with her mother...'

On no occasion have the children ever suggested they are concerned about living with me, it is a given that they have a loving home, and that is clear to see in the reports and their own applications. There has never been a need for outside involvement with reinitiating contact with me, because it is never a welfare issue, only teenagerism, which should have been dealt with by Ms Hyde and myself as parents.

(This is why I need a solicitor, the last paragraph of the letter reads like a load of nonsense to me, but it obviously means something to someone within these four walls.)

Dean Marlo

To Ruth, re: school holidays

24 June

As discussed, Hayley, Alice, Lara and I will be going on holiday to Norfolk this year. We will arrive at the Bellair Hotel on the 28th July and will depart on the 4th August.

I shall ensure that my mobile phone is switched on and Hayley, Alice and Lara will be taking their mobiles; as normal you can contact them as you please.

Yours sincerely,

Dear High Court

I would like to take this opportunity to state that I feel out of my depth without any professional representation. I would also like to confirm that I have repeatedly proved my ability to provide love and care for my children throughout.

Once again, I am in court defending myself against the Applicant's, Ms Hyde's, false allegations. I believe that I am supported by the court appointed child psychologist and my children's schools in my dedication to the stability and welfare of my children.

I have fully complied with the court order of 2004 and have clearly encouraged contact between Ms Hyde and all three children. I have never been disruptive or violent towards Ms Hyde; I have not been cautioned by the police for criminal damage, accompanied by aggressive behaviour. It was Ms Hyde who, again, brought this behaviour to our home and in front of our children.

I believe in the name of Family Justice, the court should recognise that if Ms Hyde wishes to contest the findings of Mrs Sanders' psychological report, produced at the request of Ms Hyde and endorsed by the family court, it should be achieved by her own means; it should be an issue between Ms Hyde, her legal representatives, Mrs Sanders and the family court.

Ms Hyde and her legal representatives should not be allowed to bring any further instability and emotional disruption once again into three young children's lives. These family court proceedings should be stopped so that my children can get on with their lives, unless Ms Hyde or Mrs Mason have any evidence to suggest otherwise.

I have consistently shown that I am a capable and good parent to my children; supporting their interests, achievements and day–to–day lives. Year after year, Ms Hyde tries to disrupt any normality that we have achieved.

For example: On the 16th of June, I was handed a copy of a letter from Smitch Law dated 2nd May 2007. This letter stated that Ms Hyde has instructed them that she wishes to take the two youngest children to Australia on the 2nd December for a period of 3 weeks.

This means Alice and Lara will miss 2 weeks and 3 days off school. (No holiday for Hayley.) The year 2008 will be an important year for both girls; Lara is very focused on preparing for her Eleven-plus, while Alice's attitude at school has been poor this year and she will not benefit from time out of school if she is to make up for her behaviour.

I would like to express my disappointment with Ms Hyde's request and the lack of consideration with the children's school attendance. It is not that I have a problem with Ms Hyde taking the children to Australia. Unfortunately, the timing appears to suit Ms Hyde and not the two children she wants to take with her.

At every hearing I have attended in the Family Courts, Ms Hyde has always made requests for changes to the consistency of the yearly schedule, and not within reason. Via her legal representatives, Ms Hyde appears to be able to bully and intimidate the situation in order to grant her whims, and, in their representation, the law firm show no care to any child's wellbeing, nor any repercussions that may occur as a result in the children's lives, due to their professional representation of their client's demands.

As I prepare to stand before you in London, I cannot help but think once again this seems an unnecessary use of public funding, when Ms Hyde need not have involved a solicitor, but contacted me directly with a simple letter of request. (As the issue appears to have moved on from contesting and contact, to Ms Hyde's holiday plans.) Ms Hyde has taken the children abroad previously, and I have several letters from her, outside of Smitch Law's purview, with requests for extra days, change of weekends and so on.

I have made no problems in the past with the children holidaying with their mother and I have complied with all requests and arrangements as necessary to suit Ms Hyde, while trying to maintain some consistency and stability within the schedule as ordered by the Family Courts.

I believe that the Family Courts should reinforce to Ms Hyde that she is to keep to the order and schedule of 2004, and focus on her parenting of our children.

Courts in London

25th June 2007 / High Courts of Justice Family Division Principal Registry London
Mother's application – residency and holiday
Alice's application – party to proceedings

Judge Justice Millar orders Alice and Lara to be assigned a Guardian from Cafcass.

A date is set for the final hearing, 22nd July 2007.

Ms Hyde and Mr Marlo to serve statements by 6th July 2007 and 20th July 2007, respectively.

Ms Hyde's application to remove the children to Australia for a holiday over the period December 2007/January 2008 be issued by 6th July 2007, and supported by evidence and documents. Mr Marlo, having confirmed to the court today that it is not the principle, but the dates, of the proposed holiday that would form the basis of any opposition by him, do file any evidence in response by 20th July 2007.

Court records be amended to show Mr Marlo as acting in person.

Case to be sent back to the Town Family County Courts.

Smitch Law do seek as a matter of urgency a date from the Town County Court for the final hearing of this matter, with a time estimate of two days.

Yesterday, Alice had briefly popped in unannounced at home to say hello. As I was walking into the Royal Courts, I felt a piece of paper in my suit pocket. It read: 'I love you dad and good luck at court. I do want to live with you love Alice'. This was thoughtful of Alice but, at the same time, made being here feel even more insane.

The scale of being before a judge in the County Court compared to the High Court is horrific. I felt more out of my depth than ever.

There was flutter about the entire building, though, and it wasn't for Mrs Mason's broomstick parked out front – rumour was Paul McCartney's divorce hearing was taking place across the hall.

(I never saw him, and I didn't see it in the papers later, but the thought was surreal enough, of my common-garden-estate-lad self being at court the same time as a Beatle.)

I was happy to see that it was raining today, as it meant that Lara's sports day was postponed. Lara would have been in a situation where neither of her parents were there to support her, as we were both in the High Court, London.

No mention of Mrs Sanders and her report; just Mrs Mason and Smitch Law's barrister claiming father has a problem with their client taking her children on holiday.

The judge talked with me for several minutes, she was polite and stated that she understood my concerns for the children's time out of school. Apart from that brief encounter, I sat there, wondering how much this has all cost.

We had a publicly funded child psychologist report lingering in the air, and I was listening to a barrister tell the high court judge that I continually make mother's contact with her children problematic.

I will never understand this family court procedure, whereby a barrister, or from my experience Mrs Mason, can make unfounded accusations, and by doing so they have already set the scene of the courtroom hearing, in the judges' eyes.

(It was nice not to be frowned at, or frothed at, or belittled by a judge, simply because they have come across 'bad fathers' like me before. I was relieved to not have a penal notice thrown at me, but maybe some prison time would have done me some good – it's fun to fantasise being away from all of this bullshit for a moment, anyway.)

From Mr Rowe MP

25 June

Dear Mr Marlo,

Further to our recent meeting in London, please find enclosed a copy of a letter I have received from the minister of State at the Ministry of Justice.

Hopefully you will find the Minister's comments to be of interest. If I can be of any further assistance, please let me know. Be assured that I am anxious to help you as much as I can.

Beverly and I are most grateful for the appreciation you have shown to us. It's always nice to be thanked. Best wishes.

Yours sincerely,

Dear Mr Rowe,

Thank you for meeting with me on 13 June, with your constituent Mr Marlo.

As Minister responsible for Family Justice, it was useful for me to hear about Mr Marlo's experience of the Family Courts. I understand cases involving whom a child should live with or have contact with after parental separation, such as Mr Marlo's, can be very distressing.

At the meeting, I referred to the provision within the Children Act 1989 for the court to restrict a party in making any further applications without the leave of the court. As I explained, I cannot provide Mr Marlo with legal advice, or comment on his particular case, but I agreed to provide you with some general details about the provision and these are provided below.

Section 91 of the Children Act 1989 states at paragraph 14:

'On disposing of any application for an order under this Act, the court may (whether or not it makes any other order in response to the application) order that no application for an order under this Act of any specified kind may be made with respect to the child concerned by any person named in the order without leave of the court.'

There is no guidance in the Children Act 1989 setting out how such applications should be dealt with. This has been developed by case law. In summary, the power to make an order under Section 91 (14) of the Children Act 1989 is generally seen as an option of last resort in the face of repeated and unreasonable applications.

I hope this clarifies the matter and I enclose a copy of this letter for you to send to Mr Marlo should you wish to do so.

Minister for Family Justice

(Approved by the Minister of State and signed in her absence.)

Email from CLG

30 June

Dear Mr Marlo,

I received your phone message. I have not received a draft of the order from Smitch Law. Perhaps they have decided not to send it to me. They have no real obligation to do so. In these circumstances you may have to wait for the court order.

As I said before, you can be assured that Mrs Justice Millar will take care to ensure that the order is correct before it is drawn up by the court staff.

Sorry to be unable to assist any further.

Regards,

Kevin Briggs

A conversation with Northview

3 July

I phoned Northview Grove to request a meeting concerning Alice. I was given an appointment with Mr Caldwell. (Although I had mentioned a couple of local youth organisations for Alice to talk to, she snubbed the idea.)

We talked about addressing Alice's behaviour within the school. Mr Caldwell stated that we had only 2 weeks left of term and suggested that we make a start with Alice's behaviour, if necessary, in the new term.

Mr Caldwell said that in his experience many children grow up a lot over the summer holidays and that Alice's behaviour should level out. I expressed that the lingering court hearings can't help Alice's mentality, and that she needs to feel settled at home.

Mr Caldwell and I agreed that perhaps Alice would never be a model pupil, but working together we could eliminate or minimise the behaviour Alice had shown over the past several months and help her to catch up on her education.

I left the school feeling very positive.

Northview; Exclusion

4 July

Dear Mr Marlo,
Pupil: Alice Marlo, 8OK
I am writing to inform you that I have today excluded from school your daughter for two school day(s) from Thursday, 5 July to Friday, 6 July, 2007. Alice should return to school on Monday, 9 July, 2007 following an interview with Mrs Tran/ Mrs Hewitt.
The reason for Alice's exclusion is repeated failure to follow instructions or comply with reasonable requests.
Mrs Tran/ Mrs Hewitt will talk to you and Alice about the situation Monday, 9 July, 2007 at 8.40am. If this is not convenient, please contact the school to arrange an alternative appointment.
We regard it as an essential part of the exclusion that Alice is not to be on or near the school site at any time during the exclusion period.
Yours sincerely,

I received a phone call from Alice to say that she had been suspended. Shocked (but the meeting with Mr Caldwell had gone so well!) I asked Alice why. Alice stated that initially she had been asked to remove her shoes for P.E. and had replied that her shoes take an hour to take off and put on, so she wouldn't. I closed my eyes for a second, pained at Alice's attitude, because I can hear she does not see the problem with how she's acted. In the background, someone was getting irate, telling Alice to get off the receptionist's phone. Alice replied, 'I am just arranging for my dad to pick me up, after you have suspended me again.'

Five minutes later, Northview called to formerly explain why Alice had been excluded and needed picking up.

Alice got in the car with this letter, but was not interested in talking about school and instead repeated that she does want to live with me, but she also wants to stay at her mother's at the moment. I said 'Alice' disapprovingly, because we've talked about this in circles, and in response Alice said, 'Dad', drawing out the syllable with attitude.

Ms Hyde's C2 Form (Application to Court)

5 July

The order(s) or direction(s) you are applying for
I am seeking a specific issue order that I may take the children out of the jurisdiction to Australia for three weeks in November/December 2007 for the purposes of a holiday.
Your reason(s) for applying and any plans for the child(ren)
I wish to be able to take the children to Australia for three weeks at the end of November/beginning of December 2007 for the purposes of a holiday and to see my family.

Already, the dates have changed from when she first informed me about this holiday. Has she asked Lara if she wants to spend her birthday in Australia and miss her Nan's birthday?

Dean Marlo

Further disruptions

6-9 July

Friday 6th
It is Ruth's contact weekend, and all the children are at their mother's.
Saturday 7th
Hayley called to say she was sleeping over at a friend's tonight and would probably
be home tomorrow. I told her to have a nice time and got back to work.

At around 6.30pm, my phone rang and it was Ruth, angrily asking me to come and
collect 'my daughter'. I asked what has happened, and she replied, 'Fucking Alice!' was
being disruptive and has told her to 'fuck off'. I told Ruth I would talk to Alice, because
we are supposed to be trying to keep to a routine with Alice's living habits.

As I called Alice's mobile, she didn't pick up. Unsure what to do, I waited, still hoping
whatever the problem is could be resolved without me contributing to the notion of Alice
flitting between homes. After about five minutes, Alice rang, and when I asked if she was
alright, Alice said her mother had blown up over nothing; she was going to stay in her
room and keep out of her mother's way.

Not liking the frequent verbal abuse that happens in Ruth's vicinity but feeling that
Alice's solution was probably the best one, I told her to have a quiet night and to call me
if she needs me.
Sunday 8th
I heard nothing more from Alice, so hoped Ruth had calmed down, or at least did
not go into Alice's room to reinitiate the argument.

Today, I had a lot of paperwork to do in the office; Sully had settled herself down in
the chair opposite. Alice came home at around lunchtime and I received a text from
Hayley, saying she is staying at her mother's tonight.
Monday 9th
I headed to the reintegration meeting with Alice at Northview; Ruth could not attend.
It went about as expected, Alice signed the agreement to follow school rules and went to
class.

As I was leaving, it was inquired as to why Hayley is not at school. I informed the
school Hayley had stayed with her mother last night, and I was unaware of why she was
not present. I got a similar call from Riverbank, and another in the afternoon to say Lara
had been brought in at lunchtime.

After school, Alice phoned to say she is staying at her mother's, but Hayley came
home. Both Hayley and Lara looked tired and agreed to have an early night.

Northview; Alice; Exclusion

10 July

Dear Mr Marlo,

Pupil: Alice Marlo, 8OK

I am writing to inform you that I have today excluded from school your daughter for three school day(s) from Wednesday, 11 July to Friday, 13 July, 2007. Alice should return to school on Monday, 16 July, 2007 following an interview with Mrs Hewitt.

The reason for Alice's exclusion is repeated failure to follow instructions or comply with reasonable requests. Mrs Tran/Mrs Hewitt will talk to you and Alice about the situation Monday, 16 July, 2007 at 8.40am.

Yours sincerely,

Mrs Mason sends Ms Hyde's Statement

11 July

We enclose herewith copy statement of our client dated 9th July 2007, receipt of which please acknowledge.

I, Ruth Hyde, *make this statement believing it to be true and knowing that it will be placed before the court in evidence.*

I make this statement in accordance with the order of the Honourable Mrs Justice Millar dated 25th June 2007.

I can confirm that it is my wish that there should be a Shared Residence Order in respect of Alice and Lara.

For the past four to five months Alice has been spending the majority of her time with me and I have continued to see Lara in accordance with the previous court order made on the 5th August 2004 by the Town County Court.

I would refer the court to my earlier statements but I do not feel the need to go over old ground and repeat what I have said earlier.

My only wish is that the children are happy and settled and that both of them have boundaries and know when they are going to see each parent.

Alice has been going through quite difficult times recently and I understand that she is confused about where she would wish to live. As I have said, for the last few months, she has spent the majority of the time with me although I have always encouraged her to see the respondent as I believe it very important that the children have a relationship with both parents.

Alice is now at an age where I believe she is at a cross road in her life and it is very important that the respondent and I work together to ensure that she matures into a caring young woman who is able to do well at school and enjoy relationships with her family and also her friends.

Alice's behaviour at school has been of concern and I think that she is confused about what she is feeling and what to say without upsetting either myself or the respondent.

My own view would be that it would be sensible for Alice and Lara to enjoy a Shared Residence Order whereby every other weekend Alice and Lara are with me as they have been for the last 7 years, from after school on Friday through to start of school on Monday morning, and in addition Alice to spend each Tuesday and Thursday evening with me overnight as I understand from speaking with her that these are her wishes.

In respect of Lara, I believe that she would like to spend Thursday night with myself when she has spent the proceeding weekend with me and on week 2 when she has spent the weekend with her father, she would spend Tuesday night with me; again from speaking with her I believe that these are her wishes and cause little disruption to her routine. I am happy to be flexible with these nights on occasions if special events occur.

I would also wish for Alice and Lara to spend half of the school holidays with me as they have done for the last 7 years.

My own view is that these arrangements would work very well, that the children would be spending time with both myself and their father and that in the past Shared Residence has worked although the arrangements were that the children spent blocks of periods of time with one parent rather than these proposals which effectively shares the week.

I believe that both Alice and Lara need to be aware that an order will be in place so that this will encourage Alice to spend time with the respondent rather than going backwards and forwards when the mood takes her.

As I work as a carer sometimes doing shift work, it is important to me that I know when the children are going to be with me so that I can organise my working hours around them.

The respondent and I only live a short distance apart from each other and I believe that Shared Residence is a realistic option and it would show the children that they have two homes with two parents that love them very much.

Dean Marlo

Second statement and supporting documents

11 July

I, Ruth Hyde, make this statement believing it to be true and knowing that it will be placed before the court in evidence.

I make this statement in support of my application to remove Hayley, Alice and Lara from the jurisdiction of England and Wales for the purpose of a holiday to Australia for three weeks in December 2007.

I wish to take Hayley, Alice and Lara to Australia for a period of three weeks to visit my sister and to travel around Australia.

There is now produced to me marked 'RH1' a copy of an itinerary that I have prepared on the basis that I would be able to take the children to Australia leaving on the 6 December 2007 and returning to the UK on Friday 21 December 2007.

I would wish to spend some time with my sister and then take the children to Sydney.

I understand that the school and the respondent have concerns about the children being taken out of school but I am prepared for Lara to have weekly private tuition to cover the Eleven-plus curriculum which she will commence next year.

There is now produced to me marked 'RH2' a copy of a letter from Mr Church, the Headteacher of Lara's school, dated the 5 July 2007, together with a letter from Northview Grove School dated 9 July in respect of the school's position in taking the children out of school.

I understand that the school are prepared to grant a leave of absence for up to ten days in one year but a third week would not be authorised.

I firmly believe that the trip to Australia would be of enormous benefit to the children, my sister is a geologist and we are planning to visit the aquarium together with the Opera House. I am fortunate enough to have a sister who lives in Australia so we are able to travel there but I do need to book my flights as soon as possible as the cost increases the nearer the flights are booked to the dates of the intended travel.

I would ask the court to grant my application so that the children and I can enjoy a holiday in Australia.

5.7.2007

Dear Sir or Madam,

Thank you for your letter of 4.7.07 regarding Ruth Hyde/ Lara Marlo.

At present, Riverbank School authorises holiday absence during term time up to a period of ten school days, after which the absence is 'unauthorised'.

We make it very clear to our parents, however, that any holiday absence is not in the interest of the child's education, especially since today's curriculum requirements are very full, and 'missed' work is extremely difficult to catch up on.

Both authorised and unauthorised absences are clearly recorded in the attendance register. Once the ten days have been used, every absence due to holiday purposes is recorded as 'unauthorised', and checked by a visiting Educational Welfare Officer on a termly basis.

Yours sincerely,

Mr Church, Headteacher

10.7.2007

Dear Sir/Madam,

Thank you for your letter on behalf of Ms Hyde requesting three weeks' leave for Hayley and Alice Marlo to visit Australia.

My response is determined by the Pupil Registration Regulations 1995 – amended 1997, whereby I have discretion, acting on behalf of the Governing Body, to grant leave of absence up to 10 days in the school year only.

I am happy to grant therefore two weeks for the girls to visit Australia but could not under these regulations grant a third week, which would be unauthorised. If absence is not authorised and the holiday taken anyway the case will have to be referred to the Education Welfare Service who may issue a penalty notice for £100 to each parent for each child taken out of school. Therefore, Ms Hyde would have to decide as a parent responsible for the education of her children about her application for a third week.

Alice Marlo's attendance to date in this academic year has only been 78.2% and Hayley Marlo's for the same period 85.75%. Both of these are well below the level of 94% and therefore strictly speaking insufficient for leave to be granted. I do, however, believe the girls would benefit from a holiday to Australia for two weeks.

Yours faithfully,

Mrs Tran, Headteacher

I am thankful, since the idea was first proposed, that it no longer encompasses Lara's and Ma's birthdays if it is going to be granted by the court; it's just another way to completely destabilise any normality the children have. Ruth knows the children have always enjoyed their Christmas time, and a holiday during this period clearly shows she has not considered the children's wishes, let alone what would actually be best for them concerning school.

Ruth's asking the courts to hurry up in order to save her a few pounds on a flight to Australia; I had to wait for months to get into court to see my children after she withheld contact. Swings and roundabouts. Ruth is working, lives in a four bedroom house, proposing to take a holiday to Australia for three weeks – she is the one receiving Legal Aid. (Which was misused to contest a report that legal aid paid for and now to book Ruth's holiday.)

The children's attendance alone should indicate that it is not a good idea and Ruth should be booking the trip in the summer holiday next year.

From Northview Grove Head

13 July

Dear Mr Marlo,

Following my conversation this morning with Ms Hyde regarding Alice's reintegration into school for the final week of term, the following has been agreed:

Alice will attend on a reduced timetable in the first instance to ensure that the reintegration programme is both successful and secure; when the school has sufficient evidence that this has been successful, she will be immediately returned to a full–time programme; if, during the reintegration, Alice continues to display unacceptable behaviour we shall have no choice but exclude her again.

Meanwhile, we are investigating all opportunities for Alice in terms of additional support from the Behaviour Support Unit and any other avenues that could offer Alice help to move forward.

These issues have all been discussed with Mrs Tran, Headteacher. If you wish to discuss these matters further, please make an appointment.

Yours sincerely,

Mrs Hewitt

Assistant Headteacher

Court – another application

17th July 2007 / Town Family County Courts
Mother's application – Holiday!

Judge Neely orders case to be listed for Directions 26th July, with the guardian and legal representatives to attend the hearing.

Mrs Mason writes to me

18 July

We enclose herewith by way of service upon you, our client's Notice of Amendment of Public Funding Certificate, receipt of which please acknowledge.

We also write with regard to the draft schedule for 2007/2008 which was handed to you at court on the 27th June 2007.

Can you please confirm by 4pm on the 27th July 2007 that the schedule is agreed or alternatively provide us with a counter schedule which we can discuss with our client. If we do not hear from you by 4pm on the 27th July 2007, we will advise our client that you have agreed the schedule as drawn.

We would recommend that you seek your own independent legal advice with regard to these issues.

The attached Legal Aid Notice of Extension/Amendment of Certificate's description is – Applicant to receive General Family Help in relation to proceedings, whether proposed or issued, to remove a child/children from the jurisdiction.

My applications for Legal Aid have been to stop abuse, harassment and instability, which are clearly less important issues than the provision for a holiday.

Although, it is only Melissa's help and endeavours to keep things on a level playing field that has prevented Mrs Mason from dictating a schedule to suit her client; even so, it makes little difference to the attitude of Mrs Mason or the harassment of the schedules and my life.

Another incident

18 July

In an attempt to establish some form of routine for Alice, as a compromise, Ruth, Alice and I agreed that Alice would stay overnight at Ruth's on Thursdays.

This week, Ruth couldn't make it on the Thursday so it was changed to today, Wednesday. When I took Alice at 7pm, as requested by Ruth, there was no one in, and she did not answer her phone. We went back at 7.30pm and there was still no one there, and she was not answering neither Alice nor my calls, but Alice had a key and said she would go in and wait.

My phone rang at nearly 12am, waking me up, and I answered to loud voices, crackling from the volume. I could make out Ruth, predominantly, demanding I collect Alice 'right fucking now', and Alice in the background shouting for me to come for her.

Getting up immediately, I drove to Ruth's and found Alice waiting for me outside on the curb, wiping at her eyes. While driving home, I asked what had happened; Alice said her mother had been another hour almost before coming home, but they still went swimming and got a takeout. After they'd eaten Alice had made herself a cup of tea and put 'Big Brother' on the TV. At around 11.30pm, her mother had sat down on the sofa with her, and asked Alice to change the channel.

At this point, Alice admitted she shouldn't have gone on about it, however because Alice refused to change the channel when her mother asked her to do so, they had an argument. Alice then said her mother had sat on her, so she couldn't move, and bent her thumb back to the point she was screaming that it hurt. As soon as her mother let go, Alice had called me which resulted in her mother trying to take her phone to talk to me.

I checked Alice's thumb over; nothing looked broken but it was red and slightly swollen.

Alice settled down in her room, I popped my head in on Hayley and Lara – both asleep – and headed for the office. I wasn't going to sleep after a night like this.

Dean Marlo

Mrs Mason writes to the Psychologist

19 July

I enclose a copy of an order dated 17th July 2007, which I have received from the Town County Court. Please note that you will be required to attend court on the 5th and 6th September with regard to these matters and I would be grateful if you would please confirm that the dates are in your diary.

I will be able to contact you nearer the time to confirm whether you just need to attend one day or whether you will need to attend to hear the evidence of the parents as well.

My Statement (July)

I, Dean Marlo, will say as follows:

I make this statement believing its content to be true, knowing that it will be placed before the court in accordance with the order of the Honourable Mrs Justice Millar, dated 25 June 2007, in response to Ms Hyde's proposals as contained in her statement dated 9 July 2007.

I do not refer in this statement to Ms Hyde's previously proposed trip to Australia as I covered this in my previous position statement, accessible by the court.

I do not believe that it would be in the children's best interests for there to be a Shared Residence Order in respect of Alice and Lara, and rely on the content of previous statements filed in these protracted proceedings as well as the content of Mrs Sanders' report and addendum report, in support of my belief.

I am dismayed to once again to report an incident of abuse regarding one of our children in Ms Hyde's care, and ask the court to take into consideration that while I believe Alice will 'come round', as she has in the past, and resume staying contact with Ms Hyde, I do not know when this will be.

Over the past 4 to 5 months, Alice has continued to test boundaries set to try to help her to modify her behaviour. Alice has 'flitted' between her mother and I, primarily, as I see it, as a response to my parental attempts to maintain healthy boundaries.

I do not believe it is helpful for Alice to be able to phone Ms Hyde and be immediately collected by her; Ms Hyde does not talk to Alice about whatever problem has occurred at home, nor does she try to support me as a parent. It is counterproductive and giving Alice the wrong message.

Lara is thriving on the stability that the regular pattern the current order has provided.

Like Ms Hyde, I refer to my earlier statements and do not intend to repeat their content in this statement. I too wish for the children to be happy and settled, to maintain appropriate boundaries and ensure that they know when they are going to see each parent. I agree entirely with Ms Hyde that it is very important that she and I work together for all of our children's sake.

Unfortunately, Alice's behaviour at school has occasionally been volatile and disruptive. I believe that she needs to settle down at home and talk to a children's organisation, separate from the Family Courts.

I am extremely concerned for Alice. I refer below to an incident that took place last night (18 July 2007) and from which, Alice's account of, sounds as though Alice's challenging behaviour at school is a repeat of the behaviours that are displayed towards her, while staying with her mother.

Recently, Ms Hyde, Alice and I agreed that Alice would spend one night a week at Ms Hyde's on Thursdays. This week, Ms Hyde could not do Thursday so it was changed to Wednesday at 7pm. When I took Alice at 7pm, Ms Hyde was not there and did not answer her phone. We went back at 7.30pm and there was still no one there, but Alice had a key and said she would go in and wait.

I received a phone call at about 11.45pm and heard a terrible commotion with, firstly, Ms Hyde demanding I collect Alice, and Alice shouting for me to come and collect her.

I understand an incident arose because Alice was up late watching 'Big Brother' at 11.30pm and refused to change the channel when Ms Hyde asked her to do so. As a result of this, Alice states that her mother sat on her and bent her thumb back; she is now again stating that she will not go for contact because her mother has been violent towards her.

Regardless of which version of events the court believes, Ms Hyde needs parenting classes and help for dealing with conflicts calmly.

The school informed me that following a discussion with Ms Hyde, for the last two weeks of term Alice has only been required to attend lessons dependent upon which teacher is taking those lessons and whether that teacher is one that Alice gets on with. To me, letting Alice off certain lessons is not necessarily the best way forward, as this is just reinforcing to Alice that if she doesn't like something, she can behave in a volatile way, disrupt the class and she will then get out of it. Alice needs to know that she has to deal with the consequences of her behaviour.

I have already stated I do not believe a Shared Residence Order to be in the children's best interests. Alice has previously told me that she would like to continue to spend one night a week, during the week, with her mother and I have no difficulty with that.

In respect of Lara, however, I believe that she does not want the contact order to change. In particular with regard to staying overnight during the school week with Ms Hyde (and which I believe from what Lara has said to me, she and her mother have already talked about) causes Lara some worry about being late for school. I attach exhibit marked 'DM1' an attendance sheet prepared by Lara's school, showing three occasions when Lara has been taken in to school late this term after contact at Ms Hyde's. I would like to suggest that instead of staying overnight with Ms Hyde, Lara goes home with her mother after school but returns to me at, for example, 7pm on the days suggested by Ms Hyde, with the provision that it is Lara's wish to have such contact.

I am in agreement for Alice and Lara to spend half of the school holidays with Ms Hyde, and am hopeful Alice will settle into this again.

I believe that Lara should continue to spend alternate weekends with Ms Hyde, half of the school holidays and that if she is to spend time during school term weekdays, this should not be overnight. Lara has been thriving on the routine that has been in place over the last nearly three years. She has received yet another exceptionally good school report at the end of this term.

There has been flexibility in the arrangements for the children, and I agree that this is necessary. I believe that the annual swap of weekends and halves of school holidays is easy to implement but difficulties have arisen when, for example, I have planned an activity for a weekend in accordance with the court order and Ms Hyde then seeks a late change to the weekend. As in the past, I will accommodate Ms Hyde's requests for alterations as often as possible.

We ought really to be able to make arrangements so that they fall into our respective half of the school holidays and weekends when the children are due to be with us. If they cannot, all that I would ask is that any necessary changes are notified to the other parent in writing at the earliest possible opportunity.

As Ms Hyde does, I believe that an order being in place will encourage Alice not to 'flit' between us, however, as her parents, it will be up to us to do our best to ensure that Alice complies with any order.

Ms Hyde has also phoned me a number of times, telling me that Alice is being rude to her, playing her up and disrupting the house, requesting that I go and collect Alice. I believe that if Alice, in accordance with a court order, is with one or other of us, the other parent should not intervene, unless Alice is in danger, which will of course be dependent on the circumstances at the time.

I believe that as well as the children benefitting from a stable home life and knowing what is expected when, both Ms Hyde and I need to be able to know when we can work. Naturally, there are times when last minute arrangements for childcare need to be made, for example, if one of the children is too unwell to attend school.

For the above reasons, I believe that the children staying with Ms Hyde on alternate weekends and for half of the school holidays, together with Alice staying overnight one night during the week and Lara having teatime contact during the week from after school to for example 7pm, will be best.

I am extremely concerned that we do not all slide backwards into the kinds of difficulties that led up to the ending of the Shared Residence Order in 2004. I agree with Ms Hyde that the children need to continue to know that they have two homes and two parents who love them very much, this is without question. What the children require is stability, consistency and an end to proceedings.

Court – Cafcass appointed

24th July 2007 / Town Family County Courts

Judge Neely assigns Alex Moyer of Cafcass as Alice and Lara's Guardian.

Somehow, these court proceedings have been going on for a year – I'm not sure how much more of the farce and constant worry I can take. It's looming over all of our lives; the goal post of a final hearing, of settling down as a family, is constantly being moved.

Ms Hyde could have enjoyed more contact time with her children and we could have been friendly, but due to her fluctuating mental state, she is polarised and determined to demonise and hurt me in any way she can, including using our children as a means to carry on her animosity towards me.

Court – here we go again

26th July 2007 / Venray Family County Courts.
Mother's application – Australia holiday in school term.

Judge Recorder Jadin orders final hearing dates 5th and 6th September be vacated; Ms Hyde and Bernard Craven to file statements by 9th August 2007; Mr Marlo's reply to these statements be sent by 23rd August 2007; the guardian to file her report concerning Ms Hyde's proposed holiday by 3rd September 2007. Proceedings listed for the 5th September 2007.

I have never been *opposed* to Ms Hyde taking the children on holiday and I firmly believe I've shown throughout the hearings I am there representing the welfare of my children. However, we now have a guardian solely to discuss whether the children should go on holiday during term time, against regulations and in an important year for all the children – Hayley for her GCSEs, Alice who needs to regain some stability at home and in school, and Lara preparing for the Eleven-plus.

Even though Hayley has made it clear she doesn't want to go, she is at the same time upset not to be going on holiday with her sisters; it's an absurd situation for us to be in court for.

The Hearing.

As I sat in the waiting room at 9.30am, a woman came through the door. The woman introduced herself to me as Miss Curtis, the solicitor acting on behalf of the children's guardian; she explained that Ms Moyer from Cafcass was unavailable for today's hearing.

Miss Curtis asked me what objection I had to the children going to Australia, and I informed her that my concerns were the timing of the holiday, which I explain in more detail in my statement for the hearing 25th June. She asked if I had put a statement into the court for today's hearing; I said yes, and she requested to see it.

I replied that I did not have a copy with me, and she told me that I should have sent or given both her and Smitch Law a copy. I said to her, as I have no legal representation, I was unaware of the protocol that was to be followed.

(Well, apart from the court's copy there aren't any available; Mrs Mason will have to make it up as she goes along – she is rather good at that.)

Miss Curtis asked me again what objection I had to the children going to Australia.

I explained that Hayley is afraid of flying and such a long journey puts her off, but Alice and Lara would like to go on the holiday, just not at the time Ms Hyde has chosen. Alice has said she is worried that if, as on previous holidays, she and her mother argue or have a confrontation, she would be too far from home. While Lara wants to go to Australia, she would prefer to spend the build up to Christmas at home.

Miss Curtis stated that she understood, and stood up to phone Ms Moyer. When Miss Curtis returned to the room, she informed me Ms Moyer is happy for the children to go to Australia on holiday, as proposed by their mother.

I could not believe what I had been told.

Ms Moyer has never met or talked to my children or myself, yet, as the children's guardian, she is happy to let them travel to Australia, missing 12 days of school term?

What good is a guardian to a child if they have never met or talked to each other? What good is a guardian to a child if they have no consideration for their education or stability?

Ms Hyde's barrister, Mr Porter, came into the waiting room and introduced himself to me. He asked me if I had produced a statement for the court and today's hearing, and I told him the same as I did Miss Curtis. He asked why I had not sent a copy to Smitch Law and when I tried to reply (with my well-rehearsed line of defence), in a menacing manner Mr Porter stated, 'Why not?'

Uncertain about his tact and the annoyed look on his face, I informed him that I was unaware I had to, and without a solicitor it is difficult to know what to do. He stared at me briefly, turned away and walked off; I thought 'no goodbyes', then.

(Mr Porter was not born yesterday and he knew this was not my first family court hearing; I was well aware of the procedure with statements, and, as we now both understood, I had just told him to stuff family court protocol up his arse.

It is not much of a win, but it is nice knowing I am not going to reply or send my statements to a solicitor that should not be working in family law.)

My thoughts were ended by the court usher entering and stating, to one and all, the judge was ready for us. As I walked into the court room, I noticed Mr Porter standing by the door and as I approached, Mr Porter asked me if I was agreeing to the children going to Australia or not. I said that as I am trying to be a caring and responsible parent, I do not agree with the holiday occurring in December. Mr Porter replied, 'There we have it!'

(I am sure I will have nightmares for years to come, with reoccurring thoughts of being sat there on my own, facing the Judge and to my right Ms Hyde, Mrs Mason, her assistant and yet another barrister, good old Mr Porter.)

Miss Curtis spoke to Judge Recorder Jadin (RJ from here on out) first and confirmed that the guardian was happy for the children to go to Australia, in accordance with Ms Hyde's request.

Mr Porter told Judge RJ that he is aware that the courts have Mr Marlo's statement but Mrs Mason and Miss Curtis have not been given one; Judge RJ asked the clerk to copy the one she had.

(When the clerk returned, Mrs Mason grabbed it with both hands and scuttled back to her chair, I glanced over and she looked like Gollum.)

Mr Porter continued; he had been informed by his client that Riverbank School had stated 'they had no real objection to Lara going to Australia but they could not relay this in their letter to the courts'.

Mr Church has said to me, and would be just as honest with Ms Hyde, 'Bright as Lara is, she needs to be in full attendance as this is an important year.'

As I sat in front of the judge, I once again listened to Ms Hyde's barrister convincingly make a case on behalf of his client, with misleading and inaccurate statements being made along the way.

Judge RJ replied, 'Yes, I see this is just a standard letter that is sent out.'

Mr Porter stated, 'Ms Hyde is worried because Alice is flitting from one home to another and is suffering from stress due to not knowing where she should be living.'

After several minutes I thought, 'here we go again'; Ms Hyde's barrister was there saying one thing and I am going to stand up and say the opposite. Or, at least, I wanted to stand up, interrupt Mr Porter and tell Judge RJ that this was not the case and for the past few weeks Alice had been trying to settle down and had complied with the existing court order, i.e. staying with her mother every other weekend.

Instead of banging my head against a brick wall, or getting caught shaking my head, I waited for Mr Porter to finish prattling on, until it was my turn to speak. I stood up and referred to my statement as rebuttal.

Judge RJ asked me what objections I had with Ms Hyde's proposal to take the children to Australia – do judges read the statements?

(She could have said, 'We are all here because Ms Hyde wants to take the children out of school, which could negatively impact their education, and all three children do not want to go at Christmas. It is written in your statement – you and I are the only ones that have one!')

Judge RJ then asked, 'Can you not afford proper representation?'

I replied, 'No.'

I was holding my breath at this point, wondering what this line of questioning was going to mean for me. Am I going to be humiliated for not having a solicitor? Will the judge bring an end to proceedings before the person caring for the children is exhausted and financially rinsed – what with the days off work and the worry that is compounded by these hearings – to the point I no longer can?

Judge RJ stated that there was to be a further hearing to address Ms Hyde's proposed holiday to Australia and another two-day hearing, one day set aside for Ms Hyde's barrister to cross–examine Mrs Sanders and one day for contact. Mr Porter requested that Ms Hyde's boyfriend was allowed to submit a statement to the court for the next hearing; Judge RJ agreed.

I am a calm person, but there are times that even I get upset; I have never done more than write down my frustrations, such as when I heard that Mr Craven had hurt Alice or how someone with allegations of physical abuse towards any child can be considered to hold any sort of credibility or use within these proceedings. (And that's leaving Ms Hyde *out* of the equation for once.)

Ms Hyde was cautioned for criminal damage last year and an incident of abuse towards one of the children occurred only a week ago. Yet, for so many years it has been myself and my children who have felt the full force of the Family Courts System, and not in a productive way. My judgement and ability to be a decent and honest parent to my children has been repeatedly questioned, despite there being no evidence to suggest or prove it.

After leaving the courtroom, Miss Curtis asked if we could talk about the dates for the next hearing; she said the Town Family Courts have several days available, but Ms Moyer cannot make the days in September. She went on to say that Ms Hyde would like Mr Porter to represent her in court at the next hearing, and the only time he is available is in November, therefore did I have any objection to the final two-day hearing being in November. I told Miss Curtis I just want an end to the instability and proceedings, so I agreed to sometime in November; I felt depressed over the time scale but what could I do?

When professional organisations have been asked by the Family Courts to investigate my children's lives and my own, they have supported what I have written in my statements and what I have said at the hearings. Year after year this is forgotten, so we start all over once more.

The confirmations from both my children's schools over the years have never been recognised or acknowledged and that seems to be a fundamental flaw within the family law; the Family Courts have been happy to allow the unfounded allegations and defamation of a parent to continue, regardless of the evidence that it has been one parent trying to cope with the Family Courts and an ex-partner with mental health problems, while bringing up three children in a stable, loving household.

(It's not easy when everyone is on the same page; like this, it's fucking difficult.)

Mrs Mason writes

27 July

Dear Mr Marlo,
We refer to the attendance at court on the 26ᵗʰ July 2007 and to the order made by Judge Recorder Jadin that day.
We enclose herewith a bundle of copy correspondences between ourselves and the Psychologist with regard to your children.
We would advise you that the letter of the 30ᵗʰ March 2007, which was signed by your solicitor, we enclose the medical notes of all three children which we had obtained from their GP. We understand that Melissa, who was your solicitor at the time, would be forwarding your medical notes direct.

Dear Mrs Sanders,
I write to advise that the final hearing on this matter has been listed for the 8ᵗʰ and 9ᵗʰ November 2007. Could you please confirm that you are available to attend court on those dates?

Dean Marlo

A good holiday

Despite everything going on in the background, Hayley, Alice, Lara and I had a great holiday in Norfolk; going on the rides, the pier, shopping and relaxing on the beach in the evenings. For a moment here, I almost felt like we are a normal family, with no pressure on our existence as one.

I'm still struggling with sleep, but I refused to bring any court papers with me this time around. I'm here for my children, and I hate that the family court has taken so much of that away already.

Alice's demands

7 August

Alice presented me with a piece of paper with 'I am allowing Alice Marlo my daughter to get her bellybutton pierced by a professional' written on it. There are three spaces left for signatures; Alice and her mother have already signed. I said to Alice, 'You know I am going to say this, but I think you are too young for a piercing there, and you should wait until you are older. Why not another earring?'

Alice left the room, in a huff, with the paper unsigned.

Tomorrow, I meet with Mr Rowe again...

MP to me

13 August

Dear Mr Marlo,

Following your latest appointment at my office, over the weekend I have given thought as to how I might best provide support to you in respect of the current position in relation to your former partner's application to the court for permission to remove your daughters from school for three weeks. Although, as you know, there is a dividing line between political involvement and the decisions of the court, I feel that the situation we have here is such that there is nothing to be lost by my drawing the matter to the attention to various people in Government.

I have, therefore, written to (a) the Prime Minister; (b) the Secretary of State for Children, Schools and Families; (c) the Secretary of State for Justice and Lord Chancellor; and (d) Leader of the House.

I enclose copies of all four letters. I will contact you again when I get responses. If nothing else, at least senior Government figures will be alerted to what is going on in the real world!

Please keep me posted of developments.

I also enclose a photograph of the two of us taken a few weeks' ago on the Terrace of the House of Commons. Best wishes.

Yours sincerely,

Due to feeling like I have hit the wall with instigating inquiries into the performance of the Family Courts, I told Mr Rowe that I'm going to focus on my children. While I am grateful for his support, I cannot continue to travel the endless corridors within a corrupt system. Despite mine and his best efforts, I don't believe that either of us have found any honesty, morals or standards within any of the organisations.

MP's letter, addressed to the various parties

13 August

The Government, quite rightly, disapproves of parents taking children away from school – indeed, in a move to stop this the Pupil Registration Regulations 1995 (amended 1997) places limitations on approved time off.

My purpose in writing is to draw your attention to the case of my constituent Mr Dean Marlo, who has been granted custody of his three daughters, who all are of school age. The court has granted Ms Hyde, the children's mother, certain access rights, but to all intents and purposes, Mr Marlo is a single parent.

Ms Hyde, however, thanks to Legal Aid – which is denied to Mr Marlo! – continues to pursue matters through the courts.

In her latest move, Ms Hyde has applied to the court to be granted permission to take all three daughters out of school for three weeks for a visit to Australia. While Mr Marlo acknowledges that his daughters would welcome such an extended holiday, he is very concerned at the loss of three weeks' education.

The Headteachers of the two schools attended by his daughters have also registered their opposition to so much time off school. Mr Marlo informs me, however, that the children's Guardian – who he states has never met his daughters! – has told the court that she has no objection to the children being taken out of school for three weeks!

If the Government is of the view that the Pupil Registration Regulations 1995 (amended 1997) are so important, how can it be possible for a court to even consider ruling differently? And what right does the children's Guardian have to make a recommendation without discussion with the children's father and the schools, who are seeking to uphold the best educational interests of the children as set out in the Pupil Registration Regulations?

My constituent feels that 'the system' has failed him on many occasions. Both he and I, are dismayed that the court is being urged to ignore the very regulations which Parliament has approved to safeguard the educational interests of children.

I would appreciate your comments.

Yours sincerely,

Dean Marlo

August Incident

14 August

I got a call from Alice asking me to pick her up from her mother's, due to them having a row; I agreed to meet her a few doors down.

Alice got in the car and before I drove off, I talked to her. Since it had been an argument, I told her that she should go back in and try and get on with her mother. However, Alice made it clear to me that she realised that if she did so, the situation would escalate. Alice's fear was that it would result in violence again and she decided that she was not going to let it get that far.

I let Alice know that it was responsible of her and a better way of dealing with the situation than retaliating, although her mother should not be putting her in this position in the first place.

Driving home, Alice said that she would see how her mother is tomorrow, as she wants to try with her and enjoy her holiday with Hayley and Lara.

Legal letters to me

14 August

From Mrs Mason:
We refer to the order made by Judge Recorder Jadin on the 26th July 2007 and note that we have not received your statement, which was due to be filed by 2nd August 2007.
Can you please confirm whether you have now filed that statement with the court and if so provide us with a copy.

I sent my statement to the courts before the 2nd August, same as before; what Smitch Law and Mrs Mason cannot circumvent is that I am not willing to play the solicitor game of tennis. They have personally made my life with my children a nightmare. I am not a bad father, and my family did not deserve to be treated in this way by a family law firm, a solicitor nor within the Family Courts.

How many statements am I expected to write on the same subject? Mrs Mason has a copy of my statement (curtesy of Judge Recorder Jadin) – what more can I say?

From the children's legal representatives:
TAKE NOTICE that Messrs Huffman LP have been instructed to act in the above proceedings under a substantive certificate for full representation on behalf of the Second respondent, Alice and Lara Marlo via their Guardian, Alex Moyer.

Mrs Mason with another Statement

15 August

We enclose herewith our client's statement dated 13ᵗʰ August 2007 together with the enclosures referred to, receipt of which please acknowledge.

I, Ruth Hyde, make the following statement, the contents of which are true to the best of my knowledge and belief. I understand that this statement may be placed before a court.

I make this statement in accordance with the Order of His Honour Judge Recorder Jadin, dated 26 July 2007.

I have not, as yet, received a copy of Mr Marlo's statement which should have been filed by 2 August 2007.

I make this statement to update the court concerning events which have occurred since 9 July 2007.

I can confirm that Alice has continued to spend time with me and also with Mr Marlo and I have endeavoured to encourage Alice to spend more time with Mr Marlo together with Hayley and Lara.

I have, however, been very concerned about Alice's behaviour and she has been suspended from school on two occasions shortly before the school broke up on 23 July 2007 as a result of her behaviour.

There is now produced to me marked 'RH1' a copy of a letter dated 13 July 2007, which the assistant Headteacher wrote to Mr Marlo and copied to myself in respect of Alice's behaviour at school.

I am very concerned about Alice's behaviour as I have been for some time and I am worried that she will be eventually be permanently excluded from school as a result of her behaviour.

I have tried to discuss matters with Mr Marlo but he simply isn't prepared to discuss these matters with me and I am also in discussions with the school to try and resolve these issues.

There was an incident on 18 July which involved Alice having an argument with myself.

That day Alice and I had spent an enjoyable day together going swimming and on the way back in the evening I suggested that we get a Chinese takeaway. Alice was happy with this and we went back to my home and began eating our meal. I had earlier called my boyfriend, Bernard Craven, and suggested that he come over a little bit later on to have some of the takeaway and spend some time with me after Alice had gone to bed.

We had had a very nice day and evening and Alice and I were sitting on the sofa together watching television while Bernard was eating his takeaway at the other end of the living room and doing some paperwork.

It was starting to get a little bit late so I suggested to Alice that she go upstairs to bed. Alice didn't want to go upstairs and I tried to explain to her there was something I wanted to watch on the other side and that really she should go up to her room and if she wanted she could continue to watch television upstairs.

This isn't about establishing good boundaries and bedtimes; this is about *Ms Hyde* wanting to watch something on the TV.

Alice was determined that she wasn't going upstairs and I tried to make light of the situation. I was tickling her and trying to encourage her to get up and she responded by telling me to 'fuck off'. I did not retaliate to her but continued to try and get her to go upstairs. I suggested to Alice that if she wouldn't go upstairs then I would have to tickle her and I jokingly went to sit on her lap and then got up again, I then sat directly next to Alice and tried to nudge her gently off the sofa.

(Arr good parenting tactics.)

I can't be the only person who finds this very strange to read. Almost like someone is making up a load of bullshit to justify pinning their thirteen-year-old daughter down on the sofa.

Alice then exploded and began screaming and shouting at me. She went absolutely ballistic – ('just like her father') – she was shouting at me to 'fuck off', she was saying that I was 'fucking mad' and she then grabbed my hair.

Bernard remained sitting in the corner and he did not intervene at all as he has witnessed Alice's behaviour in the past and when he tried to intervene on one occasion, she falsely accused him of hitting her.

If the only way the man can think of to intervene is to put his hands on a child, then I think it's best for all involved he stayed in the corner.

I remained calm throughout the 10 minutes that Alice was screaming and yelling. In an effort to get her to let go of my hair I used a technique which I have been shown at work which involves putting pressure on the thumb in order that she would let go of me. Alice did let go but then began accusing me of abusing her and her behaviour was absolutely unbelievable.

At no time did I retaliate. – clearly, the paragon of patience and serenity as Alice had hold of her hair for ten minutes, wait, where are we in the story? Alice went ballistic, grabbed her hair, ten minutes of shouting passes, hair still in hand, Bernard, the old bartender, was collapsed in the corner, and then she does not retaliate by using a technique used to overpower adult mental health patients. Just so I'm on the same page. – *Alice would not calm down and I explained to her that I was going to have to call the respondent to ask that he collect her and take her home. Alice kept repeating that she 'fucking hated me' and that I was a 'fucking prick'. She said that she never wanted to see me again and when I phoned Mr Marlo, he said that he would come and collect her but he didn't want to talk to me about it at all.*

Ruth has been abusing our children for 15 years, mentally and physically, my priority was to get Alice out of the situation. The distinction between Ms Hyde picking Alice up and my going to collect her, is that I am concerned for the children's welfare, whereas Ms Hyde uses Alice's defiance to further her own agenda at court. When Alice leaves our home, she does so of her own choice after refusing to talk about a situation, defying a boundary or not getting her own way; this does not end with physical violence or me preventing Alice from leaving.

Mr Marlo then collected Alice who left saying she never wanted to see me again and I spent the rest of the evening quite shaken by her behaviour.

Two days later, however, on 20 July 2007, Alice contacted me as though nothing had happened and she has continued to see me, staying at my home and carrying on as she had before.

(Alice has seen her mother all of her life behave in a nasty way, and the next day she can be as nice as pie; I am not a psychologist, but I can see the pattern.)

I was deeply disturbed by Alice's behaviour and I understand Mr Marlo has also had to put up with her behaviour towards him. It is as though she has no respect for anyone and I am very concerned as to how she can simply 'flip' over something so small as being asked to go to bed.

The children have been on holiday with Mr Marlo since 27 July through until 3 August but I have seen them since they have returned.

On Monday 6 August, the children came over to my home for a family barbeque and all three children wanted to stay. My sister and her children were visiting and were all having a lovely time so the children rang Mr Marlo to ask if they could stay the evening.

All three children stayed with me overnight and the following day Lara went home to see Mr Marlo and the dog but Hayley and Alice came to the beach hut and spent the day with us.

I am encouraged that a Guardian ad Litem has now been appointed to act on behalf of both Alice and Lara and I am hopeful that the guardian will be able to recommend some form of counselling to assist Alice with regards to her behaviour.

It concerns me that Alice's behaviour is becoming so bad that she runs the risk of being permanently excluded from school and unfortunately Mr Marlo refuses to discuss anything with me in an effort to try and resolve these matters as parents.

To/From Smitch Law

23/30 August

Dear Sirs,

With respect to copies of my statements that have been sent into the Family Courts, I have to tell you that I am reluctant to provide copies for Ms Hyde at the present time.

My reason being is that the children are on holiday with her. They all need to enjoy their holiday and I do not want to cause any kind of disruption by Ms Hyde receiving my statements (although I wish to point out that I do not believe they should cause any great upset). I simply would like the children and Ms Hyde to enjoy their summer holiday together without the court proceedings interfering. I will provide copies as soon as their holiday is over.

With regards to the schedule 2007/2008 I shall provide you with a copy of the schedule after the school holidays and any requests Ms Hyde has, can be discussed at the September hearing if necessary.

Yours faithfully,

(I still do not want to participate in the solicitor game, but I was advised by Melissa that I would have to send my statement to Smitch Law, or be in contempt of court. The above concerns come from a genuine place though, and it does no harm to wait another week. I've heard my statements are a real yawn-fest anyhow.)

30 August

We thank you for your letter dated 23rd August 2007, the contents of which we note.

Dean Marlo

From Mr MP (Enclosed MoFJ)

28 August

Dear Mr Marlo,
Please find enclosed a copy of the acknowledgement I have received from the Ministry of Justice.
They are currently investigating this matter. I will contact you again when I receive a full response. Best wishes.
Yours sincerely,

20 August

Dear Mr Rowe,
I refer to your letter of 13 August 2007 addressed to Jack Straw about family court proceedings.
Your letter was received on 17 August 2007, and the Minister aims to reply within 20 working days. However, if we anticipate a delay, I will inform you as soon as possible.
I shall also contact you again if, after considering your letter further, it appears that another Department may deal with it more appropriately.
If you would like to speak to someone in this office about your letter, please get in contact.
Yours sincerely,

My Statement to the Courts (Sept)

I, Dean Marlo, will say as follows:

I make this statement believing its content to be true and knowing that it will be placed before the court and in accordance with the order of Judge Recorder Jadin dated 26 July 2007.

I believe the children need their relationships with their mother and to be able to enjoy regular time with her. They also need stability and we all need to be relieved of the pressure of court proceedings. I am reluctant to meet the requirement of sending Ms Hyde my statement, which she would receive during the children's summer holiday with her. I feel it would only exacerbate the situation and possibly increase tension, which nobody needs and cannot be good for the children. For this reason, I have informed Smitch Law that I will provide them with my statements as soon as Ms Hyde's holiday with the children is over.

I am not trying to defy the family court in my actions I am simply delaying Ms Hyde's reaction to my statements in the hope that she can concentrate on having a good holiday time with Hayley, Alice and Lara.

As I have said before, I am unable to comment on any event that may occur at Ms Hyde's home when all or any of the children are there. I do not know what happens. I only know what the children tell me and what I am told by Ms Hyde.

More often than not, problems have occurred in the evening, usually late evening, as on the occasion 18th July, 11.45pm. Ms Hyde phoned me already inflamed and accompanied with verbal abuse aimed towards me and the situation that she found herself in. She demanded that I go straight round to hers and pick Alice up, due to her behaviour.

It is difficult to help Ms Hyde immediately with these situations owing to her aggressive attitude and the verbal abuse that she unleashes on these occasions.

As in the past, I will continue to try and assist in resolving any conflict between Ms Hyde and our children in a calm and caring way.

I have previously stated that Ms Hyde and I should be able to present a united front to all our children, so we both deal with their behaviour consistently. However, when Ms Hyde is upset, as in many circumstances, I find any productive conversation impossible.

Alice has recently led me to believe that she is now well aware of how volatile the relationship between her and her mother can be.

On the most recent occasion, 14th August, I was phoned by Alice who asked if I would pick her up from her mother's, due to having a row with her. Alice got in the car and before I drove off, I talked to Alice and told her that she should go back in and try resolve the issue with her mother. Alice made it clear to me that she realised that if she did so, the situation would escalate. Alice's fear was that it would result in violence again and she decided that she was not going to let it get that far. I took her home with me and the next day Alice returned to her mother's; Alice explained that she wants to try with her mother and enjoy her holiday with her sisters.

Ms Hyde states that Alice tells her to 'fuck off' which is not the right behaviour from

Alice if this is true. In all of Alice's problems at school over the past seven months, I have not heard any complaints about Alice using bad language and she does not use it at home with me or around her sisters.

I believe that if Alice is behaving in such away with her mother, then she is replicating the language and behaviour that she receives from her mother when they have a disagreement, which is compounded by a growing up phase that Alice is going through. Alice is already showing signs of being aware of the situation with her mother and how their relationship is affected by her mother's behaviour and, in response, Alice's behaviour towards her mother.

I feel it important to make it clear that it can be difficult to discuss with Ms Hyde how to deal with situations that have arisen; I believe that this is because of the different approaches we have. For example, on several occasions Ms Hyde has allowed Alice to break a boundary which I had set for Hayley, who is two years older.

I repeat that I agree entirely with Ms Hyde that it is very important that she and I work together. I believed that we had been doing this, with only minor difficulties regarding the coloured schedule since the order was made in August 2004. Unfortunately, last year things took a turn for the worse, with the incidents that occurred in the spring of 2006 with Alice and Ms Hyde's boyfriend Mr Craven, and between Hayley and her mother, and from there, we have gone downhill with continued court proceedings.

I hope that the Guardian will be able to assist in bringing an end to the uncertainty and emotional instability that has engulfed our children and family for so many years.

Despite having sole residency, I would be happy for Hayley, Alice and Lara to stay at their mother's, as long as it is what they want, they are happy and safe, and they are doing well in school.

The Guardian Report

3 September

Dear Mr Marlo,
Alice and Lara Marlo
Rule 9.5 Proceedings
I write to enclose, for your information, Ms Moyer's report.
Yours sincerely,
Valerie Whyte (Huffman LP)

(Before we begin, please note that errors in the below report are not from transcription issues. I also apologise, I intended to do just a full reply to this, but as you will see from the outset, I didn't make it very far.)

Introduction

The children in this family have been subjected to private law proceedings since March 2007. The court bundle documents the history of this case clearly and I will not repeat the contents unnecessarily.

Over the years there have been significant changes in their main residence. In 2000, upon separation of the parents a residence order was granted in respect of Ms Hyde, their mother. A change in circumstances – what a nice way to put a severe mental health episode that required section for thirty days and inadvertent neglect of our three children for no other reason than that Ms Hyde believed I should not have anything to do with them – *meant that residence was granted to their father Mr Marlo instead and all three children currently live with their father and visit their mother regularly.*

For the purposes of this report, I have made the following enquires:
Met with Alice Marlo on 14th & 15th August 2007.
Met with Lara Marlo on 14th & 15th August 2007.
Met with Hayley Marlo on 14th & 15th August 2007.
Unplanned, informal joint meeting between all three daughters and their mother discussing the Australian Holiday on 14th August 2007.
Met with Ruth Marlo on 10th August, 14th August & 15th August.

We were never married and I'm concerned already, at paragraph one, that these reports can't even get basic facts right.

(Due to having dyslexia and starting my own business in the early 80's, apart from the help I kindly received from someone in the offices across from me, I enrolled into an English class and was taught when writing letters, I should have the person's title and name correct, to ensure it is clear and to the point, and that spell checking is a must. When I attended these classes, it was strange but evident that I could read and write, but could not spell.)

Met with Dean Marlo on 24th August 2007.
Telephone discussion with Ms Hart and Mr Wallace at Riverbank Primary School on 20 August

2007. (Failed attempts on 21ˢᵗ August & 24ᵗʰ August.)

Telephone discussion with Mrs Hewitt at Northview Grove School on 20 August. (Failed attempts on failed attempts on 21ˢᵗ August & 24ᵗʰ August & 29ᵗʰ August.)

Read the full bundle and also the notes by previous Cafcass officers on the Cafcass file.

Telephone discussion with maternal aunt Miss Jackson on 29ᵗʰ August 2007.

Brief history of relationships and current circumstances

The parents started a relationship in 1991 and separated acrimoniously in July 1999, when the children remained in the care of their mother.

When Ms Hyde moved out, our new separated relationship as parents with three children wasn't acrimonious; we went on holiday and I babysat. I thought we were on the right road, wherein we could be friendly for the sake of our children, even though our relationship had passed. Ms Hyde changed that by withholding contact of the children from me; history indicates this was evidently due to her ongoing mental health problems, which culminated in her being sectioned several months later.

I get fed up with reading the blatant generalisation that we're a classic 'parents hate each other' scenario, because it is clearly untrue.

This guardian should have seen that Ms Hyde uses her children as weapons, and in her day to day deranged mental state, Ms Hyde becomes high on confrontations, arguing and using foul language. It is not how much she likes or dislikes me, as her behaviour I have endured over the years is being played out in the children's lives. The guardian was not there, so I guess she can write what she likes... But she is here now, and what is clear is the acrimony is at Ms Hyde's home between her and her children.

(An abusive father is not on site, so why the acrimony?)

Ms Hyde was sectioned under Section 2 of the Mental Health Act 1983 on 2 July 2000 and the children went to stay with their father.

No one likes to talk about Mrs Jackson, magistrate; grandmother; Cruella de Vil, and the day the children were placed under Police Protection because of her.

She had previous admissions at psychiatric hospitals both abroad and in the UK since 1986. (See c438 – c452 for a more detailed history on Ms Hyde's mental health). Ms Hyde has a diagnosis of Bipolar Affective Disorder.

Mr Marlo referred himself to a Drug Clinic in 1999 to address his cannabis use at the time.

Mr Marlo was granted parental responsibility in respect of all three children on 20 March 2000. A joint residence order in respect of Ms Hyde was granted the same day.

No it wasn't; I had parental responsibility and shared residency, which constituted supposedly Hayley and Alice at weekends and Lara during set times (no overnight stay until she was 5), although it never really worked out like that – if it is going to be a concise summary of the facts, I'd expect it to actually be factual.

Later that same year, on 10 October, a joint residence order was made, but Mr Marlo applied for a variation in this order in December 2003 but the order for joint residence remained.

Contact proved ongoing issues through the years and the focus of litigation with periods of Social Services involvement and the use of experts, all of which are clearly documented in the court bundles. Allegations and counter allegations have been made by both parties which are difficult to substantiate.

The schools are too hard to contact; the police line goes through to answering machine; the member of Mind has been forced to sign an NDA... Surely the solution to difficult cases isn't just to shrug and say it was too hard? My children have been abused, and Ms Hyde needs as much parenting help today as she did in 2000 because, as we've re-established, she has bipolar disorder.

Following some involvement with Social Services in 2004, the court granted a sole residence order to Mr Marlo in August in respect of his three daughters with regular contact arrangements with Ms Hyde.

What does 'some involvement' mean, and it must have been quite important as Ms Hyde lost her joint residency; surely the involvement of Social Services implies there's something going wrong in the children's residency with their mother?

All three children now remain in the care of their father with regular scheduled and unscheduled contact with their mother. They live within walking distance from each other.

The guardian has stirred the muddy waters and cherry-picked information to hand, with 'Mr Marlo referred himself to a Drug Clinic in 1999 to address his cannabis use at the time'. We are in 2007, and the guardian has been asked to provide the Family Courts with her thoughts on three children being removed from school time to go on holiday to Australia.

I did not rob a bank; I sat down and had a smoke, 8 years ago.

Reasons for application(s)

Ms Hyde would like to remove the children from the jurisdiction for the purposes of a holiday in Australia, during term time. The schools are all supporting a holiday but are concerned over the holiday being during term time, especially as both Hayley and Alice are at a crucial stage in their education.

Ms Hyde has also lodged an application for joint residence, although I have not been asked to deal with the matter in this report. However, all three children have voiced very clear views on their mother's application for shared residence and so I feel it necessary to comment on residency in this report.

(It's a good thing the children did bring it up then, given this whole report was just going to be to organise Ms Hyde's holiday plans.)

Neither parent is able to confirm who it is that suggested further assessments are required. Both parents informed me that they thought it was the other parent's idea and that they don't really want any further assessments either.

The guardian need only look at the court application – Ms Hyde applied to the courts and the judge felt it necessary the guardian comment on the views of the children about going on holiday to Australia during term time.

Summary of previous hearings/outcomes

A full bundle relating to court proceedings in respect of all three children since 2000 are available to the court and I do not purport to repeat those records, save for that all three children have been subjected to ongoing litigation for the majority of their childhood as a result of the acrimonious break–up by the parents.

(Unfortunately, the bundle has been prepared by Mrs Mason and therefore its validity is in question.)

Legal status of child

All three children live with their father under a residence order with a contact order in place dictating contact with their mother.

Children

Hayley

Fifteen–year–old Hayley is the oldest of the three sisters, with tall, medium built with long mousy brown hair. Initially Hayley refused to talk to me but gave in after both her sisters spoke to me.

Hayley was under no obligation to speak to the guardian, as she is no longer on the court order and her mother knows she does not want to fly, so isn't going on the proposed holiday anyway.

She is in her final year at school and is looking forward to leaving school, yet does not have any firm plans for her future in relation to employment or further education. However a coupe of her best friends are both deaf and she has learned British Sign Language and think she may become a sign langue interpreter.

(Usually, I'm in no position to be bringing up anyone else's grammar and spelling… However, her job is to write reports such as this and I can't help my surprise at the standard being set.)

Hayley feel she as grown up a lot in the past 12 months and says, 'I used to be just like Alice, arguing about everything when I don't get my way… f'ing and blinding but not anymore… I have calmed down a lot… I really hope Alice does too for her own good!'

Northview Grove School informed me that Hayley sometimes has a lot of verbal disagreements with Alice which will include shouting at times and they are worried about her appearing depressed a lot.

This is the first time I have heard that it is reported by Northview that Hayley and Alice have arguments at school – Alice is normally standing up for Hayley, as indicated by the child psychologist. I've a very close relationship with Hayley, and I haven't seen her depressed nor has she spoken to me with concerns; I've been in contact with Northview for both Hayley and Alice, and they've never informed me of any worries for Hayley nor Alice, only usual teenage silly attitudes and behaviour.

She appears to have a good insight into Alice's level of anger and means of dealing with that anger as being destructive and inappropriate. Hayley feels Alice is easily led and 'in with the wrong crowds'.

I had great difficulty trying to speak to somebody at Northview Grove School during the summer holidays and despite leaving many messages only managed to receive a return phone call as I finished my report of Friday 31st August at 3pm. I spoke to the Depute Head who informed me that she is very concerned about Hayley's mental health as she appears depressed and sad most of the time. She thought an expert assessment and some therapeutic help may be helpful for Hayley but recognise that Hayley is in her final year now and they are not able to provide such a service.

Hayley talks to me about what is bothering her and it is only after incidents involving her mother that I see any sadness, which is not 'most of the time' and I believe understandable, if you have read what Hayley has been through and her application to the courts at the end of 2006. If Mrs Hewitt is so concerned, why has she not mentioned it in the several times I have met with her and why bring it up at all, if apparently they are not going to provide Hayley with support?

Alice

Alice is a tall, slim, attractive thirteen–year–old, who appears at least 2 years older than her chronological age.

Why is my child being described as 'attractive' for the court? What relevance does this have?

She has long dark blond hair and a pierced eyebrow. She has very low self–esteem and made lots of references to herself being 'a bit dumb….' during our meeting. Alice described some of the anger management classes she had in the past but feel they were fruitless and said all the had to do was complete sheets of paperwork similar to the Cafcass 'Needs, wishes and feelings pack' I had given her. Alice described herself as stubborn to such a degree that she would do things just to spite others, such as when she is told she cannot have something or do something; she will deliberately do that even if she had no intention to in the first place.

Northview Grove also confirmed this view when they informed me Alice's behaviour has always been challenging but the past 6 months prior to the end of the 2006/2007 academic years has seen a dramatic increase in her violent outburst, truanting and general oppositional and defiant behaviours.

Alice's behaviour has not 'always' been challenging and it totally discredits Alice by relaying as such. May 2006 was the beginning of some trouble, but again, Alice's reports were improving by the end of the year; in 2007, Alice began flitting between homes, where she found she was able to break boundaries and have a completely different lifestyle at her mother's. Coupled with several abusive incidents involving her mother, Alice's attitude became worse; these were not 'violent outbursts', these were uniform issues and truanting from of lessons.

They felt Alice should have a psychological assessment of her mental health needs as they have come at a crossroad and feel her behaviour has become untenable at school.

Northview Grove School informed me that they have occasionally overheard both Alice and Hayley talk to one or the other parent on their mobile phones during they day offering reassurances by saying 'of course I love you dad/mum…' and feel that the children are carrying a burden by constantly having to reassure the adults of their affections. This was also an issue highlighted in Mrs Sanders' reports.

My children do not call to reassure me – I don't know where this has come from, and the implication of the emotional manipulation going on is hurtful and shocking to read. I'm at work during the day and when the children are at their mother's they get on with their lives. Hayley, Alice, Lara or myself contacting each other, like families do, and saying 'I love you' is not a sinister and controlling statement, it is normal when you're saying goodbye/goodnight to someone you love.

I've been accused of being 'emotionally flat' and unable to perceive my daughters' complex emotional needs, yet showing affection is made out to be abnormal.

Laral

The youngest sister, Laral is a very bright, resilient young girl of medium built with long mousy blond hair. She is very clear goals and visions for her future and told me that she started collecting books and information on becoming a vet in the future and plans to go to Australia to study and set up her own practise on day. She has a very deep love for animal and has a number of pets at both her mum and dad's homes.

She loves complicated jigsaws, are a high achiever at school and 'one of the clever clogs in my class' she told me. Her school reports and teacher comments confirms this.

Laral would really like to go to Australia now to see her aunt but also feel that if she does not get the chance now she will almost definitely get the opportunity when she is older to go and work and study in Australia.

Physical, emotional and educational needs (Children Act 1989, Sec 1.3(b))

All three children require stability and security as they have all suffered emotionally from the 7 years of litigation process.

Alice in particular have learned to express her views through her behaviour rather than talking calmly, about it and it can be argued that it is a result of the way in which she has seen her parents resolve conflict.

(The way she has seen *one* of her parents resolve conflict, where is the guardian's evidence that I have behaved as Ms Hyde has?)

Hayley being that little bit older have come to realise that resolving conflict has a greater chance of success if communicating calmly although she still resorts to loud verbal disagreements with her sister at school.

Lara in particular is a high achiever and is considered gifted, whereas both Alice and Hayley are considered average. Alice is said to try hard at times but due to many exclusions and some truanting, along with many absences it is felt that Alice's education has suffered. Alice describes herself as 'stupid and dumb'. Her reading and writing age is well below her chronological age.

Maybe I really am the crazy one amongst all these people, but this to me is something concerning that the guardian, Northview, Ms Hyde and I, need to support Alice on. Low self-esteem isn't going to help Alice with her education or within herself.

(I've been there, dyslexic and struggling like hell, with teachers telling me I'm stupid – I know Alice just needs to find ways to apply herself, even when things are difficult at first.)

It is imperative that Alice receives some support at school to prevent her from loosing out more on her education.

Age, sex, background and relevant characteristics (Children Act 1989, Sec 1.3(d))

Lara is an almost 10-year-old, girl of white UK background and no particular religious preference.

Alice is a 13-year-old girl of white UK background and no particular religious persuasion.

Hayley is a 15-year-old girl of white UK background and practises no religion.

Ascertainable wishes and feelings of the child concerned (considered in the light of his/her age and understanding) (Children Act 1989, Sec 1.3(a)).

Hayley, Lara and Alice all expressed a clear wish for the cessation of proceedings and for their parents to stop arguing and to try and get on for their sake. All three children have said they do not want any further assessments and were adamant that they did not want more people drawn into their family life.

Hayley

Hayley would really like to go to Australia for a holiday with her mother as she misses her aunt and would like to see her again, however is aware her aunt will be visiting her again, however is aware her aunt will be visiting her during the Summer Holidays. Hayley is anxious about flying, citing the 9/11 plane high jacking as the reason for her fears. Hayley said, 'I am really not bothered when we go as long as it does not interfere with my final year at school,' and therefore feel that next year's summer holidays are the best time. Hayley also stated that if they did happen to go before Christmas as her mother proposed, she want to be back before Christmas as she enjoys the build up to Christmas with her father. Hayley is aware her mother wants them to go in the Australian summer but feel that she would be just as happy to go in the Australian winter, as long as she gets to go at some stage. She said she prefers to have her presents in England on Christmas day rather than being away from home.

Hayley does not want her mother to have shared residence as she feels it will serve no purpose, nor further assessments. She voiced strong opinions against the court process and ongoing involvement of professionals in her life and want the proceedings to conclude. She feels that she can't trust her mother not to make future applications to vary contact or in relation to custody as, 'They keep telling us it's the last time and we don't have to go back to court and then mum goes and make another application!' Hayley also stated that she will herself not abide by the residence order if her mother was granted one as she will stay with whom she want to and won't let an order stop her from doing so.

Can someone explain to the guardian that Ms Hyde's application is for Alice and Lara only, and Hayley was discharged from all orders at any rate? Although, I appreciate Hayley's comments, because she has summarised what happens and what could happen to Lara in the future.

I explained to Hayley the option of a section 91(4) Children Act 1989 order to prevent either parent from making further applications in the near future without permission of the court. Hayley did not believe that her mother will abide by such an order.

(I guess that's the difference between living in a situation and assessing it – I believe Hayley's absolutely right.)

Alice

Regarding the Australia holiday Alice said she '…would not mind going to Australia and don't care when as long as it's not over Christmas or my birthday' and at the same time expressed serious reservations about going. She described her mother as 'unpredictable' and showed insight into how her own behaviour 'sometimes triggers off her mother's anger'.

The writing is on the wall; the guardian is recording the children's feelings, yet I still cannot be confident that her report will mean the conclusion of court proceedings.

She is genuinely concerned that she will be too far away from home in the event she has an argument with her mother as she won't be able to just call her dad to collect her. Apparently she has been collected and returned early from previous holidays as a result of their fall outs. Alice said in an ideal world, 'I wish my mum and dad could just get on well enough so dad could come with us… he can stay in a hotel nearby and if I fall out with mum and stay with him… maybe we can all share the time together that way and dad won't have to miss out on seeing us!'

Alice also expressed strong objection to her mother being granted shared residence and said that if her mother is granted residence as well she '… will just do the exact opposite of what she wants me to do and if she tells me I HAVE to stay with her I will go to dad's… I know myself too well and I know that is what I will do… I always seem to do the opposite of what people want… I don't know why… this is just who I am!'

Lara

Lara told me there is 'something big happening soon and we are not allowed to tell mum!' She told me they are moving home soon to larger accommodation nearby. They will live only one street away from their mother instead of 10 minutes' walk away. I asked why this has to be kept a secret from her mother and she said, 'Mum causes trouble and we can't tell her things… they just don't get on!'

It's hard to read that this is how it comes across to Lara; I've never said to the children they 'are not 'allowed' to tell their mother things. Hayley and Alice are old enough to remember incidents at several homes, and understand the domino cause and effect their mother can have, making judgements for themselves on what to say to her. It's no fault of Lara's, but these reports – heck, the Family Courts – do not want to hear explanations; they practically vie for an excuse to slander my position as a parent.

I do struggle. Renting leases only last a year because of my position, and paying some landlord £700 a month does not allow me to put any savings together. As it stands with the court interference as well – my focus has not truly been on work and the pressure has worn me down. Ms Hyde has directly caused incidents at every single one of our homes, without justification; I do not want to risk losing being able to rent a property because Ms Hyde has caused an incident or written a letter against me. I will of course inform her the day we move, and the new house is literally round the corner from hers – I'm not hiding, but after many years, my defence mechanism has trickled down to the children.

Lara voiced similar concerns over the issue of shared residence to that of her sisters. Lara would really like to go to Australia with her mother as she said she likes flying but at the same time she was very dismissing saying 'I don't care if we can't go this year because I know I will be able to go one day when I am adult!' like her sisters, she did not want to be away from home over Christmas and feel that she should be home with her dad for the two weeks running up to Christmas as 'it's the best time ever… dad gets really exited as he loves Christmas… he's like a big kid and we do lots of nice things.'

Lara has a close affinity to her maternal aunt as she feels they both share the same level of intelligence and focus in their lives and want to go and live with her aunt in Australia while studying a veterinary degree once she has left school.

Lara too felt the court process was interfering in her life and said she was happy with the current contact arrangements as she gets to see her mother as much as she likes. She too does not want any other experts to assess them as she feels it will serve no purpose. Lara is very mature for her age and like her older sisters stated that she did not want her mother to share residence with her father and in an ideal world her perfect contact arrangement would be to come and go between both homes as much as she likes. Lara also that she would like to go to her mum's for tea once a week when her sister aren't there.

When discussing the plan I may recommend to the court I asked Lara to write down what her ideal plan would be. Lara wrote a poem for the judge to reflect the plan she would like for her life and I quote it below:

(My letter to the judge in the poem – this poem is the same as my plan)

It doesn't bother me; wherever I may be; as long as I can see; whoever I want to see; whenever that may be; all my pets will stick by me; that's why I love them so dearly; my sisters and me; stand together and plea; for all you out there to see; we just want to be; a normal family; so if you're too blind to see; then I hope one day you will be; out of my life completely.

The likely effect on Lara, Alice and Hayley of any change in his/her circumstances (Children Act 1989, Sec 1.3(c))

All three girls have expressed a strong wish to retain the current custody and contact arrangements and do not want their mother to share residence with their father. They feel, and I support this view, that their mother is likely to undermine their placement with their father if this is to happen.

Now that another expert has confirmed it, can Ms Hyde and Mrs Mason stop proposing the narrative that I am alienating the children from their mother?

Lara, Alice and Hayley have all been involved with litigation for the past 7 years, since Lara was only 2 years old. All three sisters have come to a point where they are reluctant to trust that adults will (i) take their wishes/feelings into considering; or (ii) act in their best interest. They have lost faith in the court process to and feel that there have been empty promises of no further litigation by both parents and other experts in the past, yet litigation has been ongoing.

(A round of applause for Mrs Mason and whoever is approving her applications.)

The schools are clear that all three children are more settled since they have been in permanent residence with their father and that their attendance appears to be more punctual. Occasionally, on a Monday they may be late for school and these seem to coincide with the weekends that they stay with their mother.

Changing their circumstances now will quite likely cause all three children to lose complete faith in adults and render them more vulnerable than ever. Giving their mother shared residence with their father will no doubt give her more clout to undermine their placement with Mr Marlo which has clearly provided them with some stability and security since 2004.

Neither adult is able to discuss the children's needs or support each other's parenting styles, therefore having shared residence will cause increase in an already very acrimonious relationship between the parents and all three children will suffer significant harm through this.

Taking the children out of school during term time for a holiday abroad is clearly not in their best interest, especially as Lara is approaching Eleven-plus; Hayley in her final year and Alice approaching her GCSE year. Whilst they would benefit from such a trip abroad they will have more benefit from going during the British Summer Holidays as it will (i) not interfere with their contact arrangements with their father; (ii) not interfere with the school work, and (iii) not affect their attendance.

How many paragraphs has it taken, to state the obvious?

Alice in particular could have increased difficulties if taken to Australia outside school holidays.

Any harm which he/she has suffered or is at risk of suffering (Children Act 1989, Sec 1.3 (e))

As suggested earlier all three girls have already suffered great significant harm through the acrimonious break–up and ongoing acrimonious relationship between ten parents and ongoing litigation over the past 7 years.

They have witnessed verbal and physical violence and on occasion suffered physical injury as a result of their mother's aggression which is believed to be related to her mental health.

While the guardian has spent the whole report indicating the parents are just as bad as each other, and the children have said it is not their contact with me that is a problem, it is how much time and when they stay at their mother's – and their mother forcing contact after abusive incidents – we come to the root of the issues: how Ms Hyde's mental health affects her and her parenting.

Continuing litigation, which in itself cause further fuel between parents as they draw the children into their arguments and accuse each other of various improper parenting, are adding to the children's harm.

When a parent is calling out abuse of their children, for which 'improper parenting' is a wholly inadequate descriptor, it is not the harmful part of that situation.

Parents and other relevant adults

Mr Marlo

Mr Marlo has no representation during these proceedings for financial reasons.

Mr Marlo did not reply to any of my phone messages and it was not until I managed to get his mobile number from one of his daughters that I was able to make contact and arrange a visit. He was clearly frustrated by the proceedings and wanted an end to it all, however, happy to talk to me during our meeting.

The stress of the situation has clearly affected him emotionally as he felt the need to apologise for getting welled–up when discussing the children and the damage ongoing litigation has probably caused them.

I am informed by Northview Grove School that Mr Marlo refuses to get involved in any attempts by the school to address Alice's behaviour and will not attend the school for meetings and in particular refuse to meet at the same time as Ms Hyde.

It's absolute rubbish! I have been in contact with Northview in person, through letters and on the phone; the context to me not meeting at the same time as Ms Hyde is because, as discussed at length, Ms Hyde historically chooses to blame me or take her frustrations out on me. This would not be conducive in helping Alice at school, nor do I believe that because I am my children's father, I should be expected to endure such abuse.

However Mr Marlo is a very involved parent at Laral's school often helping out on school trips/events or assisting on sports days.

I did the same with Hayley and Alice when they were younger; secondary school is a totally different scenario as a parent than having a child at primary school.

From the court bundle, my single meeting of him and discussions with the school and the children it is clear that Mr Marlo suffers from low affect and occasionally needs reassurance that his children will always be there for him. He deeply loves all three daughters and feels that Alice's behaviour is nowhere near as bad as her mother described it. He feels she is mostly misunderstood and worries that her mother undermines him when she collects Alice for visits when she has been punished by her father. He explained to me that Alice will phone her mother to collect her if he tells her off for something or ground her and she will then be allowed to do whatever it is her father grounded her at her mother's house. He is particularly concerned over allowing the children to stay out late or visit unsuitable friends.

Once more, the accusation comes up that I need reassurance from my children – we text and call like a normal family who are separated, and other than that, when my children are at school or their mother's, I focus on work and sorting my financial situation out; due to the particular trade that I'm in, I have to fully commit to the job I'm on. I'm glad the children and I do communicate, and it has never been at a level where it is stifling or constant. Again, being a normal, caring family is presented as some sort of sinister situation.

He too objects to the idea of shared residence as he clearly feels that Ms Hyde will have more power to overturn some of the parenting decisions he makes with the children. Mr Marlo objects to any of the children being subjected to further expert assessments as he feels, 'We've all had enough… I just want to live my life without interference from courts and other people… it's difficult enough as it is.'

Mr Marlo did confirm their intention to move to larger property.

Ms Marlo showed me the contact calendar for last year which was set up according to the contact order current in place and also a proposed contact order for next year. He then showed me the contact arrangement Ms Hyde have requested for next year often putting her as having contact 3 weekends in a row when it should be every other weekend.

The guardian keeps covering points that encapsulate the larger issues for our family; Ms Hyde continues to dictate the residency order to suit herself, against both the court order and fairness. If it was the children's wishes, Ms Hyde's behaviour was reasonable and their schooling didn't suffer, the children could and would spend more time with their mother. Over time, Ms Hyde has never acted in a way to encourage the children to want her to have shared residency, which is borne out by what the children have told several professionals.

Ms Hyde

Ms Hyde is represented by Smitch Law Solicitors.

She has a history of mental health problems and a diagnosis of Bipolar Affective Disorder.

Ms Hyde was very keen to meet with me and tell me of all the families past problems proportioning all blame on Mr Marlo. She appears to continue focussing on the past, is inconsistent in what she proposes and denies having made the suggestion of further assessments. I struggled to get her to offer any outlook on the future or any suggestion on how things could be arranged to give the children a positive outlook on the future. Instead she was more concerned with Alice being the big problem and considers Alice as using her.

So, with two court experts describing communicating with Ms Hyde difficult, how am I expected to do the same? Can they now understand, that under any circumstances,

Ms Hyde's temperament makes her confrontational and clouds whatever it is we need to discuss. For years, I have not retaliated to Ms Hyde, as I am aware any response runs the risk of escalating her condition.

She fails to accept the need for Alice to see both parents pulling together and supporting each other when one punishes her and fail to accept how her actions contribute to Alice's behaviour and insecurities. I suggested that when Alice is punished by her father that she should not go and collect Alice until such a time she has completed her punishment and that the same should go for when Alice is with her.

How capable each parent or any other person, in relation to whom the Court considers the question to be relevant, is of meeting the children's needs (Children Act 1989, Sec 1.3(f))

Both parents have been locked in an ongoing acrimonious break–up for the past 7 years and neither has shown any insight into how their behaviours have affected their children. Both blame each other for the problems they are having both with each other and the children.

… And we're back to both parents are as bad as each other. There is no justice in law; there is no morality in the people who are placed in positions of protecting children. I accept that I have not dealt with every situation perfectly, I am just a human after all, but I do believe in every instance I have put my children first, and that I have never been verbally or physically abusive to anyone.

Why doesn't it matter to this guardian that Social Services have been involved; Mind; doctor's reports all indicate that Ms Hyde is physically and mentally abusive towards the children, regardless of whether she means to be. I'm not suggesting the birching table, I'm still asking for Ms Hyde to receive help!

Mr Marlo has clearly been able to offer the children some – an unnecessary toss of salt in the wound *– stability and security over the past 4 years as this is something they clearly needed and evident in school reports.*

Ms Hyde has continued to be inconsistent in her boundaries and parenting style offered to the children including undermining Mr Marlo's attempts to discipline his daughters and in particular Alice.

Ms Hyde wants to go to Australia to enjoy a sun filled holiday over Christmas and does not take into consideration the children's wishes and feelings regarding the holiday. She presents the holiday as something for the children but it is clearly a holiday to meet her own needs.

The crux of months of court proceedings, summed up in one paragraph.

Contact

Contact arrangements are to stay as they currently are per court order.

Guardian's analysis and conclusions

It is clear from my limited observations and enquiries that all three children have strong alliances with both parents and in particular are worried about their father's emotional wellbeing when they are visiting their mother.

I think all three children described anxiety and unacceptable behaviour at their mother's, which is actually concerning.

Also the children are so worried about me, if they don't go in December they'll go to Australia for three weeks in the school holidays. From what I read, Hayley's anxious about the flight, Alice is worried her mother will kick off and Lara would prefer going next year. Where is the indication they are all worried about me being alone? Lara and I have already dedicated a bottom draw for stuff she will need for a holiday in Australia; Lara has told me she does not want to go at Christmas, missing her birthday and Nan's birthday, but she is excited to go maybe in the summer.

The children will often side with the parent with whom they are residing at a particular time and are often drawn into the conflicts between the parents.

I don't have any conflicts with Ms Hyde, I am dragged into her conflicts with the children, when they report incidences of abuse and refuse contact with her. The children don't 'side' with either parent, an incident happens and the children react. She doesn't get an abusive phone call from me, a solicitor's letter or have me outside her front door shouting and screaming.

Half of the Guardian's conclusions, I have no idea where she's getting them from.

The parents are often acting in response to their own feelings rather than being child–focussed, for example when telling a child to go to the other when they have an argument, thereby punishing them by showing some rejection.

It is Ms Hyde the guardian quotes as saying that, yet I am again included in the accusation.

Miraculously, despite the trauma's Lara have had to live with the past 7 years she has shown incredible resilience, focus on her future and maturity beyond her age. I believe a large part of her resilience lies in her clearly above average intelligence.

Hayley and Alice have also been through a number of awful situations which most children never have to experience, and they have done well; they're good children, caught up in years of litigation and abuse from their mother.

Neither parent seems able to consistently put their children's needs before their own and appear to rely on the assurances from their children that they are still loved and valued. However, of the two parents, Mr Marlo is able to offer good enough parenting to Hayley, Alice and Lara.

'Good enough' – that one stings.

Whilst a holiday to Australia is a priority of Ms Hyde, none of the sisters views this proposed holiday as imperative to their well–being. It is my professional believe that the children's indication to go at a more convenient time such as the British Summer Time has a lot to do with their constant struggle to try and minimise opportunities for confrontation between the parents and by not going outside school or schedule contact times they will not offend the other parent.

Or how about three children have more common sense than Ms Hyde, Ms Mason, the guardian and the courts put together?

All three children are more concerned with keeping their parents reassured of their loyalties and love, than that of their own needs. There appears an almost role reversal in this family where the children have taken on a pseudo parenting role, and the adults are locked into juvenile adolescent type behaviours of arguing and disagreeing for the sake of it rather than being able to look at what the children really need or want. Neither parent are able to step back and let the other parent have that little bit more and it appears a continuous struggle between the parents to try and get one up against the other.

I must ask, where is the evidence that I have ever behaved like this?

I have completed my report of Friday 31st August and was just proof reading it when I received the long awaited phone call from Northview Grove School.

I'm sorry to interrupt again, but there is something devastatingly funny about the fact she's written that she was proofing this report; I've seen less mistakes in my children's homework.

The school were of the opinion that both Hayley and Alice (the latter more so) would benefit from a psychological assessment and were unaware of the current contact arrangements or that any expert reports had been done in the past or indeed what mental health diagnosis have been given to Ms Hyde. Their information on the family was limited.

Whilst there had been a number of court applications by both parents in the past 7 years, all applications since 2004 seem to have come from Ms Hyde. I believe these repeated applications have had a detrimental effect on the family dynamics and especially in relation to both parent's ability to just focus on what's best for their children rather than meeting their own needs.

She indicates it is Ms Hyde continuing the acrimony and then drags me into it too.

Whilst Alice was anxious about having anywhere to go in the event she fall out with her mother during a holiday, I am reassured from my phone discussion with maternal aunt Eleanor Jackson that she has put in place strategies that will give Alice some time out from her mother while abroad and that there are friends with children of similar ages to Alice and Hayley with whom they can socialise while in Australia.

(Let's hope by the one phone discussion Ms Moyer has had with Miss Jackson, Alice's worries about her mother being abusive are put to rest.)

Options available to the court

The court can make a shared residence order between Mr Marlo and Ms Hyde if the court deems this in the best interest of the children.

Is this all purely to ego stroke some judge? She's the children's guardian, appointed to assess the situation – why would a judge who is reading her report go against her recommendation?

The court can give permission to Ms Hyde to remove the children from the jurisdiction for the purposes of a holiday in Australia.

The range of powers available to the Court under this Act in the proceedings in question (Children Act 1989, Sec 1.3(g))

The court has a number of option and powers under these proceedings and needs to decide whether making an order is better than making no order at all in respect of either or all the children, having taken into account the welfare checklist.

Recommendation

I respectfully recommend that a holiday in Australia outside of school holidays will not be in the best interest of the children at this stage and that they would instead benefit from such a holiday at a more appropriate time such as the British Summer Holidays. I therefore recommend that such permission is granted to Ms Hyde to remove the children from the UK for the purposes of such a holiday during her allocated contact time as per contact order, during the school summer holiday period 2008.

Until I received the phone call from Northview Grove School at 3pm on Friday 31 I had considered that any further expert involvement in the family would be unnecessary and quite likely exacerbate the situation. However, while I am still not proposing any further expert assessments in these proceedings I believe that both Alice and Hayley will benefit from therapeutic services by the local Child and Family Consultation Services. I have made preliminary enquiries and they are happy to receive such a referral, however I have not had to opportunity to discuss such a referral with the children or parties in these proceedings by the time of filing my report.

It is my professional view that further expert assessment will be unnecessary and not likely to give further solutions to the family's difficulties, and instead that a therapeutic approach outside the court process may be more productive as such a process will include it's own assessment per se. I am therefore happy to proceed and make a formal referral to CFCS in respect of Alice and Hayley if the court deems this to be in their best and if the children and parents feel they are able to support any work that may come from CFCS, I would certainly recommend such an action.

No assistance with Ms Hyde's behaviour as described in this report, or assessment by her mental health team.

Whilst I have not been asked to address the issue of residence in this report I believe I have sufficient evidence to address this matter at this stage rather than wait until November when the matter is listed for a final hearing. I therefore recommend the court does not make an order for shared residence to Ms Hyde in respect of any of her children as such an order will only service to cause the children further harm under the current circumstances.

I further recommend that parent's book their holidays during the times that they are scheduled to have the children as holiday bookings outside scheduled contact times seems to cause reasons for conflict between the parents which involves the children unnecessarily.

It would also benefit the children if the schools both had a copy of my report as well as the reports prepared by Mrs Sanders in these proceedings, and if the same reports can also be made available to CFCS as well.

Lastly, but by no means the least, I recommend the court give some consideration to an order under section 91(4) of the Children Act 1989 to prevent further vexatious applications for residence and contact without the permission of the court.

Whilst speaking to Ms Moyer, I informed her that through the help of our local MP Mr Rowe, he had arranged an appointment with the minister of Family Justice, who had suggested a 91 (14) order to prevent future court applications. As I am not legally represented, Ms Moyer said she would be happy to include the suggestion in her report, as she believed proceedings have gone on for too long.

I believe my recommendations are a justifiable interreference with the rights of any adults mentioned in this report.

Alex Moyer
Children's Guardian
BA (Social Work) Honours Degree
Bsc (Psychology) Honours Degree
Psychotherapy and Psychological Counselling Diploma
Note
*Significant factual errors (**not** matters disputed by the parties) in this report should be referred to the children's Guardian. Concerns about other aspects of the report (for example, the extent of the enquires, the opinions expressed in it or matters disputed by the parties) must be addressed in court. The children's Guardian will attend court hearings unless the court orders otherwise.*

I am an honest and decent parent who has shown nothing more than concern for the welfare and stability of my children; I have tried very hard with Ms Hyde and the Family Courts year after year, showing them respect and complying with their directions.

This report just isn't accurate first of all; despite what is stated, needless wild conclusions appear to be drawn. I have no problem with the children receiving support at school, but this is the antithesis to a problem that has persisted – and will continue to persist – because no official wants to implement help, even in the face of acknowledging

Ms Hyde's bipolar disorder; her behaviour has been not only permitted but encouraged.

Dean Marlo

Case Summary (Ms Hyde's Counsel)

4 September

The court is dealing with 3 children of the parties: Hayley 15; Alice 13; Lara 9.

The parents separated in 1999, but now live close to each other, and the children attend local schools. (Mr Marlo is shortly to move house, and will be living only one street away from Ms Hyde, but has told children not to tell her of this.)

There is a long history of disputes regarding residence and shared residence orders.

In March 2000, a residence order was made to Ms Hyde. (p.1)

On 18th August 2000, HHJ Wartley made an interim joint residence order.

This order was confirmed on 10th October 2000. (p.15)

In 2000 and 2001, Ms Hyde had twice to apply for penal notices after Mr Marlo had retained the children when they should have been with her.

Penal notices and emotional trauma, hand in hand.

In November 2001 (p.20) and December 2003 (p.24), Mr Marlo tried unsuccessfully to vary the joint residence order of October 2000.

On 5th August 2004 (pp 51–53), HHJ Chips made a residence order to Mr Marlo, with contact to Ms Hyde, following a 2–day contested hearing at which both parents and the Cafcass officer gave evidence.

On 21st June 2006, Mr Marlo applied for a non–molestation order (p.54), which was compromised, with no findings or admissions, on 23rd June 2006 by each party giving an undertaking. (p.61)

(I've come to hate the profession of solicitors. The whole job is centred around finding loopholes and wording sentences to be an imitation of the truth.)

Issues around the contact the girls were having with their mother continued to arise, and on 18th July last year, Ms Hyde applied for a residence order and to enforce the contact order (p.63–65).

This was in the light of Alice having voted with her feet, and gone to live with her mother in May 2006. Ms Hyde says that Alice's behaviour while in her father's care had been deteriorating and she had got into trouble at school. (Mr Marlo says that the problems in Alice's behaviour were due to the care she received from her mother, not from him.)

There is no middle ground, there is only evidence to the statement; instead of reading the report and suggesting help for someone suffering with a bipolar disorder, Ms Hyde's counsel argues we blame each other.

At the same time, there was no real contact between Ms Hyde and Hayley, and Ms Hyde was very concerned, among other things, that the children were not attending school as regularly as they should.

In response to Ms Hyde's application for residence, a report from Mrs Sanders was commissioned by Mr Recorder Jadin on 25th August 2006. (p.118)

On 23rd October last year, Ms Hyde withdrew her application for residence (p.121). Since then, however, the case has always proceeded on the basis that her application amounted to an application for shared residence.

Child Legal Guidance then became involved, having been approached by Hayley, and they made an application on Hayley's behalf for the existing contact order to be discharged (application dated 19.12.06, at p.123a–b). A similar application was made on behalf of Alice (123j to 123l).

Consultant psychologist Mrs Sanders reported on 13th February 2007, and has since filed an addendum in April, simply confirming that she has seen the medical notes of the children and Mr Marlo, and that they do not change her views. In essence, her recommendations were that the current shared residence arrangement should remain. (p516ii.)

Unfortunately, in her initial report, Mrs Sanders had made some factual errors which greatly upset Ms Hyde (dealt with in Ms Hyde's statement on p426e). Ms Hyde also did not accept that Mrs Sanders had had the time to obtain the true views of the children.

By March this year, things had continued to deteriorate. There were real concerns about both Hayley and Alice.

Alice's GP had said that she was suffering from stress. She was sleeping poorly, and having irregular periods.

She had been disciplined at school for truancy.

Hayley had come to the attention of the police as a result of her behaviour with some other pupils.

That's a blatant lie, Hayley was not in trouble with the police.

At a hearing before HHJ Yergin on 12.3.07, counsel appeared to represent Hayley and Alice, asking that Alice be joined as a party and for that reason the matter was transferred to the High Court, where it was listed for directions on 25.06.07 before Mrs Justice Millar. Before transferring the matter, however, all parties agreed that it was clear that Hayley did not want to be subject to any orders, and all orders relating to her (save Parental Responsibiliy) were discharged.

The matter was transferred to the High Courts in London, because Mrs Mason, on behalf of Ms Hyde, contested the child psychologist report they requested. Surely, Smitch Law cannot submit a case summary that's completely inaccurate? Or does professionalism and honesty mean nothing in law?

At the High Court, Mr Marlo (in person) supported Alice being separately represented. Ms Hyde argued that her voice would be adequately heard by the appointment of a Guardian through Cafcass, and this is what was in the end done, with Alice's application to be joined as a party being adjourned generally with liberty to restore.

Having dealt with that application (which was the only reason for the matter being in the High Court), the judge transferred it back down to the County Court for a swifter hearing.

The other matter which is before the court is Ms Hyde's application to take the children to Australia for a holiday over Christmas, which will mean the children being taken out of school for 2 weeks.

In the High Court, Mr Marlo stated his position to be that he did not object to the children going to Australia in principle but he did not want them to miss school.

Therefore, the judge ordered that Ms Hyde should file detailed proposals for shared residence, and for the Australia trip (and an application re that trip) by 6th July, and Mr Marlo should respond by 20th July.

(See summary of orders sought, attached.)

Matters, having been transferred back to County Court, came (on paper) before HHJ Neely, who listed it for directions on 26th July, and for 2 days hearing on 5th and 6th September.

Sadly, those were not dates which the expert, Mrs Sanders, could make.

Therefore, at the hearing on 27th June, HHJ Chips left the Australia matter to be dealt with on the first day of the hearing, and vacated the rest of the matters to be dealt with in November, following a full report by the Guardian.

In fact, the Guardian has now concluded her reports on all matters (dated 03.09.07).

Her recommendations are that the Australia trip should take place, but in the summer of next year (para 85), and that there should not be a shared residence order (para 87). Her main recommendation is that the proceedings should conclude, as the ongoing proceedings since 2000 have caused significant harm to the children (para 52). She suggests a referral to Child and Family Consultation Services in respect of Alice and Hayley, and is willing to make that referral. (para 86). She recommends that the schools and CFCS should see her report and those of Mrs Sanders.

She raises the possibility of a section 91(14) Order.

A letter has also been received from Child Legal Guidance (dated 04.09.07), despite the appointment of a guardian, in which they purport to put forward their instructions from Hayley and Alice.

The court may wish to consider whether it is appropriate to take this into account, bearing in mind that Hayley is not a part and there are no longer any relevant orders relating to her, and that the High Court specifically chose to obtain Alice's views via a Guardian, rather than via solicitors.

Mr Porter
Counsel for Ms Hyde

Reading misleading information

4 September

I felt I had no alternative but to make an appointment with Mrs Sparrow from Northview Grove; the hearing is tomorrow and what was relayed in the guardian's report is untrue, misleading and condemned the hard work and understanding as a parent I have shown my children and both my children's schools.

Asking for Mrs Sparrow to clarify what had been relayed and written in the Guardian's report to the Family Courts, Mrs Sparrow confirmed that I had been very supportive as a parent with Northview Grove. She also arranged for herself, Mr Garrett, Mrs Hewitt, who had spoken to the Guardian, and myself to meet.

In the office, I read out from the report what had been relayed by Northview Grove to the Guardian. Mrs Hewitt stated that she did not say the things that were in the report and would phone Ms Moyer. I asked Mrs Hewitt not to contact Ms Moyer; she needed to put it in writing.

I was distressed to read her assessment of Hayley; depression in children of Hayley's age is a major concern for any parent, which is why I was surprised neither Ms Hyde or myself had been contacted by Hayley's teachers, or her Head of House, Mrs Sparrow, to get Hayley help. Shaking her head, Mrs Hewitt stated that she didn't say that either, and that she would address what she had allegedly relayed to the Guardian.

I made it clear to Mrs Hewitt on two occasions that I did not want her to phone Ms Moyer, as I do not want to be seen as interfering, but felt I had no choice and there needed to be no confusion with what is actually the truth; a letter would make clear to everyone what is being said.

Mr Garrett asked me if there was anything the school could do to rectify the situation before the hearing the next day. I replied that I would like the school to confirm in writing the aspects which the Guardian has reported Mrs Hewitt disagrees with saying, i.e. that I am a supportive parent and have been in contact with the school throughout, regarding any behavioural issues of Hayley and Alice.

Stating he will try to arrange the letter by the end of school, Mr Garrett said he would phone me to confirm it had been left in reception to collect.

Leaving, I felt drained by another meeting, misleading report and having to defend myself to get the truth told; with no one else to turn to, I called Mr Rowe to discuss my fears that once again professional people were clouding the truth with misconceptions of what was really happening within my family's lives. Fortunately, Mr Rowe said he would fit me in at the end of his consulting time today.

The Guardian's report is essential to the judge as an insight, and the judge's decisions at this hearing could bring an end to all the proceedings, which have caused so much instability and stress in the children's lives over the last 7 years.

With Mr Rowe, it is a relief to be spoken to like I am a human being and a father, while expressing the seemingly endless interference that has been allowed and encouraged to continue. At the end of the appointment, Mr Rowe stated he would contact Northview Grove, as an MP involved with many schools in the area, to discuss my situation.

Later that afternoon, Mr Rowe phoned me stating that he had 'good news and bad news'. The bad news was that the school were not going to write a letter of confirmation, as they do not want to get involved; the good news was that Northview Grove were speaking to the Guardian and addressing the issues that I had raised.

Sadly, I know that's bad-bad; I understand how it looks to an outsider. In fact, allow me to channel Smitch Law for a moment, 'Father is harassing the school because he is not happy with mother seeing her children', or something along those lines. I hope with the knowledge I had 8 years of coping with Ms Hyde's mental health issues while trying to give our children a good life, followed by 7 years of fighting for the right to be a dad to my children; the understanding that Ms Hyde is not alright, (although I sincerely wish she was) she struggles to maintain healthy routines and calm discipline, that it comes from a place of concern for my children; a necessity for the truth in order to help our family.

The Guardian states in her report that it was her opinion that any further expert involvement was unnecessary and could only exacerbate the situation. This was her opinion before she received the phone call from Mrs Hewitt.

Clearly, either Mrs Hewitt didn't inform her about my involvement over the years or the Guardian didn't relay it accurately. Neither option helps my children.

Enlightenment: Northview Grove

10 September

Over the past 4 years, I have been fully supportive and understanding with Northview Grove regarding Hayley and Alice's education, behaviour and conduct.

In May 2007, I made an appointment with Mrs Sparrow and two other teachers to discuss Hayley and Alice's behaviour. I explained my position, at the receiving end of Ms Hyde's abuse, and my beliefs as to why in particular Alice was acting out. I thought the teachers came to an understanding that I did not want to exacerbate the situation and I had made them aware of the outside factors affecting Hayley and Alice.

On one occasion, Mrs Tran phoned me to ask if Hayley could come home; she was upset and believed that her friends would get unjustifiably into trouble with the police after an incident with known bullies. Several weeks later, I found out Ms Hyde relayed to the Family Courts that the police had been called to the school, due to Hayley's behaviour, and she had been sent home because of this. I asked if it could be confirmed in writing that the police were not called due to Hayley's behaviour, however Mrs Sparrow stated Northview would not put this in writing and she was sorry but she could do no more.

In July 2007, I phoned Northview Grove to request an appointment with someone regarding Alice's behaviour. I was given an appointment with Mr Caldwell. We talked about addressing Alice's conduct and how we could change Alice's attitude to a more positive one towards school. I left the school with the impression everyone was on the same page about helping Alice. The next day, Alice called saying she had been suspended.

I have been to Northview Grove for several meetings with Mrs Tran, Mrs Sparrow, Mrs Hewitt and Ms Hyde regarding Alice's re-integrations. The appointment I had made with Mrs Sparrow where Mrs Hewitt was present, I explained I was fully behind the school in addressing Alice's behaviour; I expressed apologies to the school's receptionist for Alice's recent rudeness.

I made an appointment to discuss Mrs Hewitt's comments in the Guardian's report. This clearly was not the view of Northview Grove but Mrs Hewitt's own personal opinion. Mrs Tran took the view that Mrs Hewitt acted professionally, and what was written in the report had been misinterpreted by Ms Moyer herself. While I understand her support for her member of staff, Mrs Hewitt's comments were untrue and have the potential to prolong proceedings once again.

I understand Northview not wanting to get involved – I didn't want to have to ask. However, I have evidently been there for my children both in and out of school, and have respected the concerns from members of staff at Northview Grove. By asking for written confirmation of my visits and willingness to come into school to deal with my children's education and any situations that have occurred over the years, and that I have co-operated with Mrs Sparrow, Mr Caldwell, Mrs Hewitt and the school – there must be appointment dates proving this! – I was only asking for what any decent parent would, support from the school in relaying the facts, to ensure the welfare of the children.

From MP (Enclosed MofJ)

4 September

Dear Mr Marlo,
Please find enclosed a copy of the acknowledgement I have received from the Ministry of Justice. I had meant to give this to you when you came to my office this afternoon.
They are currently investigating this matter. I will contact you again when I receive a full response.
All best wishes for the court hearing.
Yours sincerely,

29 August

Dear Mr Rowe,
I refer to your letter of 13/08/2007 addressed to Rt Hon Minister for Family Justice, Leader of the House, about decisions of the family court on holidays.
Your letter was received on 29 August 2007, and the Minister aims to reply within 20 working days. However, if we anticipate a delay, I will inform you as soon as possible.
I shall also contact you again if, after considering your letter further, it appears that another Department may deal with it more appropriately.
If you would like to speak to someone in this office about your letter, please get in contact.
Yours sincerely,

End of an Era

Sadly, after many decades at Riverbank Primary School, and having been there for Hayley, Alice and almost all of Lara's time there, Mr Church retired as Headteacher.

I made sure to make my appreciation of his character and assistance known, and that I wished him all the best for the future.

I had to make an appointment with Mrs Irfan, the new Headteacher of Riverbank, to explain the situation of our family to her, that I have no desire to bring any trouble to the school, and will continue to provide for Lara's stability and welfare.

Dean Marlo

Court – make way

5th September 2007 / Venray Family County Courts

Judge Recorder Lowe orders, on Ms Hyde's request, for Mr Marlo to make Alice available for an extra overnight contact per week with Ms Hyde (should Alice wish). Lara to be made available for an extra evening contact per week with Ms Hyde.

Ms Hyde has court permission to remove children from the jurisdiction of the court for holidays abroad, including holidays in Australia or Canada, during their school holiday contact time, but not during term–time.

Judge Recorder Lowe makes an order under Section 91(14) preventing both parties from making an application to the court, and cancels the hearings listed for the 8th/9th November 2007.

Venray Family Court Hearing 5th Sept

I phoned the Guardian, Ms Moyer, at 8.30am and left a message for her to return my call in order to confirm that Northview Grove had been in contact. (Ms Moyer never replied.)

At 9.30am, as I sat in the court waiting room, Ms Hyde's barrister, Mr Porter, came over and asked if I agreed to the children going to their mother's once a week; I replied that this already the arrangement and I do not have a problem.

Mr Porter said, 'So you agree?'

I confirmed, yes. He then asked me if I was agreeing with Ms Hyde's schedule for 2007/2008. I informed him that I did not agree as the schedule drawn up in 2004 proved satisfactory (when followed). Mr Porter left stating he would consult his client.

The Guardian's solicitor, Mr Beltran, came over and introduced himself to me. I asked him if Ms Moyer had been in contact with him and if she was aware of amendments that needed to be made to her report. He stated that Ms Moyer had not been in touch and he was unaware of any amendments. He asked me to go into one of the rooms with him to go through the report, pointing out what I thought was incorrect; while doing this, he tried to phone Ms Moyer with no response. Mr Beltran told me, as far as he knew, Ms Moyer was of the belief that there should be no changes to the existing court order. I told him about Ms Hyde's barrister clarifying week day contact and confirmed, apart from that, I wanted the existing court order of 2004 to remain.

We were all brought before Judge Recorder Lowe.

Mr Beltran informed the judge that I have several problems with the Guardian's report, but he had not been able to contact Ms Moyer to confirm any of this as fact.

Judge Recorder Lowe looked at me with contempt.

The judge stated she has not seen the Guardian's report, and that she was unaware it had actually arrived at court. Quickly standing up, Mr Beltran apologised, saying that he had only had a copy for a short time and unfortunately, he had written notes on it so was unable to give her his copy. Mr Porter stood up and apologised, as he had also done the same. I stood and offered the judge my copy, which she took.

Mr Beltran began going through several of the issues that I had with the report; the judge stated that she would consider these while she was reading it.

It seemed unbelievable, but for some reason Mr Beltran only mentioned Northview Grove School, and not any of my concerns about the inaccurate and misleading statements made.

After several minutes, we were all asked leave to allow Judge Recorder Lowe to read the Guardian's report.

As I sat with Mr Beltran in the waiting room, he repeatedly made unsuccessful attempts to contact Ms Moyer.

The usher called us back into the courtroom and the judge stated that it was clear, reading through the report, that 'both parents do not listen to their children' and are 'more interested in arguing between themselves and bringing forth court proceedings'.

(Meanwhile, I got the sensation of leaving my own body, watching the show go on.)

The judge continued, 'The children clearly state they wish to be with their father and be at their father's for Christmas.'

This is not- not why we're here-

'The children should be with their father every Christmas day; this is what the children are saying is what they want,' Judge Recorder Lowe finished, before banishing us from the room to resolve the contact schedule for 2007/2008 and now apparently, Christmas, for her to reside over.

Without knowing my feet were moving, I found a seat in the waiting room and thought about what the judge had said concerning Christmas and couldn't believe the suggestion was even made – it is totally unfair and ridiculous. As I sat there, I felt numb; it was hard to comprehend how we had arrived at a question over where the children should be *every* Christmas day, when the basis of the application was to consider whether Ms Hyde should be given permission to take the children out of school for 12 days, and her residency.

A few minutes passed like that, me staring into the abyss in thought, then Mr Porter sat beside me and asked if we could have a quick chat. I asked if it was where the children were to be on Christmas days, and he said yes; I told him I thought it was unfair and not in the best interest of our children or Ms Hyde as a parent.

(Of course, deep down, I would love to have my children for every Christmas day, but I still felt it was wrong.)

Mr Porter stood up and told me that he would be straight back. Moments later, he returned and asked me if I was prepared to accept Ms Hyde's schedule 2007/2008. I told Mr Porter again that there is nothing wrong with the schedule drawn up in 2004, as it was designed to be an even split of weekend contact each year.

Mr Porter repeated, 'Do you agree with Ms Hyde's schedule?'

I have been reasonable and have not disagreed in any way to Ms Hyde having our children on Christmas day, for weekday contact or extra time; all I am asking in return is a schedule that ensures us no more court proceedings.

Mr Porter replied, again, 'So you do not agree to Ms Hyde's schedule?

Feeling quite exhausted for this early in the day, I shook my head and replied, 'No.'

Mr Porter turned around and walked off, not another word said.

(Where I come from, it would be considered rude to just walk off and say nothing because you could not get your own way – or succeed in the interests of your client. If anyone deserves to throw their hands up and walk away it's me, ah but that's only a fantasy for someone in my position!)

When Mr Porter returned, he suggested that Mr Beltran could work out the schedule. I turned to Mr Porter and said that he is well aware Ms Hyde's schedule is drawn up to suit herself and not for the stability or wishes of the children, and on that it is on that basis, I cannot agree.

We were all called in front of the judge. Mr Porter stood up and stated that both parents believed that the children were referring to not wanting to be away during December 2007 in Australia, and were not referring to being with their father every Christmas.

(Not that I expected it, but a modicum of respect could have been given that I didn't take the judge's strange announcement as an excuse to withhold the experience of Christmas from Ms Hyde from now on – which is what the man Smitch Law and Ms Hyde have attempted to portray me as would have done.)

With that new issue, that needn't have been brought up, out the way…

Mr Porter finished, 'Unfortunately, Mr Marlo would not agree to Ms Hyde's schedule 2007/2008.'

Swinging her disapproving gaze back in my direction, the judge stated that we would have lunch and when we resume, she wanted agreement between both parents on the schedule.

I still cannot understand why the judge did not see that I am not a parent set on being selfish or cruel towards Ms Hyde or the situation; clearly, she did not acknowledge the reasons I was unable to agree to some of Ms Hyde's requests. Has the Guardian's report not illuminated the judge in any way?

(While these proceedings cover Ms Hyde's application for joint residency, as it stands, I have sole residency and believe it should be Ms Hyde agreeing to the schedule I propose, as set out in the court order, and any alterations would be suggested by her, not dictated.)

After lunch, at 2.30pm, we were all brought before Judge Recorder Lowe again; Mr Beltran stated that he had finally been able to speak to Ms Moyer and can state that the school confirmed I have been involved in my children's education, however, Mrs Hewitt was standing by her statement that I will not attend meetings with Ms Hyde. (Which is fair enough, as long as the judge has read my statement and understands it is not out of a place of pettiness, rather to reduce the likelihood of Ms Hyde causing a scene because I am present.) He stated that other comments relating to Hayley's mental health were not made by Mrs Hewitt, as indicated and relayed in the Guardian's report, but are the words of Ms Moyer herself.

This is evidently not how this report reads. It relays that a teacher from Hayley's school, who sees Hayley often, is seriously concerned about Hayley's mental health. It deeply worries me that Ms Moyer made this statement; I believe Hayley and I are very close, and I have noticed nothing more than teenage mood swings in Hayley's wellbeing. I also think Hayley has handled both her difficult childhood and becoming a teenager very well.

The judge told us again to go out and sort the schedule 2007/2008. In particular, she addressed me, first with condemnation for 'continually bringing forth proceedings' and second, that it was about time I 'started being magnanimous'.

My feet carried me to in the waiting room and Mr Porter came over. I took out the schedule 2007/2008 that I had prepared in accordance with the court order of 2004. I asked Mr Porter to call out all the contact weekends that Ms Hyde had requested on her schedule, and began re–colouring my schedule in accordance with Ms Hyde's. All over the place but nonetheless completed, I asked Mr Porter if he was going to inform the usher that we were ready. He seemed surprised at my agreement.

When the judge had asked me to be magnanimous, I wasn't sure of its exact meaning, but I was intelligent enough to know it meant that it was me who was being asked to give way, even at the expense of the stability the existing court schedule had provided. It was not all that long ago, a different barrister in Mr Porter's position was calling for the 2004 schedule to remain. How time flies.

In response to Mr Porter's reaction, I told him that I could not understand why he seemed so surprised as 'you know, but you act like you don't know'. He stared at me blankly. Hopefully with what was a tight smile and not a tired grimace, I said I would put it another way, 'I just want to get out of here and end this façade.'

Mr Porter smiled at me and walked away.

The usher called us back into the courtroom. Speaking to the judge, Mr Porter told her that an agreement had be made and he will provide the court with Ms Hyde's schedule for 2007/2008.

I requested a 91(14) Order, which would prevent either parent (Ms Hyde – I've learnt my lesson, the only way I come back through the family court doors is by being dragged) from bringing our family back to court. Mrs Mason stood up and argued the point of the 91 (14) Order, and lost, stating to the judge that this was 'no time for the courts to step back from this family's case', and it would be 'a failing of the Family Courts to not consider the welfare of the children'.

I could do nothing, but sit there.

In the judge's summing up, she stated that I had 'no insight into Ms Hyde's mental health problems' or 'any consideration to her or my children'.

Mr Porter suggested that the judge's summing up is placed with the section 91(14) Order, as it would be a good indicator to a judge if any further applications are made. He also asked if he was permitted to request a copy of the transcript for Ms Hyde at the cost of her legal aid; Judge Recorder Lowe agreed.

I felt I was there to make the numbers up, with a minor role of agreeing to Ms Hyde's requests.

Part of me wanted to stand up and ask why I, with my primary interests being my children's welfare and the end of proceedings, should be forced to further compromise with the person whose sole interest seems to be to impede, disrupt and abuse that? The part of me still in the room sat there, just taking the dirty looks and condemnation; I again think of how this would have played out, if I had legal representation.

For some reason, it has always been one rule for them, and another for me.

A parenting thing I'd like the judge to know

I enjoy Christmas as a parent, and willingly provide the enthusiasm at this time of year because I love my children, and consider myself especially lucky to experience this time of year with them. The effort I have put into our Christmases and my children throughout the year is repaid by the joy it brings and the sense of wellbeing that the season brings.

I do feel sad each year that my children have not been brought up in a two–parent family. They have all missed out over the past eight years on the security of having both parents there. This is particularly felt on special occasions; notably on Christmas for the present opening, dinner together and relaxing knowing the people you love are around you. Whether celebrating Christmas or not, that feeling should be enjoyed by every family.

As a separated parent, it is sad to alternate time and Christmas days each year; no matter what, one parent gets up on Christmas morning to a quiet house with presents laid out and stockings full, with no cheers of joy because Santa has been. When it is my turn to have our children from 12pm on Boxing Day, it is as if our home comes alive, with my children laughing and joking; Ma and Sully tucked up with a cup of tea and biscuits; strange noises from plastic toy dogs barking and Scalextric F1 cars racing; our favourite Christmas movies playing in the background.

I am happy to join in as any decent parent does, and it makes me happy to see my children enjoying Christmas time.

In contrast, when I have our children on Christmas day and all of the above has gone by 12pm Boxing Day, it is if a black cloud comes over our home. As a responsible person and parent, I pick up the pieces, clear up the mess and get on with my life. However, like any normal parent, I am allowed to want to have my children at home but also understand that their upbringing should be split fairly.

Christmas is for children and families, in whatever forms they take; it is a time for peace, a time to remind ourselves of what is important, and why making an effort to love and care matters.

Dean Marlo

Residence and Contact Order

Before Ms Recorder Lowe, sitting at the Venray County Courts, on 5ᵗʰ September 2007; upon hearing counsel for the applicant Ms Hyde and for the children, and the respondent Mr Marlo appearing in person,

By consent (save as to the period of the section 91(14) Order in paragraph 4 below) it is ordered that:

1. The order of HHJ Chips dated 05.08.04 shall remain in force, subject to the following amendments:

a. Paragraphs 2(iii) is amended to the effect that the periods of the Easter school holiday, which the children spend with each parent shall be determined by the need for the holiday period with Ms Hyde to include Alice's birthday in 2008 and alternate years thereafter (as provided for in paragraph 2(x) of the order of HHJ Chips dated 05.08.04).

b. In addition to the contact provided for in the order of 05.08.04,

i. Mr Marlo shall make Alice available for an extra overnight contact per week (should Alice wish), which shall take place either on a Wednesday or Thursday. The choice of day shall be Ms Hyde's, and she shall notify Mr Marlo of her choice by 4pm on the Saturday preceding the day in question.

ii. Mr Marlo shall make Lara available for an extra evening contact per week with Ms Hyde. Again, Ms Hyde is to notify Mr Marlo of her choice of day (Wednesday or Thursday) by the previous Saturday, and Ms Hyde shall collect Lara from school and return her home by 8pm.

iii. Ms Hyde has permission to remove the children from the jurisdiction of the court during that part of the school summer holidays when the children are with her for the purposes of holidays abroad, including holidays in Australia or Canada.

2. The periods of contact between the children and Ms Hyde from September 2007 to August 2008 are as set out in the schedule attached hereto. In future years, Mr Marlo shall, by 31ˢᵗ May, provide to Ms Hyde a schedule setting out his understanding of the contact dates for the following year. Should Mr Marlo fail to provide such a schedule or calendar, Ms Hyde shall prepare her own and send it to Mr Marlo. Should either party object to the dates proposed by the other, both parties must use their best endeavours to negotiate agreement by the end of the summer school term. Both parties are expected to be as flexible as possible in achieving agreement in the interests of the children.

3. The hearing listed for 2 days commencing 8ᵗʰ November is vacated.

4. An Order under section 91(14), preventing either party from making further applications to the court without first obtaining the court's permission, is made in respect of both parties, and shall remain in force until 5ᵗʰ September 2010.

5. Ms Hyde has permission to obtain a transcript of today's short judgment. The cost of such transcript shall be borne by Ms Hyde's public funding certificate, the court certifying that it is a necessary and reasonable expense.

6. There be no order as to costs save detailed assessment of the publicly funded costs of Ms Hyde and the children.

The Guardian Calls

9 September

Several days after the hearing, Ms Moyer finally called me back. She apologised, telling me that she had been to the gym the night before the hearing and left her mobile there; they were not open in the morning so she picked her phone up at lunch time, which is why she could not confirm Northview Grove's comments.

This was such an important day for my three children and our family, I know mistakes happen, but you couldn't make up the level of unprofessionalism we have experienced within the Family Courts.

While it is lovely that Ms Hyde is able to offer the children holidays to places I myself could never hope to take them, (either due to the cost, flight or the wildlife) I can't help but feel that the focus of the Family Courts should be their daily welfare and stability, which, particularly for Alice, has caused issues throughout, either due to schedules or attitudes or incidents; all with Ms Hyde at the epicentre.

Mrs Mason writes to me twice

10 September

We acknowledge safe receipt of your two unsigned and undated statements which we received on the morning of 4ᵗʰ September 2007.

We refer to the hearing on the 5ᵗʰ September 2007 and trust that you have now received a copy of the order that has been drafted by our client's barrister, Mr Porter.
We would be grateful if you would please provide us with your new address in order that we can notify our client and so that we can liaise with you in the future if need be.

If Ms Hyde hadn't made such scenes in the past, I would not have been hesitant to share the address of our new rented home. As I wish to continue to co-parent our children, I have the letter typed and I will, as I have in the past, inform Ms Hyde.

It's old news, but it is strange how quickly Mrs Mason moves straight along to the next issue they can exploit. Just to make it clear for Mrs Mason and Legal Aid, we have moved into a house down the road from Ms Hyde's. Under the circumstances, neither Ms Hyde nor Mrs Mason have any reason to know the address until we have moved in.

Mrs Sanders has not attended any of the hearings, in fact, since she could not be persuaded by Mrs Mason and my lacklustre medical records to make the journey or the amendments Mrs Mason wanted to see – sole residency to Mother, Father with contact, and a penal notice might help, your Honour – the child psychologist and her report is never heard from again.

What a waste of public funding, time and turmoil in everyone's lives.

From Mr MP, Enclosed M of J

12/13 September

12 September

Dear Mr Marlo,

Please find enclosed a copy of the acknowledgement I have received from the Ministry of Justice.

They are currently investigating this matter. I will contact you again when I receive a full response. Best wishes.

Yours sincerely,

4 September

Dear Mr Rowe,

I refer to your letter of 13/08/2007 addressed to Rt Hon Minister for Family Justice, Leader of the House, about decisions of the family court on holidays.

Your letter was received on 29 August 2007, and the Minister aims to reply within 20 working days. However, if we anticipate a delay, I will inform you as soon as possible.

I shall also contact you again if, after considering your letter further, it appears that another Department may deal with it more appropriately.

If you would like to speak to someone in this office about your letter, please get in contact.

Yours sincerely,

Correspondence Officer

13 September

Dear Mr Marlo,

Please find enclosed a copy of the acknowledgement I have received from the Ministry of Justice.

They are currently investigating this matter. I will contact you again when I receive a full response. Best wishes.

Yours sincerely,

10 September

Thank you for your letter dated 13ᵗʰ August 2007 to Jack Straw. I apologise for the delay in your response. The matters you have raised fall under the responsibility of the Department for Children, Schools & Families.

I have therefore passed on your correspondence to the Department for Children, Schools & Families, with a request that they respond to you directly.

Yours sincerely,

Ministerial Correspondence Office

Record of involvement – Educational Psychologist

14 September

Pupil: Alice Marlo, 9OK
Reason for involvement:
I was asked to work with Alice due to concern about current emotional and learning difficulties. It was noted that Alice has been spending a high proportion of her time out of class, both through non-attendance and being sent out of class. Alice has been excluded from school four times in the past year. She has worked with Yvonne Tilley (Behaviour Support Tutor) and Helen Little (Assistant Educational Psychologist) recently.
Summary of Educational Psychologist work:
I carried out the following work during this visit:
Discussion with April Hayden (Learning Support); individual discussion with Alice.
Summary of key issues
We talked about Alice's current difficulties regarding conflicts with members of staff at school.
Key areas we discussed included:
Avoiding behaviour likely to provoke conflict (e.g. wearing jewellery, uniform differences); managing her response to unfairness or perceived unfairness; developing 'defensive' behaviour, aimed at avoiding getting into conflict.
Alice explained that her goal this year was not to be excluded from school. She told me that she was not very confident about this due to how she felt teachers already viewed her.
Agreed actions:
I will talk with Mitch Barley (Trainee Educational Psychologist) regarding her arranging an anger-management skills programme using assistant EP time to develop key conflict-avoidance skills.
Yours sincerely,
Gabriel Vine

Moving house

15 September

We have moved literally around the corner from Ms Hyde.

I don't have a choice; it's a landlord's market. With all the work that is coming in, it is an upgrade on our bungalow – I just hope I'm given the opportunity to provide my children with a good standard of living and a happy home life.

I made a mistake with the kittens and hope this move does not prove to be the same. On the positive side, it will show the Family Courts that I am not moving the children away from Ruth and it is closer to Northview, so less of a walk for Hayley and Alice.

Dean Marlo

From MP, a round-up response

17 September

Dear Mr Marlo,
Please find enclosed a copy of the response I have received from the Parliamentary Under–Secretary of State for Children, Young People and Families.
Hopefully you will find the minister's comments to be of interest. If I can be of any further assistance, please do not hesitate to contact me again.
Best wishes.

10 September

Dear Mr Rowe,
Thank you for your letters of 13 August to Gordon Brown, Jack Straw and Minister for Family Justice on behalf of your constituent Mr Marlo, about children being taken out of school for a holiday. I am replying as the minister responsible for school attendance.
You mention in your letter that Ms Hyde has applied to the court to be granted permission to take all three daughters out of school for three weeks for a visit to Australia. Under the Education (Pupil registration) Regulations (which came into force on 1 September 2006) it is only an authorised person (usually the head teacher) who may grant leave of absence for the purpose of family holidays during term time. Any application for leave must be made in advance by a parent with whom the pupil normally resides and the school must be satisfied that there are special circumstances that warrant the leave.
In exceptional circumstances, schools can agree more than ten school days leave of absence in a school year. Each request can only be judged on a case–by–case basis taking into account individual circumstances, such as the child's attainment, attendance and ability to catch up. Parents are not entitled to remove their children from school for a holiday as of right. If a parent does take a child out of school during term time without the Head's permission, then this will be regarded as an 'unauthorised absence' and that will be noted on the pupil's attendance record.
You raise a number of points in relation to child contact that are linked to an individual case that is currently before the courts. It is important that I or officials should not comment on the facts of such cases, in order that there can be no risk of perceived or actual interference in the independence of the judiciary. Where parents, or other parties, who are involved in cases have concerns about issues, including those such as contact and residence, it is important that they seek, and then consider, legal advice. I hope you will understand that I cannot comment on the specific details of the case. I can assure you that this is not because of any lack of concern, but because to do so would undermine the independence of the judiciary.

All I wanted was confirmation that the children should not be taken out of school during term; in the meantime, we've had two hearings and the court have already reached their decision. A dollar short and a day late.

Are the people governing this country really so out of touch that it is beyond their grasp some people cannot afford a solicitor? And in some cases, the choices come down between keeping their family warm and eating properly, and instructing a solicitor or barrister to argue the legislation already in place regarding school holidays – it's ridiculous.

434

School contact – Alice

1 October

Dear Mr Marlo,

Pupil: Alice Marlo, 9OK

I am writing to inform you that Alice will be placed in our ISC (Internal Support Centre) for a period of two days, Tuesday 2 October 2007 and Wednesday 3 October 2007, and will be working in isolation on a one-to-one basis with a member of staff.

The reason for Alice being placed in the ISC is rudeness to three different members of staff.

The ISC facility is covered by closed-circuit security for the safety of students and staff.

Alice will be returned to normal lessons after serving her time in the ISC but will continue on a report for a period of time. Should the report prove unsatisfactory, Alice may well have to return to the ISC or indeed face other sanctions, subject to circumstances.

Should you wish to discuss this matter further, please contact me at school through the usual channels.

Yours sincerely,

Alice went to her mother's for weekend contact, and is staying over tonight. Although I believe what Alice needs is consistency, I have no way to provide it as she and her mother continue to dictate her residency schedule, despite the court order being fresh off the press, which wouldn't be a problem, if Alice's education wasn't clearly suffering.

Northview; Exclusion

2 October

Dear Mr Marlo,
Pupil: Alice Marlo, 9OK
I am writing to inform you of my decision to exclude Alice for a fixed period of two days. This means that your child will not be allowed in school for this period. The exclusion begins on Wednesday 3 October and ends on Thursday 4 October 2007. Your child's exclusion expires on Thursday 4 October 2007 and we expect Alice to be back in school on Friday 5 October 2007.

Alice has been excluded for this fixed period following abusive behaviour and being placed in ISC for two days, she walked out and refused to carry out reasonable instructions and also refused to remove jewellery and co-operate with ISC staff. I realise that this exclusion may well be upsetting for you and your family, but the decision to exclude Alice has not been taken lightly.

You and Alice are requested to attend a reintegration interview with Mr Garrett at the school on Friday 5 October 2007 at 8.30am. If that is not convenient, please contact the school to arrange an alternative date and time. The purpose of the reintegration interview is to discuss how best your child's return to school can be managed. Failure to attend a reintegration interview will be a factor taken into account by a magistrates' court if, on future application, they consider whether to impose a parenting order on you.

You have a duty to ensure that your child is not present in a public place in school hours during this exclusion on Wednesday 3 October 2007 to Thursday 4 October 2007, unless there is a justifiable reason for this. I must advise you that you may receive a penalty notice from the local authority if your child is present in a public place during school hours on the specified dates. If so, it will be for you to show reasonable justification.

We will set work for your child to be completed on the days specified in the previous paragraph during the period of your child's exclusion. The work will be given to your child to bring home at the point of exclusion and topped up, if necessary, during the period of exclusion. Please ensure that work set by the school is completed and returned to us promptly for marking.

We regard it as an essential part of the exclusion that Alice is not to be on or near the school site at any time during the exclusion period.
Yours sincerely,

Schooling

4 – 10 October

Thursday 4th
I could understand Alice's behaviour at school if she was standing up to a bully, or the teacher was genuinely being unreasonable, but for petty things like uniform and attitude I don't get why Alice is putting herself in this position. Regardless, Alice has come home, and while we've talked about the work she has to do and set out times to do it, it will make little difference if she goes to school and acts the same.

Ma is still happy to come round and keep Alice and Sully company, (to feed Sully biscuits more like) which allows me to go to work, despite Alice being at home.

On the day Lara has tea at her mother's, I take Lara to school in the morning at 8.45am and work the full day, as Ruth picks Lara up from school.

I had arranged for 3 colleagues to come in and assist me on a large commercial site; it would be a rare day to push on. At 1.20pm, I received a call from Ruth, who stated that she could not make it today for Lara. I decided to ask everyone to pack up for the day as we would finish off tomorrow – and had to laugh when everyone cheered – even though I was hoping to get the job done.

I know that Ruth's behaviour would make any sane person jump up and down but, my focus was on making sure that one of us is in the playground for Lara when school finishes.

Friday 5th
Alice and I attended her re-integration meeting; I informed Ruth but she said she couldn't attend due to work commitments.

Ten minutes in, Ruth was shown into the room, and I could only be thankful it went peacefully.

Monday 8th
It's the end of Ruth's contact weekend, and all the children have been at hers.

It was nearly midday when I received a phone call from Hayley telling me that she isn't at school and is coming home, as her mother is going out. I asked if Hayley was feeling alright and she said, 'Yes, just a bit tired.'

(That means all the children had a late one last night.)

I tried to encourage Hayley to head to school after lunch, and catch her afternoon lessons at least.

When I got home from work before collecting Lara, Hayley was cooking in the kitchen.

Wednesday 10th
Ruth phoned and stated that she could not have Lara for tea on Thursday.

(I can't help but feel like the one pulled into Wonderland – day arranged the Saturday before? Father withholding contact with children?)

It's not as if I don't understand things coming up, I have tried to be reasonable with

437

Ruth since we met. However, it is the slow erosion of my being; standing in a courtroom, being condemned for my parenting as a father and my magnanimity as a person, because Ruth couldn't get on with joint residency in 2000. That's the point I've been trying to make: whether it is due to her personality or her bipolar, normal situations as two single parents have always been an uphill struggle.

It's also why it is so frustrating when the summary made is that 'both parents are as bad as each other' as it has prevented Ruth from ever acknowledging her behaviour and receiving help.

To Mr MP

8 October

Firstly, I would like to thank you for your efforts in obtaining responses to my letters.

I wrote this letter to you shortly after coming to your office on the 8th of August, but did not send it. I have since made some adjustments, and ask if you would be so kind as to read it now.

Thank you very much for your support over the years and letters regarding my family's constant involvement in the Family Courts. As you are aware, on my visit to your office on the 8th August, I had made the decision not to write to you – not to bother you – again.

Despite this, I was disappointed with the content of the letter that you received from Minister for Family Justice. As I explained to you, the Ministry did not have the courteously to reply to my letter of the 14th June 2007. I also sent a letter to the Prime Minister. Both letters were sent via recorded delivery and I do not understand why I have not received a reply, of any form, to my genuine concerns.

I know that I am just another crab in the bucket, but I believed, at least partially, in the process; the need for some sort of organisation. Naively, I thought the point of diplomatic governance was to improve the quality of life of people.

I must state again, that I am appalled and shocked by the aggression and instability that has been generated by a solicitor working within the Family Courts, and the enabling law system behind them, which is based on antiquated ideals that have never been fully addressed.

My children's future with two parents that love them has been described by Mrs Mason as 'the case from Hell' (12th March 2007).

For what my children and myself have been put through and witnessed over the years, Mrs Mason's statement was devastating. On every occasion, I have gone to the Family Courts for my children's welfare and stability, as any decent parent would.

Another of numerous examples:

I have had a barrister, who is now a judge, mislead me regarding the Headteacher of my children's school. I know that there was an attempt of an investigation and a Lord declared this barrister, this judge, did nothing wrong… However, when it is your children's lives that person has affected, and other people's lives they will impact in the future, I can no longer believe in the justice system.

I suppose the penny has dropped again, Mr Rowe, as I realise that the people who act as our ministers that I have written to, do not care enough to bring about change, while the dishonest and immoral behaviour that has been placed in three innocent children and their parents' lives, within the Family Courts and the legal system, continues.

I do believe if the Family Courts had taken a different approach in 1999, had been open to joint residency; supportive of Ms Hyde receiving help for her mental health condition; focused on what was best for the children; I would have had no need to contact

Dean Marlo

you, or any of the governmental departments, in the first place.

Instead, I have had to bear the Family Courts dismissing and ignoring the commitment I have shown throughout, and my ability to provide stability and wellbeing for my children, all while being on the receiving end of Ms Hyde's erratic behaviour. Due to the worry and pressure of the ongoing proceedings, I find myself considering whether I am able, mentally and physically, to commit myself to any more court hearings.

I do not want to upset any judge or the Family Courts, but I do feel that I consistently provide my children with love, care, meanwhile, everyone else does their level best to go against the welfare of the children.

I feel I have three choices:

One, go to the endless hearings and let Ms Hyde and Smitch Law prolong the misery that they have already placed in our lives until Lara is 16, or similarly pleads to be removed from the court order.

Two, I have considered telling my children that I have coloured in the next year's schedule in accordance with the order, opposite weekends and half school holidays. I would continue to respond to their mother's requests for changes, within reason; as in the past, I will respect the children's wishes to have additional time with their mother as and when they request – but no more court hearings. The consequences... I'd have to face them.

Three, walk away from my children and let Ms Hyde take responsibility. I know from the bottom of my heart this is not what I want nor is it what my children want or deserve, but the Family Courts have gotten me low.

We have recently had hearings in London to determine whether Ms Hyde should be allowed to take the children out of school to holiday in Australia – it is easy to forget it was supposed to be about residency, and Alice similarly being removed from the court order – and, now, Canada has been added to the list.

As a single parent, who does not receive any financial support or maintenance from the children's mother, I work hard to provide for my family. The Legal Services looked into my earnings and stated that I had a share in a limited company; this company had neither money nor any taxable profits for that end of year. I had taken a loan out for £5,000 to pay off several debts and used the remaining to take the children on holiday. The Legal Services added this loan to my earnings.

This does not come from a place of jealousy or grievance for Ms Hyde's lifestyle, it just leaves me with the question: Why am I not the parent provided Legal Aid against numerous spurious allegations?

All this worry from this unforeseen and unjustified debt comes from two misleading letters sent to the Legal Services Commission by Smitch Law, 4 years apart. The allegations made in Mrs Mason's letters were false, and could have been confirmed as inaccurate by organisations such as Company House... Information that is available to anyone. The false allegations are swiftly moved on from, yet I am the person who is left with its devastating effects and the financial instability, which can only be detrimental to the children I have responsibility for!

Over the last 7 years, it has become clear that the deceptions practiced by some law firms are making it deliberately difficult for parents to bring up their children in a safe

440

and happy atmosphere. Their practices are quite clearly destroying any chance a split family has of settling down, which would enable the parents to concentrate on their children.

These proceedings have had a detrimental effect on my family's quality of life. For years, I have had my name and character denounced and my ability to be a good parent undermined by the legal system and those working within it, without justification. Over the past 7 years, I have written many statements denying the same false allegations. Year after year, my children and I have been led down many roads within the Family Courts that lead to nowhere.

This episode has been going on since January 2006; another psychologist has seen my children and now a guardian is involved in their lives.

It seems prudent to point out that while Hayley and Alice remember some of their mother and I being together (the good, and sadly the bad) Lara has known nothing but this mess for her entire conscious life. It's not how I wanted to raise my children; Hayley will be 16 soon.

In April 2007, Judge Yergin stated that there was to be no more hearings, apart from a 2-day hearing with one day set aside for Ms Hyde's application to contest the child psychologist's report. Since Judge Yergin's ruling, I have been to 4 hearings. There have been 2 hearings where I wasn't legally represented and to this day, I would have no idea what was discussed at those hearings, if it wasn't for Melissa working pro bono.

I have had to go to the High Court in London without legal representation and have had to endure listening to a barrister convincingly relay to the judge misleading and untrue statements on behalf of their client.

When in court, it seems it is not the welfare of the children that is paramount but the stipulations of one parent by unscrupulous barristers and law firms.

I believe that the Family Courts and the legal system have failed my children and us as a family.

What is the point of the Family Courts making court orders and schedules for the parents to follow, if a solicitor can incessantly harass the schedule by repeatedly trying to change it to suit their client?

If Smitch Law's behaviour does not contravene any rules or regulations set out by the law, then perhaps those laws and regulations should be scrutinised; they are not the first law firm to exploit children's welfare for financial gain, I'm sure.

In August 2007, Smitch Law wrote to me and threatened that if I did not produce my schedule for 2008, they would advise their client that it would be her schedule that the children and I would be following. Smitch Law should not be writing to me nor advising their client concerning the schedule. Their client and I had a schedule to follow that was drawn up by Judge Chips in the court order 2004, which was easy to adhere to as it alternates, and there was no need for a middle-man to discuss alterations, as we had proven ourselves capable.

I do harp on Mr Rowe, but Ms Hyde's mental health doctor expressed that proceedings would exacerbate her condition – this I do not believe anyone has ever taken seriously; especially a self-serving solicitor.

I know it can easily be said, 'Oh no, Mr Marlo is not happy!' or, 'Because things have not gone his way, Mr Marlo is complaining!'

However, Mr Rowe, I believe you and your office know different. My concerns are genuine and meaningful, and are an insight into the goings on within our legal system and the Family Courts.

Despite all of the above, I would like to thank you once again for making the time to talk to me. As I have made clear, I am totally exhausted by the constant pressure of proceedings, but I shall take your advice and not give up with the Family Courts. I do this for the love and care as a parent for my children, in the respect I have for you and the sound advice you have given me in the past.

Rather than complaints, I would like my letters to be seen as an insight into the Family Courts and our legal system. One day, I hope they might provide a guide to the urgently needed changes required to ensure the stability and welfare that all children and their parents need and deserve.

Yours respectfully…

(I have given up hope that my complaints will make a difference, so when writing to Mr Rowe, I am instead suggesting to present my experiences as an insight into being a father in the Family Courts; who knows how to unlock the doors of sensibility and equality?)

Head Teacher (Northview Grove)

12 October

Dear Mrs Tran,

I hope that rather than being seen as criticism or complaint, this letter can be an insight into resolving Alice's recent defiant behaviour.

I would like to say that children like Alice need coaching and reassurance from adults they respect. I know it is the school's right to suspend any unruly student but, before expulsion is considered, surely there must be other courses of action that can be tried.

The majority of the teachers from Northview Grove that I have spoken to tell me Alice is a delightful child who has shown great potential. Unfortunately, during moments of insecurity, Alice resorts to outbursts of defiance.

It has been acknowledged by Alice's teachers on many occasions that Alice is not all bad, so Ms Hyde and I, as Alice's parents, believe that with an adjustment of attitude from Alice and the school, her growing up problems can be resolved.

I believe that Alice is just showing signs of what many teenagers go through. Experienced teachers of middle–school children must have seen many examples of this behaviour; continuous suspensions will do nothing for Alice's education or development towards adulthood.

I would like to take this opportunity to thank you for your time with the appointment and hope that Ms Hyde and I as parents can work together with the school for the best interests of Alice's education and development.

Yours faithfully…

Dean Marlo

Private Tuition

17 October

For:
Tuition in GCSE maths for Hayley @ £22 p/h
1 hour weekly.
Commencing Tuesday 30/10 at 6-7pm.

At Hayley's request, I arranged private tuition in GCSE maths at a tutorial centre in town.

Ruth's contact

18 - 24 October

Thursday 18th
I phoned Ruth to talk about Lara's birthday. (It probably seems early to do so, but I've learned it's best to avoid confusion.) I asked if she wanted to swap the weekend before Lara's birthday or the weekend after, as on her schedule it was one of the periods where she had given herself three weekends in a row, despite it being my year for Lara's birthday.

Ignoring my question, Ruth replied, 'To save confusion in the future, I will have Lara this year; then next year, you should have the children for all their birthdays and the following year I will.'

I told Ruth that she had Lara last year; her suggestion was unfair and unnecessary, what we need to do is keep to the court order and not create problems where there are none. Ruth hung up on me.

After school, I talked to Lara about her birthday. Lara made it clear she wanted her birthdays to stay as they have been, where she spends odd birthday years with her mother and even birthdays with me.

To achieve some form of compromise with Ruth, I asked Lara if she would like to go and sleepover at her mother's the night before her birthday and come home on her birthday morning; Lara thought for a moment and said, 'Ok dad.'

Friday 19th
It is Ruth's half term holiday between the 19th and the 24th of October, so I'm planning to work flat out during this time.

Calling Ruth, I suggested what Lara and I discussed, that she could pick Lara up after school and return Lara in the morning on Saturday for her birthday. I also told Ruth about Lara's party, which Lara wants to have at the local 'laser tag' arena.

Ruth stated she could drop Lara off at her party, and I agreed; she went on to say that if I am having Lara that weekend, she wants two days and nights in the Christmas holidays. Despite this again not being applicable due to the court order, I told Ruth I didn't mind which days she takes, however I didn't want any interference with the children's Christmas holiday time.

Monday 22nd
I phoned Ms Moyer to discuss the letter she agreed to send me and left a message for her to phone me back, which she failed to do.

Tuesday 23rd
Having heard nothing from Ms Moyer, I contacted the town Cafcass office and left a message for Ms Soto, the director, to phone me back. When she did, she asked me to write my concerns in a letter to her.

Wednesday 24th
In the post, I received a 'compliments' slip from Ms Soto, with a Cafcass booklet.

The children returned from their mother's.

Lara came into the kitchen and stated that she wanted to talk to me about her birthday. Lara stated that she was fine about going to her mother's on Friday and sleeping over, but she did not want her mother to drop her off at the party. Lara explained that when she had a party at the adventure centre with her mother last year, all of her mates were there, while she arrived 20 minutes late. Lara said that it made her feel sad and the embarrassment spoilt her party. I assured Lara I would speak to her mother about dropping her back home in the morning.

Cafcass Complaint

26 October

Please find my response below to the report made by my children's Guardian, Ms Moyer, dated 3rd September 2007.

Continually, it has been reported that Ms Hyde and my separation was acrimonious, yet in truth I babysat my children while Ms Hyde played badminton. I provided a brand-new car and money each week; as a family we went to Dinosaur World in Norfolk. It was only after several months, when Ms Hyde's demands for more money and a larger car resulted in her withholding all my contact with our children and in her instructing a solicitor. In response, I applied to the courts.

The love and care I have for my children had never been an issue previously with Ms Hyde or any organisation that has been involved with our children, due to Ms Hyde's mental health problems.

In the 90's, I smoked cannabis recreationally. With court proceedings imminent concerning some form of contact with my children, I sought professional advice. From that day, I stopped and gained medical proof of this fact. I feel it is unfair and unjust that these events are referred to, as it is irrelevant to the responsible parent I have been to this day.

The order remained but the yearly schedules were addressed via solicitors. I applied to the Family Courts to revert to the schedule as ordered, as it had been changed at the request of Ms Hyde to the point that it brought no consistency or stability to the children's day to day lives.

Allegations I have made in my statements to the family court have all been substantiated by the schools, the police, Social Services or photographic evidence. Yet, it is Ms Hyde's allegations, put forward largely in her solicitors' letters, that takes the attention of the numerous court experts. I maintain I have never acted in the manner suggested by Ms Hyde or her legal representatives.

I have been trying for years to put an end to these proceedings and reform the way they are run with the support of my MP Mr Rowe and even a cabinet minister. To me it appears that the legal system and those who profit from it are abusing Ms Hyde and her mental health, to the detriment of the three children involved.

Hayley is not covered by the current residence order, as claimed by the report; Hayley had every right to not want to talk to the guardian, as she resents being treated as if she is still under the order. (For Hayley, the court process has been in her life for nearly a decade. There have been so many examples where Hayley has been let down by the attitudes and behaviours of people in place to ensure children's welfare – Hayley just wants to be left alone, as we all do.) The court has been unable to grasp the concept but Hayley knows that I support her wishes and do not have a problem with her having a relationship with her mother, and she can stay with her mother, within reason for school, whenever she likes - as she already does.

447

The report states that Alice, age 13, has her eyebrow pierced. This is incorrect and misleading to the judge, as it is Hayley, age 15, who has her brow pierced.

Northview Grove are fully aware of Hayley and Alice's involvement with Social Services and that psychological reports have been carried out; Mrs Sanders, the child psychologist, contacted Mrs Sparrow earlier this year. Whether the findings regarding the children is relevant from the previous reports I do not know – while Ms Hyde's behaviour has not changed, the children have all grown up and experienced more, since then.

Clearly, it has been the system's ability to be used by those people within it, who profit by its use, that is the real culprit, and another three children and their parents are the victims of the machine, like many other families caught up in a game of dishonesty, instability and legal manoeuvrings, which do nothing for the children involved.

Hayley confirmed to the Guardian that her mother repeatedly brings proceedings to the Family Courts contrary to her children's wishes. It is ironic that three children are telling adults and the legal system to stop squandering their childhood, yet their involvement in their life goes on.

Any lateness and lack of attendance of the children at school should be reaffirmed to Ms Hyde as inappropriate and detrimental to the children's education.

I believe the effort I have put into bringing up my children deserves more than being described as 'providing them with some stability'.

The meaning of 'provide' is to give someone something they wanted or needed; the meaning of 'some' is an undisclosed amount, little or more but not none. Does this really sum up my parenting?

Too many fathers run away from their children, yet those who embrace their responsibilities find little help or recognition from the people who should be able to see and relay the parent's dedication, love and care for their children. I do not want a medal, I want to be allowed to be the good parent I am; this may be 'report wording' but as someone whose residency of their children may well be affected, it is hard to see how anyone would draw a good conclusion of either parent from her opinions.

I believe any parent who had been through what I have with my children would be heartbroken to see their love and dedication relayed as 'some stability'. Reading it myself, and even knowing the truth, I feel inadequate, and that there is something missing from the care I provide.

I have repeatedly tried to discuss the children's needs and wishes, while working with Ms Hyde throughout the problems her mental health issues have raised. It is reflected by the schools that the children are better focused in my residency; Judge Chips must have seen something in 2004 for Ms Hyde to lose joint residency. What good is the report to anyone if it doesn't accurately reflect the situation as it is?

At the court hearing on the 26th June, it was relayed by the guardian's solicitor that the guardian had no problems with the holiday to Australia – in spite of this meaning the children would be taken out of school for 12 days. However, in the report, Ms Moyer states that it would not be in the children's best interests 'especially as Lara is approaching her Eleven-plus, Hayley in her final year and Alice approaching her GCSE's'. The guardian was aware of the children's ages and their educational demands for their oncoming year, and yet at the hearing this was redundant.

I have continued to comply with Ms Hyde's holiday arrangements that have interfered with my contact, regardless of the fact that I have the responsibility of my children under a sole residency order. This flexibility I understand is necessary for the children's relationship with their mother and their wellbeing.

Ms Hyde has been encouraged to abuse the legal system, in a toxic symbiotic relationship, which has caused the 'significant harm' to our children. The acrimony is entirely from Ms Hyde's side; I resent the implication that by going to court with concerns for my children's welfare after abusive incidents at Ms Hyde's home, contacting Social Services or even ignoring abusive phone calls, that I have contributed or am the cause of our family's problems, as I have only responded to the consequences of something happening.

It is Ms Hyde and her legal representatives who, with Legal Aid funding, have repeatedly brought proceedings into our family's lives year after year. I do not draw my children into any disputes with their mother. I am a single parent who looks after my three daughters and goes to work, but I am penalised for making the effort. Whereas, Ms Hyde receives Legal Aid to cover the application for the purpose of a holiday during term time – incurring two family court hearings deemed necessary despite the clear defiance of both Government recommendations and what is actually best for her children.

I am always there to support my children and, in spite of all of the above, Ms Hyde, which is clear to see but not highlighted in this report; I am trying to be a caring and responsible parent regarding my children's education and nothing more.

The statement Ms Moyer could not get a hold of me I believe to be questionable. We are usually at home after school/teatime and our family and friends have found no difficulty in contacting me, I also run a business on my home phone line, I have an answering machine that gives my mobile – how come she was able to get Ms Hyde's mobile number but not mine?

I believe my children have clearly suffered in their day to day lives due to the years of ongoing court proceedings, which have been perpetrated by a financially motivated law firm, or something – I find it hard to really know what, if not for money. Any parent would find the last 7 years stressful.

I was totally shocked and dismayed to read what Northview Grove have reported to the guardian, as I've always been actively involved with the school concerning Hayley and Alice's education and behaviour – I had recently attended Alice's re-integration at Northview Grove. Ms Hyde and I agreed that we would try and defuse the situation with Alice's behaviour before it got out of hand.

I had also recently made an appointment with Mrs Sparrow from Northview Grove, where two other teachers were present. At this appointment, I explained that I was more than willing to help in addressing Alice's behaviour that the school had been experiencing over the past months.

A report in children's matters must have a high standard of professionalism, as it is vital to relay information that is correct and clear; it is left to the judge to assess, to the best of their ability, and ensure the welfare and stability of the children involved. The children have all expressed to various experts their desire to just get on with their childhoods.

I have, over many years complied with the court rulings and recommendations while having at the same time provided a stable and happy home for my children. I have tried to defuse Ms Hyde's frequently erratic and sometimes violent behaviour. And in truth, as it was in 1992, I could do nothing more than stand back, unable to calm her or find her help. Anything I did was seen as confrontational, even the love, care and support.

Over the past 2 years the conflicts as reported have been between Hayley, Alice, Ms Hyde and her boyfriend. While standing by my children after an incident with their mother, I have always observed the contact arrangements between Lara and Ms Hyde, as this is what Lara wanted. I have always avoided conflict with Ms Hyde and have openly encouraged Hayley and Alice to visit their mother, even if it was for tea once a week during the periods they refused contact.

I have not, as indicated in the report, ever told my children to go to their mother after they have misbehaved.

I have reported the incidents that have occurred between Ms Hyde and our children. Ms Hyde, her solicitors and the system, have played a large part in bringing instability, confusion and years of conflict into our family's day to day life.

What has been frustrating over the past 7 years is how, with some ease, Ms Hyde's allegations have been placed at my feet within the Family Courts. These deceptions obviously have clouded our family's true situation at every avenue and I believe that it is morally wrong for this to be acceptable. Despite Ms Hyde's numerous false assertions, I continue to be proved the mainstay, which was borne out in 2004 when I got sole residency, in Mrs Sanders' report and Ms Moyer's report.

All three children have shown great resilience with their parents separating and the non-stop proceedings.

I would be the first to agree that Lara has, through her own efforts, achieved a great deal. I find it however disappointing that Ms Moyer could only see this in Lara alone. Hayley and Alice have also achieved personal gains that are worthy of acknowledgment.

The Guardian states that taking the children outside school holidays would not be in the best interests of the children. I do not understand why the Guardian could not have reached this conclusion at the hearing held in July or why a report was necessary. By her own account, the report was rushed, which seems ironic given that proceedings are in their seventh year.

Ms Hyde's inability to adhere to the schedule is unfairly misinterpreted as partly due to my behaviour, which has never been the case.

'Seriously concerned about Hayley's mental health'.

I am deeply alarmed that this unfounded and damaging statement will serve to mislead and discredit Hayley, portraying the opposite of the responsible, caring teenager she is to all who know her well. As a caring parent, and someone who has experienced living with someone with mental health problems, Hayley has never given me any reason to worry, nor have I been made aware of anyone else's concerns over Hayley's mental wellbeing.

This statement made by the Guardian herself (and not, as her report reads, by a Deputy Head from Hayley's School) remains available to any court appointed experts or legal professionals who choose to use it in the future.

I believe that it would be more beneficial for the children if the Guardian were to recommend that Ms Hyde receive therapeutic sessions from the family service. I also believe Hayley and Alice should be asked and given the choice to talk to someone from the CFCS, or similar.

I, as a parent, want my children to have the best start into their young adult years. Hayley, as she reaches adulthood, should not be burdened with unfounded and untrue reports about her mental health. Further to this, Hayley was discharged as a party to proceedings in March 2007 – I understand asking her opinion on the holiday, but is it necessary to make remarks about Hayley's psyche, when Ms Moyer hadn't been asked to nor did she speak to Hayley herself about it.

I do not believe that it is morally acceptable for a third party or my children's schools to be made aware of the numerous unsubstantiated allegations, as included in the report. The information that the Family Courts request and may need are not the same as the needs and requests of the children's schools, or any other third party.

(I hope I am not the only one that thinks the whole suggestion is bizarre.)

As with my medical records, I have nothing to hide but it feels like a violation of privacy none the less. Why should I be looked at any different because the reader has been informed that in the 90's, I partook in the smoking of cannabis?

I would simply like Ms Hyde to settle down within her life, which I believe would be beneficial and would bring stability to our children and our family.

I am grateful and appreciate the conclusions reached in this report, as it signifies the end of proceedings, however believe the information included that she drew her opinions from, was partly inaccurate and misleading. I find it unprofessional when after being proof read, as suggested by Ms Moyer, it is also littered with mistakes in both spelling and grammar.

At the hearing on the 6th September, we were called in front of the judge at 9.45am. The judge stated she hadn't seen the Guardian's report. Both the barrister for Ms Hyde and the solicitor for the Guardian had written on their copies, so I had to give the judge my copy. To this day, it was not explained why the courts did not have a copy of the report.

Again, please know, I appreciate it has been advised 'under the circumstance' that the children remain in my residency; I am grateful. However, I hope you understand my concerns for the professionalism my family has received.

Yours faithfully…

(I ask myself why I carry on writing these letters and following up these complaints. Again, they've found no problem with my sole residency. But, I know, if this is their standard, then to do nothing would be the same as turning a blind eye to the families being lined up before the Family Courts, just to face the same misery. Whether it is the revolutionist in me, or the optimist, I have to believe that change is possible and that things can be better than they are.)

Changing plans

29/30 October

Monday 29th

Lara handed out her invitations for her party on Saturday 1st December. Unfortunately, most of Lara's friends that were coming to the party are boys who all played football for a club on weekends; it would be difficult for them to make the party in time.

A notice came through for Alice;

Dear Mr Marlo,

Pupil: Alice Marlo, 9OK

I am writing to inform you that Alice will be placed in our ISC (Internal Support Centre) for a period of one day, Tuesday 30th October 2007 and will be working in isolation on a one-to-one basis with a member of staff.

The reason for Alice being placed in the ISC is due to her truanting lessons today.

Alice will be returned to normal lessons after serving her time in the ISC but will continue on a report for a period of time. Should the report prove unsatisfactory, Alice may well have to return to the ISC or indeed face other sanctions, subject to circumstances.

Should you wish to discuss this matter further, please contact me at school through the usual channels.

Yours sincerely,

Tuesday 30th

As Hayley attended her first tutoring lesson, I discussed with Alice also attending tuition to assist her with English. I am hopeful Alice agreeing to the tuition will help her improve her confidence and attitude to other subjects as well.

I phoned the venue of Lara's party and rebooked the party for 2.45pm, as several parents informed me the football would be finished by then. I phoned Ruth and explained the reason for the change in the time of Lara's party. I told Ruth that under the circumstances would she mind dropping Lara back at mid–day, and offered, if she wanted, for her to come to Lara's party. Ruth agreed and stated that she would like to.

Tutorial Centre

31 October

Dear Mr Marlo,

I have the pleasure in offering your daughter, Alice, tuition in English on the following terms and conditions.

The fee per lesson is payable in advance by cash or cheque. Lessons not attended will be charged for.

If you have to cancel a lesson, please let us know as soon as possible. If we have to cancel a lesson we will either re-arrange it or credit you with the fees.

Books or other materials lent to you are to be returned no later than the final lesson.

Yours sincerely…

Dean Marlo

The Ruth Effect

5 - 8 November

Monday 5th
Hayley was off school on Monday following Ruth's weekend contact.
Tuesday 6th
At 4.15pm, Mr Caldwell from Northview Grove phoned me to inform me that Alice has been excluded from school tomorrow. I asked Mr Caldwell why and he replied that Alice had refused to stay in the Internal Support Centre.

Both Hayley and Alice attended their extra tuition sessions.

Up to this day, despite the recent court proceedings and new contact order for Alice to stay overnight with her mother, not once has Ruth called me to organise it, nor has Alice requested it.

Wednesday 7th
With Alice excluded from school, we arranged for Nan to come down; I made sure she knew what school work needed to be done before heading on-site. At 2pm, Alice called, stating that she is walking to her mother's. When I asked if she'd done what she needed to for school, Alice said she would finish it at her mother's.

In the evening, Lara, Sully and I left for puppy training classes. Half way through the lesson, at 8.20pm, I received a text from Alice stating that she was going to sleep at her mother's tonight. Standing to the side, I phoned Alice back to tell her that I would meet her at school at 9am tomorrow for her re–integration meeting. Alice seemed upset so I asked if she was alright.

Alice replied, 'Just forget it,' and hung up.

The class was coming to an end and thought I'd give Alice a call again when Lara and I got home.

Before I had the chance, my phone went off and it was Ruth. She told me that Alice and Hayley had fallen out, and that she also had a 'bust–up' (my heart always does a funny flip when hearing about Ruth's confrontations with the children, as I never know what level of escalation she has gone to) with Hayley, who stormed out of her house in tears.

I left Lara in the living room with Sully, practising the new tricks they'd learnt, and asked Ruth why Hayley and Alice had argued.

Ruth replied, 'Hayley has been interfering in Alice's life and that is why I also had a go at Hayley.'

I questioned how Hayley was interfering in Alice's life and Ruth stated that Hayley argued with someone that Alice had over. Ruth went on, saying she told her that she had no right to question who Alice was seeing, and that was why Hayley stormed out. Feeling uneasy at Ruth's words, at Hayley's disapproval and the fact Alice hadn't mentioned a boyfriend to me – I asked Ruth which one of Alice's friends we were talking about. Ruth stated, 'I know the young man and do not know why Hayley has made such a fuss.'

I told Ruth I would call Hayley, ask her to come home and let Ruth know.

On the phone to Hayley, some important context came to light. She informed me that the young man in question is in fact 23 years old and drives a BMW. It was strange hearing Hayley talking, saying 'the guy is a paedophile he is always hanging around school.' I looked through the list of issues I had in my head and dealing with a paedophile was not one of them; my heart sunk as I considered what the fuck I was going to do.

Hayley went on to say she was shocked to see his car parked outside of her mother's, that her mother was not in, and that Alice and this man were alone in the house. Hayley found him in Alice's room; she had a go at him, saying it wasn't right for someone his age to be seeing a 13-year-old, especially her younger sister. Hayley stated that just as she had finished saying this when Alice came into the room and an argument broke out between them.

Then her mother came home, and Hayley stopped arguing with Alice to explain to their mother the situation; their mother had a go at her, and said, 'It's none of your business.'

Disgusted, at both this 23-year-old and Ruth, I reassured Hayley that I thought it was right for her to be worried about her sister because it is not normal behaviour.

I think Alice didn't mention it to me because she knew I would not approve as if she wants to be in a relationship, I would expect it to be suitable for her age.

Hayley came home, we shared a hug and she went to see Lara. I texted Ruth to let her know that Hayley was safe and at home, but did not mention what Hayley told me. Clearly, as the man was welcome in her home with Alice, saying something would only cause an argument.

(And, truthfully, I still didn't know what to say or do. Report them both to the police? Sometimes I really do think Ms Hyde's home is a House of Horrors, out of a TV show.)

Instead, I tried Alice's number but she didn't answer.

It was about 9.15pm, we were all in bed, and Alice burst through the front door. I heard her run upstairs, and called out 'hello' as I got up to see her. She went past me with her school clothes and ran back out of the front door. Alice did not acknowledge me at all, and I saw Ruth pull away from the curb.

Thursday 8th

After taking Lara to school, I arrived at Northview Grove for Alice's 9 am appointment. Neither Alice nor Ruth were in the reception, so I phoned Ruth to ask if they were on their way. Ruth stated that she was still at work but would be there soon; I asked where Alice was and she replied that Alice was still at hers and she would pick Alice up on her way through. Mr Caldwell asked me if I would like to come into his office and wait, to which I did. While we were waiting, I mentioned my concerns about the man who drives a BMW, and is apparently known by the children around school. Mr Caldwell made a note to investigate.

At 9.25am, Ruth and Alice arrived. Ruth apologised, saying that she really had to get back to work, and suggested to Mr Caldwell that a different time for the meeting would be better for her.

Mr Caldwell stated that we must complete Alice's re–integration now.

Despite Ruth's flustering, the meeting went ahead; Alice did not say a word to me when I tried to speak to her.

From Minister of Families

8 November

Dear Mr Marlo,
I am writing to confirm receipt of your letter. I am sorry that I have been unable to contact you regarding any outcomes to your concerns as yet, but hope to be able to do so during the next week.
Yours sincerely,

Making good progress!

12 November

As you will know from previous information provided to you via the recent information leaflet on the Making Good Progress Pilot Scheme, our school is part of a national pilot that is looking at new assessment arrangements for pupils in Key Stage 2. As part of the new arrangements, pupils will be entered for single (national curriculum) level tests when they are ready: as a confirmation of the teacher's assessment that they have securely attained that level. The first single level tests will be in December this year.

The dates are: 03/12, reading; 04/12, writing; 05/12, mathematics.

No test will last longer than 50 minutes.

We believe that your daughter Lara is now working securely within level 4 in reading and mathematics. We would like to offer them the opportunity to validate that achievement through the single level tests.

We are happy to discuss this with you if you have any queries. We have already discussed this with Lara. We will assume you are happy with this arrangement unless you contact us. The results will be made available to you and your child in mid-January.

Yours sincerely,

Lara's new teacher at Riverbank

12 November

Dear Mrs Irfan,

I would like to ask if you would please take the time to thank Mr Brooks for his effort and dedication that my daughter Lara and I have seen each day this term year. Over the past few months, he has continued the high standard of teaching that I have found in Riverbank School throughout the years with all three of my daughters.

Yours and Mr Brooks' friendly and positive approach to parents and their children is very heartening to see.

Yours sincerely,

Trying to be a parent

13 November

After school finished, I tried to call Alice but she did not answer; I haven't spoken to her in nearly a week.

(I wanted to report the man to the police but I don't know his name; when I asked Hayley, she said everyone just knew him as 'that pedo'. All I can do is hope the school follow up on my concerns.)

At 5pm, I phoned Ruth with the hopes of speaking to Alice, however Ruth immediately stated that Alice did not want to talk to me. Knowing that the longer Alice keeps up the lack of communication between both myself and Hayley the worse it will be, I asked instead if Ruth was going to drop Alice round so that we can go to the tutorial centre. Ruth told me to wait. A few moments later, she came back and said that Alice was refusing to go to the centre with Hayley, so she would take her herself.

With a strange mix of relief, Alice was still willing to go to the lesson, and frustration, Ruth is enabling her to fester the bad sentiment between Hayley and Alice, I asked Ruth to talk to Alice and encourage her to resolve her problems with Hayley – who, after all, had only been looking out for her. Ruth stated that Alice has said she 'will not live in the same house as Hayley' and therefore she would be taking Alice to prevent any trouble.

At the tutorial centre at the end of the session, as Lara and I sat in the waiting room for Hayley, Alice came out of her classroom and walked straight past us without saying a word. The tutor told me Alice had refused to do anything, and that the evening's lesson had been a total waste of time.

From Northview

15 November

Dear Mr Marlo,
I am writing to inform you of a major concern that we have over Alice's behaviour.
As you will see from the accompanying letter outlining the exclusion details, Alice has, on several occasions recently, demonstrated a complete refusal to listen to and follow the instructions of very senior members of staff. When this situation is arrived at, it is impossible for us to retain a student on site as we are unable to be certain that, at times of possible danger, we will have a positive response from the student. It is vital that you discuss this aspect of Alice's behaviour with her immediately.
If there is not a substantial change in her behaviour, I fear I shall be informing you of more serious levels of intervention than have taken place already. Our duty of care for Alice's education and welfare, and the impact this has on the learning of other students, can only be undertaken with her full cooperation and communication with us.
Yours sincerely,
Mrs Tran, Headteacher

Dear Mr Marlo,
Pupil: Alice Marlo, 9OK
I am writing to inform you of my decision to exclude Alice for a fixed period of three days. This means that your child will not be allowed in school for this period. The exclusion begins on Friday 16 November and ends on Tuesday 20 November 2007. We expect Alice to be back in school on Wednesday 21 November at 8.25am.
Alice has been excluded for this fixed period for:-
Persistent disruptive behaviour; refusal to comply with reasonable instructions from two very senior members of staff; rudeness to a senior member of staff.
I realise that this exclusion may well be upsetting for you and your family, but the decision to exclude Alice has not been taken lightly.
You and Alice are requested to attend a reintegration interview with Mrs Tran/Mr Caldwell at the school on Wednesday 21 November at 12 o'clock. If that is not convenient, please contact the school to arrange an alternative date and time. The purpose of the reintegration interview is to discuss how best your child's return to school can be managed. Failure to attend a reintegration interview will be a factor taken into account by a Magistrates' Court if, on future application, they consider whether to impose a parenting order on you.
Yours sincerely,

Ruth's weekend contact

17-19 November

Alice still hasn't been home and although I've called her, we haven't had a real conversation about what happened.

I had another discussion with Mrs Tran, wherein I explained the difficulty in Ms Hyde and I not showing a unified response to Alice, and how I believe Alice's living arrangements needed to be finalised in order to curb Alice's behaviour. Mrs Tran asked why I didn't return to court (I felt that comment was ironic) and I explained, she was aware of the inaccuracies and misleading statements in the guardian's report that have emanated from Northview Grove. Apart from never wanting to visit the halls of shame ever again, I was not prepared to make an application to the courts with comments hanging over my head such as I do not play a part in my children's education or schools.

At Ruth's, things seem to have moved on; Hayley stayed at her mother's, with Alice, Sunday night.

Hayley did not go to school on Monday.

Dean Marlo

Headteacher

19 November

Dear Mrs Tran,

I feel frustrated by Alice's behaviour and the continuous suspensions that I believe have proven unsuccessful in the past.

The majority of these suspensions have been because Alice on occasions has refused to remove her jewellery or remove the hoodie from under her blazer. While I accept this is part of the school rules, the resulting confrontations and exclusions are not helping Alice.

Like many families with teenagers, this defiance of boundaries and rules is found at home as well as in school; as a parent I try to be patient as well as firm. I do not believe that constant days off school encourages a child such as Alice to conform. In reality, Alice gets bored during the day, stays up late and then lays in bed all day due to there being little to do and get up for. I see that this is not a recipe for success in a 13–year–old's life.

Again, while I appreciate the school providing Alice learning materials, her lack of understanding leaves her frustrated; this is something Ms Hyde, myself and yourselves need to make improvements on to support her. I am aware that Alice's attitude cannot be tolerated in the day–to–day running of the school, however there must be other avenues to try resolve these situations without suspensions.

I am a parent of three daughters who have always shown me love and care; it is devastating and disappointing to see Alice's behaviour and to hear the things she says – I feel I have failed her as a parent. I want so much for Alice to succeed in Northview Grove and do well in her life, but we have big issues over small matters.

I am not 'sticking up' for Alice as I appreciate her behaviour and attitude is unreasonable, and I also think Alice is aware of this too.

This may be a burden that Northview Grove feel they cannot bear, but as a caring parent I would like you to understand that on behalf of Alice's education, welfare and stability, our family and myself, I ask you please, not to give up with Alice, who I believe is and can be a genuine and caring person, because she needs that extra time and patience.

Yours sincerely,

Discussions

20 November

At 4.30pm, I phoned Alice to discuss her tuition and re–integration. Alice stated that she couldn't make up her mind, because she wanted to stay at Northview Grove but it might be best if she goes to Horizon Academy; her mother has got the application forms. Alice explained her mother told her that if she went to Horizon Academy and did not like it, she could go back to Northview Grove – who would have to take her back… As long as she lives with her mother. Or, in her words, 'Our mother lives in the Northview Grove's catchment area, and they would have to take me back.'

I told Alice that if she was to get expelled from Northview Grove it would make no difference where she was living and she needed to realise that she would not be allowed to go back to Northview. I did not mention that we live in the catchment area too.

(I never have time in the moment to stop and properly think about any of the situations that come about. The idea that Alice can not only avoid responsibility for her actions, but also *expect* forgiveness or understanding from others, is a dangerous precedent to set for anyone. Moving on to the fact that her mother is willing to enforce and support this idea – I think we've all imagined just leaving everything behind and starting anew. The problem with that ideology is that we would still be us, and therefore whatever it is we're running from, will follow sure enough. It's the same here; if Alice goes to Horizon, doesn't listen to uniform requirements, talks back to teachers and walks out of lessons, we will all be in the same position we are now.)

Alice continued talking about the pamphlet for Horizon, and eventually it was mentioned that her mother said we might have to go back to court to change where Alice is living and her address.

It's quite an important conversation, and one I'd have rather had with Alice not on a phone call. I told Alice that I have and will always stand by her wishes. (If she wants to live with her mother, while I would be sad not to see her as often, or to keep the family dynamic we'd managed to hold together, I have no desire to control any of my children.) However, I also said to Alice that she needs to be living with her mother for the right reasons, because she is loved and cared for, not in the event she might be go back to Northview – that's not the right attitude to have at all.

Regardless of whether she is going to settle down with her sisters at home, or live with her mother full time, and have weekend contact at home, Alice needs to make a decision. I do still believe that I provide Alice the best for her welfare and stability, so I told Alice that if she was going to settle down then I didn't mind her staying at her mother's a couple of nights each week, on the basis we all know where she is living permanently and she is getting on at school.

Which finally brought us round to why I actually called: to remind Alice that the effort and commitment has to start from her with regard to school rules and her attitude towards lessons. While mildly agreeing to that, Alice stated she did not want to go to her tuition class tonight. I tried to encourage Alice several times, going from reminding her it is for her benefit to eventually saying that I still have to pay for the lesson, so she should make the effort this week and we could discuss stopping the sessions after.

Alice replied, 'I don't want to go.'

I left it there.

I phoned Ruth to discuss Horizon Academy, plus Alice's tuition, and asked her to please speak to Alice. She replied, 'Alice has made her mind up.'

And that, was that.

Feeling like I spent a long time getting nowhere, I made dinner, helped Lara with some homework and took Hayley to her tuition lesson. On the way, Hayley said her mother was going to pick her up from the lesson; Ruth dropped Hayley home at 9.40pm.

Assistant Educational Psychologist Record

21 November

Visit date: 1 November 2007
Reason for involvement:
Alice is currently at risk of permanent exclusion due to non-compliance and difficult behaviour. The school are requesting short, frequent session to work with Alice to attempt to avoid further fixed term exclusions and ultimately avoid permanent exclusion.

Discussion with:
Mr Garrett (Deputy Head)
Alice is displaying challenging behaviours including 'failure to comply with reasonable requests' and 'inappropriate behaviour' within school.
Alice has difficulties in Literacy
She is artistic and shows talent in this area
Alice is 'kind and a pleasant girl' but can be 'obstinate' and by her own admission, 'likes to win battles'
Alice likes to be known as a non-conformist and likes to stand out
The ideal outcome would be for Alice to comply with school rules and authority because it is 'intrinsically what she should do' not to avoid disciplinary action. She would also spend less time wandering about the school, and more time smiling.

Main issues/concerns:
Alice has difficulty complying with school rules and does not respond well when challenged. The main concern at present is that she is at risk of permanent exclusion and is frequently excluded for fixed periods.

What I did:
I initially discussed the issue and desired outcomes with Mr Garrett, the results of which are above. I have since then worked with Alice on a number of occasions, discussing her feelings and what she would like to achieve by my input. Alice would like to avoid permanent exclusion herself, as she feels that it would adversely affect her future and realises that staying in Northview Grove would be the best outcome. We have agreed on a number of small targets and ways to achieve these all with a view to improving her chances of avoiding permanent exclusion.

Outcomes:
Since I started work with Alice, she has had at least 3 fixed term exclusions. I feel that the support I am able to provide is not sufficient to enable change. For this reason, I have contacted Secondary Behaviour Support Service, and am awaiting a reply.
Alice is becoming increasingly close to permanent exclusion and the school feel they have exhausted all avenues and cannot make any further progress until Alice agrees to comply to the school's code of conduct.
I have agreed, by request of Alice's parents, to continue to work with Alice, although I will keep this situation under review, considering the effectiveness of my input.

Plans for review:
At present, Alice is at high risk of permanent exclusion. If she avoids this, I will continue to work with her and review any progress made. I will also ask Secondary Behaviour Support to consider whether they are able to provide any support, particularly in a whole-school environment.

Dean Marlo

Re-integration

21 -25 November

Wednesday 21ˢᵗ
I woke Hayley up for school and she told me that she was too tired to go, I tried to encourage her to go in for at least half the day and offered to drop her off, however Hayley did not get up. With little option, I made breakfast, which did manage to rouse Hayley from bed but no further, informed Northview, took Lara to Riverbank early and headed to Alice's re-integration meeting.

Ruth and I both attended the meeting, but once more Alice's attitude towards the situation was flippant. In the end, Mrs Tran decided that Alice was not ready to re-attend, so she rescheduled the meeting for the following day.

Attempting to talk to Alice, I suggested she come home for dinner to discuss school and her living arrangements. Alice wasn't interested and left with Ruth.

Leaving one disaster for tomorrow, I went home to check on Hayley. I offered again to drop her to school, however she had just migrated to the sofa. Accepting the loss here too, I asked Hayley to do any homework that is due and at least try to do something productive – reading or baking, something. Unfortunately, although it would only be a half day myself, I had to go to work.

At 2.30pm, Hayley called to say she is walking round her mother's. Being on-site, there was little I could do.

It feels like Lara and I are the only people trying to keep a sane schedule, and I am grateful at least to be able to consistently provide that for Lara, where Hayley and Alice use their burgeoning independence, and Ruth, to live in chaos. I don't really know where I went wrong, but the family life we all enjoyed and had a year ago, has been turned upside down, and I really haven't got any idea of how to resolve the issues that are now imbedded into our day-to-day lives.

I got home to a letter from Mrs Mason on the doormat:
We enclose herewith Notice of Discharge of our client's Public Funding Certificate.
(The end of another great 'set' for the firm!)

In evening, at around 7.30pm, Hayley called again to say she was going swimming with her mother at her health club, and would be home around 9.30pm. I let Hayley know I didn't approve of her missing school, having stayed out late with her mother last night, and will be expecting her to go to school tomorrow.

It was after 9pm when Ruth phoned, stating Hayley wanted a shower and rather than disturb Lara and myself, she was going to stay round hers tonight.

Despite believing that this arrangement is not in the best interests of Hayley's wellbeing or her education, it wasn't so much as agreement Ruth called me for but to give me a chance to acknowledge everyone's plans – which I haven't had at times in the past and, don't get me wrong, I'm thrilled to at least be informed.

Magnanimity towards Ruth apparently means not being a parent to my children.

Thursday 22nd

Ruth and I once more sat beside Alice at her re-integration meeting, as Mrs Tran stated that Alice was close to total expulsion. Alice raised the subject of going to Horizon Academy and was told by Mrs Tran that if she were to be expelled from Northview Grove, she would not be allowed back under any circumstances and it would be unlikely she would be given a place at Horizon.

Even though it appears Hayley and Alice have reconciled, Alice is still living with her mother; it's difficult not to want to point fingers at the correlation between that and her behaviour at school. I have no chance to try help Alice as she chooses to ignore me. I've always known Ruth and I run two very different households, and for a teenager given choice, my home of boundaries and structure doesn't have the same appeal.

It was decided Alice would return to normal lessons tomorrow, because it was felt her attitude was still not appropriate to return to school today. Alice left with her mother.

Later, I received a phone call from Mrs Tran who informed me that she has seen Alice wandering the school this afternoon which is against policy; she asked me to collect Alice and told me to re-emphasize to her that she could be facing permanent expulsion.

I decided to phone Ruth first, before going to pick up Alice, to talk about what Mrs Tran had said and to ask her to make it clear to Alice once again, so she understood the seriousness of the situation. I told Ruth that I would be telling Alice the same when I pick her up.

Ruth replied, 'I will be collecting Alice; she is never going to comply with the school rules, so keeping Alice away from school is the best option until I find out how long it will be before she can be transferred to Horizon Academy.'

In disbelief, I reminded Ruth that even if Alice gets into Horizon, she will have to start following school rules, and allowing her to continue to miss so much school rather than change her behaviour isn't right. Ruth loudly and profanely disagreed, so I left it.

Friday 23rd

At 4.15pm, Lara and I were in the kitchen doing homework and working out a job, respectively, when Alice walked in through the front door with Hayley. I asked them how their day was; Hayley's was 'ok' and Alice stated she hadn't been to school, because her mother thought she needed time to cool off before she went back. Incredulous, I said to Alice that she had just had a suspension, plus an extra two days as deemed by Mrs Tran because her attitude wasn't right. I said, 'You now tell me that you have had today off school to cool off... How many days and weeks do you need to cool off before you finally realise that you must get back on track?'

Alice replied, 'I am trying.'

Now, I love all my daughters, but Alice is not making an effort.

I told Alice that I appreciate how difficult it can be at school, we've discussed how I struggle with dyslexia and in particular reading, and it must be hard for her having had so much time off. Alice interrupted me and stated she was popping round her mother's.

An hour later, Alice came home from Ruth's asking if her friend Zoe could sleepover tonight. I said to Alice, only on the basis that she goes to school on Monday and truly tries – no jewellery, uniform correct and no talking back to teachers. Probably to my own detriment, I accepted Alice's 'yes Dad, I will' and agreed.

At 6.30pm, I asked if I could speak to Zoe's aunty (who is Zoe's guardian) to confirm everything. Instead of getting her phone, Alice stated that because Zoe's aunty does not know me, Zoe could not stay. Talking quickly, Alice said that she knows she has told me that she wants to get back into the routine of every other weekend with her mother, but would I mind if she stayed at her mother's tonight; as Zoe's aunty has met her, Zoe would be allowed to sleepover.

I was reluctant to agree with Alice, but understood the situation. I told Alice to call her mother first and Alice disappeared upstairs. Minutes passed, then I heard Alice coming down the stairs, explaining to her mother that because Zoe's aunty knew her, Zoe was allowed to sleepover as long as it was at hers. Alice started arguing on the phone with her mother. Alice told her mother several times not to phone anyone and that she would be round in two minutes; Alice put the phone down.

I asked Alice what was going on and that it seemed her mother was not keen. Alice replied that her mother would 'be fine' and that she had to go as her mother was telephoning Zoe's aunty and would start trouble, and Zoe would not be able to stay at all.

(Although abnormal in a functioning situation, I did not call Ruth to confirm Alice's plan – it has been made ardently clear to me throughout the years that even in circumstances where it makes no sense, what is arranged between mother and daughter is not for me to question.)

Alice left with Zoe. Hayley had finished her homework and was baking something with Lara, which is how we spent the next half an hour, until Alice burst through the front door stating that her mother is outside and wanted a word. Putting the bowl I had been tasked with stirring down, I asked Alice what was going on.

Alice replied, 'Our mother does not want me there, it's only when it suits her.'

Bracing myself, I went to the door and Ruth said, 'What is going on?'

(That is the million-dollar question everyone is left asking when Alice and her mother organise something.)

I explained the situation with Alice, albeit slightly confused as Alice had spoken to her, and Ruth replied, 'What do you think you are doing, dropping Alice off round mine?'

I said I thought she was aware of the situation as Alice had phoned and explained, plus Alice had walked to hers.

Voice rising, Ruth stated, 'I do not want you dropping Alice off when you fucking feel like it!'

I replied, 'I am sorry that it had not actually been agreed to, but Alice left after speaking to you; I did not drop her off.'

Internally, I thought of Alice stating she is only wanted when it suits, and the many times Alice's has 'popped' to her mother's without issue.

Ruth said, 'One minute you want to meet for a coffee to discuss Alice's behaviour and how she needs to decide where she is living, and the next minute you just send her back to mine.'

(Meeting for a coffee is news to me.)

I told Ruth, that was not the situation here and she knew that; sensing Ruth was about to go off on one, I said I would speak to Alice about it and closed the door. As I returned to the kitchen, Alice, unfazed, asked me if I would talk to Zoe's aunty on the phone and see if she can stay here; after we had established the boundaries for Alice and Zoe, it was agreed that Zoe could stay.

('All went well with no trouble!')

Saturday 24th

With Zoe gone home, it was what has become a rarity these days – Hayley, Alice, Lara and I had eaten dinner and were all in the living room. In an ad break, Alice looked up from her phone and stated that she was staying at her mother's tonight.

I asked Alice what happened to trying, starting with staying with one parent on alternate weekends.

Alice replied, 'It's ok Dad, our mother asked me if I wanted to stay at hers tonight.'

Yesterday still fresh in my mind, I told Alice I think it would be best to settle down this weekend and stay at home.

Alice replied, 'But I did stay here last night and I did tell you that I would probably stay round our mother's for one night over the weekend.'

I hope the Family Courts know they set up for a 13-year-old to dictate her living arrangements, because opposition from me does not just mean enforcing boundaries as a parent, it means opposing Ruth, who will one minute tell me not to drop Alice to her when Alice wants, and the next day invite her round.

Defeated, I replied, 'Ok, but you must be back by Sunday night so we can get you set up for school.'

Alice agreed, and was soon picked up by her mother.

Sunday 25th

Several texts and at 9pm with no sign of Alice, I gave her a call. Alice picked up and said, 'Sorry Dad, I might be staying here tonight.'

I did not have the strength to argue the point, so I told Alice to make sure she was up for school.

Dean Marlo

A week's contact

26 – 30 November

Monday 26th

The tutorial centre has a programme to prepare for the Eleven-plus so, with Lara's agreement, I arranged for her to also go to tuition classes; she's really excited.

Northview called to inform me that Alice was late to school… Alice went to her mother's again after school, but came home at 6.30pm and stayed the night. She refused to talk to me about not coming home on Sunday and being late to school.

Tuesday 27th

Hayley and Lara attend tuition, Alice went to her mother's after school. I tried to call both Alice and Ruth, but didn't get through. Alice stayed overnight with Ruth.

For almost a month, Alice has been dictating where she is staying each night; I am just waiting for the Mrs Mason and Smitch Law letters to arrive, with claims and accusations and the threats of further court proceedings – however, neither Alice nor Ruth care about living with meaningful stability, as evidenced by Alice's decline at school, late nights and argumentative attitude.

Ruth has a mental health condition and whether it is that alone, or her personality, or both, it affects her daily life and how she treats our children. It is clear to see what behaviour and attitude Alice is emulating, and how that is affecting her young life already.

It is a strange juxtaposition when in Waterstones, watching Lara search through books with glee; picking out 3 activity books on the Eleven-plus, that I know she will complete, and 'White Fang' as she learns more about interpretation, comprehension and other things that I never encountered during my schooling.

(Myself and many of my friends at school were looked at as dumb, simply because we could not read – I tried but it was so frustrating; it might as well have been written in another language. We found ourselves in what was known as the D stream. We would laugh and say D was for 'no-hopers'. Luckily, I loved sports, and I was proud as punch to show Ma my A for PE each year on my report. Ma would be so pleased, it made both of our days.

With difficulty, I learned to read when I was older, as a necessity to run my own business, but I still can't spell for toffeys.)

On the occasions they used to come too, Hayley would scour the fantasy section, and Alice the art books, but for the most part, neither of them have enjoyed reading like Ma and Lara do.

I'm so proud of Lara, and glad too that she enjoys school because loving learning is a wonderful thing, and that's what worries me about Alice.

Instead of looking at being dyslexic or less academic as something she needs support to work on, she uses it as an excuse to not even try. I don't expect Alice to turn into a bookworm, or start churning out As on her maths tests, however she is capable of more than what she's currently doing.

She can read the texts her friends send her, and all three of my children know their way around a computer better than I do – those are things Alice has learned, but I don't think she's willing to look at school the same way.

I do also feel sorry for Alice because I've been there, where a teacher just doesn't want you in their class, or you always find yourself singled out for questions they know you can't answer in an instant. It is sad but true, and I'm sure some of those teachers at Northview take one look at any of Alice's behaviour and decide to make an issue.

I'm not saying they're wrong on every occasion, either, or making excuses for Alice, but she hasn't had the magical childhood I wanted my children to have, or that I hoped I could give to my children.

Wednesday 28th

I was informed that Alice was not at school today. Hayley and Alice stayed overnight at Ruth's.

Thursday 29th

Ruth picked Lara from school for tea. At 5.20pm, Ruth phoned me and stated that Lara was going to sleep at hers tonight. I asked if I could speak to Lara; Ruth told me to 'fuck off' and put the phone down. (I called Lara's mobile instead; we chatted for a minute before saying goodnight.)

Hayley, Alice and Lara stayed overnight with Ruth.

Friday 30th

It is Ruth's weekend contact, which means a full weekend of work for me.

I was on site, at around 11am, when I received a call from Ruth stating that Lara is not at school, as she was feeling sick. She passed the phone to Lara, who told me that her mother was going to drop her into school at lunchtime, when hopefully she felt better.

Hayley, Alice and Lara stayed at their mother's for the whole weekend.

Dean Marlo

Northview, something positive

28 November

Dear Mr Marlo,
Pupil: Hayley Marlo, 11TU
We have great pleasure in informing you that Hayley has now received a total of 50 House Points across her curriculum areas.
This is very good news and I am sure that you will want to congratulate Hayley on doing so well.
We hope that she will continue to work well throughout the year to build up her House Points total further.
Well done, Hayley!
Yours sincerely,

Dear Mr Rowe MP

30 November

Further to my concerns and complaint to the town office for Cafcass, I am writing to you with regards to the report that was produced by Ms Moyer and presented at the family court hearing on the 5th September 2007.

As you are aware, I believe I have every reason to ensure that the inaccurate information is removed from this professional's report. Also, I hope you would agree that misleading statements within a welfare report is not what children deserve.

For the sake of Alice and Lara not being put through any more years of instability, through the legal system, I have written to request that the inaccurate statements are rectified and it is acknowledged that their current standards are below the needs of the children and families they are supposed to help.

After 7 years of family court proceedings, reading through the Guardian's report was another tale in disbelief. Several weeks after the hearing on the 5th September, Ms Moyer visited our home twice; on both occasions she stated that she understood, and that she would write to me and the Family Courts to address the inaccuracies.

I waited until the 22nd October for Ms Moyer's letter, before I decided to phone her and left a message for her to call me back, which she failed to do. On the 23rd October, I contacted the town Cafcass office and left a message for Ms Soto, the director, to phone me back, which she did, asking me to outline several of my concerns in a letter to her. The next day, I received a compliments slip from Ms Soto with a Cafcass booklet. I hand delivered my letter to Ms Soto on the 26th October.

On the 10th November, I received a letter from Ms Soto confirming receipt of my letter and apologising that she had been unable to contact me regarding any outcomes as of yet, but she hoped she would be able to do something during the next week.

I am writing this letter on the 30th November and, as of yet, I still have not received any communication from Cafcass.

Therefore, I enclose a letter containing my full concerns with the report and ask if you would send this to the appropriate department/Ombudsman, in doing so confirming that families involved within the Family Courts need and deserve honesty and professionalism, and nothing more.

Yours respectfully…

Dean Marlo

Dear Mr Rowe, Teachers

30 November

As you are aware, I have an issue with the accuracy of the information relayed to the Guardian by a member of staff representing Northview Grove, which was presented to the Family Courts as fact.

Despite your efforts in contacting Mrs Tran, it was left to Mrs Hewitt to contact Ms Moyer and confirm that I have continually supported the school and my children with their behaviour and education.

On the 5th September 2007, I sat in the courtroom in front of the judge; the Guardian's solicitor was unable to contact Ms Moyer until 2.30pm, finally allowing him to inform the judge that Northview Grove had confirmed my commitment to the school, but Mrs Hewitt was standing by what she had told Ms Moyer.

When I spoke with Mrs Tran, I brought this to her attention; she simply took the high ground and supported a member of her staff, taking the view that Mrs Hewitt acted as a professional while relaying information to Ms Moyer, and what was written in the report had been misinterpreted. I fail to see how 'Mr Marlo refuses to get involved in any attempts by the school to address Alice's behaviour and will not attend the school for meetings' can possibly be misinterpreted.

I believe it is immoral and shameful that Northview Grove/Mrs Tran decide to hide behind a banner of 'acting as a professional' and not apologise for their involvement in the confusion that the inaccurate information caused. What was relayed on behalf of Northview Grove was not only potentially detrimental to the hearing of the 5th September 2007, but also insulted and undermined the efforts I have made to bring normality and stability into my children's lives, and my support in their schooling.

Mrs Tran has not accepted the gravity of the situation that Mrs Hewitt, on behalf of Northview Grove, placed on my family as a result of the inaccurate statements relayed. I took from Mrs Tran's approach to my complaint that she would simply like it swept under the carpet. I would like to ask if there is any way of formally requesting they rectify the inaccurate statements.

Once again, I ask you for your support in achieving some honesty and credibility from within the system; a system that has repeatedly brought doubt and instability to my family's dynamics.

Yours respectfully…

Birthdays and routines

1– 4 December

Saturday 1st

At 9.15am, Ruth dropped Lara off. We went through all the birthday motions; presents, cards, music; the lot! Ruth met us at the laser gun arena for Lara's party; we stood with the other parents and watched the children charge around. It actually went really well and everyone had a great time.

Monday 3rd

Due to the winter holidays, the tutoring sessions have been moved to Monday. Lara attended, however Hayley and Alice both went to their mother's after school. Hayley at least texted to say she didn't want to go; Alice has refused to talk about the subject besides not going. Hayley and Alice stayed at their mother's.

Tuesday 4th

Alice came home from school and stated that she was getting back into the routine of staying at her mother's on Tuesdays and Thursdays... Then Alice said that her mother could not make it this Thursday, so she was going to stay at hers tonight and tomorrow night as well this week.

Not really agreeing, but unable to have a meaningful discussion when Alice can walk out and avoid me, I instead reminded her that I do not have a problem with any contact she wants with her mother, so long as she is making an effort at school.

Alice replied, 'Dad, you are a broken record.'

At 7.45pm, Ruth called and confirmed that she was picking Lara up for tea after school tomorrow.

(It's not a funny realisation, when I think I have more involvement with Ruth now than when we had joint residency – it's like being a family in a long running episode of EastEnders, where most of the characters are at each other's throats and relationships are fucked up. Not that I watch the programme, just going based off what I've overheard when Hayley and Alice have it on.)

From Cafcass

4 December

Dear Mr Marlo,

Further to your letter of 26ᵗʰ October, I have now had the opportunity to meet with Ms Moyer to discuss her report.

In response to the issues you had raised with her following your meetings after the court hearing, she has prepared the attached response which I hope answers or explains any outstanding queries.

From my discussions with yourself and Ms Moyer and reading the report, I would agree that there are some inaccuracies and typographical errors in the report. I am in the process of correcting these, following which time I will take the unusual step of filing the amended version with the court and the legal representatives to place on record. However, none of the alterations made would have affected the final recommendation of the report.

Thank you for bringing this matter to my attention. I trust that you will be satisfied with the outcome of your comments and apologise that it has taken longer than expected to resolve this matter.

Yours sincerely,
Ms Soto
Service Manager

I am slightly concerned that it is not usual behaviour to fix the mistakes and update the court; the typographical errors are worse than a teenager's first edit and the alterations needed are for statements that directly degrade the integrity of a parent. That should mean something to any decent person. I have feelings and I have always tried my best for my children.

Believe me, I am grateful that the recommendation didn't change, but it is about the honesty of reports submitted to the Family Courts; the situation is hard enough, and parents do not deserve additional anxiety over a report that should be reliable and true.

I guess my anxiety about the accuracy in this report are borne from my experience and knowledge that one day Mrs Mason will be combing through this Guardian's findings, and, as history has shown, the judge will be informed of my lack of involvement with my children's schools. (And the rest...)

Letter from the Guardian

4 December

Following our meetings where you expressed some concerns over the contents of my report as prepared for the court, I am now putting in writing some of the things we discussed as promised.

Firstly, I accept the typing error on page 3 where I indicated your date of birth incorrectly. I believe this is a genuine typing error and not intentional.

Reading paragraph 3v I accept that it should read Ms Hyde and not Ms Marlo.

I also accept that Hayley was removed from the contact order and not as stated in my report.

Apologies for misinterpreting Hayley's hair colour. I saw her in very poor light on one occasion before writing the report and thought her hair was mousy brown, however I accept that it is lighter than initially thought.

In respect of paragraph 20, I can only reiterate what I said in the report and to you during our meetings in that I spoke to the Deputy Head. I believe this paragraph is a true reflection of our discussion. I also wish to add, as was explained to you at the final hearing, that I used the words 'mental health' to refer to an overall condition, just as doctors will refer to physical health as an overall human condition. It's a general term and by no means a diagnosis of any kind in respect of Hayley.

Paragraph 21 states Alice has a pierced eyebrow. Alice told me she had a pierced eyebrow and although I did not see it at the time, I presumed she had removed it. I have no problem with removing that sentence from my report as it was merely serving as a description of Alice.

I am not prepared to change what I state in paragraph 27 as it's the requirement of my duty to be honest and to give a clear historical picture. I understand you feel that it's not in the courts interest to know of the acrimony in the past between yourself and Ms Hyde, but in this case it was deemed relevant.

Similarly, I am not prepared to change paragraph 28 as it reflects a conversation with the school. I understand your view that both children now refute these occurrences but I am stating what I have been told during my investigation and believe this paragraph is a true reflection of the situation.

My comment in respect of paragraph 15 also stands for paragraph 26.

Whilst you believe I have incorrectly assessment Lara's affinity with her maternal aunt, I am not prepared to change my view as I believe this to be an accurate assessment as stated in paragraph 42.

I further suggest that you take your comments regarding paragraph 58 up with the school as I believe that this paragraph is a true reflection of my conversation with Mrs Hewitt.

I hope this is helpful as I understand it has been a difficult process for you and I hope that you will come to realise that my report was written based on the information in front of me, backed up with years of experience and the necessary qualifications to make the assessments that I did make. Whilst I don't expect you to necessarily agree with it, I can only hope that you would accept it was not written with the intention to harm or hurt you or any of your family members as you believe.

I would like to add that maybe in my haste I have not given you enough acknowledgement for the positive influence and stability you have offered your daughters of the years.

I had thought that my recommendations to the court will suggest the above.

I wish you all the best for the future.

Regards,

If her inclusion of the physical appearance of my daughters is necessary to include for the courts, then the description should be relayed correctly. Alice is not afraid of being direct, and wouldn't have lied about having her eyebrow pierced. I can't believe instead of being honest about getting Hayley and Alice's description confused, she's putting it on Alice; also, if she wasn't sure, she could have asked Ms Hyde or myself to confirm this detail.

Ms Moyer states here, 'in my haste I have not given you enough acknowledgement for the positive influence and stability you have offered your daughters'.

A recommendation written like this was all that was needed to remove the unnecessary ambiguity put forth by these court experts, over whether these two parents really are 'as bad as each other'. This is a letter to me, which is not the same as writing an evaluation for the courts; for it to mean anything, it needs to be written in the report, which would clarify why the children are to remain in my sole residency.

That credibility from the guardian would have been acknowledgement to the Family Courts, enabling them to concentrate on helping Ms Hyde with her bipolar disorder and parenting. Even without being one of these experts, it is clear the way she behaves towards her children and the people around her is not normal.

Contacts

5 - 8 December

Wednesday 5th

I received a copy of a note informing that Alice arrived at school at 10am today; with it came a report of Alice's attendance at school. There were 44 absences out of a total of 250 days – 35 due to illness; Hayley had 36 absences for the same period.

Ruth picked Lara up from school and dropped her back at 7pm. Hayley called and said that she is staying overnight at her mother's. It does worry me that Hayley is in the same bad routines as Alice.

Thursday 6th

Today, Alice came home from school with her friend Zoe. Again, Alice asked if Zoe could sleepover. (This is another damned if I do, damned if I don't situation; without a united front with Ruth, Alice continues to dictate her own schedule).

I replied, 'Yes, if you behave and I can talk to either Zoe's uncle or aunt before 7pm.'

Already heading towards the stairs, Alice gave a quick 'ok' before they both disappeared into Alice's bedroom. At 6.30pm, Alice and Zoe came downstairs and stated that they were going out. I told them both that before they went anywhere, I needed to speak to Zoe's uncle or aunt.

Alice said, 'Ok but we are just nipping to the shop and will be back in 15 minutes.' As Alice walked out of the front door, she asked me what time she had to be in.

I replied, 'In about 15 minutes if you want Zoe to stay.'

When almost half an hour had passed, I was worried – I didn't know whether Alice had lied to me, or if she might be in trouble. I called her several times without success.

At 8.50pm, Alice came home alone and stated that she was going to sleep at her mother's tonight. I asked where Zoe was and told Alice that she could not announce at nearly 9pm that she was going to stay at her mother's, after not coming home when she said she was going to.

Alice replied, 'I don't care,' grabbing some things for her bedroom and walking out the front door.

Never knowing how to feel after Alice has gone to her mother's, I checked in on Hayley, reminding her it was laptop off now, and on Lara, who was asleep.

Friday 7th

It was around 10am when I received a call from Northview Grove. Mrs Tran stated that Alice had turned up at school with Zoe, who has been excluded, and they both know that Zoe is not allowed on school property. As a result, the school had asked Zoe to leave the premises and were now unaware of Alice's whereabouts; Mrs Tran believed that Alice might have left school with Zoe.

Ending the call with Mrs Tran, I phoned Alice; she told me that she was at school and would talk to me later. I sent a text to Ruth, letting her know it was a possibility Alice was bunking.

It puts me in a complicated position; despite wanting to leave site to search for Alice, I have obligations to the customer and a business to run that keeps the food on the table; Alice might be at school still; I can't call the police because she's not a missing child in that sense. Mostly, I hoped I would hear from Northview.

At 3 pm, having radio silence on Alice all day, I picked Lara up from school. Alice and Zoe walked in through the door and I greeted Alice without getting a reply. When I asked Alice what had happened at school today, she still did not reply and walked up to her bedroom with Zoe. The door had been shut, even though I was following behind them, and I knocked before entering to attempt to talk to Alice.

She ignored my questions about school, but did reply when I asked if she was staying at her mother's tonight, 'I am sleeping round a friend's.'

I have no idea how to handle Alice without setting off a ticking-time bomb of her getting argumentative or walking out; it saddens me to see Alice drift down paths I can't reach her on. Not agreeing but thankful to be getting some answers from her, I queried if this had been organised with her mother and if so, which friend she is staying with just so I know.

Huffing, Alice said, 'You do not need to know,' and then asked me to leave. I said to Alice that she needs to talk to me about what she is doing and where she is staying tonight; I suspected now that Ruth wasn't aware of Alice staying out and therefore this is Alice pushing way, way beyond boundaries.

There was a slight knock at the door, before Lara came into Alice's bedroom with the house phone… It was Zoe's auntie, Maria, and she wanted to talk to me. I took the phone and I hadn't even got a 'hello' out when Maria frantically stated, 'For Christ's sake do not let your daughter out of the house with Zoe!'

Concerned, I told Maria that I believed that was their intention. Maria asked to speak to Zoe and, as I was passing the phone, Zoe shook her head, saying, 'I do not want to speak to her.'

Alice continued to grab several things and said to Zoe, 'Let's go.'

Wanting to stop Alice but not seeing a way how, I said to Alice she needed to talk to me about what's going on and I followed them downstairs.

Looking over her shoulder at me, Alice replied, 'I have nothing to say,' and slammed the door.

I was still holding the phone and told Maria that they had both just left; Maria replied that I should phone the police, and be aware that there is an order in place stating that Zoe must not contact or associate with her mother or her mother's boyfriend, who are both known heroin and crack–cocaine users. Maria explained that Zoe's mother had all five of her children taken off her and was not supposed to communicate with Zoe as she is a bad influence on her daughter; Maria suspects Zoe has seen her mother in recent weeks by arranging meetings with her through Alice's mobile.

Prior to this, I didn't know Zoe's home situation, only that her aunt was her guardian; Zoe has obviously had a difficult childhood, and Alice appears to have latched on. I am not saying that Zoe is a bad kid, or that she is solely a bad influence on Alice – Alice makes decisions fine by herself – but the negative symbiotic friendship they have struck hasn't helped.

Attempting to contact Ruth on her home and mobile number, without any success, I decided to phone the police; they took descriptions of both girls, but told me that Alice wasn't exactly a missing person and there was little they could do besides keep a lookout until she was. It was not exactly a relief, even if I understood their position, however I hoped that with more eyes we would find them before any real trouble was had.

Done talking with the police, I tried Ruth again. Thankfully, she picked up, stating she didn't know were Alice or Zoe were and that Maria had just phoned her. I let Ruth know that I called the police, and we agreed to keep in touch.

Shortly after, two officers knocked on the front door and we talked about the situation. They also asked for Alice and Zoe's description as well as Maria's phone number.

At around 8.30pm, Maria called me and stated that someone she knew had seen the girls walking up the town High Street with Zoe's mother's boyfriend. Back on the phone with the police, I informed them of where Alice and Zoe had last been seen, and that I believed they may be headed to the home of two known heroin users. The dispatcher asked why I had not gone to the address myself, which I was a bit confused about; I cannot make Alice come with me, and I don't want to have a confrontation with anyone. I told the woman that I did not want to worsen the situation and have Alice running away; she stated she would try to arrange officers to attend the property as soon as possible, but being a Friday night, the officers are tied up in town. However, she also said there's nothing stopping me from going to the house.

Calling Ruth, I let her know I was going to Zoe's mother's boyfriends, as suggested, in the hopes of finding Alice and Zoe there after they'd been seen with him in town. Ruth stated that she would like to come; just wanting to find Alice safe, I agreed to pick her up on the way through.

I headed upstairs to let Hayley know I was going to look for Alice, and found Lara in her room too, watching a DVD. I know they both love Alice and are worried about her. I explained that Alice had been seen in town and that I would be back soon.

I picked Ruth up and we drove to the address. Unfortunately, there was no one at home. Ruth phoned Maria, who gave her the boyfriend's mobile number and dialled it on speaker. He answered and said that he had left Zoe and Alice in town about an hour ago. I asked him if I could speak to Zoe's mother; he claimed he didn't know where she was.

I texted Hayley to let her know I was still looking for Alice and that she and Lara should try go to bed, although I wouldn't be home yet. Seeing not many options, I drove us around town, past the nightclubs and back around again, until 12.15am, when Ruth received a call from Bernard, stating that Alice and Zoe had just walked in.

No meaningful discussion was going to happen with Alice tonight, so I dropped Ruth to hers and returned home myself, exhausted but relieved to know Alice is safe.

Saturday 8th

Despite the situation with Alice, I still had to go to work. I texted Ruth to call me to talk about Alice. As it a Saturday, Ma was round and we agreed she would try to talk to Alice about how she is feeling.

At 8.45am, I was on site and my phone went; Ruth told me that Alice and Zoe had collected clothes from her house and Alice had said, 'I am not coming back.'

Throughout the morning, I tried to call Alice without success. My phone rang at around lunchtime, with Ruth updating me that she had contacted the police, and they advised her to call if Alice and Zoe reappeared at hers, promising if she did, they would be at hers within minutes. I couldn't take being at work any longer, so I packed up and drove home to look for Alice.

Several hours of driving around and popping back to check in with Ma passed, until my phone rang. Ruth stated Alice and Zoe had returned to hers; she managed to call the police and keep them there but the police took 20 minutes to show up… By which time, Alice and Zoe had run out the back door.

Shortly after, Ruth called again and told me the police had brought Alice back to hers and taken Zoe to the police station. She asked if I would come round to hers, as the police were with Alice now. This I did; Alice was read the riot act, and both Ruth and I talked to her about safety. Ruth told Alice she was very lucky to have two parents who love her and want what's best for her.

I left Alice at her mother's, at her request. She was flippant about the whole situation and headed up to her room without saying goodbye to me. Like when she was younger, I said the words I want her to always remember, 'I love you, Alice.'

School and incidents

12 - 14 December

Wednesday 12th
At 1pm, I received a phone call from Mrs Tran, who stated that Alice had come to school dressed inappropriately – instead of tights, Alice was wearing different coloured leggings. Mrs Tran asked me to ensure that Alice came to school dressed appropriately, and that she had tried telephoning Ms Hyde to tell her the same but she was unable to contact her at home or on her mobile. I told Mrs Tran that I would re–enforce the school uniform rules to Alice and confirm this with Ms Hyde.

Half an hour later, Mrs Tran phoned again stating that Alice was last seen walking out of school with Zoe and they have called the police. I told Mrs Tran that I would try to get in contact with Alice and be in touch.

I called Alice, and asked if she is at school. Alice said yes, but I've done this rodeo before, so I asked if she's lying to me right now. Alice said she has to go, and put the phone down. I phoned Mrs Tran back, and said that I didn't believe Alice but asked for them to check the school grounds again.

At 1.50pm, Mrs Tran rang and stated that Alice and Zoe had been seen at the traffic lights on a road nearby to Northview. I told Mrs Tran that I would drive around to try and find Alice and return her to school. Mrs Tran said that she had managed to contact Ms Hyde, and she is saying that she has given permission for Alice to leave school at lunchtimes.

Internally sighing, I told Mrs Tran that I did not approve of Alice being allowed out of school at lunch, as surely it can only serve to exacerbate Alice's poor behaviour and truancy; Mrs Tran agreed.

As I was getting into the car, I dialled Alice's number but she didn't pick up. I drove round the block a few times before pulling over to try Alice's phone again. This time she answered, and said she was walking into school, which Mrs Tran soon called and confirmed.

Thursday 13th
Lara is at Ruth's for tea after school; Alice is still avoiding my calls.

I was making dinner at around 6pm, when Ruth rang my mobile saying Alice has just kicked her bedroom door in and there is glass everywhere, and as she was in the middle of preparing dinner there would be a delay so she would return Lara at 9pm instead. I asked if everyone is okay and why Alice was upset. Ruth stated that Alice and Lara had an argument which ended with Alice punching Lara; Alice ran upstairs and after slamming her door, kicked it in. (Why a bedroom door was made of glass, do not ask me.) Continuing, Ruth claimed that Alice wanted to stay at Ma's tonight, saying, 'I don't care if she does'. I told Ruth I would talk to Alice.

As I was finding her contact, Alice rang me crying. Alice stated that she had spoken to Nan who said that it was alright with her as long as it was fine with me. I told Alice that there was no reason why she couldn't stay at home tonight, and going to Nan's was not the answer; it would also make it difficult to get to school the next morning, so, instead, we could ask Nan to stay at ours. Sniffing, Alice said that if I wouldn't take her she would walk or catch a bus, and put the phone down.

I called Ruth back, who told me that Alice had just walked out of the door and 'with the mess she has left, I do not care'. I told her that she shouldn't let Alice walk out without a care, and I would get in my car to try find her.

Ruth replied, 'If you do find Alice, do not bring her back here.'

Feeling frustrated with Ruth's attitude, I said I would be in touch and texted Hayley, who was out with friends. As I pulled out of the drive, Alice walked across the road. I got out of the car and Alice gave me hug, and she said she wasn't here to stay, just to ask me to drop her at Nan's. I told her I wasn't prepared to take her to the other side of town and asked her to come indoors to talk about what happened. Refusing, Alice walked off.

A short time later, Hayley came in and said that she had seen Alice walking towards her mother's. Hayley told me that she had said 'hello' to Alice but Alice ignored her. Not wanting to inflame the situation, I decided give it 10 minutes and then call Ruth.

I rang Ruth to see if Alice was there. Ruth told me that Alice has shut herself in her bedroom, sans door, and that she would drop Lara back at 9pm. Although I wanted to speak to Alice, I decided to simply text her 'love to you' and give her space – at least she is safe.

At 9.30pm, Lara came home. We had a hug and went to the kitchen to grab a drink before going to bed. While Lara sat at the table, I asked why she and Alice had fallen out. Lara replied she is sorry and that it was stupid, Alice had thrown a piece of pear at her which she threw back; this happened a couple of times, with some taunts, until Alice told her to 'shut up' repeatedly. Lara stated in response, she found another piece of pear and threw it at Alice, who retaliated by punching her. Their mother started shouting at Alice so she ran upstairs and slammed and kicked her bedroom door, which broke the glass into pieces.

Friday 14th

Ruth phoned and stated that she was not putting up with Alice's behaviour and was not going to be told to 'fuck off' by her. I agreed that Alice's attitude needs curbing but that she needs to get back into a routine where she is living, and give the relationship between them time to settle. Clearly, the disruption is not good for the children nor Ruth.

Ruth repeated several times that she 'wasn't going to put up with it'; I said that we both need to talk to Alice and have the same boundaries set, to which Ruth replied, 'I'm not going to fucking put up with it!'

I also received a letter from my MP;

Dear Mr Marlo,

Thank you for letters regarding further issues of concern. I am sorry to hear this, and feel that a meeting would be best to discuss them. Please contact my office to arrange an appointment.

Best wishes.

Yours sincerely…

School issues

17/18 December

Monday 17th

It was Ruth's weekend contact; at 9am, I was at work and the children were all, hopefully, at school, which is when my phone went and Ruth stated that Alice had gone to school wearing brown boots, which are against school rules, so would I take Alice some suitable shoes in. She then asked what time I was dropping Lara to hers on Thursday. Agreeing to take Alice a pair of shoes in, I replied that according to her schedule, she was supposed to pick Lara up from school on Wednesday, the last day of term. Ruth replied she had work and suggested I drop Lara to hers on Thursday at mid–day. I had no objection, so agreed to her arrangements.

Searching for shoes, I found that over the weeks, Alice has taken a large portion of her wardrobe to her mother's, including both pairs of school shoes. With a set of black trainers in hand, I phoned Northview Grove to ask if they would be acceptable for Alice to wear at school for today. Through the receptionist, Mr Garrett said that they were better than brown boots and asked me to bring them in.

At 1.30pm, Ruth called to inform me she has told Alice that she must sleep at my home tonight.

Returning with Lara after school, Alice met me in the hallway saying that she isn't going to sleep in her bedroom as it is too cold. This house has got central heating and Alice's bedroom is not cold – even so, I suggested that Alice have the portable heater, if she really wanted to warm her room. Alice replied, 'You must be kidding, I'm going to my mother's.'

I didn't argue, but it seemed a poor excuse just to stay at her mother's.

(I also expected a vehement call from Ruth, but I didn't get one.)

Tuesday 18th

After dropping Lara off at school, I arrived home to find a letter addressed to Ms Hyde; I could see that it had a Horizon Academy stamp on it, so called Ruth and informed her I had received it by mistake. Ruth replied she had requested they send us both the response to her application for Alice to go to Horizon, but she had spoken to them recently and is aware that the school is full.

At 3.45pm, Alice rang saying that she is going to sleep at home tonight and wants to get back into the routine of staying at her mother's twice a week; she wants to come home on Boxing Day with Hayley and Lara and enjoy Christmas at home. I told Alice that I looked forward to Christmas with them all.

Northview, it's about Alice

18 December

Dear Mr Marlo,
Pupil: Alice Marlo, 9OK
Due to Alice's persistent inability to comply with school rules and her constant disruption of certain lessons, we now have to convene a multi-agency meeting to initiate a Pastoral Support Plan for Alice.
This meeting will take place on Wednesday 30th January 2008 at 12am and its aim is to try and support Alice within the school and find a positive way forwards.
It is vital that you attend this meeting as your support with this plan is essential. If I can be of further assistance before the meeting, please do not hesitate to contact me.
Yours sincerely,

To the Cafcass Head

18 December

Dear Ms Soto,

Thank you for your letter dated 4th of December.

On the 23rd October 2007, you kindly returned my phone call to your office. You asked me to send you a letter outlining the issues, to which I did, and you kindly forwarded Ms Moyer's response.

I met Ms Moyer in September and informed her that I had deep concerns about the content and accuracy of her report. At this meeting, it was Ms Moyer who suggested that we went through the report starting with page two, my date of birth, and going on to changing the colour of Lara and Hayley's hair, etc. I made it clear at the time that these were not the main issues, but Ms Moyer insisted that they were inaccurate and needed to be changed.

I am disappointed with the response I have received from Cafcass and would have expected greater urgency and understanding towards a genuine parent, with a report produced for the Family Courts that has the potential to continue to mislead and misinform, bringing further disruption and instability into three children's lives.

I believe that the response I have received from Cafcass as an institution and Ms Moyer as my children's Guardian is morally unacceptable, and I shall now rely on a letter that I have sent to my MP Mr Rowe about the standard of professionalism shown.

From my experience within the Family Courts, who are involved to ensure 'a child's welfare is paramount', there has been little evidence of morals or ethical standards from some individuals and quarters, just more evidence of legal manoeuvring and manipulation, rather than meaningful decisions made for the wellbeing of the children and family. Instead of finding empathy and support, from the very beginning, it became a performance dedicated to false accusations and mislead conclusions.

I would ask you to understand that while some of the above does not apply to Cafcass, the responsibility of an accurate and unbiased reflection of the family was required – yet, this is not what has occurred. Please know that each time I went to the Family Courts, it *was* for the welfare and stability of my children and nothing more.

You say that you are going to take the unusual step of filing the amended report to the family court, and yet it is I who is left querying the unusual – in what situation does the court not benefit from a report that is accurate? Wouldn't it be beneficial for a judge to be aware of the true facts in a family's case?

In Ms Moyer's letter, paragraph 9 she writes, 'I understand you feel that it's not in the courts interest to know of the acrimony in the past between yourself and Ms Hyde.'

I have never suggested to anyone that my family's past would not be in the interests of the Family Courts, as it is evidently the most relevant. I have spent many hours, weeks and months over the last eight years preparing and writing statements to the Family Courts which relayed the day-to-day events in my children's lives and our family's dynamics. It is really absurd for Ms Moyer to make such a statement in this letter of reply; clearly once again it diverts from my genuine concerns and suggests that I am small minded to the extent that I believe that the Guardian giving the Family Courts an honest and clear historical picture of a family/our family was wrong.

Ms Moyer states that she will not change paragraphs 20/28/58 as it was 'a true reflection of my discussion with Mrs Hewitt, the Deputy Head at Northview Grove School'. However, Ms Moyer fails to mention, address or include in her suggested amendments to the Family Courts, that Northview Grove School had in fact contacted her and stated that I had been fully supportive towards the school and my children's education; which is in direct opposition with the content of paragraphs 20/28/58.

I believe I have asked politely to correct inaccurate and misleading information in a report prepared by a children's Guardian, on behalf of Cafcass and held by the Family Courts, which has been a continuation of undermining the stability within our family and my commitment to be a capable, responsible and caring parent, regardless of whether the truth, in this circumstance, changes the guardian's view.

This attitude and performance has prolonged proceedings within the Family Courts, and in itself brought its own uncertainty and insecurity into three innocent children's lives.

Correcting typographical errors does not answer, explain or amend any of the serious concerns I have. Brushing over the surface, and making further unfounded assumptions, does not address the serious misinterpretations that are within this report. I am not prepared to allow it to be left waiting; waiting for an unscrupulous solicitor and barrister to pick up and produce to a judge in the Family Courts as concrete evidence of my behaviour and attitude towards Ms Hyde, our children or our family dynamics.

Over the years, I have consistently shown my children, Ms Hyde and the Family Courts that I am happy to support the welfare and upbringing of my children.

Thank you for your time and attention with this matter.

Yours faithfully...

From Northview (forwarded)

19 December

Dear Mr Rowe MP,

I am writing with reference to a phone conversation we had months ago with regard to Mr Marlo and his family, which includes two girls at this school. I should like you to be aware that Mr Marlo has maintained contact with the school throughout the difficulties currently being experienced by the girls and has always been willing to come to the school to discuss family issues. The family situation is complex and we also on occasion meet with both the parents and sometimes with Ms Hyde, the girls' mother, on her own. Mr Marlo continues in my opinion to do his very best to support the school and his daughters.

Yours sincerely,

Mrs Tran

Headteacher

While I do appreciate the confirmation I was asking for months ago to disprove the claims made in the Ms Moyer's report, the information relayed was detrimental to proceedings at the time; this letter to Mr Rowe and myself, has little bearing on the situation.

(Regardless, I put the precious letter into my files, in the event of further proceedings.)

Dean Marlo

To MP

20 December

Please find enclosed, a letter that I have sent to Ms Soto from Cafcass. I hope that you will be prepared to assist me in contacting someone who will ensure that honesty, morals and standards are adhered to.

You are aware that I deeply do not want to complain, but I feel the injustice of false and misleading statements that exist within this Guardian's report must be addressed.

I would once again appreciate your support and help in anyway.

Yours respectfully…

Christmas

25/26 December

Christmas Day

It is their year with their mother, but Hayley, Alice and Lara all popped home to wish me a happy Christmas.

Boxing Day

At midday, Hayley, Alice and Lara returned home.

With the music on and the house feeling alive, the children, Ma and I gathered around the tree and Sully assisted everyone with opening their presents.

After tea, Hayley and Alice came into the kitchen and stated, 'You know we told you we smoke at our mother's, so can we smoke here?'

I told both of them that they should not be smoking at their age, their mother should not be encouraging them to do so and that no, they are not allowed to smoke here.

The house phone rang at 9pm and Ruth asked to speak to Alice; Alice then stated that she was going out with her mother and would be back later. The rest of us continued the festivities.

At 11:35pm, Alice walked back through the door.

Cinema

29 December

At 2.30pm Lara and I went to the cinema to watch the 'Bee Moive'. As we found our seats, I put my phone on silent.

Part way through the film, I felt my phone vibrate; I looked at the screen and Ruth's name came up. I told Lara that I wouldn't be more than a minute and went into the foyer to answer.

Ruth stated that she is going away for a few days and if there are any problems, I am to contact her on her mobile. She went on to say that she is taking the children on holiday to the Canary Islands during the half–term spring holidays, and she will be writing to the schools because the children will miss 3 or 4 days. Finally, she requested I drop the children at hers on Tuesday in the half-term holidays instead of Wednesday. I agreed to her request but asked her for confirmation in writing of the times and dates.

After the film, I told Lara that her mother had phoned to say she is going away for several days. Lara replied, 'I know, she sent me a text this morning to say she had arrived.'

I believe this is another example of Ruth's inability to be honest and straightforward with me and within our family's dynamics. It makes little difference to me where she is on holiday or the time of her arrival, but it would be reassuring if she was responsible enough to let me know before she is, presumably, out of the country.

Excerpt from a letter to Mr Rowe MP

From my written diary of events over the past 16 years, it is quite clear that Ms Hyde is rarely, if ever, brought to account for her behaviour within our family. I believe this is how Ms Hyde has managed to continue the instability and disruption within all our lives, and why my concerns for my children's welfare have morphed rather than resolved.

I do not want anyone to persecute Mrs Mason (as she has clearly done to my children's childhood and myself as a decent parent, all on the behalf of her client), I just believe that so called 'professionals', who are embroiled in the Family Courts and children's welfare, as Mrs Mason is, should be held accountable for their behaviour and performance.

It worries me that if Smitch Law's methods are not addressed, they will carry on treating other decent parents and individuals in a similarly insensitive, derogatory and aggressive manner. Furthermore, Smitch Law may not be in the minority of family law firms that act like this.

I am writing to ask for your support, because I believe we need to make the difference to children and parents in this country, caught up within a game played out by solicitors and barristers. These people have no interests in our children's long-term stability or wellbeing.

Sadly, I have been unable to find any honest or decent way of addressing the dishonest and immoral behaviour. The Family Courts and the Law Society need to look into the existing antiquated laws, ideology and performance of some individuals to ensure that legislature isn't preventing the protection of innocent children and parents.

The current climate within the Family Courts does not afford parents the chance to work together for the sake of their children to bring love and care in their new-normal as a separated family. Instead, instantly both parents are pitted against each other, with zero understanding offered to the individual family situation, and innocent children are dragged along behind.

2008

Same old

2/3 January

Wednesday 2nd

Hayley and Alice go back to school tomorrow and at midday, Alice stated that she is sleeping at her mother's tonight because all of her school stuff is at hers. I offered to drive round to pick what she needed up, but Alice said she is staying there.

Thursday 3rd

Lara had a non–pupil day today and Hayley went to school.

At 10.30am, Northview Grove called saying that Alice feels unwell and is requesting to go home. I told the school that I would phone Alice and see why she felt ill; Alice said she just felt tired and asked me to tell the school that she could go home. In reply, I told her I would come pick her up, but she said no, as she is going to walk round her mother's.

I rang Northview back; I confirmed that Alice feels ill and informed them that she will be walking to her mother's. (Which Alice would do anyway, at least this saves the truancy letter.)

I understand how difficult it has been for all of our children growing up. Alice has ended up on this path and it has made this period of parenting difficult for me, but I do not know how the Family Courts and family law, organised by professionals, could conclude such a mess. Alice's living arrangements are sporadic, again, but going back to court has never achieved anything, and I'd be reluctant (insane) to apply, anyway.

Journey

4 - 7 January

Friday 4th

At lunchtime, my phone went and it was Northview Grove. Mr Garrett explained that Zoe had turned up at the school and Alice was last seen walking out of school with her. I said I would call Alice to find out what was going on, and I did – on the phone, Alice was vague about where she was but assured me that she would be back in school after lunch, and that after school, she was going round her mother's.

I left a message for Mr Garrett, informing him that Alice would be returning to school after lunch. (To my knowledge, Ruth's agreement that Alice can leave school premises still stands.)

Half an hour later, Mr Caldwell from Northview rang, stating that Alice and Zoe had been running through the corridors in school, causing disruption as they went; including violating health and safety regulations, by pushing another student along on a hand trolley. He requested I come to the school to collect Alice. Before leaving, I called Alice to see if I could talk to her about what's going on, and she answered, but told me she was in her classroom. Sighing, I told Alice that the school had already called me and ask me to collect her.

Alice replied, 'Don't bother Dad, I am walking round my mother's after school.'

I reiterated that the school have asked me to collect her now; Alice said, 'I'll phone our mother and she will sort things out with the school. I have got to go, bye.'

I put my keys down and tried to contact Ruth, without success.

15 minutes passed, where I debated attempting to pick Alice up. My phone went off, breaking me from my thoughts; it was Mr Caldwell. He was apprehensive, suggesting Alice could walk out of school and meet back up with Zoe, and again asked me to collect her. I told Mr Caldwell that I had talked to Alice, and she was adamant that she was not coming home with me; she expected her mother to call the school to sort things out, which makes me worry that Alice would make a scene if I arrived to collect her. It might be better to give Alice permission to leave for her mother's, giving me the opportunity to drive round and meet her on the way. Mr Caldwell said he would check with reception for Ms Hyde's call first.

I tried Ruth's number again and this time she answered. I asked if Alice had rung her, which Ruth confirmed, and then I asked if Alice had mentioned that Zoe is back on the scene – Ruth said, 'No.'

I explained today's events with Alice, as reported to me by Northview Grove. In response, Ruth stated she was going home and would be collecting Lara, but she would phone Alice and the school beforehand.

Still thinking it would be worth talking to Alice, I headed to my car while trying Alice's number – this time she did not answer. As I drove to Northview Grove, Ruth called, saying she had spoken to Alice, who told her that she wasn't going to hers after school, but would be back about 9pm. I agreed that it was not acceptable, and I said I'd continue to drive around and look for Alice.

Dialling Alice's number, it rang almost to voicemail before she answered. I asked where she was, and she replied, 'Walking to the shops.'

I started driving towards the shops nearby Northview. In the meantime, I informed Alice her mother had called, and that she needed to 'touch base' with her after school before going out – despite us all knowing she should be grounded for her behaviour, I did not want to provoke Alice and have her run off with Zoe.

There was a pause, and. Alice replied, 'I am nipping round my mother's, she knows that… I've got to go now Dad.'

The next few hours were stressful, due to the fact I hadn't heard anything from Ruth nor Alice. At 4.30pm, Ruth called and informed me Alice and Zoe had turned up, taken some things and told her that they were off to the nearby city, Venray, normally an hour's drive away, and that she would be back around 9pm. Ruth said she really didn't know what to do, and I felt in the same boat. Thinking for a moment, I told Ruth to get in touch with Zoe's auntie and I would call the police.

In the space between calls, I questioned whether to actually contact the police; I really do not want to involve the police again but feel genuinely worried about Alice.

I was about to hit the last '9' when my phone rang; it was Mr Caldwell, enquiring if Alice had got home safely and if everything was alright. I gave him an update of the situation, that things weren't so good, as Alice had gone to her mother's with Zoe and had stated they were off to Venray by train.

I asked Mr Caldwell if the police were currently involved with Zoe, as, if so, I would inform them of my concerns that Alice is with her. Mr Caldwell said Mr Garrett had phoned them twice today regarding Zoe. I thanked Mr Caldwell for his call, and rang the police myself.

After explaining the situation, I was informed that if Alice's mother had told Alice that she was not allowed to go to Venray and she has now disappeared, then she is a missing person. Hearing that did not feel good. The dispatcher took Ruth's details and my own, and stated officers would visit my home and Ruth's between 5.30pm and 5.45pm.

I called Ruth and let her know the police would be contacting her soon.

While Lara is at her mother's this weekend, and I have to wonder what she thinks of Alice's behaviour, Hayley has stayed at home; Hayley was worried about Alice and had tried to call her several times.

For a couple of hours, I heard nothing. No police; no Ruth; no Alice. It wasn't until 7.45pm, when Ruth called and stated Maria had heard from Zoe's care home and that is where they are. Ruth continued, saying she had spoken to a police officer from Venray who was now dealing with the situation, and she would call again once she knew more.

Back on the phone to the local police, I informed them Alice and Zoe were safely found in Venray. They inquired as to whether I was driving to Venray to collect Alice. I hadn't thought that far, blindsided by the relief that Alice was found, but I supposed that was the only real option, so I informed them I was. I phoned Maria and asked if she would text me the address of the care home.

I spoke to Ruth, drove to Venray and picked Alice up.

As Alice got in the car, she lamented, 'Why did you have to come and pick me up, my mother said I could go to Venray and see Zoe's care home?'

Instead of wanting an answer though, Alice turned to face out the window and for the next several minutes, every time I tried to speak, Alice would interrupt with 'don't care', 'I don't want to know' or 'not interested'.

Unfortunately, I do not know if Alice is lying, or if Ruth does not remember telling Alice she could go; Ruth's mental health does affect her in that she says things, or agrees to things, and then within minutes she has no recollection.

I phoned Hayley and told her that I was with Alice and on the way home; as I pulled on to the drive Hayley was waiting and watching out of her bedroom window. It was 9.40pm by this point, and Alice requested that she be dropped at her mother's. Not seeing much option in the matter, with Alice likely walking out to her mother's – or worryingly anywhere else – I texted Ruth and dropped her off.

Another hour or so passed. As I sat in my office staring at the wall, I felt drained and tired but could not sleep. I thought hard to how I could resolve or help the situation; after all, part of my work is problem solving, yet I went through a hundred scenarios and still had no answers.

Saturday 5th

At midday, Ruth called saying Alice had just woken up, was rude and refused to tell her where she was going or when she would be back.

I called Alice and she said, 'I am going into town and our mother knows that.'

In response, I told Alice that it did not excuse her language or rudeness, that she needs to touch base with her mother and come home to talk at some point.

Alice replied, 'Whatever.'

I hoped Alice had taken the initiative, but at 5.30pm Ruth rang again; she stated Alice had turned up with Emma and wanted her to sleepover. Ruth explained that she told Alice that Emma could not sleepover due to her behaviour, and hearing that Alice had kicked–off, telling her to 'fuck off' and calling her a 'dickhead'. At this, Ruth said she told Alice that she could sleep at Emma's, but she was not having a sleep–over at hers. In turn, Alice had stormed out of her house saying that she and Emma will stay at mine – I informed Ruth this would not be the case.

Not long after, Alice came through the door with Emma, and asked if she could sleepover. I told Alice that the answer was no, and that we needed to sit down and have a talk. Alice came into the kitchen and sat down but was more interested in pleading for Emma to stay, rather than talking about her behaviour and the issues she's been having. Quickly realising that I was not going to let Emma stay, Alice stood up stating, 'I am off, you do not care.'

(Note to any future parents: sometimes your children say things that hurt you.)

About half an hour passed, and Ruth called saying that Alice had shown back up and was swearing at her while demanding that Emma stays. Ruth told Alice that she had spoken to Emma's mum, and she was coming to pick her up. As she was telling me this, she stated that Alice had walked out and slammed the front door.

Again, I felt unsure how to proceed; neither wanting Alice wandering around, nor my calling her to cause her to wander with even more defiance. I decided to wait, and sure enough Ruth called at 6.15pm, saying Alice is back at hers and is shouting loads of abuse towards her. Alice walked out of Ruth's, saying she was staying at a different friend's, Hannah's, tonight. I tried calling Alice several times but she only answered with a text to say she was at Hannah's.

Sunday 6th

At 2.30am, my phone rang – it was Alice. Alice said Hannah has been sick; she had phoned her mother to come and pick her up, but she has had too much to drink so would I please come get her. I told Alice that I would be along shortly. Instead of coming home like I asked, Alice said her mother wanted her to come home.

It was around 9am, and Ruth phoned, stating, 'You should have called to tell me that Alice was back.'

I replied that I did not call her because she was aware that Hannah had been sick and that Alice was coming home and I presumed she was still awake. Ruth said that I could have texted, and I apologised for not thinking of it at the time.

Hayley and I spent the morning pottering around together; she told me she is going to her mother's and staying over tonight – I said please have an early night so you are up for school tomorrow.

A few hours passed, until my phone went off again. Sobbing down the line, Alice asked if I would come and get her. I tried to get her to tell me what's wrong, but Alice just kept asking for me to come for her. When I picked Alice up, she was crying her eyes out and had some green liquid on her neck and t-shirt. As soon as we got home, she went straight to her bedroom.

Gathering a cereal bar and a drink, I knocked on Alice's door. I could still hear her crying, so went inside despite only receiving a muffled answer. Alice was laying on her floor and I sat down beside her as I tried to comfort her.

Alice looked at me and said, 'First of all dad, I don't want you to say anything,' which worried me immensely right away; Alice continued that she was sitting on the sofa, watching TV, when her mother started arguing with her. After a few minutes, her mother stormed off into the kitchen and came back with a bottle of Fairy Liquid. Her mother sat on Alice to prevent her from moving, shouting that she was going to 'wash that foul language out of your mouth', and then poured the soap over Alice's lips.

Alice said she struggled, managed to get away, and ran upstairs to her room, followed by her mother. Bottle still in her hand, her mother shouted at her to get out of her house now, that she would not tolerate Alice's language and attitude, and that she had 'better go live with your father'.

Alice was crying again by the end and as I gave her a hug, I suggested I run her a bath, we stick a movie on and I'll make a hot chocolate. However, Alice said she just wanted to go to bed. I understood, and told her if she needs anything, to let me know.

After a few minutes, the house phone rang; I already knew who it was. I went downstairs and listened as it clicked to the answering machine.

Ruth forwent a hello and shouted angrily, 'You can tell Alice as she is not answering her mobile, that I want the phone back that I gave to her, and I want my front door key back that Alice has. I suggest you get off your arse and drop them to me now.'

Despite wanting to address Ruth's conduct and being sickened to hear about another abusive incident, I knew that calling Ruth to discuss Alice or her behaviour towards her would, as usual, only draw me into her mania.

Ruth shouted, 'If you are going to do nothing about Alice's behaviour, I will phone Social Services!'

Huffing, Ruth ended with that she does not want Alice 'creeping' back into her house today, as Alice is aware that she is going out in the afternoon.

I texted Hayley and Lara to check they were ok. Hayley was out with friends and Lara answered she was in her room, and I tried not to think about how much I wished Lara was home, safe.

Monday 7th

Alice was up early in the morning before school; we talked about the last few months and agreed that she should speak to someone to try and resolve the issues she is having at home and at school.

I called CFCS and after explaining the situation the woman stated that an organisation called 'the Junction' deals with teenagers and could offer advice or Connexions, as the CFCS only gets involved at the referral of the child's school or the child's doctor. (Why *haven't* the school recommended CFCS for Alice?)

I phoned 'the Junction', went through the situation and was emailed several leaflets. Printing the leaflets out, I sat down with Alice and we looked through them together. After talking it out for a while, Alice said that she'd like to speak to someone from 'the Junction'.

I also emailed Connexions, to see if an appointment with someone could be set up for Alice, so that Alice has options on who to talk to.

Alice headed to school.

Shortly after Alice left, Hayley came through to door saying she didn't feel well and was too tired to go to school.

I expressed my disapproval and said to Hayley this is exactly what we talked about; she cannot stay up late and miss school the next day. Hayley said 'I know Dad' and went to bed.

Northview Grove rang in the afternoon – Alice, accidentally, squirted a drink over a teacher; it was the last straw and she has been permanently excluded. I was told to come and collect Alice.

I asked if my apologies could be relayed to the teacher concerned. Mrs Tran was surprised and stated that she had talked to Ms Hyde about the incident and she had not had the same attitude or manner that I had; she went on to say the teacher involved was getting the trousers washed and would I pay the laundry bill, I replied yes.

I tried to contact Ruth, but she didn't pick up.

With Alice at home, I hope that if she talks to someone about what has been happening at her mother's then they might be able to provide an insight, and Northview would take Alice's situation on board so that Alice can be given a chance to focus at school and improve her behaviour.

Hayley, Alice and Lara spent a peaceful night together.

From Northview Grove

7 January

Dear Mr Marlo,
Alice Marlo – 9OK
I regret to inform you of my decision to permanently exclude Alice with effect from 8 January 2008. This means that Alice will not be allowed in this school unless she is reinstated by the governing body or by an appeal panel.
I realise that this exclusion may well be upsetting for you and your family, but the decision to permanently exclude Alice has not been taken lightly. Alice has been excluded for:-
Persistently poor and disruptive behaviour, showing no respect for any authority within the school.
Complete refusal to follow reasonable requests or to work within the Code of Conduct of the school.
On the afternoon of Friday 4th January 2008, Alice totally disrupted the learning of many students, showing total disregard for the authority of senior staff and Health & Safety requirements.
You have a duty to ensure that your child is not present in a public place in school hours during the first 5 school days of this exclusion, i.e. on 8 January to 14 January, unless there is a reasonable justification. You could be prosecuted or receive a penalty notice if your child is present in a public place during school hours on those dates. It will be for you to show reasonable justification.
Alternative arrangements for Alice's education to continue will be made. For the first five school days of this exclusion, we will set work for Alice and would ask you to ensure this work is completed and returned promptly to school for marking. From the sixth school day of the exclusion onwards i.e. 15 January 2008, the local authority will provide suitable full-time education. I have informed Mr J Hill of the Local Education Authority of your child's exclusion and they will be in touch with you about arrangements for her education from the sixth school day of exclusion.
As this is a permanent exclusion, the governing body must meet to consider it. At the review meeting, you may make representations to the governing body if you wish and ask them to reinstate your child in school. The governing body have the power to reinstate your child immediately or from a specified date, or, alternatively, they have the power to uphold the exclusion in which case you may appeal against their decision to an independent Appeal Panel.
The latest date by which the governing body must meet is Tuesday, 29 January 2008.
If you wish to make representations to the governing body and wish to be accompanied by a friend or representative, please contact Mrs Clegg, clerk for the governing body at the school as soon as possible. You will, whether you choose to make representations or not, be notified by the clerk to the governing body of the time, date and location of the meeting.
Please let us know if you have a disability or special needs which would affect your ability to attend.
If you think this exclusion relates to a disability your child has, and you think discrimination has occurred, you may raise the issue with the governing body.
You have the right to see a copy of Alice's school record. Due to confidentiality restrictions, you must notify me in writing if you wish to be supplied with a copy. I will be happy to supply you with Alice's record if you request it. There may be a charge for photocopying.
You may also wish to contact the Local Education Authority, who can provide advice on what options

are available to you. Additionally, you may find it useful to contact the Advisory Centre for Education (ACE) – an independent national advice centre for parents of children in state schools. They offer information and support on state education in England and Wales, including on exclusion from school.
Yours sincerely,
Mrs Tran
Headteacher
c.c. Ms Hyde

Too tired

8 January

I woke Hayley up for school; as she got up, she complained that she was too tired to go. After the question of losing her pocket money came up, Hayley decided to attend school without a fuss. (Revealing that inner–strength that I told her she had.)

While working in the office, I received an email from Connexions:

Mr Marlo,

Thank you for your enquiry. Please find attached a copy of our referral form as discussed. I look forward to receiving your reply. Best wishes!!

Alice and I sat down and filled out the referral form for her to speak to someone.

Midday, my phone rang and I spoke to Hayley, who said she was at her mother's and was staying there until 2pm. I asked Hayley why she was not at school, and Hayley admitted she had called her mother after her first two lessons, saying she felt ill; her mother phoned the school and she had walked to hers. I told Hayley when she comes home we need to have a house meeting about school and making the effort in her last year.

There was a meeting with Mrs Tran, Ruth and myself, regarding Alice's expulsion. By this point, I understand Alice has quite the record of misbehaving, but I feel like with Alice agreeing to talk to someone, we might be able to get somewhere with her behaviour – I will plead Alice's case to remain at Northview, so we don't end up taking one step forward and five steps back.

In the evening, Alice stated she was going to stay round her mother's tonight. I couldn't believe it, because of the incident only a day a go, and we've just seen months of what this leads to. I didn't know what to say, but I don't want to stop Alice from seeing her mother, if that's what she wants. In that moment, I said, 'As long as you are sure and you are safe. If you and your mother argue, don't retaliate, go to your room.'

(In practise, this does not always work, as Ruth is unable to let arguments go and the children have said she sometimes comes into their rooms, to carry on shouting.)

Alice then said that her mother didn't finish work until 9pm, so she should be alright.

I was unaware Ruth had late evening shifts at work, and the children have obviously been left alone during this period before, or in the very least Alice has and Hayley has now caught on. Along with my concerns for Ruth's treatment of the children, both Hayley and Alice have told me they smoke and drink alcohol at their mother's; when she is at work, their friends congregate round there – now I have visions of the children partying 'til the early hours of the morning, with Ruth arriving home oblivious, despite encouraging this behaviour.

This is obviously not a good arrangement and surely not what the judge had in mind when saying that Alice could have evening contact, staying overnight once a week with Ruth. Changing residences to sleep, which is not what Alice will *actually* be doing, isn't a stable routine to be in, even if Alice doesn't have school tomorrow.

When Hayley came through the door, Alice left for her mother's. (I've noticed on several occasions this appears to be the pattern, wherein the children end up staying at their mother's usually one at a time, even Lara. It's hard to know whether this is down to their mother's stipulations, a coping mechanism for their mother's temperament, or if this is the children using their mother's disposition to their advantage.)

Hayley and I sat in the living room and in a roundabout way I asked why she is so tired after staying at her mother's – if she was not missing school, we would not need to have this house meeting. Hayley has always been honest with me, and admitted that when her mother works at night, she has her friends over; making sure they're gone before her mother returns. Concerned, I asked what happens if her mother comes home from work early and Hayley replied, 'I haven't been caught yet.'

It is usually the early morning when her friends have left and she clears up so her mother doesn't know – Hayley believes Alice has been doing the same for longer than she has.

It makes sense now why Alice has been so keen to stay at her mother's. For months I questioned where I had gone wrong, why my parenting with Alice was so challenging, and was this behaviour part of Alice growing up and dismissing the love and care she had received?

Alice, aged 13, had free reign in her mother's house; with the ability to stay up late, have friends round, drink alcohol and smoke.

I told Hayley she's coming up to leaving school and she clearly knows this behaviour is not right as she is hiding it from her mother and me; she has college to look forward to and doesn't want to get on the same path as Alice, who has made a lot of mistakes at school because of this lifestyle.

Hayley gave me a hug and said, 'I don't want to get into trouble but I'm just being a teenager Dad, and I'm not as bad as Alice.' She did agree that when she stays at her mother's in the future, she would not stay up so late or, once I made the point to her, invite her friends round without her mother's knowledge.

I thanked Hayley and said when I see Alice I will be telling her the same.

I thought about the love and care in our home, I thought about Ma and knew we could not give Hayley and Alice the same lifestyle they experience at their mother's; apart from seeing the damage unfolding, Ma and I are just not those sorts of people. While I am aware I should inform Ruth what Hayley has told me, I fear for Hayley and Alice if I do so.

From Cafcass

8 January

Dear Mr Marlo,
I am writing to acknowledge your letter which was received at this office on 24th December 2007 and I have placed this on record. I have noted the contents but this does not alter my intended action relating to submitting an amended report to the court, a copy of which I am attaching to this letter.

I am sorry that you do not feel that Family Justice System has supported your role as a parent, but I assure that Cafcass aims to put children's interests at the forefront of our work and will continue to do so. We are always pleased to receive comments and suggestions from service users as to how we can improve and if you feel able to comment about specific issues, I will record these on our internal systems.
Yours sincerely,
Ms Soto
Service Manager

Dear Sir or Madam of the Venray County Court,
Re: Hayley, Alice and Lara Marlo
The above matter appeared before Ms Recorder Lowe on 5th September 2007. Ms Moyer was the Guardian ad Litem in this matter and filed her report on 03.09.07.

Mr Marlo has raised some factual inaccuracies in the report and having read the filed document it is clear that there are also some significant typing errors.

In the circumstances, I would ask that you place the attached amended report on the court file. Any amendments made do not alter in any way the recommendation made in the report.
Yours sincerely,
Ms Soto
Service Manager

I got my highlighter back out and the 'amended' report is much the same as the first, littered with typographical errors, misleading statements and false information.

Dean Marlo

Trying to avoid bad habits

9 January

Alice rang saying she is going out with a Hannah, but she will be home tonight. I thanked her for letting me know and said I would like her to be in by 6pm for dinner, with Hannah if she wants. I also asked if she'd done her school work. Alice said, 'Some of it.' I encouraged her to finish it before heading out.

After school, Hayley stated that she was sleeping at her mother's tonight. I told Hayley to remember what we talked about and she needed to have an early night. Hayley replied, 'Yes, okay Dad.'

At 5pm, Ruth phoned and said she will be collecting Lara from school tomorrow for tea.

Alice came home on time for dinner and stayed in with Lara and me for the rest of the evening. While we were watching TV, Alice complained that Zoe is being sent away to a different care home – 300 miles away – and Alice felt bad for her, as she had phoned her in tears about being shipped off.

(I feel sorry for Zoe, and her aunt Maria; I do wonder though, if Zoe and Alice had received support, how her and Alice's behaviour could have been different.)

Making Connections

10 January

At 9.50am, I received call from the Junction, which used to be the Careers Services and now functions as a youth information centre. A 'Ms Stephanie Jones' explained who she was and asked if she could speak to Alice. I requested she call back in ten minutes, allowing me time to talk to Alice; she agreed.

I told Alice that a woman from the Junction had phoned and that she was happy to have a chat.

Alice replied, 'I do not want to talk to anyone.'

I said they are there to help, and allow her to talk to someone impartially – not like she has spoken to before, just an ear for her; this is all about giving her the chance to go through the issues that she has, which is what we discussed and she was up for regarding 'the Junction'.

Rolling her eyes, Alice said, 'Yes Dad, but not at the moment.'

I told Alice that I want what is best for her and for her to be happy; she will not resolve anything by putting off talking to the people around her who want to help.

Alice replied, 'I will talk to her but not right now…'

Alice made it clear that I was no longer welcome by repeating each time I tried to talk, 'in my time'.

Phone back against my ear, I told Ms Jones that I had reached a stumbling block because Alice was reluctant to talk right now; she said that she understood and not to worry, and asked me to pass her mobile number on to Alice. Maybe Alice would make the effort and call in her own time.

I gave Alice Ms Jones' number and said that she could phone anytime, within reason. Alice replied that she would.

Getting some office work done, at around 11.30 am Ruth called and stated Hayley was not at school, as she felt ill. In my head, I thought about Hayley's agreement to not get into this routine, and the fact I really did think she would take on board that while it might seem fun, it's not good for her.

I informed Ruth of Ms Jones' call, and that Alice hadn't spoken to her yet. I asked Ruth to encourage Alice to contact Ms Jones; Ruth said she would try.

Dean Marlo

From the Council

10 January

Dear Mr Marlo,

I have been informed that Alice was permanently excluded from Northview Grove School. I enclose a leaflet, which I hope you will find helpful.

If Alice is on School Action, or School Action Plus, is being formally assessed for a statement of Special Educational Needs, or has a statement of Special Educational Needs you have access to the Parent Partnership Service who may offer support throughout the exclusions process (see enclosed leaflet).

You will be contacted again if the exclusion is confirmed by the Governors' Disciplinary Committee, in the meantime if you have any questions please contact me.

Yours sincerely,
Children's Support Caseworker

Dear Mrs Tran (Headteacher)

10 January

May I take this opportunity to thank you for your letter dated 19th December to Mr Rowe MP.

However, I would ask you please to clarify and confirm that the current difficulties regard my daughter Alice, and not as could be suggested from your letter, 'experienced by the girls'. I am worried that such statements may be misinterpreted and has the potential to mislead the reader, a judge or a court appointed expert.

When we met on the 8th January, you made it very clear to Ms Hyde and myself, as you have to me over several months, that Hayley was a different child and the school have not experienced the same difficulties as Alice. You reiterated that Hayley had nothing to do with recent bad behaviour Alice has had in school.

In the past, I have spoken many times with Mrs Sparrow, and always found her polite and professional in dealing with Hayley and Alice's schooling. I believe that I showed Mrs Sparrow through my attitude and commitment towards my children's education and Northview Grove, that I was a caring and responsible parent. I am thankful Mrs Sparrow relayed this fact to Mrs Sanders, the family court appointed child psychologist, in January 2007.

In March 2007, Ms Hyde contested the child psychologist's report, which led to further court proceedings.

I fully appreciate that you may consider our family situation complex, but over the years I have fully informed the school of any relevant information relating to Hayley and Alice, and also changes to Alice's residency with her mother, due to Alice rebelling against boundaries that I had set as a parent.

I have only tried to simplify matters by reporting to the teachers what was going on. I am not criticising you in anyway and appreciate your letter of support concerning my conduct within school and with my children, to Mr Rowe. I, like you, want to close this matter, but I am sure you would agree that clarification is the right thing to do.

Up to 2007, Hayley and Alice had only minor problems that are common in many families, let alone with the difficult childhoods they had, which resulted in occasional detentions.

My commitment to Northview Grove, its teachers and my children's education and behaviour, has never changed.

Yours sincerely…

(It has become a bit of a habit for people to state that our family is a complex case, just to cover for themselves or a colleague.)

A letter from the Junction and Northview

11 January

Dear Mr Marlo,

Thank you for your referral of your daughter Alice to Support @ the Junction. We would like to meet her and have arranged an appointment for: 1pm on Thursday 7th February at the Junction.

The appointment will take around one and a half hours and you or another close family member are welcome to attend, although we do like to speak to young people on their own for a short while if they are comfortable with this. At this meeting, myself and my colleague Elicia Reese, will discuss with Alice what type of support she would like and the kinds of services and activities we can offer.

Unfortunately, there is no parking at the Junction, and parking spaces in the roads nearby are reserved for residents or are time restricted.

Please discuss this letter with your daughter and let us know if she will be coming to the appointment. If you have any queries or concerns feel free to call.

We look forward to meeting you both.

Best wishes,

Dana Henderson, Project worker

I asked, but Alice still hasn't called Ms Jones from the Junction, so I don't know if Alice will agree to going to this meeting; I'll bring it up to her and hopefully she will.

Dear Mr Marlo,

Permanent Exclusion of Alice Marlo, Year 9

You will have received a letter dated 7 January 2008 informing you of the decision to permanently exclude Alice. Three Governors will be meeting at the school on Thursday 24 January at 9:30 to review the exclusion. You are invited to come and also to bring Alice. You may also be accompanied by a friend or representative. A representative of the Local Authority has been invited to attend the meeting.

You may make representations to the governing body, either by coming to the meeting or in writing to the governing body. Any written information to be presented by the school at the meeting will be sent to you in advance. If you wish to provide written information, please send it to me before the meeting so that I can send it to the Governors and to the Headteacher.

Please let me know if you and Alice intend to come to the meeting and whether you will be accompanied by a friend or representative, and whether you have a disability or special needs for which we may need to make adjustments.

Yours sincerely,

Life continues

11 - 13 January

Friday 11th
It was around midday when Ruth called and stated, 'Alice is coming back to yours for the weekend.'

In response, I said no problem and asked if I could speak to Alice.

Ruth replied, 'Alice is asleep and I am going to let her lay in for as long as possible. If she is not up by 2pm, I will wake her.'

I said nothing, not that I agreed with Alice's sleep schedule.

I picked Lara up from school, and we arrived home seconds before Hayley and then Alice came through the front door. Both Hayley and Alice ransacked every kitchen cupboard for food of their liking, sitting down at the kitchen table as they organised what they were doing later and with whom.

Alice asked if could she stay at Hannah's tonight, and I told Alice that it was fine, but to call me when she is at Hannah's so I can talk to Hannah's mum or dad.

At 8.30pm Alice rang me and passed her phone to Hannah's mum; we had a chat and she told me that both Hannah and Alice were in for the night now.

Hayley had her friend Jasmine to sleepover, and Lara and I rallied for our balloon-tennis championship, which was once again a close fought match.

12th Saturday
While I was at work, Ma went into town with Lara to gather materials for their latest sewing project, and Hayley and Alice went shopping in town with their friends; Hayley had Jasmine over again and Alice had a quiet night in.

I received a letter from Ruth which read;

13 January

Dear Dean,

Just to confirm our holiday arrangements as we discussed. We are leaving on 13th February to travel to Gran Canaria and returning on 20th February. I would like the girls to come to me on the 12th February at around 4.30pm so that everything can be ready in good time for an early start the next day.

Please find enclosed flight and hotel details; as usual you can contact me on my mobile.

Hayley is determined to overcome her fear of flying, as she wants to travel when she's older and is thinking about maybe doing a gap year. I told her I would support her through it and we would try to resolve her worries before they go.

Another week

13 - 17 January

Sunday 13th

In the afternoon, Hayley came into the kitchen and told me that at 5pm she was going swimming with her mother at her health club; we chatted about school and Hayley confirmed she'd done all her homework.

Hayley walked to her mother's. Not twenty minutes later, Hayley came back through the door and stated that her mother hadn't been in and was not answering her mobile. I also tried Ruth's number for Hayley, but didn't get through.

Hayley, Alice, Lara and I sat in the living room playing a card game. Half way through a heated round of 'Go Fish', Hayley's phone rang and her mother said that she was sorry as she had forgotten about taking her swimming, but would phone when she was ready.

It was 6.30pm when Ruth arrived to pick Hayley up.

At 9pm, Lara and I were just finishing watching 'Planet Earth' and were sat in the living room. Alice came in stating that she was sleeping at her mother's tonight. I said to Alice, 'What happened to getting back into a routine?'

Alice shrugged, so I asked if she had spoken to her mother first. Alice told me her mother had asked if she wanted to stay; I kept to myself that again, no stability can be acquired, as Ruth dictates the children's contact. Leaving the room, Alice said, 'I have no school so it does not matter.'

Changing tact, I asked if she had phoned Junction – Alice replied, 'Not yet.'

Shortly after, I got an abusive call from Ruth, accusing me of telling Alice that she could sleep at hers. I informed her that Alice said she had organised it, which Ruth denied, and I reiterated that Alice needed routine now more than ever because she doesn't have the structure of school. Ruth agreed, and I told her that she should be firm with Alice and make it clear that when it is convenient, Tuesdays and Thursdays are the sleepover nights. Ruth went back to being abusive, stating she was not having Alice tonight, as she was busy, and it will be Wednesdays and Thursdays she can stay from now on. I said I would talk to Alice.

Although unhappy about it, Alice settled for the night and Hayley returned at 9.15pm.

Monday 14th

I was in the office at 11am and Alice sat down on the spare chair; she spun a few times, then said that her mother was going to phone me to confirm that she was sleeping at hers tonight. Shaking my head, I said to Alice, 'How do you expect to get into a routine, if you are not consistent from the very start?'

Alice replied, 'Our mother can't make it on Wednesday so I'm sleeping there tonight.'

At 2pm, Alice went to her mother's.

After returning from picking Lara up from school, I was preparing dinner when Hayley stated that she did not want any because she was going shopping with her mother and Alice. Hayley was dropped back at 8.15pm.

Tuesday 15th

I received a phone call from a Mrs Delgado of the Unified External Education Centre, a support school for expelled pupils. We made a home appointment for Monday 21st with Alice at 11am.

Ending the call with Mrs Delgado, I rang Ruth and told her about the appointment. Ruth insisted the meeting be held at the centre, and said she would phone them immediately to have it changed. Somehow, I managed to convince Ruth to let me speak to Mrs Delgado. I phoned Mrs Delgado back, and an appointment was made for Tuesday 22nd January at 4pm in her office. I informed Ruth of the new details.

I also called Alice, to inform her of the appointment made at the UEEC and to see if she had contacted Ms Jones from the Junction. Alice said not yet, and stated she was sleeping at her mother's tonight.

Wednesday 16th

In the afternoon, Alice returned home. At 3pm, Ruth called, saying she was going to have Lara for tea tomorrow.

I received a letter from my MP:

Dear Mr Marlo,

I hope you and your daughters are well.

Would you like me to pursue your concerns over the Guardian with Ms Soto of Cafcass? If this is the case, please phone my office to arrange an appointment at my Advice Bureau and we can discuss this further. Best wishes.

Yours sincerely,

Thursday 17th

During the day, I've been trying to get Alice to sit down with me and go through some of the work the school had provided, but she always has a reason for why she can't do it. At 3pm, Alice came out of her room saying she was going to her mother's.

Alice returned home at 7.30pm with Lara. I attempted to talk to Alice about the gravity of the situation and her behaviour. Alice replied with several poor excuses and again I said if there is support she needs that her mother and I cannot provide, she should contact Ms Jones, or someone from Connexions. This resulted in Alice announcing that she was off. (To her bedroom.)

At 9.25pm, Ruth picked Alice up.

Looking back at my parenting with Alice in the past, it is like being at the circus; one of the extras, where I have a walk on part, only to be told to sit back down. I understand that my softness, in that I do not wish to argue and will therefore put up with more than any sane person would, has contributed to the way Alice in particular behaves but, at the end of the day, I just want my children to be happy, and I never thought my lack of desire for confrontation could be turned around in the way that it has.

As Hayley, Alice and Lara have grown up, it has been Alice who decided she does not want to acknowledge that having a stable home matters; Alice behaves as she does because I am unable to properly maintain my position as her parent whilst being constantly undermined by her mother.

I have sole residency but live in fear of Ms Hyde, Mrs Mason and what another judge could decide.

Ruth's weekend contact

18 January

At breakfast Hayley asked if I would mind if she came out of school at lunchtime... I enquired as to why and she said that her mother was taking Alice to the seaside nearby at midday for the last day of the sales. I told Hayley that she should not be taking any more time off school, and that Alice is not supposed to be seen in public places during school time. Her mother is aware of this, and also should not be encouraging Hayley to miss school.

Ruth rang stating that she was putting a letter together for the Governors of Northview Grove; she indicated that she believed Alice's bad behaviour was due to her home life and her having been put through such a difficult time due to her parent's involvement with the Family Courts.

While I agree that proceedings have affected all of our children, Ruth has never truly followed a court order, which has allowed Alice to fall into the illusion that she knows more than adults do and she does not have to comply with rules.

I told Ruth that it is not an excuse for Alice pushing someone on a hand trolley, refusing to remove jewellery and wearing jumpers under her school blazer; these are teenage rebellion issues and not just the result of proceedings. Ruth argued that Alice's behaviour is a result of all the trouble over the years between us; I reminded Ruth that up to December 2006, Alice had been doing well at Northview, and it was only since then that Alice really started to misbehave and defy boundaries at home and also at school, which had been after the longest period without court involvement. As she began swearing, it was obvious we were not going to agree over this, I said 'best we leave it' and 'goodbye'.

Hayley texted saying she was with her mother after school, and came home at 8pm with multiple bags of clothes. Getting several items out, Hayley was showing me what she bought, and I asked how she had managed to go to the sales. Hayley replied that she had gone to the sick bay at lunchtime to enable her mother to collect her from school. I let her know I was disappointed she didn't listen to me this morning about how important her lessons are.

Hayley replied, 'How can you let Alice do anything and then have a go at me?'

I tried to explain she is a different child to Alice, and I do not expect her to act in this way. Hayley responded, 'So it is alright for Alice, but not for me.'

(Well, it looks like I have hit the wall again.)

Letters and arrangements

20/21 January

Sunday 20th
Hayley came home and gave me a letter from Ruth containing her February holiday arrangements, which Ruth had already put through my door on the 13th of January.

Mrs Irfan, Headteacher at Riverbank, informed me that Ms Hyde had put in a request for Lara to be out of school after the half term in February and I confirmed that I had agreed with her request. Fortunately, one of the days is a non–pupil day at Riverbank. However, it still means that Hayley will miss 3 days of school, Lara 2 and Alice, well, it hardly encourages Alice to care about getting back into school.

Monday 21st
After school, Lara was reading out loud to me in the kitchen when Alice came home. Stopping, Lara asked Alice if she could have her bracelet back that she had lent her, and Alice said no. Lara asked again, and Alice replied, 'You can have it back in three days.'

At this point, I intervened and asked Alice to return the bracelet to Lara. Alice still refused. I asked Lara to wait three days for its return and learn not to lend Alice things until she can behave reasonably.

Hayley then came home and was saying hello when Alice asked Hayley if she knew if their mother was at home. When Hayley confirmed yes, Alice left and came back through the door at 7pm.

On Alice's return, she went straight up to her bedroom; meanwhile I was in the kitchen washing up. I went up to Alice's room, knocked and asked Alice if she'd had tea at her mother's or if she'd like something to eat. Alice did not look up from her laptop, and only shook her head.

Hayley went up to her room while Lara and I were watching TV; Ruth called and asked me why Alice had told her that I was being nasty towards her. Confused, I said that no one had been 'nasty' to Alice, and I explained how first Lara and I had asked Alice to return Lara's bracelet, and she had refused. Ruth stated, 'The bracelet is not the issue here, the issue is the way you talked to Alice.'

I replied that I need to say goodbye, as I have bread in the oven. (This did not go down well, and as I put the phone down, I heard her say 'do you think you are fucking funny?') I'm just not prepared to go along with the accusation of being rude to Alice.

Ten minutes later, Alice came downstairs and sat in the front room with Lara and myself, stating that she was waiting for her mother to collect her. Lara kept quiet, as usual, but the look she gave me when Alice announced that she was going to her mother's was one I had seen many times before – Lara doesn't think highly of Alice when she's behaving like this.

I said to Alice that she needs to talk to me and not have this attitude, as I don't understand what the problem is and we can't keep going in circles.

Alice ignored me and Ruth was soon outside.

Schooling

22 January

Today, Alice, Ruth and I have the appointment with Mrs Delgado from the Unified External Education Centre (UEEC) in town.

I tried to phone Alice throughout the day with no success. Ma works part-time and was busy, so I arranged for Hayley to take care of Lara after I had collected her from school. However, as Hayley was doing extra work at school for her GCSE exams, Hayley's teacher agreed that Lara could come into Northview with her. I left Hayley working on her art and Lara with her nose buried in a book.

At 3.50pm, I was sat in the car park at the UEEC and Alice phoned me to let me know her mother was still getting ready, but they would be on their way shortly.

Heading into the building, I went into the appointment alone. I was introduced to Mrs Delgado who questioned if I was aware Ms Hyde had made a complaint to her Governors, stating that she had not been contacted concerning this appointment and so on. I told Mrs Delgado that I would be more than happy to confirm that having received the phone call from her, I immediately phoned Ms Hyde to give her details.

(This is supposed to be about Alice, what is Ruth doing?)

Twenty minutes went by, and we discussed Alice, her strengths – art, debating, leadership – and what issues I felt she had. Finally, Ruth arrived with Alice. Ruth walked in and stated to Mrs Delgado that she wasn't keen on Alice attending the Unified External Education Centre. When Mrs Delgado asked Ruth why, she said she had heard several bad things about the centre and, only the other day, her manager at work had told her how while she had been in the centre, she had to stop a child from throwing a chair across the corridor and another child swearing.

Mrs Delgado asked for the name of the woman who had come onto the centre's premises, which Ruth was reluctant to reveal; Mrs Delgado pressed on, citing a right to know who that person was and under whose authority they had been on the premises. Ruth refused to give the name, and Mrs Delgado queried where Ms Hyde worked; the room fell silent.

I looked at the clock, it was now 4.35pm. What with Ruth and Alice having been 20 minutes late and then spending 15 minutes discussing the rights and wrongs of Ruth's unnecessary comments, 35 minutes had passed without Alice and her education being considered or discussed.

It was finally agreed that Alice would visit the centre to look around on Friday 25th January at 1.30pm. As we left, there was a distinct atmosphere revolving around Ruth, and she told me that she would be taking Alice to the appointment.

Hayley and Lara attended tutoring at 6pm/7pm.

At 8pm, Ruth left on message on the answering machine saying she would be picking Lara up from school tomorrow.

MP

22 January

Dear Mr Rowe,

Thank you for your letter and in reply I am writing to you to express my disappointment with the Cafcass response and amended report regarding my family. I have responded per Ms Moyer's paragraphs in her letter 3rd December 2007. Please also find enclosed a further letter from Ms Soto, which acknowledges my worries but shows little understanding to the gravity of the situation and the importance of relaying honest and factual information to the Family Courts.

I believe that the contents of the Guardian's amended final report should be addressed accurately and professionally, and I would appreciate your integrity and any assistance you can give.

Page 2 of the amended report, my date of birth has been changed but is still incorrect. This is not an issue of equal severity to the inaccurate statements in relation to my parenting, however it is not reassuring that even basic details are not recorded properly.

Paragraph 3, Ms Moyer accepts that it should read Ms Hyde and not Ms Marlo; in the amended report it remains Ms Marlo.

Paragraph 4, please find enclosed the order 26th July 2007, which states the Guardian to file a report setting out her proposals for the 'further instruction of expert evidence and the reasons' and 'as to the application to remove to Australia'. Ms Moyer was to firstly report on Ms Hyde's proposed holiday and address Ms Hyde's concerns over Alice and Lara's contact.

It is surprising to read in the amended report Hayley's disposition is still being relayed, dishonestly, and despite not being requested. Having been removed from the court order, Hayley only spoke to Ms Moyer out of politeness and about the proposed forthcoming Australian holiday.

Hayley was not only not under order in these proceedings but also, as in the order 25th June 2007, only Alice and Lara are assigned a Guardian. Understandably, the feedback that she gave helped the Guardian obtain an overall insight, and is it not that I am suggesting Hayley shouldn't have been spoken, however Ms Moyer has made several inferences and included information about Hayley which were either false or did not pertain to the court ordered requests.

In the letter from Ms Moyer dated 3rd December, she accepts that Hayley was removed from the court order, not as written in her report... So why does her amended report still state 'all three children live with their father under a residence order'?

If Hayley's inclusion in this report is justified, then I see no point in Hayley having been put through the Family Courts process to get removed from any more proceedings. (It was agreed by Judge Yergin on 12th of March 2007 that Hayley should be able to get on with her life.)

In the first report, it is written that the Deputy Head of Northview Grove, Mrs

Hewitt, was 'very concerned about Hayley's mental health, as she appears depressed and sad most of the time.' On the day of the hearing, the Guardian's solicitor informed the Judge that the words 'mental health' were those of Ms Moyer and not from a teacher at Northview Grove. In the amended copy that Ms Soto proposes to send to the Family Courts, the paragraph now reads Mrs Hewitt is 'very concerned over Hayley's mental wellbeing as she appears depressed and sad most of the time'. I note from this paragraph that the phrase 'mental health' has been replaced with 'mental wellbeing'. This has been changed, despite Ms Moyer stating that she would not in her letter of the 3rd December as it was 'a true reflection of the conversation that she'd had with Mrs Hewitt'.

There is no evidence from Hayley's school or at home for such an assumption.

Weeks after the final hearing, Ms Moyer made an appointment to visit me; there for the first time, she explained that she had used the words 'mental health' to 'refer to an overall condition, just as a doctor refers to physical health as an overall human condition, it is a general term and by no means a diagnosis of any kind in respect of Hayley'.

This is not how the report reads, and it added additional worry that Hayley is struggling, and no one from Northview Grove School had informed either Ms Hyde or myself, or organised help for her if it was true.

As important decisions are being made by the Family Courts on the recommendations and contents of a Guardian's report, I believe that clarity and accuracy is surely not merely a requirement but essential in ensuring that the children's welfare is not undermined.

Paragraph 5, I believe, suggests to the Family Courts that this is one of 'Mr Marlo's factual inaccuracies'. As I have stated, it was Ms Moyer who insisted that Hayley's hair colour, my date of birth, etc *should* be amended in her report, as I brought the inaccuracies to her attention. I am only concerned with serious issues, such as the misleading statements and disputed words of a teacher; not petty discrepancies like the colour of Hayley's hair. (Which, in any case, should be factual if included in the first place.)

Paragraph 6, clearly the amended report remains poorly written and inaccurate.

Paragraph 13, Ms Moyer suggested that I take my comments regarding Paragraph 58 up with Northview Grove. This I have done, and now have written confirmation from Mrs Tran, Headteacher, of my full involvement with the school and in my daughters' education and wellbeing. Yet, the school's input remains the same in the report.

Paragraph 14, ultimately my worries are for the lack of care and consideration in the making of this report, and the damage to our family's dynamics that it may cause in future proceedings. (Despite the 91(14) order, I also don't believe Cafcass should be happy with lodging false information in the court.)

I have not been privileged enough to receive a copy of the judge's summing up of the hearing 5th September 2007, but I have continued with my family's life in accordance with the court order to the best of my ability, under the circumstances. It has not begun too well, but as in the past I shall stand by all of my children as any honest parent would.

It has been paramount to me as a parent to be totally involved with my children's schools, their education and behaviour; this I have done proudly, and I take joy in being able to go on school trips and help out in projects at school, in the past with Hayley and Alice, and while Lara is still at primary. Having your children at primary or secondary school is a huge part of being a parent. I have not turned it on and off when it suits.

This has been confirmed by Mr Church, previous Head at Riverbank, Mrs Hall and all of my children's teachers as they have gone through their years, as well as Mrs Sparrow, Mr Caldwell and Mrs Tran from Northview Grove.

Paragraph 15, unfortunately Ms Moyer fails to realise that relaying inaccurate and misleading information in a report prepared for the Family Courts can only harm and hurt children, their parents and family, and may, even more seriously, distort the final outcome; leading to further disruption and instability in a child's life, which has already been the case for 8 years, as she is well aware.

I do not believe a report regarding the wellbeing of children should be made 'in haste'. This was an important hearing for my children and our family, hopefully bringing an end to court involvement. If necessary for her to do her job correctly, then the appropriate thing would have been to request more time from the court. (You know I want the court hearings to *end* but if it is a question of it concluding for the right reasons, i.e. the welfare of the children, or prolonging proceedings because there have been objections and queries due to inaccuracies – we would all rather have waited.)

As you are aware, for many years I have run a small, professional construction company; since, we have earned a great deal of respect from architects, surveyors and people in the commercial and domestic sectors for our high standard of workmanship, reliability and dedication to our profession. If I, a contractor, completed an inspection of your building and relayed there were several defects requiring replacement, when in fact the building was in good condition, I would be called a disgrace to my profession and could face criminal charges. I'd probably end up named and shamed in the local gazette.

I find that in children and family matters involving the Family Courts, where you would expect honesty and straightforward conduct to be the norm, I am left with Ms Moyer saying one thing and Mrs Tran saying another.

Cafcass and the Guardians appointed have a moral duty to relay the truth and should want to fully amend any inaccuracies or misunderstandings, and be accountable and professional enough to make changes when a mistake has been made. Ms Moyer was decent to meet with me and go through her report, yet her amendments do not reflect the same amount of care.

In Mrs Soto's letter, she apologises for my feelings that the Family Justice System have failed to support me in my role as a parent, claiming that Cafcass' aim is to put children's interests at the forefront of their work. I know Ms Moyer nor Cafcass mean any harm, but I do despair for their inability properly address my concerns and reasons for raising them.

In my case, I am fortunate that the recommendation did not change, however, what if that hadn't been the outcome? What about the parents who therefore were denied contact, the children returned to residency with an abusive parent, and the feelings of the genuine parent who has been discredited?

This amended report should be returned to and the information either verified or removed, before it is lodged in court. I do believe that my family has received further injustice within the system, and the honesty and professionalism that my children deserve has once again not been at the 'forefront' of this organisation.

Yours respectfully...

Dean Marlo

Schools, Children and Families

23 January

Dear Mr Marlo,
Re: Alice Marlo
A period of tuition with UEEC has been recommended for Alice. I would like to take this opportunity to welcome her and hope the time spent with us will be productive. Details of her timetable will be discussed at your meeting on Friday 25 January with Teresa Horton, Senior Teacher.
It is a legal requirement that Alice attends regularly.
Yours sincerely,

Eastenders

23/24 January

23rd

I texted Alice and tried to call a couple of times, without any reply. After school, I said to Hayley if she sees Alice, would she please ask Alice to either ring me or answer her phone.

24th

The meeting with the Governors to decide about Alice's permanent expulsion is at 9.30am. At around 8am, Alice called saying she had been up all night worrying. I said she could have phoned me and talked through it, and that she should try have breakfast to distract her in the meantime.

Dropping Lara at Riverbank, I drove to Northview, and met Alice and Ruth at the reception door. We all signed in and sat down.

A few minutes later, Mr Milner from Learning Assistance came over. Both Ruth and Alice had prepared letters for the Governors, and I handed copies of letters that I had written to Mrs Tran several months previously, plus a statement in support of Alice. We were told that the meeting would not start for thirty minutes to allow the Governors time to read them.

Ruth announced she and Alice were going out for some fresh air, which I thought was a good idea so I went to sit in my car. From where I was parked, I watched in astonishment as Ruth and Alice stood in the alleyway, smoking cigarettes. (The alley where the students smoke before and after school, which is usually monitored by a teacher to prevent them from doing so.)

Once back in reception, Ruth and Alice sat down, both smelling like an ashtray; Ruth told Alice that she did not want her in the meeting, and that she would ask for Alice when she considered it best. Alice stated that she wanted to be there, but Ruth said no. I said Alice ought to be there, but Ruth insisted that Alice wait in reception.

It was a long meeting, with introductions done by the chairman; the school began presenting their case; questions were had by the Governors, parents and Mr Milner; Ruth and I made our representations; there were further questions; the school, parents' and LA statements were gone through... At the end, the Governors informed us they would let us know their decision the next day. As we were leaving the school, I asked Alice if she would pop round tonight for a chat; Alice agreed to.

At 6.30pm, Alice came home. Instead of having a conversation with Alice, she walked in stating, 'Me and Hayley are not allowed to watch Eastenders, Jerry Springer or anything in the living room, because you say that it is not suitable for Lara, yet our mother lets us watch anything even if Lara is there. You give Lara anything she wants – Hayley and I get nothing! I can do what I like at our mother's and get away from Lara and you.'

Ignoring the many blatant untrue baits, I told Alice that these were shallow reasons for not getting on.

521

Alice replied, 'You do not have to put up with Lara.'

I responded that Lara has done nothing to her but been a good sister; we have all stood by her throughout her behaviour over the past year.

Coming further into the room, Alice said, 'Over the past two months you have become our mother, moaning and having a go at me for nothing, and our mother has become nice and reasonable at times.'

For a moment I thought about what behaviour Alice was regarding as nice and reasonable – letting her stay up late and sleep in; allowing them to smoke – Hayley will be 16 in March and Alice 14 in April, it is an awful habit to encourage them to have at any age, let alone so young; inappropriate TV programs that sensationalise drama, arguments and treating each other badly. And then I thought of Fairy Liquid, Hayley being strangled and just the general upset the children have at their mother's, and it is difficult to hear Alice using the analogy between her mother and myself, when she knows it is untrue. Whatever thoughts I was trying to gather to get this conversation back on the path of constructive rather than Alice ranting about how unfair everything is, was interrupted by the house phone ringing.

Ruth stated she was dropping Lara off now and that she had told Alice to give Lara her bracelet back. I asked Alice for Lara's bracelet and Alice stated said it is at her mother's. The doorbell rang, Alice let Lara in and walked out onto the drive to talk to Ruth at her car. I walked up and informed Ruth Alice has said Lara's bracelet is at hers, and I thought the best thing to do would be for her to take Alice, find the bracelet and bring it back, to end the situation.

Ruth questioned Alice as to whether the bracelet was at hers. Alice confirmed it was and Ruth stated she would return shortly with it.

We headed back inside; Alice went upstairs and as I was still reeling from what Alice had said, I gave up with the idea of having a house meeting with her for another day. I joined Lara in the living room.

Lara and I did not see Ruth or Lara's bracelet that night, as she failed to return or call to tell Lara why.

Once everyone was asleep, I thought about the whole bracelet debacle itself. It is a bit like Ms Moyer and Hayley's hair colour vs a suggestion of Hayley suffering from depression; the whole family is falling out over Eastenders and bracelets, when the real issues are their actual relationships and attitudes. There is a certain amount of insanity, as I seemingly am only ever able to watch from the side-lines as choices are made and consequences play out, when the children should be good sisters, who make each other laugh and talk to each other.

Alice's letter to her school

I know I was not a perfect student at Northview Grove by far, I do understand school rules are school rules and I do understand my mistakes. But I have had a tough life and with my parents in and out of court it has been hard for me; I do not blame it on my parents I know that I do need to change for the better but I am willing to try. I know it will take a lot of hard work but I am determined to try my best for my own sake and try to comply with the school rules. Especially with the uniform one which is probably the hardest one for me but I will try my best.

Personally, I don't think I have been that bad. I am difficult and very difficult at times but I am going to try, people like my mum, dad, friends and teachers have told me I am going to be permanently excluded if I don't sort out my behaviour. I think I took it for granted and didn't think it would happen but when it did it hit me like a rock, when it came down to the crunch it did hit me hard and I thought what am I going to do with my life. I have high hopes for my future and I have lots of my life left and I don't want to waste it; I want to have a good time at college and I have a golden opportunity to do this in year 10.

I hope I haven't blown this, I wish to have a good job when I am older and be able to provide for myself with money and have a nice place to live with no help from my parents, so I can prove to myself I can achieve things. Many people have told me that I will be nothing when I am older; I just want this chance to prove these people wrong for them and myself.

I do not want to end up like people I know who live off benefits and don't have a job. I know this is going to be a hard choice to make because of all the bad stuff I have done but I am willing to change now, I have learned my lesson and will try harder than ever.

It was hard to read Alice's letter; particularly that she's been told by – many! – people that she will be nothing; Alice doesn't start fights, or become aggressive, it is mostly stupid things like uniform and backchat that got her in trouble, and she's got the potential to be anything, if she's really willing to try for it. For Alice, I really do hope Northview accept her back – I think the UEEC might reinforce negative views Alice has of herself, plus she will definitely not have the worst rap-sheet there, which could be a bad influence on her.

Letter handed to me by Ms Hyde at Northview

24 January

Dear Mrs Tran and the board of Governors,

We are writing to ask you to reconsider the school's recent decision to permanently exclude Alice.

We are requesting this for two main reasons: firstly, because there has been a well–documented context to her problems which has been largely outside her control, namely a very difficult long–term family situation which has inevitably had a major impact on her young life.

Our differences as parents have resulted in many appearances in court regarding custody and access over a seven–year period. The last twelve months have been particularly difficult for Alice with court cases in March, June and early September in the first week of school, interviews with her Guardian from Cafcass throughout the summer holidays and the school is aware that she has been visited in school on several occasions by Child Legal Guidance. In addition, we had two close family bereavements during 2007.

Secondly, Alice has had undiagnosed learning difficulties over much of her early school life, which we feel have played themselves out in her behaviour, compounded by events in her life. In December 2006, it was reported by an Education Psychologist that Alice's reading ability was four years behind average. We know that being asked to read out loud in front of the class can be a terrifying ordeal for a dyslexic child, and we felt (for a long time prior to her exclusion) that this was a possible cause of her class avoidance at times, and her acting out.

We feel that had there been some support in assessing her ability to read and in quantifying her possible dyslexia at an earlier point, there could have been a programme put in place much earlier to assist her.

It is fair to say that despite numerous requests over a period of years for learning support and counselling for Alice, such assistance really only began in Jan/Feb 07.

From speaking with a children's association, I have been told that full statutory tests for dyslexia could have been performed without delay had I requested 'statutory assessments' in writing. On many occasions over the years, I have asked for 'full' tests but there has never been any action.

Alice is now in her third year at Northview Grove and still has not had these tests, which from our perspective seem essential in eliminating possible causes of her current reading/comprehension and behavioural issues. I am sure that a review at least every 12 months would help quantify her ongoing level.

Literacy, reading, comprehension and maths are all areas where Alice has needed additional guidance. There is well–documented evidence to support the fact that children with learning difficulties, in particular where these go undiagnosed and/or unsupported, are frequently connected with behavioural problems. We feel that Alice's lack of achievement and the varied support she has received in these areas have contributed to her lack of motivation and ultimately, in part at least, to the current situation.

It is important to us, and certainly for Alice's future, that she eventually learns to take responsibility for her own actions. Possibly she does need a fresh start in a new learning environment. We recognise that this will not be easy and that, regardless of your decision here, her behavioural and learning problems are issues that will need to be discussed at length with whoever takes on responsibility for her future education.

However, in mid-November '07 I wrote to Horizon Academy to look at the possibility of Alice transferring school. On about the 18th December, I received a reply to say that they were full and Alice could be put on a waiting list, which I have done.

This week I have spoken with a family education support group and from looking at the educational guidelines there could have been a possible fresh start at a new school through an internal managed move. This option of an internal managed move was never discussed.

We had hoped Alice would have been able to go to the PRU (pupil referral units) and we were surprised and disappointed to have been told that Alice did not meet the criteria. From looking at the government guidelines and discussions with the support group, I cannot understand why she does not meet the criteria and would respectfully request reasoning behind this especially as I received no correspondence. Also, it is only an option for children up to the end of year nine and as such is a timely option for Alice.

At one of Alice's integration meetings in November, Mr Garrett said that if Alice could manage to keep on track until the end of year 9, in year 10 she would then have the option of 2 days at college, 1 day work experience and 2 days in school. This is what Alice was working towards and I had felt that this was the one option that seemed to offer an ideal solution. Naturally the permanent exclusion would prevent this from taking place. I can see that Alice has got so off track that she needs the almost one to one support, firm boundaries and small classes.

I feel that there are many occasions over the past year when conflict could have been avoided through more communication between staff – e.g. an email was sent in January 07 to all teachers about Alice's reading ability. In her summer exams, I managed to get her a reader, she sat with a small group of people like herself in a supported learning environment and there appeared to be no disruption. I had no idea that when it came to the winter exams that she would be put in the main school hall with no reader and this naturally led to conflict.

I feel that the school have tried many options, and thank them for this, but there has been a lack of consistency and continuity in areas of support. Also, having read the government guidelines it is apparent that there has been a lack of communication with parents and no opportunity for parental input to develop clear strategies. In early November, it was documented by the school that Alice was on the verge of permanent exclusion, and yet the multi-agency pastoral meeting letter arrived a month later with a meeting scheduled for the 30 January, exactly three months later. Surely this meeting was of great urgency and should have taken place before the end of the Autumn term.

Yesterday when I went to UEEC, I was appalled to discover that the school had made no mention of my name on the records provided and as a result UEEC never sent a letter to enable me to attend this important appointment; Mrs Delgado at UEEC was very apologetic. This is illustrative of the lack of communication from the school and as a parent I fail to see how I can participate fully in supporting my children to the best of my ability when I'm not kept informed.

Finally, Alice does have many good qualities that no doubt have failed to show themselves often in the school context; see past reports for art, RE, drama and geography. But she has not had an easy young life, and she is still only thirteen. For these reasons, we hope you are able to see something beyond the wilful and unruly child that presents on the surface, and to give her a final opportunity to redeem something from this situation and to move forwards.

Thank you for your consideration of this matter, I have tried to write this letter jointly but revert to first person where applicable.

Yours sincerely,

(Ack, sorry. It doesn't feel good to have Ruth write on my behalf.)

While I fully stand behind Alice receiving the dyslexia test and additional support from school, Ruth manages to make it out that there is something wrong with Alice and that the problem stems from her, which is just not the case. Up until around the middle of her second year of secondary school, Alice was doing well; receiving house points and letters home commending her work. Even the letters from Northview only indicate certain lessons or teachers where Alice would be disruptive. What Alice needed, at the start of her pushing boundaries, was a united front from Ruth and myself.

I continue to find it difficult; the root of which I would say is symptoms of Ruth's mental health condition – saying things and not remembering; mood swings; confused trains of thought. To this day I believe Ruth needs support, and this would reflect positively on our children too.

(Compared to the kinds of letters I receive from Ruth, I was surprised at how rational this was – I wonder if this is one of Mrs Mason's commissions.)

From Northview Grove

24 January

Dear Mr Marlo,

Re: Permanent Exclusion of Alice Marlo

The meeting of the governing body at the Northview Grove on 24 January 2008 considered the decision by the Headteacher Mrs Tran, to permanently exclude your daughter, Alice. The governing body carefully considered the representations made and all the available evidence. The governing body appreciated the written statement provided by the parents and the letter from Alice, but feel that a decision to overturn the exclusion would not be in the best interests of the school or of other students. The governing body has therefore decided to uphold Alice's exclusion.

The reasons for the governing body's decision are as follows:

The governing body is satisfied that there is a sufficient body of evidence to indicate that Alice's behaviour has repeatedly breached the school's behaviour policy.

The governing body note the desire of the parents to seek a statement on behavioural grounds and their belief that this should have been done earlier, but find that the school has taken all reasonable advice from external agencies and believe that this would not have changed the outcome.

Advice from Learning Assistance is that the route to this assessment would have been through co–operation with the Behaviour Support Services Tutor and Educational Psychologists, which was not forthcoming on Alice's part.

The evidence presented by the school leads us to believe that they have taken every reasonable available step to accommodate and support Alice, but with no demonstrable improvement in outcome.

You have the right to appeal against this decision. If you wish to appeal, please notify the Independent Appeal team. You must set out the reasons for your appeal in writing, and may also include reference to any disability discrimination claim you may wish to make.

An appeal would be heard by an Independent Appeal Panel, who will rehear all the facts of the case – if you have fresh evidence to present to the panel you may do so. The panel must meet no later than the 15ᵗʰ school day after the date on which your appeal is lodged.

In determining your appeal, the panel can make one of three decisions: they may uphold your child's exclusion; they may direct your child's reinstatement in school, either immediately or by a particular date; or they may decide that the exclusion should not have taken place, but that reinstatement in the school is not in the best interests of all concerned.

I would advise you contact the Advisory Centre for Education (ACE) – an independent national advice centre for parents of children in state schools who offer information and support.

The arrangements currently being made for Alice's education will continue for the time being. However, new arrangements to provide full–time education for Alice are being made and Mr Milner will liaise with you shortly about these arrangements.

Yours sincerely,

The Junction

25 January

Dear Alice,

I am writing to you to introduce myself. My name is Stephanie Jones and I work for the Junction. I spoke to your dad about some extra support for you if you would like it. He was going to ask you to contact me, however I haven't heard from you.

I have enclosed some information about what we do at the Junction and what we can offer. This might help make up your mind about getting some extra help.

We do support young people to access the right type of education and I know from your dad this seems to be an issue. If you would like to have a chat about this or any other problem, I would be more than happy to see you.

Please feel free to call me on the number disclosed.

I hope to hear from you soon.

Regards,

From the Council

25 January

Dear Mr Marlo,

I have been advised that the Governor's Disciplinary Committee of Northview Grove upheld the Headteacher's decision to permanently exclude Alice.

You have the right to appeal to an Independent Appeal Panel against this decision. Your letter should be received by 22nd February 2008 and must include the grounds for your appeal.

Yours sincerely,

Dean Marlo

Disagreements

25/26 January

Friday 25th
My phone rang at 3pm and it was Alice, stating her mother is busy on Saturday so she is going to sleep at home tomorrow night. I reminded Alice we still needed to talk about home, school and the meeting with Dana Henderson, from Connexions, plus a letter came from Ms Jones, but she said she had to go.

In the evening, I was watching Lara and Hayley play a PlayStation game in the living room. Alice came home and asked for her pocket money. I said to Alice that she can't avoid talking about her behaviour and then come in asking for money, and that I do not want to stop her pocket money but she had to show that she was getting back on track, and her behaviour around the house and towards family members had to change.

Alice replied, 'This is why I do not want to live here! I suppose Lara is getting my pocket money,' slamming the front door as she left.

At 8.30pm, Ruth called and stated, 'You are a terrible father to Alice!'

Before she could get into a full rant, I interrupted Ruth and told her Alice is well aware that I do not want to stop her pocket money, but with incidences such as at school and Lara's bracelet, it is up to Alice. Ruth and I disagreed for several minutes, and when she started to get more abusive, I said goodbye.

Saturday 26th
Midday, Ruth rang and stated that she would not be able to take Alice to her UEEC class on Tuesday or Wednesday, but she will pick Alice up after each class finishes. She went on to say that if I could not make it Tuesday and Wednesday, she would get someone else to do it. Replying that I would be available, Ruth stated, 'Alice is staying at mine tonight.'

5.30pm, I let Alice and Hannah through the front door; I asked Alice where her key was and Alice brushed past me. I said I hoped she was not coming home just to be rude. In response, Alice replied, 'You know all about being nasty.'

When I asked Alice what she meant, Alice said, 'Does my pocket money mean anything to you?'

Instead of re-treading the argument Alice tried to have with me the other day, I said, 'Let's not go down this road, I have only asked you to be reasonable.'

Walking upstairs with Hannah, Alice replied 'Whatever.'

Several minutes later, they returned, and I walked into the hall to ask Alice what she is doing tonight. In response, Alice said, 'What are you up to? What is Lara getting?'

I said, 'If you haven't got anything nice to say, then go to your room.'

Opening the front door, Alice replied, 'Don't worry, I'm leaving.'

As Alice was walking out, she turned around with more abuse about Lara; I told Alice that her attitude was unnecessary. Alice went in the direction of her mother's with Hannah behind her.

Lateness

28/29 January

Monday 28th

As Alice is at her mother's, it was organised for Ruth to take Alice to the UEEC.

Hayley has an open day at college and said she had not told her mother about it because she didn't want her mother causing a scene. I respected Hayley's choice, and to be quite honest with you, I was relieved.

I went with Hayley to her college and we explored the various different studies she could pursue. After an hour or so of walking around, Hayley had viewed all the subjects she wanted, and we headed into the carpark to go home, discussing what had interested her. Ruth appeared and stalked over to us, saying she should have been informed about the open day and invited, as she is 'Hayley's mother'.

Hayley said to her mother it was her choice, and please don't cause a scene, while in the meantime I got into the car. I know it is not cordial to say nothing to Ruth, but I didn't want my input to exacerbate the situation, as Hayley had made clear it was her decision. It didn't take long for Hayley to get into the car.

Later, Hayley came in to the living room and said to me that she was going to go to her mother's to explain why she hadn't told her about the college day, and depending on how it goes, she might sleepover.

At 10pm, I got a text from Hayley saying she was staying and goodnight.

Tuesday 29th

Northview Grove informed me Hayley did not arrive at school until 9.45am; my guess is another late night.

Just pulling up to Riverbank to collect Lara, Alice called saying, 'I can't stay in this class, I've had enough.'

There was only half an hour of Alice's lesson left, so I suggested she hold on for today and we'd discuss with Mrs Delgado for the next day. Alice stated that she was half way to the bus station and had called her mother but she couldn't pick her up.

I told Alice that I was in the playground with Lara now, and then we would be on our way.

Once in the car, Alice requested to be dropped at her mother's; I was worried about Alice being home alone for an indefinite amount of time, and asked if her mother would be there.

Alice said, 'Yes, she finished work at 2. She is going to phone Mrs Delgado when she gets in and explain that the hours 1.30pm to 3.30pm is too long for me.'

I wanted to laugh or cry out loud, but refrained from doing so, and dropped Alice at Ruth's – her car was on the drive.

I understand Alice needing time to reintegrate into the routine of school, however the lessons aren't even structured in a traditional way; if Alice is expecting to only do one hour a day, we'll spend more time getting her there and back, and I don't think it will help her focus any better. This is a slippery slope wherein Alice frequently gets her own way, when sometimes she needs to push through a difficult situation for herself. Over the weeks and months, no matter how hard I have tried, I still can't grasp how to get through to Alice.

I took Hayley to her tutoring at 6pm; Lara's teacher was away.

On the 31st of January, I wrote to Ruth:

Thank you for your letter of confirmation of your holiday arrangements with the children to the Gran Canaria; as requested I will drop the children to yours at 4.30pm on Tuesday the 12th February.

You stated you have spoken to Alice and given her a week to decide where she is living, which I agree needs to be sorted for Alice to settle down.

Please find enclosed, a cheque for £12.10 to cover for Alice's Child Benefit, from the 28th January to the 4th February.

Yours sincerely…

From MP

31 January

Dear Mr Marlo,
Thank you for your letter updating me on your case. May I suggest that we meet to discuss this further?
Please phone Beverley to arrange an appointment at my Advice Bureau.
Best wishes.
Yours sincerely,

Dean Marlo

Trying as a parent

2 - 6 February

Saturday 2nd
Midday, Ruth rang and notified me of the days that she is taking and picking up Alice from the UEEC. She also stated that Alice is getting back into a routine (I can only hope) and I am to pick Alice up from the UEEC on Monday – Alice will let me know if she finishes at 3pm or 3.30pm. This is the same time as Lara finishes school, so Alice will have to wait until Lara and I can get across town to pick her up; this in itself gives Alice the opportunity to mess around or leave before I arrive.

Monday 4th
Alice called, asking me to collect her at 3.30pm.
After picking Lara up from school, I dropped her home with Hayley on the way and drove to the UEEC. I found Alice with two friends standing outside the centre; Alice asked if we could give one of her friends a lift home and if her other friend can come over, and we drop her home later, if her mum agrees. (The friend was on the phone.) With the go ahead, I agreed to the taxi service I had been appointed. Alice and her friend went out when we arrived back home.
Leaving Hayley and Lara in the living room watching a film, we dropped Alice's friend home. On the way back, Hayley called Alice and after some discussion, Alice asked if we could pick Hayley up and drop them both to their mother's. I said that's fine but it's a school night so they need to be sensible. Alice stated Hayley told her their mother would bring them home at 9.30pm.
We picked Hayley up and I dropped them off.
As Hayley and Alice came in and said goodnight, they told me that Alice was sleeping in Hayley's room tonight. At 11.15pm, Alice woke me stating that she could not sleep and her mother was on her way round to pick her up. Knowing that saying anything would only serve to start an argument, and Alice is leaving either way, I waited with Alice for Ruth to arrive, then checked in on Hayley and Lara, who were both fast asleep.
(In stable households, the toing-and-froing wouldn't cause an issue; it would be lovely for the children to freely spend time with either parent. However, nothing about the situation at Ruth's provides consistency or stability for anyone.)

Tuesday 5th
I had a conversation with Miss Horton, a teacher from UEEC, and informed her that Alice had an appointment with 'Connexions' at 1pm on Thursday. Miss Horton was very pleased, and confirmed that she would encourage Alice to attend this meeting.
Mid-morning, Alice called and said her mother is dropping her round, and will be back to pick her up in an hour or two.
Just before 12pm, Alice's phone rang; she talked with her mother for several minutes. After ending the call, she asked me if I would drop her to her mother's, which, as I was not at work, I did.

As I was preparing dinner, I phoned Alice to see what she was up to, daring to bring up her agreeing to settle down into a routine. Alice told me that her mother has said she can stay tonight but didn't know about the rest of the week.

(I despair again. However, it is not Alice's choice but Ruth's parenting that is the problem. In the absence of any assistance being given to Ruth over the years, as I've tried to do, it seems I am unable to help Alice, even though that is the only action I can try to take. I don't want to point fingers or go back to the Family Courts because the situation we have with Alice, under normal circumstances, would have never arisen or could have been sorted out by reasonable parents.

So:

I can't go to the Family Courts, because they don't know how to handle the situation.

I can't get through to Alice, because she's nearly 14 and on her own crusade.

I can't reason with Ruth, because she has bipolar disorder and her judgement varies from day to day.)

Wednesday 6th

At breakfast, Hayley told me that she was sleeping round her mother's tonight but would return after school for parent's evening with me.

I arranged for Lara to have tea with a friend, and Lara's friend's mum kindly offered to drop Lara home at 7.30pm. After school, Hayley texted, saying she was at her mother's and would be home at 5pm/5.30pm – our first appointment was at 6pm.

In my suit and trying to avoid Sully for fear of being covered in fur, I waited until 5.45pm before calling Hayley; Hayley asked me to pick her up from her mother's, then bring her home so that she could get dressed.

I drove to Ruth's and when Hayley got in the car, I said to her that this was not the way to approach her parent's evening, with 15 minutes until our appointment.

We drove home and Hayley got changed; we managed to make the 6pm appointment with Hayley's maths teacher. Ruth turned up 5 minutes late and sat down with us. After speaking to the teacher, we left the classroom and I saw Alice in the corridor. I said hello and asked Alice if she should be on school premises.

Alice replied, 'I don't know.'

Figuring it was better if Alice stayed with us – I didn't know if Ruth had brought Alice with her or if Alice was here of her own volition – we all walked to the next appointment; as we did so, I reminded Alice that she had a meeting with Dana from 'Connexions' tomorrow.

Alice said, 'Our mother told me that Connexions is for nutters and I am not going.'

In disbelief, I turned to Ruth and said she should be encouraging Alice to go to the meeting, as it will do Alice some good to talk to someone.

Ruth replied, 'I work with the people that are sent to that place and it is not for Alice.'

I'm not really sure what job Ruth does, only that she is an expert – Connexions is there for teenagers who need help, and while Alice still hasn't contacted Ms Jones from the Junction, I believed I could get her to go to this meeting. I asked Alice again if she would please meet with Dana.

Ruth stated, 'She is not going.'

This conversation continued in and out of the appointments with most of Hayley's teachers. This is Hayley's parents evening, we shouldn't be discussing Alice right now and Ruth should not be telling Alice organisations there to help teenagers having problems are for 'nutters'. It is incredible, because I literally did not see this coming, and yet you would think with my battle scars I would have learned to expect the unexpected by now.

I said to Ruth that when I informed Miss Horton (Alice's teacher at the UEEC) of the appointment, she was keen for Alice to attend.

Scoffing, Ruth repeated, 'Alice is not fucking going.'

Realising Ruth had managed to be confrontational throughout Hayley's parents evening, I felt the need to leave. Despite having one more teacher to see – it was only P.E. – I looked to the heavens and decided that I'd had enough of Ruth's attitude; I apologised to Hayley, who was going home with Ruth anyway, and decided to go.

If I put to the side the fact that tonight should have been about Hayley and her education, it bothers me that Ruth has put Alice off seeking help. This was the first stepping stone we've really had for Alice, wherein she could confide in someone, maybe address any issues she's having, and fill that gap that I am sadly unable to, and from what I can see, her mother is unable to understand.

As Lara was getting ready for bed, Hayley and Alice came home; they both went into their bedrooms to gather some belongings, as Hayley informed me she and Alice were going swimming with their mother. When I queried swimming at this time on a school night, 8.30pm, Hayley and Alice said goodbye and that they would see me tomorrow.

(It does feel like being in a family sitcom, and I'm standing here waiting for the laugh track.)

Appointment 'Connexions'.

7 February

While Lara was eating breakfast, I called the UEEC to explain that, as far as I knew, Alice was not going to attend her appointment with Connexions and therefore should be coming into the centre today. I was speaking to Mrs Delgado, but she told me she was about to go into a meeting so had to go before we could discuss other options of support for Alice.

I dropped Lara to school and called Connexions, explaining why I believed Alice was not going to make the appointment. I asked if there was someone they could suggest I talk to about my concerns for Alice's wellbeing at the present time; they stated they would have Dana phone me.

Later that morning, Miss Horton from UEEC returned my call, and we discussed Alice's other options for support. Not long after that call ended, Dana from Connexions rang and said Ms Hyde had been into the centre this morning, and explained that it was vital Alice does not miss any time out of her classes at the UEEC, as Alice's education has suffered for too long. Dana stated that she agreed and suggested that she would make an appointment with Alice at a later date, if Alice still wished to meet.

While in principle yes, I agree, I said to Dana that Alice missing one two-hour session would not have been the end of the world and I explained my concern that this is an extension of the instability being placed in Alice's life; how Alice had said the night before her mother had told her Connexions was for 'nutters'.

Dana stated that if Alice did not want to come it was up to her... Which is sort the crux of the problem we are having, and I tried again to explain that Alice's reluctance has been created out of the perception she could be a 'nutter' if she goes there. (It's like Ruth propaganda, of course Alice isn't going to feel encouraged.) I am genuinely worried about my daughter's welfare and stability, and Ruth's comments are, I believe, a sign of poor understanding with regard to what Alice needs.

I asked Dana if I could come in at Alice's appointment time and just talk about the situation and my concerns; Dana replied Connexions is an organisation for children and they do not get involved with parents to that extent. It was a long shot, and I told Dana that I understood, but could she suggest any organisation who may be able to help. Kindly, Dana gave me several names and said she would try and make an appointment with Alice at the UEEC.

Money talks

8 February

Pulling up to collect Alice from the UEEC, Alice and six other children, who were waiting to be picked up, were standing in the carpark being watched by two teachers. I said hello to Alice and she jumped in the car. I got out to introduce myself to the teachers; one explained she was one of Alice's teachers, and I asked how Alice is doing. She said there are times when Alice tries but, on most occasions, Alice simply refuses to do her lessons and, when it suits, she will just get up and walk out of the class.

As I drove us home, I tried to get Alice to talk about how she's feeling and suggested the possibility of Dana from Connexions meeting her at the UEEC, but Alice stared resolutely out the window, not answering. I moved the conversation to what Alice was up to tonight, and thought I would leave the discussion about where she is going to live for another day.

Finally, Alice said, 'I have had a hard day, so don't talk to me about it. Can you drop me at my mother's?'

I said I would prefer her to come home so we can actually have a conversation about any of these things, across the months that it has been, and she cannot keep skipping the subject with me. Alice did not reply. I dropped Alice off at Ruth's; I said goodbye and that I love her. Alice got out of the car.

Hayley came home from school with a young lad called Conner, whom she introduced as her boyfriend. He seemed polite and they got on well together; I'm pleased for Hayley that she found someone she likes.

At 6.30pm, Alice came home and asked if she could have her pocket money. I told Alice previously, that she would get her pocket money back if she tried with Lara, at the UEEC and attended her appointment with Connexions.

Alice gave me some verbal abuse and walked out of the front door.

Another week, another letter to Ruth:

Please find enclosed, a cheque for £12.10 to cover for Alice's Child Benefit from the 5th February to the 11th February.

Yours sincerely...

From MP Rowe

8 February

Dear Mr Marlo,
Advice Bureau – 14th February
I am pleased to confirm an appointment has been made for you at Mr Rowe's Advice Bureau on 14th February at 9.30am.

Please bring with you any relevant documents or reference numbers which may be of assistance. It is important to contact Mr Rowe's office if you are unable to make this appointment or experience any difficulties as there is a great demand to see Mr Rowe, and others could be offered your appointment if you are not able to attend.

The Advice Bureau is held at a former church hall – a map is enclosed for your assistance.

Best wishes.

Yours sincerely…

Support (Connexions) – re: Alice

11 February

Dear Mr Marlo,
If I haven't heard from you or Ms Hyde within 14 days of the date of this letter, I will close her file. She can always contact us again in the future if she needs to.

Dear Alice,
I was sorry not to see you for your initial appointment here last Thursday.
I spoke to both your mum and your dad and they explained that you've just started at UEEC and you felt the time of the appointment would interfere with this. They also said you're not sure about coming to our Support Centre anyway.
That's fine Alice, young people are free to make their own choice about using our service or not. To help you decide, I could come along to see you at UEEC before your lessons start one day. I could explain a bit more about us and answer any questions you might have. Then you could decide whether you wanted to give our service a go.
If you'd like me to do this, please ask your dad or mum to call me. I will then call UEEC to arrange a day and time.
Best wishes,
Dana

Happy Holidays

12/13 February

Tuesday 12th

In the morning, Hayley came into the kitchen and stated that she was going round her mother's at 2pm and Ruth requested I drop Lara to her at 4.30pm, which I did.

Wednesday 13th

At 9am, I received a text from Alice which read, 'Hi Dad, sorry for this year I am going to get back on track. I will miss you. Love Alice'.

An hour later, Hayley called and said she had been arrested last night. Shocked, I asked Hayley what had happened.

Hayley replied, 'It was for swearing at an officer in the High Street, and our mother wants to talk to you.'

Handing the phone over, Ruth explained that Hayley was lucky she had only received a caution from the police. I asked Ruth why she had not called me and she said, 'I went to the police station but they were busy so I had to go back. It was too late and there was nothing you could've done. I'm very upset with her because she knows we're going on holiday.'

I wondered why Hayley would have been out so late, and asked what time she went to the station.

Ruth replied, 'First I went to the police station at 8pm and again at 10.30pm.

In response, I said that 8pm wasn't late, and she should have let me know. Getting agitated, she stated she had packing to do and needed to prepare for their holiday; she had told Hayley that she could phone me at the airport in the morning.

I repeated that she should have informed me and before she put the phone down, Ruth said, 'It was Hayley's right and I am informing you now.'

Dean Marlo

Dear Mr Rowe

14 February

Once again, I find my children and myself subjected to the consequences of the symptoms of a parent's reoccurring mental health problems, which have not been fully recognised or addressed by either the Family Courts nor their appointed experts. As you are aware, for me this has continually been about the welfare and stability of my children.

As evidence shows, the care I provide for my children I have had to fight for on every occasion within the Family Court System. In fact, my children and I have been on a dishonest and immoral ride, and I ask you please to find an organisation who will act responsibly towards the injustices faced, over many years, by my family. I would like to see ministers recognise and acknowledge the failures of the Family Courts, in order for improvements to be made.

Months before my daughter Alice was permanently excluded from Northview Grove School, Mrs Tran, the Headteacher, asked me why I could not go back to the Family Courts to address where Alice was living and possibly Alice's behaviour. I explained there would be little point, as the first thing that would be presented to the judge by Ms Hyde's counsel would be the inaccurate and misleading Guardian's report.

I reminded Mrs Tran that I had previously brought to her attention the false information provided to the Guardian on behalf of Northview Grove School, which stated 'Mr Marlo refuses to get involved in any attempts by the school to address Alice's behaviour and will not attend the school for meetings'. I find it ironic that the person who had relayed the misleading information was in one of the meetings which I had attended at Northview Grove School, where I expressed my concerns for Alice, and also that we were coming up to proceedings after seven years of involvement, which the whole family hoped would end the uncertainty within all our lives.

I have found little understanding to the gravity of the misleading statements within this report and the devastating effect it may have on our family in the future.

Lara has the opportunity to not spend her entire life involved with Cafcass, Guardians and psychologists, whereas Hayley and Alice have sadly spent half their lives caught up in the process.

I do not believe it is acceptable to deny a person the right to have inaccurate information removed from a report.

Yours respectfully...

Appeals Panel

18/22 February

18 February

Dear Mr Marlo and Ms Hyde,

I am writing to acknowledge receipt of your appeal against the decision to exclude Alice from Northview Grove School.

Details of the date and the venue of your appeal will be sent to you in due course.

You may wish to provide more information in addition to that already supplied with your appeal. Please note that this must be received by this office no later than 6 school days before the scheduled hearing date.

If you intend to call witnesses at the hearing then you must let me have their names, addresses and phone numbers immediately.

You can, if you wish, choose to be legally represented or accompanied by a friend at the hearing. Again, I would need the name, address and phone number of your representative. You should also advise whether Alice will be attending the hearing.

Yours sincerely,

22 February

Dear Mr Marlo and Ms Hyde,

Further to my previous letter dated 18th February 2008, with regard to the permanent exclusion of Alice from Northview Grove School.

The appeal hearing will be at 10am on Friday 7th March 2008, at the community centre, by the local motorway. Please let me know immediately if you are unable to attend on this date.

Yours sincerely,

From MP

22 February

Dear Mr Marlo,

Further to your latest appointment at my Advice Bureau, as promised I have written to Cafcass to organise a meeting – at which I would seek to accompany you – to discuss the continuing matters of your concern. I enclose a copy of my letter for your information. I will contact you again when I get a response. Clearly the situation has been allowed to drag on for far too long, with 'the system' failing you on a regular basis. I admire your perseverance in the face of so much unhappiness; I am sure that I would have given up long ago.

Please be assured that I will continue to do what I can to assist you, and your three daughters.

Best wishes.

Yours sincerely,

22 February

I write on behalf of my constituent Mr Marlo who has three daughters aged 10, 13 and 15. I have been seeking to assist Mr Marlo for several years, involving making numerous representations on his behalf and last year having a meeting in London with a government minister.

Putting it starkly, 'the system' has failed – and continues to fail – my constituent and his family.

I therefore write to request, please, a meeting with you and Mr Marlo so that we can discuss his situation. Hopefully, we may between us find a way of taking things forward in a positive way. I look forward to hearing from you.

Many thanks.

Yours sincerely,

Hayley, and Ruth CB

25/26 February

25th

At the meeting with Hayley's teachers about what college and career she is interested in, Ruth handed me a copy of a 'record of reprimand' from the police, regarding Hayley's behaviour before their holiday to Gran Canaria.

Offence(s):
Words/behaviour – harassment alarm distress
On 12/02/2008 Hayley Marlo used threatening, abusive or insulting words or behaviour or disorderly behaviour within the hearing or sight of a person likely to be caused harassment, alarm or distress thereby CONTRARY TO SECTION 5(1) AND (6) OF THE PUBLIC ORDER ACT 1986.

With the children back from their holiday, I sat down with Hayley to talk about what's going on with her behaviour and her future. Hayley has been spending the majority of her time with Conner, either in the living room, her room or out in the evenings, which I hope is not the cause of her trouble with the police.

26th

I wrote to Ruth:

Please find enclosed, a cheque for £12.10 to cover for Alice's Child Benefit from the 11th February to the 18th February.

Yours sincerely…

Cafcass to MP

5 March

Dear Mr Marlo,
Please find enclosed a copy of the acknowledgement I have received from Cafcass.
They are currently investigating this matter. I will contact you again when I receive a full response.
Best wishes.
Yours sincerely…

3 March

Dear Mr Rowe,
Thank you for your letter dated 22 February 2008 received in this office on 26 February 2008.
I have been asked to acknowledge receipt and let you know that it would not be appropriate to meet with you as this would prejudice the manager's position in the event of a review. I have therefore forwarded your letter to Mr Ivy, our Regional Complaints Manager, who will formally respond to your request for a meeting.
Yours sincerely,
Governance Support Officer

Ruth CB

6 March

Please find enclosed, a cheque for £24.20 to cover for Alice's Child Benefit, from the 18th February to the 3rd March.

Yours sincerely…

Dean Marlo

Ruth's notes

This letter was handed to me by Ruth at Alice's appeal, on the 7th March.

From reading the paperwork from Northview Grove School, it appears they have been extremely supportive and have tried, unsuccessfully, to support Alice in school, and have worked tirelessly to avoid permanently excluding her.

It appears Alice entered NGS at year 7 with no SEN provision or concerns from her primary school, Riverbank School.

In her summary statement (section 1, page 3) Mrs Tran acknowledges 'NGS was aware of complex family issues'. At the end of year 7, Alice's report records 9/14 'excellents' or 'goods' for effort; the interim report for year 8 records 11/14 'excellents' or 'goods' for effort. It is only by the end of year 8 does Alice's story start to change when this goes down to 5/14 and the interim report for year 9 is 5/14.

Why the change, what has happened? Could the changes be related to emotional difficulties? Along with these changes are multiple reports for inappropriate behaviour.

From reading the paperwork, it appears the school have attempted to tackle the inappropriate behaviour, but have not worked too hard to discover the underlying causes of this sudden change in attitude and approach from Alice. There appears to be little acknowledgement by NGS that Alice's changes could be related to her emotional stress and turmoil the family situation is causing her.

Emotional and behavioural difficulties are linked together. EBD (or BESD) is a term used when a child's ongoing behavioural difficulties appear to have their root cause in emotional or possibly social problems, deep rooted emotional difficulties may manifest in disruptive behaviour or in unusual quietness. EBD's can be so complex that outside professionals need to be involved to help the child cope with daily living and learning.

EBD (BESD) is a learning difficulty where the regularity and seriousness of a pupil's challenging behaviour is greater than average. The child may not be able to control their feelings so their learning is disrupted.

Key characteristics of EBD's are when the child:

May find it difficult to form friendships

Appear to be preoccupied and therefore find it difficult to get involved with activities

Have difficulties to keep on task

Often become tearful or throw tantrums for no apparent reason.

Have low self-esteem and often become victims or bullies

Be excessively attention seeking through either negative behaviour or clinginess

Be aggressive and disruptive

Find it difficult to conform to classroom rules and routines

Underachieve in many areas of the school curriculum

Many of these characteristics could be related to Alice.

Schools and local authorities are required to offer support to students with BESD. BESD can be very difficult for adults to deal with emotionally. Many teachers have not been trained to deal with the challenging behaviour.

Apart from the statement above written by Mrs Tran, the only other comment I can see recorded is in an email (page 9, section 1) where it asks for Alice to be put on the Educational Psychologists list to discuss her emotional state of mind. Written by hand also, 'Behaviour and emotional state (recommendation to seek further emotional support from outside agencies)'.

The EP visited on 14 September 2007 (page 10, section 1). An agreed action was to arrange 'anger management skills programme' for Alice – was this organised? There was plenty of time from September to January for this to happen. From the report, the EP appears to focus on Alice's current difficulties regarding conflicts with members of staff.

NGS had placed Alice on School Action, acknowledging the dyslexia and her learning difficulties along with the focus on the behaviour but with little acknowledgement of the emotional needs that could be causing the behaviour.

Did NGS at any time suggest involving social care or consider organising urgent counselling for Alice?

Has a Comment Assessment Framework form been completed for Alice? (This is a standard assessment for children with additional needs which can be used across all children's services.)

Have NGS staff had training to support pupils who are 'at risk' and displaying challenging behaviours? Was flexibility in the curriculum considered?

Children and young people have rights of their own, independent of those of their parents, guardians and carers. These rights should be recognised and respected. Where there is a conflict of interest between parents and children and in all decisions relating to the child's/young person's future, the child's interest must be given primary consideration.

The framework for the Assessment of Children in Need (Department of Health 2000) Levels of Vulnerability and Need would appear to place Alice at Level 3 – children with complex needs.

NGS considers they really had no option but to permanently exclude Alice from their school, was the event on the 4th January the final act and permanent exclusion is 'the last resort'?

If NGS had taken some other course of action on 4th January 2008, would this action have seriously harmed the education or welfare of the others in the school?

Has the permanent exclusion caused more harm to Alice than it will prevent other students experiencing?

With regard to supporting Alice, emotionally and educationally, I completely agree, but teachers are not parents and the challenging behaviours Alice displayed were rooted at home. If I try to enforce a boundary and Alice hides from responsibility at her mother's, who cannot seem to agree with me regarding a stable foundation of rules between us, she is going to go to school and apply the same principle, i.e. rules don't apply to me.

As Ruth's notes show, Alice was doing well, really well, up until the end of year 8; this coincided with when she started being picked up by her mother. I do not wish to cast any blame, but unless this aspect of Alice's behaviour pattern is addressed, there is not going to be much anyone can do.

I have tried to get Alice to speak to several organisations, and it truly upsets me that the courts have been involved so much and it has obviously had an overall effect on all of my children. This is not what I wanted for their childhoods at all. However, Alice has to do the talking part and I'm not sure how to help her if she won't talk to me, a counsellor or her teachers about what she needs.

From my MP

11 March

Dear Mr Marlo,
Please find enclosed a copy of the response I have received from Cafcass.
Hopefully you will find their comments to be of interest. If I can be of any further assistance, please do not hesitate to contact me again.
Best wishes.
Yours sincerely,

7 March

Dear Mr Rowe,
I am in receipt of your letter dated 22ⁿᵈ February 2008, addressed to the Cafcass Chief Executive concerning Mr Marlo. The letter has been forwarded to me to respond as the Regional Complaints Manager for Cafcass. In your letter to Mr Marlo, you suggest that a meeting with him may help to take things forward. The complex nature of this case and the previous history of Cafcass' involvement with Mr Marlo and his family would I feel militate against this being a productive course of action. I will attempt to give some reasons for this position.

In responding to you, I have spoken to the Service Manager for Cafcass, Ms Soto, who has a full working knowledge of the case. I have also read the correspondence and case records, including the welfare report submitted to the County Court on the 3ʳᵈ September 2007, regarding Mr Marlo's three daughters aged sixteen, thirteen and ten years old respectively.

To place this whole matter in some context, Mr Marlo has not made a formal complaint but requested that his concerns be treated as an 'insight and comment' upon Cafcass' services. I feel it is important to note that Cafcass have been involved with Mr Marlo and his family intermittently for several years, and there have been a number of reports prepared and Cafcass officers involved.

In June 2007, the court ordered that the children should be separately represented in the proceedings and hence a Guardian ad Litem from Cafcass was appointed, and they instructed a solicitor to act on behalf of the three girls. A Guardian is appointed to represent the children in cases where there are long running and difficult issues between their parents which have impacted upon their welfare. A Guardian is charged with representing the children formally through a solicitor and making an assessment of issues. This assessment is encompassed in a report which is used at a hearing before a judge when all parties are present and able to represent themselves.

Mr Marlo had some concerns about the content and quality of the report prepared by the Guardian in this case. He phoned the Service Manager, Ms Soto, on the 22ⁿᵈ October 2007 and at her request subsequently wrote and outlined his concerns. Ms Soto met with the Guardian to discuss her involvement and the content of her report. This led to amendments being made and a revised report being submitted to the court.

The issues before the court related to mother's applications to remove the children from the jurisdiction for a holiday in Australia during school term time, and a joint residence order. On the strength of the girls' views concerning these issues, the Guardian was able to deal with both matters in her report. Both issues were dealt with on September 5ᵗʰ 2007, by a consent order, that is, by agreement between the parties.

The outcome reflected and supported Mr Marlo's existing position that the children remained resident with him and that any holiday abroad should be in scheduled school holidays.

Mr Marlo was disappointed that the Guardian was not able to attend the hearing, but she was not available and the children were represented by their solicitor in any event. Following the hearing, the Guardian visited Mr Marlo twice at some length to discuss the report and the outcome of the proceedings. The Guardian also wrote a letter to Mr Marlo clarifying to outcome of their discussions.

Mr Marlo has subsequently spoken to Ms Soto by phone and said he feels 'let down' by the Family Justice System. He appeared to have expected more continuing social work support from Cafcass. But as an agency we do not have the remit or resource to provide continuing after court involvement. This is an area in which Cafcass is seeking to develop support services but at present we are unable to meet the expectations of families, particularly complex situations outside of our statutory obligations.

My overall assessment is that Mr Marlo has made representations about the service he has received from Cafcass and they have been responded to in an appropriate fashion. The report was amended and there were a number of discussions which allowed him to express his views and concerns.

I hope this information assists in your dealings with Mr Marlo, but if you have any further queries, please do not hesitate to contact me.

In respect of further representations from your constituents about the work of our agency, it would in my view be mutually beneficial if you were able to visit our local Cafcass office, and meet staff to discuss the challenges the service faces. At the present time, the team for your constituent is waiting for new premises to be refurbished and opened in an exciting new partnership with another child welfare agency. We anticipate moving into the premises towards the end of the summer and would welcome a visit from you to meet staff and discuss the work we do. If you would like to follow up this proposal, please let me know and I will keep you informed of developments.

Yours sincerely,

Mr Ivy

I appreciate the good press Mr Rowe attending would achieve, but I do feel that the invitation should have been written in a separate letter to the response to my letter about a report containing misleading and false information being filed at the Family Courts.

What is the point of a report if it doesn't say the truth?

This regional manager hasn't understood the gravity of the situation; I've had eight years of false information being presented as fact, which has put me under pressure to clarify the accusations, as well as having to attend court hearings for nearly a decade that have not ensured the welfare of my children.

I feel I have to continue to address my dissatisfaction with this report, as I am fully aware that at any future hearings, regardless of the overall recommendation, the misleading statements could be used to cloud whatever issue we may be having.

From the Appeal Panel

12/13 March

12 March

Dear Mr Marlo,

Further to my previous letter dated 18th February 2008, with regard to the permanent exclusion of Alice from Northview Grove School.

The appeal hearing was adjourned from 7th March and will now be heard at 9.30am on Tuesday 25th March 2008, at the community centre, by the local motorway.

Yours sincerely…

13 March

Dear Mr Marlo,

Further to my previous letter dated 12th March 2008, with regard to the permanent exclusion of Alice from Northview Grove School.

Due to unforeseen circumstances, the appeal hearing has been changed to 9.30am on Monday 21st April 2008, at the community centre, by the local motorway.

Yours sincerely…

That's nearly a whole month later! What about the child's education they're supposed to be considering in the mean time?

The last thing Alice needs is to stay out of mainstream school and remain in a setting where she is surrounded by other pupils who are non-conformist, and are likely excluded for worse things than Alice has been. I just don't see how it can benefit her education, to be influenced by other children with similar behavioural problems.

Connexions

14 March

Dear Mr Marlo,

As we haven't heard from your daughter Alice since we wrote to her on 11 February, we are assuming she has decided not to use our support service at the moment. That's fine, and we will now put her file away.

We can work with young people until they are 18 years old, so if Alice decides she would like any support in the future, please do not hesitate to get in touch.

Best wishes,

Build up

19 - 24 March

Wednesday 19th
Lara went for to tea at her mother's after school and at 8pm, she called to ask if she could stay. I said yes, and told her to have a good night.

Thursday 20th
While I was working, Mrs Hart rang to ask why Lara was not at school, and I informed her Lara stayed at her mother's last night. I called Ruth, who didn't answer, and had no choice but to assume Lara is falling down the same rabbit hole Alice did and Hayley has been lately; late nights at their mother's means a day off school.

Ruth stays up to the early hours and cannot get up in the morning; due to her mind-set, she is unable to comprehend that her behaviour is not normal - Ruth's routine is chaotic and self-serving. I am, as usual, appalled by Ruth's behaviour towards our children.

I do not think doctors or anyone can change Ruth's bipolar disorder, but it could be managed and better understood to support Ruth, protect our children and deescalate our family's position.

Sunday 23rd
At 7am, Alice phoned and asked if I was at work or at home, because she wanted to talk about something. I said I was at home and Alice walked over.

Alice informed me that she was on the pill. I asked Alice if it would be ok to make an appointment with her doctor, to make sure we are all on the same page about her health; Alice said there was no need, as her mother had spoken to the doctor and it was to help with heavy periods.

I reminded her if she needs anything, she only has to ask, like a hug, a trip to the pharmacy or a hot chocolate. Alice smiled and gave me a hug.

Monday 24th
I wrote to Ruth:
Re: School holidays 31st March – 11th April 2008.
For your clarity, your next contact will start on the 5th April at 6pm until 14th April midday.
Yours sincerely…

Schedules for Ruth

1 April

Please find enclosed the schedule for 2008/2009.

If you have any requests, would you please put this in writing and I shall be happy to look into it.

Yours sincerely…

Dean Marlo

Surprise!

4 April

I was in the office when Hayley came in and announced Conner had proposed to her, and they are engaged. I was a shocked, even though he is a nice lad, because they're both so young and have only been seeing each other a few months. (Sure, he's been over for dinner and we've gotten the dart board out for a couple of rounds, and he's got a good eye for triple 1… It all seems a bit sudden.)

Not wanting to dishearten Hayley in anyway, but feeling like I had to say, I expressed that I was happy for her but that I did not see the rush in them getting engaged, when they could just enjoy each other's company without that pressure. In response, Hayley stated she has already said yes, and has made her mind up.

Understanding this was her choice, I told her again I was happy for her and that if she needs to talk to me, she knows she can.

Hayley said, 'Thanks Dad, love you.'

I offered to have Conner round for dinner to celebrate, and congratulate them both. Hayley said she'd organise something, then flew out the door to go inform her mother.

Hayley called and said that her mother is thrilled; she has said they can have an engagement party at hers tonight, which Hayley is excited for and is now arranging.

Dear Mr MP Rowe

5 April

Once again, I would like to thank you for your efforts and commitment over many years with my family's case and myself, which has always been much appreciated.

Despite your efforts, I feel that I am left with no alternative but to sadly resign from my involvement with the Family Courts. This I believe is solely owing to the position and pressure that the Family Courts and the legal system have continually placed on my family and its dynamics.

Can it not be understood that I have had enough? Enough of trying and having it thrown verbally and physically back in my face, in and out of the Family Courts. Enough of the discrimination, conduct and performance that I have received while representing my children's welfare and stability.

I have never received acknowledgment or confirmation of the effort and commitment that I have shown my three children their entire lives. In truth, I have constantly tried to get along with Ms Hyde for the sake of our children.

The letters you have sent on my behalf to the relevant ministerial departments have been honest, straightforward and meaningful. Only requesting confirmation of procedure and appropriate performance required within the Family Courts and legal system. Unfortunately, your received responses have delivered little more than poor excuses; they have not addressed the behaviour of individuals within the justice system, Family Courts and law firms.

Ministers who are empowered to see members of our community are treated with respect, are clearly failing to uphold these ethical standards and in doing so are failing in their own duties. How can things ever change for the better if ministers will not listen or try to understand how unnecessarily hard things really are? There should not be a stone to hide behind when children's welfare is being fundamentally undermined.

In reality, all I have ever asked for was that honesty be paramount within the Family Courts and I do not believe that you or any other decent person would have asked for anything less. Eight years of trouble in my family's life, simply because I suggested that I was more than happy to be a part of my children's lives. Eight years of trouble in my family's life, simply because I stood up for my children when their welfare and stability was threatened – both by their mother and by the underhanded behaviour and performance within the Family Courts.

If I could ever get through to these individuals, I would ask them to stop using their positions and the system to draw out proceedings, with some unscrupulous solicitors and barristers trying as best as they know how to manipulate any opportunity at the expense of children and their family's wellbeing. It is evident from the performance of Smitch Law et al, it achieved nothing more than inciting disparity, resentment and accelerating any acrimony between parents, ignoring the real issues and, in doing so, installing uncertainty into children's lives.

The Family Courts need to acknowledge Ms Hyde's mental health in order to actually make a difference to our family; if a 'finger has to be pointed' then it needs to be done – I get no satisfaction from the recognition that Ms Hyde needs help, and have no interest in discrediting Ms Hyde in a court room. The benefit would be seen by our children and the ability for us all to get on with our lives.

I've never used Ms Hyde's mental health against her or made disparaging remarks to her. I understand and respect the way it affects her, out of her control, which is why I have continued to request she receive assistance when she needs it, and for the third parties involved to understand why communications break down; why the children sometimes refuse contact with their mother; how I try to be reasonable, despite Ms Hyde rarely affording me the same.

If I could ever get through to these individuals, I would tell them to realise and see that they are the cause of me. They are the cause of my letters of complaint; letters hoping to address and remove the immoral behaviour found within the Family Courts and the legal system!

In September 2007, I left the family court building in Venray mentally drained after having a year and a half of court involvement; attending 13 hearings in town, Venray and London. Throughout, my commitment to my children over the years was attacked and criticised by Mrs Mason and Ms Hyde's barrister, and ignored or dismissed by the judges, regardless of the conclusion reached once again being in my favour.

That evening I decided to stop writing the day-to-day goings on in my family's life. (Although this I couldn't fully commit to, as I am perpetually anxious about many issues that have arisen; I have realised that writing the truth down is virtually pointless. I dread to think how many hours, days and months of my life – dyslexic, struggling to spell, having everything checked by close friends – I have spent, which has at the end of the day still resulted in little understanding of the real issues that have been at the heart of our family's problems: a parent's ongoing mental health condition.

Throughout, I believe that I have been honest with my children, Ms Hyde and the Family Courts. Obviously, I felt I had to keep a record of what our children had experienced and still are experiencing. I also felt that I had to express my concerns to the appropriate government departments of the needless instability and deception that not only exists within the system, but is being permitted and encouraged.

I believe what has gone on for the last eight years is shameful and disgraceful; you are my MP, and I have written to you covering individuals and fundamental ideals within the legal system; how law firms apply the law regarding children and families; the disparity of judges' mindsets. In response, these ministers and government bodies have made it abundantly apparent that they simply do not care for children's welfare and stability, or the parents who are in the family court, in genuine need of assistance and honest guidance.

My family and friends have all been aware of my situation and the unnecessary uphill struggle my children and I have had to endure. They have been appalled by the attitude and dishonesty towards a parent that has continually been there for my children and openly promoted contact between the children and their mother, despite years of disgraceful behaviour from Ms Hyde towards her children and myself.

In 2004, the Family Courts gave me a sole residency order to carry out my role as a responsible parent. Despite showing clear evidence year after year that my only concerns and interests have been for my children, the Family Courts have clearly shown me no respect and have allowed a decent parent to be discredited at every opportunity, meanwhile my children's best interests have not been protected.

The judge at the hearing in September 2007 stated that I was uncaring and not interested in my children or their mother, or that she has mental health problems. This could not be any further from the truth, but might just have been the last straw that broke the camel's back.

This is my declaration to those who live as I do, with the success of their deceptions and behaviour towards my children:

I will have no further dealings with the immoral people whose conduct I have had cause to complain about.

I will not recognise law firms that are guilty of undermining children, their childhood and their family's dynamics.

I will not acknowledge those government bodies or ministers that continue to dismiss and stand by the performance as currently exhibited within the Family Courts and the legal system.

I have nothing left to give them; I just want to raise my children.

I believe I have the right to be left alone by those individuals who have, without good reason, truth or justification, discredited and condemned my name and character, my family and, in this case, three innocent children.

(I know that there are people out there that will laugh or tell me to get over it, but you see, Mr Rowe, this letter is not for them, this one's for me!)

When you consider what I have been put through as a caring parent, there is no wonder why so many fathers do not 'take any part in their children's lives or support their upbringing', as I believe the majority do not want to be part of the never-ending carousel of human misery.

It should be understood that for the wellbeing and future of children and their parents we need honest, sensible guidelines and the removal of inappropriate behaviour that is clearly detrimental to children, parents and family law in this country.

If I could ever get through to these people, I would tell them that my youngest daughter Lara is 10 years old, and I would like to take one of my children to primary school without unfounded interference from Ms Hyde, a law firm and the legal system.

I would like to be allowed to enjoy my role as a parent to all of my daughters without being followed by a cloud of intimidation and worry day after day, year after year.

At the end of the day, Mr Rowe, since September 1999, whatever form of contact I was to be granted with my children, Ms Hyde was not happy; she incessantly tried to disrupt or exploit and generally attempted at every opportunity to make life as difficult for me and our children as she possibly could.

The law firm and the courts merely enabled her to do so for eight years.

Once more, I would like to thank you, Beverley and colleagues for all your support for myself and my children.

Best wishes and regards to you as always.

The Division Bell

7 April

On the 5th of April, at 6pm, I dropped Lara to Ruth's for her half-term contact – Hayley and Alice had also stayed at their mother's for this period, although I was expecting Alice to pop in next week for her birthday.

I went to work yesterday and half way through this morning, I was overcome by nausea. Since about 4 this afternoon, I have been intermittently running to and from the bin to be sick, and then collapsing back on the sofa. Sully has, as always, kept me in good company, even though it was at a distance.

At 8pm, I had fallen asleep, when I was woken by Hayley, Alice and Lara who had all come through the front door sobbing. Hayley explained that there had been an incident at their mother's – now I felt sick for a totally different reason.

Hayley and their mother had an argument about Conner's stuff, and Alice had gotten involved. Their mother had been verbally abusive to her and Alice, and she grabbed Alice's arm and starting shouting in her face. I asked Lara if she had been in her room.

Lara replied, 'I was at the start but I was there when our mother grabbed Alice.'

Hayley stated that she tried to get her mother off Alice and her mother turned around and punched her in the chest and on the side of her face. Hayley showed me a cut on her inner lip and a red mark on her chest.

Lara was sobbing as I cuddled her; when I looked down at her, I had a vivid flashback of Hayley in 2000. Is this simply the way the world works?

Lara said she had been in her room with one of her friends and they could hear their mother shouting at everyone. For some reason their mother brought up Ma, which Lara described as her mother 'bad–mouthing Nan'. This continued for a while before Lara decided to stand up to her mother. Lara left her bedroom and told her mother, 'Leave Nan out of this, she has never spoken badly about you and has never wanted to get involved in any trouble.'

The argument progressed to Ruth grabbing Alice and punching Hayley twice. Hayley admitted that she was so upset, she had pushed her mother on the stairs, which caused her to slide down. This is an out of character reaction for Hayley; I do not approve of any of my children hurting or intending to harm anyone. Taking a deep breath, Lara said she knew she had to get away, despite feeling awful about leaving her friend in her room and with her mother, she ran with Hayley and Alice.

Hayley, Alice and Lara are all very shaken by their experience and have made it clear to me that they do not want to return to their mother's at the present time.

Knowing this is going to drag me back into the centre of what I just told Mr Rowe I was done with, I hugged my daughters and settled them down. We would have to go through what happened properly; I will need to contact Social Services too… I never have intentions of breaking the court order but, under the circumstances, I have been left with no choice and will once again stand against the abuse of my children.

The house phone rang throughout the evening, and the abusive voicemails played out. Our mobiles rang, too. No one wanted to answer.

CBO

8 April

In the morning, Hayley came into the kitchen and said, 'Dad I know this is the worst timing, but Connor has nowhere to live and has been sleeping on his friend's couch. Can he stay at ours?'

I told Hayley I have no problem as long as they are respectful about it, but we'll have a house meeting with Alice and Lara, to make sure they are comfortable with it too. After the house meeting, Hayley called Connor to tell him he can move in.

I received a letter from the Child Benefit Office saying that there was someone else (Ms Hyde) claiming for Hayley, Alice and Lara. As a result of this, my Child Benefit has now been suspended; in reality, this excludes me from Housing Benefits and Child Tax Credits, as well. Again, this has put me under unnecessary pressure.

Following this, over the last day all I have received is incessant phone calls from Ms Hyde threatening me that Social Services and the police are on their way round. These come with all of the verbal abuse and false accusations that always accompany Ms Hyde's phone calls. While I answered the first, and explained the children's current position – i.e. no contact at the moment – I let the answer machine handle the rest.

It is another day I find myself concerned about Ms Hyde's mental stability, and I feel that this should not be my concern alone in the interests of the welfare of our three children. How long have I asked for other organisations to take the appropriate action to ensure that Ms Hyde is not, even if it is inadvertent, jeopardising the children's safety and wellbeing?

Referral to Social Services (Are you shitting me?)

8 April

Fw: Mr Marlo
Dear Ms Hyde,
I acknowledge your referral to this department today and the information provided. I have considered the information carefully and can confirm that the Assessment and Child Protection Team will not be involved.

I note your comment about not being able to return to court, however I would strongly urge you to seek independent legal advice.
Yours sincerely,
Mr Trumpton

Letter posted through my door by Ms Hyde

8 April

As you are aware from your letter to me of 24ᵗʰ March 2008 and the court order of 5ᵗʰ September 2007, the dates for contact with the children are very clearly set out. My contact week for the Easter holidays, as per your letter and the court order, is from 5ᵗʰ April 6pm until 14ᵗʰ April midday.

As per my conversation with you on Sunday 6ᵗʰ April, and Lara's conversation with you five minutes later, we had agreed that Lara would visit you for two hours from 10am until 12pm 9ᵗʰ April 2008, to see her new rat and the dog.

I am disappointed that Lara was not returned to me yesterday after visiting your house, and that you would not answer your mobile or home phone. I decided that it was in Lara's best interests and my own because of my car accident not to risk any upset to Lara at bedtime and had hoped that you would contact me in the morning and return Lara as per the court order and our agreement as above, at 12pm.

At the time of writing this letter, 1.15pm, Lara has not been returned to me; I have tried you again on your mobile and home phone and you are not answering.

I have now taken advice from my solicitor and expect a phone call from you as soon as possible, telling me when you are going to return Lara, or I shall be left with no choice but to enforce my rightful contact with Lara through the court system.

I would also like to remind you that I am due to have the children for Alice's birthday this year as per the court order.

She has abused and assaulted our daughters *again* and the only compulsion she has is to cover for her own despicable behaviour.

There was no conversation with me; I was sick as a dog and at any rate, Lara had a friend round at Ms Hyde's at the time of the incident, and Ms Hyde gets the date wrong in her own letter.

Hayley and Alice clearly aren't as important to resume contact with as Lara – maybe it's because she knows she has abused them, and she thinks that Lara had been fine before, so why not now?

The whole thing just turns my stomach. I've got to once more witness Ms Hyde pull the wool over everyone's eyes – Mrs Mason, always lurking in the shadows happy to slither out to suck a few more pounds from the taxpayer, to defend this false depiction of a mother that Ms Hyde tries to hold up, and I've got to look forward to judges, whose heads are too far up their own arses to make heads or tails of any situation.

Both Ms Hyde and Mrs Mason should be ashamed of themselves for the abuse they have brought into three children's lives, and my own.

Clearly Ms Hyde's excuse is she has a severe mental health problem – what is Mrs Mason's excuse and family law's reasoning to allow a solicitor to harass a family year after year? Just maybe, it has been the judges' inability to look at our family's case for what it was; allowing a family law solicitor to dictate what was going on in and out of proceedings and in our day to day lives.

Diabolical

9 April

This all escalated from an argument about Connor's things; Hayley wanted them in her room, which Ms Hyde had agreed to. Hayley said Conner had dropped his stuff off and left for work; as she was taking the bags up to her room, her mother demanded they be kept in the garage – I understand why Hayley spoke up against that, but I also wish Hayley and Alice had both learned by now that continuing an argument with their mother escalates the situation unnecessarily. Apparently, Alice had added that Hayley should be able to decide for herself, and I obviously do not condone them believing they can assert the goings on in their mother's home but-

Ms Hyde could have been reasonable and either said Conner's belongings could not be moved in, or accepted that he would be in Hayley's room, so it makes sense for his stuff to be – I have no idea why it would be necessary for them to be kept in the garage. (Unless it was his moped.)

The wall: Ms Hyde is both an adult and a mother, and needed to remove herself from the situation before she felt out of control.

Hayley was seen by her GP for a cut mouth and bruised chest, as a result of her mother's behaviour.

Hayley and Alice telephoned their mother throughout the day and asked if they could pick up some of their belongings from hers, including Alice's medication. Lara said she wasn't interested in her things and would just rather not see her mother at the moment. (But asked for Hayley and Alice to give Wotsit scritches, if they see her.) At any rate, Ms Hyde refused to agree to Hayley and Alice going to hers.

After several phone calls that only served to upset everyone, Hayley called the police and asked if they would assist in accompanying Alice and herself in getting their belongings from their mother's. The police did not get back to Hayley (part of me was relieved – Ms Hyde does not need the police showing up as well to compound her mania), and she decided to spend the night with Conner at his friend's.

At 9pm, I received a call from the police stating that they couldn't get through to Hayley on her mobile and they are driving to Ms Hyde's address, ready to assist. I told the officer that Hayley was not at home, but I would bring Alice.

As Alice and I pulled up outside Ms Hyde's, the police officer explained that Ms Hyde was being verbally abusive already and that they would stay close to Alice the whole time. I left Alice with the officers and drove home, not wanting my presence to further aggravate things.

About ten minutes later, the police knocked on my front door explaining that Ms Hyde had been verbally aggressive to Alice and they feared the situation may escalate, so they have brought Alice home and will return to Ms Hyde's to collect Alice's belongings.

Alice came in crying and I reassured her; we waited for the police.

I helped the officers remove half a dozen boxes and bags from the boot of the car.

After the police left, Alice went through the things her mother had packed, since Alice had only been in her room a short period, and said, 'She has put all of my old stuff, shoes and boots with holes in and stuff I haven't worn for years!'

Ms Hyde used the police as a dust-cart and my home as a dumping ground; these items are obviously not what Alice wanted from her room.

Behind Closed Doors Part II

Birthday

It's Alice's birthday, which had a weird atmosphere to it this year, what with the upset still so fresh for all of the children.

(Ms Hyde has done herself no favours; Lara rarely leaves the room to speak to her mother on the phone, so I overhear Ms Hyde shouting at Lara, saying that she has done nothing wrong, and it is her holiday time. Whether or not, due to her illness, Ms Hyde believes she hurt Hayley and Alice in front Lara, the children have asked for some space. I understand calling Alice on her birthday, but hounding Lara for the past few days with only denial of the behaviour Lara is upset by has only served to distress all the children further, as Hayley and Alice then become protective of Lara, making everyone more emotional.)

Alice had a whole party planned at her mother's; luckily even with the short notice most of her friends have still come to our home, and it has been mostly a happy day, apart from an argument Alice had with her mother on the phone.

Dear MP – 'The Real Slim Shady'

11 April

Thank you for returning my call today and being understanding to the situation this counter–claim has once again placed my family in.

In a nutshell: for several months, Alice has lived sporadically with myself and her mother; come Alice's suspension from Northview Grove School, Alice had spent more and more days and nights at Ms Hyde's. Alice opted to live with little boundaries and the ability to stay up late and, as I have been told, smoke and drink alcohol.

I provided Ms Hyde with the Child Benefit money for Alice. Alice would tell me week after week that she was returning home and getting back on track; she made it clear that she did not what to live with her mother and was just staying round hers because she needed to take 'time-out'. In reality, Alice, aged 13 at the time, and her mother were dictating what was going on, and I had to stand back feeling helpless to be able to do anything.

Almost immediately, I was being told of many incidences that were occurring at Ms Hyde's home, and felt very concerned for Alice over this time. (Although I also felt that my hands were tied.) Alice went to stay at her mother's on the 2nd January and, on the 6th of January, Alice and her mother had an argument, and Alice returned home. At that time, Alice and I made an appointment for Alice with Connexions. For several weeks, Alice did not stay with Ms Hyde, but returned after being influenced by the lifestyle her mother allows – Ms Hyde later cancelled Alice's appointment.

On the 7th April there was another incident at Ms Hyde's property. Once again, all three children witnessed more verbal abuse and aggressive behaviour from their mother, which resulted in Alice being grabbed, Hayley being punched twice and all three children feeling it necessary to leave her property.

It is my hope that Alice can get back on track and be allowed to use the next two years left in school to make up for the year lost.

I would like to thank you for your effort and time in assisting my family with this matter. I apologise for taking up your time with this, but I was already at my wits end with the Family Courts, and my children are still being abused.

Yours respectfully…

To Child Benefit Office, MP and PM

11/18/20 April

11 April

Dear Sir/Madam,

Thank you for returning my call.

Due to an incident at their mother's property, all three children involved in the case number provided above have returned to my residency full time, until such a time as they feel comfortable with returning to their mother's for contact, as set out in the court order September 2007.

Thank you for your effort in assisting my family with this matter.

Yours faithfully...

18 April

Dear Mr Rowe,

Please find enclosed, a letter that I propose to present at Alice's appeal against permanent expulsion on Monday 21st April.

I would appreciate it if you could provide me with a letter for the committee of the many difficult years our family (Alice) has faced, and, if you would also be so kind, to confirm my dedication to my family and my ability to be a competent, caring father.

This confirmation, which will only be used at Alice's appeal, I am asking for as a genuine parent and assure you that I am trying my best in the hope that my daughter can complete her education fulltime in the mainstream schooling system.

I believe that it is vital to any young person's emotional stability to experience and enjoy a normal education and relationship with their friends, teachers and school.

Yours respectfully...

20 April

Dear PM,

May I firstly thank you for reading this letter, which I hope you will acknowledge by return. I have also enclosed a copy of a letter that I sent to you on the 14th June 2007, which I have not received a response to.

I would like to ask if you would kindly recognise on my behalf the genuine effort, honesty and commitment that I have received from Mr Rowe in his role as a Member of Parliament.

I am sure you would agree that we must find time to recognise and commend Mr Rowe and likeminded MPs for their dedication as not only a government official but likewise to their constituents.

I do hope you consider my sincere request worthy of your attention and assure you of my best intentions at all times.

Yours respectfully...

Dean Marlo

Panel Member

21 April

It is a fact that all three of our children have continually been placed in a difficult position by ongoing court proceedings. As the middle daughter, Alice appears to have been affected more than her two sisters.

Before Alice even became a teenager, she made several life changing decisions. Alice saw the option of living with a parent with no boundaries; as a result, Alice became tired, irritable, rude and defiant to individuals and rules. I believe that, without support, children that go down this path may stay on the road of personal self–destruction. Given the opportunity, anyone can regain their self–respect, which becomes evident when they are dealing with people and life itself.

Over the last year, I have been especially concerned, but my involvement had to remain at a distance from my normal relationship with my daughter Alice; I understand that Alice, owing to her age, would not take advice from me and as I did not want to make our relationship confrontational, or have Alice pull away, I offered advice and support when I could.

In the last 3 months, since being expelled from school, I believe that Alice has seen a lot about life and has realised the consequences of her actions and behaviour. By her own account, Alice has shown me that she no longer wishes to continue on the path she was on. Alice has been attending the UEEC and the teachers there I have always found to be polite, helpful and patient with the difficult children who attend the centre; many of these children are sadly a lot further down the road than Alice.

Alice has experienced the lifestyle of some of the children that attend UEEC and has lived in an unstable household for periods of time. Alice has realised that her behaviour and attitude has set her on a path towards a person she doesn't want to be. Many teenagers experience the process differently, some acting out, and this was amplified by the situations going on at home, but Alice is considerate and capable, who does not deserve to be defined by her actions at thirteen.

My daughter is clearly at a crossroads in her childhood. I hope that you can see reason in Alice's case, and take into consideration that some young individuals need all the available support to give them the determination to regain their self–respect and position within their community, and wider society.

Alice has associated with children that have not received or have refused the love, care and support needed by every child, which has led her to realise that these friends are living on the very edges of society; constantly running away and being involved with the police and court system. She does not want to become another vulnerable young person.

I would ask you to reconsider Alice's expulsion from Northview Grove on the strength of Alice's acknowledgment of her previously unacceptable attitude and the knowledge of the ongoing support and care Alice receives from her family.

Yours respectfully…

From MP

21 April

To whom it may concern,
Re: Mr Dean Marlo and Alice Marlo
Mr Marlo is a remarkable man. A lesser person would have cracked a long time ago – or simply walked away and left the State to look after his three daughters, at considerable cost to the public purse.

My Advice Bureau and casework through correspondence over the past 11 years has seen an endless stream of mothers whose husbands or partners have abandoned them and their children. It is a shameful indictment on the male of the species.

Occasionally, the person left to bring up the family is the father. Mr Marlo has done so, against all the odds, with 'the system' seemingly conspiring to knock him down at regular intervals. It is not for me to comment about the mother of his three daughters, although the fact that she appears to have recourse to public funds to undertake court proceedings, whereas Mr Marlo has to fend for himself is an unfairness which I have tried to correct – even to the extent of the two of us having a meeting in London with the then Minister for Family Justice.

I have sought to help Mr Marlo and his family for several years. I know from our regular meetings that he cares deeply about his daughters, whom he loves dearly. I have no hesitation in saying that I consider him to be a competent, caring father who is dedicated to his family.

Every school, of course, experiences pupils who cause concern. Whatever the case is against Alice Marlo, I would ask that the family's circumstances are taken fully into account – and for those considering Alice's future to ask themselves whether permanent exclusion is in her best interests?

Every child matters, the Government tells us. I believe every child should enjoy a normal education and relationship with their friends, teachers and schools. That is Mr Marlo's plea. It is one I endorse.
Yours sincerely,

Alice's Tribunal

21 April

Dropping Lara at Riverbank, I drove to the community centre with Alice for her tribunal. Due to the events of the 7th of April, Alice told me she had texted her mother and asked her not to come, as Alice did not want to see her. I did not speak to Ms Hyde about it, I left it up to Alice. (I'm at my wits end with Ms Hyde.) Just in case, on the way, I said to Alice, if your mother is there, don't let it make you upset and try to focus on the day.

When we arrived, Ms Hyde was inside reception waiting for us. She tried to talk to Alice but she ignored her. We all signed in and sat down; a woman then walked in, holding what must have been a six-week-old baby, and approached us.

Ms Hyde stated, 'This is Ariel and Georgia, who are coming in with us, as Ariel is a family friend.'

I saw Alice swing around to look at me in disbelief, and I did not necessarily agree with a stranger joining us for Alice's meeting, nor the baby in her arms, but I had better things to think about, like Alice's permanent exclusion; not that Ms Hyde had offered the courtesy of asking if I minded. I believe this is a personal and family situation, however saying anything at this stage would only serve to distract from Alice, so I just accepted Ariel sitting down next to Ms Hyde.

Once the tribunal introductions had been made, as babies do, Georgia started crying, and Ms Hyde asked the Chairman if he would mind pausing the proceedings while Ariel leaves to settle the baby down. The Chairman agreed, and after five to ten minutes of us all listening to the baby cry through the other side of the door, one of the panel members stated, 'Are we really waiting for a baby to stop crying to continue?'

With the spell broken, the Chairman said that Ms Hyde's attendee would have to remain outside, so that we could get on.

After hearing all our representations for Alice, we were informed the panel will write with their conclusions in the coming days.

As we all walked back into the reception, Ms Hyde handed me a letter.

From Ms Hyde (true colours)

21 April

18 April

Dear Mr Marlo,

It is with regret that I have to write to you in this tone, but in the complete absence of your willingness to communicate either via telephone – home or mobile/ letter last one sent 8/4/08 or email I simply have no choice left.

I left you nine years ago for very valid reasons and put up with 8 years of domestic abuse/ violence, both physical, verbal and mental abuse as you can well remember.

Whilst I feel extremely sorry for you that your own childhood included both physical and sexual abuse it is time to move on and either get help with your problems or sort yourself out; I said this to you when I was living with you and tried to get you to come to 'relate', I paid my £5 but you refused to come.

They told me that they couldn't help unless you were willing to attend.

Not only is it an accumulation of awful things to say to or about a person, it's all lies – or at least, she has it confused who endured 8 years of whom, eroded daily by verbal and mental abuse not only myself, but physical, mental and verbal abuse of our three beautiful children as well.

She has recently assaulted our daughter and has sat down to write the several letters I have received. It is evident that Ms Hyde's bipolar disorder leaves her distorting the truth and facts. For example, I was not sexually abused as a child; according to her medical records, she was. If Ms Hyde has to write a letter, it should not be the tale of two cities that I was an abusive man, nor her own delusions about my childhood – this is about our three children, who have come home again speaking of violence and being screamed at by their mother.

If you read about the subject of domestic abuse/ violence, you will understand that many times this abuse is carried forward to the next generation unless the cycle is stopped/ broken.

(Is it possible to die from irony?)

This is exactly what is happening to our family. The time has come for this to stop.

I was involved in a very serious car accident on 5ᵗʰ April resulting in severe whiplash all down my left-hand side and have been off work for two weeks. As it goes, I am still in pain and have spoken with the physio who says it will be 4-6 weeks before I can do any sport, light exercise only and plenty of rest.

(What I wouldn't give for one of those judges and a psychologist to have been a fly on the wall in Ms Hyde's home on April 7ᵗʰ. Being right-handed, her swing obviously wasn't affected by her injury. I can't articulate the culmination of *years* of abuse, and I am still reading this self-victimisation after she hurt her daughters, *again*.)

The accident wasn't my fault, a male driver pulled out in front of me from the verge as I was going 30mph up a hill in the early morning with a clear road ahead.

I was lucky that my airbags came out and I had put 4 new Good Year Tyres on the week before, as my car was due its MOT in May.

Why does this read like a statement to the police? My interests are solely on the welfare and happiness of my children, and I don't need to read about the circumstances of her accident. This is just another reflection of her manic mind and cold personality; she is writing this to explain why Hayley, Alice and Lara came home in tears, two days into their Easter holidays with their mother.

Two days after this, 7/4/08 when all 3 girls knew very well that I was feeling very sore/stiff and achy, I had to put up with the incidents of Monday night.

They have all been reported to the Domestic Hate Team and further harassment all week by Hayley and Alice (mostly Alice), coming round in gangs of friends hammering on my door, screaming abuse and texting me nasty messages. (Kept.)

So 16-year-old Hayley, 14-year-old Alice and 10-year-old Lara are on a Domestic Hate Team list. Her own children. She lost control and is willing to condemn the children?

This has resulted in the landlord – who is, let's not forget, the one, the only, Mrs Jackson! – asking me to change the locks, which I have done, but there is also a large hole in the bathroom door that either Hayley or Alice has done which I am going to have to foot the bill for because I don't want to prosecute them. I have been advised to prosecute in the hope that they will learn that their behaviour is wrong.

The accusation of a hole in the bathroom door is new.

Instead, I am going to write to each of them as I have been advised to do by the police, a warning letter that if any such abusive/aggressive/destructive behaviour should occur again in my house, I will have no hesitation in prosecuting.

The last incident was 16/04/08 from Alice and then again from Hayley on Thursday 17/4/08 when I rang the home number (new) to have telephone contact with Lara.

I am not prepared any more to put up with the verbal/physical abuse from yourself, Hayley or Alice any more.

It made me sick the first time it was written about me, and it does to this day. However, seeing Hayley and Alice being described in the same way... I am overcome by the injustice of it all.

Also, my home number hasn't changed in almost 10 years, since I moved out of my office space. It's simply a delusional detail.

The worst part of the incident for me on the 7/4/08 was when I was lying at the bottom of the stairs in agony and all 3 children chanted 'crocodile tears' and laughed – even Lara.

I have vivid memories of Hayley as young as 2, being taunted by the very words, and I have no doubt Ms Hyde continued to use it when the children were upset. This to me is not evil children, but vindicated children. I'm not saying it was right, but I understand what saying that to their mother must have meant to them – to all of them, *even Lara.*

These comments and this behaviour do not come from children who are sound of mind, and the words 'crocodile tears' are exactly what you used to say to me after you hit me or pulled my hair.

I'm sorry to keep repeating myself, especially 17 years after my story begins, but I never raised a hand to Ms Hyde, nor retaliated nor initiated any form of verbal, physical or mental abuse. I'm not an abusive man. I just want to be a dad to my children. It's all I've ever wanted. I am, as usual, only in existence to be Ms Hyde's reusable scapegoat for her own abhorrent behaviour.

For these reasons and many more I am prepared to stand up in once again in court and speak the truth as I have always done in the hope that our 3 beautiful children will have the chance to get the help that they need, and have the best chance to grow up and have normal, healthy relationships with their family, friends and partners and their own children.

If something is not done, they will end up as dysfunctional people, like yourself.

Thanks to Ms Hyde, Hayley is 2 years away from being all grown up – her chances to be normal were stolen by a mother who would not accept help for her mental condition, and a solicitor more interested in lining their pockets. There is no relationship that Ms Hyde has with anyone that is healthy.

I run my own business; I do my utmost to take good care of our children; the children all have lots of friends; we have family dinners; I've got close friends who respect I'm a man with an ex-partner determined to make my life miserable, and they support me however they can. Lara is the head of her school council, preparing for her Eleven-plus. Alice is going to a different school, and while not traditionally academic, she has lots of interests and is not going to be tied down by the mistakes of her younger self. Hayley has been in the newspaper as part of her signing choir, a group she has several friends in, and though her grades are not the highest in the class, she's willing to work and is going to college.

So… She can stick her dysfunction up her arse, we're all trying, but when has she ever?

This I find very sad as it is not all their fault.

Good to know she believes our children are not 'all' to blame.

Children learn from their parents, and since you have had sole custody over the last 4 years, the children's behaviour has grown steadily worse, resulting in Alice being permanently excluded from school on January 7th 2008, and Hayley being arrested for continual swearing at a police officer in a public place (McDonalds) on February 12th 2008, the day before we were due to fly off on holiday to Gran Canaria.

It's so difficult to get further than a paragraph without feeling the need to fact check every single statement she makes.

I have done my best to show our children a calm, loving home; until Ms Hyde appeared to kick the van, my sole residency was the most stable year of the children's lives. (As reflected by their schools.)

Also, 'the children's' is too general – Lara has never been trouble, or in trouble for that matter. Lara said to me that she felt like a line had been crossed in herself on the 7th of April, as she has literally never voluntarily involved herself in an argument with her mother before. To continue being the bearer of bad news, both when Alice was excluded and when Hayley was arrested, the children were in Ms Hyde's care. I'm not expecting her to take any responsibility, she doesn't do that, but I thought it was worth mentioning for the people who, like me, can't believe this is her defence as a mother who split her child's lip.

I think that the family problem is further compounded by the fact that Hayley and Alice have both told me that they smoke hash/weed which in young people causes mood swings and paranoia (adults as well).

I would never encourage Hayley or Alice to smoke in general, let alone use any kind of drugs. This is another horrible accusation that Ms Hyde's clearly building up for Mrs Mason to use, wherein I'm letting my two teenage daughters do drugs?

I know that it was true for you as you have been a heavy hash/weed smoker throughout the 8 years that I lived with you and the 5 years that I knew you before I lived with you.

I smoked a couple of joints in the evening after work and once the children were in bed. I quit in 1999, when I was preparing to get parental rights and this whole shit show in the Family Courts Theatre drew its curtains.

I met Ms Hyde in 1990; this is another random false detail that she has convinced herself is true.

I have given the children leaflets and spoken to them at length and discussed the harmful effects of the THC in cannabis but to no avail.

Lara is still only a 10-year-old child and has had to witness the most terrible things in her life so far which is so unfair.

Lara is terrified of Alice at times as you are well aware because at your house you have given her a lock on her door with a key, so that she can lock herself away from Alice when Alice becomes angry/verbally abusive/aggressive and physically violent. This is simply not fair on Lara and not right.

The rented property we live in is an older build; the doors upstairs have big keyholes, which is a novelty, and why Lara asked for the key to her room. The reason I gave Lara a key to her room was because I trusted her, and it would give her some responsibility in a safe way. I have a master key but still, and to this day, I know of only two occasions she used it - both were to cheat in hide and seek.

Ms Hyde shouldn't be making these kinds of allegations about Alice when it is her own behaviour she is describing. She has over many years been able to throw accusations about what is going on in a home where she does not live, while dismissing what happens within her own four walls; she makes the worst out of anything she is thinking or any situation.

On top of this, you are withholding contact from me the right to be with my youngest daughter.

You are such a 'control freak' it is sad to see that none of the children are allowed to exercise 'personal choice' in your household it simply doesn't exist.

I am asking you once again that you maintain the contact set out clearly in the court order and make Lara available for her next contact, weekend Friday 15/4/08 after school until Monday on 28/4/08 and for tea on 23/4/08 collect from school.

In addition I have lost my whole week Easter holiday contact with Lara which I will never be able to regain.

Time is something that is always lost forever.

To make up for the 7 nights I have missed of the Easter Holidays, I am requesting that I have Lara for the whole of the May half term week from after school Friday 23rd May 2008 until 12pm June 2nd 2008. This is 4 nights.

It's funny that she was talking about a 'control freak' and 'personal choice'; is she giving Lara any here?

The remaining 3 nights I will take later on in the year and will give you at least 2 weeks notice as per the court order.

Form C1A Children Act 1989, Section 3 Part 6, Page 5: ABDUCTION. 'Child abduction' is the wrongful removal of a child from any person having, or entitled to, lawful control of that child.

Hayley, Alice and Lara walked out of Ms Hyde's house to our home. If they wanted to see or stay with Ms Hyde, they are all aware it is their decision I stand behind.

What actually was child abduction, was in 2000 when Ms Hyde walked into my home and took Lara, then returned later for Hayley, as she was at the time withholding my contact of Alice. Guess what, I've read the Children Act 1989, because most of it applied to what she was doing to me!

It really is something, to read Ms Hyde's demands for contact, when the reason the children are refusing is because she abused them. I know her mental health clouds her memory and what she has written is what she believes. It saddens me that the years of abuse my children and I have endured have been allowed to continue, despite the symptoms of Ms Hyde's condition being clear in her judgement and actions.

When I rang on 16/4/08 and Alice answered, she refused to let me speak with Lara and let rip more verbal abuse, saying 'she doesn't want to speak to you', Alice then said the same thing when I asked to speak to yourself.

In court you have been told time and time again not to put the children – any of them in that position and this it is the parents who must communicate important matters.

Over the last 9 years, you have never observed a court order if you have felt that you want to do something else; they seem to be hardly worth the paper that they are written on.

(Aye, the court orders are a joke.)

I have applied back to court for my rightful contact times as set out clearly in the order and shall be asking that this time there is a contact order with a power of arrest in the hope that this will keep the continuity and stability for the children; something that you feel is unimportant.

The penal notice is back on the board, what have I done again? Oh, stood by my children like a decent parent would, both literally and emotionally, because I care about them.

I would also ask that you stop harassing me for sexual favours as you have done over the past 9 years. The last 2 occasions being Hayley's college open day 28/01/08, in the car park when you said I could have the child benefit for Alice if I gave you a hand job; I told you again to get lost and that I had a steady boyfriend of 5 years, let alone from the fact that I think it is an abnormal request, and not from someone sound of mind.

In my mind, there are no lines that Ms Hyde hasn't crossed, yet a new letter can come along and I feel my knees buckle as I am blindsided by another false accusation I didn't think possible or see coming.

Also, what kind of sick person asks for a sexual favour at their child's college interview?

Previous to this, the night when Alice ran away and turned up back at my house at 12pm. We had been in your car round town looking in all the clubs and pubs and then we went for a curry. When you drove me home, even though you knew that my boyfriend/partner was there, you drove me round the estate harassing me yet again to have sex with you. (I have reported these comments to the Doctor.)

Our child was missing. We did not have a curry. I did not ask for anything.

I would expect a reply to this very serious letter within 7 days of the postmark on this letter and will be sending it recorded delivery.

I will also be sending copies to the judge at the County Court/my solicitor at Smitch Law/Mrs Irfan at Riverbank School/Mrs Tran at Northview Grove and Mrs Delgado at UEEC.

Yours sincerely,

Ruth Hyde

With no evidence provided, that's the entire town informed about Ms Hyde's delusional version of me; from child abuse to child abuser, asking for sex and abducting children. I've also figured out why so many parts of this are written so strangely – it's not only a letter to me vindicating Ms Hyde, but it will also end up in Mrs Mason's court bundle with so many allegations against me a judge would be hard pressed to appraise either parent's credibility.

Ms Hyde still wants people around my children and myself to frown and disapprove of the conduct she is suggesting I am capable of. I am well versed on what Ms Hyde's mentality is towards me, and the harassment I have felt over her deranged comments and stories over the years has worn me down.

Mrs Jackson seemingly forewarned me in 1991 that her daughter continually made-up terrible stores about people. Well, after 17 years of false allegations, delusional stories and defamation of my character, I would agree with her. It is a pity Mrs Jackson failed to ever relay this to the Family Courts.

I did not want her to stand up in court and suggest what she had to me, just to tell the truth. In 2000, her daughter had sole residency of our children, was having a manic episode and there was ongoing court involvement; Mrs Jackson knew her daughter could not cope with Hayley, Alice and Lara. She should have made the effort to ensure the Family Courts were fully aware of her daughter's behaviour and condition, for the wellbeing and safety of her daughter and grandchildren.

(They say nightmares happen when you are asleep… I keep waking up in one.)

Parstons Solicitors

22 April

Dear Melissa,

I am writing to you and I am asking for your help.

Please find enclosed, a letter that Ms Hyde handed to me at Alice's permanent exclusion appeal on the 21st of April.

I am deeply concerned about the content and false allegations that are implied by Ms Hyde in this letter regarding my children and myself. Once again, I deny the personal allegations made about me and cannot express to you enough the unnecessary stress and worry this has brought into my life. I feel totally appalled and abused by its suggestions and the stories relayed.

It is particularly worrying that Ms Hyde is proposing to send copies of this letter to Mrs Irfan, Headteacher of Riverbank Primary School, Mrs Tran Headteacher of Northview Grove, and Mrs Delgado, Headteacher of UEEC.

For years, as you know, my children and I have had to put up with false allegations from Ms Hyde being placed within our lives, our community and also within the Family Courts. The continuation of Ms Hyde's behaviour and actions towards our children and myself is appalling, exhausting and dehumanising.

I quite honestly have had enough and do not believe that my children and I deserve to be persecuted and treated in such a manner.

Will you please help, as I believe that this has gone on for far too long and it is eroding my children's wellbeing and my own.

Yours sincerely…

The Appeal Panel Concludes

23 April

Dear Mr Marlo,
Alice Marlo, Northview Grove School
Following the hearing of your appeal by the Independent Appeal Panel constituted by the County Council on Monday 21 April 2008, against the decision of the Governing Body of Northview Grove School not to reinstate Alice Marlo, I am writing to advise you of the Panel's decision.
After careful and lengthy consideration of your representations, both oral and written, together with the representations of the school and Local Authority and in light of the available evidence, the Panel has unanimously decided to uphold the exclusion and Alice's school record will reflect this.
Upon conclusion of the evidence and testimony stage, the first issue for the Panel to decide was whether on the balance of probabilities Alice had done what she was alleged to have done. The Headteacher, Mrs Tran, confirmed in response to questions from the Chairman of the Panel that Alice's permanent exclusion was based on a cumulative series of incidents rather than a single one-off incident. The Panel reconsidered the school's case at pages 1-270 of the bundle, together with extra documents that were provided on the day of appeal and satisfied itself that there were many incidents from January 2006 that went towards the Headteacher's final decision to permanently exclude.
The Headteacher summarised Alice's behaviour in a log at pages 109 to 113 of the bundle that records a significant number of incidents throughout Alice's time at Northview Grove. You broadly accepted the facts as detailed and consequently the Panel considered that document to be of assistance to it. The Panel also considered in more detail the several incidents that resulted in periods of fixed term exclusion, namely: 06/03/07; 26/04/07; 04/07/07; 10/07/07; 02/10/07; 08/10/07; 07/11/07 and 12/11/07 and the incidents that resulted in periods of internal seclusion as detailed in the log.
The Panel was satisfied there was evidence of persistent disruptive behaviour which together resulted in serious breaches of the school's behaviour codes. They further accepted that a number of incidents were sufficient in themselves for the school to have genuine concern for the continued safety of staff and other children on the premises.
The Panel therefore accepted on the balance of probabilities that Alice had done what she was alleged to have done in each of the incidents previously detailed.
The Panel went on to consider the basis of the Headteacher's decision and the procedures followed and whether the Headteacher and Governing Body complied with the law and had regard to the Secretary of State's guidance on exclusion in deciding, respectively, to exclude Alice and not to direct that she be reinstated. The Panel considered the accepted procedure and format had been followed correctly and that the process was lawful.
The Panel went on to consider the school's published behaviour and discipline policy, as they are required to do. They considered that it was properly drafted and made clear what the possible sanctions for misbehaviour were, including the ultimate sanction of permanent exclusion. Having consulted the policy, the Panel were entirely satisfied that previous fixed term exclusions were an appropriate response to earlier incidents and that at all times the school's policy documents were followed where circumstances reasonably allowed.

The Panel would have found it of assistance to view the school's Special Educational Needs Policy and would have expected to have seen a detailed Pastoral Support Plan for Alice; particularly in light of the assistance Alice was receiving from both the school and other agencies. Nevertheless, they heard testimony from all parties and were satisfied that Educational Psychologist and her department followed a clear programme of appropriate intervention at all stages. Consequently, the Panel did not consider themselves disadvantaged by the lack of a specific PSP.

Due to the nature of the incidents under consideration, it was not necessary for the Panel to consider the fairness of the exclusion in relation to the treatment of other pupils involved in the incidents.

The Panel considered whether, in its opinion, permanent exclusion was proportionate. Mindful that Alice is being supported with School Action Plus, and that every effort should be made to avoid excluding a pupil with Special Educational Needs, the Panel looked carefully at the range of strategies employed to assist Alice. The school detailed a number of strategies which resulted in Alice's academic and personal welfare being properly addressed.

Having reconsidered the evidence in detail, the Panel unanimously concluded that the incidents for which Alice was excluded seriously breached the school's published policies. Mindful of your representations, the Panel nevertheless found that the degree of disregard for school rules was so serious that permanent exclusion had been proportionate.

Balancing the interests of Alice as an excluded pupil and those of the whole school community suggested to the Panel that reinstatement would not be the most sensible outcome in this case, and Alice would benefit from a fresh start at another school. In making this decision, the Panel considered the representations from the school that should Alice be reinstated there would be a degree of risk to the safety, welfare and morale of the whole school community. In summary, therefore, the Panel unanimously decided to uphold the Headteacher's decision to permanently exclude Alice.

The Panel's decision is binding on you, the Governing Body of Northview Grove School and the Local Authority.

The alternative arrangements put in place for Alice's future education will continue for the time being; but Mr Milner from the Local Authority will be in touch with you to discuss the next stages.

A copy of this letter will be added to Alice's school record for future reference.

Yours sincerely,

Clerk to the Independent Appeal Panel

Progress Report – Hayley's Maths Tutor

24 April

Hayley is a very pleasant girl who has a good attitude towards her work; she is always willing to try a problem first, rather than waiting for me to show her what to do. Due to this, she is making good progress. Yours sincerely,

Fledgling relationships

24 April

After a few weeks of being in each other's pockets, as a parent I could see the strain it was putting on Hayley and Connor's fledgling relationship. I suggested that perhaps they would be happier if they had more time to themselves, to have their own lives as well as their relationship, so maybe Connor should think about looking for a flat.

I left Hayley and Connor to talk about it, and offered my support if they wanted it.

It didn't take long before Hayley came to me and admitted that she felt it was too much too soon, and that she thought they would be happier with their own place anyway. I told Hayley she didn't need to move out as well if she didn't want to, or put pressure on her relationship with Connor, and with the emotional turbulence of the past few weeks, she needs to try to relax and enjoy the time. Hayley gave me a hug and returned to her room.

Dear Ms Hyde,

25 April

I am writing to inform you that Lara has stated that she does not wish to come for weekend contact or Thursday tea contact with you at the present time.

Lara has confirmed her feelings to you on several occasions when you have talked to her on the phone.

I feel that I have been left with no other option but to take Lara out of school today and go to the appropriate organisation.

Yours sincerely…

Attempts

26 April

A mutual friend of Hayley and Connor has a room he's renting out, and Hayley helped Connor move in. I think the space will do them some good, and give them time to sort through their feelings.

While Hayley and Alice have always had lots of stuff in both mine and their mother's homes, they still wanted to retrieve some belongings from their mother's; I tried to tell them to let things calm down and give it time, but they were both adamant.

Hayley informed me that she had spoken to her mother, who said she and Alice could collect some things at 11.30am, but that they were not allowed inside her house together. Hayley and Alice hesitantly agreed to this.

Several times over the next hours, Ms Hyde rang Hayley to rearrange the time, which culminated in Hayley no longer being given permission to go round. It was arranged for Hayley to collect her things another day. Hearing this, Hayley went out with Conner.

The next minute, Alice stated she is going to phone the police to see if they will escort her again. I looked to the heavens, preparing myself to say let's not aggravate the situation by showing up with the police, but Alice flew out the room. As I climbed the stairs, I could hear Alice talking to what I could only presume was the police; having now reached the landing, I thought my best option was to retreat, find Lara and Sully, and wait to see what happens.

Lara was showing me some tricks that she'd taught Sully when Alice came in; she asked Lara if there was anything from her room she wanted Alice to bring home. Shaking her head, Lara said no. Lara admitted the only thing she really missed was Wotsit. I asked Alice what the situation with the police was, and she said they would try to send a couple of officers over at the time her mother had agreed.

I said to Alice, hopefully her mother will be calm and as long as she just goes to her room and gathers her belongings, there shouldn't be a problem.

With no sign of the police, reluctantly, Alice walked to her mother's.

When Alice called to ask me to pick her up, she was waiting outside the neighbours with some bags. As I pulled to the curb, Ms Hyde's front door swung open. Hurriedly, Alice got in the car and said that her mother kicked off immediately, and was going on about 'getting your dad arrested'.

Ms Hyde was advancing, shouting, and I drove away, reassuring Alice and telling her not to worry, even though I was.

From Ms Hyde

9 May

Dear Dean,

As you are aware Alice's appointment for her teeth extraction had to be postponed for the third time because of the first tribunal to the 15th April 10.00am; for some reason you declined to take her to this appointment and I had to cancel it giving 24hrs notice otherwise I would have lost my £20 deposit. The following appointment was made for Thursday 15th May at 10am. I know you are aware of this appointment but can you please ensure that Alice has nothing to eat or drink for four hours before; if you are not going to attend this appointment please can you have the courtesy to let me know with a minimum of 24hrs otherwise I will again lose my £20 deposit. It is very important that Alice attends this appointment as something should have been done approximately 2 years ago concerning her teeth.

I have spoken with the orthodontists and they can confirm that the x–rays needed for the operation have been sent. They have said that they would like to see Alice within a month of the operations so that she can discuss the ongoing treatment to rectify her dental problems.

When Alice came to live with me for five months last year she severe tooth ache in June and I was appalled when I went to the centre for a check up that she had not been taken by yourself for a check up for 18 months and they had deregistered her on the computer. I then registered her with my own dentist where she had a check up and was found to be needing 6 fillings, these were done over a period of time. I really feel that you have neglected to look after Alice's dental health and ask you again to make sure that Alice attends her appointments.

Whilst on this subject I would like to urge you to attend Hayley's dental requirements following her loss of her retainer which has resulted in her front teeth becoming crooked again. I have said to Hayley many times that I am prepared to go halves with you on the cost which she tells me is approximately £40.

Finally, while on the subject I am sure that Lara needs a check up and I wondered whether you could let me know that she has been or has an appointment.

Yours sincerely,

Another letter primed for Mrs Mason to place in her court bundle.

I feel I am getting cynical, but I have reached the outer limits. I am worn down and tired of the abuse, of never having the opportunity to settle down and being constantly bombarded by Ms Hyde's presence, personality and bipolar disorder.

While Mrs Mason, the Family Courts and family law have been having a jolly, three children have been left to deal with one of their parents with severe bipolar disorder.

The children needing to go to the dentist is part of being a parent, and Hayley, Alice and Lara have always had regular check-ups, contrary to what Ms Hyde says; Alice has a phobia of the dentist – there would have been 10 more pages to the book if I had included all of the times spent trying to coerce Alice to the dentist – which Ms Hyde is aware of, and this made it more difficult to get her to go, resulting in the fillings needed.

If it truly had been 18 months since the last dentist appointment, and Ms Hyde is so concerned, why had she not taken Alice herself or written me a letter in this vein before?

Adjusting

May

Hayley has been staying with Connor for the past several weeks, and she has not been home to see Alice, Lara, Ma or myself – except on a Friday, for her pocket money.

I have been trying to do more hours at work, since my Child Benefits are still suspended, and not having that top-up to my finances is just another thing on the list to worry about.

I asked Hayley if she would help me out by being at home, at least once a week, with Lara so I could return to site after dropping Lara home from school – on these occasions it would be because Ma can't make it, but I also emphasised to Hayley that she should spend some time with Lara anyway, as they used to be so close and I know Hayley growing up has been hard for Lara to adjust to.

Week after week, Hayley never came and would either make a flimsy excuse, or we simply did not see her… Until Friday rolled back around, and Hayley would be there for her pocket money.

Dean Marlo

Court – another ghost hearing

14th May 2008 / Venray Family County Courts
Mother's application – Contact with Alice and Lara

Judge Recorder Shelton directs the application of Ms Hyde to be treated as permission to issue an application for contact to Alice and Lara, including a penal notice on Mr Marlo to be attached to the order made in the proceedings dated 05/09/07.

Notice of this application to be served by the court to Mr Marlo and the hearing adjourned until 11th June 2008 at 10am.

This hearing was with legal representatives only - i.e. I was not informed or represented.

I won't let Lara be forced to go like Hayley was in 2000. The courts have worn me down and I no longer fear the repercussions of standing by my children.

It is great to see the justice system at work, what with the police being involved with Ms Hyde for assault and I'm the one with a penal notice application against me.

(I don't want to go to prison, but if that's the hill the Family Courts want to die on… I'm not putting another one of my children through that and give in 'without a fight'.

If a judge is reading, it's only a lyric! Even now, as I sit here writing the word 'fight', I know this could be an example of my violent tendencies, but I guess 'I am whatever you say I am'.)

Ms Hyde's application to the courts

Incidents of abuse, violence or harm

7/4/08 – In the context of an argument (Hayley's fiancé of three days moved his belongings into my house against my request to them both) Hayley called me a 'fucking wanker' and as a result of this and other verbal abuse from both Hayley and Alice I asked Hayley and her fiancé to leave the house and stay with her father or her fiancé's parents. Hayley pushed me on my bad shoulder (I had been in a serious road traffic accident early on 5/4/08) all three of my children knew very well that I was injured – I am still suffering from whiplash and pulled ligaments two weeks on. I pushed her away from me telling her to stop it and that I was in pain. She immediately pushed me again and I fell on my bad shoulder into the banisters half way down the stairs, tripped and rolled the rest of the way down the stairs. When I looked up all three children were laughing and chanting 'crocodile tears'.

Involvement of the child(ren)

I can't make an informed judgement here, as I have only seen my eldest two children, Hayley and Alice since, in the context of the incidents of intimidation.

I don't believe that Hayley intended for me to fall down the stairs, however her behaviour was reckless, disregarding my injury and the children reacted afterwards cruelly. I am receiving ongoing treatment for my injury which was aggravated by my fall.

I called the police after the children had left the house, partly because I have been in a comparable situation before and so has my partner, where allegations were subsequently made by the children, always after seeing their father, which greatly distorted the facts & truth.

My youngest daughter Lara had a friend over to play during these events and appeared traumatised. I had to call his parents straight away to collect him.

This incident happened in the context of several years of verbal abuse and occasional less serious physical incidents.

I believe that verbal abuse will definitely continue and that there is always an occasional risk of physical incidents, especially now the two elder children are becoming fully grown. I should add that in the week since the incident of 7/4/08 there have been several incidents of severe intimidation by Hayley and Alice (mostly Alice) with groups of their friends coming round to the house. This has resulted in me having to change the locks on my house at the request of my landlord.

Contact with my youngest daughter Lara has been withheld by their father since/against the official court order (part 6) ABDUCTION.

Witnesses

Conner Farley

Bernard Craven

Steve (Lara's school friend)

None of these people would appear in court as they would all wish to remain neutral.

Medical treatment or other assessment of the children

Cafcass and a guardian were appointed in the high court last June.

My middle daughter Alice has seen an educational psychologist over the last year. She was permanently excluded from school January 7th 2008 and is now at UEEC where her behaviour is up and down. She is often not willing to engage at all. We think she may have a very slight learning difficulty connected with dyslexia. Preliminary tests have been carried out.

Abduction

Please give the following information:

Your reason for believing that the child(ren) may be abducted

Whether the child(ren) have previously been the subject of a threatened abduction, an attempted abduction or have been abducted.

Whether the police or any other organisation has been involved in any alleged previous incident identified above.

Whether each child has their own passport and who has that passport at the moment.

Having read the notes relating to abduction this is exactly what Mr Dean Marlo has done to my youngest daughter Lara. He is withholding any form of contact including by phone contrary to a court order.

He has done this many times with my other two children as well.

Please see court order enclosed.

Steps or order required to protect you and the children

A court order with a power of arrest for my youngest daughter Lara Marlo so that regular contact with myself can take place and that the court order will be observed by Mr Dean Marlo (father).

All three children to be put on the child protection register.

Attending the Court

No disabilities but a separate/private waiting room would be helpful.

None of the witnesses will give evidence, as in the past, because they are either too frightened of threatening behaviour or they wish to remain neutral.

For the major incident of 7/4/08 one witness is my daughter's boyfriend and he wishes to remain neutral.

The second witness is my partner of 5 years and he wishes to remain neutral.

The third witness is my youngest daughter's best friend at school who we have to play and stay over on a very regular basis and have done since both children were 4. It would be unfair to question him, aged 10.

Signed,

Ruth Hyde, 18/04/08

This whole application is difficult to read, from the allegations to the way Ms Hyde reports events. She has blamed everyone for the current contact arrangements, apart from the way her actions have made the children feel.

The witness box makes me laugh too;

Conner dropped his things off and left before the argument started between Hayley and her mother; the only thing he was witness to was leaving his belongings with Hayley at the front door. Steve was in Lara's bedroom the whole time and even though he heard the verbal altercations, he didn't see what happened. (Is he neutral or too frightened to come forward?) Bernard was downstairs and came out of the front room to find Ms Hyde at the bottom of the stairs, per the children's account, and Ms Hyde's lack of mention in her statement, and we know from his previous actions, he's hardly credible.

Again, I am accused of abducting Lara, which is completely untrue and a serious allegation to make in an application; meanwhile, no mention of Alice's contact (other than the fact that Alice is still governed by the '07 order) so I suppose the court will assume she is acting of her own volition, but will they ask why? Why the children are refusing contact and why now, after years of following the order regardless of what her sisters are doing, Lara feels unsafe at her mother's?

The people that assess the court applications, along with Mrs Mason, have 17 years of serious allegations purported by Ms Hyde; evidence has never been produced for a judge to act on these statements, and yet the long line of false accusations continue. It appears to be a means of stating the worst to increase the likelihood of the courts approving her application – a father abducting a child from her mother is certainly a different hearing to the children are refusing contact due to their mother assaulting them.

Dear Mr MP

15 May

Thank you very much for your letter of the 21st April 2008, which was considerate of you and much appreciated.

Sadly, the Appeal Panel upheld the Governors' decision to permanently expel Alice from mainstream education. Since January this year, Alice has attended the UEEC from 1.15pm until 3.30pm.

Child Benefit

Since the 1st April 2008, my child benefit has been suspended which means I have had to look after and support three children as a single parent; trying to provide money for school dinners, school activities, petrol – to take Lara to school and in order to work – clothes, food shopping and financing our home, all on £161.35 per week from Working and Child Tax Credits. Please understand that I am grateful to receive this money. With circumstances as they are, I have not been able to work properly and to go shopping for four people with £40 makes it impossible to provide adequately for us all.

Once again, the recurring inappropriate behaviour from one parent has resulted in the system placing a genuine parent in an untenable position.

I have written to you in the past about the help and support that could be given by an appointed Welfare Officer. Not only would this Welfare Officer offer support to both parents and their children, they would also know first-hand of any development in the family's dynamics, and also be able to clearly relay the information to the Family Courts or, if necessary, an organisation such as the Child Benefit Office.

My point being, there would be more than enough money within the system for an organisation that would not only support the families that needed it but would be able to communicate with the Family Courts directly, cutting out the dishonest legal game and immoral continuation of the needless misery in a family's life.

I would like to ask if there is any minister who can justify to me the deplorable way my children, many other children and families have been treated by those working within the system?

If we as people of our community act inappropriately at our work place or when out on the streets, we run the risk of reprimand, caution, arrest or being sent to jail.

I would like to ask the Minister for Family Justice what right has the system or individuals working within the system have to ignore and dismiss the inappropriate behaviour and performance that is having a serious detrimental effect on children and families every day?

Ministers who are empowered to ensure that honesty, morals and standards are upheld are simply failing children, their families and our communities.

Those law firms which are found to be profiteering, misleading and dishonest, with no regards to the children and families involved, should be told to clean up their act or have no further dealings within family law. This is what happens when you're a person on the street in society, why is it any different, and arguably less accountable, for people working within the system?

I only ever received letters from government departments with poor excuses and misleading paragraphs that reject the heart of the issue or twist the perception to the point they justify immoral behaviour, even in children's matters.

The court order, September 2007

Due to the alleged violent incident at Ms Hyde's house on the 7th April, Hayley, Alice and Lara have refused to go their mother's for contact. This incident has once again caused me worry, not only for my children's welfare but also the possibility of prolonging our involvement within the Family Courts.

I am reluctant to go back to court to address the court order, as I have already indicated my children and I have endured enough of the façade, which has only led us more or less to where we began: there is an incident at mother's home involving a mother and her children, the children return to me upset, I stand by their position to not visit their mother at the present time, I get a penal notice-

If this must indeed return to court, I believe that under the circumstances and the position the legal system and Family Courts have placed my family in for many years, I should receive Legal Aid to provide me with professional representation to remove the uncertainty that has been placed in my family's life year after year, due to Ms Hyde's behaviour and inability to get on with her contact with her children. The system does not want to change for an ongoing case, so I am forced into the reality of needing a solicitor to navigate the legal blockades in the hope of finally bringing my children some peace and stability.

It is sad that the Family Courts are unable to recognise and accept the difference between a genuine parent and a parent that suffers with reoccurring mental health problems, and understand that despite the children's mother frequently acting in an unacceptable and aggressive way, I have not tried in any way to prejudice or encourage the children not to see their mother. This still remains today.

This has not been a domestic dispute, as has been played out for 8 years within the Family Courts by some unscrupulous law firm, a solicitor and multiple barristers.

With no apologies

I believe Smitch Law Solicitors are guilty of milking the Legal Aid purse and more importantly, robbing three young children of any normalcy that existed in their lives and childhood.

Melissa / Parstons Solicitors

Unfortunately, my solicitor for many years, Melissa, has left Parstons. Since the end of 2006, Melissa has given me free advice, help and guidance; for this, I will be eternally grateful and appreciate all Melissa has ever done for my children and myself.

It is clear that, as with Ms Hyde's behaviour towards our children over the years and the performance of those working within the Family Courts, between them, they believe they can behave as they wish as long as it is behind closed doors.

I have never encouraged or provoked the dishonest and inappropriate behaviour that my family have received, and I would like to see justice for my children, and all children in this country. The genuine efforts of people like Melissa should also be recognised and her approach to family law should be looked at as an example.

The major failures in my family's case should be worthy of bringing to the attention of the House of Parliament, to stress that children and their family values are being eroded by the behaviour and attitude that is endorsed within the system.

I also believe it worthy of telling it as it is - that when ethical codes are clearly being breached and the appropriate Government departments are informed of this, they are dismissive and do their utmost to defend an unsubstantiated opinion.

In 1999, I suggested that I could bring some stability into my three children's lives.

My willingness to fulfil my role as a parent to my children has resulted in nine years of the waste of time and resources for numerous judges, courtrooms, solicitors, barristers, psychologists, Guardians–

And the list goes on, with Legal Aid and myself footing the bill.

I kindly urge you to bring to the attention of MPs in the House of Parliament the needless, detrimental and harmful behaviour towards honest and decent parents that not only exists within the legal system and Family Courts, but is perpetuated without truth or justification.

The families and children of our communities need our ministers to act and make meaningful changes to the mechanisms that run the system.

Acknowledging and condemning the inappropriate and immoral behaviour, would be a step in the right direction.

Further, please find enclosed, a letter that I received from Ms Hyde at Alice's tribunal of 21st April.

I am deeply concerned about the content and false allegations that are implied by Ms Hyde in this letter towards my children and myself; I feel totally appalled and abused by its suggestions and the story that it relays.

I am appalled that Ms Hyde states in her letter that she is forwarding it to the Headteacher's of all the children's schools; Mrs Irfan, of Riverbank, has already informed me that she has received a copy.

Thank you again for your time and serious consideration to my thoughts based on my experiences.

Yours respectfully...

From Ms Hyde

21 May

Dear Mr Marlo,

I am very disappointed that you have not replied in full to my letter of 18th April.

I clearly asked you page 7, paragraph 1 to have Lara for the whole of the May half term, starting after school of Friday 23rd May until 12pm June 2nd to make up for the week I lost in the Easter holidays. In addition to this contact, you have not made Lara available for teatimes during the week (Wednesday or Thursday after school, my choice) as per the court order.

You have also changed your phone number without informing me either verbally or in writing. I only found out because Alice mentioned that you might be changing back to your original number a while ago. Also, I noticed the new name and number on your van as it is always parked on the road.

I find the lack of communication from yourself is unacceptable. You refuse to communicate either verbally by email or in writing. Any court order can only function with good communication and this has been emphasised so many times in court and yet you still disregard it.

Having read the account of the incident at my house you seem to find it acceptable to condone bad behaviour when you see it take place at my house; this is no different from the past when you have actively encouraged abusive and disruptive behaviour towards me. You have always brought the children into the arena and used them as your mouthpiece; your inability to deal with our problems without involving the children has done them no favours and it is high time you learnt that this approach is disruptive for them.

Finally, you took possession of the Riverbank School photos and delivered them back at the last minute, depriving me of any opportunity to view them. This is a lack of common courtesy and I think deliberate on your part. Fortunately, the school rang me and I was able to obtain copies.

I need an answer by return in writing as to whether or not Lara is coming for half term either on Friday 23rd May as requested or Wednesday 28th May at 12pm as per the original court order.

Yours sincerely,

CBO Calling

23 May

I received a phone call from the Child Benefit Office; they informed me that they had all the information and evidence that they needed, as sent in by Ms Hyde and myself, so there would be a committee hearing on the 6th June, when a decision would be made as to who would be receiving the Child Benefit in the future for Hayley, Alice and Lara.

(It's not like I've got children to look after in that period or that I've had sole residency since 2004… They don't even owe Ms Hyde from periods of Alice living at hers, although I suppose Ms Hyde wouldn't have included my letters and cheques in her 'evidence'.

The worst thing about this is, weeks, months, ago, whenever Ms Hyde made the initial call, the domino she set in motion would never fall and leave her in a difficult position; she is unaffected, wholly, by the months she has placed me in financial hardship, while I provide for our children. And, either they rule in my favour, in which case that one phone call wasted everyone's time except hers, or they rule in her favour, and the children are not having contact due to an abusive incident, so I guess she'd be getting paid for *not* having the responsibility of her children.)

Mr Rowe to me

27 May

Dear Mr Marlo,

Further to your phone call this morning, I have written to (a) the Secretary of State for Justice and (b) Minister for Family Justice. I enclose copies of both letters, which you will note are basically the same. I will contact you again when I get responses.

In the meantime, I must repeat the advice which I gave you today, namely that you must attend the court hearing. I appreciate that such hearings are most unpleasant for you, but I feel that if you are not there then this will work against you.

I also repeat my further suggestion that you seek legal advice, although I appreciate that this is probably not a realistic option because of the cost involved.

Please keep me advised of how things develop. Best wishes.

Yours sincerely…

27 May

Dear Minister,

You will recall that when you were the Minister responsible for Family Justice I had a meeting with you and my constituent Mr Dean Marlo who has experienced several years of court proceedings against him by the mother of his three daughters, for whom he has custody.

You may recall that the mother, Ms Hyde, suffers from mental health problems. Regrettably, she has been extensively funded with Legal Aid to pursue regular court proceedings against Mr Marlo. My constituent is not a wealthy man, but he is denied Legal Aid. It is thus a very unlevel playing field whenever matters get into court.

Why should Mr Marlo continue to be subjected to legal proceedings with the public purse funding Ms Hyde? It seems like a nice little earner for the firm of solicitors involved! But what of fairness and justice for Mr Marlo?

Mr Marlo contacted me today to advise me of the latest court action against him. I enclose a copy of the Notice served on him. He states that he had no knowledge of the hearing on 14th May. I have advised him to seek legal advice for the resumed hearing on 11th June, but he says he simply cannot afford legal advice – and by going to court he will lose a day's pay. That said, I have urged him to attend the court hearing.

The 'system' is clearly working against my constituent and his three daughters; is causing him and them considerable distress; and I now have a bulging file as evidence of my efforts to help Mr Marlo in the face of regular legal action by solicitors who are being handsomely paid by the public purse.

I would welcome your comments.

Yours sincerely,

Dean Marlo

Hayley visiting

2 June

Hayley informed me that she is going to go to her mother's to ask for an apology. Although we were both concerned how her mother will react, it showed Hayley was still willing to try with her mother. I said if she needed me to, I can come and pick her up.

It did not take long before Hayley returned; she was sobbing. Between her crying, she told me that her mother denied punching her, and had called her 'a wicked child' for pushing her down the stairs. I gave Hayley a hug, and as I have throughout her life, I told not to take what her mother says to heart. Hayley nodded but there were still tears in her eyes, and she went on to say that her mother also said, 'I cannot be alone with you, due to your lies.'

I felt sad for Hayley, and how she has been put through this emotional and physical abuse from her mother for her whole life; she still went back round there to attempt to have a relationship with her. Yet, again, she is instead devastated by her mother's attitude towards her.

MoJ to Mr Rowe MP, and my reply

4/9 June

4 June

Dear Mr Marlo,
Please find enclosed a copy of the acknowledgement I have received from the Ministry of Justice.
They are currently investigating this matter. I will contact you again when I receive a full response.
Best wishes.
Yours sincerely,
PS. Thank you for your most recent letter which I hope to deal with in the coming week.

2 June

Dear Mr Rowe,
I refer to your letter of 27 May addressed to The Rt. Hon Secretary of State, about Legal Aid.
Your letter was received on 29 May and the Minister aims to reply within 20 working days. However, if we anticipate a delay, I will inform you as soon as possible.
I shall also contact you again if, after considering your letter further, it appears that another department may deal with it more appropriately.
Yours sincerely,

9 June

Dear Mr Rowe,
Thank you very much for your letter of the 4th June and the copy of acknowledgement from the Ministry of Justice.

Please find enclosed a copy of a letter that I am taking with me to the family court hearing on 11th June 2008.

I feel once again I must express to you that many aspects of our legal system are unwarranted, unfair and promotes an un-level playing field, as I have experienced, simply because I have tried to get back to work to provide for my children and give them a decent standard of living. For this, I have continually been discriminated against concerning Legal Aid, resulting in me not having the ability to be professionally represented as I have been threatened, pursued and drained by the Family Court System.

Penal Notice
In 2000, my solicitor told me that if the Family Courts granted me any form of contact with my children, and Ms Hyde decided that she would not comply with the order, then the judge would be reluctant to place a penal notice on a parent that was the mainstay in their children's lives. It must mean something different when the 'mainstay' is a father; this threat has been levelled against me constantly.

Why as a parent do I live my live in fear of a prison sentence when I have committed no crime? This burden must be seen as unacceptable and unjust.

Order 91(14) September 2007
After your own efforts, we were told on good authority that an order 91(14) would

599

allow our children/family to have a break from family court involvement and lengthy court proceedings. Yet, within 9 months, we are bordering on square one again with Cafcass involvement and a penal notice.

Maintenance

I feel it unjust that Ms Hyde, as a parent, makes no contribution in the way of any maintenance for the upbringing of our children, despite, I believe, it being required by law. (Although certainly it would bring further grief in my life, even though I have the legal right, it is hard when the person is making your life difficult already.) In my children's case, no one is interested in the fact that in the last 4 years, since I have had sole residency, Ms Hyde has paid no maintenance towards her children's upkeep.

In addition to this, Ms Hyde is able to repeatedly use the Legal Aid purse to bring instability into our children's lives.

I know, have spoken to and am aware of parents, predominantly fathers, who are troubled by being refused contact or involvement with their children. Yet these parents are hounded into paying maintenance for their children that they are not allowed to see or have little to no input towards. Of course, not every case is the same – there are some horrific parents out there, I am also aware of this – generalising a law in a way that persecutes innocent people is not just or effective.

I do not have any issues with Ms Hyde improving her standard of living. However, I firmly believe that fathers and mothers should be treated equally regarding maintenance, Legal Aid and abuse of any kind.

Legal Aid

In 2002, Smitch Law, on behalf of their client, wrote to the Legal Aid Department questioning my entitlement for Legal Aid. This was regarding the hearing for Joint Residency of Hayley, Alice and Lara, which was brought about after Ms Hyde had been sectioned for the fourth time under the Mental Health Act.

I strongly believe that because of the malicious interference of Smitch Law, at Ms Hyde's behest, my financial aid was wrongly rescinded causing me extra worry of financial hardship. After the hearing, I received Joint Residency of my children along with a bill for £800, plus VAT.

Not exactly the best send off from the family court – having £800 debt and residency of three children is a good thing right?

Once again in 2006, Smitch Law placed uncertainty in our lives as a family by challenging my receipt of Legal Aid. Not only had I the worry of more court proceedings, Alice flitting between homes and a Ms Hyde sized boot dent in my van door, but also the strain of having to pay for any representation.

I have not sat back and lived on benefits; I have worked to raise my three daughters. Once again, I feel that I am being unfairly punished for this.

You understand then, my fear that future legal bills will result in placing me into a bankruptcy situation, and I have the worry of further proceedings, without any help from Legal Aid for legal representation.

Yours respectfully…

Letters by Lara to the Judge

Dear Sir/Madam,

I am writing to inform you why I am not going to see my mother on Thursdays for tea and weekends.

I am refusing to go because of a recent incident involving my mother punching my sister in the face, this has made me scared and afraid of being there; another reason is she has insulted my nan who has done nothing to her and has not got involved with my mother in any way, she has only been my loving Nan who has always been there for me. Her doing this has made me really upset.

Finally this is not my dad's choice, or my sisters making me say this, please listen to what I am saying and what I want. This is what I want others to see. So even if she says 'I'm taking Lara' I will always refuse until such time I feel secure round my mother's. I believe that I should be off the court order and be free to choose whether I should go round there such as if she has made me upset or if she is scaring me I don't have to go round hers until I feel secure.

Please read these letters out during court and let my mother know how I feel.

Yours faithfully,

L Marlo

To Sir/Madam,

This is my second letter concerning recent things my mother has said. To start with I am always going to the phone to answer her calls even though I don't want to talk to her; she is constantly hanging up on the phone just because I am telling the truth and I am extremely upset that she hangs up in the middle of the sentence when I am trying to speak.

I would also like to raise that I do not want to go round hers for the summer holidays and not until I feel ready.

Another thing that she does that really annoys me is that she calls me up and then asks me if I am going round hers when she knows how I feel and I think she does it to waste time because like I said in the first letter I am in no situation that I feel secure enough to go round hers. One of my best friends was round her house when the incident took place and I was sitting on my bed when she started talking a load of rubbish about my Nan. That's when I had to say to him, 'I need to go and stick up for my Nan and my Dad and my sisters'. He sat in my room listening to all of us pointing out truth from lies and lies from truth. If the police get involved and they place a penal notice on my dad and they try to take me to my mother's I shall do the following: sit in the middle of the floor and tell the police why I am not willing to go there and if I don't make it clear enough they shall be getting both of these letters.

I hope now after you have received both of these letters you will stop believing my mother's ridiculous and cruel lies that have hurt and disrupted my life so far. I believe that I should be off the court order and be free to choose whether I should go round there such as if she has made me upset or if she is scaring me I don't have to go round hers until I feel secure.

Please read these letters out during court and let my mother know how I feel.

Yours faithfully,

L Marlo

Dean Marlo

To the Family Courts – From Hayley

10 June

Dear Sir/Madam,

I am writing to inform you about the incident which happened recently which has come to the point where I would not like to visit or have contact with my mother.

On the 7th of April 2008, I asked my mother if my fiancé could stay round her house for a couple of days, which she had let him for the past few days and bring some of his belongings. When my fiancé dropped his clothes and belongings to the house, she replied I could put them in the garage, which I was not happy with as they could be in my bedroom. I asked why they could not be in my room, which is when my mother started shouting.

Alice got involved and agreed with me that his things should be in my bedroom. This then turned into a big argument, which I ended up calling our mother an abusive name down stairs.

She then came upstairs and started on Alice. Shouting and arguing inches from her face and grabbing her arm which by then Lara had come out of her room and was standing behind me.

I was getting scared for Alice so I pulled our mother's arm, my mother turned round and punched me in the chest then my mouth. I was totally shocked by her actions and felt my lip it was swollen and bleeding on the inside of my mouth.

At that point our mother had started to walk half way down the stairs so I followed after her. I wanted to hit her but I controlled my anger and pushed her lightly, she then pretended to fall the last three steps, ending up sitting on the floor. She then got up and went into the kitchen crying.

We all collected our things and went back to our dad's. Me, Alice and Lara were all in shock and crying when this incident happened.

I have taken my mum back into my life so many times when she has hit me in the past and I haven't reported it but this is the last time and I would not like to see my mother ever again.

She has also hurt my dad and Nan so much which has an effect on our family when my mum starts telling lies.

I have written this letter to explain how I feel and I hope you understand my feelings towards my mother.

Dear Judge,

11 June

It is with much sadness and regret that I find my family once again back in the Family Courts.

I believe that Ms Hyde's application for permission to apply for a penal notice to be placed on me to be an unreasonable and an unjust request, as it is Ms Hyde's behaviour that has resulted in our children's reluctance to have contact with their her and comply with the court order. I do feel that the application for a penal notice is just another attempt by Ms Hyde to cloud the issue and undermine my ability to provide the love, care and support that our children need.

Throughout our family's involvement in the court process, it has been made quite clear that Ms Hyde has repeatedly shown her inability to get on with our children in her contact time, and has found it very difficult to maintain consistency and care in our children's lives. This I believe is due to Ms Hyde's failure to calmly evaluate a situation and her aggressive response, behaviour and attitude towards her children and others.

As Hayley is no longer under a court order, I would ask the Family Courts to recognise that the non–compliance of Alice and Lara of the court order is entirely due to Ms Hyde's behaviour towards her children while in her contact time.

I have done my utmost to comply with judges' wishes and court orders but once again, as a caring parent I must listen to my children's concerns for their welfare and happiness.

It is my opinion that the application by Ms Hyde is not only detrimental to our family but also a waste of court time and resources; Ms Hyde has allegedly assaulted her eldest daughter, which was witnessed by her two younger daughters, causing them to not wish to visit their mother. While the abusive behaviour has never been addressed, I would like you to note that, in past incidents, given time, the children return to their mother's, which negates the necessity for court enforcement of the order or harassment of me, as the parent who had three crying children appear at the door two days into their half-term contact with their mother.

Whatever form of contact I was awarded with my children, Ms Hyde has tried to disrupt and exploit it, or make life as difficult for our children and myself as she possibly could.

The content and false allegations that are implied by Ms Hyde in her correspondence and her application are deeply concerning, and I believe that her unfounded accusations are another symptom of her on-going mental health condition.

I once again deny the personal allegations made about me and cannot express to you enough the stress and worry Ms Hyde has brought into my life; I feel totally appalled and abused by the suggestions and stories relayed. These unsubstantiated statements have been passed on to the Headteachers at all three of our children's schools by Ms Hyde.

For years, my children and I have had to put up with false allegations from Ms Hyde being placed within our lives, our community and also within the Family Courts. I feel totally victimised by the continuation of Ms Hyde's behaviour and actions towards my children and myself, and do not believe that my children and I deserve to be persecuted and treated in such a manner.

I do not want to get involved with any more litigation with Ms Hyde or more proceedings within the Family Courts; my children and I have had enough, and I ask the Family Courts to recognise this.

I am not the person that Ms Hyde portrays and do not act towards her in any detrimental way, as a person or regarding her relationships with her daughters. I therefore ask that the court order of September 2007 remain in place for Alice and Lara, with contact resuming at the children's requests.

Yours faithfully...

Courts – the applicant is an abuser, your Honour

11th June 2008 / Venray Family County Courts
Mother's application – give back the children

Judge Daggett hears from counsel for the applicant Ms Hyde and Mr Beltran, solicitor for Cafcass.

The court directs Ms Hyde does have permission to proceed with her application to attach a penal notice to the Order of the 5th September 2007; Ms Hyde and Mr Marlo file statements, and the children's newly appointed Guardian, Ms Dowling, to file a report.

Case listed for the 28th July 2008.

(I reckon they are getting pissed off in the prison block, having to keep making my bed up, only for me not to check in.)

Following all the disruption in their lives, Alice has become very anxious and in the past week has refused to go anywhere if I am not also present. Upon Alice's insistence and worries, she wanted to come to the court hearing with me and maybe explain to the judge exactly what was going on, as she felt like her views had not been properly addressed in the past. Alice's anxiety has created a new set of problems that I am struggling to handle; I didn't want Alice to come to court, but, as over the past year, it is difficult to reason with Alice and I did not want to intensify any of the emotional turmoil she is going through.

Unfortunately, in court I explained to Alice, there was no time for me to ask the judge for permission for her to speak, as proceedings had been set out for the next hearing.

I didn't really do much else, what with having no representation and just the letter I'd written to the judge. (I am still waiting for the pen to be mightier than the sword.)

At the end of the hearing, Judge Daggett asked me if I would like to withdraw the letter I'd handed in, which I did. I am not a legal person, but it was my understanding that when Judge Daggett addressed Ms Hyde's barrister and requested a statement be made, and I was told to make a statement in reply – essentially, whatever was in my letter would have to wait for the statements.

With the next court date expected for the end of July, I explained to the court the children and I were going on holiday for a week starting on the 18th August, to ensure this period is not selected if the hearing is moved back.

Dean Marlo

From HM Revenue and Customs

11 June

Enquiry:
You have told us that since 8 April 2008 Hayley, Alice and Lara have been with you full time.

Ms Hyde has told us Hayley and Lara are with her every other weekend, Friday to Monday sometimes staying overnight during the week, and that from the end of December 2007, Alice has lived with her fulltime.

In order for us to confirm that Hayley, Alice and Lara are living with you, please send a letter from Social Services, the educational establishments that Hayley, Alice and Lara attend or your general practitioner.

If we do not receive a reply within 14 days from the date of this letter, a decision will be made using the information we hold.

Another institution Ms Hyde has blatantly lied to, using them for her own gains.

NGS (Copy to Mr Marlo)

13 June

Dear Ms Hyde,
Thank you for your letter regarding Hayley's GCSE examination. The examinations office at Northview Grove School have already notified the examination board of Hayley's special circumstances. Any decision regarding this is made entirely by the examination board taking each case into consideration at the time of marking the papers.
Yours sincerely,

She tries to pull the caring mother card, as though she was not the one to upset and disrupt Hayley during her exams. Due to what had happened in April, I'd been in contact with all the children's schools, but particularly for Hayley, because Hayley was clearly not in the same mindset she was before the incident, and she didn't deserve her mother's behaviour to affect the outcomes of her exams.

This is just another letter, prepped for Mrs Mason's court bundle.

Dean Marlo

From UEEC (forwarded to me)

20 June

Dear Ms Hyde,
With reference to our recent conversation, I can confirm Alice's attendances for the Summer Term 2008
are as follows:
Summer, term 1 (14 April 2008 - 23 May 2008) –
Sessions offered, 28
Sessions attended, 25
Summer, term 2 (2 June 2008 - 23 July 2008) –
Sessions offered, 18
Sessions attended, 1

What this information actually reveals but does not have the context for, is Alice's anxiety. This has resulted in Alice sitting in my van while I work rather than going to the UEEC, which I know is not ideal; Alice and I are trying to help her resolve her worries, but with the looming court proceedings, I don't see how any of us are supposed to cope or focus on the future.

(I lack faith in the Family Courts, but we still have to get through the proceedings to be able to pick up the pieces and start again.)

Mrs Mason's jaws are on the doorframe

20 June

We refer to your attendance at court on the 11th June, informing that the hearing date has been moved to 21st August 2008.

We should be grateful if you would please provide us with a copy of the letter that you handed to Judge Daggett that day in order that we may have full disclosure.

Alice & Lara have been appointed their own solicitor, Legal Aid funded, and a Guardian.

We enclose herewith a copy of our client's Statement dated 25th June 2008, together with exhibits referred to, receipt of which please acknowledge.

I informed the court the children and I go on holiday on the 18th of August and, as for Mrs Mason's request, she is fully aware of court protocol and has no right to request the letter I retracted in any case; she will have full disclosure through my statement, as requested by the judge.

Ms Hyde's Statement

I, Ruth Hyde, in the County Court make this statement believing it to be true and knowing that it will be placed before the court in evidence.

I make this statement in accordance with the Order of Judge Daggett dated 11th June 2008.

I would first of all like to say how very sad that I am to be in this position again and having to seek the assistance of the court in order to be able to maintain a relationship with my children.

I had hoped that the last order made on 5th September 2007 would mean an end to court proceedings but this has not been possible.

It is simply impossible to deal with Mr Marlo. He refuses to speak to me at all, he doesn't keep me informed about anything to do with the children and just after the hearing in September 2007, he moved to his current address. Mr Marlo did not inform me of his intended move and I only heard from the children. Since Mr Marlo and I separated in 1999 he has moved six times and I understand he may also be moving again.

During 2007, Alice actually lived with me for six months due to disagreements with Mr Marlo. After the hearing in September, Alice went back to her usual behaviour of wanting to come and live with me whenever she had a disagreement with Mr Marlo and lived with me from December 2007 until 6 April 2008 with no contact at all with Mr Marlo except for a few phone calls and a couple of visits when she went for tea earlier this year. I did encourage Alice to see and speak with Mr Marlo but she was adamant that she would not do so.

When Alice was living with me, I discovered that she had not been to the dentist for 18 months and it was necessary for me to register her at my dentist. Alice had six fillings last summer when I took her to the dentist. The dentist stated that Alice needed to have some teeth removed and an appointment was made for December 2007. Unfortunately Alice would not go to that appointment but later Alice stated that she would go and I booked a further appointment. Unfortunately Mr Marlo has failed to take Alice to the dentist and she is in dire need of further treatment. Mr Marlo does not seem to believe that it is important for Alice to go to the dentist despite the fact that he knows she needs to have teeth removed.

In December 2007 Alice ran away from school on two occasions and on one occasion attempted to get to Venray to stay with a friend who was living in a care home. On the other occasion I believe that she was somewhere in town but she arrived back at my home at midnight. Mr Marlo and I went out in his car that evening looking for her by driving around town and going to her friends' homes.

Her behaviour at school was getting worse and Alice was finally excluded from school on 8 January 2008. There is now produced to me and marked 'RHY1' a copy of a letter dated 7 January 2008 from Northview Grove School confirming that Alice has been permanently excluded from school. The letter explains that Alice was excluded for persistently poor and disruptive behaviour, showing no respect for any authority within the school, a complete refusal to follow reasonable requests or to work and also showing a total disregard for the authority of senior staff and Health & Safety requirements.

I was devastated by Alice's exclusion from the school and worked very hard to try and have Alice re-instated. Unfortunately, however, despite an appeal to the Independent Appeal Panel, the school have refused to allow Alice to return.

After Alice was excluded from school I attempted on numerous occasions to speak with Mr Marlo about how we could work together and try and help Alice. As usual, Mr Marlo refused to discuss anything with me at all and I felt that he was simply trying to blame me for Alice's behaviour and bringing up my past mental health problems. I had been trying to explain to Mr Marlo for years beforehand that Alice's behaviour was of great concern to me but he simply stated, when he did speak with me, that Alice did not behave like that when she was with him and that it was all my fault.

Clearly, as can be seen from the letter from Northview Grove, Alice's behaviour is not just when she is with me but with other people. I want Mr Marlo to try and accept that Alice needs a great deal of help and guidance and that we should all be working together to ensure that Alice is allowed back at school.

Alice is just 14 years of age and I fear that if she does not return to main stream school shortly then her education will come to an end.

Since the middle of February 2008 Alice has been registered at the Unified External Education Centre. Unfortunately, Alice has not been attending school for the last month. Alice just has to attend for two hours every day but has only attended one session in the last four weeks. There is now produced to me and marked 'RHY2' a copy of a letter from the County Council dated 20 June 2008 confirming Alice's attendance. I am extremely upset that Mr Marlo is unable to ensure that Alice goes to the UEEC. Mr Marlo refuses to discuss anything at all with me concerning the children and the first I knew about Alice's non–attendance was when I received the letter from the UEEC referred to above.

My own view is that Mr Marlo cannot bear it when the children and I are close and getting on. I believe that he finds it very difficult when Alice has chosen to spend time with me rather than him and he will say that this is because I do not have any boundaries and Alice can 'get away with murder'. This is complete nonsense. Mr Marlo and I have very different parenting ideas. I want my children to grow up knowing right from wrong and to have respect for other people. I do set boundaries for the children and I will not tolerate bad behaviour. Unfortunately Mr Marlo does not have the same views about bringing up the children. He constantly undermines me as a mother. He always refers to me as 'the mother' and the children now refer to me as this when I call them. Mr Marlo encourages the children to disrespect me, he involves the children in these court proceedings and I believe he is doing all he can to destroy my relationship with the children. I find this totally unacceptable. Mr Marlo actually brought Alice to the last hearing on 11 June 2008 which I think was inappropriate and there was no need for her to be there.

In February 2008 Hayley was arrested by the police for being abusive to a police officer. The children and I were due to go to Gran Canaria on holiday and the girls arrived the day before we were meant to fly. Hayley had had an argument with Mr Marlo before coming to my home and after supper Hayley wanted to go out. I didn't want Hayley to go out but she was insistent. At about 8pm I received a call from the police to say that Hayley had been arrested and I went down to the police station. Hayley was eventually released from the police station at 1am and we were due to leave at 8am to catch the plane. Hayley asked me not to tell Mr Marlo what had happened as she knew that he would be very angry and she wanted to tell him in her own time. The police officer at the station assured her that in view of her age it was up to her if she wanted to tell her father or not. She had been frightened by her arrest and the hours that she had spent in the police cell and during her time in custody she caused cuts and bruises to her fists because she was punching the concrete walls of the cells in sheer frustration. When Hayley was arrested she asked the police to phone me rather than her father because she knew how her father would react.

After Hayley was released by the police, I told her that I would have to tell Mr Marlo but I agreed that we would ring him on the way to the airport as by this time it was 1am and far too late to call. I was concerned that Mr Marlo might do something to prevent us from travelling. I knew that he would go ballistic and the children and I were looking forward to our holidays.

I did phone Mr Marlo on the way to the airport to tell him that Hayley had been arrested. Mr Marlo immediately became agitated and aggressive. I simply told Mr Marlo that it had been dealt with and that I was informing him of what had happened and that he could discuss it with Hayley when she returned from holiday. Mr Marlo was getting more and more annoyed so I had to end the phone call. I felt that I had done what I should have done by telling Mr Marlo as he had a right to know which is more than he has ever done in keeping me informed of important matters relating to our children.

There have been some problems with regard to my contact with the children but there have been some really happy times. There are now produced to me and marked 'RHY3' photographs taken of the children and I during Christmas 2007, Lara's birthday in December 2007, our holiday in Gran Canaria in February 2008 and around Hayley's birthday in March 2008. I think that these photographs show that the children and I have had some really enjoyable times which is why I am so surprised at the letters the children were meant to have written to the court.

Just last Mother's Day in March 2008 all three children sent me beautiful cards and Lara made her own. There is now produced to me and marked 'RHY4' copies of these cards. I believe that they show how much the children love me and I am sure that Mr Marlo is doing his very best to try and turn the children against me.

Matters really came to a head in early March 2008. The children were due to see me on the weekend of 1/2 March 2008 and Mother's Day was on Sunday 2 March 2008. Lara contacted me to say that it was her dog's birthday on 1 March 2008 and she wanted to spend the day with Mr Marlo. I did suggest that Lara could spend the day with her dog and Mr Marlo on the 1 March 2008 but that I did want her to spend time with me on Mother's Day. Mr Marlo, as always, does not encourage the children to spend time with me despite the fact that there is a court order and I find this very frustrating. I would expect him to support me and tell the children that they need to have a relationship with their mother but he refuses to do so. All of the children are very aware of the respondent's feelings towards me and I believe that they have been affected by this.

On Friday 4 April 2008 Hayley came to see me with her boyfriend and she asked if she could stay. Hayley had only earlier got engaged to her boyfriend that evening. I told Hayley to ring Mr Marlo to tell him that she was intending to stay the night with me and she did so. Alice was living with me at that time so she was in the house and Lara was at Mr Marlo's as she was not due to come for contact until 6pm on 5 April 2008.

On 5 April 2008 I was involved in a serious car accident which resulted in my car being written off and I suffered very bad whiplash. I was prescribed pain killers which I continue to take.

Lara came for contact on the Saturday evening. Hayley and her fiancé went out for the evening and Lara and I sat down to watch a DVD together. Alice and Lara were having an argument and that evening Alice decided to go and stay with Mr Marlo. This was quite surprising given that Alice hadn't wanted to see him for weeks beforehand. Alice then returned to me on the Sunday.

Hayley's fiancé stayed on the Friday evening and Saturday evening and spent much of Sunday lounging around. Hayley asked me if her fiancé could stay again on the Sunday night and I agreed but I was still feeling very shaken by the accident and I wasn't happy that Hayley's fiancé was staying another night.

On 7 April 2008 I noticed that there were five bin bags outside the front door and Hayley told me that her fiancé was moving in. I told Hayley that he could not move in but Hayley completely ignored me and walked upstairs with the five bin bags. Alice then got involved and said that if Hayley wanted her fiancé to move in then she could make that decision. I told Alice that it wasn't anything to do with her and that it was my decision for Hayley's fiancé not to move in.

I didn't want to have an argument with Alice so I started to walk down the stairs and went into the kitchen. Hayley then followed me into the kitchen and screamed at me 'you fucking wanker'. I told Hayley that she was not to speak to me like that and I asked her to leave. She walked upstairs and I followed her and told her that I would not tolerate her behaviour and that she would have to leave. Alice then became involved again and started shouting. Hayley then grabbed my left arm which was incredibly painful due to my accident. I admit to pushing Hayley away from me but I did not punch her in the chest. As part of my employment I am trained in dealing with confrontational situations and maintaining personal space. My reaction would be to push Hayley away and walk away and not at any time would I punch her. I did not punch Hayley either in the chest or in the face and she had no injuries at all.

I then walked back to the top of the stairs and Hayley and Alice were screaming abuse at me. I was facing both girls and had my back to the stairs. Suddenly, without any warning at all Hayley pushed me in my upper chest causing me to fall down the stairs. I landed in a heap at the bottom of the stairs and was very shaken. I burst into tears and was in a great deal of pain. When I looked up the stairs all three children were laughing at me and shouting 'crocodile tears'.

The children then ran down the stairs and out of the house. After a couple of hours I decided to call the police to report what had happened. The police finally arrived at 3am and I explained to them what had happened. The police advised me that I should prosecute Hayley for what she had done but I was not willing to do so. I didn't want to get Hayley into trouble, as she had already been with the police in February 2008 because of her behaviour towards the police and I didn't want to make matters any worse. I knew that Hayley wanted to go to college and I didn't want anything to prevent her from doing so.

I have not seen Lara since she left the house with Hayley and Alice on 7 April 2008. This is the longest time that I have not seen Lara and I am finding it incredibly difficult.

Mr Marlo wrote a letter to me on 25 April 2008 which he hand delivered which is now produced and marked 'RHY5'. In this letter he states that Lara does not want to see me and that he was taking Lara out of school that day to take her to the 'appropriate organisation'. I have no idea what organisation Mr Marlo was meaning but in the past he has contacted Child Legal Guidance, Mind (Connexions) and Social Services. The school did confirm to me, however, that Lara did not attend school on 25 April 2008. I don't think it is appropriate for Mr Marlo to act in this manner.

Mr Marlo refuses to respond to any correspondence that I send to him or answer his phone if I try and call him. There is now produced to me and marked 'RHY6' copies of various letters that I have sent to Mr Marlo which he has not even acknowledged. I have attempted to communicate with him in, I believe, a courteous manner but he simply won't respond.

I have attempted to speak with Lara every week but she has been quite abusive on the phone which is completely out of character for her. I did speak with Lara on Wednesday 18 June 2008 and she was very much calmer. I explained that I wanted to see her as did my parents but I would not force her to come if she didn't want to. I suggested that she came over for tea and I told her how much I loved her and how much her grandparents loved her.

On 27 April 2008 I was arrested by the police for assaulting Hayley. I believe that Hayley waited for about 9 days before she went to the police to make the allegation that I had assaulted her. I am sure that Mr Marlo would have encouraged Hayley to go to the police and I am now having to deal with police investigations. I have co-operated fully with the police and I have explained exactly what happened on the evening of 7 April 2008. I told the police of my discussions with the police at my home on 7 April 2008 and the fact that I did not want to prosecute Hayley for pushing me down the stairs.

I am due to return to the police station on 3 July 2008 when a decision will be made as to whether a prosecution will be made. I understand that they will have to make a decision by 2 July 2008 as to whether a prosecution should take place.

If I am convicted of assaulting Hayley then I will lose my job and I will not be able to work in my current field in the future.

Since the incident on 7 April 2008 I have seen Hayley on two occasions, the last time being on 2 June 2008. She came to my home on her own saying she wanted an apology from me for punching her in the face. I told Hayley that I had not punched her in the face and that it was inexcusable of her to push me down the stairs. I told Hayley that I was happy to see her but I could not see her on my own because I did not want her making further false allegations. Hayley did not apologise to me for her behaviour on 7 April 2008 and she left the house in tears. Since then, Hayley has sent me very hurtful texts such as 'You fuck my life up every time. Thanks. I really do hate you for what you have done to me in my life.' (Sent on 3 June 2008.) Alice has also been sending me abusive texts which I find incredibly hurtful.

I am completely worn down by the behaviour of all of the children and while I accept that Hayley and Alice are of an age to decide whether they wish to see me, I believe that there does need to be a court order to ensure that I am able to have a relationship with Lara. Without a court order I know that I will not be able to have a relationship with Lara. I do not accept that it would be best for Lara not to have a relationship with me or her extended family. Lara has always been a very calm child and has come for contact whatever has been happening with the other two children. She has managed to keep outside of the quarrels involving Hayley and Alice and we have always enjoyed a very close relationship.

I am fearful that Lara is now been encouraged by Mr Marlo and her sisters not to have contact with me and to act in the way that she has done recently. Lara's behaviour is completely out of character and I am worried that she is copying Hayley and Alice in relation to their behaviour.

Mr Marlo needs to accept that all the children need to have a relationship with both of their parents. I accept that the children should remain living with Mr Marlo which is where they wish to be but I feel that they do need the input of a mother.

I love my children very much, they have my extended family who love them and wish to be involved in their lives and I find it very upsetting that the children, at the moment, are not able to enjoy a relationship with me and my family.

I feel that the past 9 years have been a war between Mr Marlo and I. This has not been of my making. I simply want to be able to see the children and to have a civil relationship with Mr Marlo which would enable us to speak with each about matters relating to our children. I know that if the children could see that Mr Marlo and I were able to work together then matters would calm down. Sadly, Mr Marlo is unwilling to do anything conciliatory despite me attempting to deal with matters in this manner.

My last recourse has been to make an application to the court to enforce the contact order that was made in September 2007 in relation to Lara. My only wish is to be able to have a relationship with my children and for the court to enforce the order that was made last year.

Mr Marlo has shown time and time again that he is unwilling to comply with court orders. He refuses to provide me with a schedule for my contact for the year as he should do by the 31 May each year. No matter how many times I ask Mr Marlo to provide me with the schedule he refuses to do so. It is incredibly frustrating for me as I am unable to make any plans in respect of the children including booking holidays.

The children should be able to have a relationship with both their parents, they should be able to enjoy spending time with their mother and their father and their extended families and I am very upset that at the moment the children do not have any contact with me or my family.

I am asking the court to confirm the contact order made in September 2007 in relation to Lara and attach a penal notice to the order to ensure that my contact can take place.

To Judge Chips

20 June

I am writing to you for two reasons, firstly because you granted me sole residency of my three daughters in 2004 (Case Number above) and secondly, as you were the judge at the hearing in Venray on the 26th July 2007.

I raised my concerns to you that I had not received any communication in writing regarding the forthcoming hearing from neither the Family Courts nor Smitch Law. I am once again worried that I am not being kept informed or treated fairly as I, up to the 20th June, have only received one letter on the 23rd May from the Family Courts as conformation of a hearing on the 11th June 2008.

I was shocked to read on the order from the Family Courts on the 14th May 2008, 'Mr Marlo not attending'. The truth is I did not attend because I was unaware of the hearing taking place.

After the hearing on the 11th June 2008 with Judge Daggett, a date for the next hearing was suggested for the end of July; I explained at the time that between the 18th and the 25th of August, the children and I would be on holiday, in case the date was pushed back.

Subsequently, I was informed by Smitch Law that the hearing date had changed to 21st August 2008. As I have stated, I did inform the court of the children's holiday and can only apologise for any inconvenience this may cause; I do not believe the children should miss out on their holiday in order for court hearings to proceed.

I would like to confirm that on the 20th of June, I received a letter of conformation of this date.

Yours faithfully…

Gathering supporting evidence

24 June

From UEEC:

Dear Mr Marlo,

I can confirm that the records we hold show that you have sole residency of your daughters, one of whom is Alice who is a pupil at this centre. On occasion when we have tutored Alice at home, it has been at your address.

Yours sincerely…

From the children's doctor – at a cost of £5:

Hayley Marlo

Alice Marlo

Lara Marlo

I write with regard to the above-mentioned children who are currently registered at this surgery with the aforementioned address. I understand that this is their father's address and this is where they currently reside. I hope this information is useful to you. Should there be anything further questions, please do not hesitate to be in contact.

Yours sincerely,

From Mr Rowe to CBO

26 June

Dear Mr Marlo,

As always, it is disheartening and upsetting to learn that your ex–partner continues to distress you via 'the system' that is supposed to support you and your children.

I have written on your behalf to request that the Child Benefit you are entitled to should be reinstated as a matter of urgency. A copy is enclosed for information. Hopefully this may help towards a speedy conclusion.

Beverly also informs me you have experienced a knock–on effect with your Council Tax. Once you have dropped off the relevant paperwork, I will also pursue this for you. Best wishes.

Yours sincerely,

Dear Sirs,

My constituent Mr Marlo has contacted me due to the severe financial hardship he and his three children have been placed under since Child Benefit was ceased, pending investigation.

Due to Mr Marlo's former partner making claims that she has main custody of the children, your office stopped payments to him. I am advised that details of the court ruling providing Mr Marlo with the custody of his children has already been sent to you by him.

Additionally, supporting evidence has been sent by Mr Marlo in response to your request for additional proof on behalf of Alice and Lara. Copies of these are also enclosed for your information.

I have been assisting Mr Marlo for many years so am able to vouch for both his integrity and support for his children.

Due to the immense financial pressure the family are now enduring I would be grateful for a speedy conclusion to your investigation. Thank you.

Yours sincerely…

Dean Marlo

Falling apart

Alice is having problems with anxiety, having panic attacks when I go out to work, or to drop Lara at school, or to go anywhere. She's refusing to go to the UEEC, however, I've managed to arrange with the school for her to have some lessons at home. This is not always successful.

Hayley's attitude has been distant, and she has been spending more time with her fiancé, building up to staying at his place most nights for the past months, which I'll admit inside I'm not thrilled about; she's 16, Conner is 17 and they've still so much to figure out about life and adulthood, I don't understand the need to rush into an engagement, and I think she is wrapped up in what a lot of young people get engulfed by: their first love. Outwardly, of course, Conner has always been welcome to stay over, has dinner with us, when Hayley chooses to be in for it, and I generally have no problem with him.

On top of this distance, Hayley has shown a habit of only returning home to request pocket money, which I have spoken to her several times about.

This weekend, having not seen or heard from Hayley (besides a few short texts) for a week, when Hayley appeared in the kitchen for her pocket money, I reminded her that I had asked for her to help out and if she was not prepared to do so, then I would not be giving her any pocket money.

I expected for Hayley to be upset, but to talk about it and come to an understanding; like a prequel to having a job, she could earn her pocket money by looking after Lara for a couple of hours.

I did not expect for Hayley to say, 'That's how it is, is it?' and walk out the front door.

I texted Hayley that evening, just a simple 'I love you and have a good night'. I do not like confrontation in general and I don't want to be falling out with Hayley – this is uncharted territory in our relationship, as Hayley and I have always been on the same page.

On Saturday, Hayley came home and everything seemed fine, as she said hello and went into her room. Minutes later, Hayley was coming back down the stairs with her laptop under her arm and a backpack that looked stuffed to the brim. She stated, 'If I find out anyone has been in my room then there will be trouble.'

I asked Hayley what she meant.

Hayley said, 'If anyone goes in there, I will move out.'

Shocked by her statement and as Hayley was going out anyway, I said, 'If you have nothing nice to say, please leave.'

Hayley responded, 'I am.'

And that was pretty much the end of the conversation, with Hayley going out the door.

Lara came downstairs and said that Hayley had taken her laptop charger with her. Sighing to myself, I wished that I had a time machine to go back and do everything differently. I opened the front door and called out to Hayley, who was across the road, walking towards the bus stop. I crossed over and asked if she had taken Lara's charger

618

and Hayley replied, 'I can't find mine.'

I said that she cannot just take Lara's and should tidy her room to find her own; she rifled through her bag for the charger, handed it over and silently walked off.

I have Lara in tears at the end of every phone call with her mother, Alice sitting in my works van while I'm on-site with anxiety and Hayley has walked out over threatening trouble (no one has been in her room, or would, we have a household where everyone respects each other's space); we're in the middle of court proceedings, and I don't know how to stop the wheel from spinning, before we've all fallen out of it.

That night, I received a text from Hayley saying that she is staying at Conner's. It was good to hear from her, even though the text was frosty.

Dean Marlo

HM Revenue & Customs

30 June

Dear Mr Marlo,
About your Child Benefit
We stopped paying your Child Benefit for Hayley, Alice and Lara because we got a claim from Ms Hyde.
Our enquiries are now finished. We can continue to pay you Child Benefit for Hayley, Alice and Lara.
About our decision
We accept that you satisfy the rules for entitlement to Child Benefit. However, when two people claim Child Benefit for the same child, we cannot pay benefit to both of them in the same week.
Where we use the term child or children, we also include young person or young people.
When we received a claim from Ms Hyde on 25 March 2008, we were already paying Child Benefit to you. The law allows you to keep the benefit for up to three weeks following the week in which the claim was made. That is up to Sunday 20 April 2008.
Where two people have claimed Child Benefit for the same child for the same period, they can agree between themselves who will get the Child Benefit. If they cannot agree and the care of the child is shared, a person acting on behalf of the Commissioners for HM Revenue & Customs has to decide, at their discretion, who should get the benefit.
When making their decision, the person acting on behalf of the Commissioners for HM Revenue & Customs looks at:
The pattern of care and living arrangements for the child
Any court orders in force covering arrangements for the child's care
The child's official address
Where the child's personal possessions are kept
Where the child would stay if they were ill
If it is sufficiently clear that one person has the main responsibility, the level of financial support from other state benefits for the child if the Child Benefit claim was disallowed (such as Income Support)
We have considered that you both have care and responsibility for Hayley, Alice and Lara. Information provided confirms that the care is shared between you. We therefore agree that you both satisfy the conditions for Child Benefit however, the benefit can only be paid to one person for a child.
From 21 April 2008, we have decided that you can continue to receive the Child Benefit for Hayley, Alice and Lara.
We will pay the money we owe you direct into your chosen account.
Yours sincerely,

Huffman LP (children's solicitor) writes to me

2 July

I refer to the above matter and your phone call to me indicating you are unable to attend the Hearing on the 21st August. I would be grateful if you would let me know if you have spoken to the court about this and what the court has said.

I would appreciate hearing from you.

I had told everyone involved that we were on holiday in August, yet, due to incompetence or lack of care, that's the exact week the hearing was booked for.

Hayley's College Interview

7 July

Hayley has asked her mother for her passport, for her college interview, which is required for identification, but Ms Hyde has refused to hand it over. As a result, we had to contact the college to ask if the copy I have of Hayley's birth certificate will suffice.

I am so proud of Hayley; she's going to be studying science with a focus on sport and nutrition – I think she'd make a great primary school PE teacher.

Before Hayley's college interview, Hayley and I arranged to have a coffee in town.

At 10am, Hayley's interview time, I was there alone to wish her good luck; Ms Hyde did show up, but it was after Hayley had come out and she did not bring Hayley's passport.

Reply to Ms Hyde's statement

8 July

Paragraph 4 – I can only reject Ms Hyde's accusations that I do not discuss children matters with her or fail to communicate.

Please find letters of communication that I have had with Ms Hyde in 2007 and 2008, marked 'DM'; I believe they show Ms Hyde and I communicating and generally making arrangements without fuss or bother.

It is unfortunate that the children and I, over the past 8 years, have not had a home to call our own. But either by circumstances or by being better situated for walking or travelling to school, every property I have rented all three children have happily made their home and we all have many fond memories from each one. As a parent, I would like to say that it was not ideal, but the children and I have made the best of our situation.

DM1a – Ms Hyde requests to take our children on holiday, 07/06/07-12/06/07, requiring the children to miss 4 days out of school, which I agreed to and dropped Lara off as desired by Ms Hyde. While on holiday, it was requested they stay for an extended time; the children missed an additional 3 days of school. Although unhappy with the children missing school, without fuss or argument, I agreed.

DM1b – Ms Hyde planned to take our children to the Gran Canaria, 13/02/08-20/02/08, requesting her contact to start on the 12th February to help with holiday arrangements. This I agreed to, which meant losing two days in my holiday contact time, and the children also missing four days out of the start of school term.

DM1c – Ms Hyde requests half towards Alice's Birthday present that she brought her, which I paid by cheque (DM1ca).

DM2 – Schedule 2008/2009 provided to Ms Hyde 1st April 2008.

DM3 – Lara is a very happy, intelligent and stable young person.

DM4a/b/c – Letters from Riverbank School, Northview Grove and UEEC.

DM5 – My letter handed to the Judge on the day of the hearing 11th June 2008.

Paragraph 5 – Unfortunately, most parents have disagreements with their children, but to my knowledge I have had only one serious disagreement with Alice, where Alice was trying to test the boundaries at home, as many children do.

Alice, aged 12-years-old, asked if she could stay at a friend's overnight, which it turned out was actually at the Grandfather of the friend's home, and he, for whatever reason, had a 'tag' placed by the police. I said no and what followed was 30 minutes of verbal confrontation from Alice, resulting in me still saying no, and Alice telephoning her mother to come and pick her up, to which she did.

At the time, Alice refused to talk to me, however Ms Hyde called daily making abusive demands such as I empty Alice's bedroom and bring it all to her house, and requesting Alice's Child Benefit. As the weeks went on, Ms Hyde continued her verbal abuse on the whole family, finally culminating in Ms Hyde visiting our home and causing criminal damage, for which she was cautioned by the police.

For 4 weeks, Alice stayed with her mother, returning home after having a disagreement with her.

From 5th September 2007 up to the 7th November 2007, things appeared to be going fine. Lara was having tea after school when Ms Hyde could make it and despite Alice not requesting an overnight stay with her mother during the week, all three children were going to their mother's for every other weekend contact.

On 7th November 2007, Hayley and Alice had an argument while at Ms Hyde's home; this was regarding a 23-year-old man who Alice had apparently been seeing at her mother's for several weeks. When Hayley arrived at her mother's and found Alice, 13, alone with him, she told him she thought his relationship with Alice was inappropriate; Alice had argued with Hayley, and their mother had yelled at Hayley for 'wrongly getting involved'.

I knew nothing of Alice's relationship with this man, who should be on a register; I was appalled when I spoke to Ms Hyde, who said she knew the man, confirmed she had told Hayley off and that Hayley had left. I reassured Hayley that I thought it was right for her to be worried about her sister and the age of the person her sister was seeing alone at her mother's house.

For the next few days, Alice gave me the cold shoulder and refused to pick up her phone or talk to me. This, I believe, is because Alice knows I do not approve of the age of the man involved and that she would have to have a conversation where I shatter her teenage illusions, and remind her that a ten-year age gap at 13 is paedophilia, or in the very least, has the potential to leave Alice taken advantage of. Alice, already knowing her mother was on her side, used her mother to avoid what she didn't want to hear.

After several days of telephoning Alice, she answered her phone and agreed to come round. Alice stated that she needed 'time out' from Hayley, while I tried to explain to Alice that Hayley, her sister, was just looking out for her, Alice was having none of it.

From the 7th of November 2007 through to the 26th of December 2007, I only saw Alice when she would pop home maybe once a week or when I went to Northview Grove School regarding her behaviour and attitude.

With referral to paragraphs 7 to 12 re Alice's behaviour, by Ms Hyde's own admission, Alice was in her care for this period. During this time, I was worried about Alice's welfare and behaviour, but could only offer parental advice and support to Alice at a distance, when she was prepared to listen. This attitude shift took me completely by surprise and I found parenting Alice difficult.

For Christmas and New Year, Alice was at home. Then, on the 2nd January, Alice stated that her uniform was at her mother's, so she was going to school from her mother's in the morning. The next few days, Alice would phone me stating that she was sleeping at her mother's that night.

At 9.30am, 6th January, I received a distressing phone call from Alice. I picked Alice up; she was emotionally and physically drained, and stated that she had been arguing with her mother when she had pinned her down, trying to pour dish soap in her mouth. Reassuring Alice, we talked about finding someone for her to speak to about how she feels and what was going on in her life. With Alice's agreement, the following day I approached an organisation called 'the Junction', Alice had the opportunity to speak to someone from the Junction and an appointment was made for Alice with a different organisation, Connexions, on the 7th of February.

On the 8th of January, Alice stated that she was staying overnight at her mother's, which I believe was due once again to Alice being influenced by her mother to live with little boundaries. Alice popped home to see me on several occasions over the weeks and I could see that Alice was becoming more and more unbalanced. I urged Alice to speak to someone from the Junction, and to attend the appointment with 'Connexions'. Alice reassured me that she would.

On the 7th of February, I received a phone call from 'Connexions', explaining that Ms Hyde had come into the centre and cancelled Alice's appointment stating that her education was more important.

Alice was attending the UEEC from 1.15pm to 3.30pm. Miss Horton, assistant manager at UEEC, was aware of this interview and had viewed it as being positive for Alice.

I was being told of many incidents that were occurring at Ms Hyde's home and felt very concerned for Alice over this time, however I felt helpless as to what to do. In reality, Alice was only aged thirteen and she and her mother were dictating what was going on. When Alice would answer her phone or pop in, I talked with her about the situation, and each time Alice made it clear that she did not want to live with her mother, she wants to get back on track and return home.

Alice stayed sporadically at her mother's from 8th January 2008 to the 7th April 2008; during these periods, I provided Ms Hyde with the Child Benefit money for Alice. On the 7th April there was an alleged incident, wherein Ms Hyde grabbed Alice and punched Hayley twice, the result being the children's reluctance to visit their mother at the present time.

Paragraph 6 – All our children have had regular check–ups with the dentist, as is routine as a parent; if she believed that the children were not being taken to the dentist, then she has had every opportunity to contact the children's dentist to check for herself.

Ms Hyde states that an appointment was made for Alice in December 2007, however unfortunately Alice would not go. Ms Hyde states that another appointment was made, but unfortunately, I failed to take her. Alice is terrified of the dentist, to which Ms Hyde is fully aware. I do work hard with Alice to address her anxieties for the dentist and will continue to do so to sort out the problems Alice has with her teeth.

Paragraph 7 – When I collected Alice from Venray that evening, Alice asked me why I had done so when her mother had said she was allowed to go.

Mrs Tran from Northview Grove School would confirm that I attended Alice's reintegration meetings with or without Ms Hyde, and I tried my utmost to communicate with Alice, Ms Hyde and the school to address Alice's behaviour and prevent Alice from being expelled. This I had to do while having limited contact with Alice, however I did not take Ms Hyde to court to enforce the contact order, as while I may not like any of Alice's decisions during these periods, I respected her choice to live with her mother.

Paragraph 9 – I reject Ms Hyde's accusation that I refused to discuss Alice's behaviour with her.

On one occasion, re Alice's total expulsion, Ms Hyde was suggesting in her statement to the appeal panel that Alice's behaviour was due to the effect the family court proceedings had on her. Ms Hyde got abusive with me simply because I would not agree entirely with her view.

Alice, her mother and I know that Alice's behaviour was not primarily a result of the Family Courts; Alice's poor behaviour over this period was a result of a lack of boundaries and discipline in Alice's childhood. I witnessed Alice move from home to home and become more unbalanced, and Alice was clearly unsure which lifestyle she wished to have – attending school on time, rewards for good work, age-appropriate activities and curfews. In the eyes of a 13-year-old, who thought of herself as much older, to smoke and drink alcohol while at her mother's was obviously the fun option.

Paragraph 13 – RHY2 Is not a letter from UEEC as stated.

Paragraph 14 – I do not and have never discouraged the children from having a relationship with their mother. There has never been any evidence to suggest this, and the opposite is suggested by Mrs Sanders', the child psychologist, reports and via Cafcass. In fact, amongst other things, both reports concluded that it was Ms Hyde who wished to continue the acrimony between her and myself.

As the children have gotten older, Ms Hyde has repeatedly shown her inability to assess and react to a situation in a controlled and calm manner, which came to the forefront once again on the 7th April, resulting in further allegations of physical and verbal abuse towards our children. I stand by my children's feelings and wishes, and believe their experiences to be true, both from my knowledge of Ms Hyde, the image they took of Hayley's lip and seeing the cut in person. The question the court and Ms Hyde recurrently desire me to answer, is an explanation of why I am reassuring my children after an abusive incident.

(Are we ready to talk about how abusive behaviours are seen to be more acceptable if it is a female perpetrator? I'll say it again for the people at the back, abuse doesn't have a gender – that is how it should be viewed and policed. If we get into it, the response should be proportional; sadly, a large number of abusers are male, who need to be dealt with more effectively to prevent this cycle of abusive boys turning into abusive men that we're still in, but also to not undermine, mince words or ignore female abusers. Can we just sort things out so the people who need help actually receive it, or is that too radical a concept?)

Alice has been suffering from anxiety and since she did not have a guardian or a solicitor, she wanted to present to the court her feelings in June 2008. I reluctantly agreed.

Paragraph 15 & 16 – Hayley and I rarely have disagreements; she was excited before she went to her mother's to go on holiday the following day.

As a responsible parent, I admit that I would not be happy with my daughter getting arrested, disappointed, yes, but as for me 'going ballistic', it is not a phrase my daughter ever uses nor a condition I have ever experienced. I fear this is another example of Ms Hyde's imagination and self–motivated fictional writing.

Ms Hyde states that she was told by the police at 8pm of Hayley's arrest. When I was told the following day, I thought that Ms Hyde should have informed me, and told her as much; I made no issue of the situation and would certainly never have interfered with Ms Hyde's and our children's holiday plans. I find it an absurd suggestion that I would attempt to do so.

Paragraph 18 – I am unaware of any problems concerning Ms Hyde's contact set out in the order 2007, until these proceedings. Hayley and Alice stayed with their mother as they wanted to, which Ms Hyde was happy with, and Lara followed the court order, requesting extra time as she wished.

Paragraph 19 – I have never discouraged our children from having a relationship with their mother, this is apparent from the photos Ms Hyde has supplied to the court, as well as by her own admission, that when Hayley and Alice have refused contact, Lara has continued to do so. Why would I be withholding contact of Hayley and Alice, but not Lara? And now in this hearing, it is reversed, wherein Hayley and Alice are choosing not to have contact, but I am supposedly withholding Lara?

Ms Hyde refers to the letters that the children have written to the court and simply refuses to acknowledge that our three children have always had their own minds and thoughts which are influenced by what is going on in their lives.

Paragraph 20 – As all the children visited their mother on Mother's Day and gave her cards which were much appreciated, mentioned in Paragraph 19, I see no evidence of my lack of support or me discouraging the children from having a relationship with their mother. Lara, being the child she is, wanted to make her Mother's Day card, we went to the shop to buy the materials to make it special; when Hayley and Alice requested extra pocket money to go into town to get their mother a present, I was happy to provide it.

Paragraph 21/ 22 – I was not there so I am unable to comment.

Paragraph 23 – I do not believe that Ms Hyde's account is accurate. I made an appointment with 'Connexions' to see if Alice could receive some emotional support. On the date of the meeting, Alice had returned to Ms Hyde's and Ms Hyde personally cancelled the appointment.

I dispute that Alice had been reluctant to see me, rather she had been getting on with her life at her mother's with few boundaries; smoking and drinking alcohol without question, as I was informed of the goings on by Hayley and Lara, and which I could see in Alice's behaviour changes and tiredness when we did have contact.

Paragraph 24-27 – To the majority of the paragraphs, I cannot fully comment because I was not there; I can only go based on what the children say happens and what I know Ms Hyde has been capable of in the past. On this occasion, all of the children came home emotionally upset, and Hayley had a cut lip and a sore chest.

Paragraph 28 – Ms Hyde's suggestion that she did not prosecute Hayley so as not to jeopardise her going to college is extraordinary, when on several occasions since 7th April, Hayley has asked her mother for her passport for ID purposes for her college interview, but Ms Hyde has refused to hand it over.

Before Hayley's college interview, Hayley and I arranged to have a coffee in town. At 10am, Hayley's interview time, I was there alone to wish her good luck; Ms Hyde arrived 30 minutes late and without Hayley's passport.

Paragraph 29 – Lara has chosen not to have contact with her mother since 7th April, owing to the distress Lara has felt concerning her mother's behaviour and actions. Sadly, Lara has become quite worked up when she has spoken to her mother on the phone since. However, as I try to calm Lara down after these calls, she tells me this is because, similar to Hayley, Lara has asked her mother for an apology, and she has either denied it happened or told Lara to move on.

Again, the reason Ms Hyde does not have contact with Lara is solely due to her behaviour and attitude towards her children, which has nothing to do with me.

Paragraph 30 – My letter, 'RHY5', states that Lara doesn't want to see her *at the present time*. I believe this letter clearly indicates that whatever the circumstances, I still communicate with Ms Hyde, and at no point have indicated Ms Hyde will not see her children.

Due to the alleged violent incident and the distress, not for the first time, I had to make a decision as to what was best. As it was an abusive incident and Lara was adamant about not seeing her mother, I took her to Social Services. Hayley just wanted to get on with her life and her fiancé, and Alice was resolute that she would not be following any court order from now on.

Paragraph 31 – I communicate with Ms Hyde whenever possible but I refuse to be drawn into Ms Hyde's verbal abuse, behaviour or actions.

I deny the personal allegations made by Ms Hyde in her letter 'RHY6', handed to me at Alice's exclusion appeal hearing on the 21st April. I once again felt that due to the content of the letter, if I replied it would have only exacerbated the acrimony that Ms Hyde continues to incite.

Paragraph 32 – Ms Hyde has phone contact with Lara, despite Lara often ending the calls upset.

Ms Hyde appears to conveniently forget that Lara has witnessed her behaviour, during severe incidents and attitude towards herself, her sisters, dad and nan; she seems to expect her relationship with Lara to be unaffected by this.

Paragraph 33 – On the children's return from their mother's on the 7th April, Hayley showed me her cut lip. At no time did I try to make Hayley go to the police or make an allegation that Hayley had been assaulted. I left it as a matter for Hayley to decide for herself that I would support her through.

(I love that based on my prior history of reporting immoral, abusive or dishonest behaviour, and obviously coming up with changes, acknowledgement and reprimand for those involved, I'm egging Hayley on to call the police – their caution for criminal damage against Ms Hyde in court still landed me with an undertaking and the judge's comment that both parents are as bad as each other!)

I did not interfere with Hayley or the incident nor at any time have I harassed, by phone or contact, Ms Hyde over the allegation that she has assaulted one of our daughters.

Paragraph 34/35 – As responsible people, we all have to make life saving and job changing decisions every day, whether it be to get up for work, take the children to school on time, or look left and right when crossing the road. If Ms Hyde did physically assault her daughter, then I believe that Ms Hyde had the same opportunity as we all do, to consider the consequences of her behaviour and actions towards her daughter, children and other people.

(Unless, her mental health condition affects her decision making in an ongoing manner, wherein she needs support, check-ins, medication, something, to ensure that she is capable of handling all the responsibilities, the fun and the difficult, that come with being a parent.)

Paragraph 36 – Once again, I believe Ms Hyde had the opportunity to make up ground with Hayley yet she used the opportunity to tell Hayley that she could not see her alone in case Hayley made further false allegations. Ms Hyde states that Hayley left her house in tears, which she appears to show no empathy or remorse for; then that Hayley started sending her very hurtful texts, apparently unaware why Hayley was upset with her at all.

Paragraph 37 – I honestly believe that neither I nor the Family Courts have ever denied Ms Hyde the opportunity to have a good relationship with her daughters. It is Ms Hyde's behaviour alone that disrupts her relationship with them, the continuity within their sibling relationships and the compliance with the court orders.

Paragraph 38 – Neither I, nor Hayley nor Alice, have ever discouraged Lara from seeing or contacting her mother in anyway. Lara is a bright and intelligent child, and her thoughts and beliefs are her own. These are taken from her experiences in life, as in any normal child.

Paragraph 39-42 – The past 8 years of family court proceedings have impacted on my life and I have for the past several years tried my utmost to bring an end to the instability that Ms Hyde has been able to promote, and the misery that constant proceedings can bring into a family's dynamics.

On good authority, I was told that the 91(14) Order placed on the order in September 2007 was introduced to give our children and family a break from repeated court involvement. Yet, here we are once more, due to Ms Hyde's dissatisfaction with the children's reluctance to have contact, as a direct result of her behaviour; Ms Hyde is allowed to bring us, within 9 months, back into the Family Court System.

Paragraph 43 – I have complied with court orders and any adjustments with regards to additional contact as requested by Ms Hyde or the children over many years. I delivered the schedule 2008/09 to Ms Hyde's home.

Paragraph 45 – I would urge the Family Courts not to attach a penal notice to any directions/court orders that they deem necessary to make, on a parent who is the mainstay in their children's lives. I would also ask the courts to recognise a parent who has constantly made his children's welfare and stability paramount, and, despite repeated provocations, has kept a level head and has been a calming influence in their lives throughout.

I believe that the best way forward would be to revert to the existing contact order, on the understanding that I have never discouraged the children from having contact with their mother. For the precedent that Hayley and Alice already have, and Ms Hyde has accepted, they can continue to have contact with their mother per their discretion to do so, as long as it is not a detriment to their education or overall wellbeing. For Lara, each contact visit would be with Lara's consent and the assurance of Lara's welfare and safety.

I do not see my conduct as of 'doing all I can to destroy a mother's relationship with her children', nor do I believe that I am the person that Ms Hyde portrays; since meeting her, I have never acted towards her in any detrimental way, as a person or regarding her relationships with her daughters.

It has to be understood and acknowledged that Ms Hyde needs to address her behaviour, and this may require some form of outside support. Consequently, I believe that her relationships with her daughters would resume as she wishes and perhaps even improve.

Although it is written in Ms Hyde's statement that she agrees that Alice can decide where she wants to live, Alice is still party to the court order and I will therefore comments as follows on Alice and Lara:

Lara is a happy go lucky child who tries her best in any task or challenge that she is asked to do. She is sociable and enjoys taking part and having fun with her friends. Like any normal child, Lara enjoys being loved and cared for and responds by returning the love and care she receives.

Coming to the end of year 5, Lara has well above her expected grades for her year and SAT's testing; 5c in reading and writing, and 5b in maths.

For several months, in the face of what has been happening in the background, Lara has been working hard to prepare for year 6 ahead and to sit her Eleven-plus examination in November 2008, to which Lara has set her mind to try to pass, and it is a joy to see her flourish through her own hard work. Lara has, without doubt, continued to excel in her schoolwork and I believe her effort and commitment over many years should not be compromised in anyway.

As many parents with adolescent children will confirm, everyone deals with this time in their lives in their own way. Upon reaching this age, Alice has, on occasions, become confrontational and distant from the loving and caring child she is, and, on occasions, Alice has tried to see how far she could challenge the boundaries.

Now permanently excluded from her school and away from her usual friends, Alice now understands that it was as a result of her behaviour. Alice has not given up and I see the determination in Alice to make something out of the situation she finds herself in, and she will be a better person for realising and acknowledging her mistakes, in her attitude and actions.

Alice is growing up and I believe beginning to understand that the effort you put into life is normally rewarded in some way.

Once again, Alice is a loving child and I believe Ms Hyde could regain her relationship with her daughter if she addressed her behaviour when having contact with her children.

From HMRC to MP

10 July

Dear Mr Marlo,

Please find enclosed a copy of the response I have received from HM Revenue and Customs. Hopefully you will find their comments to be of interest. If I can be further assistance, please let me know. Best wishes.

Yours sincerely,

23 July

Dear Mr Rowe,

Thank you for your letter dated 26 June 2008.

As you may be aware, to be entitled to Child Benefit for any week, a person must satisfy one of two conditions. Either that the child is living with them in the week or that they are paying towards the child's support at least to the amount of the Child Benefit which would be paid. In cases where a child spends time with each person, we consider that both may satisfy the conditions for Child Benefit, for that child.

Child Benefit law does not allow payment of benefit to be made to more than one person, for any child in the same week. Similarly, we are unable to split the benefit payments between parents, as the law does not allow benefit to be apportioned, nor can we pay benefit to two customers on an alternative week basis.

Child Benefit does provide the facility for the parties to decide between them who should receive the Child Benefit. Should they not be able to reach an agreement, as in this particular case, then it falls on to an officer of HM Revenue & Customs acting for the Commissioners for HM Revenue & Customs to impose a decision. As this is a discretionary decision, it does not carry the right of appeal.

It is often very difficult to decide in whose favour discretion should be exercised. There are no hard and fast rules governing the decision and each case is decided on its own merits.

Looking specifically at Mr Marlo's case, I can confirm that a claim was received from another person, in respect of the children Mr Marlo received Child Benefit for. Enquires were necessary with both customers to establish the situation regarding the children's care. Whilst these enquires were carried out, payment of benefit was suspended, which is normal practice, to protect both customers.

I am pleased to say that our enquires have been completed, and it has been decided that Child Benefit will continue to be paid to Mr Marlo. A letter notifying him of this was sent to him on 30 June, and payments were reinstated.

I would like to thank you for bringing this case to my attention, and giving me the opportunity to explain the situation.

Yours sincerely,

Customer relations manager

Dear Mr Rowe,

14 July

I would like to request an urgent appointment with the Minister for Family Justice before the 28th July 2008 if this is possible, please. I hope after reading my letter you would agree it is shameful that the Family Courts gave permission for Ms Hyde's application and that they believe threatening to imprison an honest and decent parent is the answer.

Please find enclosed my statement for the hearing on the 28th July 2008. I believe that as you are my MP, you should be aware of its content and what is going on; it should not be me alone who faces the Family Courts and Ms Hyde's entourage of legal representation. Someone has got to be there for the people who have no one. (Even if it is only in spirit.)

I have had no legal advice or legal help with this statement or these new court proceedings, and I once again feel totally out of my depth within the court system and its protocol.

In 2004, you told me that I should accept whatever decision the judge made concerning the residency of my children and just get on with my life, to which is what I have been trying to do with sole residency.

Eight years of Family Courts involvement, with 36 hearings and orders. Please find enclosed, copies of orders and directions.

From my own experiences and listening to other parents, I hope you would agree that many single parents who are mothers want their children to have a relationship with their father, and would welcome the father playing a role in the upbringing of their children. In 1999, I suggested that I was more than happy to bring some stability and care into my children's lives, as any parent would. The relationship I had with the children's mother had come to an end, but it did not mean my responsibility as a parent to our children had to end too.

Inside the Family Courts and out, Ms Hyde has incessantly denounced my name and character; I am not the parent or the person that Ms Hyde has, over the years, portrayed me as. Clearly, the Family Courts will not recognise, accept or acknowledge the lack of evidence for Ms Hyde's assertions, nor the wealth of evidence I have been able to provide confirming the opposite.

I have never wanted, and still do not want, to take on the entire Family Courts cavalry; I am only relaying what has happened in my family's case. The majority of these 'professionals' are parents themselves, and I am shocked by the lack of empathy they show for the children who have had their lives partially defined by the playground politics of unscrupulous individuals.

Ever since I met Ms Hyde, she has wanted to argue, row and have a dispute (this is influenced by her mental health condition) and, when we were together, she always had my support as someone who loved her, wanted nothing more than for us to be a family, and for her to receive help when her behaviour deteriorated.

Within the walls of the Family Courts, Ms Hyde has been allowed to escalate, repeatedly relying on the legal system to facilitate new ways to disrupt my life; engaging a law firm, solicitor and barristers to represent her feelings of dissatisfaction and acrimony.

Please find enclosed, a copy of the letter I handed into the Family Courts on the 11th June 2008 and withdrew. Several days later, I received a letter from Smitch Law requesting a copy of my original letter that the judge gave back to me. On the 16th June, I spoke to the children's solicitor from Huffman LP about the forthcoming dates for the hearing, and she informed me that Mrs Mason had phoned her office requesting a copy of my letter.

Judge Daggett clearly stated that Ms Hyde was to produce her own statement to which I was to reply; my original letter of the 11th June having been withdrawn from the court records and, therefore, Mrs Mason and Smitch Law had no right to be making this request. To me, it reads as underhanded, attempting to, as lawyers do I suppose, find ways to justify any concerns I raised, and to assist their client in writing her statement.

Smitch Law's conduct is dishonest and their intentions have nothing to do with the welfare and stability of the children involved. I ask once again, please, for you to achieve some form of accountability for those actively inciting the misery, and stand up for a parent and their children, who have continually paid the consequences of Smitch Law crossing the ethical codes that exist to ensure children's welfare.

Smitch Law, a Lord and the Law Society would say that they have broken no law, but I would say their behaviour is corrupt and immoral in children's matters, and on that basis, perhaps it is the laws these people are following in the first place that are wrong, if this is acceptable. For the families who are sadly forced to rely on the sensibility of the Family Court System, the whole performance is unnecessary and detrimental; those needing help are not believed, and those requiring support do not receive it.

(Where does all that money go? In the gills of apathetic sharks.)

The Child Benefit Office and the 'someone else is also claiming' conundrum, reoccurring 1st April 2004, 20th June 2006 and 2nd April 2008.

On the 2nd April 2008, I received a letter from the Child Benefit Office, stating that 'someone else' is also claiming Child Benefit for all three children. Due to the suspension, my monthly financial income has been reduced by almost £200, with no way of me addressing this short fall. The only money I received per week was the £161.35 from working and Child TC, which is more than appreciated but inadequate to see our family of four through the week.

On Friday 23rd May, I received a phone call from the Child Benefit Office informing me there would be a committee hearing on the 6th June, where a decision would be made as to who would be receiving the Child Benefit in the future for Hayley, Alice and Lara.

On 11th June 2008, I received a letter from the Child Benefit Office requesting I provide a letter from either Social Services, an educational establishment or the GP, 'in order for them to confirm' that Hayley, Alice and Lara are living with me, despite them having a copy of the existing court order in force.

Calling Social Services, I was told that as a 'case' was not open on my children or the family, they could not relay this information. Reluctantly, I approached Lara's and Alice's schools, but as UEEC was aware of Alice's prior housing habits, I was unsure if it would be enough. Riverbank were happy to write a letter, but this only covered Lara; Northview Grove informed that they did not want to be involved in any disputes, and would not provide a letter. I did not want to bring this to Hayley's college doorstep, so I approached the children's GP, who was happy to provide me with a letter of confirmation that all three children were registered at my address – at the cost of £5.

On the 30th June, I received a letter from the Child Benefit Office stating that the Child Benefit for all three children has been reinstated.

As a parent, I have genuinely struggled over this time to make ends meet.

May I take this opportunity to thank you for your efforts and concerns by way of letters to the Child Benefit Office, and your help in resolving this matter for my family.

As you are aware, I have found no way of addressing the discrimination and dishonesty that has, without justification, impacted my children's lives and my own. I am left with the belief that ministers responsible within our society and democracy are either not listening or do not care for the jobs they are empowered to do – clearly my family and many other families and children are suffering as a result.

I do not think that my family's case is anything for the Family Courts to be proud of, and believe that it is time that the minister for Family Justice addressed the disparity seen in my case, which is sadly not isolated, and that regularly occurs within the Family Courts and our legal system.

Again, I ask, if possible, please, for you to arrange an urgent appointment with the Family Justice Minister, before the 28th July 2008 - your support on the day, as always, would be much appreciated. The Family Courts are once again not listening and ignoring the evidence that has been provided to them over many years. I find the Family Courts facilitate and appease Ms Hyde, at the expense of the children involved and our family's wellbeing.

I know that it is short notice to request an appointment, but my liberty is at stake and the threat of removing my ability to be there for my children. I do not believe that it can be deemed a reasonable response to state that they cannot get involved due to the case being 'live', as it has made no difference to my ministers' responses to my letters and concerns regarding the behaviour and performance my family have received within the Family Court System.

(They seem to want to wait for the penal notice to take effect, the children to be forced to return to an abusive household, wherein Ms Hyde denies ever touching Hayley and cannot be in the same room alone with her for fear of false allegations; Alice's relationship with her mother has not improved with telephone contact; Lara's ready to stage a protest; I will already be in handcuffs, and unable to write my letter of complaint – which is the outcome Mrs Mason and her client have constantly tried to achieve.)

I once again thank you Mr Rowe for all you have done to help and assist me in my family's case, and also ensure you of my best intentions at all times.

Yours respectfully…

Still gathering – Summer

15/16 July

15 July

Dear Mr Marlo,

I have pleasure in offering your daughter, Lara, tuition in Eleven-plus preparation on the following terms and conditions.

The £22 fee per lesson is payable in advance by cash or cheque. Lessons not attended will be charged for.

If you have to cancel a lesson, please let us know as soon as possible. If we have to cancel a lesson, we will either re-arrange it or credit you with the fees.

Books or other materials lent to you are to be returned no later than the final lesson.

Yours sincerely…

16 July

Dear Mr Marlo,

Further to our conversation, the Teacher Assessments for Lara Marlo are detailed below.

Year 5 Teacher Assessments for Lara Marlo – Summer Term 2008

Reading – 5c

Writing – 5c

Math – 5b

Yours sincerely,

Mrs Irfan

16 July

To whom it may concern:

Alice Marlo

I write with regard to the above mentioned girl who is registered at our GP practice. Her father has asked that I write to confirm that she has attended the surgery on a number of occasions with panic attacks. These consultations occurred on the 18th June and the 3rd July 2008.

Should there be anything further you wish to discuss please do not hesitate to be in contact.

Yours sincerely,

Letter from Lara

16 July

To Judge,

If you believe that I should visit my mother and that she cares for me; you don't have to sit there and listen and watch the way my mother acts. At the age of 10 I have seen a lot of things I shouldn't have. I am constantly being in fear that she is going to lash out at me after she's had a go at one of my sisters or watch her pulling my sister across the floor or punching them. Even when my sisters are not there, I get shouted at for things like asking for help on my homework. I hope you do realise my school work is important to me and I have high expectations of myself to passing the Eleven-plus. If you honestly think that my mother cares, she doesn't. She can't even be bothered to get up in the mornings on time to take me to school; and as a result I often don't have breakfast.

I hope now you will listen to me as I feel comfortable, I get to school on time and I have a decent breakfast round my dad's.

I hope that I will be taken off the court order and I can be free to stay with my dad as I wish and I will be able to grow up like any normal child.

Yours faithfully,
Lara Marlo

Letter by Alice to the judge

I would like to be taken off the court order because of all the incidents that have happened while I have been with my mother, e.g. one of the latest, 7th April 2008, when my mother hit Hayley (my sister) in the chest and then again in her face which made Hayley's lip bleed. (Picture attached)

There have been many incidents and this last one has made me think that I don't want to live with my mother. The circumstances might have been different, but the whole time she has denied the incident that me and my little sister (Lara aged 10) witnessed. I think that it is just bad that my mother could hit one of her daughters and not just that as well hit her in front of my youngest sister.

All the incidents that have taken place she has never once said sorry and I feel that there are only a certain amount of chances that a person can give. She has still not apologised for the latest incident. She obviously does not care because she should have said sorry girls I didn't mean any of this but instead she has just made our lives HELL.

i.e. there have been other incidents since like my bus pass when my mother insisted that she had handed it in to my school and they had recorded it. this had been a long time without my bus pass so I said to my mother you can keep my pass I am ordering a new one. Then a few days later I had a phone call saying that it had turned up in one of her friend's cars.

The phone calls I have had of my mother saying that I need to watch out and then me saying why and her hanging up.

Trying to get my personal possessions back has been the hardest. I had been asking her for some time if I could have my stuff back and she had kept saying no. I had hardly anything to wear so I called the police to try and get my stuff back. I went round her house because I needed my pills that I was meant to take every day but she would not let me have them. The police went with me on the 9th April 2008 and the police officer involved said to me we will go in the house but be calm. I replied all I want is my stuff back, I didn't want no hassle. This was days before my birthday and she knew I just wanted to get on with my life but she just kicked off and the officer had to get me out of her house. I didn't manage to get anything apart from my pills.

A few weeks had passed so my sister (Hayley) rang my mother up and said could Alice and me come round and pick up some of our things. She agreed but said 'you both are not allowed in my house together'. So we said we would go in separately. It was arranged that we would go to get our stuff at 11.30 but we had several phone calls arranging the time to 12pm then 12.45pm and at around 1pm she just changed her mind for no reason saying that Hayley could not come round but I could. So I went round there and started putting my stuff in bags. As soon as I got in the door she kicked off saying how rude I was and then saying 'I am going to get your dad arrested'. This made me feel very upset because my dad has not done anything to deserve this.

She has kept saying that the police and social services are going to come round to our home which has made our lives up and down, having to stay in when all the times she has said they were going to come round they never did.

I hope you take this letter into consideration because I am 14 and I just want to get on with the rest of my life. Me and my sisters don't need to see or be affected by the aggressive behaviour that happens round our mother's on a regular basis.

Yours truly,

Daughter

17 July

Although I hardly see Hayley, and she often does not answer or return my calls, Hayley rang to ask if I knew anyone who needed a labourer, as Conner is looking for work.

I told Hayley I could take him on for a couple of days a week; I thought it would be an opportunity to see more of Hayley and check that she's doing alright. It has allowed Hayley and Alice to talk for a bit as well, as I know that while Hayley has been getting on with her life, she hasn't spoken to neither Alice nor Lara much.

I pick Conner up in the mornings and have a coffee with Hayley when I drop him home, which is nice routine to have.

Huffman LP writes to me and the Courts

18 July

Dear Mr Marlo,
I refer to the above proceedings and enclose copy letter which has today been faxed to the court. We shall keep you updated of the outcome.

We refer to the above matter whereby we represent Ms Dowling, the children's Guardian.
The matter is currently listed before the court on the 28th July and the 21st August for a two–hour hearing. Ms Dowling would like the opportunity to meet with the children during the school holiday period and to undertake her report.
Furthermore, the above-mentioned dates are not convenient to Ms Dowling or myself.
We can confirm we have spoken to the parties regarding this course of action which is accepted as a way forward.
We can confirm we have sought the available dates of counsel for Ms Hyde and Ms Dowling and we would be grateful it the matter could be listed in September 2008, after the children have returned to school and the Guardian has had opportunity to prepare a report in this matter.
We can confirm all parties are available on the following dates, 22/23/24/25 September.
We would therefore be grateful if the matter could be listed for a two-hour hearing on either of the above dates with the hearings on 28th July and 21st August being vacated.
We enclose the copy correspondence from Mrs Mason agreeing to the above proposed course of action and we have corresponded with Mr Marlo, who is a litigant in person and does not anticipate any difficulties in that regard.

Dean Marlo

From MP

24/31 July

24 July

Dear Mr Marlo,

Please find enclosed a copy of the response I have received from the Parliamentary Under-Secretary of State at the Ministry of Justice.

Hopefully, you will find the Minister's comments to be of interest. If I can be of any further assistance, please let me know.

Best wishes. Yours sincerely,

17 July 2008

Dear Mr Rowe,

Thank you for your letter of 27 May, concerning your constituent, Mr Marlo, who has been involved in protracted legal proceedings regarding contact with his children. I am replying as the Minister with responsibility for legal aid. I have also received a copy of the letter sent from Mr Marlo to the Rt Hon Minister for Family Justice.

You say that Mr Marlo is not eligible for legal aid and simply cannot afford to defend the regular court proceedings brought against him by his former partner, who is eligible for legal aid. Decisions about funding in civil cases are entirely a matter for the Legal Services Commission (LSC). This is an independent and separate from the Government. As such, neither the Justice Secretary nor I intervene in or comment on decisions made about the grant of public funding in individual cases. It is important that these decisions are, and are seen to be, free from political and government influence. That said, it might be helpful if I set out how the legal aid scheme operates.

Generally, legal aid in civil cases is available to anyone who qualifies, provided that the case is within the scope of the scheme. Each application is considered on an individual basis and is subject to statutory tests of the applicant's means and the merits of the case. The rules for scope and qualification are in legislation or other documents laid before Parliament.

Those in receipt of Income Support, income based Job Seeker's Allowance, or Guarantee State pension credit, automatically qualify financially for legal aid. Otherwise, they can obtain 'free' (or non-contributory assistance) if they have a gross monthly income of less than £2,530, a monthly disposable income below £300 and disposable capital of £3,000 or less. If their monthly disposable income is between £301 and £698, or disposable capital between £3,000 and £8,000, they will be offered funding on the basis that they agree to pay contributions towards their legal costs. Applicants can check their eligibility for legal aid by using the eligibility calculator on the LSC's website.

In addition to qualifying financially, an applicant must also show that they have reasonable grounds for taking, defending or being a party to proceedings, and that it is reasonable, in the particular circumstances of the case, for legal aid to be granted. The LSC must consider, for example, whether the case has a reasonable chance of success, whether the benefits of litigation would outweigh the cost to public funds, and whether the applicant would gain any significant personal benefit from proceeding, bearing in mind any liability to repay the costs if successful. These factors are similar to those that would influence a privately paying client of moderate means when considering whether to become involved in proceedings.

If Ms Hyde continues to pass the means and merits tests therefore, her actions will continue to be funded. However, legal aid is granted on the strength of the information provided by the applicant, their solicitor and counsel's opinion where there is one. To maintain a balanced view, it is open to any interested party to make representations to the LSC about a person's eligibility for funding. However, although it is open to anyone to make such representations, this does not mean that representation will automatically lead to the funding certificate being discharged. The LSC must comply with set procedures before it can reach a decision about the status of a certificate. Representations have to be put to the legally aided client, who is given a chance to explain the situation. If the LSC is satisfied, it must allow the certificate to remain open.

In respect of Mr Marlo's eligibility, legal aid is intended to help the least well-off in society with the costs of their legal advice. The government recognises that those who have capital or income in excess of the limits might still not be able to readily afford legal representation, and may feel that the system is unfair. However, there are many competing priorities for Legal Aid and a threshold must be set.

However, for those who do not qualify for Legal Aid and need legal assistance, Citizen's Advice and Law Centres and Advice Agencies can give legal advice themselves and refer clients to a pro bono organisation for representation. To find the nearest one, your constituent can refer to the phone book or visit the 'advice guide' website. Law centres and advice agencies are in the Community Legal Services directory, which is available from Community Legal Advice.

Community Legal Advice is a national phone advice line and website service, run by the LSC for people using the courts of England and Wales is also available. It provides an advice service for people with civil law problems (including family and personal matters) such as welfare benefits, debt, housing, employment or educational issues.

I enclose a copy of this letter for you to pass on to your constituent, Mr Marlo, should you wish to do so.

31 July

Dear Mr Marlo,

Thank you for the copy of your court summons regarding your Council Tax Arrears. I am sorry for the delay in replying to your letter. I have noticed that the court hearing would have taken place by now, and I am therefore writing to see if I can still offer any assistance. If this is the case, please let my office know. Best wishes.

Yours sincerely…

Dean Marlo

From Smitch

4 August

We refer to the court order dated 11 June 2008 and note that we have not heard from you with regard to your statement which was due to be filed by 4pm on 2 July 2008. Could you please confirm whether you are intending to file such a statement and if so, provide us with a copy.

Court – just directions folks

5th August 2008 / Venray Family County Courts

The matter is listed to be heard on 23rd September 2008 at the Venray County Court.

Dean Marlo

Mrs Mason writes to me

6 August

We enclose herewith Notice of issue of our client's Pubic Funding Certificate, receipt of which please acknowledge.

(I thought I would get my secretary straight on it – I often wonder what I'm supposed to do with these letters… I know it's the process because I haven't got a solicitor, but to me it is absurd and only achieves putting salt in my lack of Legal Aid wounds.

The certificate is marked as 'emergency' granted as 'full representation', dated 9th June 2008. A second certificate, dated 29th July 2008, marked as 'substantive' and 'full representation, as applicant to be represented on an application to vary or discharge a contact order'.

Ms Hyde has a solicitor, the Guardian has a solicitor, the children have a solicitor, and I'll be representing myself. Is this family law's level playing field?)

Tutankhamun

7 August

Lara has a wide range of interests, but she has always been particularly fascinated about the ancient Egyptians; the hieroglyphs; the mysteries still being solved by archaeologists and historians.

As a treat for doing so well at school this year, we booked tickets to go to London and see the Tutankhamun & the Golden Age of Pharaohs exhibit at the O2.

Hayley wasn't interested in coming and with Alice, we have been trying to get her to stay for periods with Ma, to work on her reliance on me being around; she loves her nan and it was a good opportunity to break the dependence. Alice also felt that London itself would do her anxiety no favours.

Lara and I had a really good time looking at the artefacts up close.

It was like a little bubble universe we dipped into for a day, where we got to be a child and a parent enjoying something together.

Dean Marlo

Witness Care Team

27 August

Mr Dean Marlo,
Re: Ruth Hyde
Court Name: Town Magistrates Court
Date of Hearing: 26th August, 2008
I am writing to you with reference to the statement your daughter made in relation to the incident which occurred on 7 April 2008 at Ms Hyde's property.
The defendant named above was charged with the offence;
Assault by beating (Battery)
After considering all the evidence in the case, the Crown Prosecution Service has offered no evidence in respect of the charges against the defendant. However, the defendant has agreed to be bound over to keep the peace and be of good behaviour for a period of 9 months in the sum of £100. This means that the case is now concluded but should the defendant commit an offence during the specified period of the bind over, the above sum of money will be forfeited and this case will be put back before the court.
The standard to which a case has to be proved in the criminal courts is very high and the Crown Prosecution Service has to have a realistic chance of conviction in order to continue a case to trial.
Although you may be disappointed with the outcome of the case, your daughter's contribution in assisting us to put this case before the court was very important and is greatly appreciated. Providing a statement to the police is crucial to the criminal justice process and I hope that, if necessary, you both will be willing to assist us again in the future.
If you feel that you and your daughter require further advice or support, please do not hesitate to contact Victim Support or any of the other organisations detailed on the list I have included with this letter, who will be able to assist you.
On behalf of the Prosecution Team, I would like to take this opportunity to thank you for providing a statement to the police and for your assistance in this case.
Yours sincerely,

No evidence – three witnesses, and Alice took a picture of Hayley's lip outside Ms Hyde's house after the incident occurred!

From CPS

27 August

Dear Miss H Marlo,

R —v— Ruth Hyde

Ruth Hyde has been charged with an offence of Battery upon you. Police have sent us the file relating to the case because the Crown Prosecution Service is responsible for deciding whether or not this case should be prosecuted. As the Crown prosecutor in charge of the case, I have to make that decision.

When deciding whether or not to prosecute, I have to follow the guidance set out in the Code for Crown prosecutors. The Code sets out two tests that have to be applied by Crown prosecutors to ensure that our decisions are both fair and consistent. The enclosed leaflet explains what the tests are and how Crown prosecutors apply the Code for Crown prosecutions to each case.

The defendant was made aware of the seriousness of his conduct when he attended court. He accepts that his behaviour fell below acceptable standards and accordingly he agreed to be bound over to keep the peace. This means that if he commits a further offence or breaches the peace within the next nine months the magistrates will take some or all of the £100 bindover as well as dealing with the new offense.

I hope that this letter, together with the leaflet, assists you in understanding what has happened in this case and how I came to my decision.

If you have any queries relating to this letter or any other matter, please write to the address shown below.

Yours sincerely,

I really wish I could say I was joking; the Crown Prosecution obviously didn't bother to change the template on the battery letter from he/him to she/her. I'm somewhat devastated by this, because it just feels like as usual, Ms Hyde's abuse of our children is demeaned and acceptable. I don't know why it is acceptable for a woman, when a man, rightfully, would not get away with punching their child in the face as the latest conclusion of 16 years of dreadful, condemnable and avoidable behaviour.

This whole thing is driving me crazy, but Ms Hyde can and will simply fold the top of this letter and it will read that I am the one being charged.

I know Hayley was upset to read it because police involvement at this level would have finally been some comeuppance for her mother's treatment of her. Ms Hyde continues to deny the incident to this day, and Hayley should have felt validated by professionals that her mother should not be punching anyone, let alone her daughter.

For me, I at least hope that the courts will take the police charging Ms Hyde with battery seriously, and acknowledge the concerns that I have for my children and for once back me as a parent trying to bring normality and happiness to their lives. That is, unless they skip the names at the top of the letter and presume this is another case of a father's disgraceful behaviour and after assaulting his daughter, he will lose any rights he had.

Ms Hyde can commit battery against her child and not even the Crown Prosecutor really gives a fuck. I despair with justice, and the illusion the system has cultivated.

Dean Marlo

It really does sadden me, that it has come to the charge of battery on one of our children before Ms Hyde's inability to cope and unacceptable conduct towards them to be taken seriously in the Family Courts – or at least, I hope it will now be evident and the Family Courts will approach our family with the appropriate level of intervention, which is to get Ms Hyde assistance, and stop blaming the children or myself when contact breaks down.

From the Police (via Hayley's solicitor)

27/30 August

27 August

Dear Hayley Marlo,
I am writing simply to confirm that your bail has been extended and that you are now due to return to the Police Station on 11 September 2008 at 9.00pm.
It is very important that you comply with your bail. Failure to answer your bail is a criminal offence and could result in your arrest and prosecution and could be detrimental to your chances of further bail.
Please can you phone me in a few days before you are due to return to the police station. I will try and find out from the officer dealing what will happen and it may save you an unnecessary journey if the case is not proceeding or the bail date is to be changed. If you are due to return to the police station at the weekend, please be sure to call no later than the Friday before so I can confirm the attendance of a representative from this office. It would be helpful if you could let me have a contact number for you in any event.
If the matter is to proceed I or one of my colleagues will arrange to meet you in the reception area of the police station as above. I would advise you not to report to the front office until we are there.
Should you have any queries in the meantime, please do not hesitate to contact me.
Yours sincerely,

Despite saying she didn't want to compromise Hayley's position at college or her future, Ruth went forward with the charges she brought against Hayley.

The letters for Hayley are still addressed to our home, and I drop her a text when one comes through. She has discussed the police situation with me, and it is unbelievable to me that Ms Hyde would put her daughter in this position, after the behaviour she has subjected her children to their whole lives.

Hayley puts on a brave face but I know she is worried about what is going to happen.

30 August

Dear Hayley Marlo,
Further to your recent arrest and subsequent detention at the police station, I am writing to confirm that you are due to return to the police station on 3rd October 2008 at 1pm.
It is very important that you comply with your bail. Failure to answer to your bail is a criminal offence and could result in your arrest and prosecution and could be detrimental to your chances of further bail.
Yours sincerely,

Dean Marlo

Thoughts and prayers

On the 11th of June, it was arranged that a hearing would be held on the 28th July; I informed on the day that the children and I would be on holiday on the 18th August for a week.

I then received a notification for a revised hearing date, 21st August as well as the 28th of July.

Subsequently, I received a letter from a court official from Venray County Court, informing the new date for the hearing was to be 23rd September, as the previous dates were not convenient to the Guardian or myself. The letter requests all parties be present at 9am, despite the hearing not starting until 10am. I take Lara to school every morning and I am not prepared to disrupt her breakfast time and school day by needlessly arriving at court an hour early, when I don't even have a legal representative to meet.

This seems to be just another endless continuation of proceedings, which have done nothing to address the real issue of Ms Hyde's behaviour towards her children. The court fails to recognise the instability and upset that someone with bipolar disorder, to the extent Ms Hyde suffers with, can bring to a family's dynamics, especially when assisted by a law firm that shows no concern for the children involved. Who is running the Family Courts – arrogant judges or unscrupulous law firms?

All I have tried to do is fit in running my small business around raising my children, to provide them with a good standard of living. I have always put them first, as any decent parent would.

With regard to the letter forwarded to me by Mr Rowe from the MoJ, I will not dwell on the misery needlessly placed in my children's childhoods by the Family Courts over the past eight years... But to reply to him, even in this small way, there is a 91(14) order, placed to prevent parties from repeated and protracted court hearings. Yet, to a family law firm and the Legal Services Commission, this – and the reasons it was ordered in the first place – appears to be meaningless.

My children's childhood and my position as their parent has been in a dishonest and unnecessary game, with practitioners using the law to the advantage of their client, regardless of if their actions stand in opposition to the stability and welfare of children.

I can (have had to, to carry on) accept the unfairness to myself, but I cannot accept a system that continually, without reason, truth or justification, places my position as the mainstay in my children's lives in an untenable position. I have always stood by my children as a parent, and I do not believe the Family Courts have shown three children the respect they deserve, nor the appropriate consideration to parents standing in a courtroom.

I would like to leave the MoJ with this thought:

I wake up every day with the worry and threat of a penal notice and prison, and I cannot afford the advice of legal representation; then I get up, be a dad to my daughters and run my business.

650

Huffman LP writes to me

3 September

Further to correspondence in this matter, I write to advise that Ms Dowling has been directed by the court to undertake the wishes and feelings report on behalf of the children. Unfortunately, Ms Dowling has had difficulty in getting in touch with you. I therefore suggest that perhaps you could attend our offices on the 17th September at 10am in order to meet Ms Dowling and discuss this with her.

Please could you contact me upon receipt of this letter to confirm the appointment, or alternatively to make a different arrangement.

Letter to Huffman LP for the judge

To the Judge,

To be honest, I think that this has gone on too long and it's not good for any of us. We just need to get on with our lives and I think that the court order should say that we live with our dad because of all the upset our mother brings to our lives and if in the future she accepts EVERYTHING that she has done to us then we can get in contact with her if need be but at the moment we are strong to what we say and we do not want a relationship with her because of the lies and violence in her home.

Lara has her Eleven-plus coming up soon and I am sorting myself out at school because of my GCSEs and I have got into college and doing well there. I think that if we have to go and see our mother, our lives will be up and down again and we don't need it not when we are back on track because we as children need to know where we stand.

We have suffered for the times our mother has kicked off and we are just fed up of all of it. I understand that children should have a relationship with both parents but not if you felt at risk and are at risk at their home. Let's just say Lara went back to my mother's what would happen if Lara got hurt round there, what would happen then should she still have to put up with it like I have had to because the judges have sent us back round there and look what happens, one of us gets hurt time and time again it's not right!

Yours truly,
Alice Marlo

Court – life wasting away

19th September 2008 / Venray Family County Courts

Judge Neely orders upon reading Huffman LP's letter and upon parties agreeing, the hearing be adjourned and a new date set for 12th November 2008.

After court, the Guardian Ms Dowling visited Alice, Lara and myself at home. She spoke to the children by themselves, and I believe they made it clear that they did not want contact at the present time, as they still feel upset about the incident, and their mother's denial and attitude has not changed.

I told Ms Dowling that I thought for the time being telephone contact should continue, with hopefully normal contact resuming in the future every other weekend. This is what has happened with Hayley and Alice when incidents have occurred at Ms Hyde's in the past, and I believe what the children need is time and peace – to get on with their lives and repair the relationships with their mother without the stress of court involvement or experts and more hearings.

Also, I mentioned that it would still be beneficial for Ms Hyde to receiving some form of parenting help, because the court needs to recognise that Ms Hyde has a long-term mental health condition; this will affect the children for the rest of their childhoods and as adults. Ms Dowling nodded and said she understood.

With Ms Dowling gone and the prospect of hearings for months to come, Alice announced she was going out with friends, and agreed when I said she had to be in at 8 pm. Lara set up the PlayStation, ready to lose an hour to a fantasy world and I sat down next to Sully to watch.

Dean Marlo

Huffman LP to me and the County Courts

22 September

Dear Mr Marlo,
I write to enclose copy letter I have sent to the court, the contents of which are self-explanatory.

We write further to our letter of the 19th September requesting that the hearing be adjourned and relisted on 12th of November 2008. However, matters have taken a further turn and we are now writing to ask whether it would be possible for the matter to be listed in front of a Circuit Judge tomorrow, 23rd September, for a 30-minute directions hearing.

Ms Dowling was hoping to do some work with Lara and her father to facilitate some contact between Lara and her mother, but it does appear from the meeting between the Guardian, I and Lara on Friday afternoon that it is not going to be possible at this stage to organise contact between Lara and her mother.

Ms Dowling is at a loss to how to progress this matter and to that end, Mrs Mason from Smitch Law, who represents Ms Hyde, and ourselves are of the view it would be extremely helpful to have a directions hearing listed before a Circuit Judge when matters could be discussed further. We would be very grateful if the matter could be listed for 30 minutes on the 23rd September, and we apologise for causing inconvenience to the Court by asking for the matter to be relisted at this late stage.

We look forward to hearing from you as a matter of urgency.
Yours faithfully,

Lara watched her mother punch her eldest sister in the face, and lived on many occasions with the fear of her mother becoming verbally and physically aggressive towards her too; what is wrong with these people? Children are being abused – they just carry on as if it does not matter – not only physically but also emotionally... Is it only when men behave like this, that it has an effect on the wellbeing of a child?

Whichever solicitor, this was about Ms Hyde getting contact with her children, unscrupulous and uncaring individuals making a sham out of a family's situation and family law. None of them have ever considered that Ms Hyde needs help with her condition.

If anything was urgent Huffman LP, the Guardian, Smitch Law and Mrs Mason, it would be to ensure the safety and wellbeing of the children involved, and not taking a parent back to court, suggesting I am refusing contact of Lara with her mother and threatening another penal notice.

Lara has grown up with her mother's volatile parenting, and the only reason there were not more incidents between Ruth and all of her children, was that Lara had learned how to deal with her mother – not that these children's professionals care, to them it is perfectly normal for a child to be seen and not heard, and to hide from their mother when she becomes abusive towards her sisters and herself.

In a way that no other professionals seem to be able to fathom, Lara understands that her mother's behaviour has a pattern, and it is not going to stop. Lara could also see the impact her mother's attitude had on Alice, and knew that it was not right. The children's Guardian and solicitors are more focussed on the fact that a mother is not having contact with her child, rather than listening to why the child does not want contact with her mother.

Lara's decision has nothing to do with me; I supported her having extra time with her mother and never stopped her from going even when Hayley and Alice were not having contact in the past, and my concerns for her welfare were the same as they are now.

It took me four months to get a family court hearing to see my children when Ms Hyde refused me contact. Ms Hyde has had years of recorded disruptive and aggressive behaviour towards her children. Despite this, the children's solicitor and Mrs Mason ask the family court for an urgent hearing the next day.

It is Lara's choice to refuse contact with her mother at the moment. Lara told the Guardian the reasons why, yet Ms Dowling 'is at a loss'. Was the Guardian at a loss because she could not persuade a young child to have contact with a parent that was abusing her sisters and herself, or was the Guardian at a loss because of the disgraceful behaviour of a parent towards their three young children?

(I know the answer and it isn't the right one.)

I guess I am off to court to be awarded a penal notice for not forcing Lara to have contact with her abusive mother.

Dean Marlo

Court – Another day, another dollar

22nd September 2008 / Venray County Courts

Notification, Judge Neely orders hearing for directions 23rd September 2008 at 10am.

Court – Did you exchange a walk–on part in the war?

Application be adjourned to a review direction hearing before His Honour Judge Neely on 9th February 2009 at 10am, time estimate 1 hour at Venray County Courts.

Vanya Roshan, Family Support Worker, be requested to work with Lara Marlo to address the issue of contact between Lara and her mother. Such work not to commence until after Lara has sat her Eleven-plus exam at the end of November.

There be letterbox contact between Ms Hyde and Lara by way of short letters and cards. All correspondence to be sent via Lara's solicitor and seen by Ms Dowling, her Guardian, beforehand.

There be phone contact between Ms Hyde and Lara 3 times per week on Sunday, Tuesday and Thursday between 7pm and 7.30pm.

The hearing on 12th November 2008 be vacated.

When it rains

Come 11.30am, I had been rained off site and headed for home.

When I arrived, Ma was sitting with Sully in the kitchen.

Ma asked if I had heard from Hayley and I said no; Ma said she had been trying but had no luck until yesterday when Hayley phoned, and asked if they could meet in town. Ma was happy to and jumped on the bus.

Ma explained she waited 30 minutes outside the post office without Hayley picking up her phone. As Ma was walking off, Hayley ran up to her, stating that she was sorry and had to go, but could she borrow some money. Ma told Hayley that she did not have any money until Thursday, when her pension is paid into her bank.

Hayley said 'ok, goodbye' and walked off.

I know Hayley is going through a selfish teenage stage, but it's not nice to know your mum has been stood up, and the only reason Hayley had met with her nan was to ask for money.

The disagreement between Hayley and I was over a few words, yet we've ended up the most distant we've ever been, and I struggle to comprehend how we can all regain what we had.

Ma was upset; Hayley had never let her down. Up to this time, Hayley would change her plans just to see her nan. I feel let down by Hayley's behaviour.

I care for Ma, as she loves me as her son and Hayley, Alice and Lara as her grandchildren; I know with Ma's attributes and qualities, she is also a mother figure to them. I don't know where any of us would have been without her.

Hayley moving out

1 November

Hayley came home and stated that she is moving out to live with Conner.

I didn't mention what Ma had told me, and even though it hurt that she wanted to move out, I put a brave face on.

I gave her a hug and said, 'Look Hay, your room will always be here and I hope you and Conner come and see us regularly.'

Hayley said of course, sorted out some things from her room and I helped move the larger pieces of furniture in the van to the flat Conner lived in with one of his friends.

I'm not thrilled about Hayley's new living arrangements, but she is happy and excited to be living with her fiancé and going to college; that's the most important thing.

A thought to parents and parents to be-

Make sure you are there and enjoy your time with your children, because it soon disappears.

(I would give up my sword, horse and castle to go back ten years.)

Eleven–plus

22 November

Despite everything going on in the background, Lara has been working hard to prepare, with the hopes of being accepted into the Grammar School if she passes the Eleven-plus.

Yesterday, Ms Hyde spoke to Lara on the phone; I heard Lara say to her mother thank you for the good luck, but she did not want to see her in the morning as she wanted to be focussed on the test. This resulted in Lara holding the phone away from her ear for several minutes, only managing to cut in with 'no' and 'you're not listening to me'. She ended the call frustrated and said to me she hopes her mother does not come tomorrow.

(After reassuring Lara, I thought I would give Ms Hyde a call but, as I went through how the conversation would go in my mind, I decided to not ring her and just hope she does as Lara has requested. At the end of the day, no one has put Ms Hyde in this position but herself – I know in normal situations, I should be encouraging Lara. However, if this is how Lara feels, and with the denial of her mother that the incident even happened, I do not believe it is in Lara's best interests to have another adult undermine her.)

We drove to the exam centre, listening to Lara's favourite music and sat in the car for a few minutes, where I gave Lara a small teddy for her desk and wished her good luck. Just as Lara was prepping herself to go in, Ms Hyde appeared. She began talking to Lara through the car window.

Lara held my hand, gave it a squeeze and said I love you, before getting out the car. I said one last good luck, and watched as Ms Hyde moved out of the way of Lara's door.

Staring straight ahead, Lara ignored Ms Hyde and walked into the exam hall; Ms Hyde followed after her, trying to engage. Lara did not stop, she kept on walking until she was inside the building. Normally, Lara would do one last wave but she did not turn back. I took the opportunity to drive away before Ms Hyde could come back towards me.

When I picked Lara up after, I asked her it went. She said, 'I'm not sure, Dad,' and it was sad to see her confidence so knocked. I said as a treat we would go into town to a coffee shop, for a proper hot chocolate. That got a smile, and we headed off.

From the doctor

27 November

To whom it may concern,
Alice Marlo attended surgery today with her father, Mr Marlo, stating that her panic attacks are much improved but she is still finding it difficult to attend school. At present, her father is working half an hour away, and she feels that she does not have the confidence to be in school without the knowledge that Mr Marlo is nearby to fetch her should she need him. She is working on strategies to try and improve this.
I hope this letter explains why she has not been to school in the recent past, but should there be any further questions, please do not hesitate to be in touch.
Yours sincerely,

Alice becoming dependent on me following the incident in April makes it difficult to have quality time with Lara and plan any outings, such as badminton or the pier, because Alice either does not want to go, or we have to leave early. I do not blame Alice for what's going on, I'm trying to understand how to help, but it has added to the strain of daily life, and I am coping with another set of requirements to balance.

When Alice's anxiety started getting bad, I arranged with the UEEC for Alice to have home tutoring on some days. Now, despite Alice having less panic attacks, she does not even want the lessons at home, unless I am there.

Dean Marlo

Huffman LP write to me

8 December

I write further to the Hearing on the 23rd September whereby it was envisaged that the Welfare Worker from Cafcass do some work with Lara, with a view to letterbox contact taking place.

I can confirm that unfortunately Vanya Roshan of Cafcass has advised Ms Dowling that the he is unable to start any new work now until the New Year, and therefore we have asked the court whether or not they feel an urgent direction hearing should take place in this matter in order to address these issues.

I have also tried to make contact with Vanya Roshan to enquire as to timescales and I will of course revert to you at the earliest opportunity. This letter is simply to put you on notice that there may be an urgent directions listed in the very near future.

If you have any queries, we recommend that you seek independent legal advice.

Lara feels strongly about not living with her mother at the present time. The telephone contact she does have is hardly productive, largely due to Lara not wanting to talk and her mother not listening when she does.

Lara has said that no one has told her that it was awful her mother had behaved in that way. It makes me feel sad that adults can't see the genuine distress Lara feels towards her mother, and not even respect her feelings enough to say parents shouldn't hit their children.

2009

Dean Marlo

Phone calls

11 January

I received a call from Ms Hyde stating that it is disgraceful I have allowed my daughter to be homeless after she split up with her fiancé – I tried to explain that the last I heard from Hayley, it could only have been last week, everything was going well, and she hadn't contacted me to say otherwise. Ms Hyde did not hear this though, and continued to shout about how useless of a father I am, and how fortunate Hayley is to have her mother. At this point, I put the phone down.

I tried Hayley's number but she did not pick up.

From Huffman, disbelief

12 January

Dear Mr Marlo,
I have been asked by the guardian, Ms Dowling, to write to you regarding Hayley's belongings. I am instructed that Hayley would like to arrange a time and date with you to pick up her belongings from your house and that she would be accompanied by Ms Dowling, guardian.
I wonder if you would be so good as to contact me directly to arrange a time and date for Hayley and the guardian, Ms Dowling, to come to your home for Hayley to pick up her personal belongings.
I look forward to hearing from you regarding this matter.

I couldn't believe what I was reading when I received this letter. Hayley has never not been welcome home, and I helped Hayley load the van to take her belongings to Conner's. It hurt to see it even suggested that there would be a need for a guardian to attend with her.

I'm not sure why it is Alice and Lara's Guardian and solicitor who are once again involving Hayley in the proceedings.

In her entire lifetime, Hayley and I have had this one argument which has led to the current state of our relationship – as she had only moved into a room, essentially, with Conner, she couldn't take everything with her. I have not withheld her belongings, but feel it would be a mistake to allow her to completely tear her bedroom apart now, and further remove the idea of Hayley having a place at home, as she's always had.

I texted Hayley so we can arrange a time for her to come over and that I did not believe it was necessary for Ms Dowling to attend.

(I hate to bring it up, but this letter arrived the day after I received an abusive call from Ms Hyde… The police at hers and the Guardian is at mine, I can see the set-up she is going for.)

Hayley did not get back to me.

Dean Marlo

From Ms Hyde

18 January

Dear Dean,

I have tried calling you to speak with you as regards the children's dental health but you have not returned any of my calls.

I am just writing to let you know that Alice has an appointment with the dentist on Wednesday 28th January 2009 at 12:10pm. It is some time since she has been and a regular check-up will hopefully prevent a repeat of the round of fillings that she had to undergo at the last visit. Her last visit was October 07 and unless she has been recently there is dental and orthodontic work outstanding from that period.

If this appointment is not suitable for you, please will you rebook at a time convenient to you and Alice. Also, I would like to ask you to make sure that Lara has a regular check up for the same reasons; if Lara has not been for a while, she may need re-registering which I can do so that all 3 children are with the same dentist.

For your information Hayley is registered and has an appointment in February for a check-up. Finally, I'd just like to say that this is not for my benefit it is for the children's dental health so please would you try and make sure the appointment is kept for Alice and one is made for Lara and let me know.

Thank you.

Regards,

Guardian Report (through Huffman LP)

6 February

Dear Mr Marlo
Lara and Alice Marlo
9.5 Proceedings
Please find enclosed a copy of Ms Dowling's, the Guardian, report dated 3 February by way of service upon you.
Yours sincerely,
Valerie Whyte
Associate, Solicitor–Advocate

Introduction

I have not been ordered to submit a report in respect of this hearing but I feel that it is essential that the court is made aware of the concerns that I have in respect of this case.

This case came back before the court on the 11th June 2008. Ms Hyde made an application to enforce the contact order made at County Court on the 5th September 2007. This awarded her contact with Alice and Lara every other weekend, one night during the week and during school holidays.

Unfortunately, due to a difficult incident which took place at Ms Hyde's home on the 7th April 2008 these contact arrangements broke down. There was an argument during which Ms Hyde physically assaulted her eldest daughter, Hayley. This matter was reported to the police and Ms Hyde was arrested on the 27th April 2008.

She subsequently appeared in the Town Magistrates Court for this offence and received a bind over to keep the peace.

Following the 7th April Lara has refused to have any face-to-face contact with her mother. Alice has visited the house on one occasion to collect some of her belongings. Phone contact has been very difficult with both children feeling compelled to talk to their mother but actually not really engaging. Ms Hyde has also attempted letter box contact with her youngest daughter Lara and has in fact sent letters to the school. These allegedly have not been opened by Lara and thrown away. Ms Hyde informed me that she had obtained this information from the school.

In June 2008, the relationship between Hayley and her father broke down and she subsequently moved into her mother's home where she remains to date. She alleges that she has made several attempts to retrieve her belongings from her father's home but to date although some have been returned, she claims that he refuses to return the rest. Those belongings that were given back Hayley claims arrived at her mother's home in black plastic bags. She maintains that all attempts by herself to resolve the situation with her father have been rejected and he has told her that he does not want to have a relationship with her while she is living at her mother's.

I have seen no evidence to substantiate these claims but from my meetings with Hayley it is very clear that she is very distressed about the loss of her relationship with her father, paternal grandmother and her siblings. On the 12th January, I asked the solicitor of the children to write to Mr Marlo about Hayley's belongings which she did, but to date she has had no response.

Dean Marlo

On the 23rd September 2008 this matter was back in front of the court. His Honour Judge Neely made a direction that Vanya Roshan, Family Support Worker from Cafcass, should undertake work with Lara to address the issue of contact between her and her mother. Unfortunately, this work has not yet commenced as at the time Vanya did not have the capacity to take on further work. On the 8th December, the children's solicitor wrote to the court informing them that Vanya Roshan could not begin work until at the earliest the New Year. Consequently, the status quo remains the same with Lara and her mother only having phone contact on a weekly basis.

Issues of concern

I am very concerned about the lack of direct contact between Lara and her mother. I accept that Lara states that she does not want contact but believe that even if she did, this would not be encouraged by her father and sister Alice. From my limited involvement with Mr Marlo and Alice, I have formed the opinion that there is considerable animosity towards Ms Hyde and therefore any contact between Lara and her mother is actively discouraged.

Alice has been excluded from main stream education and was for a time attending the UEEC. Her attendance here has been spasmodic. I am informed that Mr Marlo has refused home tuition for her. The UEEC have made arrangements for her to attend after school hours, because her behaviour around the other pupils is very disruptive. Alice's attendance is improving but still erratic. The school have considered a referral to the Education Welfare Office.

Conclusion

I have to acknowledge that for a considerable period of time I have felt very uncertain as to the way forward in this case. The continued difficulties that exist between the parents in this case and their inability to resolve these without involving the children is seriously very worrying.

I have finally managed to get agreement for Vanya Roshan to undertake work with Lara Marlo but this needs to start now as he is only available until April. I have liaised with him and agreed that I will introduce him to Lara the week beginning 9th February.

It is my view that this matter should be listed for a final hearing sometime in April when Vanya has completed his work.

Billie Dowling
Children's Guardian

A belief, idea or thought does not make it real and the only suggestion to relay in a report should be factual, with supporting evidence; otherwise, as we have got, it is a written description of their own opinions, by someone who might have seen you for 30 minutes to an hour – I would still like to know if any of them can see they have not gained an understanding of anything.

Has she forgotten already what she wrote in her introduction, regarding Ms Hyde physically assaulting her daughter - surely, she is aware that Lara witnessed the assault? Again, this is not a situation of two parents' inability to resolve issues without involving the children.

Clearly, the experts are not prepared to put themselves in any of the children's position, watching a parent behave in that way – even if it has become normalised, this was another level wherein all three children were involved.

Why now, after all these years, would I say to Hayley that I don't want a relationship with her if she lives with her mother? Bearing in mind, up to this year, Hayley has been a loving, caring daughter and we were very close, due in part to what has happened throughout her upbringing. This whole process restarted because Hayley had been assaulted by her mother, and I once again stood by her. Over the past two years, Alice has flitted like a bird between our homes, but now I'm turning my back on my eldest daughter?

Hayley sometimes popped in, but our relationship is not as close as it used to be. Although deeply saddening to me, I am of the view Hayley is a young student, getting on with her life. It is shocking to see what the Guardian has taken away from the situation.

Ms Dowling has no evidence of the above, nor justification to relay to a judge that I would discourage Lara's contact with her mother – my only stance is to support my children's wishes and feelings, and I do not interfere with any of my children's relationships with their mother.

Unfortunately, the recent turmoil has resulted in Alice suffering from anxiety and panic attacks; this has reflected in her schooling, but she has been doing her best to cope with the new challenges this has brought, as have I. Do they think I'm not aware of the consequences this may have for Alice as she misses out on her education (limited as it already is) and how it generally affects her day-to-day life? It's not easy for Alice, and it's not easy as a parent to see her struggle, and not be able to help.

Alice and Lara have their own issues with reconciling with Hayley because she recanted to them that her mother had hit her, once she was living back round there. In the very least, I want for my children to be good siblings, but somehow, we've not even ended up there.

Dean Marlo

Council, Schooling

6 February

Dear Mr Marlo,
I am writing in response to your telephone call to the Unified External Education Centre today when you spoke to Mrs Delgado to request a record of Alice's attendance and an acknowledgement of your support of that attendance.
We are enclosing a copy of Alice's attendance which has improved this half term. Last half term it was 32%, this half term it is 65%. We acknowledge as a Service that you have supported this increase in attendance.
Yours sincerely,

Settling dust

8 February

Hayley came home with a friend and asked me for some bin bags before heading up to her room. About half an hour later, Hayley and her friend left with several bags.

Since Hayley moved in with her mother, she has visited twice to sort things out – I have tried to make it constructive, but on both occasions, Hayley decided to begin complaining about Alice and Lara, and how unfair the situation is. I told her to concentrate on how we are all going to move forward, however, whether it is teenagerism or a new side to Hayley that I don't recognise, Hayley would not let it go, and we still haven't resolved anything.

Alice called her Guardian to ask if she would be able to go to the hearing with me, and maybe speak to the judge herself. Ms Dowling told Alice that there have been occasions where a child has been asked by a judge for their views directly, and if she feels strongly about her views being heard, she could go. I would have preferred for Alice to have gone to school, but Alice wanted to see an end of court involvement in her and her family's lives, and confirmed with Ms Dowling that she wanted to attend.

I understand that children have no place in the Family Courts; I'd really rather Alice not come, as it served no purpose last time and I don't even want to be there. However, with her anxiety and everything else going on, I don't have the energy to tell Alice she can't. At the same time, this is about Alice and Lara – why wouldn't she want to be heard? The Family Courts process has consumed both of their lives, meanwhile the children all had to cope living with a parent that has a mental health condition.

A doctor and a psychologist have relayed concerns of severe mania, and aggressive outbursts. If the judges can just ignore their appointed experts, then why not talk to a young member of the family and hear some home truths from someone that was living there and through it.

Dear Judge Neely

I feel that I should be allowed to come to court with my dad because no one except me, Hayley, Lara and our mother have been there and knows what really goes on when she kicks off and we shouldn't have to be put through this as kids.

When I met my Guardian, she said that I can go to court.

I had to phone the police and ask if they would come round with me so I could get my stuff without any trouble as I explained to the police she would not let me have my tablets to which I had to take daily and she new that full well, before I entered her house the police officer said to me that if she kicked off I would have to be taken straight out because it would be conceded a breach of the peace which not even five minutes later they had to do because she kicked off and I had to be taken out of her property and the police officer said my mother was totally out of control, our mother had pre boxed some stuff up to which the police had to go back round there and pick up when I got it, it was old boots and jeans with holes in.

After this occasion I have tried over 20 times to get my stuff from our mother's. since being in the Family Courts again my guardian has made no effort even though when I met her we discussed this issue and she told me she would sort it out and she hasn't been in contact since and this was September 2008 so I have tried to contact her and have left her a voicemail to get back to me and still to this day I have had nothing.

Yours faithfully,
Alice Marlo

Lara's class teacher

9 February

Lara is a very able girl who consistently achieves a high standard of work in all curriculum areas. Although she has always been well focused in school, since September she has become more involved in and responsible for her own learning, actively working to improve her skills and knowledge.

She responds positively to challenges and shows independence and commitment to meeting homework deadlines and working towards curriculum targets set. She has ambitions for her secondary schooling and is working hard to achieve them, both at home and at school. She is predicted to attain Level 5 in all three areas tested by the end of Key Stage 2 SATs.

Her sense of responsibility and her ability to think independently make Lara an ideal leader of the School Council. From being a class representative last year, Lara has this year taken over the 'top job'. She and her fellow councillors are responsible for helping the school achieve Healthy School and Environment awards, and Lara has proved extremely reliable in attending and leading meetings, producing minutes and rotas, and generally being 'right-hand-man' to the Deputy Head who oversees the Council's work.

Lara has a secure friendship group and is on good terms with all of her peers. She is adaptable and has the ability to work productively alongside anyone in the class. She is an open and friendly girl, with a good sense of humour who, while being perfectly aware of difficulties and shortcomings, nevertheless tends to look for the best in people and situations.

Yours sincerely,

Court – here we go again

9th February 2009 / Venray County Courts

Judge Neely orders Family Support Worker Vanya Roshan to undertake work with Lara, and the Guardian Ms Dowling to file an addendum report to deal with the work undertaken by Vanya Roshan. Matter listed for review on 22nd April 2009.

At the very start of the Hearing, Alice & Lara's solicitor Mrs Whyte stood up and stated to the judge, 'Mr Marlo has brought Alice to court again your Honour.'

I stood up and told the judge and Mrs Whyte that Alice has come to court for the second time, under the approval of her Guardian Ms Dowling.

Mrs Mason stood and said, 'This is a young child being brought to court your Honour; this young child, your Honour, is 13-years-old and court is not a place for a young person.'

As Judge Neely rose in his chair and started his rant. I thought 'do not shoot the messenger' – knowing I already had two targets on my back, placed there by Mrs Mason and Mrs Whyte.

The judge turned to me and stated, 'If you ask a child Mr Marlo, you will find they do not want to be brought to court hearings.'

(Why not actually ask Alice, your honour, or is it easier to talk down to someone?)

Mrs Mason lied to the judge, and Mrs Whyte knew that Alice had spoken to her Guardian about attending, which was what Alice saw as permission.

Mrs Mason, who has been Ms Hyde's solicitor since the year 2000, should by now know the ages of the children involved, and Alice is 14; she is going to be 15 in April. The information Mrs Mason gave the judge was not a professional mistake, it was a deliberate attempt to mislead the judge and further demean the opinion of me as a father.

(Needless to say, Judge Neely frowned and frothed at the mouth. You know when a bully looks at you from across the room, and you do not know whether to look at the floor or the ceiling tiles; ether way, I could feel Judge Neely trying to catch my eye.)

Venray court order, HHJ Neely

9 February

The Court Orders:
That Vanya Roshan, Family Support Worker, do undertake work with Lara Marlo to address the issue of contact between Lara and her mother. Such work is to commence forthwith.
That there be indirect contact between the Applicant and Lara by way of short cards and letters, such correspondence to be sent via Lara's solicitor and seen by her Guardian beforehand, and further that there be telephone contact between the Applicant and Lara three times a week on a Sunday, Tuesday and Thursday between 7pm and 7.30pm.
The Guardian do file an addendum report to deal with the work undertaken by Neil Shade and to file such report by 4pm on Monday 6 April 2009.
The matter is listed for a review on 22 April 2009 at 10am before His Honour Judge Neely, at Venray County Court.
Costs in the application.

What the judges never say but know, is that whatever form of residence they give to Ms Hyde, it ends up with another abusive incident and the children refusing contact. This has escalated from Hayley in 2000, to Alice in 2004 and now Lara in 2008 – surely, they can see the pattern? The Family Courts are fully committed to organising penal notices for me, yet are unable to commit to helping a parent cope with her bipolar disorder and her children.

Tens of thousands of pounds spent on a family court sham, when a fraction of the cost could have been spent on supporting Ms Hyde and hopefully bringing stability into three children's, and their parents', lives. This has got to be better than the Family Courts ensemble denying Ms Hyde has an ongoing mental health condition, dismissing the evidence, accepting multiple applications from a self-serving law firm, and using inaccurate reports to guide them.

Dean Marlo

From Riverbank Headteacher

10 February

To whom it may concern,
I wish to confirm that the school has passed on any letters received from Ms Hyde to Lara Marlo, and that on at least two occasions she has been observed opening them. The school has not seen or known any occasions when she has thrown these letters away unopened.
Yours sincerely,

Meeting changes

11 February

At 10:20am, I received a call from Mrs Whyte from Huffman LP, requesting I bring Lara to the Cafcass office at 4pm today. When I asked why, she stated, 'Ms Dowling felt you were a bit stressed when you left court the other day, and it would be better for everyone if Lara was brought into the Cafcass office.'

(Stressed, or, sick to death with these professionals being paid to make a muddle of a family's dynamics and continuing the dishonesty and unethical performance within the Family Courts. Out of the blue, on the 6th February I had received a Guardian's report with false and misleading statements that was superfluous and once again detrimental.)

I told Mrs Whyte that it was an unreasonable request, as Lara was told she would meet Vanya at home after school. When Mrs Whyte stated 'it would be better for everyone', she was evidently not thinking about Lara's best interests, as she has been at school all day, it is cold and she needs to come home, have a hot meal and settle down in the warm, and not be dragged across town to satisfy Mrs Whyte, Ms Dowling, Judge Neely or an abusive parent.

I told Mrs Whyte that the appointment was made for Lara at home and that is where she will be. After several minutes of silence and a discussion going on in the background Mrs Whyte conceded and said Vanya will visit Lara at home at 4pm.

I asked Mrs Whyte while she was on the phone if she could explain why she felt it necessary to say to the judge that Alice is in court again, and she replied, 'Alice had been in court two times as you told the judge, and Alice should not be at court.'

I reminded Mrs Whyte that it was in fact Ms Dowling who had told Alice that she could attend the hearing.

Mrs Whyte agreed, but said that Ms Dowling should not have told Alice that she could go, and the judge had said Alice should not be coming to court.

Feeling emotionally exhausted by the phone call and revisiting the memories of the day in court, I queried why, as she was there to represent Alice, did she not correct Mrs Mason when she was misleading the judge about Alice's age; I reminded her that Alice is 14, nearly 15.

Mrs Whyte replied, 'Well, Ms Mason does not know Alice's age either.'

Is this the attitude from a children's solicitor, if Mrs Mason does not know then it does not matter if Mrs Whyte does not know?

Mrs Whyte said, 'I am sorry you feel I did not represent Alice in the right way.'

I asked for her apology in writing for implying to the judge that Alice has been attending court on many occasions, and for not correcting Mrs Mason on Alice's age when she was manipulating the judge. I was surprised when she said she would.

I hope the letter will aid me if the accusation comes up by Mrs Mason that it was for my own personal reasons that Alice was in court.

(It is a pain in the arse trying to gather supporting evidence, and I'd rather just move on with my life, but I don't know what else to do to defend myself and my children from the dishonesty that persists behind the Family Courts' doors.)

Sometimes I think I am going crazy; an allegation is made in court, I go into defence mode gathering evidence to disprove the statement; when we go back into court, the allegation is forgotten and the evidence dismissed, and we move right along to the next false allegation or manipulative suggestion.

Huffman LP to me, twice

11 February

Further to our attendance at court on 9th February, please note that the matter has now been listed for a review hearing on the 22nd April 2009 at 10am, before his Honour Judge Neely, with a time estimated of one hour.

If for any reason there are problems with the setting up of further meeting between Lara and Mr Roshan, please contact me to let me know and I will do my best to sort any difficulties.

Further to our phone conversation I write, as requested by you, to apologise for having given Alice's wrong age when we were in court before his Honour Judge Neely. According to the records, I have Alice's date of birth as 1994 which means that she is 14, not 13 as I stated in court, but equally that she is not 15 as you stated to me on the phone today.

Why do they always have to have the last word? I only asked for confirmation that in court representing Alice, she failed to ensure the judge was not mislead by Mrs Mason.

The point really is that it was stated before a judge that a 13-year-old is attending court, and not that I said Alice is 'nearly 15' on the phone. I think it would be fair to say Alice acts like a 14-year-old and not a 13-year-old; as any child and parent knows, coming up to 15 is a big step up from 13.

(I feel shocked as I sit here in the midst of all this bullshit and think that in two months, Alice will be 15 years old, and I have genuine tears in my eyes when I consider of all the time wasted, and the upset and trouble in all of my children's lives.)

UEEC, Alice's School

12 February

Dear Mr Marlo,
I understand that you have requested confirmation that when Alice's educational programme has involved teaching within the home, you have been supportive of this programme.
We acknowledge as a service that you have supported this programme.
Yours sincerely,

I am still collecting evidence that will mean nothing to a judge, as they simply brush aside the numerous false allegations made, or hand me another penal notice.

(On a serious note, apart from looking after Alice and Lara; trying to run my business; preparing and collecting evidence for the Family Courts; hiding from Ms Hyde; worrying that Smitch Law and Mrs Mason will be accompanied by something new up their sleeve and a judge in their pocket - I'm exhausted.)

Dear HH Judge Neely

14 February

I have had no legal help in preparing my reply to Ms Dowling's report or this forthcoming hearing.

I feel I must bring to your attention not only the despair that is being placed unnecessarily into our family dynamic, also the dismay I have when reading the Guardian's report submitted to the Family Courts for the hearing on the 9th February 2009.

I am totally appalled and exhausted with the on goings in my family's case within the Family Courts. In the name of common sense, honesty, morals and standards, please would you intervene and ensure that these proceedings are dealt with professionally, honestly and justly, so that the welfare and stability of the children involved is paramount.

The report submitted by Ms Dowling had not been ordered by the court, as Vanya Roshan, the Family Support Worker, was unable to start work with Lara until February, and the Guardian therefore had not spoken to or seen us as a family since September 2008. (Except when Alice called on the 8th February, to ask if she could attend court.) I find once again an inaccurate and misleading report has been presented that only be considered misleading within the Family Courts.

I would like to ask your Honour, for good reason, that Cafcass and all solicitors are asked to step back to allow Vanya Roshan to do his work with Lara, allowing Ms Hyde and myself to come back to court for a final hearing date. When Vanya Roshan has had time with Lara, the Guardian can submit a report based on his findings that has some meaning to Lara, some relevance to the situation our children find themselves in, an insight into our family's dynamics and the way forward. If, in the meantime, Lara wishes to reinitiate contact with her mother, as I have for her sisters in the past, I will respect her choice to do so.

I am not standing up against Ms Hyde, I am standing by my daughters because they are morally right and their reasons are justifiable.

Lara has had her first session with Vanya Roshan and I ask your Honour to recognise and acknowledge my cooperation with Vanya and the Family Courts, and my endeavour to resolve these proceedings.

I would like to clarify several misleading statements made at the hearing 9th February 2009; I bring these matters up as I believe that honesty and fairness must be maintained.

I have enclosed letters in my statements from UEEC and Riverbank School, which could have been obtained by Ms Dowling and Mrs Mason, instead of false information being included in Ms Hyde's statement and the Guardian's report. In doing so, I would ask politely for law firms and appointed organisations to behave in a moral manner as they are dealing with children's welfare, and this should be reflected in their conduct.

Please find enclosed, a letter from Alice's School UEEC stating that I have been fully supportive of Alice's home tutoring. Also, a letter with Alice's attendance at UEEC and

681

a letter from her GP, explaining the reasons for her missed time.

Please find enclosed, a letter from Lara's Headteacher, stating that the school has not seen or know of any occasions when Lara has thrown letters from Ms Hyde away. In fact, the school confirms on two occasions Lara has been observed opening them.

Please find enclosed, a letter from Lara's teacher regarding her disposition in school.

It has never been my intentions to get on the wrong side of the Family Courts or the legal system. In 1999, I went to the Family Courts to obtain contact with my children and to relay that I was able and willing to play my part in their upbringing. Throughout, the only thing I have been guilty of is trying to be an honest and decent parent.

I believe it to be shameful that in 2009 – after ten years and 36 hearings – a children's Guardian from Cafcass can make some absurd conclusions.

We still live 100 meters away from Ms Hyde's house, and I have never brought trouble to her door; Hayley and Alice used to happily walk between our homes. In every case, the incidences of alleged abuse have arisen while the children were in their mother's care; despite the numerous allegations, from carpet burns on Alice's back, to Hayley being taken to the ground and strangled, I have remained calm and responsible; I have listened to our children and in the interests of their welfare and stability, I have done nothing more than stand by them. This is not vengeance against a mother, this is me supporting the emotional and physical wellbeing of my three children.

I have never discouraged my children from seeing their mother, or suggested that Lara would not be getting involved with the Family Support Worker. I hope you will consider this when appraising the Guardian's report and my reply.

Yours respectfully…

To HH Judge Neely: Guardian report

14 February

Please find below my reply to the Guardian, Ms Dowling's, report.

I received the report at 2pm Friday the 6th February, at very short notice.

Ms Dowling takes the opinion that Alice, my middle child, and myself would actively discourage Lara from having contact with her mother; this opinion is based on limited involvement that took place nearly five months ago, and does not take into consideration previous incidents, wherein Hayley and Alice would refuse contact while Lara would continue to do so.

Once again it is clear reading the report that it contains needlessly inaccurate and misleading statements and opinions with little or no substance, disgracefully trying to imply that both parents' behaviour is as bad as each other.

Lara has made it clear that she does not want contact at the present time with a parent that she has witnessed physically assaulting her sister. Cafcass have made arrangements to try and help regain contact, yet Lara is not even told what is going on in her life.

Regarding specific paragraphs of the report:

(4) Ms Dowling states that Ms Hyde has sent letters to the school, which Lara had not opened but thrown away, and that this information was obtained from Lara's school.

I have been in contact with the Headteacher from Lara's school, who informs me that neither she nor any of her staff have relayed such information. Instead, she mentioned to me that on one occasion Ms Hyde requested that a member of staff was there to watch Lara open the letter and have her read it in front of them. Lara did feel embarrassed and anxious over this, and mentioned it to me at the time. However, when I asked Lara if she wanted me to have a quiet word with the Headteacher, Lara said, 'Forget it Dad,' so I did not bring it up again.

Lara has brought several cards home from her mother, and they have been put on top of the fridge as she did not want to keep them in her room; Lara's letters from her mother are personal letters to her and nothing to do with me, Lara has grown up with this understanding and so have I.

I cannot understand why Ms Dowling felt the necessity to write a report with misleading and unfounded statements about Lara's conduct as well as my own; this statement was in fact false, callous and an injustice to Lara and her character.

I also bring to your attention that Ms Hyde visited Lara's school and requested that the Headteacher take Lara out of her class, where Lara was working, so that she could speak to her. The Headteacher asked Lara if she would like to leave her class, but Lara stated that she wanted to get on with her work. This is contrary to the order, which indicates letterbox contact, and Lara has had every opportunity to respond to Ms Hyde, if she desired to. I believe it shows a lack of understanding on Ms Hyde's part for our children's feelings, and this is the reason why this division has been prolonged.

(5) Hayley left home over a silly disagreement over pocket money and then moved in

with her fiancé. I am shocked as a parent that it could be suggested that I would behave in the way described by Ms Dowling towards Hayley, my eldest daughter, who I not only love, but have endured 10 years of hearings trying to ensure the best for her.

I do not believe we are the first family to have a disagreement; I am heartbroken over the distance that has come between Hayley and myself, over money. I am also sickened by the Guardian's use of the difficulties that Hayley and myself are having, and believe that it is shameful behaviour to include misleading information about Hayley, who is not governed by a court order, in proceedings covering Lara's contact with her mother.

Also, I find it quite unbelievable that the Guardian does not understand that the upset between the three sisters has nothing to do with myself, and equally, the relationship between myself and Hayley does not impact Lara's relationship with her mother.

The key things here are that Ms Hyde is alleged by the children to have punched Hayley in the chest and face and has been arrested and bound over to keep the peace, which has resulted in Lara's reluctance to have contact. Hayley and I had a disagreement over pocket money and Hayley, who did not tell me the relationship with her fiancé had ended, moved into her mother's instead of coming home. That was her choice, even though she knows her room is as she left it and she has always been welcome, and despite the concerns I have for her in her mother's residence.

(6) I have never prevented Hayley from collecting her possessions, so I saw no need to reply to a letter asking me to do so. I simply refuse to engage in the game that has been facilitated by the legal system over the past ten years.

From my recollection of the meeting with Ms Dowling, Alice, Lara and I, repeatedly made it clear that we had all had enough of the insatiability that the endless hearings had placed in all our lives. I honestly believe all I expressed to the Guardian at our meeting was genuine exhaustion with Ms Hyde's behaviour towards our children, and the years of proceedings that seemed never-ending in its depletion of my family's dynamics.

I find it very difficult to understand why the Guardian stated 'for a considerable period of time' she has felt 'very uncertain as to the way forward in this case'. It was unfortunate that Vanya Roshan was unable to start work with Lara in December as arranged, but Lara has never stated she would not see the support worker.

(The Guardian had nothing to tell the courts about Lara; Alice's views were clear, so let's throw Hayley into the mix and her relationship with her father.)

For 16 years, Hayley showed me the love and care any parent would be proud of; she was calm and happy to join in and have fun no matter what we were doing. Hayley and Alice would always be there wanting to help with Lara, when they were all younger; at home, going to nursery or on holiday to Disney, Skegness or the caravan park. We were a tight knit family and that was complemented by Ma, who gave nothing less than all of her love and care.

I feel that the worry expressed by the Guardian about the 'continued difficulties between the parents' would be better suspended until she has received Vanya Roshan's findings after working with Lara, before making an uninformed and unsubstantiated opinion. Despite her treatment of our children, I have acquiesced to Ms Hyde's requests and demands; the evidence of which has been clearly documented over the last 36 family court hearings.

What worries me, as a parent, is the repeated lack of respect, consideration and understanding of all of the family members by professionals preparing and presenting reports to the Family Courts.

The facts in this case:

1. Lara saw her mother physically assault her sister.

2. Since then, Lara has not wanted to resume contact at the present time with her mother.

3. 23rd September, your Honour ordered for the Family Support Worker Vanya Roshan to work with Lara in December 2008, however this was cancelled.

4. Meeting with Vanya Roshan reappointed for week starting 9th February 2009.

5. I support any work carried out by Vanya Roshan regarding re–establishing Lara's contact with Ms Hyde; Lara continues phone contact and to open any letters received; as in the past, she has a mobile which she can call her mother on any time, and if she wants to see her mother, she is free to do so. Lara knows this.

It should have been at the forefront of everyone's mind, after ten years of family court involvement and numerus experts – which have achieved nothing but uncertainty for us as a family – it is time for the Family Courts to stand back and let this family try to get on without their involvement.

Allowing Ms Hyde and Smitch Law to constantly bring proceedings has proved to not be the answer.

Ms Hyde may be able to settle down with her children and if not, under our family's circumstances, Alice and Lara are old enough to decide for themselves. If any abuse towards the children occurs (which never stopped, with ten years of court involvement) Social Services and the police are there to ensure the welfare of Hayley, Alice and Lara.

In the event that Ms Hyde has letters or evidence from the schools, police reports or organisations such as Social Services, concerned about my behaviour towards my children, then the Family Courts could be there to assist.

The process of gaining hearings needs overhauling, starting with the basics – family law solicitors must ensure evidence is provided with any applications to the court to start proceedings, their client's written statements are factual and any information in the bundle is relevant and does not stray from the interests of the children.

As I have had to do, a solicitor should be focussing on gathering evidence to support their client, not trying to dictate a family's daily lives, or bring them to the Family Courts based on their client's hearsay, despite hiding behind the veil of acting in the best interests of their client, they had a moral obligation to the stability and welfare of children.

(Even though I do not like solicitors in principle, I understand they are always going to be a part of the system; the point is, if there was another Melissa at the other side of the table, things would not have played out over ten years.)

In one of Ms Hyde's most recent applications to start proceedings, she states that I have kidnapped Lara – this was overseen by Mrs Mason (and publicly funded.) When I had Melissa as my solicitor, she would read through my statements and applications to ensure what I was writing had relevance, meaning and the evidence to prove it.

I am told that our family's case is complex... Yes, I can imagine any family's case would be if you ignore the facts and dismiss the truth.

Dear Melissa

15 February

Thank you for your email address and thanks again for getting back to me. I hope that you are well and I am sorry to ask for your advice. I have lost faith in the system again, and need your advice please.

In brief:

Ms Hyde assaulted Hayley in April 2008.

Hayley, Alice and Lara refused to have contact with Ms Hyde.

Ms Hyde brought proceedings to the courts in June and September 2008.

Alice and Lara were appointed a Cafcass Guardian and a solicitor, and a Family Support Worker was due to begin work with Lara to re-establish contact. A hearing was listed for 9th February 2009.

Before the hearing in September 2008, the Guardian informed Alice that she can go to court with me, if she wished.

At court on the 9th February 2009, Alice's solicitor stood up and stated to the judge 'Mr Marlo has brought Alice to court again your Honour.' I stood and stated Alice has been to court twice. Mrs Mason stood and said, 'This is a young child being brought to court your Honour, this young child, your Honour, is 13 years old and court is not a place for this young person.'

Alice will be 15 in April.

Alice's solicitor made no contact prior to Alice being at the hearing to say she did not agree with the Guardian about Alice attending. She did not mention it to me or Alice; I do not believe a solicitor should be misleading a judge nor misrepresenting Alice, her client.

Mrs Mason has been representing Ms Hyde regarding our three children for 9 years, and she stated that Alice was 13 to the judge. This is either further unprofessional behaviour from this solicitor in her attempt to influence the judge by gaining weight to her dissatisfaction by deliberately misleading them – or just another example of her careless conduct.

Alice's solicitor and Mrs Mason clearly conspired to shame me for allowing Alice to come to court – further clouding the judge's perception.

Please could you tell me what age a child would be permitted to accompany a parent in the Family Courts, if the child wished to? Also, can Alice change her solicitor?

Contact

23/28 February

Monday 23rd
I received a call from Hayley and we chatted for a bit; she asked if I was at work, and when I said no she said she would pop in.

Hayley didn't stay long, but said there were some things from her room she wanted to get. I left her to it and a few minutes later she came back down. I said I hoped to see her on my birthday, and Hayley replied, 'Of course, Dad,' and left.

Saturday 28th
Alice and Lara made me breakfast and I had a lovely day with them, Ma and Sully. Hayley popped in with a card; I was pleased to see her and we agreed to meet on her birthday.

Dean Marlo

To Ms Hyde

3 March

Re: Lara's Secondary School Admission 2009

On the 2nd March, I received the confirmation letter from the School Admissions that Lara has been offered a place at Horizon Academy.

As you are aware, Lara is happy with this placement and is looking forward to going Horizon Academy in September.

Would you please put Alice's and Lara's passport through our door or arrange for me to pick them up, within the next couple of days.

Yours sincerely,

From Melissa, SHE'S BACK

3 March

Dear Dean,
Sorry for the delay in replying fully to you.
I am also sorry to hear that the cycle has, yet again, repeated itself.
You ask two questions:
At what age can a child accompany a parent to court?
Can Alice change her solicitor?
1. Only rarely in the local County Courts should a child attend at court. It generally does not happen. Of course, it could have been Alice's opportunity to see her mother. Judges are usually displeased when children attend at court and it is something that is actively discouraged. Sometimes judges will ask to see children and I have known children to be collected from school and lunchtime and taken to talk to the Judge; this very, very rarely happens, though. In some of the main courts, the children will attend at court to meet with the Cafcass Officer, to try to speed the process up. This tends to happen more in London. Of course, again, Alice may have wanted to go to court to see her solicitor.
2. It is difficult for children to change their solicitor. I have only had one case where I acted for the parents and the child was separately represented and where the child attended at court and made loud noises about changing their solicitor (age 15). A report was ordered by the judge to inform the court as to whether or not that child was competent to instruct a solicitor of their own choosing. The report said that they were not and so they had to keep that solicitor.
It seems to me what Alice needs to do really is speak to her Guardian. Has there been any recent contact since your email to me? Does Alice have anyone at school she can voice her concerns to, and who may help her to make contact with either the Guardian or the solicitor?
One word of warning Dean, recent changes to Children Law jeopardise Lara remaining with you unless you are seen by the judge as doing all you can to actively promote her relationship and contact with her mother.
I do hope the above is of help to you. If you have any further questions, please email me.
Kind regards,

Dean Marlo

The birthday sketch

Along with a few presents, I got Hayley a card, put some cash inside in it and waited for Hayley's call to let me know where she wanted to go. I gave Hayley until 10am, then rang her and she said she was busy, so she would see me another day.

Dear MP

31 March

Please find enclosed, a letter I have written to Gordon Brown PM. I hope you will be able to assist me by sending this letter to him.

Yours respectfully...

Dear Mr Brown PM,

I went to the family court hearing in February 2009 with a clear mind and the understanding that with the help of a Family Support Worker, we may have been able to resolve our family's issues and family court proceedings. Yet, I find once again the resentment towards an honest and decent father still exists and attempts to falsely discredit my behaviour and character remain. This is at any cost.

The animosity shown towards me as a parent from within the system is unnecessary, immoral and totally shameful. It would be overwhelming and shocking to anyone, as it has been for me, to have never acted in the way that I am continually portrayed within the Family Courts.

For 9 years, the same law firm have had the ability to twist the truth or situation to suit themselves and their client; clearly crossing the line of ethical conduct on many occasions and, without doubt, bullying their way through proceedings and openly showing no regard to the welfare and stability of the children involved.

The warmongering must be stopped and the Family Courts must make it clear to professional people involved in family matters and children's welfare that it is not acceptable for law firms, barristers, solicitors or Guardians to be morally lacking in their attitude, behaviour and performance, and that false or misleading statements will not be tolerated. It should be made very clear that such behaviour is not in the best interests of the children involved and a family's dynamics.

I believe that it is the responsibility of our government ministers to ensure that honesty, morals and standards are being upheld, and to take action when it is clear that these values are not.

By those I have explained my experience to, I am frequently asked, after another 5 years of proceedings, what was the point of the Family Courts granting me sole residency of my three children, when at any opportunity they have played along, sat back and allowed a decent parent to be persecuted without truth, good reason or evidence?

I have shown that my only concerns are for my children. It is shameful that in 2009, after ten years and 36 hearings, a Guardian from Cafcass can report that I would 'actively discourage' my daughters' contact with their mother.

We currently live 100 meters away from Ms Hyde's home and I have never brought upheaval to her door; when I was granted sole residency I did not move to Scotland, we have always lived within a 5-minute drive from Ms Hyde.

The penny needs to drop and I am asking you as the Prime Minister not to sit back when people are being unjustly persecuted. I hope you will confirm that this is not what democracy or society is about; I need my ministers to agree that enough is enough, as I personally cannot accept any more of the dishonesty from within the system.

I ask for your support in ensuring that my case is looked into, as I believe what is clear is the disparity and the animosity found in families is being inflamed by unscrupulous law firms, with priorities set only for their finances or status.

Below I have listed only several situations, and must make clear that I am attempting to allow you to grasp the position our children and myself are recurrently placed in, and it is not point fingers. Professionals within the Family Courts treat me like a criminal, yet;

I have not been the parent that has had Social Services involved due to being physically violent towards our 10–year–old daughter in 2004.

I have not been the parent shouting and screaming outside my former partner's various homes, and being charged with criminal damage in 2006.

I have not been the parent bound over to keep the peace after being charged with the offence 'Assault by beating (Battery)' on our 16-year-old daughter in 2008.

I am not the parent that has ever discouraged our children from seeing the other parent or her family, despite my unaddressed concerns for their welfare.

My family and many other families need and deserve the appropriate departments to make clear to unscrupulous law firms, judges and children's organisations, that their behaviour is detrimental to a child's welfare and their family's stability. Those found to be conducting themselves inappropriately within 'children's matters' should be removed from the court proceedings and not permitted to work within family law again, without acknowledgement of wrongdoing and improvement of their behaviour.

This behaviour is not accepted outside of a courtroom; can anyone please tell me why it appears to be acceptable within the Family Courts? Or is it not acceptable, but no one can be bothered to address it?

I shall be making a stand for honesty, morals and standards within the Family Courts at the hearing on the 22nd April 2009. I am not asking you to support me in my case, but to support my belief that I should expect nothing more than the compliance to standards from professionals working in children matters.

I will never understand or accept why when writing to government ministers and the appropriate departments, doors are shut, communications are closed or I am sent up the garden path. My local MP has been fully supportive, yet finds his hands to be tied; not receiving meaningful responses to his attempts to address the issues that he is aware of, and he fully appreciates that the performance my family have received from within the Family Courts should not be acceptable.

It must be realised and practiced that for separated mothers and fathers, getting on is the best thing we as parents can do for our children. Sadly, in some circumstances the other parent has proven themselves to be irresponsible, abusive or absent, and the appropriate support should be in place to help or protect the parent who does have responsibility of the children, and the children themselves.

Criticisms are aimed at the Family Courts, but underlining their decision–making and actions are deceitful and misleading law firms and organisations that continue to make this process needlessly difficult. How can a judge ever assess children's best interests if legal representatives on behalf of their client can be dishonest and misleading in their conduct, or if reports can contain allegations without investigating to see if the information is true?

Legal Aid and Smitch Law's profiteering, 2000-2009.

Throughout these hearings, Smitch Law have been, and are being, paid handsomely to, as far as I can see, prolong their involvement with my family's case. I would like to point out that the only person not getting paid at these hearings is the person that has the responsibility to provide financially for their children.

I believe the law firm in question should be named and shamed for their menacing attitude towards a single parent with three young children. The thousands of pounds they have gained in my family's case over 9 years, by being misleading and playing the system as best as they know how, with clear disregard for any child involved, should be retrieved, and their dishonest earnings donated to set up an organisation that will ensure the behaviour and performance already endured by families by unscrupulous law firms and the Family Courts, never resurfaces in children and family matters again.

Unfortunately, we find there are some dishonest people in all walks of life who misuse their position; when this is brought to the attention of the appropriate organisation it should be investigated, lessons learnt and reassurances made to that this behaviour will not be tolerated.

Cafcass 2009

I was of the understanding the current court proceedings were about trying to regain contact between my youngest daughter and her mother.

Clearly, the Guardian made the effort to receive and relay the false information to the Family Courts in her report. Yet, the Guardian made no effort to ensure what she was relaying to a judge was in fact accurate or worthy of inclusion in a report that had not been requested; filled with unfounded allegations, it has once again achieved nothing more than clouding our family's dynamics and misleading a judge.

I would be grateful if you would assist me in gaining an appointment with the Directors of Cafcass and myself, as I believe that they have a responsibility to ensure honesty, morals and ethical standards are being practiced and maintained, when working in children's matters and family cases within the Family Courts.

Huffman LP / Mrs Whyte, Alice and Lara's solicitor.

At court on the 9th February, at the very start of the hearing, Alice's solicitor Mrs Whyte stood up and stated to the Judge, 'Mr Marlo has brought Alice to court again your Honour.' I stood up and told the judge that this is at Alice's request and that day was her second attendance in court. Then Mrs Mason from Smitch Law stood up and told the judge, 'This is a young child being brought to court your Honour; this young child, your Honour, is 13-years-old and court is not a place for a young person.'

The judge turned to me and stated, 'If you ask a child Mr Marlo, you will find they do not want to be brought to family court hearings.'

At the time, Mrs Whyte did not voice any issues or explain that it may be detrimental in the judge's eyes for Alice to be there, regardless of how strongly she feels. It also does not take into account Alice's recent struggles with anxiety, and her previous determination, which has not gone away, to do what she wants to do.

Why did Mrs Whyte not simply call Alice or myself before the hearing on the 9th February and relay it would be considered inappropriate for Alice to attend the court? If Mrs Whyte, as Alice's acting solicitor, was concerned that Alice, as she relayed to the judge, was 'at court again', why did she not just communicate in any way?

Sitting before Judge Neely, Mrs Whyte knew full-well that Ms Dowling and Alice had spoken, agreeing that Alice could come; Mrs Whyte did not bother to inform Judge Neely of this fact.

This solicitor did not have the decency to prevent this situation from being used as a weapon against a parent, who was standing in a courtroom again because of Ms Hyde's despicable behaviour towards our children.

Before the hearings in September 2008, I made it clear that I did not believe Alice should be coming to the court, which is why Alice talked with her Guardian.

Alice wanted to attend court due to witnessing her mother being physically abusive in April 2008; questioning why things are never sorted out, what with court orders being a part of her life; the Guardian encouraging Alice to make her views heard by the judge.

Evidently, Mrs Whyte allowed Judge Neely to get the impression that it was for my own personal reasons that I was bringing Alice into the hearings. Mrs Whyte should have brought this issue up with Alice and her Guardian before the hearing day and if not, she should have addressed the issue with the Guardian and Alice before we were called to see Judge Neely.

Smitch Law

Alice is 14 years old, and will be 15 at the beginning of April.

Mrs Mason from Smitch Law has been representing Ms Hyde regarding our 3 children since 2000, yet Mrs Mason stated to the judge that Alice was 13-years-old. This is either another example of the immoral behaviour by this solicitor, in her attempt to influence the judge, giving weight to her client's dissatisfaction and point by being deliberately misleading about Alice's age, or it is just careless and unprofessional conduct in children's matters.

Over the past 9 years, the Family Courts, as an organisation, have done nothing to address or express disapproval, condemn or criticize the dishonest and detrimental performance of this solicitor and law firm, as felt by my family and has been brought to their attention. Smitch Law and the legal system have needlessly put my family thought hell, simply because I was happy to assist in my children's upbringing and childhood. They have played a game of deception, harassment and persecution towards myself and three innocent young children. It has been my family's experience, with approval from the system, that the intimidation and deception practiced by this family law firm is impeccable and unquestionable; any excuse is used to defend this conduct.

Why is the system allowing this behaviour within the Family Courts?

What has been achieved over the last 10 years:

My respect and compliance with the Family Courts has been disregarded.

My dignity and trust have been lost.

My ability to be a parent has been condemned and denounced.

Total persecution of three children's childhoods.

Years of interference and false allegations, without truth, justification or evidence, which could only have a devastating effect on children's stability and wellbeing.

Any form of contact I have been awarded with my children through the Family Courts, Smitch Law has unerringly tried to disrupt, exploit and generally make bringing up three children as difficult for me as a parent as they could. These individuals are using the legal system to torment and intimidate separated parents and their children.

My faith in the system and Family Courts has broken down completely, and this is solely due my experiences of unethical, unprofessional and callous people working in children matters and the departments set up to ensure standards are kept.

My undertaking and responsibility to raise my three daughters as a single parent has been manipulated and disrupted at any opportunity. I believe I have tried very hard to get on with my children's mother, to provide for my children, and comply with the Family Court's directions.

However, there comes a time in any person's life when the abuse must stop and the respect once held is gone.

As I have stated, I shall attend the hearing on the 22nd of April 2009 as requested by the Family Courts, but due to the ongoing erosion of my very self, by unscrupulous family law professionals, this will be my last visit to the Family Courts.

Yours respectfully...

Dean Marlo

Huffman LP writes

14 April

Dear Mr Marlo,

You will remember when we were last in court that Ms Dowling was ordered to file an addendum report on the work undertaken by Vanya Roshan by 4pm on 6th April 2009. Unfortunately, Vanya is currently on holiday and she has not been able to speak to him. She will do so once he returns from holiday on the 20th April, with a view to filling and serving her report on 21st April. I will do my best to get this to you on this date.

I have written to Mrs Mason to inform them of the same and I will have written to the court to inform them of the difficulty as well.

I apologise for the late filing of this report.

The hearing on the 22nd April currently remains listed before his Honour Judge Neely at Venray County Court.

MP Rowe writes to me

16 April

Further to your visit to my office this afternoon, I confirm that I have received your letter and enclosures which you requested that I send to the Prime Minister. I will do so.

I feel that you have been badly let down by 'the system', with the result that you and your daughters have suffered appallingly. I regret that, despite my best endeavours, I have not been able to provide you with the outcome which you and your family deserve.

Your case is one which I feel should be subjected to a thorough, independent, investigation – under the chairmanship, I suggest, of a respected High Court Judge – to determine how things have been allowed to drag on for so long, with you left to fend for yourself without legal assistance while the mother of your children has been able to pursue, courtesy of the public purse, claim upon claim against you which must in total have cost many thousands of pounds.

In addition to writing to the Prime Minister, if you wish I am also prepared to contact the Secretary of State for Justice to request that your case is placed before a High Court Judge for a detailed review of what has occurred over the past decade.

Good luck with the next hearing in court. Best wishes.

Yours sincerely…

Dean Marlo

To MP

20 April

Any honest and decent person would be as appalled and dismayed by the unprofessional conduct from a Cafcass Guardian and children's solicitor, who have the responsibility to ensure that their conduct is in the best interests of any child involved in family court proceedings. I believe it is an example of the amateurish behaviour and performance, where individuals show no regard to children's welfare and stability, and only prolong the uncertainty and confusion in a child's life.

I realise, sadly, this has turned the pressure on Lara, who has been made aware by her mother that it is her contact she is seeking, not that with Alice, who although is technically on the court order, had requested removal previously and has not been mentioned throughout, regarding the importance of her re-initiating contact with her mother. Perhaps it is accepted that I have raised my children as their own people, whose feelings and wishes will be respected, and therefore Alice can repair her relationship with her mother whenever she so chooses. The same applies to Hayley and myself; the situation hurts me greatly, and all I can do is be there when Hayley does allow me into her life.

Without any communication from the Guardian or solicitor, on Friday the 6th February at 2pm, I received a letter from Huffman LP; the letter contained the Guardian's unrequested report, based on a meeting had 5 months previously, and without Vanya, Family Support Worker, having started work with Lara.

The report was full of misleading and false statements. Once again, allegations are made without fact or evidence. The report clarifies no matters, and only added to the false allegations floating around in the family court building.

At the hearing on the 9th February 2009 the Guardian *was* ordered by the Family Courts to file what is now an addendum report by 4pm on the 6th April 2009.

I have heard nothing from anyone involved.

On the 14th April I received the letter attached, stating Ms Dowling has been unable to talk to the Family Support Worker, as he was currently on holiday. I would suggest that this is not a case of difficulty, but clearly professional incompetence in children's matters. Once again, my children, on this occasion Lara, and I have complied with family court requests and directions. Without fail, Lara has once a week for almost two months talked with the Vanya for approximately one and a half hours per meeting after school.

Lara wants to get on with her life, and be a normal child.

I just want out of the Family Courts show.

Yours respectfully…

Dear Mr Rowe,

20 April

May I thank you once again for making yourself available to see and talk to me with little notice; I also thank you for your letter of the 16th April 2009, and your endeavours to assist me in my requests to question the resentment, hostility and persecution I have received from within the Family Courts and legal system.

The unethical behaviour that has been practiced within the Family Courts for many years, I believe, has had a direct and detrimental effect on children, families and society as a whole.

I do hope that the Prime Minister will hear alarm bells, because my family's 10–year ordeal would be devastating for any child and their family's dynamics.

I would also appreciate your assistance in contacting the Secretary of State for Justice, as I believe injustices have been allowed to continue within the system and in my family's lives; a child's welfare and stability has not been paramount, and this cannot be seen as acceptable.

Over the past 10 years, within the Family Courts, the same law firm has been jumping up and down with shouts and cries of 'this family is dysfunctional' and 'the children are at risk and vulnerable' – meanwhile these same people year after year have then been misleading, dishonest and immoral; they have abused the system and let down three children, while denying their own client help, which would have been to everyone's benefit.

I have been here for my children all their lives, and the only people who have had a problem with my care and commitment to my daughters have been within the walls of the Family Courts, based on Ms Hyde's baseless accusations. I have done my utmost to be a good parent to my three children, and for that, each time I have been called into family court proceedings, I am treated like a criminal; like a piece of dirt!

When corruption and deceit is evident within the playground (the system) it must be rooted out, removed and not tolerated; the point surely being to allow people to live their lives without persecution, prejudice or trepidation.

I would like to make it very clear that you and others within the process, have made every effort and taken the care to pursue my requests to write to or speak to ministers responsible for various departments.

You have provided my family and myself with the outcome that I have asked you for and that is being honest, straightforward and moral. For this, I will be forever grateful.

Yours respectfully and with kind regards…

Dean Marlo

Council, Alice's School Service

21 April

Dear Mr Marlo,
Further to our conversation today, I can now confirm, in writing, Alice's attendance for last term.
The first half of the term to 13 February 2009 was 68% and the second half of the term to 3 April 2009 was 90%.
If you need any further details, please do not hesitate to contact me.
Yours sincerely,

Huffman LP enclose to me

21 April

Lara and Alice Marlo - 9.5 Proceedings
I write to enclose, by way of service upon you, Ms Dowling's position statement together with exhibit. We apologise for the late filing of this document.
Yours sincerely,
Valerie Whyte, Associate, Solicitor–Advocate

Introduction
There have been proceedings in relation to this family throughout the whole of Lara's life. In April 2008, Ms Hyde re–issued proceedings as contact with all children had broken down. This was following an incident when it was alleged that Ms Hyde was assaulted by Hayley. Ms Hyde has since been bound over by the Criminal Court in relation to the assault on Hayley.

When I first became involved with these children, as previously mentioned, there was no face-to-face contact between Ms Hyde and any of the girls. On my first meeting with Mr Marlo, Alice Marlo and Lara Marlo, Alice and Lara were adamant they wanted no contact with their mother. Hayley was not present at this meeting yet Lara and Alice stated that Hayley was also clear she did not want contact.

In April 2008, Hayley left the family home.

(In April 2008, Ms Hyde punched Hayley and all three children left *her* home.)

She claims that her father told her to choose between the family and her boyfriend. Due to the fact that Hayley chose to continue her relationship, her father allegedly told her to leave. Initially she went to live with her boyfriend at a friend's home then when this arrangement broke down both Hayley and her boyfriend became homeless. Hayley gravitated back to her mother's home where she continues to live to date. She is not subject to these proceedings.

The problem with this not being my first Cafcass rodeo, is I don't know how much of what is written here is actually what Hayley said, and how much is the Guardian's own opinion on what she has been told by Ms Hyde.

Hayley argued with me over pocket money, and left to live with her fiancé – which over the last few weeks she'd spent most of her time doing. Hayley popped in occasionally, and while I stayed in contact, attempts to meet up for a coffee usually ended in disappointment on my end, as Hayley would phone to say she could not make it. I gave Conner a job, before he found more permanent work. As her dad it hurt, but she was living her life with her fiancé, which usually eclipses all else in a young person's life.

Hayley did not call me or tell me that she was homeless; I believe Hayley was drawn to Ms Hyde's lifestyle, as well as being the only child currently having contact, rather than come home.

I just need to end the court involvement and that's what I have to focus on, as well as continuing to look after Alice and Lara. To me, it seems Hayley is getting on with her life, and I have to accept that, while resolving to try harder to fix the relationship with her once the courts are out of our lives.

I wish the court would understand, no one is more devastated by the breakdown of Hayley and my relationship than I am. While I would like for us to be as close as we were not even half a year ago, I cannot make Hayley's choices for her.

The court ordered for Cafcass to undertake work with Lara and this began on 11 February 2009. Vanya Roshan has undertaken seven sessions with Lara, all of which have taken place in the family home, and Vanya and Lara have spent the time together on their own.

Lara's wishes and feelings

From the feedback, it is clear that Lara has maintained her position of wanting no contact with her mother. This is no direct contact. She states that her mother in the past has had no time for her, not encouraged her and that she has witnessed violence from her mother towards their sisters. She states that she dreads the weekly phone calls as her mother repeats the same things and will not listen to anything that Lara has to say.

Lara sees living with her father as very positive. He has time for her, he puts her first and gives her confidence.

Analysis

It is my view that this position is totally entrenched. The relationship between the parents has totally broken down and the children, over the years, have got caught in the middle of this. Both parents believe that their actions are in the best interest of the children but in fact what has happened is that the children have found themselves in the position of having to take sides and their own sibling relationships suffer.

Let's blame the parents, who have put these three children in a position of having to pick sides, which has resulted in the children making false allegations of violence and witnessing abuse from their mother; Hayley punched herself in the face, cutting her lip, and Alice dragged herself along the floor, leaving carpet burns on her back.

No one has ever listened to Lara when they ask how she feels; incidents like watching her mother cause criminal damage outside of her home or Hayley being punched in the mouth by her mother are mentioned in passing, as though Lara wouldn't be affected. Emotionally, Lara had to manage what she has seen and heard her sisters go through her entire life. Again, I do feel strongly that the incidents Lara has witnessed should not be ignored or dismissed; as Lara's Dad, I of course comforted her and we talked about her mother's behaviour, but the Guardian had the opportunity to reassure Lara as well.

I believe if the Guardian had taken this approach with Lara witnessing an abusive parent and talked through each incident she has witnessed, Ms Dowling might have realised that Lara should not be subject to such behaviour, as her sisters have sadly grown up with; her mother needs help with her bipolar and coping with her children.

I ask for the evidence that suggests I behave as Ms Hyde does and how it can be justified that by standing beside my children after they have been abused, it can be reported: 'both parents believe that their actions are in the best interest of the children'.

The current position is that Hayley has no contact with Lara and Alice.

The situation has become very complicated regarding everyone's relationships with each other. Ms Hyde has still not apologised, and that is what Alice and Lara are maintaining they need, acknowledgement of her wrong doing and space, before their relationships with their mother can be repaired. At the same time, when Hayley walked out, she did not answer Alice or Lara when they texted; now, she has gone back to their mother's, which Alice and Lara feel betrayed by because their mother has stated that by

Hayley's return, it is proof they were lying; their mother still hasn't apologised and this is about their mother treating Hayley wrong. Yet, somehow, the take away is always that both parents are just as bad as each other.

Ms Hyde wants Hayley to see her father and have contact with her sisters, and therefore encourages Hayley to keep trying. This always leads to disappointment for Hayley and inevitably she gets very hurt. Ruth's response to this is to become angry and protest about how unfairly Hayley is being treated. This is all done in front of Hayley and leads to Hayley getting caught up in her mother's rage. It does not seem to me as if the situation is allowed to settle and for the children to find their own space to repair their relationships. This for me evidences the enmeshed situation within this family and within which the children find themselves.

Finally, a statement that does relate to our family; this situation hasn't been allowed to settle and Ms Hyde has not given Alice and Lara space, which has kept everyone's emotional level high, and resulted in even Ms Hyde's contact via calling devolving into arguments and upset.

As usual, phrases like 'caught up in her mother's rage' casually describe Ms Hyde's opinion that Hayley is being treated unfairly – does taking out her rage on Hayley not bother anyone else?

I wish there was a book, or an 'ask the audience' in real time to explain how to deal with all the situations I've got going on at once; mend my relationship with Hayley; handle Alice's anxiety; reassure Alice and Lara that their mother's behaviour is wrong; prepare for the family court hearings that are corrupt and a sham-

No work has been completed in relation to Alice. This was not ordered on 9 February 2009. Alice has, however, made her position clear over time which is that she does not want indirect or direct contact with her mother.

Again, the hypocrisy is incredible. If Ms Hyde's relationships with all her children are so important, why has she not insisted work with Alice as well, to make sure I'm not abducting or manipulating her too?

The order of 9 February 2009 paragraph 2 referred to indirect contact from mother to Lara by way of short cards and letters to be sent via Lara's solicitor, to date none have been received.

No, Ms Hyde is too busy giving Lara social anxiety by making her read out letters in front of a teacher and it does not matter if Ms Hyde is visiting Lara's school in violation of the court order, which states that the letters should be passed through Lara's solicitor or guardian. I cannot but wonder, if I, as a father, was visiting my daughter's school after assaulting one of them, would I have been encouraged to do so, or swiftly arrested, cautioned by the police with a restraining order and penal notice from a judge? And would everyone be understanding, forgiving, and support Lara in having contact with me, if this was the case?

Conclusions

The work has been completed with Vanya Roshan. Throughout the records that I have, Lara has been adamant that she wants no direct contact with her mother. I attach to this statement, as Exhibit BW1 a letter prepared by Lara for the court and other documents relating to her wishes and feelings which further evidence her position.

I feel that Lara is very clear that she needs a final resolution to this matter. I do not believe that forcing her to attend contact with her mother would be in her best interests and could result in her becoming isolated from her father and Alice or being placed in a position where she has to keep secrets.

Ms Dowling states she has included a letter from Lara relating to her wishes and feelings which is further evidence of her position, and then two lines down she throws into the cauldron that it would not be in her best interests due to her becoming isolated from her father and Alice or being placed in a position where she has to keep secrets – where is her evidence of this?

Also, can she not gaslight my 11-year-old? At the beginning, she lists what Lara has discussed with her support worker; one of her issues is that her mother will not listen to anything she has to say – and Ms Dowling just turns this around that Lara's view is coached, or that when Lara is ready to see her mother, I will disown her, or she will have to hide it from me.

There is no evidence of any of these situations, and the much more real possibility is overlooked, that during the next argument during her mother's contact, Lara could be the one being assaulted.

This situation with court intervention has continued throughout Lara's lifetime and it continues without permanent resolution for her. Resolution is something Lara desperately needs and I would encourage.

Exhibit - Lara's Cafcass booklet:

Dear Judge,

I would like to tell you that I have had enough of my mother and guardians visiting me. My mother has caused me terror and upset during this last year because of me watching her punch Hayley and the very upsetting phone calls. I am upset to talk to her let alone see her. Every Sunday, Tuesday and Thursday, I dread her call to me. I would like to tell you that I want to get on with my life and not have to see or speak to her again.

Please listen to me as this has gone beyond my comfort zone. Thank you,

Dad – always tries to pick people up from situations they don't want to be in.

Alice – bit of a grump; still friendly most of the time.

Hayley – she has pushed away her family that have always tried for her.

Nan – always there to try and help.

Mum – she doesn't want to hear what I say and ignores me.

Lara – I like to help people.

What I wish to happen...

I wish I didn't have to see my mum. I wish court stuff would be over so I can get on with my life. I wish the court won't put it off and say to play happy families again. I wish the court would help get Alice back into mainstream school.

My needs...

I need court stuff to be out of my life forever.

If my mum is not being nice down the phone I have the right to hang up.

My feelings...

I feel angry and upset with Mum and Hayley for being liars. I feel stupid about myself for trusting them for so long.

What I told my Cafcass worker...

Everything I've listed

HH Judge Neely,

22 April

I have had no legal help in preparing my reply to the guardian's position statement or for this forthcoming hearing.

Firstly, I enclose letters of fact from UEEC and Riverbank School, some of which I have already sent to you; in doing so, I request the removal of the false statements made, and would ask politely for law firms and appointed organisations to behave in a moral and honest manner, as they are dealing with children under family law.

There are two letters from Alice's school, UEEC, stating that I have been fully supportive of Alice's home tutoring, together with a letter of Alice's attendance at UEEC. The first letter regarding Lara is from her Headteacher, disputing the Guardian's claims, as the school does not know of any occasions where Lara has thrown these letters away. The second is from Lara's year 6 teacher.

At the hearing of the 9th February 2009, Mrs Mason informed you that Alice was 13-years-old; Alice's solicitor did not correct her. I would like to bring to you attention that Alice was in fact 14-years-old at the time, and is now 15.

Despite Hayley not being party to these proceedings, Ms Dowling continues to bring Hayley into her reports with unconfirmed statements; I fail to see why Ms Dowling did not also talk to me about my relationship with Hayley, as she felt the need to include it. In any case, I refute what has been written about Hayley, her being unable to retrieve her belongings and my relationship with her.

Ms Dowling has had no contact with Alice and Lara since September 2008, yet her report appears to be based on her involvement with Hayley.

The Guardian was not asked to comment on my relationship with Hayley, nor do I need her involvement to bridge the gap that has come between Hayley and myself; as Hayley is the oldest, she has been conscious of proceedings the longest, and has had to deal with the court process for a large portion of her life. I cannot believe her comments to Ms Dowling, and I equally cannot believe that my daughter would lie, with the context of these proceedings carrying on in her family's life again.

Hayley and I have been in contact, although some attempts to see each other have not happened. While deeply upsetting to me as I love my daughter, I still have two children to look after, a business to run and hearings to attend, and I will not/cannot force Hayley to have contact with me if that is not what she wants.

I believe that it has been fully documented that throughout our children's lives, there have been incidents at Ms Hyde's home, and Hayley and Alice have refused to visit. Ms Hyde then applies back to the Family Courts and, just like this time, it does not matter how this mother treats her children, no attempts have been made to resolve why incidents turn abusive when involving Ms Hyde; it appears it is easier to declare 'both parents are as bad as each other'.

I would like to make it clear that I have never been in trouble with the police; I have run the same business for nearly 30 years and have the respect of customers across the county; my children's school, their friends' parents, my friends, family and neighbours can, and have on several occasions, accounted for my character.

I entered the Family Courts with the intention of being a good dad to my children, and nothing more.

While most of Ms Dowling's statements appear to disparage my commitment to my children and my ability to be a good father, it is remarked upon almost offhand that 'Hayley is caught up in her mother's rage'. I feel I must bring to your attention her choice of word being 'rage', which I feel the semantics of again do not present the picture of Ms Hyde's current mental health being stable. Previous reports have indicated court proceedings would exacerbate this. Our children, all their lives, have been caught in the path of their mother's mania; they have been saying so for the past 9 years.

Based on opinion, which I believe I have proven on several occasions lacks credibility, instead of seeking ways to resolve our family's involvement with the Family Courts again, i.e. comment on Lara and Alice's wishes and feelings, and make reasonable suggestions, the Cafcass Guardian has further mixed up our the situation, for no justifiable or ethical reasons.

There is no evidence that I have ever discouraged our children from seeing their mother, nor will there ever be. I firmly believe what the children, myself and our family need is an end to proceedings, with a view that, as all three children know and Hayley and Alice have in the past, when Alice and Lara wish to resume contact with their mother, they can.

Yours respectfully...

My Position Statement

I hoped that after the family court hearings in 2007 our family would be able to settle down and move on in our lives and away from court proceedings. Sadly, due to an incident at Ms Hyde's home in April 2008, this has not been the case.

I would like to re-confirm that over the past 9 years, I have facilitated Ms Hyde's requests and tried very hard within the Family Courts, year after year, showing respect and complying with directions.

There is no evidence that I have ever discouraged our children from seeing or contacting their mother; the children have had their own mobiles for years, and have every opportunity to visit their mother. I believe it is shameful that, without truth or good reason, the opposite can be suggested.

I believe that Lara is very clear in her mind and that her feelings are her own; Lara wants to do her best at school, giving her greater options in secondary school and setting her up for a bright future in an interesting career. Despite witnessing the incident of 2008, Lara is reluctant but has never refused to speak to her mother on the phone, and I believe if this continues over time, things will settle down, then relationships with their mother can and will be rebuilt – as Hayley has done, and Alice has in the past.

However, on several occasions, Lara has been deeply upset after phone contact with her mother, and it is my opinion that if Ms Hyde does not change her attitude, the healing process will take longer. This is in Ms Hyde's hands.

I believe that phone contact is important and ask the court to consider phone contact initially twice a week, with the understanding and acknowledgement by myself, that once Ms Hyde has started rebuilding her relationship with Lara, it will be up to Lara and Ms Hyde when she/Lara phone each other, bridges are built and contact re–established.

I believe that our whole family, children and parents alike, are exhausted after 10 years of family court proceedings. Everyone desperately needs the conclusion and ability to get on with our lives.

This in itself may be the answer to being able to get on with each other, being allowed to move on and rebuild our family's dynamics.

For these reasons, I ask the Courts to consider making a new order, with phone contact between Ms Hyde and Lara, twice a week, and the reintroduction of the order September 2007, at Lara's pace.

The Family Courts were not the cause of our family's initial problems, they just failed to address a parent with a serious mental health condition; took part in and permitted deformation of a good parent while prolonging misery in three children's lives.

The tax payer has been unethically rinsed the through Legal Aid, making a bunch of solicitors and barristers richer, while the Family Courts kept their significance intact and fucked over another family.

(Look on the bright side, they are 'all right Jack'.)

Dean Marlo

Court – Removing a child

22nd April 2009 / Venray County Courts

Judge Neely orders Alice be removed as a party to these proceedings.

Ms Dowling, if so advised, shall file and serve position statement by 9.30 am on the 27th April 2009.

Ms Hyde and Mr Marlo shall file and serve position statements by 4pm on 24th April 2009.

Final hearing ordered for the 27th April 2009 at 10.30am, time estimate of 1 day.

Smitch Law shall lodge with the court two trial bundles by 9.30am on 24th April 2009, and also provide Mr Marlo with a bundle by 4pm on the same day.

Alice has firmly established, since the age of 12, that she can and will live with whomever she pleases, and her input has been largely ignored in every letter and by all involved.

It is sad, because Alice tends to take over the phone from Lara when she has been reduced to tears by a conversation with her mother. I am left comforting Lara, while trying to get Alice either talk to her mother calmly or say goodbye, as she is protective of Lara, but this comes through as arguing and retaliating with her mother on the phone. Neither of which, crying or arguing, is helping repair the relationships with their mother. From what Lara has mentioned to me about these conversations, not only is her mother still denying the incident at hers last year, she has claims that because Hayley is living with her, Alice and Lara are 'liars' and that Lara needs to 'move on'.

This has, of course, not helped to encourage Hayley, Alice and Lara to reconcile, because Ms Hyde uses Hayley as an excuse, and can only see Hayley, Alice and Lara's reactions and behaviour, instead of her own.

For Lara, it is particularly difficult, because while Hayley is free to live where she likes, the same now going for Alice, Lara feels under pressure by the thought of court ordered contact. The decisions of everyone last year, really come down to having the consequences land on Lara, who witnessed her mother punch Hayley, has spoken to all the court appointed officials, has spoken to her mother and gotten nowhere, and was very hurt when Hayley moved in with her mother and began stating the incident didn't happen.

If a penal notice is ordered on me, and Lara refuses to have contact with her mother, I may end up in prison, and what is that going to do for Lara's emotional state? Even if no-one explicitly told her, 'if you do not go to your mother's, then your dad will be arrested', if I am arrested and she is the only one on the court order – Lara is smart and learned 2+2 many years ago. Both Hayley and Alice have reported their mother threatening them with having their dad arrested in the past, on different occasions, so it is not farfetched that Ms Hyde would finish her round of abuse of us all, emotionally, physically and mentally.

(It's a bad situation for everyone's relationships, and the wires keep fraying further apart rather than being repaired, but how to fix things without invalidating anyone's feelings or ignoring abusive behaviour?)

I have sat down with Lara and talked through the situation with her mother; Lara explained that when Hayley and Alice fell out with their mother, she would be left alone with her, and where before she felt she could keep out of the way, now she could find herself as involved as they were. All of Lara's life she has witnessed verbal and physical abuse by her mother; she is constantly late for school and instead of Ms Hyde, it is Lara and I who are both not only concerned about her wellbeing but also that her education will suffer.

With tears in her eyes, Lara stated none of the people trying to make the decision for her will be at her mother's when she kicks off – as in the past, Ms Hyde's mental state fluctuates and she will not reach out for help herself; it will be whoever is in her contact who will have to deal with it.

In 1992, Ruth and I sat with our new baby Hayley and we were both the happiest parents in the world. At the time, I thought about the challenges of being a parent but nothing could have prepared me for the outside involvement when trying to bring my children up.

To this day, I still feel sad when I think of the weeks, months and years wasted in my children's childhood by immoral, dishonest and corrupt people working in family law.

More letters from Lara

Dear Judge,
I have NOTHING in common with my mother and I wish that I didn't have to talk to her. She upsets me every time she calls and I cry every time. Not only physically has she upset me but mentally too; all my life I have lived with her shouting and hitting my sisters, quite frankly I've had enough. Not only has she hurt me by shouting but also she has been nasty, unwilling to hear my point of view and has told many lies about incidents that I have witnessed. Please read this letter and put my view into action, as I hate having to cry every Tuesday, Thursday and Sunday. Don't make me have to get upset and allow me to move on and get on with my life.
Yours truly,
Lara Marlo

To Judge,
I am writing to you to tell you the reasons why I do not feel comfortable around my mother's. To start with I am scared of her. As I am sure you know, I watched as my mother punched Hayley. My friend was round and I would never ever feel safe having any friends round or even being there myself.
Secondly, my mother calls me up and she says that all she wants to do is say hello; she says that but after I do not wish to sit and hear her saying the same thing as I often start to get quite annoyed.
I think that before you start to try and get me back to a place that I don't feel happy or comfortable in – you should consider these things:
I am happy and enjoying my childhood around my dad's.
I need to be allowed to get on with my friends and school work.
I do not need harassing calls from my mother
Please consider that this is what I want.
Yours sincerely,

Lara is an intelligent child, but she is still a child; her view is very polarised and I know that – I am not expecting the Court to agree with Lara's feelings, only understand why she feels this way, put measures in place to ensure Lara is being listened to and perhaps finally get Ms Hyde parenting help. The Court is capable of not agreeing with Lara and not undermining her at the same time.

When a parent or adult compromises a child, there is nothing outside forces can do to remedy the situation. Lara and her mother need to sort this out themselves, and the court need to recognise that this will take time; pressurising a child to return is only going to result in resentment and probably rebellion, which in her mother's household, could mean further abuse of our children.

I really do wish the Family Courts would get away from the idea that I've ever prevented any of the children from seeing their mother or that I would disown them if they do – that's a new one, but hurts just the same. This has frequently been used as a stalling mechanism and has prevented Ms Hyde from getting help, and the children from having a good relationship with their mother.

I am only standing up for my children, as I would expect Ms Hyde to if the children had come home accusing me of punching one of them. Smitch Law would love to be in that position; it would be unquestionable as to the outcome of proceedings.

(I can hear the words of Mrs Mason bouncing around the family court walls, 'This should not take long, your Uranus.'

There would have been one hearing and I would have lost my contact with my children... And it wouldn't be over a year later.)

What our family needs, and has always needed, is recognition and understanding from the Family Courts of Ms Hyde's need for support with her mental health and parenting, and an end to proceedings.

No one has been able to repair their relationships with court hearings hanging over all of our heads.

Mrs Mason writes (with package)

23 April

After dropping Lara off at school, I drove home to find the postman had left a parcel at my door.

I opened the package and found four folders and a letter.

(Nearly finding myself collapsed on the floor, looking at Sully for courage, at seeing 4 full folders of documents, I wasted five minutes trying to convince Sully to have a look and take on at least one of the folders, but she only turned her head to one side; it's just me against the entire Smitch Law shiver of sharks.)

We refer to the forthcoming hearing on Monday 27th April and we enclose herewith a trial bundle for your use at the hearing.

Your and our client's Position Statement will need to be included once they have been filed.

I took the first folder and started reading. I worked through the day and, after Lara and Alice went to bed, the night on my responses to the bundle… It was not until the early morning, when I reached for the second folder, I saw a separate letter attached, and it read:—

For the urgent attention of HH Judge Neely in the County Court.

We refer to the order made by HH Judge Neely on the 22nd April 2009, and enclose herewith two trial bundles for the above hearing, one for the Judge and one as a witness bundle.

Tiredness and disbelief set in at the same time. That was enough. I left the additional two folders in the packaging, deciding I would find out who they were addressed to in the morning; as I jumped into bed, I thought hopefully not me.

(Arr, goodnight cruel world.)

Each folder consisted of one hundred and two pages; not one showed evidence that I had any part to play in the children's and family's problems. There were copies of old court orders, reminders to the judge of previous notifications of several Penal Notices on me, solicitors' letters and pictures of Ms Hyde with her children in happy times.

I sat there in front of the four folders, with four hundred pages of the same bullshit. Immoral and corrupt people, making themselves in charge and taking over children's lives and abusing parents along the way.

I am raising my children, working hard on building sites, trying to make ends meet, and Mrs Mason is being paid by Legal Aid to present four copies of rubbish, which they then mistakenly sent the Judge's copy to me – well I think so, it's so confusing. I am overwhelmed by the court process itself, before even considering the most important aspect: the welfare of my children. Yet, I find I am sitting here surrounded by a nightmare.

(I checked again, and yes, it is not a copy; Smith Law headed-paper and addressed to the judge.)

Huffman LP writes to Alice

23 April

Following the Court Hearing on the 22ⁿᵈ April 2009, I can confirm that his honour Judge Neely, has released you from the proceedings and made no order in respect of yourself.

As you know, Ms Dowling is well aware of your views in relation to Lara but if there are any other points that you would wish to make and the children's barrister to present to the judge on Monday, please let me have those comments in writing or by email. I will ensure that the barrister gets your comments so that I too can present them to the court.

I know you are concerned that Ms Dowling told you many months ago that it was right for you to come to court. That information was not correct and you may remember that I said to you when I met with you on the 10ᵗʰ June 2008, and several times at court and in a phone conversation since then, that you should not come to court but that instead you should attend school.

There is no purpose to you attending court at the final hearing on Monday 27ᵗʰ April and in any event the court would not normally ask a child of your age to come to court. My understanding is that his honour Judge Neely made it very clear in court to your father that he did not want you to attend the hearing this Monday.

I take this opportunity of wishing you all the best for your future now that proceedings in relation to you have come to an end.

Mrs Whyte goes through how many times she told Alice that it was not appropriate for her to be at court, after Alice had attended twice. It is a pity that she could not waste the judge's time by telling him that the Guardian had told Alice she could go.

To Mrs Whyte's point about Alice attending school, she has no idea what kind of school Alice is attending – it is not a school by any stretch of the imagination, it is a centre were uncontrollable and disobedient children attend; most with no mum's or dad's in sight; brought in and taken away by taxi; despite the efforts of the teaching assistants, the children's few hours at the centre are unproductive, with many walking out and meeting up again in town.

Whether it has been due to Alice's lifestyle over the past year, her exclusion from mainstream school or the incident at her mother's with Hayley, maybe all three, I am a parent with a child that has anxiety and suffers from panic attacks. We have worked together to improve Alice's attendance at school, and she is doing better, but it's not plain sailing.

Mrs Whyte confirms to Alice that she has been released from proceedings and asks Alice if she has any comments that she and the barrister can present to the judge – at a hearing where Alice would not be party to the proceedings, and after Alice has already written two letters explaining her views.

Due to Alice's involvement over many years with court experts, and the fact her Guardian stated if she felt that her voice and views were not being heard by the judge, then she should go to court; Judge Neely had Alice at the court hearing and he had the opportunity to talk with Alice. Out of the blue, maybe, but this is a family with past aggressive incidents involving a mother and her children, and another opportunity for the Family Courts to step in and stop the abuse. As the judges make up the rules as they go along, what harm would it have done? He could have prevented an abusive parent from carrying on; he'd probably make the local gazette with headlines: Judge steps in and saves abused children.

(He is such a fucking hero – but, no movement from Judge Neely… I just have memories of his wild staring eyes.)

I am constantly reminded within the Family Court's four walls, that this is a complex case, yet when Judge Neely had the ability to talk to someone imbedded in the family's day to day lives, he gets on his high chair, stares round the room to find someone to throw his toys at – finding me, he, with all of his wisdom, states, 'If you ask a child Mr Marlo, you will find they do not want to be brought to family court hearings.'

(All hail Judge Neely. If he had asked me, I would have told him I did not want to be there, either.)

If Judge Neely believed this was a complex case with 10 years of litigation and Family Courts involvement, he had read the children's letters (hopefully), he could have taken the step of speaking to Alice and find out first-hand what had brought about the latest incident, and, consequently, the family back to the courts.

Again, I find a judge that is detached from truly finding out what is going on; Judge Neely is clearly unable to grasp that he had an opportunity to try and address Ms Hyde's behaviour towards her children and aggressive outbursts, which are related to her bipolar disorder. Instead, it is Lara who has to be monitored, with another court expert in her life.

(What would I know? I have only been living with Ms Hyde's disorder for 18 years, and watched my children for 17 years do the same.)

Anyway, Judge Neely had the Guardian's report to guide him… The very same report that resulted in me making calls, requesting confirmation letters and ensuring that they are in court before the judge.

I know I have no hope of convincing Judge Neely that this is about my children and nothing more. It was never my intention to complain about anyone's behaviour or any court reports; 9 years ago, I was shocked by the deceitful harassment and the level of discrimination that existed within family law and the Family Court's – to this day, I am still shocked.

What do I do?

Go along with a report that suggests my lack of responsibility towards my children, or write a letter to the judge with the evidence that disproves the assertions?

At each hearing, as with this one, it made no difference to the judge, as there was no mention of the false information presented to the court. If I am a criminal, then I should be treated like one! If not, I am almost to the point of begging to be left alone, so that we as a family are allowed to get on with our lives.

From Smitch – Chronology

24 April

As always, these documents are in original form, factual inaccuracies, mistakes an' all.

We enclose herewith chronology and our client's position statement as directed.

1986 – Parties begin their relationship.
1991 – Parties first cohabit.
March 1992 – Hayley Marlo born, child of both parties.
July 1993 – Ms Hyde sectioned for 1 month.
April 1994 – Alice Marlo born, child of both parties.
June 1995 – Mother sectioned then discharged.
December 1997 – Lara Marlo born, child of both parties.
December 1997 – Ms Hyde is admitted to the Hills.
1999 – Parties separate.
24 March 2000 – Court orders: Mr Marlo is granted PR for all three children; residence order for all three children in favour of Ms Hyde; contact order for Mr Marlo.
2 July 2000 – Ms Hyde sectioned.
20 July 2000 – Mr Marlo applies for a residence order.
18 August 2000 – Interim joint residence order.
22 August 2000 – Ms Hyde applies for a penal notice as Mr Marlo failed to return Hayley to her mother.
24 August 2000 – Mr Marlo ordered to return Hayley to her mother. A penal notice is attached to the 18th August 2000 Order.
10 October 2000 – Interim joint residence order confirmed.
27 October 2001 – Ms Hyde applies for a penal notice for the second time after Mr Marlo retains the children.
5 November 2001 – Mr Marlo applies to vary the joint residence order; the application is unsuccessful.
19 November 2001 – Court refuses to vary the joint residence order.
18 December 2003 – Mr Marlo applies to vary the joint residence order.
15 January 2004 – The application is adjourned to 19th February 2004, for the purpose of approving a schedule of contact.
11 February 2004 – Ms Hyde applies for a residence order and for Mr Marlo to have a contact order.
19 February 2004 – Directions appointment, Ms Hyde and Mr Marlo to file statements and also for a Cafcass officer to file a statement. Matter listed for a final hearing 25th June 2004.
27 February 2004 – Ms Hyde applies for a penal notice to be attached to the joint residence order.
2 March 2004 – Court orders the application to be heard before a circuit judge on 19th March 2004.
19 March 2004 – Application for penal notice is adjourned generally. Joint residence confirmed.
27 April 2004 – Ms Hyde applies to enforce the shared residence order of 19th March 2004.
28 April 2004 – Mr Marlo applies for a variation of the shared residence order.

29 April 2004 – Interim residence order made in favour of Mr Marlo. Contact order made in favour of mother.

24 June 2004 – Final hearing adjourned to 5ᵗʰ August 2004.

5 August 2004 – Residence order for all three children is made in favour of Mr Marlo, with a contact order made in favour of Ms Hyde. This was following a 2-day contested hearing, including evidence from a Cafcass officer.

April – July 2006 – Alice moves to live with Ms Hyde.

May 2006 – Alice returns to live with her father. Ms Hyde having no real contact with Hayley.

21 June – Mr Marlo applies for a non–molestation order. Hearing is adjourned until 23ʳᵈ June 2006.

23 June 2006 – Application for non–molestation order is compromised, with no findings or admissions, each party gave an undertaking.

18 July 2006 – Ms Hyde applies for a residence order and to enforce the contact order.

10 August 2006 – Mr Marlo files supplemental information, alleging harm.

25 August 2006 – Report from psychologist Mrs Sanders commissioned.

23 October 2006 – Ms Hyde withdraws her residence application. Since this time, the case has proceeded on the basis that her application amounted to an application for shared residence.

19 December 2006 – Child Legal Guidance makes an application for Hayley for discharge of a contact order and to be joined as a party in the proceedings. Child Legal Guidance makes an application for Alice for a discharge of the contact order.

Early January 2007 – mid August 2007 – Alice moves to live with Ms Hyde. Ms Hyde suggests mediation to Mr Marlo to discuss issues around the children but he refuses to mediate.

13 February 2007 – Report of psychologist Mrs Sanders filed.

16 February 2007 – Court orders: Hayley and Alice's application for discharge of care orders adjourned until 13ᵗʰ March 2007. Report of Mrs Sanders to be disclosed to representatives of Hayley and Alice.

March 2007 – Alice diagnosed as suffering from stress, sleeping poorly and having irregular periods. Alice also disciplined at school far truancy. Hayley comes to the attention of the police as a result of her behaviour at school.

12 March 2007 – Counsel, for Hayley and Alice, requests for Alice to be joined as a party to the proceedings. Matter transferred to the High Court. All parties agree that Hayley did not want to be subject to any orders, therefore al orders relating to her (save PR) were discharged.

April 2007 – Addendum report of psychologist Mrs Sanders filed, confirming that she has viewed the children's and Mr Marlo's medical notes and they do not change her views as recorded in her report dated 13ᵗʰ February 2007.

25 June 2007 – High Court directions hearing: Mr Marlo (in person) supports Alice being separately represented. Ms Hyde supports the appointment of a Guardian instead. A Guardian is appointed and Alice's application to be joined as a party is adjourned generally with liberty to restore. Ms Hyde's application to take the children to Australia for two weeks over Christmas is heard. Mr Marlo does not object to the holiday in principle but did not want them to miss school. Justice Millar orders Ms Hyde to file a statement by 6ᵗʰ July 2007; detailed proposals for shared residence; detailed proposals for the Australia trip; an application for the Australia trip; Mr Marlo to respond by 20ᵗʰ July 2007. Case then transferred back to the County Court.

17 July 2007 – Directions hearing in front of HHJ Neely, who lists the case for a 2-day hearing on 5ᵗʰ and 6ᵗʰ September 2007, and for directions on 26ᵗʰ July 2007.

24 July 2007 – Guardian, Ms Moyer appointed.

26 July 2007 – Matter before HHJ Chips ordered that the Australia trip application be dealt with on 5th September 2007. The second day be vacated, and the rest of the matters to be dealt with following a full report from the Guardian November 2007.

3 September 2007 – Guardian completes her report. She recommend; the Australia trip should take place but in the summer of 2008; there should not be a joint residence order; all three children should remain living with their father; proceedings should not continue as the ongoing proceedings since 2000 have caused significant harm to the children; a referral to Child and Family Consultation Service should be made for Alice and Hayley, and she is happy to make that referral; the schools and the CFCS should see her report and those of Mrs Sanders; a section 91(14) order should be considered.

4 September 2007 – Letter received from Child Legal Guidance, putting forward the instructions of Hayley and Alice, despite the appointment of the guardian.

5 September 2007 – Final order made, with a section 91(14) order made, preventing either party from making further applications to the court without leave of the court. All three children are residing with Mr Marlo and Ms Hyde has a defined contact order. Proceedings now relate to Alice and Lara only.

October 2007 – 7 April 2008 – Alice spending time living with both her mother and father.

January 2008 – Alice permanently excluded from school.

February 2008 – Alice registered at Unified External Education Centre and has to attend for one hour each day.

7 April 2008 – Argument between Ms Hyde and Hayley and Alice. Scuffle led to Ms Hyde falling down the stairs. Lara was also present. All three children left Ms Hyde's home.

19 April 2008 – Ms Hyde applies for enforcement of contact with Alice and Lara.

27 April 2008 – Ms Hyde arrested on suspicion of assaulting Hayley on 7th April 2008. Ms Hyde on police bail. Hayley continuing to have contact with her mother.

April 2008 – Ms Hyde sought leave of the court to enforce the court order made in September 2007.

14 May 2008 – Ms Hyde obtained leave for a penal notice application and directions given for Mr Marlo and, the Guardian, Ms Dowling, to be served with the application.

11 June 2008 – Ms Hyde is given permission to proceed with her application. Ms Hyde and Mr Marlo to file statements of evidence. Ms Dowling to prepare a wishes and feelings report of the children.

July 2008 – Ms Hyde accepts a bind over in relation to incident with Hayley.

5 August 2008 – Matter listed on 23rd September 2008.

19 September 2008 – Matter adjourned until 12 November 2008.

23 September 2008 – Application to be adjourned until 9th February 2009. Family Support Worker to work with Lara on the issue of contact with her mother. Hearing on 12 November 2008 is vacated.

January 2009 – Hayley moves to live with her mother.

3 February 2009 – Report of Guardian Ms Dowling raising concerns about lack of direct contact between Lara and her mother. Ms Dowling accepts that Lara does not want contact but believe that even if she did this would not be encouraged by Mr Marlo or her sister Alice. Ms Dowling confirms she has formed the opinion that there is considerable animosity towards Ms Hyde and therefore any contact between Lara and her mother is actively discouraged.

21 April 2009 – Report of guardian, Ms Dowling, filed, stating that Lara should not be forced to attend contact. Proceedings should be resolved.

22 April 2009 – Court orders; Alice removed as a party to proceedings; listed final hearing on 27th April 2009; Ms Hyde & Mr Marlo to file position statements; the Guardian to file a position statement.

Ms Hyde's Position Statement (written by counsel)

Ms Hyde has had the opportunity of considering the latest report of the Guardian, received on the afternoon of 21 April 2009, and the previous report, dated 3 February 2009.

Throughout the proceedings which commenced in 1999, Lara has always had regular contact with both Ms Hyde and Mr Marlo. Even during periods when there were problems with Hayley and Alice, Lara has always maintained a relationship with both of her parents. This position changed in April 2008 and since that time Lara has not had any direct contact (save for phone contact) with Ms Hyde or her family.

Ms Hyde has always encouraged all three children to have a relationship with their father. Mr Marlo has made it clear through his actions that he is unwilling to do the same.

Since January 2009, Hayley has been living with Ms Hyde. Hayley has tried, with the encouragement of her mother, to see Mr Marlo but with little success. Hayley has been trying to retrieve her belongings from the home of Mr Marlo but has not been allowed to do so. At the hearing on 9 February 2009, it was agreed that Ms Dowling would attend with Hayley to collect the belongings. This has not happened with Mr Marlo refusing to allow Ms Dowling to attend at his home. Ms Hyde has asked Vanya Roshan, Family Support Worker, to assist but again he has been unable to retrieve the belongings with Hayley.

Ms Hyde firmly believes that in the past the fact that court orders have been in place which have defined when Lara will see each parent has enabled Lara to have a relationship with both her parents without feeling that she is somehow letting Mr Marlo down. Since the order was suspended last year, there has been no contact other than the weekly phone calls.

Ms Hyde is disappointed that it has taken over a year for the court to deal with her application. She accepts that it is unsettling for everyone to have the proceedings ongoing but feels that Lara's position has become more entrenched due to the length of time that has now lapsed.

In the Guardian's first report, she clearly states how concerned she is about the lack of direct contact between Ms Hyde and Lara, and that she felt that both Mr Marlo and Alice were putting Lara in a difficult position. Ms Hyde agrees fully with this statement and is therefore surprised and disappointed to read the addendum report dated 21 April 2009 and Ms Dowling's comments therein.

Ms Hyde has always had a great deal of involvement in Lara's life. She has hundreds of photographs showing family days out, holidays abroad and these are evidence of the very close relationship that Lara had with her mother and her large extended family. Lara was always very close to her maternal grandmother and her Auntie and she was fortunate enough to have enjoyed many family get togethers during the first 10 years of her life. All that has now stopped.

Lara has been unable to have relationship with her elder sister, Hayley and Ms Hyde feels that this is detrimental for both of the children.

Ms Hyde believes that no child will have a balanced, happy and settled life when they are unable to enjoy a relationship with both of their parents. Ms Hyde accepts that Lara should continue to live with Mr Marlo but she is desperate to reinstate her relationship with Lara.

Ms Hyde has attempted over the last year to keep her contact going with Lara via the phone calls made each week. Unfortunately, there have been difficulties even with phone contact. Often when Ms Hyde rings at the appointed time the phone is engaged or in fax mode. On other occasions, Alice will answer and will be rude and aggressive. The Lara that speaks to Ms Hyde now is not the Lara that Ms Hyde knows and she is extremely concerned about her emotional state.

Ms Hyde is at a loss to understand how Lara can simply blank out all of the good times that she has had with her mother but feels very strongly that Mr Marlo and also Alice have been instrumental in Lara's change in attitude.

Ms Hyde is asking the court to consider making an order for direct contact. Initially, Ms Hyde would suggest Lara coming for tea midweek for a few hours. In time, Ms Hyde would hope that the previous position could be reinstated i.e., alternate weekends, tea midweek and half of the school holidays.

If the court finds, having heard the evidence, that there should be no direct contact then Ms Hyde will have to accept that albeit unhappily but she would like the door to be left open to enable Lara, if she wishes, to make contact herself.

Finally, Ms Hyde does have concerns about the lack of communication between Mr Marlo and herself regarding issues relating to the children. Mr Marlo refuses to involve Ms Hyde in issues relating to the children's welfare. By way of example, both Alice and Lara are not receiving regular dental treatment and appointments that have been made were cancelled. Ms Hyde would also wish to be told if the children are unwell or if Mr Marlo is taking the children abroad for any reason at all.

Response to Smitch

(I know we've all been through this before but everyone strap back into the carousel, because here we go again…)

I must dispute both the accuracy and honesty of the chronology and Ms Hyde's position statement.

The chronology provided by Smitch Law states that the parties began their relationship in 1986. I met Ms Hyde for the first time in 1990; she was delivering sandwiches on an industrial estate where I was running my construction business.

In 1991, Ms Hyde came to my door with her arm bandaged in a sling, stating she had been assaulted by her boyfriend, was going bankrupt and had nowhere else to go. I believed Ms Hyde had gone through a hard time, and she began cohabiting with me. Shortly after, our relationship commenced.

I do not know why it has been suggested Ms Hyde and I started our relationship, 4 years before we had even met.

Honestly, it is exhausting to continue to see misleading statements, which appear to have no reason for even being suggested. Current issues need addressing so our family can get on with living, yet this is the level of consistency Ms Hyde and professionalism Smitch Law conduct themselves with.

Since the matters were largely dealt with at the time, I am not going to comment on the rest of the period up to 2004, such as why the applications came up. While I understand the nature of a chronology is to allow for ease of reading, several applications, wherein Ms Hyde was applying for enforcement of the order, for example, were the results of incidences between Ms Hyde and her children.

In January 2006, there was an abusive incident at Ms Hyde's home, wherein Alice was pushed by Ms Hyde's boyfriend, and Hayley was left with a bruised arm trying to help her sister; despite her sisters walking out of Ms Hyde's home and refusing contact, Lara went for contact with Ms Hyde. Police incident no: 20060106–XXXX.

14th February 2006, while Hayley and Alice refused contact with their mother, Lara went for the half term holiday contact.

31st March 2006, over the weeks, contact is re–established and Ms Hyde, Hayley and Alice agree to a sleepover. At 9pm, I received a phone call from the police stating that Ms Hyde has made allegations that our two oldest daughters had been violent towards her and were now missing.

13th May 2006, Alice, aged 12, requested to sleep a 15-year-old friend's Grandfather's house. After making further inquiries, it came to light the man was on police tag, and I therefore said that Alice could not go to the sleepover. This eventually culminated in Alice calling Ms Hyde to pick her up, which she did.

This had not happened before, and I was shocked by Alice's behaviour. For a period after this argument, Alice gave me the cold shoulder. I did not apply to court, as I believed this was centred around a, Alice mixing with the wrong friends at school and b, Alice testing the boundaries as many young growing children do, from time to time.

While I attempted to contact Alice during this time, I, as I have done for Hayley in the current situation, had to respect her wishes, and could only attempt to care for Alice's wellbeing from afar, meeting or talking to her when she would allow. When in a household where both parents live under the same roof, and disagreements such as this happen, it is resolved swiftly because the child, usually sulking in their room, will have to talk to their parents and move on. Unfortunately, having two households where total avoidance can be achieved has obviously affected all three of our children, for various reasons, some justified, some not.

I have clearly encouraged Lara to have a good relationship with her mother, which Ms Hyde indicates in her statement, with Lara having ten years of some happy memoires.

From the several Guardian's reports, it is clear that the breakdown of Ms Hyde's relationship with Lara is a direct result of her own behaviour towards all of the children; most recently, during the argument overheard by Lara and her witnessing her mother use violence against Hayley, which Smitch Law described only as 'a scuffle led to Ms Hyde falling down the stairs'. The next parts of the chronology discuss Ms Hyde's charging and bind over, yet you would be remiss for not knowing what for.

I do not believe anyone, but in particular the Family Courts, who are there to ensure the welfare and stability of children, should accept the minimisation, dismissal or omittance of any form of abusive behaviour. This should be strongly addressed, to protect the children involved from further harm.

It has been well documented that Ms Hyde suffers from a mental health condition, which is seen to affect her daily life; it does not constitute blame, but these incidences are happening none-the-less and the only person who has never altered their behaviour is Ms Hyde.

On the day of the incident in 2008, Lara walked through our front door sobbing and distressed; she relayed to me that she had watched her mother punch Hayley in the face. Sadly, all three children had been subject to abuse in their own way – Alice was grabbed by her mother, then Hayley tried to intervene and was subsequently hit, and Lara witnessed this happen – I was not there, but knew that the first thing I needed to do was contact an organisation for my girls to talk to. I wish I could say that it was only for their emotional and mental wellbeing, but unfortunately after ten years of this, I had to also think about the potential of court hearings; if I wait to take the children, and try to be a dad first, I could be accused of coaching their views.

I think the greatest tragedy of these proceedings, again, was that the children were hurt, and that is still not the focus of the Guardian, solicitors, barristers or judges.

This is not the first incident Lara has witnessed; however, I believe that having grown up in that environment at her mother's, unlike her sisters, Lara has always tried to remain out of the way or removed herself from the situation.

Ms Hyde states that Lara has had no direct contact with her family, which is false. Those who have contacted the children, some cousins and their step-aunt, have met with Alice and Lara; once again, I remind the court all three children have their own mobiles, and can and do contact who they like, including both Ms Hyde and her extended family if they so wish.

Up to the middle of January 2009, Hayley had been calling round our home and talking with Alice and Lara; Hayley has retained her relationship with her Nan and her uncle Rob.

It is claimed that it was ordered at court for Ms Dowling to accompany Hayley to our home to collect the belongings she couldn't take while living with Conner (due to the size of their flat) – this never happened and I will attach the court order of the 9th February. The fact that such a blatant lie can be included suggests to me that Mrs Mason is counting on judges not looking through the bundle to check that what is written in the position statement is true, relying on the honesty and integrity of a family law shark… Which begs the question: what is the point in any of this process, when the only thing that truly makes a difference to your ability to be a parent to your children, is your funding to have a solicitor and barrister deceive on your behalf?

I have heard nothing from Vanya Roshan regarding Hayley's belongings, but Hayley has come herself, taking bits and pieces as she's wanted to.

While these proceedings pertain to re-establishing contact between Ms Hyde and Lara, I find it shameful that lies about Hayley have been included to imply credibility to Ms Hyde's latest narrative, instead of the truth: Ms Hyde has not made amends with Lara due to her own attitude and behaviour, on the day of the incident, before and since.

(Spoiler alert: the chronology and attached bundle were the last communication I received from family law firm Smitch Law, and Mrs Mason – it was long overdue. I would have held a party if I had known at the time.)

Lingchi - To the Court

Dear Sir,

I am writing this letter to you in my own words as I am not allowed to come to the court to speak for myself.

I know that I am 17 and I am not on the court order but I would like you to know exactly what has been happening these past months which has affected me.

Since Christmas, I had mainly good conversations with Nan on the phone and I went to visit her a couple of times. When I spoke to Lara in March/April she told me that I was lying and that Nan hadn't called me. I then called Nan which ended up getting into an argument and she ended up hanging up on me. I then sent a text to her saying: 'Thank you 4 disowning me I thought we was family no matter what love you Nan hopefully you will all realise what you all are throwing away.'

Which she then replied: 'I am ashamed of you Hayley what you and your mother have done to this family and continued doing it I'll always love you but I'll never forgive you for turning into your mother.' I feel really upset that my Nan feels she cannot have a relationship with her granddaughter without involving all the family problems; yet Alice and Lara can still have their Nan.

I have said sorry to Dad, Alice, Lara and Nan for the way I was last year and I understand now the way I was acting wasn't right but they still won't forgive me. Dad and Nan have said they can't have a relationship with me, while I'm living with enemy (Mum).

I have had hardly any contact since before Christmas although I did go round with my college stuff as I thought Dad would be interested in what I was doing like he always used to be, but he wasn't that interested and it was always awkward because of Alice and Lara and I always ended upset from arguing. I went round to Dad's on Christmas Eve to try and make up with them all again and I took round three small cards which I know weren't the normal cards that I would usually give them. Dad wouldn't let me in the house and I ended up coming back home crying my eyes out because it seemed like none of them cared, I also didn't get a Christmas card off Dad, Alice or Lara all I got in return was 'what sort of card was that'. Even though I didn't get a card off them Nan did send me a Christmas card which made me feel a little better that one of them still cared. Dad said all my life that when I was old enough to drive he would buy me a car etc and when it came to around that time in December and I wanted a car for when I turned 17. Mum asked me if I wanted Dad involved but I told her that he didn't care and didn't want anything to do with anything else I was doing. But like Mum always does she called Dad and asked him about being involved with my car and we never got a reply from that day. It came to Dad's birthday in February Nan called me a few days before and asked if I was sending Dad a card I replied no why was I going to give him a card when he hadn't even bothered with me for all these months. Nan told me that I should and Mum was telling me that I should, so I got Dad a card it wasn't the same card as I would usually get him for his birthday but I thought it was a card that he would like. I went round to his house and Dad answered the door he ended up inviting me in which wasn't normal as he didn't want anything to do with me for months, I told him Mum was waiting for me and he said you better go then which I did. But he messed up my head so much I didn't understand why he wanted something to do with me now but not before. Then came my birthday in March I wasn't expecting a card or anything because Dad's card wasn't a proper one but I did get one which I was surprised about. Now that I have been disowned by Dad, Nan, Alice and Lara I can understand how Alice felt when she lived at Mum's, I realise how nasty me and Lara was towards her just like what they are doing to me now but it is ten times worse or it feels like it anyway.

Me and Lara were like two peas in a pod we liked all the same things she looked up to me and now she wants nothing to do with me I wish she would come and meet me just me and her to let me explain she will grow up one day and do things like I did.

My belongings and my stuff – I had tried to talk to Dad about it like an adult and I don't want to take everything we could of talked about what I could of had and what I couldn't of had but he had decided that there was only one bag of stuff that is mine from my room and to be fair my room at Dad's was bigger than your average room and Dad brought us all lots of things.

Everything in my room meant something to me and I hope that I will one day get all of my things that I love back.

It has been so long since I have been in my room at Dad's it is difficult for me to remember exactly what was in my room these are some things I can remember: laptop (pictures and information), BMX, wardrobe, c-d player, motor bike things, books, teddies, covers (wolf and panther), desk, all my toys, dolls house, personal items, shoes.

I will admit that I did say quite a few nasty things to both Alice and Lara on the phone when I have tried to speak to them and I regret the things I said, but there is one thing from one of the phone conversations that I had with Lara that I thought was a bit odd which she said to me: 'if I hurt my best friend and then turned around the next day and tried to be friends with them, they would say no'. It didn't make any sense to me as I have done nothing to Lara at all.

Things that Alice and Lara have said to Mum on the phone about Mum not feeding Lara most of the things that I have heard them say have been lies Mum and Dad are good parents in their own ways and Lara and Mum were always together doing things (going to the zoo, swimming and bike riding) when we went to Mum's. Me and Alice would be doing our own things or have our little arguments we all had such a good time round Mum's yes we did have our ups and downs but what family doesn't. I wish that Alice and Lara could realise that Mum is always here for us no matter what and at least she is still making the effort with her other two children even though they say they don't want anything to do with her. I wish they could feel how I feel with a parent who isn't even showing they care one bit.

Yours sincerely,
Hayley Marlo

Court – denouement

27th April 2009 / Venray County Courts

We were brought in, and Mrs Mason spoke to the judge for a good 30 minutes going over the case. I heard the judge state that Mrs Mason's chronology had been 'very helpful' and I found myself imagining a laugh track playing in the background. Then, I was called to the stand.

Ms Hyde's barrister began his cross-examination of me by making various false statements, such as that I 'blame Ms Hyde for everything'. Then he said, 'It has been well documented you are verbally and physically abusive to Ms Hyde. It also appears, and I must agree with my client, you have been single handedly trying to destroy the relationships of a mother and her children, and now you are manipulating Lara to have no contact with her mother, as you did with the two oldest children in the past. Having returned to your residency, Alice now refuses contact with her mother, despite living with my client for extended periods in the past. As I have been told and understand, you are now determined to destroy your own relationship with your eldest daughter.' He stared at me and asked, 'What is going on Mr Marlo?'

I was too numb to move. He continued, heedless, 'It is clear that all three children know how to press their mother's buttons and are very confrontational.'

I could not hold my tongue any longer; the false allegations towards me I am conditioned to, but using or suggesting that my children incited the abuse and assaults… I cannot remember what I said, even if it was a word, more of a 'haiyaa', but whatever I said, the judge just frowned at me.

It was as if on the 7th April 2008, Ms Hyde had not assaulted Hayley; Ms Hyde had not been arrested and bound over by the police; the children hadn't vacated Ms Hyde's residence because of this incident, regardless of Hayley's reparations with her mother now. The courts had already acted oblivious to another example of Ms Hyde's unacceptable behaviour towards her children, and instead wanted to further condemn a family trying to get on with their lives. It is not my desire to question the all-seeing Family Courts oracles, however it is also counter-intuitive to ignore the cause of proceedings in the first place. My cross-examination went on until the judge called for lunch.

As I sat in my car with a sausage roll, which I couldn't stomach and had gone cold, yet I was somehow still covered in crumbs, I thought about the morning and how Ruth's barrister had emotionally ripped me apart, and how I felt just as set upon as I did 9 years ago. I felt completely battered by the accusations made, without any evidence, thrown out there and for what purpose? So the judge can cherry pick and choose what part of the accusations to pay attention to, if not all, as they look across the courtroom for any movement, an angry glance or shaking of a head. It is very difficult not to react at all, as I would say the human response to hearing deformation of yourself and your family would be to call out the lies, but that is not the process. You sit in the stand and they tear you apart, and the evidence that should be relevant to proceedings is dismissed, as the picture is painted to the judge via the barrister's opening speech. He certainly ticked all the boxes of being a Smitch Law derivative; I wanted to refute all of his statements, but knew that I did not have the similar legal knowledge to counter in any meaningful way.

These barristers are trained in the art of being ruthless, with no regard to the fact that you are a human being, or a parent with concerns and not, as they are trying to imply, a fucking criminal. Ms Hyde assaulted Hayley and Alice; the children and I have had over a year of court proceedings, again; Lara has had a stranger coming to see her once a week and I am cross-examined, by a person who does not know me or my family's dynamics, but makes comments and unfounded allegations all the same, knowing full well the process is demoralising, hurtful and emotionally driven.

It is wrong to make parents feel like this in the Family Courts.

I wanted to leave, just turn the car key and drive home, but a part of me feared the consequences and what it would mean for Lara, Alice and myself if I do not comply... Hoping things might turn for the better, I dragged myself back into the building.

The hearing resumed at 1.30pm; with all of my worrying and anxiety, I had only now thought about having to leave to be on time for when Lara comes out of school. As I walked back into the courtroom, I asked Mrs Whyte how long she thought proceedings would take this afternoon, and she replied, 'As long as the judge feels it necessary.'

In response, I explained, 'I have to pick Lara up from school, and I thought this was about what's best for Lara?'

From the other side of the courtroom, Ms Hyde *scoffed*.

The camel's back snapped. The person who a year ago had assaulted Hayley, scoffed in the face of Lara's wellbeing. I could not suppress my feelings of disgust and shock to the façade that was once again being played out within the Family Courts, under the banner of 'a child's welfare and stability is paramount'. I felt I had no option but to remove myself from the dishonesty that was, and had been for many years, detrimental to my children and their childhood; for my own sake, I could not face Ms Hyde's derision for Lara. I have always been waiting in the playground for her, on time, ready for when she gets out, and I was not about to falter because the Family Courts want to chase their tail on whether or not a child will be affected by witnessing abuse, or argue semantics of whether the children are a bunch of pathological liars while Ms Hyde can do no wrong.

I stood up. I walked out of the courtroom.

As I headed back down the corridor, I heard the door fly open and someone state, 'You must return, as we cannot finish without you here.'

I replied, not turning around, 'I'm going to pick my daughter up from school.'

Despite finally feeling liberated by walking out, I had little more to add; then one thought came flooding through and I said:

'You can all fuck off.'

(I know, my aggressive tendency shining through.)

Ten years put into five words.

When walking in, I had no intention of walking out, but it is a fitting end to the misery my children and I, as their parent, have felt and been put through just to be a family.

Ouroboros

The day of that hearing will live with me for the rest of my life. And I know that there are some people who will shun me for walking out of the family court building; for not persevering and for proving Ms Hyde's point that I just will not cooperate.

After picking Lara up, I decided to put all the boxes of tapes, containing recorded telephone conversations I'd had with Ms Hyde over the past decade, and the folders, which documented the events and involvement of all the organisations as a chronology to the injustice and abuse of a family, in the loft. I want to cut all my ties with the misery that has been, and move on. (Deep down, part of me was still worried that this wasn't the end, so I could not throw away the years of evidence I had gathered.)

Mrs Mason and Smitch Law's barristers, as well as judges, spent years on the defamation of an honest parent's character. The judges failed to recognise or care that a mother had a mental health problem, and were bamboozled by a law firm and associated solicitor and barristers, who were condoning Ms Hyde's behaviour and dismissing all the incidents she and the children were involved in. The court ignored any information which exposed the blatant lies Ms Hyde put forward through her legal representatives.

The judges never followed through on the mental health practitioner's advice to monitor Ms Hyde and ensure her medication is being taken – as early on as 2000. They did not try and help her improve her behaviour towards her children, despite the involvement of Social Services and the police on many occasions while the children were in her residency.

I have never withheld contact from Ms Hyde. In incidences where Ms Hyde had been physically abusive towards the children, they were understandably reluctant to return. I would be failing as a parent to further distress my children and undermine their welfare, just as the courts have done.

Ms Hyde would not try and sort things out with her daughters, or understand their need for time and space; she would run straight to her solicitor and be allowed to drag our family back into the Family Courts.

I have no criminal record and multiple character witnesses – ranging from neighbours at the time Ms Hyde and I were together, to Riverbank School, who remained impartial throughout and were the only organisation that were solely concerned with the children's welfare – which repeatedly confirmed to the Family Courts that I was a loving, caring dad to my children and not abusive or defamatory towards Ms Hyde.

I was repeatedly set up by Smitch Law as the unreasonable parent, and the difficult parent, that would not let Ms Hyde have peace with her children. This was completely untrue.

It did not matter what had gone on between Ms Hyde and her children, we were in court to listen to Smitch Law and, based on that, the judge would decide what direction the whole family would be going.

Year after year, at every hearing, there were professionals in a position to try and get Ms Hyde help, which would have benefitted Ms Hyde herself and the children, a long time ago. Unfortunately, said professionals chose to turn the Family Courts into a dishonest and shameless theatre.

38 court hearings, 13 judges and 10 years of hell for a family.

For all of the might and the self–importance of this organisation, they simply slandered a good parent and squandered the childhoods of three young children.

The judges demonstrated little to no understanding or care for someone with mental health problems or the impacts of the illness on the children's day-to-day lives.

The professionalism you would expect from this organisation clearly falls below any ethical or reasonable standards, and the individuals involved should be brought to account. We should be assured by the Family Justice Department that this unethical behaviour will not be accepted, even when behind closed doors.

The majority of the families in this country are lucky, and through hard work and resilience manage to stay together. However, for those families that are not together, for whatever reason, I ask mothers and fathers please do not put your children through this injustice and unhappiness; be responsible for your children – don't go to Family Courts expecting to find honesty or decency. As parents, we do not always get it right, but our children deserve to have in their lives any decent Mum or Dad.

It really is up to us.

The Injustice to Children & Families: provided by the Family Courts Theatre

For weeks, I lived with the fear of the police knocking on the door under court directions, and finding myself behind bars, in prison, for putting Lara's welfare and stability first.

To date, the Family Courts have had no communication with me to inform of the outcome of their hearing on the 27th April 2009 and, from my experience with the behaviour of several judges over the years, I conclude that this is just another example of the disrespectful behaviour and unprofessional performance that my family has received all the way through from this unscrupulous organisation.

If not for my love for my children, the determination to stand up for family justice and the importance of decent parents in their children's lives, I would have walked away from the very start; rather than face the bias and corruption, the behaviour of judges and the mindless self–importance of several individuals in children matters.

What is the point, if a judge is not there to be honest and true, showing an impartial judgement to any actual evidence put before them?

Ms Hyde went from sole residency, to joint residency to contact, and yet the sole residency I was granted, they allowed to be abused without evidence at any opportunity.

The Law Society

There is a crime here, and that is harassment of a decent parent and the detrimental effect this law firm has had on three young children and their parents, over nine years.

All of the above could have been avoided, and the Legal Aid stockpile accumulated over the years must be at a good £100,000 plus; a decade down the line, our family is back inside the Family Courts walls with the same problem, a mother behaving inappropriately towards her children.

Whatever the circumstance, childhood is not easy. The system has needlessly put three children through additional pressure and upset. This is not family justice. The 'justice' part of the equation seems to be greatly inflated; if the departments did not use the word, then perhaps they would not receive letters of complaint when it becomes clear it does not mean anything to the organisation or how they practice – come to think of it, they should rebrand entirely, as the families involved do appear to be irrelevant to the cause as well.

Accountability and honesty from people working in the system:

Those who fail to learn from history are forced to repeat it; let us hope mothers and fathers can one day be treated equally as parents to their children, and it is acknowledged from the heart of our system, we have got it wrong, lessons need to be learnt and it's time for change, with a different approach to family justice and family law. Mothers and fathers are 'parents' to their children, and are both able and equal in fulfilling the task regardless of gender.

If we do not stand up for ourselves and the prejudices facing many people, nothing will change. Everything that has benefitted society from a social, environmental or educational point of view has been fought for, against a majority inside the constitutional walls, by protest. It would be nice, for once, to actually break the cycle and properly address the numerous systemic issues, so that instead of talking about equality as a distant dream, we can avoid another generation challenged by discrimination and all of the prejudices that exist today.

However, we cannot hope to change the ignorant view point of the population if the governance does not try to set an example.

It is shocking to me that the UK attempts to mediate on an international scale, when internally there is not much to idolise about the mechanics of our democracy. The way children are treated by the individuals who practice family law is immoral; if even elected MPs can question the integrity of the Family Courts and the injustices being playout over many years, and be told to keep their nose out of the affairs of the legal system, what hope have the rest of us got?

It should be seen as a privilege to work in government and departments tasked with shaping our society for the good of everyone, yet we find unethical behaviour is protected by their own. How can an organisation with the most responsibility and power, be held the least accountable?

I just asked for honesty and integrity, and received nothing in return.

We not only owe it to ourselves to change; we also owe it to the people who are genuinely wronged by our system and our current society's values towards each other.

From my MP

8 May

Dear Mr Marlo,

I am sorry to hear from my colleagues that you had another unhappy experience in court, but I am very disappointed that you felt it necessary to walk out of the hearing. However, I can well understand how upset you must have been.

As ever, I am keen to do all I can to help you. That said, I am not a lawyer and the court system would not take kindly to me becoming openly involved in their deliberations. That does not stop me raising your case with the Justice Secretary, in the same way as I did previously with the Rt Hon Minister for Family Justice MP.

As promised, I have written to draw his attention to your case and to request that he agrees to meet the two of us. I enclose a copy of my letter for your information. I will contact you again when I get a response.

I also enclose a note which I have just received from BBC Radio 4 asking me if I can put forward any story in my constituency which they could investigate. Would you like me to see if they would be interested in your story? We have nothing to lose.

Best wishes.

Yours sincerely…

Dear Justice Secretary,

I would be most grateful if you would kindly agree to meet me and my constituent Mr Dean Marlo who, over several years now, has been dragged through the Family Courts in respect of matters relating to his three daughters for whom he is the legal guardian.

What has happened shames Britain's legal system! It also reveals how one firm of solicitors have, thank you very much, made a fortune by using the legal system – with lots of Legal Aid courtesy of the public system! – to hound Mr Marlo.

Their client is mother of the three children. Suffice to say her situation is such that she is not the parent with whom the children live; it is not necessary to labour that point but you can draw your own conclusions as to why this is. Notwithstanding, she is granted Legal Aid at every turn. My constituent is a conscientious, hard–working man who has had his life ruined by the manner in which the legal system has operated against him.

'The system' has failed him. He is an astonishing man, who battles on as best he can – in the face of all that the legal profession throws at him, and despite the failure of the courts – without any recourse to legal assistance because (a) he cannot afford legal representation and (b) he is not entitled to Legal Aid, whereas the mother of the three children is – he somehow continues to provide loving care for his daughters.

Where is the justice here? Where is the level playing field? How can this be fair?

What is happening to Mr Marlo is wrong, wrong, wrong.

You are the Secretary of State for Justice. My constituent is being denied justice. His three daughters have for several years been caught up in the failures of the legal system and those engaged in preparing reports etc for the court hearings.

What has happened (and continues to happen) to Mr Marlo is an outrage. The legal profession should hang its head in shame for allowing this state of affairs to happen. I therefore ask, please, that you agree to meet Mr Marlo and myself so that you can personally consider his case. I look forward to hearing from you. Many thanks.

Yours sincerely...

To MP and a solicitor

11 May

Dear Mr Rowe,

I know my dad has written to you for many years and I would like you to know how my sister Lara and myself are treated.

I have written this letter for my sister and myself not with the help of my dad or for my dad but for my family.

Yours faithfully,

Alice Marlo

Dear Mrs Whyte,

I am writing to you on behalf of my sister Lara and myself.

We both believe that it is disgraceful that you have not bothered to write to us concerning the last hearing. Lara is 11 years old and she has been left not knowing what is going on.

After doing all of that work with Vanya you and Lara's Guardian have shown no care for the young person you represented in the court. You both have just dropped Lara and that is not right.

You have just left Lara not knowing what is going on and just think she can get on with her life. What a load of rubbish about Lara's wellbeing.

I know that I have been quickly taken off the court order without fuss which I find strange considering what has been said about me this year and over the years, despite not being on the court order I believe I should still be told what is going on in my life and yes my sister Lara's life.

My dad told me that he left court early to collect Lara from school and that the courts were annoyed at him for this.

Just like me when I was younger the only person's life that is made sad is the young person that is not being met by a parent (like our school friends) that has always been there for them after school, this may mean nothing to you, but it has to us.

I believe you and the Guardian were representing Lara and me at the start of these court hearings and you should have made things clear to us both about the outcome.

I believe it is disgraceful that you can tell lies about me and tell me one thing and do another, and not even bother to write to us so we can get on with our lives and put an end to another court hearing.

My sister and I would like to get on with our lives and once again put this court hearing to an end in our lives, but how can we do this if we are not told by the people representing us in court what has gone on and why?

Alice Marlo

From Mrs Whyte

19 May

Dear Alice and Lara,

Many thanks for your letter of 15 May 2009. The reason why I have not previously written to you both is because I usually prefer to receive the court order prior to writing to you with the details. I do have the order now.

With regard to you Alice, the court has agreed that there is to be no order in relation to yourself.

With regard to you Lara, you are to have telephone contact with your mum twice a week and to exchange cards and letters with her. If any further contact can be agreed between you and your mum then that is absolutely fine with the court for there to be such contact.

That sets out the main body of the court order, particularly with regard to the important points for you both.

This therefore does now bring matters to an end and I am going to proceed to close this file.

I wish you both all the very best for the future.

With kind regards,

Mrs Whyte was there for the hearing, the judge would have made clear what his order was on that day, and yet she had no communication by phone or letter concerning the outcome of the hearing with her clients, Alice and Lara, for over three weeks.

On the 9th February 2009, Mrs Whyte sat in court and allowed Mrs Mason to falsely relay to the judge that Alice was 13-years-old; within two months Alice, 15, was taken off the court order.

It just does not make any sense, because this information could have been relayed with one phone call: Alice is off the court order, and Lara is to have letterbox contact. Mrs Whyte was well aware I was not there when the judge was summing up and gave his final order – I guess that was my doing – but under the circumstances, she should have been in contact with Alice and Lara that day, to ensure peace of mind for her clients. I have been there and Melissa would phone me on the day.

'Then that is absolutely fine with the court,' which proves a sad fact, that the Family Courts merely dismiss and excuse the abuse towards children. When does verbal and physical abuse of children become 'absolutely fine'?

It is written in family law that a child's (Lara's) feelings should be heard and paramount in the court's directions, yet this is not the reality.

It's a strange topsy-turvy way to run an organisation, while proclaiming a child's welfare is paramount; it appears to be about what legal representatives and the judge want, and the children's welfare comes in a close second or maybe third – either way, it's last.

From MP to Alice

26 May

Dear Miss Marlo,

Thank you for the correspondence you have sent to me on behalf of your sister and your family. It is of great credit to you. It brought me great sadness at the manner in which you have all been treated.

I have written to your solicitor to seek an explanation. A copy of my letter is enclosed for your assistance. I hope that you will be able to gain the representation which you are entitled to.

When I receive a response, I will contact you again but, in the meantime, should you still remain unhappy with the service you have received then you may wish to contact Child Legal Guidance, who will be able to give you further advice.

Best wishes.

Yours sincerely…

Dear Mrs Whyte,

My constituent, Miss Alice Marlo, has sent me a copy of her correspondence to you concerning herself and her sister, Lara Marlo, following the continuing legal challenges this family has endured for years. I have to say I am amazed how well the family have managed to cope with a system that would have destroyed many.

I would be grateful for your response to why she feels that her wishes and comments are not been correctly put across in a court of law. Thank you.

Yours sincerely,

Dear Mr Rowe, from Alice

1 June

Thank you for your letter. I enclose a letter Lara and I have received from Mrs Whyte.

Mrs Whyte's reason or excuse has nothing to do with treating Lara and myself with some consideration and respect with all that we as children have been put through and the fact that we had made it clear to everyone involved, the Cafcass guardian, Vanya the family support worker and Mrs Whyte herself, that we had enough of the court and all of the upset and uncertainty that has always followed when our mother takes our dad back to court because she has hit us or kicked off and we have had to leave and did not want to see her.

We are only children but we know now that lies can be told about us in the family court and no one cares but I would have thought that Mrs Whyte and the Cafcass guardian would have made the effort by communicating with us to reassure us after the hearing and put an end to the worry and concerns both Lara and myself have had over the past 12 months and that had been expressed by Lara and myself to both Mrs Whyte and the Cafcass guardian.

Our solicitor and the Cafcass guardian did nothing to reassure Lara and myself after the hearing, they just allowed us to keep worrying about what was going on in our lives.

We should have been contacted and reassured after the hearing of what was going on by the people representing us or Lara in court.

When Lara and I met Ms Dowling, she stated that if we did not go to our mother's the court could choose to send our dad to prison. We are children and Lara and I watched our mother punch our oldest sister in the face cutting Hayley's lip. Since this happed Lara and I have had another year involved with the courts including Cafcass and solicitors. All of the things my mother has done and once again the courts have turn it on to my dad.

The Cafcass guardian encouraged me to attend court so I could tell the judge my feelings and tell him what happened at our mother's and the reason why we walked out again and did not want to see her. The judge did not want to hear the truth and I witnessed all of the legal people ganging up on my dad making lies up to make my dad look bad. They even dragged me into their lies and used me against my dad.

I saw every one putting my dad down but he had done nothing, our mother punched Hayley in the face and our dad was there for us. He did not start trouble with our mother he just looked after us.

Thanks for Child Legal Guidance's number, after talking to my dad about how Mrs Whyte has acted and seeing how my dad was treated in court I decided to try and get on with my life and do not want to get involved with any more legal people. I am not going to give them the opportunity to abuse me like they have my dad for years.

In court no one tells our mother her behaviour is wrong they just turn everything onto my dad so my mother keeps abusing us because she thinks it is ok and then tells us how the courts have said that our dad's behaviour is disgraceful.

Our mother needed help with her behaviour years ago but the court would rather tell lies instead of helping our mother with her behaviour and our time spent with her.

What Lara and I have learnt is with the court and judge and legal people one lie covers another lie.

Yours faithfully,

Moving time again

3 June

With the hearings consuming my life for the past year, I just haven't been focussed on work – the house we're renting is far too big, and Hayley has said she is not coming home.

For the time being, we're moving into a 3-bedroom terraced house with no drive; we have to park in a car park and walk up the road. It's not ideal, but I need smaller outgoings to get back on top of work and my finances.

Alice can't wait to reorganise a new room, and Lara is looking forward to using the move to clear out some of her old things and get ready for secondary school.

(Sadly, Lara did not pass the Eleven-plus.

We read the email wrong and spent five minutes celebrating and cheering, before the crushing realisation Lara had been off getting a place by 20 or so people. I felt awful; the rollercoaster of emotions was only intensified by the guilt and questions of my involvement in what has happened over the past year, and although pointless to dwell on impossible choices made in the past – what if I had just said to Lara, look lov, you have to continue your contact with your mother. Would that have changed everything? It is with extreme sadness that deep down I wonder if I really have been the problem in all of my children's lives all along – what if I had given up when Ms Hyde walked out?

Despite my introspection, with pride I can say that Lara has taken it well and has said, 'Whatever school I go to, I'm going to do the best I can.'

With the reputation of her sisters, and mother, at Northview, Lara chose to go to Horizon Academy; I understood and we put it as her first choice. It was nice to have the ability to actually talk to Lara about where she wants to go to school, as Hayley, Alice and I never had that option, with Ms Hyde dictating everything.)

From MP Rowe

19 June

Dear Mr Marlo,
Please find enclosed a copy of the response I have received from Huffman LP.
Hopefully, you will find their comments to be of interest. If I can be of any further assistance, please let me know. Best wishes.
Yours sincerely...

Dear Mr Rowe,
Re: Alice and Lara Marlo – 9.5 Proceedings
Many thanks for your letter of 15 May 2009. It is quite correct to say that for Alice Marlo and her sister, Lara, this has been a really difficult situation.
I replied to Alice's letter of 15 May 2009 confirming that the court made no order in relation to Alice and in relation to Lara, that she has phone contact with her mother twice a week and to exchange cards and letter with her. Any other contact arranged between Lara and her mother is absolutely fine with the court.
Lara and Alice were represented by their Guardian, Ms Dowling, although it is true to say that at Alice's age she would have been separately represented if her views were different from the Guardian. In actual fact, her views were exactly the same as the Guardian's views and that is why the court ultimately agreed that there should be no order for contact between herself and her mother.
As stated above, I replied to Alice's letter on 19 May 2009, but I am not enclosing a copy of that letter because, clearly, that is confidential between the children and myself but I have set out for you basically what was said in that correspondence.
I know that Alice and Lara have both found this matter difficult to deal with but proceedings have now come to an end and the court has ordered that there are to be no further applications by either parent unless the court grants leave for them to bring further applications.
I now hope that this is the end to the litigation for Alice and Lara, and that they can get on with enjoying their lives.
With kind regards.
Yours sincerely,
Mrs Whyte

MP to Alice

3 July

Dear Miss Marlo,
Thank you for your letter and the copy of the letter you received from Huffman LP Solicitors, which I
read with interest. I appreciate your continued concerns. I continue to assist your father. Best wishes.
Yours sincerely,

From MoJ to Mr Rowe

Dear Dean,
Please find enclosed a copy of the response I have received from the Parliamentary Under-Secretary of State for the Ministry of Justice.
Hopefully you will find the Minister's comments to be of interest. If I can be of any further assistance please let me know.
Best wishes,

30 June

Dear Mr Rowe,
Eligibility for Legal Aid
Thank you for your letter of 8 May to the Justice Secretary, about your constituent Mr Dean Marlo, whose ex–partner is entitled to Legal Aid to pursue a family matter while he is not. I am replying as the minister responsible for Legal Aid.

I should begin by explaining that the decisions about Legal Aid funding in civil cases are a matter for the Legal Services Commission (LSC), which is responsible for administering the Legal Aid scheme. You will therefore appreciate that neither ministers nor government officials intervene in or comment on decisions made about the grant of funding in individual cases. It is important that these decisions are, and are seen to be, free from political and government influence. That said, it might be helpful if I explain how the Legal Aid scheme operates in England and Wales.

Generally, Legal Aid funding is available to anyone who qualifies, provided that the case is within the scope of the Legal Aid scheme through the Community Legal Service. Each application is considered on an individual basis and is subject to the statutory test of the applicant's means. In addition to qualifying financially, an applicant must also show that the merits of the case justify the grant of public funding. The application is considered against criteria specific to the type of case; these criteria are set out in a document called the Funding Code. Broadly speaking, the test is designed to measure, taking all circumstances into account, whether a privately paying client of moderate means would be prepared to spend his or her own money on taking the case. The LSC must consider, for example, the prospects of success, any alternative sources of funding, and any other circumstances such as wider public interest or overwhelming importance to the applicant.

Those in receipt of Income Support, income-based JobSeeker's Allowance, or Guarantee State Pension Credit, or income related Employment Support Allowance automatically qualify financially for Legal Aid. Otherwise, they can obtain 'free', or non–contributory assistance, if they have a gross monthly income of less than £2,657, a monthly disposable income below £315 and disposable capital of £3,000 or less. If their monthly disposable income is between £316 and £733, or disposable capital between £3,000 and £8,000, they will be offered funding on the basis that they agree to pay contributions towards their legal costs. Applicants can check their eligibility for Legal Aid by using the eligibility calculator on the LSC's website.

Legal Aid is granted on the strength of the information provided by the applicant, their solicitor and counsel's opinion where there is one. To maintain a balanced view, it is open to any interested party to make representations to the LSC about a person's eligibility for funding. However, although it is open to anyone to make such representations, this does not mean that representation will automatically lead to the funding certificate being discharged. The LSC must comply with set procedures before it can reach a decision about the status of a certificate. Representations have to be put to the legally aided client, who is given a chance to explain the situation. If the LSC is satisfied, it must allow the certificate to remain open.

The LSC cannot withdraw funding on speculation or rumour and can only act on facts. It has limited ability to investigate allegations which are not supported by evidence. It is also important to bear in mind that, in litigation, there can be more than one side of the story. In all cases, but particularly when considering the entitlement to Legal Aid, this continues throughout the life of the case. The legally aided client's solicitor is also obliged to ensure that it remains reasonable for the legally aided client to continue to receive funding. They must inform the LSC if, at any point, funding is no longer warranted. A solicitor using Legal Aid has an obligation to safeguard the Legal Aid Fund. A solicitor is required to inform the LSC if:

Their client has refused an offer of settlement which the solicitor considers to be reasonable;

They suspect the client is abusing the scheme by requiring that the proceedings be conducted unreasonably;

They have doubts about whether to continue to act for the client; or

They believe that the client no longer has reasonable grounds for being involved in proceedings.

The LSC will then decide whether or not the case continues to justify the grant of funding.

I am, of course, aware that some people who are facing court proceedings might nevertheless not be eligible for Legal Aid funding. The financial eligibility criteria are designed to focus our limited resources on priority cases and vulnerable clients. The government recognises that those who have capital or income in excess of the limits might still not be able to readily afford legal representation, and may feel that the system is unfair. However there are many competing priorities for Legal Aid and a threshold must be set.

You mention that Mr Marlo is not eligible for Legal Aid and that he is struggling to meet his legal fees. Advice for those who do not qualify for Legal Aid and need legal assistance can be obtained from Citizen's Advice and Law Centres. Advice Centres can give legal advice themselves and refer clients to a pro bono organisation for free representation.

Community Legal Advice is a national phone advice line and website service, run by the LSC for people using the courts of England and Wales is also available. It provides an advice service for people with civil law problems (including family and personal matters) such as welfare benefits, debt, housing, employment or educational issues.

I hope this letter clarifies the situation and I have enclosed a copy for you to forward to Mr Marlo, should you wish to do so. I am happy to meet you but I should make it clear that the confidentiality provisions under Section 20 of the Access to Justice Act 1999 restricts the disclosure of information to a third party, as such no detailed information about the legal aid application of Mr Marlo's ex–partner can be discussed without her consent. Please contact my Diary Secretary to make the necessary arrangements if you still do so.

Yours sincerely,

Secretary for MoJ

Dean Marlo

From Legal Services Commission

20 July

Dear Mr Marlo,
Legal Aid Cert No.   *: XXXXX*
Debt   *: £5,450.85*

This debt has now been interfaced from our central data base onto our collection's system, with regard to the amount paid to Messrs Parstons Solicitors, which represents the liability you owe as your Public Funding Certificate was revoked.

Please ensure that you contact this office within the next seven days to prevent recovery action.

Yours sincerely,

Debt Recovery Unit

MP to me and LSC

28 July

Dear Mr Marlo,
Further to your visit to my office and the conversation you had with my secretary Beverly, I understand that you have received a Legal Aid bill. I have therefore written to the Legal Aid Services Commission to ask for a breakdown of this bill. Please find enclosed a copy of my letter. I will contact you again when I receive a response. Best wishes.
Yours sincerely,

I write on behalf of Mr Marlo who has received a bill for £5450.85. I have been assisting Mr Marlo with his case for a number of years and am keen to assist him further.
I would be grateful if you could please provide me with a breakdown of how this figure has been reached. Thank you.
Yours sincerely,

Dean Marlo

From Tax Credit Office

13 August

Dear Mr Marlo

We need some more information from you regarding your tax credits claim.

Your child Alice Marlo is currently included in more than one claim. There is an overlap in responsibility dates for this child. In your claim, you have stated a responsibility start date of 29 April 2004, the other claimant has stated a start date of their responsibility of 12 January 2007 and end date of 25 May 2009.

From Legal Services Commission

3 September

Dear Mr Marlo,
Legal Aid Cert No. : *XXXXX*
Debt : *£5,050.17*
I am disappointed to note that I have not received a response to my last letter to you.
Please ensure that you contact this office within the next seven days to prevent further recovery action.
Yours sincerely,
Debt Recovery Unit

From Mr MP Rowe

3 September

Dear Mr Marlo,
Please find enclosed a copy of the response I have received from the Community Legal Services for your information. If I can be of any further assistance, please let me know.

7 August

Dear Mr Rowe,
Your constituent: Mr Dean Marlo
Thank you for your letter dated 28ᵗʰ July 2009. Please note that this letter has been passed to myself as Director of Recovery Services.

In supplying you with the information you had requested, it may be useful if I provide you with a brief background of your constituent's case. When the debt interfaced from our central database onto our collection's system, the amount of the bills paid to the solicitors were £5,450.85 viz. Messrs Parstons Solicitors, which represents the liability owed by Mr Marlo, as his certificate had been revoked (he was deemed ineligible for public funding).

Without rehearsing the precise operation of the billing procedure to you, Mr Marlo would have been advised by his solicitor when their bill was being prepared for taxation and he should have been informed of this process in accordance with Legal Aid regulations by Parstons. A detailed breakdown would have been sent to him. If he has not received a detailed bill, he may wish to contact his former solicitors for a copy. However, our Debt Recovery Unit's approach for payment should not have been unexpected, (I note that your client has moved address, without informing ourselves, this may have resulted in him not receiving the papers from his solicitors, as they too may not have been advised of his move.)

I have had an opportunity to examine the file in detail and note that the court has taxed the costs in this matter, which was sealed on the 17ᵗʰ March 2009. A copy is enclosed. Moreover, it was noted by me that the sum allowed was £5,170.00 and not as shown on our database, therefore I have made the necessary adjustment and confirmed that they have further reduced the bill by £119.83, bringing the correct total liability owed by Mr Marlo to £5,050.17. I apologise on their behalf for the confusion that this may have caused to him.

I conclude that the outstanding balance of £5,050.17 is correct and shall be referring this matter back to my Debt Recovery Team to continue with collection, thus I should be obliged if you would kindly inform your constituent that they will be contacting him in the near future seeking repayment.

I hope this has been of assistance, and enclose a copy of this letter for you to give to Mr Marlo, if you wish.

Yours sincerely,
Director of Recovery Services

From Horizon Academy

10 September

Dear Mr Marlo,
Re: Lara Marlo 7HD
I have received Lara's records from Riverbank Primary School and they contain a copy of a court order regarding mother's contact with her. I am not sure whether this is still current or has lapsed.
I would be grateful if this could be clarified please by contacting the Assistant Head of House.
Yours sincerely,

Dean Marlo

To Horizon Academy

15 September

Re: Lara Marlo 7HD

Further to your letter of the 10th September 2009 and the conversation I have had with the Assistant Head of House. I have had sole residency of Lara since 2004. I confirm that it was decided by the Family Courts in April 2009 that Lara has letterbox contact and it is her choice whether she has weekend contact with her mother.

If you have any questions concerning the above, please do not hesitate to contact me. Yours faithfully…

Post-it note, signed, From Hell

25 September

Dear Dean,
Please find enclosed copy of the judge's summing up that you missed. I shall be writing to you shortly with my own concerns.
Regards,
Ruth

HHJ NEELY
The court is concerned with Lara Marlo born December 1997, she is 11 years old. She is the daughter of Ruth Hyde and Dean Marlo. She has two siblings who are relevant to these proceedings: Hayley born in 1992 and Alice born in 1994.
The issue before the court is whether and to what extent the court should order Lara to have contact to her mother; she currently lives with her father. In relation to Ms Hyde, she, represented by Smitch Law, makes a number of suggestions. Firstly, that work which was carried out by Vanya Roshan through Cafcass should be continued and completed. Secondly, that there is no reason why there should not be contact that is by way of tea or something of that sort on a regular basis. Thirdly, another possibility raised was that a visit should occur, as it were, supervised by possibly a Family Support Worker, somebody similar, or possibly a Guardian.
The father who attended in person, but left court halfway through cross–examination, suggests that there should be phone contact only. The Guardian Ms Dowling, and their legal representative, supports the view that currently the contact to Ms Hyde should be phone contact and letter contact and that there should be no further direct contact at the present time. She also supports the continuing of the 91(14) Order, made as long ago as September 2007, I will deal with that in a moment.
The hearing has lasted the best part of a day. I have read the bundle which has been helpfully supplied by Smitch Law together with a number of other documents. There have been a numerous materials including letters from the children setting out their different perspectives. I have heard evidence from Ms Hyde. I have heard evidence from Mr Marlo but curtailed because he left at lunchtime halfway through cross–examination. I have heard evidence from Ms Dowling, the Guardian.
The history can be shortly stated. The parents lived together for a number of years before finally co–habiting in 1991. They have three daughters, Hayley, Alice and Lara, the parents separated in about 1999. From almost the time of their separation and certainly since March of 2000, there have been ongoing proceedings between these parents involving their children. It is true to say that there was a period of about two years when there appears to have been a pause as far as the proceedings were concerned. However there have been innumerable applications made by both parents as a result of the care provided to their children. The children have lived variously with both parents and in different combinations.
Effectively, what appears to happen is that a child will live with one parent, a difficulty will then arise and the children then 'up–sticks' and goes with the other parent until a difficulty arises and then the same situation presents itself and both parents blame the other. It is quite impossible in a complicated and difficult family dynamic as this to begin to unravel what is, even by family court standards, a very unusual

749

and difficult case to understand. However, it is an unhappy one because it was hoped when Recorder Lowe made an order in September 2007, that essentially the parents had been able to sort out the arrangements for their children, but all was not well.

There were difficulties with Alice who in due course ran away from school and eventually was permanently excluded. In February of last year, Hayley was arrested and then on the 7th April last year, an incident occurred at the maternal home when Ms Hyde was involved in a tussle with her daughter, Hayley, she was arrested. Indeed, I believe she was bound over to keep the peace as a result. However, the practical effect was that Hayley left the home with Lara and has gone to live with her father. Lara remained with her father and has not seen her mother since. By June 2008, Hayley had another difficulty with her father and returned to live with her mother where she currently remains.

Therefore, the current situation is that Hayley remains with her mother and has very limited contact with her siblings and as far as I can tell no contact with her father. Alice and Lara live with their father and they have no contact with their mother. Alice, on any view, has been a troubled young woman and has been through a number of difficult periods and it is generally agreed, I think, has not been perhaps helpful to the breakdown in the relationship between Lara and Ms Hyde.

The situation so far as the evidence is concerned is that Ms Hyde gave evidence. She told me that she felt that all the children fed up with proceedings. That appears to be something upon which all parties agree, and that she and Lara needed finality and space. However she, Ms Hyde, did not agree with the suggestions of the children because she thought that it could be detrimental.

She said that she has had regular contact with Lara by way of phone and the incident on the 7th April 2008 appears to have been a constant theme. I do not get the impression that it was mentioned in every phone call but certainly seemed to be mentioned in most of the phone calls. Ms Hyde apologised and said that she was sorry that it happened, she is told by Lara that she does not believe her and that she, her mother, is lying.

It is clear that the view is one which emanates, if not from Lara's direct perception it is certainly not ameliorated by Mr Marlo's perception, nor have I heard direct evidence about Alice's perception either. There are phone–calls that are reasonable. One was last Thursday, but then one on Sunday was not a good phone–call. She does not really understand how the certain current situation has arisen and feels powerless. A view which I can understand actually well since it seems to me that on the face of it, there is no good reason at all why Lara should not have contact with her mother. She tells her father that she is frightened of her mother's conduct and it is clear that what occurred on the 7th April last year was undignified and very unhelpful. Whether it really should have led to the sort of fracture and schism that it has, I rather doubt, but it is typical of the way in which this family has from time to time operated. Something occurs and then a schism follows it. Subsequently, there is a further reconciliation. It is very unhelpful and very corrosive to the children and very damaging to the adults too. It is perfectly obvious having listened to both Ms Hyde and Mr Marlo, they have been wounded considerably by what has occurred over the years.

Therefore, by and large, I accept the genuineness of what Ms Hyde told me. It seemed to me she was sensible and positive. However, it was equally clear that there were moments when I do not think she really understood the way in which Lara and the children generally look at their parent's perspectives as between the two of them. It seemed to me that whereas she had apologised, the apology was perhaps not sufficient with Lara even though I think Ms Hyde felt that she had done sufficient. Ultimately, it is not something which I can do much about.

I then heard from Mr Marlo who took the view, I have no doubt based on experience, that time and space will heal the rift as indeed has always happened in the past and that he took the view that the contact should simply be phone contact only at the moment.

He became increasingly anxious that during the course of cross–examination where he clearly identified that Ms Hyde as the guilty party and that he has done absolutely nothing wrong. He became very animated when he was being questioned; it seemed to me perfectly properly about what he had done for example to repair the relationship with Hayley. He did not seem to think that it was relevant and missed the point entirely. However, in my view the way he had conducted himself with Hayley last summer was pretty deplorable and actually has done nothing really to repair the relationship which she seeks. He after all is the adult; Hayley was only born in 1992. He has done nothing about it and it seemed to me to be quite illustrative of the way in which he approaches the relationships he has with his children. As I commented and the Guardian agreed, 'You are either with me, or you are against me'; that seemed to me to be his approach generally to his children.

I listened with care to Ms Dowling. I understood her frustration as to how this case could really be dealt with. She took the view that Alice had not been helpful in the dynamics of the case. She told me that, to use her words, the way Hayley was treated last year, 'It was quite shocking'. Mr Marlo would never acknowledge Alice now, nor indeed any responsibility for what had occurred. She took the view that the children were forced to take sides. She did not endorse that the current arrangements are in the children's best interests.

A number of things had occurred to her when requesting a way forward. Indeed, as I was listening to Mr Marlo's evidence, I wondered myself whether I should be invoking a Section 37 report and some sort of public law order. However, the effect of that of course would be devastating as far as Lara is concerned and she would, in my judgment, be alienated from her mother whom she would blame because it would be my decision and not hers. Hayley will find herself in the care system and having regard to the positive aspects of the parenting, that would be a most unhelpful development.

The Guardian was critical of both parents. She took the view that they lacked insight and that the damage that had been caused to the children was a result of their parents' entrenchment. However, she tried to balance what was in the children's best interests, in Lara's best interest at the current time. It seemed to me that there having been work carried out with Vanya Roshan, that is why these proceedings were delayed, that the result of that was to hear clearly what Lara's views were. I was quite affected by that because it was quite evident both from the live evidence and from the evidence which I have seen in the papers that Lara, who is an intelligent girl, has an articulate view of where she currently is. It might not be a view that I share, but nonetheless, she holds it sincerely herself.

Mr Marlo's evidence was not satisfactory. It seemed to me that he had some fairly unreconstructed views as to how parents should conduct themselves. When pressed, he was difficult, but on the plus side, it is clear that he believes in his children. He supports them and in all other aspects, other than in a relationship with their mother, he appears to be a good parent.

My conclusions very sadly are these. I do not find this an easy case. I suspect that Ms Hyde understands and indeed did say when she started giving evidence that the options for the court are extremely limited. I could take a punitive approach and attach a penal notice. In my view, that would be disadvantageous to Lara. I would have to be prepared to follow it through and make a committal order. The effect on these children, if I did that (because I think there is every prospect Mr Marlo would not comply), would be absolutely devastating. I do not think there is any particular reason why Lara should not be having direct contact with her mother today and that is what makes it so difficult and so upsetting and so unfair. However, on the other hand, I cannot change the last decade, as it has been years now, of the difficulties between these parents and of their respective children. It is a very involved background.

I hope that there will be some reparation in the future. I suspect on the past form, there will be. I have had regard to Lara's best interests. Her welfare is of paramount consideration and of course I apply the welfare checklist. It seems to me that the best I can do at the present time is for an order for indirect contact by way of letters and cards. That there should be the phone contact twice a week which, quite surprisingly, Mr Marlo supports and I think the order should have a preamble upon the court considering contact to the mother, Ms Hyde, is in Lara's best interests. It seems to me that is the best I can currently do in order to encourage her, at some stage in the future, to have direct contact with Ms Hyde. It seems to me to order any other type of contact would be simply to prolong the proceedings which neither parent seeks and the Guardian does not support. With a heavy heart that is the order that I make.

On the 5th September 2007, Recorder Lowe made a Section 91(14) order until the 5th September 2010, so for another 18 months or thereabouts. I have heard no submissions by either of the applicants as to whether I should amend that order. My current view is that I do not propose to do so. Does anybody have any submissions?

End of judgement

Dear ministers, we do not need this poison any more

I look back at all the hours and nights I spent in an attempt to write meaningful letters to address the injustice, dishonesty and hurt that my children have been put through, and I am disappointed the most justice I have felt was walking out of that building.

For nine years, the same law firm have acted purely on information provided by their client; no evidence of any misconduct on my behalf has ever been given to the Family Courts in the 38 hearings in my children's case; no police cautions or transcripts; no letters from nurseries, schools or any organisation objecting to my behaviour or that suggest I have ever discouraged our children's contact with their mother; no phone bill, detailing my harassment of Ms Hyde; no tapes of phone calls; nothing.

Ministers, the Family Courts and the appropriate organisations should address family law as a whole, wherein children's welfare and stability actually is paramount, and not just a tag line, and unscrupulous law firms are reprimanded and addressed, as they are clearly profiteering off acting in a detrimental way towards family dynamics.

Honest and decent people deserve to be told why they can be forced to live for years with threats to their children's welfare, and their own wellbeing, when dealing with the Family Courts.

I am genuinely worried about the £5,000 plus the Legal Commission have recently informed me that I owe them, due to this law firm writing to the Legal Aid Commission and making unfounded and inaccurate accusations about my person and finances. I found the MoJ's explanation of how thoroughly the LSC ensures the fairness of their decisions to be an insult; checking Company House would have taken two minutes, and disproven Smitch Law's claims.

The removal of my Legal Aid once again allowed this law firm to bully me, my family's ability to get on and court proceedings; deceitfully using the law for their own gains and immorally playing the system to the best of their ability.

This law firm got rid of the opposition so they could behave as they wished, behind closed doors, trying to manipulate and deceive as they have over the past 9 years, and as they did at the very start, in 2000, by suggesting to the judge that I was aggressive and extremely violent. (To this day there is still no evidence to suggest or support that I am or ever was the person this solicitor implied, on behalf of their client.)

These are children and family matters and I was a single parent with three young children to support. I worked part time so that I could be there for my children at breakfast, the start of school and returned from work to collect them after school. Working part time to be there for my children meant my income was low and I did rely on Family/Working Tax credits and Housing Benefits to try and make ends meet.

(I firmly believe without running my own business, I would not have residency of my children at all; missing days for years to attend hearings, the time to prepare for court dates and meeting with various organisations? It wouldn't happen for most employees.)

Despite this, the Legal Aid Board found that I was ineligible and now inform me I will have to pay back all the Legal Aid I received since 2004.

I was not playing a game with my children's childhood within the Family Courts, financed by Legal Aid. If this had been the case, I would have told my children in 2006 that enough was enough; that I was done with mental abuse from the legal system, just for being there for them. Even without Legal Aid or representation, I attended the hearings.

I honestly believe that if I had walked out of my children's lives at any stage, they would have no doubt ended up in care, as three more young people lost to another system that does not know how to deal with them.

One of the symptoms of Ms Hyde's bipolar, is that she cannot see or feel when she is becoming ill; she has no idea or realisation of her behaviour towards others and those close to her, such as her children; she will not accept the impact, emotionally and physically, her behaviour has on her children, who love her.

Ms Hyde can become aggressive, destructive and violent over the most insignificant situation or communications. When Ms Hyde and I cohabitated, I tried my best for 8 years to help her come to terms with her illness, without outside help as Ms Hyde would refuse any support. I received little to no assistance from Mrs Jackson, who would rather dismiss that her daughter had a problem or was having an episode. The first time I experienced Ms Hyde's full mania, I was led to believe it was the first time her mental health had gotten so bad - neither Ms Hyde nor Mrs Jackson thought it was relevant to mention her problematic attitude growing up or her two episodes while travelling before we met.

Out of all of this, what breaks me up is that I genuinely loved and cared for Ms Hyde, in and out of hospital, as well as our three children; I still wanted to find her help, at the time to keep our family together and after our relationship ended, I would have had no problem remaining friendly with Ms Hyde, to raise our children as two parents who love them, separated.

I believe I have shown throughout that my children's welfare and stability has been paramount; only to find, all of my love, care, honesty and decency to be unjustifiably dismissed within the Family Courts.

After years of caring for someone with mental health problems, looking after three children and trying to work for the good of our family, suffering years of witnessing my children be abused, and myself being verbally abused, subject to aggressive behaviour, and so many unsubstantiated accusations, only to go to the Family Courts and then be treated like a common criminal, like dirt... I have felt like a shell of a man, and a father, and can only dream of how great our children's childhood should have been, if we had joint residency from the beginning, and Ms Hyde was receiving support. When she was becoming ill, I would have taken care of the children while she received help, and I would never have withheld or stopped them from seeing her. I believe I gave my children a good childhood, but there is so much we could have done differently as parents, if the Family Courts were not at the forefront and Smitch Law on the side-lines.

I feel my children and family have been let down badly by the Family Court System. Each time I have been in the Family Courts, they have given their permission for the hearings to turn into a battlefield. I have repeatedly defended my family from an unscrupulous law firm, who have no care for the children involved and abused their client's mental health to enrich themselves.

Mr Rowe and I met with the Minister for Family Justice, and wrote twice to the Minister of Justice. While she initially suggested the Order 91(14), and the MoJ responded, nothing has been done to address the dishonest, immoral and unethical behaviour towards children that my family's case highlights, which has already been allowed to continue for so many years.

Despite feeling let down again by the response, I knew I needed to concentrate on Lara starting secondary school, Alice attending UEEC and also trying to get out of debt, due to having been consumed for the last year in proceedings supposedly regarding Lara's welfare.

It should be a given that ministers and people empowered by law will hear the issues raised about the performance of those working within the system, but in particular children and family matters, where the proceedings regard the welfare of children.

When asked, it should be regarded as part of their duty to investigate concerns raised by the people moving through the system; to ensure that ethical standards are met, and people are treated with impartiality and respect, regardless of gender, race, disability or sexuality. If rights are nothing more than the words on the page they're printed on, then I would request the people are made aware of this, so that we can finally get everyone to agree, the legislation does not reflect the real world and something needs to be done, starting at the most powerful end of the scale, to change that.

What has held so much justice back is a lack of accountability. How can we move forward, without acknowledging the wrongs? And the rights – although, there is far less to praise than there is to criticise.

Will the Family Court System be magnanimous, and confirm that it is ethically and morally right for judges to ensure evidence, fact and truth are the standard for all involved, and that any false information relayed, any questionable conduct seen, is condemned for its wrongful place in justice.

The judge states in the transcript from the Hearing 27th April 2009, 'I do not think that there is any particular reason why Lara should not be having direct contact with her mother today and that is what makes it so difficult and so upsetting and so unfair.'

I think this judge should be ashamed of himself. No child should be born with an amnesty given from the family court or the Justice System to a parent or parents, allowing them over many years to be aggressive, violent and detrimental to their children's welfare and stability, as the Family Courts clearly have.

I ask the Family Justice Minister and the Family Courts to get off their high–chairs and realise the reality is there are unscrupulous law firms working in children and family matters that are unethical in their conduct; there are guardians who misrepresent the children they are supposed to support; dishonest barristers turn into heartless judges; even with evidence, judges do not condemn child abuse.

It must be deemed as immoral in our democracy to do nothing when cases such as this are brought to ministers' attention, and an independent investigation is necessary and should be carried out.

2010 Onwards…

From MP Rowe

7 January 2010

Dear Mr Marlo,

Further to your phone call to my office, as requested please find enclosed a copy of my letter to the Prime Minister. This is the same format as the correspondence I previously sent to the Justice Secretary, as you have asked.

I hope that it may be possible to finally get someone to more than just listen but to take action towards resolving the appalling manner in which you and your daughters have been treated.

I have at all times always done my best. I am truly sorry that my various representations have so far not achieved the outcome which you seek and deserve.

Best wishes.

Yours sincerely…

Dear Mr Brown,

My constituent Mr Dean Marlo has experienced several years of court proceedings against him by the mother of his three daughters, for whom he has custody.

The mother, Ms Hyde, suffers from mental health problems. Regrettably, she has been extensively funded with Legal Aid to pursue regular court proceedings against Mr Marlo. My constituent is not a wealthy man, but he is denied Legal Aid. It is thus a very unlevel playing field whenever matters get into court.

Why should Mr Marlo continue to be subjected to legal proceedings with the public purse funding Ms Hyde? It seems like a nice littler earner for the firm of solicitors involved! But what of fairness and justice for Mr Marlo?

Mr Marlo contacted me last year to advise me of the latest court action against him. He states that he had no knowledge of the hearing on 14th May 2009. I have advised him to seek legal advice, but he says he simply cannot afford legal advice – and by going to court he lost a day's pay.

The 'system' is clearly working against my constituent and his three daughters; is causing him and them considerable distress; and I now have a bulging file as evidence of my efforts to help Mr Marlo in the face of regular legal action by solicitors who are being handsomely paid by the public purse.

I would welcome your comments! What is happening is not fair nor just.

Yours sincerely…

The last shot

15 January 2010

Dear Mr Rowe,

I am making this complaint about Ms Dowling due to her behaviour and performance dealing with my daughters Alice and Lara and our family's case within the Family Courts.

The Guardian's report 3rd February 2009:

Ms Dowling states that her report had not been ordered, but submitted to inform the Court of her opinions on our family's situation. This I do not have a problem with.

What I do object to, is the concerns expressed being based on a one-hour conversation five months prior, and Ms Dowling not having the decency to speak to the children and myself properly before writing such unfounded and unsubstantiated remarks about a family's dynamics and individuals within the family.

Prior to a Guardian being appointed and on the strength of her wanting to have her voice heard, Alice attended a hearing. After Ms Dowling was appointed, Alice asked if she could attend the next hearing; Ms Dowling told Alice that if she felt that strongly, then she should, and ask the judge if she could explain how she felt and the reasons why. Without any further communication or advice from the Guardian, Alice attended another hearing.

It was clear two solicitors were prepared to discredit my conduct to the judge for bringing Alice to the hearings. The children's solicitor did not represent Alice's views nor did she confirm that Alice's guardian had said she could attend as she felt so strongly, and did nothing even when it was clear that Alice was being used as a weapon within proceedings by Mrs Mason.

Please find enclosed, conformation from both Lara and Alice's schools that the information relayed by Ms Dowling was misleading and false.

Alice and Lara's appointed Guardian uses Hayley in her report and relays unsubstantiated allegations without care or consideration; Hayley and I repairing our relationship is something that is between us, and has no bearing on the incident last year, nor on Alice and Lara's own relationships with their mother and Hayley.

Hayley has never not been welcome at home, and has come to get her things as she has wanted to. While we have met for a coffee and spoken on the phone, Hayley is a young person getting on with her life and social circle; I cannot and do not want to make Hayley's choices for her.

I find it incredible once again to have Ms Hyde's behaviour shifted onto me. After the physical incident at Ms Hyde's home, Hayley and Alice asked for some personal belongings, and Ms Hyde told them no. Alice went into her mother's with the police to get her things.

From Alice to Lara, it is written by Ms Dowling that Ms Hyde has attempted letterbox contact, and these have allegedly not been opened by Lara and thrown away; it is said Ms Hyde was told this by Riverbank Primary.

On 23rd September 2008, the court ordered: 'there be letterbox contact between Applicant (Ms Hyde) and Lara by way of short letters and cards. All correspondence to be sent via Lara's solicitor and seen by her Guardian beforehand.'

On 9th February 2009: 'there be indirect contact between the Applicant (Ms Hyde) and Lara by way of short cards and letters, such correspondence to be sent via Lara's solicitor and seen by her Guardian beforehand...'

Presumably, it is not frivolously written that Lara's representatives read what Ms Hyde is sending to her; it serves the purpose of protecting Lara in case of manipulation, emotional abuse or alienation. It also allows Lara to maintain contact on her terms and give her space to reconcile with what's happened to her relationship with her mother before re-establishing visiting contact – which, I believe, may have already occurred, had Ms Hyde not been able to take our family back to court.

I don't have the order made on the 27th of April 2009 (they never bothered to send it to me), but in the judge's summing up he states: '...an order for indirect contact by way of letters and cards.'

Assuming the stipulation for the letters to be passed through Lara's solicitor or Guardian has been removed as of April 27th, it does not excuse Ms Hyde attempting to contact Lara through her school, and is another example of how she is sabotaging her relationship with Lara in order to have Riverbank be an audience. Lara has asked for space and time; Ms Hyde has called her a liar. The courts previously ordered letters be passed through a representative of Lara's; Ms Hyde has dropped letters to Riverbank and through our door.

I don't get any pleasure from quoting the court order, nor from the discord in the children's relationships with their mother. I'd still like to think that if Ms Hyde received meaningful support for her mental health and parenting, there would be a chance of normality in everyone's lives. This is the fundamental point, which could never be recognised by the Family Courts; I want Ms Hyde to receive help and for both our relationships with our children to thrive. Instead, I've spent years defending against false allegations and an unscrupulous law firm at the helm of an antiquated system.

Ms Hyde has never abided by any court order, which should make it evident that she has also never wanted to cooperate with me as two equal parents, as she has had control, regardless of our separation. It is an impossible situation; Ms Hyde's mental health has diminished any hope of our family achieving a sense of normality, and by now I'm not shocked or surprised, I just can't believe how long it has been allowed to go on for. She has been able to manipulate every part of our lives for a decade, while the Family Courts wound her up and watched her go.

Across the course of ten years, Ms Hyde went from a loving family home with three beautiful children, to full contact, sole residency, shared residency, joint residency, contact, contact with two children ordered, contact with one child ordered and finally letterbox contact.

Is our family situation really that complex for the experts and judges? They were the ones making all these orders!

Again, I could not believe the lies being written about Lara too, and I contacted the Headteacher of Riverbank, who informed me that neither she nor any of her staff have relayed such information. Instead, she additionally informed me that on one occasion, Ms Hyde asked a member of staff to have Lara open the letter and read it in front of the teacher, and that the school had carried out her request.

To make such statements about a child or their family in a self-decided report, without investigating and confirming the information is true, I believe is not the conduct expected of a children's Guardian or an organisation like Cafcass.

Ms Dowling takes the opinion that Alice and I would actively discourage Lara's contact with her mother; I have stood by my children's wishes, and the only times there were issues with Ms Hyde's contact was after an incident between Ms Hyde and the children. I would consider myself a failure of a dad and a person if I minimised or ignored Ms Hyde's abusive behaviour towards the children. Despite my fears, I have never told Lara she cannot or should not talk to or see her mother; I have not protested in any way to Lara working with a Family Support Worker; nor have I ever heard Alice advising Lara not to. As in the past, when Lara continued her contact even though Alice and Hayley didn't, Lara's decisions are her own, and she has not been influenced by her sisters throughout.

It is saddening to read that even Alice is being blamed for the consequences of Ms Hyde's behaviour.

The judge could see that I was of the view time would heal the relationship, as it had done for Hayley and Alice in the past, and that based on Lara's present reservations about contact, it should be telephone only. As Lara has pointed out to me and the Guardian, she sometimes cannot have a conversation with her mother without becoming upset by something she has said – upon that healthy basis, they consider that being forced to go round there is going to magically fix how Ms Hyde's behaviour has impacted all of her children.

How does discrediting Alice and I with false allegations help to re-establish Lara's contact with her mother? Once again, a child expert does not appear to realise that Ms Hyde, as she did in 2000, needs help with her parenting, to show her how to deescalate situations and remove herself, before she loses control and takes it out on her children. However, the suggestion that Ms Hyde needs help with her parenting doesn't even surface.

Instead of concentrating on organising help for a mother with her aggression and behaviour towards her children, the Guardian wants to play the same game as the Family Courts: Ms Hyde has acted 'undignified and unhelpful', during a 'tussle', but the parents must be as bad as each other. I am not trying to make Ms Hyde the identified patient, and I am not claiming to have not made my own mistakes as a parent, but this all cycles back to an incident of unacceptable physical abuse by Ms Hyde. It is a reflection of the past ten years.

(Again, I cannot help but think of how the incident would be relayed if I had 'tussled' with my daughter, causing a cut lip. None of the tone and sadness and confusion how to proceed would be even considered, as it would be identified as child abuse and I wouldn't have seen my children again; I'd definitely have met my prison bunk.)

Yet, the children's Guardian decided to relay false information about my daughters and myself. Ms Hyde does not get help; incidences reoccur and the cycle revolves. Sadly, our children have witnessed it all before, and I ask you to understand that Ms Hyde's behaviour has orchestrated how our children's and family's life has been for too many years, in and out of the Family Courts.

As for the accusations of continued difficulties with both parents, I would like to bring to Cafcass' attention that I have done nothing but facilitate Ms Hyde's requests and demands for the past eight years - evidence of which has been clearly documented over the last 38 family court hearings.

As a parent who has had to rely on the Family Courts and all its affiliated organisations, there is a repeated lack of respect, consideration and understanding of all the family members.

The facts of what brought us back before the court for this past year (as pertaining to Lara, who proceedings now solely cover):

1.   Lara saw her mother physically assault her sister.

2.   Since then, Lara has not wanted to resume contact at the present time with her mother.

3.   On 23rd September, Family Support Worker Vanya was ordered to start work, to which he did once weekly for seven weeks starting 11th February 2009.

4.   I support any work carried out regarding re–establishing Lara's contact with Ms Hyde, outside of the Family Courts process.

On the day of the hearing in April 2009, a barrister from Ms Hyde's Law Firm handed me a copy of a letter to the judge from Hayley. It was shocking to me that Hayley would, of her own volition, involve herself in proceedings, as she wanted to see the end of court involvement along with the rest of us. I must compare this with the one Hayley wrote before court last year, and cannot help but believe Ms Hyde has influenced Hayley's writing of this letter.

Also, I believe that neither Smitch Law nor Ms Dowling should have involved Hayley, immorally using my eldest daughter as a weapon in court, as some form of justification to shift attention away from what happened on the 7th April 2008.

As a parent, I had letters from Cafcass to organise the removal of any items Hayley had left at home, meanwhile Hayley and I talked and met for coffee occasionally; Hayley acted like many teenagers do – she had her fiancé and not a lot else mattered. It was hard as her dad who loves her to see and live with, but from talking to other parents, I believed this was an unfortunate phase that some children go through. Additionally, Hayley was emotionally upset by everything that had already happened with her mother; I understood.

Why was this not recognised by a professional children's organisation such as Cafcass and their employed Guardian?

Hayley's emotional behaviour and personal upset was used to indicate my failings as a father, when unfortunately raising children doesn't come with a road map nor a magic wand. The original disagreement was about money too, which is not uncommon in families with teenagers who like to go out with their friends/boyfriends/girlfriends, the only difference is that any situation brought about is turned into the smoking gun, meanwhile the Family Courts and children's organisations want to defend their 9 years of judgements by comparing physically abusing your child to having a disagreement. There was no bad language, no aggression. Hayley walked out and that in itself is hard to live with, and the best I can do is be here for Hayley when she needs me.

Cafcass have been asked by the Family Courts to make arrangements to try and help regain contact, yet the young person whose life is being manoeuvred, Lara, is not even told what is going on by her Guardian, who hadn't contacted her since September 2008.

I believe that this children's Guardian should have been able to see the whole family were exhausted living with Ms Hyde's mania, her attitude towards our children and our family dynamics for too many years, and that we were struggling once again to cope with Ms Hyde and her unacceptable behaviour.

I ask, could all involved not just have been honest and respectful in their conduct and performances towards three young children? Their mother evidently suffers with mental health problems and within the Family Courts, this was not news. If I can do a brief search and find information, couldn't Mrs Mason, the Guardians, a judge or someone else involved?

The appointed experts should have realised that Ms Hyde struggled to cope with three young children, and having teenagers was always going to be challenging, as it is for any parent. However, Ms Hyde has shown signs over the years that this challenge was going to get harder for her, particularly as she needs help with conflict resolution and remaining calm, but this support never came, neither for Ms Hyde's mental health condition nor for her parenting of our children.

The behaviour my family has received within the Family Courts is shameful and would be for any parent who had shown that their only concerns are for their children's welfare and stability.

Where we have ended up, is with everyone's relationships fractured.

Trying to reinitiate contact with Ms Hyde before addressing these problems, leaves Lara primed for the same abusive cycle Hayley and Alice have grown up with, which Ms Hyde fails to recognise for herself and why the involvement of these experts is vital in understanding and enforcing the support Ms Hyde needs.

I believe that Cafcass should by now have had the notion that it was time to help Ms Hyde with her parenting and, for the sake of our children and our family's dynamics, stop a law firm from inflaming Ms Hyde's condition, which has already prolonged the suffering of our family through the courts for years – leaving everyone disjointed and achieving nothing.

I have not mentioned it, however it is on my mind nonetheless; what about the stress of the threat of going to prison? Judges dip into the pail of 'Community Chest' cards, hoping to read 'go straight to jail, do not pass go'. I feel despair at the knowledge that, as a father, I am merely a removable piece in the Family Courts version of 'Monopoly'.

From MP Rowe – Full circle

21 January 2010

Dear Mr Marlo,
Please find enclosed a copy of the acknowledgement I have received from 10 Downing Street. As I expected, sadly, my letter has been forwarded to the Ministry of Justice for them to answer. They are currently investigating the matter. I will contact you again when I receive a full response.
Best wishes.
Yours sincerely…

Dear Mr Rowe MP,
I am writing on behalf of the Prime Minister to thank you for your letter of 7 January, on behalf of your constituent Mr Dean Marlo.
The Prime Minister has asked me to arrange for a Minister in the Ministry of Justice to reply to you direct.
Yours sincerely,

MP Rowe RE: MoJ

10 February 2010

Dear Mr Marlo,

Please find enclosed a copy of the response I have received from the Parliamentary Under–Secretary of State at the Ministry of Justice.

Hopefully you will find the Minister's comments to be of interest. If I can be of any further assistance, please let me know.

Best wishes.

Yours sincerely…

7 February 2010

Dear Mr Rowe,

Eligibility of Legal Aid

Thank you for your letter of 7 January to the Prime Minister concerning your constituent Mr Marlo, whose ex–partner is entitled to Legal Aid to pursue a family matter while he is not. Your letter has been transferred to this department for a response as both the Justice Secretary and I have ministerial responsibility for Legal Aid in England and Wales.

I have looked carefully at this again in the light of your letter but I do not think I can usefully add to my letter of 30 June last. I attach a copy for convenience. You will know from that letter that I cannot in any event comment on the grant of Legal Aid funding in an individual case. This is quite properly a matter for the Legal Services Commission (LSC) which administers the Legal Aid Scheme. I also outlined the process that enables any interested party to make representations to the LSC about a person's eligibility for funding. The aim of this is to maintain a balanced view and ensure that the LSC can take into account all relevant information in deciding on Legal Aid funding.

My offer remains open to discuss these matters with you if you would find it helpful subject, of course, to the confidentially restrictions mentioned in my earlier letter. If you wish to pursue this please contact my office to make the necessary arrangements. I have enclosed a copy of this correspondence for you to forward to Mr Marlo, should you wish to do so.

Yours,

The Neely on my neck

After the last hearing of the 27th April 2009, I have been concentrating on Alice and Lara's schooling, organising work around my children and getting on with my life.

Out of the blue, on the 25th September 2009, I received the note from Ms Hyde through my door, stating 'Please find enclosed copy of the judge's summing up that you missed'.

Having looked through the contents of this letter, I was shocked and dismayed by Judge Neely's findings, beliefs and explanations. At the time, I could not bring myself to address the transcript and the dishonesty written within.

What is the point of all of the family court process, when a judge relays behaviour and conduct of a family and family members which are not true, and there is no evidence to support what he states. Judge Neely uses unsubstantiated claims and turns them into a reason for his ridiculous and meaningless understanding of our family and what has gone on over the 10 years within the Family Courts.

'…a child will live with one parent, a difficulty will then arise and the children then 'up–sticks' and goes with the other parent until a difficulty arises and then the same situation presents itself and both parents blame the other…'

It's been a decade of explaining and defending, while a series of professionals decide their own narrative. Only Alice changed households on a whim, and again the missed point of when Hayley and Alice would refuse contact and Lara continued, was due to abusive incidents at their mother's; this is not a case of unruly children playing their parents, or of two parents proportioning blame. Yet, Judge Neely has made his conclusions, once more a generalisation of opinions rather than objectively considering the important aspects of our family's dynamics.

Judge Neely clearly expresses no understanding to the gravity and distress of a young child, who has witnessed the assault of her eldest sister, another in the years of aggressive and unacceptable conduct by her mother. When and how Hayley and Alice choose to repair their relationships with their mother is down to them, and Lara's feelings and choices are just as valid as theirs.

This is not about one parent blaming the other parent, this has always been about Ms Hyde's behaviour and actions towards our children.

Once again within the Family Courts, Judge Neely discredits, with no evidence, our family and I believe uses Lara as a weapon when he states, 'I could take a punitive approach and attach a penal notice. In my view that would be disadvantageous to Lara. I would have to be prepared to follow it though and make a committal order. The effect on these children, if I did that (because I think there would have been is every prospect Mr Marlo would not comply), would be absolutely devastating.'

Judge Neely accepts sending a father to prison for doing nothing would be seen by Lara as devastating, yet he is blind to the physical and mental abuse as detailed by every quarter and now three children.

Judge Neely needs to understand that there are children within families that are being physically and mentally abused. It is from this that a child, of their own choice, comes to a decision that at the present time and under the circumstances, they need a break from the instability and domestic trouble that occurs when contact takes place with one of their parents. These children's actions and beliefs come from their experiences and their understanding of their parents; moving from home to home, and their knowledge of two home settings.

Moreover, the Family Courts ordered a Family Support Worker, Lara has attended all of the sessions, and yet they are not listening at all. Judge Neely treats Lara's resistance to reconnect with her mother as condescending drivel, like it does not still imply a mother's difficulty in connecting with her children. Lara's feelings are trivialised by her mother, which is why contact is still not taking place; our daughters are three very different people, and Lara does not want contact until she believes her mother's sincerity in an apology. This requires work on Ms Hyde's part to change her attitude, receive help – something! However, Ms Hyde has continued to deny the existence of the incident in 2008, except that Lara, Alice and Hayley should be ashamed of *their* behaviour. Do the experts understand the problem with that, for the emotional manipulation that it is? Because Lara might not know what emotional manipulation means, but she knows it's not right, and it doesn't feel good to be called a liar by her mother and that she is the one who should be sorry for her behaviour on the day.

Mrs Mason famously once said, 'This is no time for the courts to step back from this family's case.'

Yet that is all they have done, for years, allowing a parent with severe mental health problems to abuse their children and an unscrupulous law firm to exploit and manipulate our family situation.

Judge Neely came to his own conclusions, with the help of several poorly written Guardians' reports, and Mrs Mason's influence throughout proceedings.

Mrs Mason used all her experience to treat three children and myself as objects, to be used and abused. Judge Neely's final assessment was to seriously consider putting me in jail, but then uses Lara as an excuse not to follow through with his intentions.

My one question to Judge Neely would be: are you fucking serious?

I would have thought that due to it being made clear by the Guardian and the forgotten psychologist reports, I am Lara's mainstay.

And my crime? Standing by my children and walking out of a ten-year Family Courts farce...

My summing up of their conduct would be: Shameful!

Ms Hyde's mental health history is well documented, of course it has a bearing on the situation. Instead of recommending some support and help with Ms Hyde's parenting and behaviour towards her children, Judge Neely makes up stories to suit his own beliefs. He was clearly happy to listen to Ms Hyde, who wasn't having contact because she punched her daughter, and Smitch Law, who lead him up the garden path. Judge Neely expresses his disapproval of me without evidence, truth or reason.

I do not believe Judge Neely nor Smitch Law would have found it so easy to behave in this way if I had been legally represented, which is crazy because by the formula the Family Courts have cultivated, I know I would be adding another shark to the mix, and it's not like Melissa having a moral compass kept Mrs Mason's teeth at bay.

Should I stand up for honesty and decency, and ask the system to show compassion to those who have been badly let down by those empowered to act in a moral and just way towards children and families? Or should I live with the misery, say nothing, and allow other innocent children and parents to suffer as my family has?

To pay no attention to this deplorable behaviour in children and family matters would be an injustice to those children and families that have suffered over the years at the hands of unethical and immoral behaviour and performances within the Family Court System.

Our ministers owe it to the innocent lives that have been irrevocably changed by the failings of organisations and the system to meaningfully investigate and introduce changes.

To MP

15 February 2010

Firstly, I would like to send you my regards and hope you are well.

I have enclosed several letters and ask you kindly once again for your consideration and assistance with the unnecessary injustice, discrimination and persecution placed on my family's dynamics, my children's childhood and my parenthood.

I spoke to Beverly on the phone several weeks ago, and told her I would like to make an appointment with my doctor to talk about the anxiety and stress that I feel, due to all the dishonesty and persecution as a parent I have received from within the Family Courts over the past ten years. As I explained, I am apprehensive to make the appointment with my doctor in the fear that Mrs Mason may find out and, if so, will find way to twist the truth and use it against me and my family within the Family Courts.

Thank you for your assistance and consideration with this matter.

Yours respectfully…

Dear Mr Rowe, Order 91(14)

15 February 2010

On the 7th April 2008, all three of my children came through the door two days into Ms Hyde's half term holiday contact, in tears and describing an incident of assault on Hayley. Two weeks later, on the 24th April 2008, Ms Hyde, assisted by Smitch Law, funded by Legal Aid, made another application to the Family Courts, even though Ms Hyde had just physically assaulted her eldest daughter at her home and despite the Order 91(14) being in place; she was granted Legal Aid to pursue the application, evidently meeting the LSC's checklist for eligibility and the Courts believing her to application to be justified.

Through these new proceedings, in 2008 and 2009, I was given a copy of Ms Hyde's application to the Family Courts. She relays that there was an incident at her home, along with police officers' names and a case number. (After the children left her home in April 2008, Ms Hyde called the police, on Hayley for pushing her down the stairs, and Social Services, to start the ball rolling on her claiming I had 'ABDUCTED' Lara.) Ms Hyde wilfully omits the argument between herself, Hayley and Alice beforehand, or that she struck Hayley twice.

Section 3 of a court application requests 'if as a result of any incidence of domestic abuse, other harm or risk to you or the children there is, has been or there is pending and known involvement with the police, provide details and identify'. Ms Hyde fails to relay having been charged by the police with criminal damage for her actions at my children's home in 2006, which again Lara witnessed.

She did include, 'Social Services on and off for 6 years'.

As far as I am aware, Social Services have only actively gotten involved with our family on one occasion; in April 2004, after the children had stayed overnight with their mother, Alice received carpet burns to her back, where the skin had been taken right off. It came to light that Ms Hyde had been aggressive and violent with both Hayley and Alice, but no further action was taken by Social Services. (After full intervention by Smitch Law.)

After the incident 7th April 2008, I once again felt concerned about Ms Hyde's behaviour, mental stability and the threatening phone calls from her that followed. I took Lara to Social Services so she could talk to someone if she needed, and explain why she did not want contact with her mother. (Sadly, I also knew that a defence for Ms Hyde could be erected by suggesting I am or have coached the children's views – oh wait, the Guardian believed that anyway.) I relayed to Social Services that my children and I were available at any time. They have not been in touch since.

I do not believe Ms Hyde's behaviour should have been my concern alone. This was yet another violent incident by someone that has a history of mental health problems, described as: lacking in judgment, signs of being aggressive, assertive, disconcerted, talking very fast and clearly not taking in what is being said to her. So far, all my family have received from those empowered with the responsibility of protecting children, is an inability to grasp the fact that it has been Ms Hyde's behaviour towards her children that has orchestrated the last ten years within the Family Courts.

What my family have received from within the Family Court System is a law firm (public funded for ten years), judges and the system itself manipulating the process and dishonestly condemning a parent who not only was supportive of getting Ms Hyde help to ensure our children have a good relationship with both parents, but who also put up with the abuse just to be a dad to my children.

Sexism is a prevalent issue, and we have no doubt far larger strides as men to make things not only equal, but protect vulnerable parties who do not yet have a voice inside the system because of the way it was set up. However, my case is not isolated, and what is even more sickening to me is that throughout, undeniably because she is a mother and I am a father, her behaviour towards the children has been accepted, swept under the rug or outright justified by people championing children's welfare.

I do not believe anyone involved would have been so lenient, forgiving or uncaring, if it had been me pulling Alice across the floor, strangling Hayley or even showing up at Ms Hyde's home, to kick her car and make a scene. I recorded the incidences I was aware of and witnessed, but only the children know the true extent of what was going on living with a parent with manic mood swings.

The whole point, and the only focus for the Family Courts, should be children's welfare – there is no barometer for acceptable abuse.

Judge Yergin sent our family's case to the High Court London in 2007, because Ms Hyde contested the child psychologist's report she and her legal representatives had requested. This once again started the Family Courts process and the melt down and misery of our family dynamics.

At the hearing in London, Smitch Law insisted Alice and Lara needed a Guardian and so it was ordered they would have one. Our case was then transferred from our home town to a court with new judges and a 70-mile round trip. I phoned Melissa and told her that our case had been moved to Venray, and Melissa explained this was a calculated move by Mrs Mason, as she probably felt she would have no success with proceedings back in our home town. (Thinking they could try their luck with a different set of cards, jokers and judges.) I told Melissa I drop Lara off at school at 8.50, it will take me an hour to an hour and a half depending on the traffic to get to court – it was ridiculous to put a parent under so much pressure just getting to a hearing.

How can Mrs Mason, from a family law firm, manipulate where the hearing should be taking place?

(Our town has a Family Courts – I know it is shit but we've got one. Also, I guess Mrs Mason's ally the Fat Controller, Emperor Baxter, has retired or lost his mind completely; placing a penal notice on himself and is too scared to leave his home in fear of being sent to prison… Or maybe he has finally got that number one spot on live at the Apollo? – He was a funny man, to some.)

It was not as a result of any inappropriate behaviour of the parent who had been given the responsibility of the children's wellbeing since 2004; Cafcass involvement had nothing to do with any incidence of abuse or harm to my children on my behalf or as a result of my parenting.

Our attendance at the High Courts in London, and Cafcass involvement in 2007, was only because Ms Hyde contested the child psychologist report and, in the end, became about sorting Ms Hyde's holiday arrangements. Neither case, Australia nor Canada, ever happened; we didn't get that far before another abusive incident between a mother and her children occurred.

The Family Courts have let my children and family down. It has been their inability and that of their judges to address in anyway Ms Hyde's parenting, behaviour and ongoing mental health problems, which has or is making Ms Hyde's time with her children challenging. They have failed to investigate the incidences with the children that have resulted in further abuse, police involvement and other children's organisations being involved.

In Ms Hyde's application, she relays the involvement of Family-in-Focus, and Mind/Connexions. However, she fails to state that while Alice and I organised for her to speak to the Junction and Connexions more than once, Ms Hyde cancelled the appointment and discouraged Alice from speaking to someone.

While Alice was staying at her mother's for periods of time, I was of course worried; Alice would explain that her mother would start arguing, then she would shout and scream for up to an hour, running in and out of several rooms, bursting through doors and working herself into a frenzy. Being brought up with this in her life, Alice gave Ms Hyde as good has she received in an argument. This, in a young child, meant Alice would end up emotionally and mentally exhausted.

Hayley and Lara as children did not have the same temperament as Alice, and would nearly always settle for a peaceful life and keep out of the way, this sadly changed for Hayley as she grew up and became a teenager. However, during altercations between her mother and her sisters, Hayley was protective of Alice and Lara, and would become involved by coming to Alice's defence. In saying this, I believe that unfortunately Hayley's current attitude is part of a teenage growing up process that some children go through, and I believe Hayley in time will regain her composure and stability.

After every confrontation, I do not get involved apart from listening to my children, being there for them and understanding their requests to not have contact with their mother at the present time.

Telephone contact happens, but the children and Ms Hyde still argue over the incident. This, I am well aware is not healthy; Ms Hyde demanded telephone contact, and that is always where the conversations end up. Largely, because within hours of the children returning home, tears and bloodied lip and all, their mother was on the phone denying any aggressive behaviour on her part and demanding an apology from them.

(And all the above has blocked any way forward to repair her relationship with Alice or Lara.)

Often, I wonder if I am the one losing my mind, when I consider how openly Ms Hyde shoots herself in the foot. According to Ms Hyde, with the children running out the door, she called the police on Hayley, Social Services to already level accusations against me, a Hate Team, to report Hayley, Alice and Lara; presumably, Lara's friend's parent collects him, and they are informed of her version of events; she wrote a letter, claiming it had been prearranged for Lara to visit Sully and Ratthew, her new pet, and that I had not brought Lara back. Next, she's back on the phone to Mrs Mason, and together the courts sign off on another year of everyone's lives.

None of the above befits someone apologetic for their actions or looking to emotionally reassure her children, and to see Ms Hyde encouraged to carry on, all it did was finally crush what little respect for the Family Courts I had left.

Ms Hyde relates her version of the domestic incident at her home, but fails to take responsibility for hurting her daughters; Hayley went to the GP with a cut inside her mouth and a sore chest. I am not condoning Hayley or Alice's behaviour beforehand, swearing at their mother and dictating living arrangements, however Ms Hyde's inability to be calm with her children once again resulted in verbal and physical abuse, our children not wanting contact and another opportunity for Ms Hyde to go to her law firm and take our family back to court - all the while not recognising it is her behaviour that stops the children from wanting to have contact with her.

The Family Courts, having done nothing to assuage this notion, then put the blame on anything else rather than addressing the problems with Ms Hyde's attitude, mental health and the resulting behaviour toward her children. This has been the case over the last 10 years.

Ms Hyde's dissatisfaction should not be sufficient for an unscrupulous law firm to repeatedly bring cases to the Family Courts, for the courts to grant their applications, and then act in such a way that they show no ethical regards to the children involved and their welfare, or that of their client.

Ms Hyde fails to include Hayley, Alice and Lara as witnesses, but does include Conner, who dropped his bags off and left, Bernard, who was downstairs at the time, and Lara's friend Steve, who Lara had left in her bedroom.

It is written by Ms Hyde that Alice was excluded from school, but omitted it had been while she was in Ms Hyde's care. Prior to the friend's grandfather's tag argument and towards the end of 2007, Alice was doing well at school; something clearly changed in Alice's lifestyle.

Alice did not have an easy time in her childhood with her mother, coupled with the everyday choices and problems that come with being a teenager, Alice became rebellious. At age 13, Alice chose to live in an environment that did not have consistency or structure, and the girls have all said, even Lara who would have been younger than ten, their mother allowed them to stay up late and drink alcohol, which must have contributed to Alice's difficulties at school. (Barring Alice's dyslexia, but there was support there in that aspect, it was just that Alice was not in the right place of mind to accept it.)

All of this, is aside from the daily eroding emotional abuse, verbal confrontations and physical incidents.

Alice has since grown up a lot and turned her life around; she now regularly attends UEEC and is expected to attain good grades in her GCSE subjects, especially in art where she is predicted to get an A.

None of our children have ever had their contact withheld by me. It has always been their decision, based on the behaviour of their mother, and there has never been any evidence to suggest otherwise.

Abduction of a child.

It took me so long to prepare a response to this application, partly because I was once more blindsided by the acceptability of the accusations that can be suggested to the Family Courts, without evidence.

It is wrong when an accusation of abduction of the children can be made, when proceedings have come about due to a violent incident as Ms Hyde's home, between her and the children, while contact within the court order was being observed.

When Ms Hyde walked into my house and took Lara in 2000, there was so much hurt and confusion as to why it was even happening, I felt sick and I called the police. Thankfully, I have never had to experience the devastation that must be felt by a parent who has had their child truly abducted. The fact that Ms Hyde cannot understand the weight of her accusations further indicates her lack of compassion and understanding that she needs some help.

Ms Hyde is unaware her behaviour crosses any decent or ethical line, which is recognised in a report from a mental health doctor and diagnosed as severe bipolar disorder. This report was presented by Mrs Mason to the Family Courts in 2000, so she is well aware of her client's disposition. This application has been written under the supervision of Mrs Mason, and she too treats abduction as something that can be used without consideration or meaning, and bantered about as if it means nothing to those children and parents who are placed in such a deplorable position.

I felt emotionally shocked and drained as I read through Ms Hyde's admissions, as it brought home all the sadness I had felt for Ruth, Hayley, Alice and Lara.

With each line and paragraph, the tears rained, to the extent I had to put the papers down several times because I could not see.

As I continued through Mrs Mason's bundle of 2000, I got to Mrs Jackson's input, and the above process began all over again. The reason why Mrs Mason had the audacity to present a report from a doctor which described Ms Hyde's severe bipolar episodes, was because it included the accusations of Mrs Jackson; the implication that I was abusive to both Ms Hyde and our children, and the cause of Ms Hyde's condition.

I have to accept (I do not know why) the false allegations from Ms Hyde, despite the thought of abusing my children or being accused of doing so was, and still is, unbearable.

I realise now that all of Mrs Mason's inclusions, effects and deceitful behaviour cumulates in her knowledge that she could not do anything to defend Ms Hyde's past behaviour or mental health record, but she can imply that I am no better as a person or parent to look after the children than her client.

I cannot express the tears, hurt and misery Mrs Mason has placed in my life, and yet I continue to pick myself up for the sake of my children and start again.

Where was Mrs Mason's commitment to the wellbeing of her client and in addition her obligation to ensuring any action a family law solicitor takes must be in the interests of the children? Is Mrs Mason and this law firm complying with any ethical codes, and are they acting within a standard expected from a family law firm?

Is it not unjust and unreasonable to force any child to visit somewhere where they have witnessed physical violence over many years, and again with this incident towards their elder sister? Even before Ms Hyde raised a fist to Hayley, she grabbed Alice and was shouting in her face, which is not right for a child to be put through or to witness.

In her application, Ms Hyde requests that all three children should be put on the 'Child Protection Register'.

It is deliberately misleading in an application, to imply she is so fearful for the children in my residency; there has never been any evidence of violence or abuse in my household, and this must be seen as scandalous and detrimental to the children and myself as a parent, who has done nothing more than try to support and love my children.

Ms Hyde states her witnesses are 'too frightened' to testify; I have never threatened anyone, nor have I even been cautioned by the police for anything, let alone violent behaviour, so the wording she has chosen here is to do nothing more than imply to the judge that I am intimidating: a 10 year old, my daughter's ex-fiancé and Ms Hyde's own boyfriend – first, what the fuck? Second, I haven't seen Connor since before Hayley broke it off with him. Third, I've never met the man; he's sat next to Ms Hyde at a couple of hearings, but if I was really that way inclined, I'd have done something when he pushed Alice across the room.

(If I am aggressive as suggested, I am very good at controlling it. I guess this will mean nothing, as I am told by the judge and Mrs Mason that I am still a violent man.)

Mrs Mason is up to the challenge of deceiving the family court process by being dishonest and manipulative on behalf of her client, rather than the interests, welfare and stability of the children within the court order. Their client's representation has been constructed in such a way as to shift attention from the root of the issue, or any questionable behaviour on Ms Hyde's part, and imply, as thoroughly as they can, that it is my conduct that should be in question, which is morally wrong as it is a blatant attempt to manipulate and distract from the real issues of the children's welfare and assisting a parent in receiving help for their ongoing bipolar disorder.

I have said it before, but Mrs Mason does not act as a compassionate human being, she continues to act like an oppressor and bully.

Where is the justification within this application to the Family Courts to bring further proceedings back into our family's life, and make redundant the Order 91(14)? Where is there evidence provided for any of her assertions?

In response to her application, the judge in 2008 saw fit to grant permission for Ms Hyde to proceed with the attempt to attach a penal notice to my name – how, ethically, was that justified?

Repeatedly, the Family Courts have judged me to be the responsible parent, granting me sole residency in 2004. How is it then, that I am also the parent with 3 Penal Notices attached to orders, and a 4th or 5th applied for? Either the Family Courts have horrifically misjudged, or they are enabling the harassment of a decent parent, for no reason.

As has been for the past 10 years, I was working, getting on with my life, while my children were on half term contact with their mother. On the 7th April 2008, I was on the settee feeling ill, when the incident at Ms Hyde's took place.

Never have I spoken to or advised any of our children not to have contact with their mother, before or after any of the many incidents. I do not encourage or provoke Ms Hyde's behaviour towards our children or our family's dynamics, yet hearing after hearing, the reasons why we are back in court is placed on my parenting or me.

I hope by reading the above you understand that this is not about one parent blaming the other parent, and see that children and families need honest support, help and level–headed guidance from those working within children and family matters. To this day, I am asking for Ms Hyde to receive some form of help, to try and ensure the happiness and safety of all our children.

It needs to be ensured that children and their families are treated morally and compassionately, and the behaviour and performance by those working within this system reflects the true meaning of 'a child's welfare and stability is paramount'.

Thank you for your assistance and consideration with this matter.

Yours respectfully…

Another Dear Mr Rowe,

15 February 2010

I have £5,050.17 owed to the LSC, and I still do not know how I am going to pay for it. The reality is, I could not afford a solicitor for one day, let alone paying back Legal Aid since 2004.

It is hard to deal with the personal persecution that has been placed in my life; I have been hammered for being there for my children.

Over the past ten years, I have brought my children up sadly relying each week on Child Benefit, Family & Working Tax Credits and some help from Housing Benefits with our rent.

As a single father, I was no different to any other single parent with three young children. I have tried to install work ethics in my children's lives, and despite a one-day job taking me two days, I was without fail there for my children before school, after school and to spend time with them. This I was proud and glad to do, as a dad. Clearly, I was not going to earn a full salary, but what I did earn made all the difference to us day-to-day.

When Smitch Law first contacted the LSC about my eligibility for Legal Aid, my accountant could not understand the dismissal of years of low income, and the next time, Melissa could not understand why I was not being treated fairly by the Legal Aid Board.

Ms Hyde has never made the effort financially or paid any maintenance towards our children's upbringing, but nothing is said. (As you know, I do not want anything from Ms Hyde other than to get on with raising our children with love and care, but the principle of the matter remains.) Yet, Ms Hyde is given Legal Aid to bring proceedings forward, due to her own behaviour towards our children.

I believe it is shameful, with all that my children and I have been put through by the Family Court System, that I, as a parent with the financial responsibility of my two children who are still at home, Lara 12 and Alice 15, can find our family's financial position to be threatened by the Legal Services Commission.

I ask the Legal Services Commission understand that I am mentally and physically exhausted over what my children and I have experienced within the ten years of family court proceedings; what is more, I do not have £5,000 to spare to pay this debt.

Thank you for your assistance and consideration with this matter.

Yours respectfully…

On the up and up

1 May 2010

With the ability to dedicate more of my time to work, we're doing much better financially than last year and have moved into a nicer rented house in a cul-de-sac, with a garage and big garden. Lara has been asking about getting ping-pong table and I finally think we have the space to do it!

About a week after we moved in, there was a knock on the door.

I was greeted by two plain clothed police officers, who requested they come and inquired as to whether Alice was home.

Concerned and wondering what this could be about, I invited them into the living room where the officers explained there had been a sting operation, regarding a 26-year-old man, and a string of offences involving over ten girls under sixteen, regarding pictures and online conversations dating back to 2006. Alice was one of the girls.

I felt sick to my stomach. This was the man Hayley found in Alice's bedroom at Ms Hyde's in 2007.

Alice was out with friends, but when I gave her a call she came home to talk to the officers.

When I checked in with Alice after the police had left, she told me they requested she write a statement, and maybe appear in court. Alice said she didn't want to get involved and with her anxiety, she wouldn't be able to anyway.

I asked Alice if she wanted to talk about it and if not, if there was someone we could get in touch with; Alice said that the man didn't do anything to her and she is fine. (Whether that is due to Alice's naivety, I don't know, but I can only hope she takes on board the gravity of the situation and talks to me if she needs to.)

Dean Marlo

Still my MP

Firstly, may I congratulate you in gaining a further term as the MP for my constituency; this once again can only benefit the area and our community. It is to your credit that I have seen first-hand the effort, support and commitment you show your constituents. For this, I thank you and have the utmost respect.

Thank you for your letter 30th March 2010 and your sincere support, advice and time spent on asking ministers to act responsibly and morally, regarding my complaints as a parent with the dishonest and immoral performances found in child and family matters within the Family Courts and legal system.

I really must ask, when is the right time for government ministers of relevant departments to get involved with legal or family court matters?

These internal bodies have never carried out an honest investigation into the serious breach of ethical and moral conduct within the Family Courts. They have asked for information and evidence; when provided, they simply dismiss and rewrite what went on to suit themselves and defend the unnecessary and unscrupulous conduct brought to their attention. The performances that my family have received, to which I have felt necessary to report, would be detrimental to any child, parent and their family's dynamics.

At the moment, I am unable to make any sense of the persecution and bullying that my family, children's childhood and my parenthood have endured. I have not visited my doctor, because I do not think in all honesty my doctor can help with this state of mind. What I require is justice; those people responsible to be brought to account and changes made to ensure no family goes through this in the future.

If we now have a listening Government and Prime Minister, one that acts honestly and honourably, they can put things right for many children and families of the future, and the families that have been let down badly by the Family Court System can finally begin the healing process.

This would be with the knowledge that other children and their parents would not be put through the 'behind closed doors' performance that currently takes place.

An independent investigation should be made into the attitudes and ethics of those working within the Family Court System, and the legal system as a whole. The government should make it clear that this conduct will not be tolerated; the examples from my family's story alone deserve to be condemned, and I ask them to look meaningfully at this case and see how a family has been handled by the dishonest process. I ask them to see how a family was professionally manipulated and pressured to almost breaking point.

The mighty pen, with honesty, morals and decency attached, stood no chance against the immoral behaviour from people working within the Family Court System. I have been writing to you as my MP for a decade, and I hope you understand why I cannot forgive those people who, for no good reason, lied and cheated three young, innocent children out of a stable and happy childhood. It has been their unethical actions that have tarnished my children's childhood and my parenthood over the past 10 years.

Curtain Call

There is a 'Chapter 12' in this true story, and I can only hope that the government, the system and ministers can see the injustice. My hands should not be forced by the continuation of the corruption, or undermined by those empowered to ensure standards are kept.

It is difficult to live with the knowledge that the legal system, Family Courts and so-called professional people working in children and family matters, can show no care or consideration, nor remorse, for their part in the misery they indorsed.

It should not be too much to expect or ask from the Family Courts; honesty, morals and standards. Yet, here I am, again, asking.

Please find enclosed, two letters regarding Lara and her performance in her first year at Horizon Academy - I could not be prouder. I know you, Beverly and all concerned will be as pleased for Lara as I am.

Thank you, as always, for your time.

Yours sincerely....

Child Support Agency

3 - 4 April 2013

Dear Mr Marlo,
Child maintenance arrears reinstated
We previously decided that we would not collect £429.22 that you owed for the period from 27/08/1999 to 25/01/2001 in child maintenance until a later time. The arrears are owed for maintenance for:
Alice Marlo, born 1994.
Lara Marlo, born 1997.
We made this decision because of your circumstances at that time.
However, we have now decided that you do have to pay this amount. This means that you now owe £429.22 in child maintenance arrears.
Please call us now and pay what you owe. You can pay by credit and debit card over the phone.
Yours sincerely,
Centre Manager

Dear Mr Marlo,
We previously told you that we closed your child maintenance case from 26/01/2001 for:
Alice Marlo, born 1994.
Lara Marlo, born 1997.
Although you are no longer required to make regular child maintenance payments, you still owe arrears that built up in the past. We have looked at your case and found that you owe a total of £429.22.
We may not have contacted you for some time about your case but we are required to collect all outstanding arrears. You now need to pay what you owe.
Please call us now on the number at the top of this letter to discuss how you can pay what you owe.
If you need to see how this arrears amount has been worked out, please call us on the number at the top of this letter. We will then provide you with this detail in writing. If you do not contact us, we will assume that you do not need this information.

What can we do if you don't pay your arrears?
If you are employed, we can take action to deduct the money you owe directly from your wages or pension.

We can also take further action, including:

Action through the courts – *failing to pay child maintenance can lead to court action and you may have to pay the legal costs involved.*

Seizing goods to pay your arrears – *in England and Wales, items you own can be seized and sold by bailiffs. In Scotland, items may be attached by Sheriff Officers and sold at auction. You may also have to pay the costs of this action.*

Making deductions from accounts – *amounts can be taken from one of your accounts and you may be charged a fee for each deduction.*

It's not too late to pay.
To avoid these actions, please call us now on the number at the top of this letter and arrange to pay in

full what you owe. You can pay over the phone using your credit or debit card.
Yours sincerely,
Centre Manager

Dear Mr Marlo,
Your case closed on the 26/01/2001 however this closure has left an arrears amount of £429.22 owing from the past.
Please call me on the number at the top of this letter to make a credit/debit card payment to clear these arrears.
If this is not possible, please complete and return the enclosed Direct Debit form and we will arrange to take a monthly payment of £35.77 to clear the arrears.
Please find enclosed a new Direct Debit form for you to complete and return to us by 11/04/2013.
Yours sincerely,
Debt Manager

Is it really 2013, and are they seriously suggesting they are chasing child maintenance that they will then pass on to Ms Hyde? I wonder if Ms Hyde will be receiving a letter regarding maintenance, since I have had sole residency, from 2004.

Dean Marlo

Requesting experience at a hospital

19 April 2013

My name is Lara and I am writing to you to ask if it could be arranged for me to spend a day at your biochemistry lab.

I am fifteen years old and attend Horizon Academy in town. I have been predicted to gain A in biology, chemistry, physics and maths, however have personal goals of A* throughout.

I am very interested in biochemistry and would be grateful to have the opportunity to further my understanding and knowledge in a biochemistry lab and also as a profession.

Thank you for your attention with my letter and I hope this can be arranged in the near future.

Yours faithfully,

Lara Marlo

Dear Sir MP

2 September 2013

May I firstly say that I hope you are well and apologise for writing to you about this matter. I have received a letter from the CSA and I am attempting to clarify the details regarding residency of my daughters with them, but I am concerned that the truth will be distorted and the CSA misinformed.

On the 3rd April 2013, I received a letter from CSA stating that I owe £429.22 from 27th August 1999 to 25th Jan 2001.

This letter has been on my mind for the past 4 months, and has brought me nothing but unnecessary worry. Not only the amount, but also getting involved yet again with another organisation that I feel may persecute me for being there for my children.

In 2000, I had several phone conversations with the CSA and they confirmed to me that there was no payment outstanding; I had been giving Ms Hyde money for the children above the amount the CSA indicated I would have to pay. (I was also paying for the vehicle for Ms Hyde to use with the children; I wanted to provide for my children, however I could.)

After the hearing in October 2000, I sent the CSA a copy of the joint residency order and in 2004, I sent them a copy of my sole residency order.

As a family and single parent, we have found it hard but what makes it harder is the fact I have not been treated equally and Ms Hyde spent ten years disrupting our children's residency under the pretence of a responsible parent to three young children.

I would ask you please to confirm to the CSA that you are aware of my family, and the circumstances of our case are made clear to them.

Yours sincerely...

Dean Marlo

From MP Rowe

2 September 2013

Thank you for your letter regarding the difficulties you are experiencing with the Child Support Agency. I suggest that we meet to discuss this further. I have therefore made you an appointment at my Advice Bureau on Wednesday 13th November, at 9am, at my constituency office. If this is not convenient, please phone my office.

I appreciate that this is some time away, but unfortunately, I am unable to make you an earlier appointment as my prior Advice Bureau are all fully booked. I would point out that I have more opportunities for residents to meet me than any other MP in the area.

If you would like to phone my office and provide them with your phone number, Beverly could phone you if a cancellation becomes available. Best wishes.

Yours sincerely…

Dear Sir MP – Fourteen years on

3 September 2013

Ms Hyde has been permitted to bring so much trouble and instability into three children's lives, year after year; with an open door to the Family Courts throughout and a law firm that was clearly hell-bent on inflaming any situation, with no consideration to the children's welfare and stability.

Many of the hearings were farcical and were made a mockery of by the immoral behaviour and conduct of some individuals working within family law.

Families and their children do not deserve law firms who have a burning desire to win a case, no matter what the cost; parents and children deserve honesty, morals and standards to be carried out by all working in the system.

For me it was a sentence for ten years. It was like being on trial, with months and years of volatility. After weeks of being treated like a criminal within the Family Courts, the hearing would lose sight of the children and spend the time trying any way possible to skirt the issues our family have.

I went to the Family Courts in November 1999 for contact with my children, to inform the Family Courts that I was there for them as a father, and that my only concerns were for their welfare – nothing more.

Whatever I provided for my children, their mother continually destabilised any normality we achieved. I have been left feeling bullied and isolated, exhausted and drained from defending my children and myself to 13 judges in 38 hearings over 10 years within the Family Courts. I also provided several organisations with evidence of the serious inappropriate and underhanded behaviour going on within the Family Courts and 'children matters', and I was dismissed.

The Family Courts, with some help, entangled three young children into a shameful process that provided needless instability, uncertainty and turmoil in their young lives.

At the hearing on the 27th April 2009, at the Venray Family Courts, I'd had enough and could not cope with the abuse, corruption, and dishonesty that had been placed in my children's lives and my own, discrediting my ability to be a decent parent and father to my children. My children's best interests meant nothing to these individuals and their attitude and conduct made that perfectly clear.

I am not angry Sir Rowe, I am totally burnt out.

For 4 years, I have been unable to think about what went on, or to look through ten years of persecution and torment; chewed up and spat–out, for being there for my children, mentally manipulated by the system because I cared; threatened with prison because there was no good reason for the Mrs Mason to get her client's own way.

If the police had come for me, I would have rather gone to prison than step foot inside another family court building – like so many other fathers, we should not be made to feel like this.

To be treated so dishonestly and have witnessed the detrimental effect on three young children and their childhood, will never go away. However, acknowledgment and condemnation from the system, an honest attempt to investigate and resolve the issues within, would at least make it easier to sleep at night.

I would like the opportunity to ask this government and the Prime Minister, Deputy Prime Minister and Family Justice Minister, if they will instigate a comprehensive investigation into the way my family was treated and the operation of family law.

As in any organisation, democracy or society, people working in family law who demonstrate no consideration for their ethical conduct or behaviour must be held accountable, for the good of children and their families, communities and the credibility of the profession they represent. Law should not be beyond reproach, and any evidence of inappropriate conduct should not be ignored or dismissed.

I ask you once again, if you would kindly endorse that my family's involvement 1999-2009 within the Family Court System be investigated and write a letter on my behalf to the departments responsible.

Yours sincerely...

To the Child Support Agency

2 September 2013

In reply to your letters of the 3rd & 4th April 2013;

On separating from Ms Hyde in July 1999, I gave Ms Hyde £160 a week via cheque; organised and financed a brand-new Ford Fiesta car for her to take our children to school and for her/their personal use. I was paying an additional £125.13 per month for the car.

Come September 1999, Ms Hyde started to demand more money each week and insisted that I take the car back, and get her a bigger car. I told Ms Hyde that I could not afford to, and from that time Ms Hyde refused me any form of contact with our children. I continued to make payments into Ms Hyde's bank and she carried on using the car.

Despite all my efforts, I had no alternative but to contact a solicitor and apply to the County Courts for contact with my children. In November 1999, my solicitor made an application to the courts and the hearing was set for March 2000. At this hearing, I gained a contact order for my three children, every other weekend and half of all school holidays.

On the 2nd of July 2000, Ms Hyde was sectioned under the Mental Health Act for the fourth time. I had full residency of the children until their mother was released in August, where the children resided with their mother and I on a weekly basis, up to October 2000 when a joint residency order was granted – 6-week residency each with alternate weekends. Ms Hyde had the Child Benefit for two of our children and I had Child Benefit for one.

In August 2004, I was given sole residency of our three children.

As a family and single parent, we have found it hard, but what made it harder was the fact that Ms Hyde repeatedly applied for the Child Benefit for which she was not entitled, and has never contributed with any financial support since 2004 or the children's sole residency with me.

Yours sincerely…

Dean Marlo

To/from Sir MP

5/11 September 2013

Dear Sir Rowe,

Thank you for your letter and the appointment to see you on the 13ᵗʰ November. I enclose both my home and mobile number if a cancellation becomes available.

Also please find enclosed several of Lara's school reports and Alice's GCSE results, to which as a parent I am very proud. I know you would agree that they show the effort Alice and Lara have put into their school life, as well as the standard of education Lara is receiving from Horizon Academy.

Once again, thank you.

Kind regards...

11 September 2013

Dear Mr Marlo,

Thank you for your letter providing me with your phone numbers just in case a cancellation becomes available. This is appreciated.

I am delighted to hear that your daughters are doing so well. Best wishes.

Yours sincerely...

From Sir Rowe

5 November 2013

Dear Mr Marlo,

I am pleased to confirm an appointment has been made for you at Sir Rowe's Advice Bureau on 13th November at 9am.

Please bring with you any relevant documents or reference numbers which may be of assistance. In addition, please complete and send back the attached Consent Form or bring it on the day. Without it, Sir Rowe will not be able to represent you.

It is important to contact Sir Rowe's office if you are unable to make this appointment or experience any difficulties as there is a great demand to see Sir Rowe, and others could be offered your appointment if you are unable to attend.

The Advice Bureau is held in a former church hall. A map is enclosed for your assistance. Best wishes.

Yours sincerely,

Beverly

Dean Marlo

Dear MP Rowe

13 November 2013

Thank you for seeing me this morning; I am confirming in writing what we discussed. On the 13th of September 2013, I received a phone call from someone at the CSA. They asked me several security questions, then stated that they had been forwarded my letter; cases like mine are now dealt with in Scotland and she had my response, but was unaware of the contents of the letter I had received from the CSA. It was requested I inform them what the letter stated, and I explained it said I owed monies from 1999 to 2001, coming in at £429.22.

I was told the matter would be looked into 'next week'. I asked if I could have their name, phone number and extension if possible; they told me that their name was June, and gave me a contact number.

I have still not received any response from the CSA, although their letter of the 3rd April 2013 threatens me with:

Deducting the money I owe directly from my wages.

Action through the courts.

Seizing goods to pay the arrears.

I have still not received any reasonable response from the CSA regarding my letter of 2nd September 2013, or a sensible explanation from the CSA after the nonsense phone call I received on the 13th September.

'As someone who is liable to pay child maintenance, if you change your address and don't tell us within seven days, you may be subject to criminal proceedings and fined up to £1,000.'

Owing to my family's position throughout the years, I have always kept the organisations involved up to date with my new addresses. I am familiar with the process because, unfortunately, my financial position has been a struggle, and I have lived in rented accommodation with my children on yearly leases.

Sir Rowe, I am not a criminal and I have never behaved in any way to suggest that I am. I should not feel victimised or persecuted, yet once again I do.

I ask you please for your advice and help concerning living with a system that appears to be hell-bent on kicking you when you are already down.

Kind regards,

Another for Rowe

13 November 2013

I also kindly ask for your advice and assistance in obtaining a meeting, as I believe I would like to go in front of the Parliament Select Committee and challenge the apparent viewpoint that everything within family law is working smoothly.

Is it morally right and ethically acceptable for you to be told not to interfere or question the conduct of people working in the legal system? Is that not why we vote in representatives, as constituents, to offer insight into the way the authorities are governing?

No honest and decent person would endorse the behaviour and attitude my family unjustly received and had to endure from the legal system. Yet, the Family Courts, the MoJ and the Law Society just brush their behaviour under the carpet, endorsing their contempt and lack of respect for the support a family desperately needed.

As a family we deserve closure; as people in a society, we deserve acknowledgement and reparations to ensure that families do not continue to suffer in this way.

Kind regards...

Dean Marlo

From MP Rowe to CSA

15 November 2013

Dear Mr Marlo,

It was a pleasure to meet you again, especially with the wonderful news of how well your daughters are doing. If you need any proof of what a good father you are, your daughters are it. You looked in good health and were in fine spirits.

Please find enclosed a copy of my letter to the Child Support Agency requesting that the debt they are claiming against you be 'written off' as we discussed. I hope that in this case the Agency can see the sense that (a) you were providing the care for your children at this time and that (b) it relates to more than ten years ago.

When I receive a response, I will contact you again. Best wishes.

Yours sincerely,

Dear Senior Resolution Manager,

Mr Marlo has been to see me following a demand he received from the Child Support Agency for a debt of £429.22 being claimed against him which related to more than ten years ago!

My constituent strongly disputes this liability as he had paid maintenance and had joint custody for a short period which became sole custody, from 2000. He therefore incurred all costs for the care of his three daughters.

Mr Marlo has had no contact throughout the past decade or more from the Child Support Agency querying liability or custody.

I have been seeking to assist Mr Marlo for around ten years. The demand you have sent him has shocked me, as it has my constituent. I would be grateful, therefore, if you can look into this historic and I would say unfair demand on Mr Marlo who, having brought up his daughters with great fatherly dedication, is now effectively being penalised.

I suggest that after such a long time the amount demanded is 'written off' on the basis that it is time expired; if it was ever justified in the first place.

Thank you.

Yours sincerely…

CSA

11 December 2013

Dear Mr Marlo,

I am writing further to a letter we have received from Sir Rowe MP, your member of parliament, and our phone conversation of 28 November.

You are concerned that we have asked you to pay £429.22 child maintenance arrears in respect of your three daughters, when you advise they have been living with you since 1999. I have looked into your case and can now provide information on this issue.

Ms Hyde applied for child maintenance for your daughters, Hayley, Alice and Lara in August 1999. On 23 November, we worked out you should pay £18.67 a week. At that time, Ms Hyde was obliged to apply for child maintenance as she was receiving a benefit.

We reviewed your maintenance payments on 22 December 1999 and worked out that you should have been paying £5.20 a week from 8 October 1999. This was because you had informed us of new housing costs.

We completed a further review in May 2001, when we worked out you did not have to pay any child maintenance from 26 January 2001 as Hayley was now living with you. At this time, you owed child maintenance arrears of £429.22.

When I phoned you on 28 November, I explained that my investigation into your case had shown that we should have reviewed your maintenance payments in April 2000, when you told us that you had shared care of the children. We have now worked out that you did not have to pay any child maintenance from 7 April 2000.

Additionally, Child Benefit records show you started receiving child benefit for all three children from October 2004. Therefore, we have closed your case from 22 October 2004. We have sent you notification of these decisions separately. I am sorry for the delay in completing this action.

The new maintenance calculation reduced the arrears of £429.22 by £186.45. The remaining £242.77 is due for the period 27 August 1999 to 31 March 2000. As you and Ms Hyde have previously confirmed you were making voluntary maintenance payments in excess of the maintenance due at that time, we have adjusted these arrears from your account. This means you no longer owe any child maintenance.

If you have any further queries you can contact us.

If you do not believe this response satisfactorily deals with your complaint, you can, within the next six months, write to the Client Service Director. Where the Client Service Director is unable to resolve the complaint to your satisfaction, it will be referred to our Complaints Review Team for further consideration.

Yours sincerely,

Dean Marlo

MP Rowe with CSA news

17 December 2013

Dear Mr Marlo,
Some good news! Please find enclosed a copy of the response I have received from the Child Support Agency.
Hopefully you will find their comments to be of interest. If I can be of any further assistance, please let me know.
Best wishes.
Yours sincerely,

11 December 2013

Dear Sir Rowe MP,
Thank you for your letter of 15 November regarding Mr Marlo, your constituent.
Mr Marlo is concerned that we have asked him to pay £429.22 child maintenance arrears in respect of his three daughters, when he advises they have been living with him since 1999. I have looked into Mr Marlo's case and can now provide information on the issue.
Ms Hyde applied for child maintenance from Mr Marlo for their daughters, Hayley, Alice and Lara in August 1999. On 23 November 1999, we worked out Mr Marlo should pay £18.67 a week. At that time, Ms Hyde was obliged to apply for child maintenance as she was receiving a benefit.
We reviewed Mr Marlo's maintenance payments on 22 December 1999 and worked out he should have been paying £5.20 a week from 8 October 1999. This was because he had informed us of new housing costs.
We completed a further review in May 2001, when we worked out Mr Marlo did not have to pay any child maintenance from 26 January 2001 as Hayley was now living with him. At the time, he owed child maintenance arrears of £429.22.
My colleague phoned your office on 28 November and explained that her investigation into Mr Marlo's case had shown that we should have reviewed his maintenance payments in April 2000, when he told us that he had shared care of the children. We have now worked out that Mr Marlo did not have to pay any child maintenance from 7 April 2000.
Additionally, child benefit records show that Mr Marlo started receiving child benefit for all three children from October 2004. I am sorry for the delay in completing this action.

Dear Sir Rowe,

6 January 2014

Thank you for your letters, support and efforts regarding the Child Support Agency's demands for child maintenance 1999-2001.

I am of course pleased with the CSA's decision, but feel disturbed by the fact that from the beginning of April 2013, the CSA were writing requesting I pay 'now' to avoid legal action and advising me to complete a Direct Debit bank form.

In the April letter, they state they have looked at my case and found that I owed a total of £429.22. In the letter I received 11th December 2013, it states they should have reviewed my maintenance payments in April 2000 and have *now* (December 2013) worked out that I did not have to pay any child maintenance from April 2000, and the new maintenance calculation reduced the arrears from £429.22 to £242.77.

Look, Sir Rowe, I still do not believe I owe the CSA anything and what has gone on here is not right in any way but, as you are aware, harsher things have happened in my honest attempts to be a dad to my three daughters.

As always, sincerely thank you, and kind regards…

Semi-logue

Since walking out of court, I have just happily gotten on with my children, without being made to feel like a criminal, living under the shadow of prison and solicitor involvement in my life. All I have done is be there for my children, and, in the end, the Family Courts still wanted to see me behind bars. For years I've been aware that I was being suffocated by Ms Hyde, Mrs Mason, barristers, judges and the sadness my children and I were subject to.

I am sure you can imagine my relief when they finally broke the camel's back, and I had the courage to walk out and say goodbye to the cruel culture that manifests within the Family Courts.

Collectively, under the banner of family justice, for ten years they stole from and interfered in my children's childhoods and my parenting, which can't be seen as acceptable.

Since 2008, Alice, Lara and I have lived happily at home together. Lara chose to not reinitiate contact with her mother; to this day, Lara has had no desire to do so. At the time, Lara told me that I might be getting some calls from her mother because she was not going to answer the house phone anymore and just wanted to focus on her education. To Lara's credit, she achieved mostly A* across her GSCEs.

Hayley and I meet up for coffees and talk on the phone; our relationship isn't as close as it should be, but I am happy to say she is successful and busy, enjoying her life.

In 2013, I helped Alice afford the deposit for a flat, which she has since decided to rent out, and move back home with Lara and me.

It was devastating, to lose Ma in 2014; Ma was a beloved Mum and Nan. Ma was old-school and you could not but love a person that was so kind, caring and loving.

I have been able to put the ten years of court involvement to the back of my mind, and only feel sad when I think Ma was a lovely person and she did not deserve to see her grandchildren and son treated in this way.

Ma, you made our world a better place, thank you, we love you and miss you to this day.

I still run the same company, and by working hard, in 2015 I gained a mortgage on a property to call home.

(Although pleased and grateful to still be able to work to earn that kind of money, this is something I could have achieved – or even, paid off my home from 2000 – years ago, were it not for being persecuted and abused by the family justice system.)

Several years later, Alice regained contact with her mother and continues the relationship to this day, which I've never had a problem with.

Hayley and Alice, as in the past, have a relationship with their mother and both understand it is not stable.

In 2017, Lara moved out with her boyfriend; when the relationship ended in 2019, Lara moved back home.

I am very proud of my children, and I cherish the love and care that they show me.

The family court judges missed 38 opportunities to help my family and a parent with reoccurring mental health problems – it should have been joint residency from the beginning.

The court experts missed so many opportunities to help Ms Hyde and our children; they need to take a step back and reassess how to approach families, and understand that hearsay and poor assessment do nothing for children's welfare. They played a part in making a case 'complex', exacerbating the suggestion that I was just another bad father and ex-partner.

More understanding and support needs to be provided both for any parent suffering from a mental health condition, and for those affected around them.

In truth, it did not matter what form of residence the judges gave me, there would always be a problem, manifested by Ms Hyde and her law firm – this, they also failed to recognise. I was given the responsibility of my three children through sole residency in 2004; they then allowed that decision to be undermined, harassed, and discredited for years. Addressing Ms Hyde's long-term mental health problems may have resulted in nothing, and the outcome may have been what we have today, but at least an attempt to make a difference might have prevented over ten years of uncertainty and turmoil in three children's lives.

The real shame and proof of failure of the Family Courts is that had Ms Hyde received help, we could have been friendly and raised our children under a joint residency order that actually made being parents and providing for their childhoods an enjoyable experience together, even though we are separated.

Clearly, this could never be achieved with the existing attitude and environment of family law, in addition to solicitors such as Mrs Mason, who frankly showed complete contempt for children's welfare, a total lack of consideration for a person with a mental health condition and disregard for ethical codes of practise – if you still have a solicitor and the Family Courts involved after ten years, they are clearly prolonging their involvement, manipulating the system and profiteering from the misery that they have been able to propagate.

How many judges to change a lightbulb?

23rd June 2006 / Town County Courts
Mr Marlo's application, criminal damage – Judge Baxter orders parents not to communicate or go to each other's homes.

28th July 2006 / Town Family County Courts
Ms Hyde's application, residency of Alice and Lara – Judge Neely orders hearing listed for the 8th August 2006 be re–listed for the 25th August 2006.

25th August 2006 / Town Family County Courts
Ms Hyde's application – at the request of Ms Hyde and her legal representative, Judge Recorder Jadin orders medical records of family to be sent to the courts; parents to file statements; a letter of instruction be sent to a child psychologist to assess the children and family. Hearing date set for 4th January 2007.

6th October 2006 / Town Family County Courts
Ms Hyde's application – Upon reading a letter from Smitch Law, Judge Randall orders a hearing for the 23rd October 2006 to consider the current directions and time table.

23rd October 2006 / Town Family County Courts
Ms Hyde's application – Ms Hyde withdraws her application for sole residency. Smitch Law request Mr Marlo's bill for the child psychologist be put onto Ms Hyde's Legal Aid. Judge Neely agrees. Child Psychologist to complete her report and provide it to the Courts by 16th February 2007. A further hearing to be set after 1st March 2007.

9th January 2007 / Town Family County Courts
Application made by Children's Legal Centre – Hayley to be removed from the court order.

24th January 2007 / Town Family County Courts.
Application made by Children's Legal Centre – Alice to be removed from the court order.

6th February 2007 / Town Family County Courts
Judge Baxter orders the CLC's application to be heard on 16th February 2007.

16th February 2007 / Town Family County Courts
Ms Hyde's application – Judge Yergin orders disclosure of the child psychiatrist report to the solicitors; a position statement be made by both parents by 2nd March 2007; the application for contact orders for Hayley and Alice adjourned until 12th March.

12th March 2007 / Town Family County Courts
Ms Hyde's application – Ms Hyde contests child psychologist's report. Judge Yergin orders for the case to be transferred to the Principal Registry of the Family Division in London. Hayley be discharged from the court order. An availability order is made by 2nd April 2007 that the medical records and letters of instruction are filed to all concerned parties. Hearing listed for a final 2–day hearing on 9th April 2007.

21st May 2007 / Town Family County Courts
A hearing was held with only legal representatives present. Mr Marlo had no legal representation, and therefore wasn't represented.

25th June 2007 / Royal Courts of Justice, Principal Registry of the Family Division London

Judge Justice Millar assigns a Guardian from Cafcass for Alice and Lara; Alice's application for removal from the court order is adjourned. Ms Hyde's statement be sent to the Courts by 6th July 2007; Mr Marlo's statement and response to be sent by 20th July 2007. Ms Hyde's application to remove children to Australia for a holiday over the period December 2007/January 2008, be issued by 6th July 2007 and supported by evidence and documents; Mr Marlo's reply filed by 20th July 2007.

Smitch Law seek, as a matter of urgency, a date from the Town County Court for a final hearing, time estimate 2-days.

17th July 2007 / Town County Courts

Judge Neely orders the case be listed for directions from Judge Chips on 26th July 2007, at the Venray County Court. The Guardian, or their legal representatives, to attend the hearing.

24th July 2007 / Town County Courts

Judge Neely appoints Ms Moyer from Cafcass as Alice and Lara's Guardian.

26th July 2007 / Venray County Courts

Ms Hyde's application – holiday to Australia. Judge Chips orders Ms Hyde and her partner to file statements by 9th August 2007; Mr Marlo's statement by 2nd August and response by 23rd August 2007. The Guardian to file her report concerning an interim position statement and Ms Hyde's proposed holiday, by 3rd September 2007. Proceedings listed for the 5th September 2007 and final hearing date set 8th and 9th November 2007.

5th September 2007 / Venray County Courts

Judge Recorder Lowe orders HHJ Chips' order to remain in force, amended for Mr Marlo to make Alice available for an extra overnight contact per week with mother (should Alice wish). Lara to be made available for an extra evening contact per week with mother. Ms Hyde has permission to remove children from the jurisdiction of the court for holidays abroad, including holidays in Australia or Canada, during their school holiday contact time but not during term–time.

Judge Recorder Lowe places an order under Section 91(14), preventing either party from making further applications to the Courts and cancels the hearing listed for the 8th and 9th November 2007.

14th May 2008 / Venray County Courts

Ms Hyde's application, contact with Alice and Lara – Judge Recorder Shelton orders, upon hearing from Ms Hyde in person, Mr Marlo not attending, permission to issue an application for contact to Alice and Lara, including for a penal notice to be attached to the order made 05/09/07. Application is adjourned to 11th June 2008, time estimate 30 minutes at the Venray County Courts.

11th June 2008 / Venray County Courts

Judge Daggett, upon hearing from counsel for Ms Hyde, Mr Marlo and the children's Guardian, gives permission to Ms Hyde to proceed with her application to attach a penal notice to the order of the 5th September 2007. Ms Hyde do file and serve on the children's Guardian a statement of evidence by 25th June 2008, and Mr Marlo to file a statement in reply by 2nd July 2008. Case listed on the 28th July 2008, for a time estimate of half a day at the Venray County Courts.

5th August 2008 / Venray Family County Courts

Courts order the matter is listed to be heard on 23rd September 2008 at the Venray County Court.

23rd September 2008 / Venray County Courts

Judge Neely orders the application be adjourned to a review direction before 9th February 2009; a Family Support Worker be requested to work with Lara to address the issue of contact between Lara and Ms Hyde, such work is not to commence until after Lara has sat her Eleven-plus exam at the end of November. There be letterbox contact between Ms Hyde and Lara by way of short cards and letters, such correspondence to be sent via Lara's solicitor and seen by her Guardian beforehand, and phone contact three times a week on Sunday, Tuesday and Thursday between 7pm and 7.30pm. The hearing on the 12th November 2008 be vacated.

9th February 2009 / Venray County Courts

Judge Neely orders a Family Support Worker to undertake with Lara to address the issue of contact between Lara and mother; there be indirect contact between Ms Hyde and Lara by way of short cards and letters, such correspondence to be sent via Lara's solicitor and seen by her Guardian beforehand, and phone contact three times a week on Sunday, Tuesday and Thursday between 7pm and 7.30pm. The Guardian do file an addendum report to deal with the work undertaken by the Family Support Worker and to file such report by Monday 6th April 2009. The matter is listed for a review on 22nd April 2009.

22nd April 2009 / Venray County Courts

Judge Neely orders Alice Marlo be removed as a party to these proceedings.

The application be listed for final hearing with a time estimate of 1 day before Judge Neely on the 27th April 2009. Ms Hyde and Mr Marlo shall file and serve position statements by 24th April 2009. The Guardian, if so advised, shall file and serve position statement by 9.30 am on the 27th April 2009.

Smitch Law shall lodge with the Court two trial bundles and provide a bundle to Mr Marlo by the 24th April 2009.

27th April 2009 / Venray County Courts

I attended the hearing in the morning, but after lunch I could not suppress my feelings of distress and shock to the façade that was once again being played out within the Family Courts and under the banner of 'a child's welfare and stability is paramount'.

The Family Courts have made no communication with me to inform me of the outcome of the hearing 27th April 2009, although Ms Hyde passed along Judge Neely's summary. From my family's experience with the behaviour of several judges over the past ten years, I would conclude that this is another example of disrespectful and unprofessional performance that my family has received.

Since proceedings began in November 1999, across ten years, there have been 13 judges involved with our case and 38 hearings – 23 of those in just three years.

Epilogue - Lara

I have always considered myself to be incredibly fortunate to have an amazing Dad. What really made my childhood special was the effort Dad put in every day, in so many ways. I know now as an adult this isn't easy to do, even without court proceedings in the background and the efforts of a vengeful ex-partner.

I could come up with millions of examples of my dad as a parent and the ways he was thoughtful, loving and fun… Like me spending way too long demanding to be called Harry Potter, and him accepting his assignment as Hagrid with the same level of enthusiasm as Robin Williams would a character, or trips to the bookstore, and finding the time to sit with me, despite how hard I know he finds reading. My favourite film for a long time was Jurassic Park; on movie nights, we would make dens out of the sofa cushions and Dad had a proper music setup, so he would pull the bass over - when Roberta did her roar, I could feel my sofa foundations rattle.

Our home in 2000 was beautiful, and although we never got the 'roads and cars map' carpet in any of our other houses, we still made each one a home.

Any work, art, stories and pictures, by Hayley, Alice and myself, were put on the walls; the office, the kitchen, the living room. We decorated with photos next to terrible drawings, some kept in the loop from when we were younger. Every kind of project; sewing, woodwork, glitter bombs, science experiments, questionable garden food and bathroom potions, baking, you name it, he was there to be a part of it or ready to head to the library, the shops, if necessary, to get more information, equipment or ingredients. He helped with homework, and we helped each other with spelling.

Sometimes we would come home from school, and Dad had set up a 'Treasure Hunt' where we would have to figure out riddles to find the prize, usually the latest magazines we were following or a small toy. We had the best Halloween, Easter, Christmas and birthday parties on any estate – in summer, we'd all be out on the trampoline and running about in large scale water-bomb fights. With my friends, Dad played a game called 'Zombie', which was basically 'manhunt' but he had to act like a zombie; we would rush to tidy up just to fit in a game.

Dad's music taste is varied and extensive; so much of my music taste, my desire to be a drummer and subsequently getting lessons, comes from the number of albums we'd listen to. Our homes were alive with music and we'd all be dancing horribly, except Alice who actually took lessons. Dad tailored several cassette tapes for each of us with our favourite songs on – I still have one of mine!

Dad loves nature, and we would walk around the local woodland areas with our dogs and have picnics in the nature reserve; at one of our homes, there was a family of hedgehogs we would leave food out for.

I was probably the only kid at primary school who genuinely loved it when I could have Dad come in and help the class out, either on school trips or for construction (memorably in Year 4, when Dad taught the class and Mr Wallace, who literally never let it go, 'measure twice, cut once') and I was also the only one who would have people begging to be in my group, because Dad was guaranteed to be the most fun.

It's been over a decade since I stood in my primary school playground, and it took me this long to thank Dad for always being there, even though there were people who clearly believed what they had been told by Ms Hyde about him and his parenting, and how it must have felt, to be waiting for me to come out, with the eyes and judgement of the entire playground of mums – who really, didn't have a clue - on him.

For the most part, the Family Courts was an ambiguous shape in my understanding; it looked like Dad in a suit, but not the one he'd wear to Murdock's, and heartfelt hugs in the playground; it was talking to strangers and filling out pamphlets.

(As a side note, if you are overcome by something cringy you did as a child, remember I wrote a *poem* about my *pets* during my parents' *custody battle*. I had no clue what the stakes were, *clearly*, to me it was a given I'd live with Dad.)

Despite being raised in the same households, Hayley, Alice and I had very different experiences, especially with Ms Hyde. Alice would question our mother's erratic behaviour, Hayley would step in to defend Alice, and I would hide in my room. The dice would roll on how the argument would end. After, Ms Hyde would either still be pissed off, about to get pissed, or she would start being nice to *me*.

On the many occasions Hayley and Alice left for Dad's, I would feel guilty for remaining in her residency; for not sticking up for them. I was a coward, looking to not get into trouble with her myself, and instead took advantage of the times when she was clearly being emotionally manipulative, like being allowed to watch a horror movie, to stay up late with her, drinking wine, getting Wotsit and having kittens.

I already knew it wasn't a matter of if, it was *when* the abuse got worse for me.

Seeing her every other weekend, and how erratic that actually was, it is evident Ms Hyde could not be consistent; not her moods, her timing, her lifestyle or her care. She would flip over nothing, change rules on a whim, be late for every appointment we ever had, and it's a miracle she's only ever had one car accident with the way she used to drive.

I'll always remember one of the speeding tickets Ms Hyde received and the picture attached proving the car's number plate; at the time, she had a Volvo with seats in the boot, which is where Alice and I were plastered by the sheer velocity we were travelling - no seat belts. We found it funny at the time but, like so many absurd situations with Ms Hyde, it was dumb luck that no one got seriously hurt.

There wasn't a single holiday with her that went off without incident; in these cases, I mean Hayley or Alice, or Hayley and Alice, running away *from* Ms Hyde following arguments, in France, Spain and Cornwall. On one all inclusive, she spent so long in the bar, Hayley, Alice and I had our own 'favourite' bartender, and there's a photo of us standing behind the bar with them pretending to make drinks. In Egypt - the only holiday I went on without Hayley and Alice – I tried a shisha pipe for the first time in a room with Ms Hyde and a bunch of middle-aged men, and two of them made offers to marry me. Ms Hyde had found one man's offer of a few camels amusing, and told me I ought to be flattered. (I was uncomfortable and went back to puffing the strawberry flavoured pipe; again, it's scary how differently situations could have gone.)

When I was younger, I already had a plan to go to university; I was a curious child, yes, but I just wanted to get away from, what I can now recognise as, Ms Hyde's

802

interference. As harsh as it is to say, even Australia had nothing to do with her step-sister, although it would have been convenient and saved me accommodation fees, it's that as a country, there isn't one much further from Ms Hyde!

(To date, I wonder if my only actual solution is a name and scenery change.)

Often, I would be waiting in the playground after school on a Friday, sometimes I was told to move to the reception, as it was not safe for me to wait there, and she would finally arrive. On the drive home, I would be told I am going to a friend's on the Saturday; on Sunday we would have lunch at Cruella de Vil's, which meant we spent most of the day, unsupervised, on the farm. This was a lot of fun, but it boggles me that to everyone around her at the time, she was stating that she wasn't *allowed* to see us because of Dad's 'tyranny' over the court order.

Remembering my bedroom at hers, nothing sticks out from my obsessions at 10 – no music, games, clothes, themes. Around a year after the incident of '08, she dropped a box of my belongings on our porch (unlike Hayley and Alice, I never wanted nor retrieved anything from Ms Hyde's house – although I had considered if I could get away with it if I saw Wotsit) and I didn't recognise *anything*. I donated everything to a charity shop.

This is not to say that I did not also have good times with Ms Hyde; nothing is ever so simple. It is just that the 'good times' are only ever broad strokes. It was Wotsit; the occasional avocado and Bousin on a tray with a cup of tea; going to the adventure centre.

There just aren't any small moments, to me important ones, where she fostered a feeling, a moral or a memory for me. She does not encompass what the word *mum* means; I have always been grateful for Nan, and Dad is an amazing parent, not worrying about adhered to gender roles.

I did not miss her with an ache, when I'd left.

Fundamentally, she does not respect boundaries or treat anyone like an actual person. I believe that she is incapable of loving unless there is something in it for her, and that the times she was a good mother, was because she *benefited* out of the situation. Dad never saw us as bargaining chips or bragging rights – he was proud to be our Dad, and genuinely loved us. She took Dad to court for 10 years to demand residency, but, when we were there, a lot of the time she didn't want us to be; she just didn't want Dad to care for us, either.

In April 2008, after we'd walked out, she called to yell at me about why I wasn't there for her holiday contact. It hurt to be called a liar; I stood there watching it happen, left my best friend Steve sitting in my room, never got the opportunity to say goodbye to Wotsit and then had to explain everything to Guardians, who, when asked, informed me that if the court decides I have to return to contact with my mother and I refuse, Dad may go to prison – it was my residency she was after. All the negative things that were happening at that time, and the majority throughout our childhoods, were because of her, and she *was* lying. I would get so frustrated at not being understood or heard, being talked over and listening to insults about Dad and Alice, I would end her calls in tears.

The more she talked at me though, the more I questioned past events and the more I realised she encapsulates a lot of the traits I never want to be; self-centred, cruel and severely lacking in empathy.

I've now read the letters she posted to Dad around this period multiple times, and I don't think I've made it through once without having to stop and in disbelief consider the narratives she spins, and the people she's willing to throw under the bus to save her own face. Part of this may be due to her bipolar disorder, which I do not hold against her, but to have this level of consistent harassment, defamation and commitment to the court process, I mostly conclude that, at a cellular level, she is just not a nice person.

The argument of 'I am your *mother*' is interesting, because at the time I was saying 'we are your *daughters*' with the same amount of emphasis on 'how could you do this?'.

After the incident, I had the foresight the answer to my previous question of 'when' was: *imminently*.

From a relatively young age, I was told I was doing above average at school and was expected to hit benchmarks for older children. However, like the frankly terrible slam poetry I submitted to the judges indicates, I was just a kid. There was a lot about Ms Hyde's behaviour and treatment that I didn't process or understand, and, due to the literal development of my child brain, I could only see it in a ridged perspective (it's not for me to argue it was the right perspective nonetheless, you've read the books): she shouldn't have hit Hayley and the word 'sorry' wouldn't be enough to reassure me.

Her actual apology to me was 'I am sorry that is what you think happened' or variants thereabouts.

In Year 5 and Year 6, I was held in at lunchtimes and taken out of lessons to either open a card filled with empty sentiments or be talked to by my teachers about regretting my decision to not have contact. No other adult than Dad ever said that how she behaved was wrong and, I'll be honest, that fucked me up a bit.

These cards, like the petering out phone calls, were sporadic from the get go, and have, to my not insignificant relief, reduced to only birthdays and Christmas; while I may sound ungrateful, she has continued to raze my boundaries and I don't want *anything* from her. I have tried not to live in fear of having her interact with me, and it's like a stranger somehow having more right to your feelings than you do. I have never cashed a cheque she has sent for my birthday or Christmas on the principle I will not be bought, nor will I give her any satisfaction in even thinking she has a part *in* my life.

I want what I wanted at 10, to be left alone; to thrive without her.

Around a year later, I received a postcard from Ms Hyde which informed me my guinea pig had died and the vet had advised her to write to me. She was still calling, leaving messages on the answer machine. A short time after Alice had reconciled with Ms Hyde, she came home with a handful of photographs, picking some out of me that she said I could have. There was a goofy looking one of me holding Wotsit as a kitten and, unbidden, I asked how she was. Alice told me she'd died years ago. I'd already mourned Wotsit's loss once, feeling guilty about not saying goodbye and not being able to explain that I wouldn't be seeing her any more. At the time, the phone calls had stopped but I received the occasional card through my door, and again, I couldn't believe Ms Hyde would feel the need to tell me about the 'Grade 2 listed building' she has purchased, and not the death of my cat.

I felt lost, when Hayley went out and just… Didn't come home. We were close and similar. As three siblings, we usually got closer after incidents; when things didn't fully escalate, there would still be smacking, shouting and many 'crocodile tears'.

When Hayley moved back in with Ms Hyde, that wasn't the issue; Alice had done it intermittently in the previous years, I just adjusted to the new scenario. (I couldn't see it when I was younger; Alice was difficult to live with, because she was going through so much, and although regrets are pointless, if I could go back, I would be a better sister to her.) However, hearing Hayley say that I was a 'selfish little bitch', that 'Mum never did anything to you anyway' and 'you need to move on from last year, nothing happened', I realised I did not recognise this person who had my sister's face and voice. Reading her letter to court in 2009 was heart-breaking, and again made me wonder how Dad managed to survive everything that happened in our family. I missed her with a fierce ache, which at first made me think I was unwell, and would later recognise as *grief*, that diminished the more decisions she made and attitude she had.

Starting secondary school is nerve-wracking for anyone. I thought by going to Horizon, I'd have a clean slate with the teachers and the school. I could be judged on my own merits and, as the court proceedings had concluded, I still wasn't having contact with Ms Hyde, which significantly reduced the general chaos that clung to our family's daily lives. However, of course, Ms Hyde had to approach Horizon continuing to claim I had been abducted; that Dad has alienated me from her; to pass on messages of 'I am your mum, and I miss you'. I'd had enough of the teacher sit-down-and-hear-me-impart-my-wisdoms-about-your-relationship-with-your-mother talks.

The truth is, despite kicking her heels in about contact with me for the first year or so, tapering off for her holidays and such, which I do believe comes from the part that sees herself as a mother, she didn't really want me there. Like Bernard's boating days, her numerous holidays and her general attitude towards us, we were just objects she could show off and use to gain attention for herself when it suited; make sure to smile for the family portrait and don't worry about what happens behind closed doors.

Within my first week, I got called into my Head of House's office, to check I was 'doing ok at home' and that there wasn't something I needed to discuss. I couldn't believe it at the time, I was livid. Ms Hyde herself burnt any bridges we could have met on.

Witnessing Ms Hyde punching Hayley, and participating in the argument beforehand, crossed a line within me, her phone calls gave me phone anxiety ('thanks mom') and her harassment of me, through both my schools, under the guise of caring, turned my feelings towards her from red to grey. I wasn't even angry anymore, I was devasted that she would not leave me alone. I had already put so much pressure on myself to do well at Horizon, even though what I desperately wanted was to be normal, average, to keep my head down, but the irony was normal had never been on the table – from Ms Hyde's orchestration of my childhood, her abuse of my sisters, my dad and me, to after, not letting me move on, her words picking old scabs and introducing new (not good) thoughts… She emotionally emptied me.

To my friends, when we exchanged our TragicBackstories™, I gave Ms Hyde's actions more power, and she became my own personal bogeyman.

(I still don't know when she will pop up, but I know she won't respect me and will try to act like I haven't deliberately had radio silence for over a decade and a half.)

Losing some of my rose-tinted gaze of childhood and cutting out someone toxic, was just another life lesson I'd learned early, and the best I could do was not let her attempts to manipulate me or the situation succeed. As far as I could tell, the only reason Dad hadn't been punished was *because I achieved above average at school.* I became terrified of failure. Every exam I took suddenly became life or death in my head and I treated any test as necessary to excel in; I feared a low mark of any form in every subject, a detention or missed homework was unacceptable, as I thought if I slipped up, even once, I would be giving Ms Hyde a reason to take Dad back to court.

I didn't realise until around thirteen how much her interacting with my school, lying, and calling up, less so over the years, affected me, but I felt it all the time. It pissed me off how much she was still influencing me, despite my attempts to distance myself from the personality mutations one goes through in her proximity.

I'd be going about my day- then, she'd call, or I'd be summoned into the school office, or a week before my birthday I get that sinking feeling of anxiety, that she could arrive at any time, and anything could happen. That reminder, an unavoidable anchor to my childhood with Ms Hyde, throws me for a loop every time; that all my parts, everything I've built and fought for since, loses meaning. It returns me to feeling young, vulnerable, and unable to make her stop – I hate that there's nothing I can do about it.

By the time we lost Nan and I reached college, I was burnt out.

Ms Hyde never had the conversation with me that she had a mental health condition, and knowing that the Jekyll and Hyde like personality shifts, mood swings, smacked thighs and grabbed wrists, were not because we were bad children, would have gone a long way. Her mental health is out of her control, the fault I find in her is that she has never *tried* to get help, to manage her condition, attempt to be a better mum, or genuinely apologise for the, maybe genuinely inadvertent, hurt her actions and words caused – to Dad, Nan, Hayley, Alice and anyone else in the vicinity of our family. I do now at least understand, somewhat, why she behaves this way.

Sadly, from what I overhear from Alice, I do not believe Ms Hyde is a genuine parent to neither Hayley nor Alice, despite them both having reinitiated their relationships with her long ago. She hasn't changed; after 15 years that's pretty disheartening.

I still have phone anxiety, look twice before crossing the road, and thrice before unlocking the front door.

I've considered police involvement before, filing for harassment maybe, at 10 I'd definitely watched too much TV and wanted a restraining order. But the situation was and is delicate. I have never tried to initiate contact, and it feels like a door that will swing back and hit me in the face if I write a letter now formally requesting she kindly fuck off. There's also her mental health to consider, and Alice's relationship with her; I do not want to make Alice's life difficult or upset Ms Hyde, despite how little she deserves the consideration.

Completing Part Two marks almost 15 years without contact with her, of my own volition, and the last conversation we had can only have ended in me asking to be left alone. She remains blind to the pain she caused everyone, and lives a self-centred and superficial lifestyle, heedless to those who may get in her way. I am resolute that I made the right decision for myself to not end up as someone I resent, by finding Ms Hyde unforgivable and moving on in my life without her; not because I didn't care about my mum, but because there are so many awful things she did, and that I feared she would do, both in my own experiences and that of everyone in my family by proxy. I wouldn't like the person I'd have become, either, under her influence. (And that was before I'd read Dad's folders!)

I still think, despite now knowing the background context, I had an amazing childhood, and that is without doubt down to Dad and Nan. I can't convey the enormity of the small things to the big moments, where I was happy, learning, exploring and unaware of the reality going on above my head. I hope, throughout this journey, you've been able to see some of these good moments, too.

While Ms Hyde had a leading role, reading through the folders and mountains of paperwork that Dad faced was overwhelming. I'd be scanning a document and come across another wild accusation, or horrific allegation, with solicitors lying and judges making a complete mess of our family situation. I couldn't believe how much of a catastrophe there was at every possible avenue. If the systemic prejudices and failures didn't exist, there wouldn't have been 10 years of this madness.

Mrs Mason, and Smitch Law, show why integrity matters. She gilded an abusive mother, was ready to condemn a genuine father to jail, and didn't care that living in Ms Hyde's household, even temporarily or for short periods, was having a detrimental effect on three children. People who need the attitude Mrs Mason took would have genuine evidence to the numerous accusations – there are abusers out there, it's just in our case, she and her client were the ones doing the abusing.

It is incredible to me that Dad had been writing all of this down, receiving these letters and organising statements etc, whilst doing all the things he was, as a Dad. (He wasn't even in his final form!) It saddens me that, even though I didn't see it, he was under so much pressure and stress, when he should have been able to enjoy our family life.

Stereotypes and systemic discrimination doomed our family the moment Ms Hyde refused Dad contact with us. The fact Dad is a man did not stop him from being a good parent, and the fact that Ms Hyde is a woman did not mean she was a good parent. A mother was abusive and a father was nurturing. We can't keep letting antiquated ideals stop honest people from living their lives. Judge Baxter personally almost made it so the next three years of my life, until I was 5, I didn't live with my sisters properly and only saw my dad for set hours. They talk of alienation – if Judge Baxter believed Ms Hyde would behave unfavourably to 'losing' sole residence of her children, and did not wish to see Dad had every right to be a parent to his children, then it was either an immediate indication her mental health was not stable, or she is, frankly, selfish and heartless, to not see how much it hurt Dad not to have a part in our lives. Either way, his answer should have been joint residency.

Ms Hyde's bipolar disorder totally stumped the Family Courts; that was the barrier between our parents getting along, together and separated, and the reason there were so many incidents throughout Hayley, Alice and my childhoods. Whether it was a failure of the time in that mental health was still stigmatized, or it was a sexism issue, wherein it was unfathomable to the elders of the right honourable Courts that a man, a father, could be more than the stereotypes of a gender, and be nurturing, caring and loving, they condoned the abuse of every family member for 10 years, longer if Dad hadn't walked. Then, their conclusion was that Ms Hyde had done no wrong. (It's been three years of writing and I'm still fucking flabbergasted.)

I could not have asked Judge Neely to write a better summary that encapsulated the faults in the system and how laughably out of touch those involved are to the actual human beings standing in front of them. In a truly impressive show of form, Dad ended our family's involvement in the Family Courts where he started: with concerns for Ms Hyde's mental health, the need to stand by his children after they'd been abused and the threat of prison – with the very real possibility of boots flying through the door, being held against the wall, again, and not having any right to protest, because a penal notice had been issued. The judge is right, I would have blamed Ms Hyde had Dad been imprisoned – who else's fault would it be? Dad had never stopped us from seeing our mother, and each of us not wanting contact with her has been down to the treatment of us in *her* house, by *her*.

I can't understand Judge Neely's heavy heart, nor his conclusions drawn about both Dad and Ms Hyde. It is maddening, when people can openly get away with generally being awful. I don't think any of the individuals involved had ever lived with someone who has an unmanaged mental health condition, or in particular the mania associated with bipolar; at times she was scary, wasn't in control of herself, and she could be cruel.

(No disrespect or hate to anyone suffering from any form of mental health condition – we are the sum of our parts, and it's merely that Ms Hyde adds up to 'no good' in every possible aspect.)

Of course we were protective of Dad, that's what happens when you love someone and they've been treated unfairly. Ms Hyde did not hide her derision of him, and that is why without someone else holding her accountable for her behaviour and providing support through monitoring, three children and her ex-partner bore the brunt of severe, life-long bipolar disorder.

I've responded to each of the accusations through Dad's old letters to my own thoughts added through his words, and it still doesn't feel like justice enough or that we've adequately explained just how easily the Family Courts could have helped or how unjust Dad was treated.

I know good people exist within the system – if there was ever a cry for them to assemble, this is it – but they are not the majority or the moving force, and, if they are speaking out, it is being swallowed by the sea of corruption.

What matters is the effort someone puts in, whether or not they want to try to be a better parent, and the care taken to make every day something special, as well as love and patience through the pleasant (and not so pleasant) experiences of having children. Nobody gets it right all the time; these are not qualities found only in mums or just if you are a dad.

At the end of the day, I hope what can be learned by our experiences detailed within Behind Closed Doors is that greater support and understanding is always needed; joint residency should be the norm unless evidence is provided otherwise; personal egos, agendas or gain should be kept far away from the Family Courts and those working in family law. All of these things require foundational changes in the way the system is set up, and consistent effort to ensure those empowered to administer justice are not abusing their position.

Epilogue – Dean

An open letter to: PM Rishi Sunak, Minister for Family Justice - The DCA - The Law Society - The Bar – Legal Complaints Service (Office of Supervision of Solicitors)

A proper administration of justice and one of those fundamental tenets, a pillar of fairness, is to ensure honesty, morals and standards are paramount in any investigation carried out by those who find themselves with the responsibility and privilege of overseeing justice.

Ken Burns wrote, 'It is very difficult to dispel ignorance, if you retain arrogance', and it is from mine and sadly many other families' experiences that this arrogance, dishonesty and self-serving, has undermined our whole justice system and eroded the importance of family values.

Lara and I hope that what our family endured - and other children and their parents suffer, in the hands of shameless people involved - as relayed in 'Behind Closed Doors Part One and Two', will serve as an insight into the harm and damage to a family's dynamics, if practices, such as those demonstrated throughout family law by judges, law firms and their solicitors, continue unchallenged.

Over the years, during the relationship with my children's mother, we did have many happy occasions; despite time and time again being concerned and coming to the realisation that a member of our family had mental health problems.

In 1993, when Ms Hyde became ill and was detained in hospital, I was shocked and scared by the experience of living with someone losing their mind through manic episodes over many months; my only thoughts were for her wellbeing and our young daughter Hayley.

I researched the effects, causes and symptoms of someone suffering with a mental health condition, in an attempt to help Ms Hyde and keep our family together. In doing so, I found myself living with someone not coping with their manic state, and with no help from outside sources, she was able, depending on her mania, to verbally and physically abuse our children and myself over many years.

As I entered the Family Courts process, it was not only to regain contact with my children but I also went in with the understanding that the courts would ensure that the welfare of children came first, and they would be protected by family law and the Children's Act. Yet, blinded by dishonesty, self-importance and greed, there are self-serving, corrupt and immoral individuals and organisations, all touting antiquated family law legislation, which doesn't help families.

So many judges missed the fact that they were in a position to recognise a parent with mental health problems and provide help for them, though support groups and the NHS, which would have prevented ten years of proceedings and ensured the welfare and stability of three children's childhoods.

A solicitor, with the help of several highly paid barristers, turned the residency of our children into a sham, bringing unethical and immoral behaviour to the forefront of a family's situation. Throughout the hearings I attended, they served to discriminate and victimize me as a father, relaying defamation and championing my inability to be an honest and decent person towards my children and their mother.

This family law solicitor found it easy to hound me as a parent and person, acting and behaving like a bully, which had an impact on my children's lives and drained me to the core.

This law firm's constant involvement diminished the likelihood of two parents ever getting on. Profiteering tens of thousands of pounds, they set themselves up for a good lifestyle and reputation, at the expense, in this case, of three innocent children, their own client's mental health and a father's ability to focus on being a parent. Instead of securing support for their client, for the benefit of the three children in her care, they chose to harass the person who had, for years, endured living with someone with a severe mental health condition and was already under the cosh of her mentality concerning contact of my children. Under the guise of family justice and family law, they instigated financial hardship, years of court applications, numerous penal notices and the manipulation of any schedule of contact.

As parents entering the Family Courts process, we find barristers pleading their client's case with the desire and aim of getting their client what they want, regardless of the outcome in a child's life. This cannot be seen as acceptable, and a child's welfare should never be placed in this position.

Children's wellbeing should be evaluated and judged on evidence of both parents' ability to provide and care for them, and not in the capacity of a solicitor or barrister to undermine the children, judges and parents within family law and the Family Courts System.

Where is the respect for children? Where is the moral intent from those who practise family law?

It is a sad fact that for decades the welfare and stability of children's lives have been dictated by ruthless, uncaring and immoral people, who have been allowed to make a mockery out of family justice and family values.

It's just another farce, with barristers and the rest boycotting court proceedings; wearing the yellow ribbon; asking the government for more taxpayers' money so people can be legally represented… Honestly, I have seen more diamond rings, gold chains and Rolex watches inside a courtroom, than in a high-class jeweller's shop window! (Not forgetting the expensive suits and dresses, all necessary costumes for the act.)

My point is, they all seem to be doing very well off the back of injustice and harm to innocent children and their parents.

We have had decades of 'dysfunctional' and stressed families, but in how many of those cases were decent fathers repeatedly demonized for their inability to be there for their children? In truth, how many children have been let down and prevented from having a relationship with their dad, by the discrimination, injustice and exploitation of their fathers?

Coupled with the bias found in the Family Court System, if this solicitor had been successful in their attempts to discredit me and grind me down to the point that I'd walked (ran) away, I would have become another bad father for the statistics, regardless of the love and care I have for my children.

I have had four penal notices placed on my liberty by one family law solicitor; she did not care for the possible repercussions in three children's lives by her actions, she was prepared to see a father behind bars, to allow her to continue to manipulate her client's position.

It sends a cold shiver down my spine when I think of all of the good times I have shared with my children, that simply would not have happened, if I did not have the love and strength to overcome the distain shown to me as a father by family law and the people who are implementing the process within family justice. The system lets down families who are in need of assistance and protection of the court, and those who are genuinely there for their children - it is a failure across the board.

We deserve confirmation that family law and its ensemble will conduct themselves in compliance with honesty, morals and standards, and that ethical codes of practice will be followed, for the sake of the children involved. Anyone working within the system must understand that their behaviour, attitude and determination should solely be in the interests of the children's welfare, and not their own status or capacity to profiteer from unscrupulous behaviour on behalf of their clients.

We need to acknowledge and address the discrimination and challenges brought to the attention of the people who we elect to lead us; government ministers who are placed to serve, should be making fair legislation for the good of the people and the wider environment. This is about accountability to allow us to move forward and make the positive changes needed.

I hope you agree that we need meaningful commitment from our justice system to ensure no future parent is treated in this manner through the Family Courts, as many already have. A parent to a child is what it means, a parent; both have the ability to enhance their children's lives and upbringing.

The white elephant here is a parent has a mental health condition and she, along with her children, was let down by the system that should have been there to help.

To finish, I'd like to firstly thank you for getting to the end of our story, and secondly thank the people who showed decency, honesty and respect to three children and myself over many years.

Special thanks to:

Ma, for always being there as a loving Nan and Mum.

Mr Church, the children's Headteacher at their primary school for over a decade, who was honest and caring in his approach to the welfare of children.

Mrs Hart, the primary school secretary and governor, who was caring, kind and understanding with all of the children and their parents.

Melissa, who, through her integrity as a person, outshone any of her fellow practitioners of law, and indeed the Family Courts.

Mr Ellwood from Cafcass, who saw through the lies and manipulation that was being presented to him.

Judge Chips, for also seeing through a law firm's attempts to mislead and disregard the interests of the children involved.

Finally, my MP, who genuinely worked hard to address my children's and my own injustices.

Without the love, care and compassion of the people above, I without doubt would have not been allowed to see my children, and the very special times we did have together that were magical, priceless and happy, would not have happened.

Thank you, to you all.

For the past 10 or so years, I have felt emotionally drained by the subject; with a sense of failure for not pursuing the injustices my family found within family law and trying to help other children and their parents.

In 2019, we had a loft clear out and Lara asked if I minded if she looked through the folders and paperwork I had kept – Lara was shocked and suggested compiling everything in order… Which quickly spiralled into a novel, that was already hitting the half-a-million-words mark before we'd even reached 2006, and finally Part Two. Here we are, four years later at the end of our story. A special thanks to Lara for tirelessly co-writing both Behind Closed Doors Part One and Part Two.

From the beginning, we both agreed when relaying the contents of the folders, our intentions were to highlight the desperately needed changes in family law and the Family Court System, because parents should be treated objectively, equally and in the interests of a family's dynamics and the children involved.

The Family Courts are harbouring unethical people and it is their behaviour that has let parents down, and failed to ensure that a child's welfare is paramount. The process is corrupt, defunct, where the unscrupulous hide behind closed doors, protected by their own, believing they are elite and beyond reproach.

The immoral behaviour found within family law needs to be acknowledged, shamed and condemned, and the same efforts and determination used to inflame and divide families, needs to be administered to put things right.

On behalf of all of the families exploited by family law, we would like those individuals and organisations involved to be magnanimous, to recognise their immoral behaviour; the hurt and pain that has been unleashed across generations, and understand that it is unacceptable to continue to turn parents and their children on the carousel of human misery that is the Family Court System.

Thanks again for reading.

Printed in Great Britain
by Amazon

20355072R00464